Seventh Edition

D0427864

Three Genres
The Writing of Poetry, Fiction, and Drama

STEPHEN MINOT
University of California, Riverside

Prentice
Hall

UPPER SADDLE RIVER, NEW JERSEY 07458

Library of Congress Cataloging-in-Publication Data

Minot, Stephen.
Three genres: the writing of poetry, fiction, and drama/Stephen Minot.—7th ed.
    p. cm.
  Includes indexes.
  ISBN 0-13-042099-9
    1. Creative writing.   I. Title.
  PN145. M5
  808'02—dc21   2002020584

Editor-in-Chief: Leah Jewell
Senior Acquisitions Editor: Carrie Brandon
Editorial Assistant: Jennifer Migueis
Production Editor: Maureen Benicasa
Prepress and Manufacturing Buyer: Sherry Lewis
Marketing Manager: Rachel Falk
Marketing Assistant: Christine Moodie
Text Permissions Specialist: Mary Dalton-Holfman
Image Permissions Coordinator: Carolyn Gauntt
Cover Designer: Robert Farrar-Wagner
Cover Art: Virginia S. Minot

This book was set in 10/12 Palatino by DM Cradle Associates
and was printed and bound by Courier Companies, Inc.
Covers were printed by Phoenix Color Corp.

For permission to use copyrighted material, grateful acknowledgment
is made to the copyright holders on pages 447-449, which are considered
an extension of this copyright page.

 © 2003 by Pearson Education, Inc.
Upper Saddle River, New Jersey 07458

Printed in the United States of America

10 9 8 7 6 5 4

ISBN 0-13-042099-9

Pearson Education LTD., London
Pearson Education Australia PTY, Limited, Sydney
Pearson Education Singapore, Pte. Ltd
Pearson Education North Asia Ltd, Hong Kong
Pearson Education Canada, Ltd., Toronto
Pearson Educación de Mexico, S.A. de C.V.
Pearson Education-Japan, Tokyo
Pearson Education Malaysia, Pte. Ltd
Pearson Education, Upper Saddle River, New Jersey

To Ginny
Special thanks for editorial assistance through seven editions
and now for the artwork that graces the cover.
   All this with cheerful patience.
Love abounds!

CONTENTS

PREFACE

FOR STUDENTS

What Are Your Goals?

Most readers skip prefaces; they want to plunge right in. That will come. If you want to make the most of this text, read this preface. First, here is an important question only you can answer: Why are you interested in creative writing?

There are many possible motives. Writing—and especially imaginative writing—is not a science. Everyone approaches it for slightly different reasons. Your answer, though, will determine how you use this text. Here are three of the most common reasons people become involved in creative writing.

1. For many, learning more about literature is the goal. There is no better way to increase your understanding of poetry, fiction, or drama than to write them. Learning by doing is effective in all the arts. And in sports, too. Those who have spent time learning to play the violin have a special understanding of classical music. And what better way is there to appreciate soccer or baseball than to play it? If you write a sonnet or a short story or a play, you will become a better reader.

2. Others hope that creative writing will become a long-term avocation. A great majority of those in creative writing classes or adult workshops don't plan to make writing their primary vocation. They are like those who play a musical instrument seriously but without any intention of joining the Boston Symphony. They devote time to improving their skills, they take part in workshop groups, they may publish from time to time; but writing remains an avocation, not a vocation.

3. For a smaller group, writing has become a central commitment. It is not an easy route. College students may have to slight other courses. When they graduate, they will probably have to enter another field to earn enough to eat and pay the rent. In spite of these challenges, they identify

themselves as *poet, writer,* or *dramatist.* To support this notion, they must allot a portion of each day to reading contemporary fiction, poetry, or drama in a close, professional way. They attend readings and conferences, but most important, they write regularly. In short, they are immersed in a particular genre—not just their own work but the best of what is being published as well.

Which group do you fall into? If you are just beginning, you may well be in a fourth category: those who are testing the field. They aren't sure just how important writing may become in their lives, but they know that they are not going to find out simply by wondering. They are determined not to become one of those wistfully passive adults who keep saying, "I've always wanted to write."

It may be that you will begin with high expectations and will discover after graduation that you are really a reader rather than a writer. But you will have lost nothing because you will have become a far more perceptive reader than you were before. The pleasure you take in reading will be greater.

Or perhaps you will begin with a commitment to one genre and find that your real talent and interest lie in another. Writers, unlike ballet dancers and atomic physicists, don't have to start early and stay on a single track. In writing, anything is possible at any stage and at any age. No aptitude test or teacher can predict how much talent and commitment will develop until you have a body of work to show.

What This Textbook Can't Do

Reading this textbook hastily won't be of much help. Don't try skimming. It is essential that you take extra time to study the poems, stories, and plays. The text will show you what to look for, but it is no substitute for close, analytical reading of the literary examples themselves. Ultimately, they are your teachers.

Next, allow time to write and revise your own work. This or any text can't be a substitute for the effort of actually writing poetry, fiction, and drama. There is a fundamental difference between *content* texts, such as those in literature, history, philosophy, or political science, and *process* texts. Content texts can be read at a steady pace. They provide facts and concepts. Process texts, such as those in the creative and performing arts, guide your creative efforts. You learn by doing. *Doing* in this case means writing.

Finally, this textbook will not try to persuade you that every step of the way will be fun. Workshop sessions are often the most enjoyable classes on campus, but much of the time you will be on your own. Creative writing is more than just tapping into some bubbling well of inspiration. Good writing takes effort. What this text can do is make that effort more rewarding. And it certainly will speed the process of development.

How to Get the Most from This Text

You bought this book. Here are five ways to make it a good investment:

• In the poetry section, spend extra time on Chapter 2, "Plunging In." Almost every poem will be used later to illustrate different poetic techniques. You will be returning to them repeatedly. The special effort you make on Chapter 2 will make the entire section more meaningful.

• There are six stories in the fiction section and three plays in the drama section. Allow extra time for them, just as you did for the poems in Chapter 2. Don't wait passively for the text to analyze them. The analysis of literary concepts won't mean much unless you become familiar with the work being discussed. Study each of these closely before going on.

• Try to use the terms introduced in this text accurately and often. Some will be new to you, but when you start to use them in discussions, they will become familiar and helpful. They will help you to be precise in discussing literary works.

• If some section seems unclear or puzzling, get help. Talk it over with your teacher or someone else using the text. Or e-mail me at *s.minot@juno.com*.

• Mark up your book with legible, helpful marginal notes. Link the concepts and approaches with works you have read. Underline passages that are important. Tests have shown that those who take reading notes improve their comprehension. They convert passive reading into active involvement.

All this will take you a little more time than it would simply to read a textbook from beginning to end. But creative writing is not a skill that can be mastered in ten easy steps. It is a slow process of growth—growth both in your understanding of what literature has to offer and in your ability to create new work with your own individual stamp.

FOR TEACHERS

Why a New Edition?

I, too, hate them. All those marginal notes lost, favorite works dropped for no good reason, new works to deal with, old syllabi made obsolete. And for what? Surely six editions were more than enough. Isn't a seventh edging on redundancy?

For all that, there are justifications. First, although excellent literature is timeless, students are not. Their needs and expectations change. A work that draws them into the world of literature one decade will strike students in the next educational "generation" as naive or pedestrian. Yes, we who are involved with literature do proselytize. We want to use works that will attract today's students while giving them enough complexity to stretch their abilities.

Second, analysis and examples that seem highly effective in manuscript don't always fare as well as expected when tested in many classrooms. *Three Genres* has been adopted in all 50 states and in a great variety of institutions. There are good reasons for every change in each edition, but the ultimate test is in a multitude of classrooms. I depend on teacher response.

Third, although the text is new for each succeeding class of students, it becomes more than familiar for those of us who use it regularly. We as teachers need fresh examples, fresh approaches to the art of writing.

The Mechanics of a New Edition

No, it's not just a matter of shuffling chapters. At best, it is a two-year process. The first step is to elicit feedback. Four formal critiques from teachers are commissioned by the publisher. These are anonymous and represent different types of schools in different sections of the country. In addition, I maintain a file of comments I have received. Opinions vary, of course, and sometimes contradict each other.

Decisions have to be made. The diagram of the relationship between similes, metaphors, and symbols, for example (page 67), has just as many enthusiasts as detractors. Do the "seven deadly sins" of fiction intimidate more than they help? It depends on whom you ask. Will Murray Schisgal's satiric play in this edition offend some? Stay tuned. Ultimately, I have to make a series of judgments.

Then there is the matter of permissions. In many cases, even works that are retained have to be renegotiated. Some agents and certain publishers are unrealistic about what is a fair permission fee. A few authors have badly inflated egos. Bargaining is a slow and frustrating process. It takes six months.

Then comes the actual writing. By revising about one-third of the text and replacing one-third of the examples, I try to strike a balance between change and continuity. At best, this process takes another six months.

It then takes another full year from the time the completed manuscript is delivered to the publisher to the date on which the book is available. My wife and I proofread the manuscript, the edited manuscript, and the page proofs in addition to the work of the in-house proofreaders. (Even after these nine professional proofreadings, every new edition contains at least two elusive typos!) This is all a long, time-consuming process, but we hope that it results in a text that meets the needs of both teachers and students.

What's New This Time?

1. *A troubleshooting guide*: the new Appendix A, provides topics in all three genres that often give trouble. Each genre is listed separately, and the topics

with page references are arranged alphabetically. Students can use this guide to review areas they are unsure of, and, equally important, instructors can recommend specific pages for review when writing their comments. These should help students in their revisions and also suggest topics for the next conference.

2. *An expanded poetry selection* gives a greater variety of poems, including an example and explanatory section on the pantoum.

3. *Brief comments and questions on the Poems in Chapter 2* have been added to each poem in order to arouse interest and help students who are reading these poems for the first time.

4. *An expanded fiction section* includes an additional story, giving a greater range of tonal effects and style.

5. *A new chapter on dialogue in fiction* shows various approaches as well as uses.

6. *A new play by Murray Schisgal* (author of *Luv* and co-author of the award-winning script for *Tootsie*) is included in the drama section.

7. *An expanded Glossary-Index* includes definitions of a greater range of literary terms.

The Instructor's Manual will once again be available upon adoption of the text. It contains suggestions for syllabi as well as exercises for individual topics. I urge teachers to contact the publisher for a copy of this helpful resource that has been prepared especially for them.

Full Use of *Three Genres*

A number of instructors have assigned *Three Genres* as an optional or supplemental text. This may be helpful with advanced classes, but the text has not been designed for casual browsing. The most effective way to justify its adoption is to assign specific chapters on specific days and ask students to discuss some of the techniques covered in that section. If supplemental anthologies are used, they will help students apply the approaches described here to additional works. This encourages students to use this text actively rather than merely as a resource.

A Companion Text

Literary Nonfiction: The Fourth Genre is my new text, also published by Prentice Hall, designed to meet the phenomenal growth of interest in this type of writing. It can be used as a companion to *Three Genres*, serving as a natural introduction to poetry, fiction, or drama; or it can be used independently in courses that focus exclusively in creative or literary nonfiction.

Literary Nonfiction carefully distinguishes literary prose from the factual essay and argumentation papers students are used to writing. It guides them through a variety of approaches such as personal experience, a sense of place, and character studies and analyzes structural strategies such as contrasts, incremental evidence, and linkage by image. Unlike other texts in the field, it explains how literary nonfiction can serve as a natural transition to poetry, fiction, or drama. My intent is to place literary nonfiction in the context of all creative writing.

Originally *Literary Nonfiction* was conceived as a replacement for the drama section of *Three genres*. Soon, however, it was clear that a separate volume would provide instructors with greater flexibility. Hearing about your experience with either of these texts by letter or e-mail (s.minot@juno.com) will be of great value and much appreciated.

Special Thanks

I owe sincere thanks to my senior acquisitions editor, Carrie Brandon, who has gone out of her way to establish good working relations with the publisher. I am also indebted to my production editor, Maureen Benicasa.

Thanks also to sharp readers of the Sixth Edition who e-mailed errata. High on the list are Philip Schneider of Washington State University, L. Currivon of Leeward Community College, Hawaii, and Ed Phar (and his 50 students) at DeVry Institute of Technology in Arizona. I'm also grateful to a number of anonymous critics for their thoughtful suggestions: Laurie Kutchins, James Madison University; W. David LeNoir, Western Kentucky University; Howard Kerner; Andrew Furman, Florida Atlantic University; and Elizabeth Bruton, Catawba Valley Community College.

Finally, I owe an immeasurable debt to my wife, Virginia S. Minot, who in the past three decades has proofread 25 typescripts, galleys, and page proofs for the various editions of this text as well as the same for novels and story collections. All this without so much as a sigh of protest—at least within earshot. I am particularly pleased that this year her print collage has been used for the cover of both this edition and that of *Literary Nonfiction*. Her contributions have been immeasurable.

Stephen Minot

1

WHAT MAKES A POEM A POEM?

Five distinguishing characteristics of poetry: use of the poetic line, images, the sound of words, poetic rhythms, and thematic density. Simple versus sophisticated poetry. Using poetic conventions to achieve true originality.

Yes, but is it really a poem? This question keeps coming up whenever we discuss poetry—particularly contemporary work—but we rarely take the time to answer it. Defining poetry seems difficult because the **genre**[1] includes such an astonishing variety of forms and approaches. Types vary from lengthy Greek **epics** to three-line **haiku**, from complex **metrical** schemes to the apparent formlessness of some **free verse**.

In spite of this variation, however, there are certain basic characteristics shared by all poetry. These not only help to distinguish poetry from **prose**, they suggest special assets that have drawn men and women to this genre since before there were written languages. As readers, we have come to expect these qualities unconsciously. When one or more are missing, we may sense the lack without knowing exactly what is wrong. As writers, however, that vague sense is not enough. We have to identify just what aspect has been ignored.

There are five fundamental qualities that distinguish *poetry* from *prose*:

- utilizing the **line** as the primary unit rather than the sentence
- a heightened use of **images**
- greater attention to the *sound* of words
- development of **rhythm**
- creating **density** by implying far more than is stated directly

Poems differ in the degree to which they make use of these five characteristics. Although all poems rely on the line as a basic unit of composition,

1. Words in **boldface** are defined in the Glossary-Index.

even that aspect can be either highly pronounced or barely noticeable. The use of the other four characteristics varies as well. But they remain the core of what makes poetry fundamentally different from prose. Because these distinctions are so important for both readers and writers of poetry, each deserves a close look, both here and in subsequent chapters.

The Poetic Line

When you write prose, the length of the line is determined simply by the size of the paper you are using. If your work is published, your editor, not you, will determine the length of the lines. The length will vary depending on whether the work is printed in magazine columns or book pages. The prose writer, then, works with sentences and leaves line length to others.

Not so with poetry. The poet determines where each line is to break. Line length is a part of the art form. For a printer to change the length of the lines would be as outrageous as revising the wording itself. This first characteristic, then, is embedded in the very definition of the genre.

The importance of the line in poetry is more than just a matter of definition. It is for most poets the basic unit of composition. When we write prose, we naturally think in terms of sentences; but when we turn to poetry, we usually move line by line.

Most poems also use sentences and are usually punctuated in the conventional manner, but the effect of the grammatical structure is muted by the use of lines. Only occasionally are lines complete sentences in themselves. When too many lines end with a period they tend to create the singsong effect we associate with nursery rhymes and comic verse. Instead, the sentence structure and the idea or feeling expressed often continue smoothly into the next line. These are called **enjambment**, or **run-on lines**. This double use of line length and grammatical structure is unique to poetry.

The importance of the line in poetry is fundamental and it actually preceded the written word. Epics such as the *Iliad* and the *Odyssey* apparently were memorized and recited before they were written, and the rhythm of spoken lines was an essential aid to memorization. So was **rhyme**. Even today there are individuals who have memorized their native epics without being able to read or write.

As soon as poetry was recorded on the page, there was less need for memory aids. But poetry has never lost its roots in the spoken language, nor its reliance on the line. This is why most poets keep reading their work aloud as they compose so that they can hear as well as see the lines as they develop. It also accounts for the increasing popularity of poetry readings and the availability of videocassette recordings at most libraries.

With metered verse, the length of the line is determined at the outset. **Meter** is based on a recurring pattern of stressed and unstressed syllables in each line, so the length of the line is determined in advance by the poet's choice of a metrical scheme. Writing a metered poem does not mean giving up control; it merely means that the choice is made at the beginning of the poem rather than line by line. Meter is a structuring of natural speech rhythms, just as formal dance steps are agreed-upon patterns drawn from improvised dancing.

Free verse is like free-style dancing in that it has no preset structure. The length and nature of each line are determined as the poem develops. But, again, as in free-style dancing, those variations can be extremely important. They can be used to control the pace of reading, to emphasize a key image, to establish rhythms, and sometimes even to shape the printed poem in some significant way.

Both metered and free-verse poems are organized by lines. For many poets, the patterning of lines becomes a kind of signature, an identifiable **style** by which his or her work becomes distinct from all others.

Control over the line is an invaluable asset of the poet, a privilege not shared by writers of prose. It is an absolute distinction that differentiates all verse from all prose.

The remaining four characteristics of poetry are not as absolute. One can find poems that do not make use of them all. But they are qualities that we associate with the genre. They help to define poetry and distinguish it from prose.

The Use of Images

The second characteristic of poetry is its heightened use of **imagery.** We think of images as objects we can see, but actually the term includes anything we can respond to with one of the five senses—sights, sounds, tastes, tactile sensations, and even smells. That may seem like a wide net, but think of all the **abstractions** it excludes—words like *love, hate, democracy, liberty, good, bad,* and *death.* Indeed, *life* itself is an abstraction.

Essays tend to be rooted in abstractions. Philosophical works, for example, often explore the nature of good, evil, or truth. They use abstractions to describe abstractions. Economic papers analyzing the gross national product, poverty, or profit margins do the same. → How so?

Many poems also deal with abstract themes, but they usually translate those broad concepts into objects we can see or respond to through one of the senses. The abstraction *desire,* for example, is too general to have an impact on a reader. We know what it means, but only intellectually. The poet Philip Appleman helps us to *feel* an aspect of desire by comparing it with the ocean's undertow. (The poem is on page 43.) We all know what *rage* is when we read about it in a news item, but the word is too common and too abstract to have emotional impact. Dorothy Barresi creates that impact by plunging us into a bizarre and violent dream scene of rage in her poem "Mystery" (page 39).

Images can be used by themselves or to create **similes, metaphors,** and **symbols.** More about that later. The point here is that most poetry is rooted in objects we can see or respond to through the other senses. Poetry is by nature *sensate*—a genre of the senses.

Heightened Use of Sound

When we recall how poetry began by being spoken, chanted, or sung, it's clear why it frequently makes more use of the sound of language than does prose. It is no accident that the word *verse* applies not only to poetry but to the sung portion of a song, that *ballad* describes both narrative poems and songs that tell stories, and that a *refrain* is a repeated line in either a poem or a song. Poetry is never far from voice.

For those who have not read much poetry, **rhyme** may seem to be the primary way of linking words by sound. This is natural enough since we have heard rhyme used in jingles, nursery rhymes, and simple ballads. Ending two or more lines with matching sounds is relatively easy to do. But when rhyme is too regular it becomes obtrusive. It can easily take over, sounding like a monotonous drum beat dominating more subtle aspects of a poem. Because of this, those poets who do use rhyme almost always adopt various ways of muting it, techniques that will be described in Chapter 5.

In addition to rhyme there are two other ways of linking words by sound: by matching the initial letter ("*green* as *grass*") or by selecting words in which internal syllables echo each other ("*trees* and *leaves*"). The paired words, of course, must appear close enough to each other so that the reader can hear the linkage.

"Fern Hill" by DylanThomas is a good example of an unrhymed poem that nonetheless ripples with sound linkages. The poet is describing with dreamlike phrasing his memories of his childhood on a beautiful farm in Wales. Here are three of the 54 lines. I have circled several of the linkages in sound.

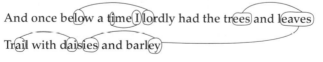

And once below a time I lordly had the trees and leaves

Trail with daisies and barley

Down the rivers of the windfall light.

The poem is printed in its entirety on page 21. You may wish to turn to it now and discover for yourself how intricate sound linkages can be, even in poetry that is not rhymed.

Prose can also appeal to the ear. We hear the effect of sound occasionally in oratory and sermons where repetition of initial sounds and repeated phrases create effects similar to those in the sample from "Fern Hill." Significant pauses sometimes provide an effect resembling that of spacing in a printed poem. But these techniques are rare in prose. The conscious, regular use of the sound of language is a characteristic that is far more common in verse.

Poetic Rhythms

Rhythm in language is like the beat in music. It can be as pronounced as the drum in a martial band or as subtle as a string quartet.

Because words—especially in English—are made up of **stressed** and unstressed syllables, it is a fairly simple matter to create regular patterns of these stresses. Some of those systems have become regularized as metrical schemes. Here are two lines taken from Richard Wilbur's "The Pardon":

[handwritten: Ta-tum]

[handwritten: U – unstressed I – stressed]

U I U I U I U I U I
In my kind world the dead were out of range

U I U I U I U I U I
And I could not forgive the sad or strange

There are five stressed syllables (I) in each line and five unstressed (U). If you read those lines in a normal manner, you will hardly notice the stress, so for purposes of analysis, you may wish to read them aloud with exaggerated stress.

If we group them in pairs of unstressed and stressed syllables, the rhythm sounds like ta-*TUM*, ta-*TUM*, ta-*TUM*. Traditional patterns like these are called **meter**, and I will return to metrics in Chapter 6. Although these particular lines are unusual in their regularity, I use them here simply as an example of how language can be infused with a regular rhythmical system without being made to sound artificial.

Although metrics dominated British and American poetry for some five hundred years, looser systems referred to as **free verse** have dominated the genre since the 1930s. The phrase *free verse* did not come into general use until after 1900, but nonmetrical rhythms have been used for centuries. Samples of what we now call free verse can be found as far back as the Song of Songs, one of the books of the Old Testament.

Starting in the 1980s, there has been a renewed interest in metrical schemes. This revival of metrics is generally referred to as the **new formalism**. Poets disagree, often vehemently, on whether or not this is a good development, but behind the debate is the fact that both free and metered verse are ways of infusing language with rhythms not generally found in prose. Only by trying both approaches can you determine which approach you find the most rewarding.

Nonmetrical rhythms can be created in many ways. Some poets develop a recurring pattern based on the number of syllables in each line. The **haiku** is about the shortest example of this, with five syllables in the first line, seven in the second, and five in the third. Thomas' "Fern Hill" is a much more complex example of **syllabics**, and I will return to both it and the haiku in Chapter 6.

Other poets arrange long and short lines on the page in such a way as to highlight certain phrases or even trip the reader. The poems by Denise Levertov (page 27) and E. E. Cummings (page 30) in Chapter 2 are good examples. I will be analyzing these techniques in greater detail in Chapter 8, "Free-Verse Patterns." I mention them here simply as an overview of the range of rhythmical techniques available to the poet.

Density

The fifth and final characteristic is **density**. Fiction is loose and wordy by comparison with poetry. One reason we read poetry more slowly and often repeatedly is that it usually implies much more than the immediate, surface meaning. Both the statement and the emotions are frequently layered with **overtones**.

The resistance some feel to reading a new poem comes from the fact that poetry often takes more effort to appreciate than an article or even a short story. Reading poetry takes practice, just as coming to appreciate classical music does. But there is a special reward in coming to know a work that gives pleasure from repeated reading. A poem of substance is something one can return to many times.

When we turn to writing poetry, we may have to spend hours, often spaced over several days, going over draft after draft to achieve this density. The process may seem slow, but the reward comes when we have the feeling that we have revealed more in a few lines than a prose writer could have developed in pages.

The fact that poems are concentrated does not mean they necessarily have to be short. Long **epic** poems like the *Iliad* and *Beowulf* deal with mythic and historical events that unify a culture. In our own age, epic tales are more frequently presented in the form of novels or films. Still, poets like Robinson Jeffers and Vikram Seth have written with the same goals. George Keithley's *The Donner Party,* a book-length poetic retelling of a doomed group of American pioneers, became a bestseller. But in spite of their length, these works still have greater density than prose. One cannot read them at the same rapid pace as one does a novel.

Book-length poems are rare these days. Contemporary poets have turned increasingly to their own experiences and feelings. Even when they are exploring broad aspects of the human condition, they tend to draw on their own lives, implying the general through material that is personal and specific.

One way poetry achieves density is through the use of words and phrases that are evocative. All words have **denotative** meanings—their literal definition; but most have **connotative** meanings as well—their associations.

Waking, for example, denotes literally the end of sleep, but it can also imply (or connote) awareness, as in "I suddenly woke to the idea that. . . . " *Sleep* has, in addition to its literal meaning, the connotations of death. So when Theodore Roethke begins "The Waking" (page 29) with the statement, "I wake to sleep," we recognize, at least on second reading, that he is describing how he plunges abruptly into life's experiences while knowing full well that he is mortal and will ultimately die. Notice, however, that it took me 19 words to explain rather clumsily in prose what he communicates in four.

Density like this is often achieved through comparisons known as **similes** and **metaphors**, and through **symbols**—all of which will be discussed in Chapter 4. What is important here is the fact that all these devices are not mere decoration; they are ways of making language suggest far more than its literal meaning.

When we read a poem, we necessarily slow down. We do this partly because of the density. We're looking for all those implications and overtones that often don't exist in prose. We are also responding to the sound of language. Even if we are reading silently, we tend to hear the lines as if they were being read aloud. There's no "speed reading" with poetry.

Evaluating a poem is even more deliberate than reading. Anyone can say, "I like it" or "I don't like it," but those judgments tend to be as subjective as one's preference for a particular ice cream. A good critic doesn't treat a poem like a dessert. Poets (and serious readers) examine what works and what doesn't. To do this, we have to take a close look at all five of poetry's characteristics: the use of the line, the sound of language, the rhythms, the images, and the degree of density.

When you start writing poetry, the most fertile sources to consider will be your own experiences and your feelings about those experiences. What is important to you can be shared with others if you are truly honest. But poetry isn't simply a collection of feelings spilled out on the page like journal entries. Useful as journals are, their entries are no more than snapshots that some artists take to recall specific scenes. A poem, like a painting, is an artistic construction. No matter how personal the subject matter may be, a poem is a verbal and auditory art that makes special use of the line, vivid images, the sound and rhythms of language, and compression of statement known as density. These are not only the recurring characteristics of poetry, they are the special assets of the genre that poets keep working to develop. They form the core of the chapters that follow.

Simple versus Sophisticated Poetry

What is a *good* poem? This question invites a second: Good for what? If a poem is intended for a mass market—as greeting cards are—it should have a positive message and be phrased in unvaried metrical lines with a regular rhyme scheme. Both the sentiments and phrasing should be familiar, not fresh or startling. To be "good," a mass-market poem should soothe, not probe.

Poems that are **literary**, however, are intended for readers who are looking for an entirely different experience. They want poetry that opens up and explores different aspects of the human experience. They enjoy word-play and subtle use of sound and rhythm. They are willing to deal with dis-turbing insights. They expect the language to be fresh and don't mind if it is sometimes challenging. Some like poems that emphasize language itself, playing with words in complicated ways; others prefer work that focuses on what it is to be a human being.

There are problems, however, with calling this kind of poem *literary*. For one thing, the term seems a bit pretentious when applied to contemporary work. Besides, we then face the problem of defining *literary*. Our problems are compounded when we call it "good" poetry. This seems like a value judgment and implies that popular, mass-market verse is "bad." It is as sub-jective as calling classical music "good" and popular music "bad." There is no quicker way to plunge a group of two or more into an afternoon of fruit-less bickering.

The best solution is to borrow two terms from the language of science. To a biologist, simple forms of life are *simple* and complex forms are *sophist-icated*. Thus, the bird is no better in any objective sense than the jellyfish, but it is far more sophisticated in that its potential as a living creature is greater. The organism is more complex.

In writing—as in nature—**simple** and **sophisticated** are not absolutes. They represent a scale with an infinite number of points. The clever comic verse of poets like Ogden Nash and Dorothy Parker are certainly more sophisticated than most nursery rhymes but less sophisticated than the poems of, say, Dylan Thomas. The works of an individual poet will also vary. The fact that someone is able to write highly sophisticated work that is dense in meaning and complex in treatment does not mean that he or she can't also write comic verse or light satiric pieces as well.

Should all poetry be sophisticated? Of course not. We still enjoy 14th- and 15th-century Scottish **ballads**, metrical tales of adventure and passion; and millions have been delighted with more recent ballads by poets like Rudyard Kipling and Robert Service. Today we have the highly popular work of Rod McKuen, and the verses of Hallmark cards have reached more readers than T. S. Eliot and Robert Frost combined. And we all enjoy **occasional verse**—poems written for special occasions such as weddings or birthdays. Writing popular but essentially forgettable verse like that is an honest craft that requires practice. There are "how-to" books that help those who want to succeed at it, but this textbook is not one of them.

Sophisticated writing—poetry as well as fiction and drama—is the subject of this text. Such work offers fresh insights, new ways of looking at our lives. But it is not necessarily cluttered or obscure. Sometimes a three-line haiku manages to convey more than a long and intricate work. Complexity of meaning is not always achieved by using unfamiliar words, obscure literary references, or complex metrical schemes.

Verse, incidentally, is a broad term that includes simple work intended for mass readership as well as more sophisticated work. Although *verse* is often used as a synonym for **poetry**, many prefer to reserve the word *poetry* for sophisticated verse.

Joyce Kilmer's "Trees" has been used many times in battles over what is and what is not "good" poetry. Let's stay clear of that futile debate and instead take a cool, objective look at what makes it an excellent example of highly popular simple verse. Here are the first three of its six stanzas.

> I think I shall never see
> A poem lovely as a tree.
>
> A tree whose hungry mouth is pressed
> Against the earth's sweet flowing breast;
>
> A tree that looks at God all day
> And lifts her leafy arms to pray; . . .

What can we say objectively about these six lines? First, they clearly are not prose. They are written as verse. The length of the lines is an immediate giveaway: the pattern has been set by the writer. Further, we can hear some kind of regular rhythm simply by reading it aloud. And the intentional use of sound is unmistakable: the lines are grouped in pairs that end with the same sounds to form rhyming **couplets**. Further, because trees don't literally have hungry mouths, we must conclude that a **metaphor** is being used. That's four of the five characteristics we associate with verse.

We can also identify the work as a sample of relatively simple verse. As with nursery rhymes, there is great regularity to the rhythm and to the rhyme. Without knowing anything about the meter, one can detect four distinct beats to each line, and every rhyme is an exact matching of sound landing on a stressed syllable. This regularity creates a singsong effect. Like the beat in a marching band, it dominates.

Conspicuously missing, however, is density. There is nothing new or insightful about the assertion that trees are beautiful. The poet is repeating a commonly held view, a **truism**. Seeing the tree as a praying figure is somewhat **hackneyed**. We can't say that the poem is "bad," since it has given pleasure to millions of readers. But we can say that both the poetic techniques and the assertion it makes are on a simple level.

By way of contrast, here in its entirety is a two-line poem by Ezra Pound:

In a Station of the Metro

The apparition of these faces in the crowd;
Petals on a wet, black bough.

If this were printed in a solid line like prose, we would probably assume that it was merely a fragment—perhaps from a journal—and skip over it quickly. But because it is presented with a title and in two lines, we are assured at the outset that this is a poem and that it is intended to be read with some care. As with "Trees," the very shape of the work on the page has influenced the way we will read it.

How seriously should we take it? After a single reading it is clear that this is not a comic jingle, nor is it a conventional statement about the beauty of nature. No truism, it is a fresh and vivid picture. The wording is intriguing: how can a crowd in the Paris subway (or any subway) be seen like an "apparition," and in what way might the faces resemble "petals on a wet, black bough"?

Let's take a close look. What are the overtones that come to mind? An "apparition" is a sudden, ghostlike appearance, dark and perhaps ominous. As for those petals, they have been torn loose in a rainstorm (the bough is wet) and plastered on a "black bough." It's a dark picture. We like to think of commuters in the subway as purposely traveling by their own choice, in control of their lives; but what choice do petals have when blown loose in a storm and plastered on a wet bough? None.

It would be a mistake to read more into the poem than this. The mood is dark and the suggestion about the lives of commuters is bleak. Perhaps there are other occasions in which we are victims of forces beyond our control, but the poem doesn't say so. It is not making any grand statement about our lives. It is a quick glimpse in which our notion of what it is to be a commuter is nudged. If, after studying the poem, you find yourself waiting silently in a crowd, you may well view the scene in a different, more vivid way than you would have otherwise. Rather than being soothed with a truism, your outlook has been enhanced.

There is no rhyme in this poem, but like the lines from "Fern Hill" quoted earlier, it has a number of linkages in sound. "Crowd" and "bough" echo the same sound in what is known as a **slant rhyme**. The second line has two linked pairs: the *e* sound in "petals and "wet" and that heavy *b* in "black" and "bough." Unlike most prose passages, these lines are linked together not only with meaning but with sound.

The essential difference between this poem and "Trees" is that Kilmer makes a conventional or commonplace assertion about trees in general, while Pound gives us a unique insight drawn from a very specific scene. In addition, the two poems represent a difference in technique that often distinguishes simple from sophisticated work: Kilmer employs rigid metrical and rhyme schemes, while Pound mutes both the rhymes and the sound linkages so that they do not become obtrusive. As we will see, there is a tendency in sophisticated poetry to mute the impact of both meter and rhyme even when the work is regularly rhymed and metered. "Trees," like much mass-market verse, actually stresses them.

Simple verse has various functions. In the case of **ballads**, it entertains by presenting a simple story, often a lament, in a rhythmical manner. Ballads can be and frequently are put to music. Greeting-card verse soothes by rephrasing conventional beliefs and sentiments. **Occasional verse** can enliven or memorialize special occasions such as weddings or birthdays.

Sophisticated poetry, on the other hand, provides more lasting rewards: it gives us pleasure through fresh insights, genuine feelings, and the subtle use of form. It may startle us into seeing the world and ourselves in a different light. When it speaks to us, we don't throw it away after the first reading. We savor it.

Conventions versus Individuality

Are there poetic rules? No. But that doesn't mean that anything goes. There are **conventions** that poets make use of in an infinite number of ways.

An artistic convention is any pattern or device that is used in a large number of works. As we have seen, the poet's control over line length is one of the conventions that differentiates poetry from prose. Beginning each line with a capital letter is a convention that some poets use and others do not. Heightened use of images to create metaphors and symbols is another.

The use of **meter**—patterns of stressed and unstressed syllables, discussed in Chapter 6—is a more precise convention. It is highly regarded by some poets like Robert Frost and Richard Wilbur. Another convention unique to poetry is rhythmical patterns created by line length and vertical spacing. This device is one of the characteristics of **free verse**. It is preferred by poets like E. E. Cummings and Denise Levertov. **Rhyme** is also a convention enjoyed by some and not by others. Traditional forms like the **sonnet, haiku,** and **villanelle**—described later—are all conventions worth considering.

Every art form has its conventions. Those familiar with popular music, for example, distinguish blues from bluegrass and rock from jazz. Artists distinguish realists from impressionists, surrealists, and minimalists. Within each category there are usually subdivisions. Familiarity with basic terms makes conversation about music or art more precise and enjoyable even for the casual listener. Those who compose music or who paint use these conventions to shape their own work and to develop their own individuality.

Without being familiar with poetic conventions, the would-be poet runs the risk of merely writing prose in short lines. Such work may be sincere, but so can the efforts of a violinist who refuses to practice. On the other hand, allowing poetic conventions to stifle individuality and genuine feeling can make the work sterile. As we have seen, heavy-handed use of rhythm and a blatant rhyme scheme help to make Joyce Kilmer's "Trees" poetically simple. It is *conventional* in the precise sense that it adheres to a number of conventions in a rigid and wooden manner.

As with any creative art, the first step is to explore and then practice the conventions of the genre. There is no freedom in ignorance. Only if you have actually written a sonnet or a typographically innovative free-verse poem are you really free to decide which approach is best for you.

Practicing poets base their decisions partly on personal preference and partly on the needs of a particular poem. They can do this only when they are at home with various techniques.

The following ten chapters deal with the conventions of the craft and, equally important, ways of muting those conventions so that they stay in the background. These chapters will also help you to read poetry with greater insight. This is essential if you are to learn directly from the limitless body of published poetry.

As you study the various options open to you and apply them to your own creative work, you will find yourself developing your own individual **voice** as a poet. This will reflect what is unique in you—your specific feelings and insights.

2

PLUNGING IN:

Reading as the First Step

*Why poets read poetry. Why it is essential that you study these poems
before reading the following chapters. Active versus passive reading. How
to increase your pleasure. The poems themselves.*

Musicians listen to music. Scriptwriters study films. Novelists read fiction.
Poets read poetry. It's as simple as that. One problem is that many of those
who would like to write poetry have listened to more music and seen more
films than they have read or listened to poems.

The reason poets read, aside from the pleasure, is that like any art form
poetry cannot be created by following a series of rules or instructions.
Creativity is not a science or a computer program. The poet relies on having
in memory a backlog of many works. These provide a sense of what is possible in the genre.

For some, there will be a real temptation to skip over this chapter and get
to "the real stuff." Wrong! *This* is the real stuff, these poems. The chapters
that follow will suggest ways to read the real stuff with greater insight and
how to draw on published work when creating your own. If you skip over
this chapter, you will be like an absentminded gardener who waters and fer-
tilizes the plot but has forgotten to plant the seed. This book will speed your
development, but poetry itself is the essential first step.

Active versus Passive Reading

Much of our daily reading is passive. Our eyes pass over the newspaper like
a grazing cow, pausing and moving on without much thought. During the
day words wash over us in the form of headlines, street signs, and instructions. Even in the evening when we have a chance to read what we want, we
often turn to a magazine article, story, or novel as entertainment.

This was true even before television, but the tube has influenced us all. TV dramas emphasize the visual over the verbal, and their scene changes are rapid. Like all dramas, they eliminate the chance to review poignant segments. Many lack subtlety or insight.

Poetry requires an entirely different approach. Since it tends to be dense in meaning and implication, a single casual reading often seems confusing. The subtleties of word choice, rhythms, and the sound of language slip by unnoticed. It's easy to blame the poem when the fault is more often the way one reads. You can't enjoy the scenery if you're driving at top speed.

Active or deliberate reading is important if we are going to enjoy a poem. And it is essential if we plan to write poetry. Every poem can teach us something, but only if we take the time to study it. Here are some tips on how to shift from passive to active reading:

- Slow down. The poem will remain a blur if you read it as fast as a newspaper article or a short story.
- Give it multiple readings. Three at least: one aloud for the sound and rhythm, one deliberately line by line for analysis, and a third time at a normal pace again.
- Go back to puzzling lines or phrases. Use your dictionary when needed. (I prefer an electronic dictionary for speed and helpful word origins.)
- Use a pencil. If the book is your own, underline what you like and circle what puzzles you. If you have looked up a new word, pencil in a brief definition. If you are using a borrowed copy, consider photocopying the pages.

It will take you about an hour to read the poems in this chapter. I suggest that you break your time into two half-hour sessions. Taking legible notes will help you in two ways: they will help you to review the poem later, and in addition the act of writing down your impressions and questions will ensure that your reading is active, not passive.

Almost every poem in this chapter will be discussed in some way in the chapters that follow. You may want to review the poem when it is referred to in the analytical chapters (page references will always be given), but even if you don't in every case, you will have the tremendous advantage of recalling at least in general terms the poem as a whole.

I have provided brief comments or questions at the end of each poem to help you study the work effectively. They are intended only to get you thinking about the poem analytically. Remember, though, that analysis is only a part of the reading process. After you have examined the characteristics of the poem, give it one more reading just for the pleasure of it. If you are by yourself, try reading it aloud. Another approach is to go over this chapter with one or two friends, taking turns reading aloud and discussing each poem in turn.

If you have not enjoyed much poetry in the past, relax. There is something here for everyone—some humor, some **pathos**, and plenty of insight to make you think about your own life and experience. Some are by men and about an equal number by women. The poems include a wide range of types, both metered and free, and the poets represent a variety of ethnic and racial backgrounds. Of course there will be poems you don't like. Like people you meet at a party, they won't all be your type. But remember this: a poet can learn from every conscientiously composed work.

Read, enjoy, and take notes. When we return to these poems in the chapters that follow, they will be familiar. That familiarity will help you as you begin to compose your own work.

Design

ROBERT FROST

I found a dimpled spider, fat and white,   a
On a white heal-all, holding up a moth   b
Like a white piece of rigid satin cloth—   b
Assorted characters of death and blight   a
Mixed ready to begin the morning right,   a   5
Like the ingredients of a witches' broth—   b
A snow-drop spider, a flower like froth,   b
And dead wings carried like a paper kite.   a

What had that flower to do with being white,   a
The wayside blue and innocent heal-all?   c   10
What brought the kindred spider to that height,   a
Then steered the white moth thither in the night?   a
What but design of darkness to appall?—   c
If design govern in a thing so small.   c

Because this is a **sonnet**, it has a regular rhyme scheme. Why is this less obtrusive than the rhyme in "Trees" (page 9)? How is the poet using "appall" in the next to last line?

As the Cold Deepens

ELIZABETH W. HOLDEN

She is eighty-six
and her friends are dying.
"They're dropping like flies," she grumbles
and I see black winged bodies crumbling
on window sills when we open our summer house.   5

Flies all over!
Brushing them onto the floor, sweeping
them up, we drop black mounds into the bag.
"What a mess!" my mother declares.

I think of flies   10
how they live in a weightless armor
tough, resistant like a finger nail.

My mother is almost weightless now,
her flesh shrinks back toward bone.
Braced in her metal walker   15
she haunts the halls, prowls
the margin of her day, indomitable
erect in this support
that fuses steel with self.

At noon the flies mass on the sills   20
flying up and down the pane
pressing for sun.
What buzzing agitates the air
as the swarm becomes a single drive
a scramble up, a dizzy spin.   25

It is hard to hold the light
which grows weaker every day.
The temperature is falling
The glass is cold.

In how many different ways is the speaker's mother compared with flies? What
is being suggested by the two references to temperature at the end of the poem?

Domestic Animals

LINDA PASTAN

The animals in this house
have dream claws and teeth
and shadow the rooms
at night, their furled tails dangerous.
In the morning, all sweet slobber   5
the dog may yawn, the cat
make cat sounds deep
in its furred throat.
And who would guess

how they wait for dark   10
when into the green
jungle of our sleep
they insinuate
themselves, releasing
their terrible hunger.   15

This poem appears to be about animals, but what is implied about us humans by the phrase "the green / jungle of our sleep"?

The Gift

CAROLE OLES

Thinking she was the gift
they began to package it early.
They waxed its smile
they lowered its eyes
they tuned its ears to the telephone   5
they curled its hair
they straightened its teeth
they taught it to bury its wishbone
they poured honey down its throat
they made it say yes yes and yes   10
they sat on its thumbs.

That box has my name on it,
said the man. *It's for me.*
And they were not surprised.
While they blew kisses and winked   15
he took it home. He put it on a table
where his friends could examine it
saying *dance* saying *faster.*
He plunged its tunnels
he burned his name deeper.   20
Later he put it on a platform
under the lights
saying *push* saying *harder*
saying *just what I wanted*
you've given me a son.   25

Describe the tone of this poem. (Review **tone** in the Glossary/Index.) What is the poet implying when she uses "it" for the subject?

Anger Sweetened

MOLLY PEACOCK

What we don't forget is what we don't say.
I mourn the leaps of anger covered
by quizzical looks, grasshoppers covered
by coagulating chocolate. Each word,
like a leggy thing that would have sprung away,   5
we caught and candified so it would stay
spindly and alarmed, poised in our presence,
dead, but in the shape of its old essence.
We must eat them now. We must eat the words
we should have let go but preserved, thinking   10
to hide them. They were as small as insects blinking
in our hands, but now they are stiff and shirred
with sweet to twice their size, so what we gagged
will gag us now that we are so enraged.

"What we don't say" is vividly pictured in a series of **metaphors**. Circle them. Now take a close look at the last two lines: how is the word "gag" used in two different ways?

Sonnet 29

WILLIAM SHAKESPEARE

When in disgrace with fortune and men's eyes,
I all alone beweep my outcast state,
And trouble deaf heaven with my bootless⁰ cries,
And look upon my self and curse my fate,
Wishing me like to one more rich in hope,   5
Featured like him, like him with friends possessed,
Desiring this man's art, and that man's scope,
With what I most enjoy contented least,
Yet in these thoughts my self almost despising,
Haply I think on thee, and then my state,   10
Like to the lark at break of day arising
From sullen earth, sings hymns at heaven's gate,
　　For thy sweet love remembered such wealth brings,
　　That then I scorn to change my state with kings.

⁰ *bootless*: useless

Like many **sonnets**, the **tone** shifts after the first eight lines, providing a vivid contrast with that of the last six. Study the **rhyme** scheme here and compare it with that in "Anger Sweetened" (page 18), a contemporary sonnet.

After Spring

CHORA

After spring sunset 5
Mist rises from the river 7
Spreading like a flood 5

Haiku

ETHERIDGE KNIGHT

1

Eastern guard tower
glints in sunset; convicts rest
like lizards on rocks.

4

To write a blues song
is to regiment riots
and pluck gems from graves.

5

A bare pecan tree
slips a pencil shadow down
a moonlit snow slope.

Haikus in English traditionally have five syllables in the first and third lines and seven in the middle line. They also tend to draw on some aspect of nature and state or imply a particular season. Which of these conform to all three **conventions**? Look closely.

What the Mirror Said

LUCILLE CLIFTON

listen,
you a wonder,
you a city
of a woman.
you got a geography   5
of your own.
listen,
somebody need a map
to understand you.
somebody need directions   10
to move around you.
listen,
woman,
you not a noplace
anonymous   15
girl;
mister with his hands on you
he got his hands on
some
damn   20
body!

The **tone** of this poem echoes informal speech. Pick out phrases that are
common in speech but avoided in formal writing. Although the poem
appears to be formless on first reading, it actually has a **refrain** that gives it
structure. What is it?

River Sound Remembered

W. S. MERWIN

That day the huge water drowned all voices until
It seemed a kind of silence unbroken
By anything: A time unto itself and still;

So that when I turned away from its roaring, down
The path over the gully, and there were   5
Dogs barking as always at the edge of town,

Car horns and the cries of children coming
As though for the first time through the fading light
Of the winter dusk, my ears still sang

Like shells with the swinging current, and   10
Its flood echoing in me held for long
About me the same silence, by whose sound

I could hear only the quiet under the day
With the land noises floating there far-off and still;
So that even in my mind now turning away   15

From having listened absently but for so long
It will be the seethe and drag of the river
That I will hear longer than any mortal song.

There is a fundamental contrast in this poem: the sound of the river and what Merwin describes in the last line as "any mortal song." What do these represent? What is the **rhyme** scheme? Which stanzas do not have true rhymes?

Fern Hill

DYLAN THOMAS

Now as I was young and easy under the apple boughs
About the lilting house and happy as the grass was green,
       The night above the dingle starry,
         Time let me hail and climb
      Golden in the heydays of his eyes,   5
And honoured among wagons I was prince of the apple towns
And once below a time I lordly had the trees and leaves
       Trail with daisies and barley
      Down the rivers of the windfall light.

And as I was green and carefree, famous among the barns   10
About the happy yard and singing as the farm was home,
       In the sun that is young once only,
        Time let me play and be
      Golden in the mercy of his means,
And green and golden I was huntsman and herdsman, the calves   15
Sang to my horn, the foxes on the hills barked clear and cold,
        And the sabbath rang slowly
      In the pebbles of the holy streams.

All the sun long it was running, it was lovely, the hay
Fields high as the house, the tunes from the chimneys, it was air   20
        And playing, lovely and watery
              And fire green as grass.
        And nightly under the simple stars
As I rode to sleep the owls were bearing the farm away,
All the moon long I heard, blessed among stables, the nightjars   25
        Flying with the ricks, and the horses
              Flashing into the dark.

And then to awake, and the farm, like a wanderer white
With the dew, come back, the cock on his shoulder: it was all
        Shining, it was Adam and maiden,   30
            The sky gathered again
        And the sun grew round that very day.
So it must have been after the birth of the simple light
In the first, spinning place, the spellbound horses walking warm
        Out of the whinnying green stable   35
            On to the fields of praise.

And honoured among foxes and pheasants by the gay house
Under the new made clouds and happy as the heart was long
        In the sun born over and over,
           I ran my heedless ways,   40
          My wishes raced through the house-high hay
And nothing I cared, at my sky blue trades, that time allows
In all his tuneful turning so few and such morning songs
        Before the children green and golden
          Follow him out of grace,   45

Nothing I cared, in the lamb white days, that time would take me
Up to the swallow thronged loft by the shadow of my hand,
        In the moon that is always rising,
          Nor that riding to sleep
        I should hear him fly with the high fields   50
And wake to the farm forever fled from the childless land.
Oh as I was young and easy in the mercy of his means,
        Time held me green and dying
      Though I sang in my chains like the sea.

We have already examined how Thomas links words by sound (page 4). Pick out more examples in every **stanza**. Much of this poem is a dreamlike memory of an ideal childhood, but the **tone** shifts dramatically in the last four lines. What does he mean by "Time held me green and dying"? *Hint:* Notice how he uses the word "green" in each of the six **stanzas**.

Always the One Who Loves His Father Most

CLEMENT LONG

Always the one who loves his father most,
the one the father loves the most in turn,
will fight against his father as he must.
Neither knows what he will come to learn.

The one the father loves the most in turn
tells the father no and no and no,
but neither knows what he will come to learn
nor cares a lot what that could be, and so

tells his father no and no and no,
is ignorant of what the years will teach
nor cares a lot what that could be, and so
unties the knot that matters most, while each

is ignorant of what the years will teach,
they'll learn how pride—if each lives out his years—
unties the knot that matters most, while each
will feel a sadness, feel the midnight fears.

They'll learn how pride—if each lives out his years—
will lose the aging other as a friend,
will feel a sadness, feel the midnight fears.
The child and then the father, world without end,

will lose the aging other as a friend.
And then the child of that one, too, will grow—
the child and then the father, world without end—
in turn to fight his father, *comme il faut,*

will fight against his father, as he must,
always, the one who loves his father most.

This is a **pantoum**, a verse form explained in detail in Chapter 7. For now, focus on the way lines 2 and 4 in each **stanza** are repeated as lines 1 and 3 in the next stanza. Can you see a relationship between this series of repetitions and the **theme** of the poem?

The Narrow Mind

DICK ALLEN

It lives in a small backwater, and it doesn't know
Much more than dragonflies and darning needles.
The plash and galump of a frog. What it wonders
Is how do I get through another day.
It feeds on what's been whispered to it   5
In secret meetings at dusk, and what's proclaimed
By flights of crows. It likes
Lying on a sunlit log or wading
To shore with its fellows—where it seeks
Places it hasn't any trouble squeezing into.   10
What it demands, the few times it demands,
Is never to be shaken. But if that happens,
It wants the right to reassert itself.
And will die for that right. You can find it
By heading west at sunset, its spot   15
Marked by bubbles rising to the surface.
The brighter you are, the more likely it will greet you
With suspicion, so to get close to it
You must tell it stories that it wants to hear.
If you would expand it, if you would lift it out,   20
First consider its age and if it's strong enough
To live anywhere else. Elsewise.
You either must row around it or overwhelm it
With goodness and mercy and bribes.

Poets generally title their poems with an **image**—something that can be seen
or perceived with one of the other senses. Robert Frost's "Design" (page 15)
is an exception, and so is this poem. In each case, though, the theme of the
poem is implied through visual details. To appreciate "The Narrow Mind"
fully, describe in a paragraph of prose an imaginary person who illustrates
Allen's description.

We Real Cool

GWENDOLYN BROOKS

The Pool Players.
Seven at the Golden Shovel.
We real cool. We
Left school. We

Lurk late. We
Strike straight. We

Sing sin. We
Thin gin. We

Jazz June. We
Die soon.

Like Dick Allen's "The Narrow Mind" (page 24), this is a poem that takes a strong stand. It is an argument in verse. The phrasing is a precursor of rap music. What are the advantages of using this approach rather than more conventional phrasing?

This Winter Day

MAYA ANGELOU

The kitchen in its readiness
white green and orange things
leak their blood selves in the soup.

Ritual sacrifice that snaps
an odor at my nose and starts   5
my tongue to march
slipping in the liquid of its drip.

The day, silver striped
in rain, is balked against
my window and the soup.   10

This poem draws on several of the five senses. Identify them. Notice also that the theme suggests a contrast. What is being contrasted with what?

The Dolphin

MAURYA SIMON

Just off the Santa Monica Pier,
a dolphin swam in tight circles
for hours, having lost its power
to echolocate a wiser course.

No matter that photographers,   5
marine biologists, and reporters

with their mini-cams and prayers
tried to will it from its torment:

the dolphin churned and turned
with dizzy ardor, as if devotion   10
to repetition could set it straight,
could help it navigate to freedom.

Was it toxins spewed in the ocean
that sent its brain to spinning,
or do dolphins, just like humans,   15
go off the deep end, either with

or without reason? Exhausted,
finally, the dolphin drowned.
On t.v. it looked as still as time.
But it keeps circling in my mind.   20

"The Dolphin" illustrates how an actual news event can serve as the source of a poem. The dolphin, however, is not the true concern of the poem; it is us. How does the phrase "like humans" explain why, in the last stanza, the narrator can't let go of the scene?

The Black Snake

MARY OLIVER

When the black snake
flashed onto the morning road,
and the truck could not swerve—
death, that is how it happens.

Now he lies looped and useless   5
as an old bicycle tire.
I stop the car
and carry him into the bushes.

He is as cool and gleaming
as a braided whip, he is as beautiful and quiet   10
as a dead brother.
I leave him under the leaves

and drive on, thinking
about *death:* its suddenness,
its terrible weight,   15
its certain coming. Yet under

reason burns a brighter fire, which the bones
have always preferred.
It is the story of endless good fortune.
It says to oblivion: not me!   20

It is the light at the center of every cell.
It is what sent the snake coiling and flowing forward
happily all spring through the green leaves before
he came to the road.

Like "The Dolphin," this poem appears to be based on a true event. It differs, however, in that more analysis is included. Notice where the poem departs from the event and then offers two different responses to the dead snake.

The Bay at West Falmouth

BARBARA HOWES

Serenity of mind poises
Like a gull swinging in air,
At ease, sculptured, held there
For a moment so long-drawn-out all time pauses.

The heart's serenity is like the gold   5
Geometry of sunlight: motion shafting
Down through green dimensions, rung below rung
Of incandescence, out of which grace unfolds.

Watching that wind schooling the bay, the helter-skelter
Of trees juggling air, waves signalling the sun   10
To signal light, brings peace; as our being open
To love does, near this serenity of water.

Note that this poem opens and closes with the **abstract** word "serenity." Find and circle the concrete nouns that are used to help us see and feel this serenity.

Merritt Parkway

DENISE LEVERTOV

       As if it were
forever that they move, that we
      keep moving—
            Under a wan sky where
        as the lights went on a star   5
             pierced the haze & now
       follows steadily
              a constant
     above our six lanes
     the dreamlike continuum . . .   10

And the people—ourselves!
    the humans from inside the
    cars, apparent
    only at gasoline stops
                  unsure,   15
      eyeing each other
           drink coffee hastily at the
        slot machines & hurry
   back to the cars
       vanish   20
       into them forever, to
       keep moving—

Houses now & then beyond the
sealed road, the trees / trees, bushes
passing by, passing   25
      the cars that
          keep moving ahead of
    us, past us, pressing behind us
              and
          over left, those that come   30
       toward us shining too brightly
moving relentlessly

      in six lanes, gliding
     north & south, speeding with
a slurred sound—   35

This is a **free-verse** poem that uses **line** length to suggest the motion of cars on a six-lane highway. Notice the repetition of the word "moving." **Sound** is also used for effect. To hear this, pick out and circle the repeated *s* sounds in the last five lines that highlight the final phrase, "slurred sound."

On a Maine Beach

ROBLEY WILSON

Look, in these pools, how rocks are like worn change
Keeping the ocean's mint-mark; barnacles
Miser on them; societies of snails
Hunch on their rims and think small thoughts whose strange
Salt logics rust like a mainspring, small dreams   5
Pinwheeling to a point and going dumb,
Small equations whose euphemistic sum
Stands for mortality. A thousand times
Tides swallow up such pools, shellfish and stone
Show green and yellow shade in groves of weed;   10
Rocks shrink, barnacles drink, snails think they bleed
In their trapped world. Here, when the sea is gone,
We find old coins glowing under the sky,
Barnacles counting them, snails spending slow
Round lifetimes half-awake. Beach rhythms flow   15
In circles. Perfections teach us to die.

Like Robert Frost's "Design" (page 15), this poem is rooted in a close examination of a specific scene from nature. Notice how references to money ("coins")
and time ("mainspring") expand the theme to comment on our mortality.

The Waking

THEODORE ROETHKE

I wake to sleep, and take my waking slow.
I feel my fate in what I cannot fear.
I learn by going where I have to go.

We think by feeling. What is there to know?
I hear my being dance from ear to ear.   5
I wake to sleep, and take my waking slow.

Of those so close beside me, which are you?
God bless the Ground! I shall walk softly there,
And learn by going where I have to go.

Light takes the Tree; but who can tell us how?   10
The lowly worm climbs up a winding stair;
I wake to sleep, and take my waking slow.

Great Nature has another thing to do
To you and me; so take the lively air,
And, lovely, learn by going where to go.   15

This shaking keeps me steady. I should know.
What falls away is always. And is near.
I wake to sleep, and take my waking slow.
I learn by going where I have to go.

Like Robley Wilson's "On a Maine Beach" (page 28), this poem deals with our mortality. But notice that neither poem relies on **abstract** words like "life" or "death." Roethke uses "wake" to suggest birth and "sleep" for death. They are easier to comprehend. What is implied with the repeated phrase "learn by going where I have to go"?

"Buffalo Bill's"

E. E. CUMMINGS — images

Buffalo Bill's
defunct
          who used to
          ride a watersmooth-silver
                              stallion   5

and break onetwothreefourfive pigeonsjustlikethat

Jesus

he was a handsome man
               and what i want to know is
how do you like your blueeyed boy   10
Mister Death

Here is an extreme version of typography similar to that in Denise Levertov's "Merritt Parkway" (page 27). What is being suggested by running words together in line 6? ("Pigeons" refers to clay pigeons used for target practice.)

Coast to Coast

PHILIP APPLEMAN

The bird that shook the earth at J.F.K.
goes blind to milkweed, riverbanks, the wrecks
of elm trees full of liquor and decay—
and jars the earth again at L.A.X.

Once, on two-lane roads, our crazy drives   5
across the country tallied every mile
in graves or gardens: glimpses in our lives
to make the busy continent worthwhile.

Friendly, then, the smell of woods and fields,
the flash of finches and the scud of crows,   10
the rub of asphalt underneath our wheels
as tangible as sand between the toes.

From orchards out to prairies, then to cactus,
the rock and mud and clay were in our bones:
as birches turned to oak, then eucalyptus,   15
we learned our lover's body stone by stone.

Now, going home we're blind again, seven
miles above the earth on chartered wings:
in a pressurized and air-conditioned heaven
the open road's a song nobody sings.   20

This poem is based on a contrast. His preference is unmistakable, but it is presented indirectly through the details he uses. If you circle the phrases that imply a strong preference for driving and a disdain for flying, you will see how opinions can be presented in poetry indirectly through images rather than stated analytically as they often are in essays.

Is It Well-Lighted, Papa?

JAMES BERTRAM

Is it well-lighted, Papa—this place
where you have gone to escape and erase
dreams gone dry and bare-teethed critics' remarks
that tormented you like the old man's sharks?
Do we dare term your suicide disgrace?   5

Clean, like your prose, the bell tolled and the chase
no longer, you knew, was "El Campion's" race.
A final shotgun sentence rings truly stark.
       Is it well-lighted, Papa?

Weak man or strong man? Why can't we embrace   10
the truth: a fawn with a grizzly bear face.
For despite your indelible machismo mark,
you always told us how you feared the dark.
       Is it well-lighted, Papa?

Notice how the question posed in the title is repeated as a **refrain** in each of the three stanzas. The poem is a **rondeau**, and the use of refrains is one of its elements. For further analysis of the form, see page 100. For now, however, focus on the way the refrain highlights the key question the way a repeated chorus does in some song lyrics. As for the subject, notice the many references to Ernest Hemingway and his work.

Morning Swim

MAXINE KUMIN

Into my empty head there come
a cotton beach, a dock wherefrom

I set out, oily and nude
through mist, in chilly solitude.

There was no line, no roof or floor   5
to tell the water from the air.

Night fog thick as terry cloth
closed me in its fuzzy growth.

I hung my bathrobe on two pegs.
I took the lake between my legs.   10

Invaded and invader, I
went overhand on that flat sky.

Fish twitched beneath me, quick and tame.
In their green zone they sang my name

and in the rhythm of the swim   15
I hummed a two-four-time slow hymn.

I hummed *Abide with Me.* The beat
rose in the fine thrash of my feet,

rose in the bubbles I put out
slantwise, trailing through my mouth.   20

My bones drank water; water fell
through all my doors. I was the well

that fed the lake that met my sea
in which I sang *Abide with Me.*

Rhyming couplets (see **Stanza**) are often avoided in serious verse because of the risk of creating a singsong effect. Notice how Kumin mutes the rhyme by having the sentences continue into the next line. Take a close look at "the beat" on line 17. How many different rhythms does that describe?

Practice

TIMOTHY STEELE

The basketball you walk around the court
Produces a hard, stinging, clean report.
You pause and crouch and, after feinting, swoop
Around a ghost defender to the hoop
And rise and lay the ball in off the board.   5
Solitude, plainly, is its own reward.

The game that you've conceived engrosses you.
The ball rolls off; you chase it down, renew
The dribble to the level of your waist.
Insuring that a sneaker's tightly laced,   10
You kneel—then, up again, weave easily
Through obstacles that you alone can see.

And so I drop the hands I'd just now cupped
To call you home. Why should I interrupt?
Can I be sure that dinner's ready yet?   15
A jumpshot settles, snapping, through the net;
The backboard's stanchion keeps the ball in play,
Returning it to you on the ricochet.

Writing a poem about sports is a daunting challenge. Popular **ballads** like "Casey at the Bat" are fun but not substantial. Steele's approach here is to avoid a game and focus on the motion of a single basketball player. His concern is to capture the grace of the action and the intensity of involvement. Notice that the poem is not presented through the eyes of the player. Why not?

Lizards and Snakes

ANTHONY HECHT

On the summer road that ran by our front porch
    Lizards and snakes came out to sun.
It was hot as a stove out there, enough to scorch
    A buzzard's foot. Still, it was fun
To lie in the dust and spy on them. Near but remote,   5
    They snoozed in the carriage ruts, a smile
In the set of the jaw, a fierce pulse in the throat
Working away like Jack Doyle's after he'd run the mile.

Aunt Martha had an unfair prejudice
    Against them (as well as being cold   10

Toward bats.) She was pretty inflexible in this,
Being a spinster and all, and old.
So we used to slip them into her knitting box.
    In the evening she'd bring in things to mend
And a nice surprise would slide out from under the socks.   15
It broadened her life, as Joe said. Joe was my friend.

But we never did it again after the day
    Of the big wind when you could hear the trees
Creak like rockingchairs. She was looking away
    Off, and kept saying, "Sweet Jesus, please   20
Don't let him hear me. He's as like as twins.
    He can crack us like lice with his fingernail.
I can see him plain as a pikestaff. Look how he grins
And swings the scaly horror of his folded tail."

This is a **narrative poem**. That is, it tells a story. It appears at first to be a simple, amusing tale, drawing on a childhood memory. But the light tone ends dramatically in the last stanza. What do the boys learn about Aunt Martha's beliefs and fears?

The Pardon

RICHARD WILBUR

My dog lay dead five days without a grave
In the thick of summer, hid in a clump of pine
And a jungle of grass and honeysuckle-vine.
I who had loved him while he kept alive

Went only close enough to where he was   5
To sniff the heavy honeysuckle-smell
Twined with another odour heavier still
And hear the flies' intolerable buzz.

Well, I was ten and very much afraid.
In my kind world the dead were out of range   10
And I could not forgive the sad or strange
In beast or man. My father took the spade

And buried him. Last night I saw the grass
Slowly divide (it was the same scene
But now it glowed a fierce and mortal green)   15
And saw the dog emerging. I confess

I felt afraid again, but still he came
In the carnal sun, clothed in a hymn of flies,
And death was breeding in his lively eyes.
I started in to cry and call his name,   20

Asking forgiveness of his tongueless head.
. . . I dreamt the past was never past redeeming:
But whether this was false or honest dreaming
I beg death's pardon now. And mourn the dead.

Like "Lizards and Snakes" (the preceding poem), this is a narrative poem
and appears to be taken from a childhood memory. But the dream described
in the fourth stanza presents more complex themes. Why does the narrator
feel guilty, and how does he or she seek redemption?

Those Winter Sundays

ROBERT HAYDEN

Sundays too my father got up early
and put his clothes on in the blueblack cold,
then with cracked hands that ached
from labor in the weekday weather made
banked fires blaze. No one ever thanked him.   5

I'd wake and hear the cold splintering, breaking.
When the rooms were warm, he'd call,
and slowly I would rise and dress,
fearing the chronic angers of that house,

Speaking indifferently to him,   10
who had driven out the cold
and polished my good shoes as well.
What did I know, what did I know
of love's austere and lonely offices?

This is a poem in tribute to the speaker's father, but notice how far it is from
greeting-card verse. Circle the realistic details that give this work the feel of
authentic memory. If you are not sure how he is using "austere and lonely
offices," look up "offices" in a good dictionary. It has interesting uses and
derivations.

Balances

NIKKI GIOVANNI

[handwritten: line margin is tipped]
[handwritten: →]

in life
one is always
balancing
[handwritten: whole]

like we juggle our mothers
against our fathers   5
[handwritten: young]

or one teacher
against another
(only to balance our grade average)
[handwritten: growing]

3 grains salt
to one ounce truth   10
[handwritten: concept of truth]

our sweet black essence
or the funky honkies down the street
[handwritten: race-balance]

and lately i've begun wondering
if you're trying to tell me something
[handwritten: what poem is really about]

we used to talk all night   15
and do things alone together

and i've begun

(as a reaction to a feeling)
to balance
the pleasure of loneliness   20
against the pain
of loving you
[handwritten: Scale is tipped / Having to balence]

Read this poem aloud, pausing at each double space. Notice that while Giovanni uses no punctuation, the spaces are used to cue the reader when to pause. The first half of the poem reads like an arbitrary list of examples illustrating the statement in the first three lines; but with "lately i've begun wondering" we learn the **occasion** (the specific cause) for the narrator's interest in balances.

Rhymes for Old Age

CHASE TWICHELL

The wind's untiring saxophone
keens at the glass.
The lamp sheds a monochrome

of stainless steel and linens,
the nurse in her snowy dress   5
firm in her regimens.

The form in the bed
is a soul diminished
to a fledgling, fed
on the tentative balm of spring,   10
sketch for an angel, half-finished,
shoulder blades the stubs of wings.

Darkened with glaucoma,
the room floats on the retina.
The long vowel of *coma*   15
broods in the breath, part vapor.
What has become of the penetralia?
Eau de cologne sanctifies the diaper.

Flood and drag, the undertow.
One slips into it undressed,   20
as into first love, the vertigo
that shrinks to a keepsake of passion.
Sky's amethyst
lies with a sponge in the basin.

In theme, this poem is similar to Elizabeth Holden's "As the Cold Deepens"
(page 15), but the condition of the old woman is worse and the **metaphors**
used are more demanding. Each **stanza** has a word you may want to look up
in a good dictionary not just for the meaning but for the **overtones** that are
suggested: in the first stanza, "keens"; in the second "fledgling"; in the third
"penetralia"; and in the last "vertigo." Ask yourself two questions: In what
ways is an old and dying woman like a fledgling? And how can descent into
death be like descent into "first love"?

Names of Horses

DONALD HALL

All winter your brute shoulders strained against collars, padding
and steerhide over the ash hames, to haul
sledges of cordwood for drying through spring and summer,
for the Glenwood stove next winter, and for the simmering range.

In April you pulled cartloads of manure to spread on the fields,   5
dark manure of Holsteins, and knobs of your own clustered with oats.

All summer you mowed the grass in meadow and hayfield, the mowing machine
    machine
clacking beside you, while the sun walked high in the morning;

and after noon's heat, you pulled a clawed rake through the same acres,
gathering stacks, and dragged the wagon from stack to stack,   10
and the built hayrack back, uphill to the chaffy barn,
three loads of hay a day, hanging wide from the hayrack.

Sundays you trotted the two miles to church with the light load
of a leather quartertop buggy, and grazed in the sound of hymns.
Generation on generation, your neck rubbed the window sill   15
of the stall, smoothing the wood as the sea smooths glass.

When you were old and lame, when your shoulders hurt bending to graze,
one October the man who fed you and kept you, and harnessed you every
    morning,
led you through corn stubble to sandy ground above Eagle Pond,
and dug a hole beside you where you stood shuddering in your skin,   20

and lay the shotgun's muzzle in the boneless hollow behind your ear,
and fired the slug into your brain, and felled you into your grave,
shoveling sand to cover you, setting goldenrod upright above you,
where by next summer a dent in the ground made your monument.

For a hundred and fifty years, in the pasture of dead horses,   25
roots of pine trees pushed through the pale curves of your ribs,
yellow blossoms flourished above you in autumn, and in winter
frost heaved your bones in the ground—old toilers, soil makers:

O Roger, Mackerel, Riley, Ned, Nellie, Chester, Lady Ghost.

The subject of this poem is clearly farm horses, but the **theme** is broader than that. Take a close look at the **tone** of this tribute and ask yourself whether it might be applied to people. What kinds of people come to mind? Turning to the poem's organization, circle the words that suggest seasons. What period of time is covered? Finally, can you speculate why the poet may have purposely chosen long, slow-moving lines for this particular subject?

A Secret Life

STEPHEN DUNN

Why you need to have one
is not much more mysterious than
why you don't say what you think

at the birth of an ugly baby.
Or, you've just made love   5
and feel you'd rather have been
in a dark booth where your partner
was nodding, whispering yes, yes,
you're brilliant. The secret life
begins early, is kept alive   10
by all that's unpopular
in you, all that you know
a Baptist, say, or some other
accountant would object to.
It becomes what you'd most protect   15
if the government said you can protect
one thing, all else is ours.
When you write late at night
it's like a small fire
in a clearing, it's what   20
radiates and what can hurt
if you get too close to it.
It's why your silence is a kind of truth.
Even when you speak to your best friend,
the one who'll never betray you,   25
you always leave out one thing;
a secret life is that important.

Consider (but do not reveal) one or two opinions or feelings you would not
tell anyone. Then take a close look at the **simile** on line 19 suggesting that
these secrets are "like a small fire." List all the characteristics of a fire that
might also apply to your private world.

Mystery

DOROTHY BARRESI

Their words harden in the turning air,
little earrings of light.
I saw, I hate, you never.
Ashtrays and pillows begin to orbit the room.
Whatever furniture they have   5
rears up on hind legs and howls.

Not even the stove's clock
can catch its breath when they argue.
Its arms windmill, making

the seasons slip a cog.   10
A buckeye tree in the yard goes
green to burnt orange in a matter of minutes.
Their dog turns suddenly old and blind
and cannot read the book of a dead sparrow
held open in its paws.   15

Later, the couple kiss
like guests on a television talk show,
expecting nothing.
Whatever they fought about is a mystery to them now.
The wife heads for the kitchen,   20
sets back the clock, while her husband
demagnetizes the steak knives.
Even their dog remembers its old trick
as it romps in the dark yard.
Play dead, then retrieve, retrieve,   25
the calm rising all around the house
like a blood pressure.

This is a highly visual poem. Underline all the dreamlike details that
suggest the intensity of their argument. What about the future for this
couple? What is suggested at the end about calm "rising . . . like a blood
pressure"?

Grandmother

PAULA GUNN ALLEN

Out of her own body she pushed
silver thread, light, air
and carried it carefully on the dark, flying
where nothing moved.

Out of her body she extruded   5
shining wire, life, and wove the light
on the void

From beyond time,
beyond oak trees and bright clear water flow,
she was given the work of weaving the strands   10
of her body, her pain, her vision
into creation, and the gift of having created,
to disappear.

After her,
the women and the men weave blankets into tales of life,   15
memories of light and ladders,
infinity-eyes, and rain.
After her I sit on my laddered rain-bearing rug
and mend the tear with string.

Notice that this poem is not just about the grandmother but also her descendants including, in the last two lines, the narrator. If you circle the key images—"silver thread," "shining wire," "weaving," and mending—you will see how the poem strings together the generations of Native Americans.

Chrysalis

JUDY KRONENFELD

An invisible visitor slipped in
and led you away,
as we closed ranks around your bed,
thinking at last you're sleeping,
at last some sleep   5

After we were shouted out in a swirl of white,
the grenade of tears bursting in my chest,
I came back briefly to admire
his clean work: just your chrysalis
on the bed, like a drained glass   10
left on a hotel room table

Now I send memory to the well
with its cup of bone
wanting to fill it to the brim
but the pump is frozen   15
and the water is stone

First you're not there
sitting on the couch
then the couch is gone
the room   20
the house

Notice how one **image** frequently leads to one that is similar in some way. The dry quality of a chrysalis is compared with "a drained glass" in line 10. Trace how that glass leads to several closely related images in the third stanza. Notice too how the "invisible visitor" in the first line of the poem is echoed with the stages of invisibility in the last stanza.

The Paradise of Wings

Theodore Deppe

My grandfather called it
the Paradise of Wings, a clearing
hidden in blue hills where thousands
of geese gleaned stubbled corn
beside a tapered lake. His favorite walk—   5
shared with me as a secret—made of that place,
those burnished wings, a sort of gift.

That fall, when flocks funneled above our house,
he'd hoist my sister to his lap
so I could go alone, be his eyes and ears.   10
I'd wait in a blind of scrub oak, calculate
the time to break from hiding, then whirl
my arms until the low sky rose in a wide arc
to settle out of sight behind the ridge.

One day my sister stumbled from the house,   15
panic in her face as she ran to me.
Though Grandfather stopped at the front steps
we ran all the way to the valley
I'd sworn to keep secret.
She made me promise   20
never to leave her alone with him,

told me just enough so that I, too,
feared his hands. Light kept draining
from black water, leaving in its place
an opaque stillness   25
where geese stood about on shelves of rotting ice
and my sister's hate
was the only living thing in paradise.

This poem demonstrates the fact that any subject, no matter how personal, can be handled in poetry. But note too that the poem is carefully structured. Compare the tone of the first stanza with that of the last one. Which visual details (**images**) account for the differences? Also notice how there are two entirely different kinds of secrets in this poem. How do they differ?

Desire

PHILIP APPLEMAN

1

The body
tugged like a tide, a pull
stronger than
the attraction of stars.

2

Moons   5
circling their planets,
planets
rounding their suns.

3

Nothing is what
we cannot imagine: 10
all that we know we know
moves in the muscles.

4

Undertow:
I reach for you,
oceans away.   15

It is not easy to write a love poem that doesn't sound **hackneyed**. The first step is to find a fresh and original **metaphor** that will bring originality and sense of authenticity to a well-used subject. Appleman uses the tide right from the start. Notice how it is developed in the second stanza (the moon causes the tides) and echoed once again with the sea images in the last stanza. The final stanza, by the way, is like a **haiku** in its simplicity, even though it doesn't follow the traditional syllable count. (See page 107 for comparisons.)

The Mapmaker's Daughter

ANITA ENDREZZE

the geography of love is terra infirma

it is a paper boat
navigated by mates
with stars in their eyes

cartographers of the fiery unknown   5

it is the woman's sure hand
at the helm of twilight, the salt
compass of her desire

the map of longing is at the edge
of two distant bodies   10

it is the rain that launches thirst
it is the palm leaf floating on waters
far from shore

the secret passage into the interior
is in my intemperate estuary   15

the sweet and languorous flowering
is in the caliber of your hands .

the circular motion of our journeying
is the radius of sky and sea, deep
territories we name   20
after ourselves

This is another love poem. Like "Desire," it uses a series of fresh images. It also uses the sea in many ways. But the construction of this poem is more complex and its style is both more sensual and more dreamlike. Underline each of the nouns that refer to the sea and to boats. Notice how each forms a **metaphor** related to some aspect of love.

The brief comments and questions after each poem are intended to help you read the work analytically—as a poet might. No doubt you preferred some poems to others, and you may wish to mark or photocopy those that are your favorites. But remember that you can learn from any carefully composed poem.

As we return to these poems in later chapters, keep in mind that this text is not intended to shape your preferences. That's up to you. Instead, the intent is to help you read a wide range of poems with greater perception and insight. Your ability to create new and effective work on your own depends largely on your understanding of what the genre has to offer.

3

SOURCES:

Where Poems Come From

Looking closely at what you see and hear. Drawing on friends and relations. Probing your true feelings. Examining ambivalence. Playing with language. Avoiding pitfalls. How to jump-start your creative ability.

Most contemporary poets draw directly or indirectly from personal experience. This requires being particularly sensitive to what we see and hear.

Unfortunately, it is all too easy to get through the day without examining the world around us. We tend to rush from one project to the next without allowing time for reflection. In addition, some have the feeling that their lives are too dull and uneventful to be of interest.

When you start writing poetry, make a conscious effort to look closely at the day's events—what you see and hear. And don't ignore your past. Keep in mind that every life is unique; our experiences and our reactions to those experiences are as individual as our fingerprints. In the process of writing, you will be sharpening your ability to reflect on your life, present and past, and to examine your true feelings.

To become a good observer, you may have to downshift. Consider the sign that marks many railroad crossings: Stop, Look, and Listen. Stop, for example, and look at the way flower petals have been plastered against a wet, black bough after a storm. That's what Ezra Pound did, remember? The poem is on page 10 if you need to review it. What made it a poem was not just the visual aspect; it was also the connection he made between those petals and the human faces in a subway station. He stopped, looked, and let his mind make a sudden leap, a connection.

It is similar in some ways to a vision Barbara Howes had while standing on the beach. By way of review, here is the first of three stanzas (the entire poem is on page 27):

> Serenity of mind poises
> Like a gull swinging in air.
> At ease, sculptured, held there
> For a moment so long-drawn-out all time pauses.

We can be fairly certain that Howes didn't start out planning to write a poem about serenity. Poets don't usually begin by reflecting on an **abstraction**. The stimulus for that poem was almost certainly the sight of a gull poised on an air current. We can't know for sure, of course, but the title, "The Bay at West Falmouth," is rooted in a specific place, not an abstraction.

Fortunately for us, she wasn't the sort to shout out the obvious, "Hey, isn't that pretty!" or to start fumbling for her camera. Instead, she took the time to let that visual **image**, the gull, stimulate her imagination. To her it seemed like a sculpture, and like many sculptures, it seemed to make time pause.

At some point in the writing a further insight came to Howes. That scene, she writes,

> . . . brings peace; as our being open
> to love does. . . .

Where did that poem come from? The gull. But it took a poet's imagination to let that vision suggest a sculpture, a pause in time, serenity, and eventually the concept of being "open to love."

This is not to suggest that the poem came to her in final form as she stood at the edge of the bay at West Falmouth, Massachusetts. It's almost never that easy. She probably worked over successive drafts in the weeks that followed. Poems often evolve slowly, occasionally frustratingly, as one searches for the right phrasing. But our concern here is for the moment of conception. The gull for Barbara Howes provided that initial stimulus, just as those faces in the Paris subway did for Ezra Pound.

Not all poems, of course, spring from a single visual impression, but if you look over the samples in the previous chapter, you will see a number of examples: a rock pool for Robley Wilson in "On a Maine Beach" (page 28), a solitary basketball player for Timothy Steele in "Practice" (page 33), and a river in flood for W. S. Merwin in "River Sound Remembered" (page 20).

Visual impressions rank high among poets, but don't ignore the other senses. Sounds that launch poems may take the form of a fragment of music, an adult crying, glass breaking. Tactile sensations range from a frosty glass of lemonade to a dentist's drill. While taste and smells are less often used, occasionally they can provide an intense stimulus. The first source of poetry, then, is all about you in the form of sensory impressions.

Draw on Friends and Relatives

This second source of poetry may not strike you as abruptly. Insights about friends and relatives sometimes creep up on you. But there is plenty to work with when you consider the full range: parents, stepparents, grandparents, siblings, aunts, uncles, teachers, employers, classmates, roommates, spouses, lovers, even dogs and cats. The relationships you have with these people (and animals) are rarely simple. Often they are charged. Greeting cards, of course, also deal with many of these categories, but with cartoonlike simplicity. **Sophisticated** poems deal with real or as-if-real people and reveal complex emotions that are often mixed. They probe what is unique in relationships.

Nikki Giovanni's "Balances" (page 36) might seem on first reading to have begun with the abstraction of the title. In the first two of nine irregular **stanzas**, she presents the topic and gives a couple of examples:

> in life
> one is always
> balancing
>
> like we juggle our mothers
> against our fathers
>
> or one teacher
> against another

That, however, is only a preamble. At the end of the poem we find out what is really on her mind:

> and I've begun
> (as a reaction to a feeling)
> to balance
> the pleasure of loneliness
> against the pain
> of loving you

What started off appearing to be a generalized little commentary on how one balances relationships turns out to be a reconsideration of a very specific relationship. The poem describes how the speaker has to weigh loneliness against the pain involved in maintaining her love for the other individual. Although the true concern is withheld until the end of the poem, it was probably the starting point in her mind, the stimulus that started her writing.

Anthony Hecht's "Lizards and Snakes" (page 33) appears to be based on a childhood friendship. We have to say "appears" because we don't know for sure how much of this came from the *poet's* own experience, but clearly the *narrator* is reporting a very specific event.

It begins in the **style** of a simple **anecdote**, a humorous account about tricks the narrator used to play on his Aunt Martha with his friend Joe. In the third stanza, however, the boys are jolted into a realization that the aunt is in fact terrified of lizards, seeing them as images of the devil. In this way the poem reveals a change in a relationship—the unconscious cruelty of the boys abruptly shifting to one of compassion.

Changes in attitude or perception lend themselves to poetry because they often provide dramatic impact. Sometimes they produce a real jolt. This is certainly the case in Theodore Deppe's "The Paradise of Wings" (page 42). The first stanza presents what appears to be a warm relationship between a boy and his grandfather. They even share a secret: a hidden clearing where geese come to feed on corn.

In the concluding two stanzas, however, the boy and his sister are shocked into realizing the true nature of the grandfather, and at the end they are left with fear and hate. The poem has its genesis in a terrible shattering of trust, the end of innocence for them both.

Poems like this raise the question of how revealing you can be when basing a poem on someone you know. If you feel that the poem could embarrass or even hurt certain readers, consider asking them in advance. You can explain that the apparent speaker in a narrative poem is not necessarily the poet.

But if seeking permission is awkward or impossible, or if you find that the closeness to actual people is intimidating you in the writing process, feel free to disguise some of the physical details. Change locations, events, or even the sex of a particular character. Remember that when writing poetry (or fiction for that matter) your first loyalty is to the art form. Your goal is to write the best piece you can. Unlike the journalist, you have no obligation whatever to report accurately the events or physical details that initiated the work. After all, the reason we call these genres "creative" is that they are indeed inventive. Poems, stories, and plays are often generated by personal experience, but they should never be bound by it.

Probing Your True Feelings

We think we know what we feel, but we're not always right. Sometimes we confuse what we think we *ought* to feel with our true emotions. In general, leave those socially approved and conventional sentiments to Hallmark cards. That's their specialty. As a poet, exercise the courage to explore your *un*conventional feelings.

As Stephen Dunn points out, we all have secrets we choose not to reveal. Here, as a reminder, is the opening of his poem "A Secret Life" (page 38):

> Why you need to have one
> is not much more mysterious than
> why you don't say what you think
> at the birth of an ugly baby.

If you keep a private journal (strongly recommended), consider making a list of things you honestly feel but don't tell anyone. If you do so, as Dunn recommends, "late at night," you may understand how such secrets are "like a small fire." They burn "if you get too close," but they may also serve as the genesis of new poems.

Linda Pastan explores our secret lives in an entirely different way in "Domestic Animals" (page 16). Volumes of very simple verse have been written on the virtues of both cats and dogs, but Pastan points out that sweet as they are by day, they

> . . . wait for dark
> when into the green
> jungle of our sleep
> they insinuate
> themselves, releasing
> their terrible hunger.

Notice how different that poem would be if she wrote "*their* sleep" rather than "*our* sleep." She is not just saying that domestic animals have their secret wild side, she is implying that we do too. When poets probe their most private thoughts and feelings, they may find themselves in what Pastan describes as "the green / jungle of our sleep."

Examining Ambivalence— both values

Ambivalence is a crucial element in many poems. It comes from *ambi-*, meaning "both" (as in *ambidextrous*) and *valence*, from the same root as "value." It describes a combining of two quite different emotions—love and hate, fear and desire, courage and cowardice.

Don't confuse this with a change in outlook such as we saw in Anthony Hecht's "Lizards and Snakes" (page 33) where the first view of the boy's aunt is altered by what they overhear, or Theodore Deppe's "The Paradise of Wings" (page 42) in which the initial impression of the grandfather is dramatically reversed. With ambivalence the two conflicting emotions or attitudes occur simultaneously.

Feelings of love are often charged with ambivalence. Nikki Giovanni describes it clearly in "Balances" (page 36). At the end of that poem the narrator finds herself caught between "the pleasure of loneliness" and "the pain / of loving you."

Molly Peacock describes a type of ambivalence all of us have felt in "Anger Sweetened" (page 18). The two forces in this case are our desire to be polite and our longing to express exactly what we feel. "What we don't forget," the poem states in the first line, "is what we don't say." The ambivalence we feel about being courteous is an almost daily experience.

When casting about for a subject that might generate a poem, consider your mixed feelings. And be honest about them! Few student poets make the mistake of attempting love poems that are simple expressions of unalloyed affection. We've heard enough of that in routine song lyrics. But tributes to older people like grandparents sometimes take on that same simple approach in spite of good intentions. Watch out too for the inverse, the expression of unalloyed hostility. Parents are often the target, as are former lovers and suburban life. If you are emotionally unprepared to include some ambivalent feelings, you are probably too close to the subject. Spare us!

Another risk is dealing with widely supported causes. Campaigns against drugs, street violence, and war are best treated in posters and television spots, not sophisticated poetry. The only way to handle these topics is to present them with striking **ambivalence** the way Gwendolyn Brooks does in "We Real Cool" (page 24). Every evil, after all, has its secret appeal.

Playing with Language

Although many poems spring from what the poet has seen and felt and from relationships with others, another important factor is sheer love of language.

All creative writers pay close attention to how they use words, but poets often take a particular delight in fresh and ingenious phrasing. They assume that their work is going to be read more deliberately than prose and so feel free to push language into new configurations.

E. E. Cummings is a good example. Here once again is "Buffalo Bill's," a poetic tribute to the skill and grace of a great performer from the past:

> Buffalo Bill's
> defunct
>   who used to
>   ride a watersmooth-silver
>   stallion

and break onetwothreefourfive pigeonsjustlikethat

>>>>>>>>>>>>>>>>>>>>>>>>Jesus

he was a handsome man

>>>>>>>>>>>>>and what i want to know is
how do you like your blueeyed boy
Mister Death

The historical Buffalo Bill was a showman, so it is most appropriate that the poet use some showy tricks himself. He runs words together to create the ripple effect of Buffalo Bill's rapid firing, and Cummings personifies death in a way that is both colloquial in style and serious in theme. What a waste, the poem seems to ask, to have a man of such dazzling ability lost to the stillness of death.

Or take the fanciful phrasing in almost any section of Dylan Thomas' "Fern Hill" (page 21). We have already looked at the way he plays with the sound of words throughout that poem. In addition, he uses phrasing that suggests the *feel* of a scene even when it doesn't make sense in a literal manner. Here is one of many examples:

> All the sun long it was running, it was lovely, the hay
> Fields high as the house, the tunes from the chimneys, it was air
> And playing, lovely and watery
> And fire green as grass.

Logical? It's not the logic of prose, but the images bounce off each other to give a sense of delight and wonder. Translated into literal prose it might come out like this:

> All day long the sun shone and I raced about. Life was lovely as I played in the fields with hay that seemed as tall as houses. The metal chimney pots squeaked in the wind but I heard them as tunes. My life was as free as air and filled with playing. Everything in my world was lovely and as fluid as water. I was as lively as fire and as supple as a green sprout.

Each image is accounted for in this prose version, but all the joy and whimsy have been squeezed out.

Perhaps it has never occurred to you that you can actually have fun with language. If so, here is an exercise that will start you thinking about language in a nonintellectual way—that is, in a poetic way. Buy a journal, a separate notebook for poetic "sketching," and carefully draw at the top of a fresh page these two shapes:

If each shape had a name, which one would be Kepick and which Oona? Write the name you have selected under each figure and then record these choices: If they are a couple, which is the man? If one is a brand of gasoline and the other a type of oil, which is which?

Suppose one is a melon and the other a lemon? And now listen to them: one is a drum and the other a violin. Too easy? One is a saxophone and the other a trumpet; one is the wind and the other a dog's bark. It is an odd and significant fact that 19 out of 20 people will give identical answers. This is a set of shared associations that is of particular interest to poets.

Thinking of them once again as a couple, make up four nonsense words that are harmonious with Oona and four for Kepick. Now try a few lines of very free and whimsical verse describing Oona and Kepick with your newly invented words used as nouns, verbs, or modifiers. (Surely it would be appropriate if Ooona looked feenly in the shane, but how does she feel when Kepick kacks his bip and zabots all the lovely leems?)

There is no end to this. It won't lead directly to sophisticated poetry, but it will help you to hear the music in language. The two should not be confused, but poems often have as much to do with sound, rhythm, and overtones as they do with making statements.

Avoiding Pitfalls

You can think of these pitfalls as the seven deadly sins of poetry, though some find the phrase intimidating. In any case, they are types of poetry that keep showing up in creative writing classes. You will save yourself hours of futile revision time and will improve the quality of any workshop course you may take if you can stay clear of them.

- *The Impenetrable-Haze Poem.* The conscientious reader struggles from line to line without detecting any direction or coherence. Individual images may seem to make sense, but nothing hangs together. The work as a whole does not suggest a theme that any two people can agree on.

Why is obscurity so common among beginning poets? For some, it's a result of never having learned how to read complex and demanding poetry.

Their inability gives them the feeling that if they write carelessly and without purpose, others will be able to make sense of it. A frequent defense: "It means whatever you want it to mean." That's another way of saying it doesn't mean anything

Another cause for obscurity is shyness. The writer is reluctant to reveal genuine feelings or experiences and hides behind a barrier of fuzzy language. As I have noted before, it takes courage to share what is really important to you. Keep in mind that while complexity is often necessary, obscurity cuts you off from your readers.

- *Truth-in-a-Nutshell.* When a poem tries to define truth, beauty, love, or evil in the abstract, it is apt to sound like a little essay in short lines. It also tends to be boring for lack of a personal element. We're all for truth and beauty and all opposed to evil, so why remind us once again? Abstractions are always risky, but they can serve if you focus on a very specific truth that your readers haven't considered before. Stephen Dunn's "A Secret Life" (page 38) is a good example, as is Molly Peacock's "Anger Sweetened" (page 18). Beauty too has to be focused on a specific example such as the gull in Barbara Howes' "The Bay at West Falmouth" (page 27). The most fruitful approach is to start with a specific **image** as she does and *imply* the abstract.

- *Oh-Poor-Miserable-Me!* Sadly, it is young poets who seem to be most tempted by this misuse of poetry. In some cases it reflects genuine despondency, and those feelings deserve a sensitive response. But a poem that is based on unrelenting self-pity belongs in a psychiatrist's office, not a writing class. Unrelenting self-pity becomes repetitious like a song that repeats the same note over and over.

For some, self-lamentation can become addictive. Since kind classmates are reluctant to be critical, the writer is insulated against negative evaluations. The best approach for the group is to separate the poet from implied speaker with comments like, "We could identify more fully with the narrator if the poem provided some relief or balance." Mature writers know that for a poem to be effective as a literary work it must be presented with some restraint, subtlety, and at least a touch of objectivity.

- *The Marching-Band Poem.* Every poem should have some type of rhythmical effect, but unvaried **meter**—especially when combined with a blatant **rhyme scheme**—tends to dominate the work. It becomes obtrusive. We're used to a hand-clapping beat and predictable rhyme endings in nursery rhymes, greeting-card verse, and some ballads, but the subtleties of sophisticated poetry are drowned out by heavy-handed rhythms and rhymes. Later we will look at specific ways to mute these auditory aspects.

- *Hark, the Antique-Language Poem.* Lo, yonder bovine ruminates 'twixt bosky dell and halcyon copse. No, it never gets this bad. But watch out for those time-honored yet dated contractions such as *o'er* and *oft* as substitutes for *over* and *often*. They are particularly tempting when one first tries metered verse. Sometimes they're sprinkled in like chocolate jimmies to make a work seem profound. Resist the urge. Every age has its own linguistic flavor, and like it or not, you're writing for the twenty-first century.

• *The Wailing-Violin Poem*. Genuine feelings are the stuff of good poetry, but when the reader's emotions are manipulated to evoke tears, the poem is no longer sincere. Honest sentiment focuses on the specific and is true to the poet's feelings. **Sentimentality** supercharges those feelings simply to produce a surge of emotions.

Elizabeth Holden could have set those violins wailing when she described a woman of 86 who sees her friends dying in "As the Cold Deepens" (page 15). Instead, she focuses on the image of flies and links that image with the mother. As readers, we sympathize, but we don't feel our emotions being manipulated.

• *The Collective-Group Poem*. We all resent being included in sweeping generalizations about "all women," "all men," "all students," "all Americans," "all parents," or all anything. Poems that make assertions about such groups are offensive at best and prejudicial at worst. Each of us, after all, is an individual. Poems generate a sense of authenticity when focused on a single such individual.

Holden's poem is not about elderly women as a class, it is about a particular woman in a particular place facing old age. "Lizards and Snakes," by Anthony Hecht (page 23), is not a sweeping statement about how all young boys are thoughtless and cruel; it is a narrative about two specific boys on "the day / Of the big wind. ..." Hecht, like Holden, starts with the specific and draws implications from that.

Don't let these warnings inhibit you. If you review the first few lines of the poems in Chapter 2, you will see that your options are almost limitless. Just make sure that the subject matter you are working with is rooted in a personal experience, observation, or insight that is important to you.

Six Ways to Jump-Start a New Poem

Don't stare at a fresh sheet of paper, hoping it will give you a topic. Paper doesn't talk. Your new poem has to come out of you. Here are six ways to locate the material that is already within you. It's all there, waiting to be given fresh words.

1. Let other poets get you in the mood. Review about ten poems in Chapter 2. Ask yourself, "Where did that come from?" You won't ever know for sure, but just asking the question will stimulate you to look in the same area.

2. If you have been keeping a journal, use it. Look over those scraps of impressions, insights, fantasies, feelings, dreams, stray lines of verse. If you haven't started one yet, buy a notebook for such musings. Carry it with you; add to it at odd times.

3. Draw on your five senses. List very briefly those objects you saw today that you will remember five years from now (a good exercise for your journal). What is it about those objects that makes them memorable? Try the same for last summer. Reach back for visual impressions from your childhood. Why have they stuck when thousands of other details slipped through the sieve of memory?

Do the same for sounds. Music may well come to mind first, but don't forget the voice or laugh of a particular person, the sounds of mechanical objects like a car, truck, or motorcycle, or the natural sounds of wind or rain. Describe these with fresh language—no babbling brooks, breathless calms, or howling gales.

Try the same for memorable sensations of touch, taste, and smell. Some may be pleasant, but others will be rancid or bitter. All sense data have the potential of generating a poem.

4. Recall some of the most vivid experiences you have had in the past two years. We're shifting here from things seen or heard to episodes that might be developed in narrative form. What makes them vivid? Often the event may be minor, but the emotions it generated are memorable. Keep an eye out for samples of **ambivalence**—opposite reactions existing at the same time.

Do the same for the dramatic events of your childhood. Did any of them change your attitude? Did they help you to see things in a different light?

Now ask yourself some tough questions about your own life. (Remember, no one is listening!) When were you truly frightened? Would what frightened you then frighten you now? Were you ever deeply ashamed? As you look back, was the shame justified? Did you learn anything from it? Have you ever had a moment of elation that turned to disappointment or even depression?

5. Consider your friends and relations. Can you see in any of them contradictions that are worth exploring? Have you ever had to act as a parent to your parent or other older person? What did it feel like? Is there anyone you once hated whom you now understand or perhaps even like? Whose death would really hurt you? Why that person and not others? When dealing with your relationships with others, look closely to see if there is some type of ambivalence worth developing. It may not be as dramatic as love mixed with hatred; it may be a blend of admiration and resentment, respect and disapproval, pleasure and displeasure.

6. As soon as you select a topic that might serve as the kernel of a poem, start writing. Get phrases down even before you are sure. Then lines. At this

stage, don't worry about the order. Postpone that until later in the process. Lines that come to you early may end up at the end of a developed poem. Phrases you originally put down in a cluster may eventually be separated. Stay loose. Don't rush it. Keep trying different versions. Let the developing poem speak to you as it takes shape.

Keep in mind that most of your writing and your training as a student has been prose. The same is true for your reading. As I pointed out earlier, prose is wordy compared with poetry and makes little use of the sound of language or rhythmical effect. As you work on a new poem, compress your language and keep reading it out loud to hear the sound of what you are writing. At first you will have to compose somewhat intuitively. In later chapters, however, we will be examining techniques of rhythm and the sound of words that will give you a broader range of options from which to choose. For now, it is enough to remember that poetry is not just an outpouring of feelings; it is an art form in which sound, shape, and implication are all blended into the whole.

4

IMAGES:

The Essential Element

*Images defined and contrasted with abstractions. The impact of strong nouns.
Images used as figures of speech: similes and metaphors. Other figures of
speech. The cliché: a dying simile. The image as symbol. Building image clusters. Playing with images in your journal. Moving from play to serious work.*

Images, as I pointed out earlier, are words that we can respond to with any
of the five senses. Usually they are objects we can see, but they can also be
sounds, textures, odors, and occasionally even tastes. Images are also
referred to as **concrete** nouns, though it is strange to think of the delicate
scent of a rose set in concrete.

The opposite of an image is an abstraction. **Abstractions** are concepts
that the mind must grasp intellectually. *War*, *peace*, *love*, *democracy*, and even
the word *abstraction* itself are abstract.

There is nothing reprehensible about abstractions. Civilization (itself an
abstraction) depends on them. Mathematics, for example, contains an entire
language of abstractions called numbers. We can't see or feel *five*; we can't
weigh it or stroke it. But the concept is essential if you are going to build a
house or a satellite. Philosophers spend their lives dealing with truth,
knowledge, and ethics—all abstractions.

Poets also deal with abstractions. In this very volume you have read
poems titled "Practice," "The Pardon," "Balances," "Mystery," and "Desire."
Try taking a photograph of any of those! In each case, however, the poet has
translated those chilly abstract concepts into sight and sound. In "Practice"
(page 33) we both see and hear a solitary basketball player; in the "The
Pardon" (page 34) we not only see a dead dog, we smell him and we hear
"the flies' intolerable buzz." In each of these poems, an abstraction has been
made vivid with data for our senses.

If you are in doubt about whether a word is abstract or concrete, ask
yourself whether it refers to something you can see, hear, taste, smell, or feel.

How much does truth weigh? What are the dimensions of death? How big a box do you need to contain happiness?

I have been describing images as the opposite of abstractions, but actually they are points on a continuum. *Serenity*, for example, is an abstraction that, like all true abstractions, cannot be seen or heard. You can't weigh it or put it in a cage. *Bird* is more concrete, but it is still rather general. We know it has feathers and wings, but there is a big difference between a hummingbird and an ostrich. *A gull* is more specific, and "a gull swinging in air, / At ease, sculptured, held there . . ." is a fully developed image. We not only see a specific bird, we see it "swinging in air." As you probably remember from Chapter 2, this image is taken from Barbara Howes' poem "The Bay at West Falmouth" (page 27). If you have forgotten how she links that image not only with "the heart's serenity" but to "being open / to love," review it now so that my analysis does not remain abstract.

Here are some other examples showing the continuum between highly abstract words or concepts and images that a poet might use. In fact, poets *have* used these images in poems you have read just recently. See if you can recall them:

> *Reliability* is abstraction.
>
> *A workhorse* is one way to make that abstraction visible.
>
> *Ned*, a specific farm horse that has worked for a lifetime until death, is a far more concrete image.
>
> *Chance* is an abstraction.
>
> Seeing a *white spider on a white flower* gives us a visual picture.
>
> Seeing a *white spider on a white flower holding a white moth* is a once-in-a-lifetime chance occurrence that is so unusual as to raise questions about whether there is some design in the natural world.
>
> *Anger* is an abstraction.
>
> *Anger sweetened* gives promise of an image—a teaser of sorts.
>
> But when we are told that things we didn't say because of politeness end up like insects in our stomachs, we have a memorably repulsive image.

The Impact of Strong Nouns

As you can see from these examples, a concrete noun has to be specific in order to serve as an effective image. Because poetry relies so heavily on what we see and hear, it is important to select nouns that have impact whenever possible.

In most cases, finding just the right noun means that you won't have to modify it with an **adjective.** Whenever you do use an adjective, check to make sure that you can't find another noun that doesn't need to be modified. Here is

use sparingly

a list of nouns that are modified because they don't exactly describe the object. On the right is a single noun that is more precise and so has greater impact.

avoid adverbs

a large stream	a river	*less is more*
almost a hurricane	a gale	
a small lake	a pond	
a loud voice	a shout	
extreme fear	terror	
excessively thrifty	miserly	

There is nothing wrong with adjectives as such. There are occasions when they provide just the shade of meaning you are trying to express. But think of them as fine-tuning. In many first-draft poems, half of the modifiers could be removed. Examine each one critically.

Finding the right noun also requires being absolutely sure about the meaning. This is less likely to be a problem with most concrete nouns, but less familiar abstract nouns may require special attention. We all have words in our passive vocabulary that we understand well enough when we are reading but not well enough to use in speech or writing. Look these up. You may be surprised at the precise meaning.

If you have a computer, seriously consider adding an electronic dictionary. These, unlike spell checkers, provide full definitions without leaving the document you are working on. The Random House Electronic Dictionary has the particular advantage of including derivations. Because it is so much quicker than flipping through the pages of a dictionary, you will find yourself using the electronic dictionary much more often. You will expand your vocabulary as well.

Don't hesitate to make your nouns describe specific people, places, or objects. We have already seen how Dylan Thomas' "Fern Hill" focuses on a specific farm, not farms in general, and Barbara Howes' "The Bay at West Falmouth" gives the strong impression of describing a specific event in a specific place. W. W. Merwin goes even farther in "River Sound Remembered" (page 20) when he starts out with "That day the huge water drowned all voices. . . ." He's not talking about rivers in general; he's recalling a specific time of a flood. "That day" even implies that we were there and remember it too.

These examples are further evidence of how many poems start with the specific and, with that as a base, go on to suggest more general insights.

Images as Figures of Speech

Until now I have been describing images used simply as descriptive details—things seen, heard, felt, smelled, and tasted. Images also serve as the concrete element in almost any **figure of speech**. In fact, some poets and critics use the word *image* exclusively for examples of figurative language.

Figures of speech most commonly take the form of the **simile** and the **metaphor**. These are both comparisons, the simile linking the two elements explicitly with *like* or *as*, and the metaphor implying the relationship.

Here are four similes from three different poems you read in Chapter 2. I have already quoted from the first two poems several times without having to explain similes or metaphors. That shows how familiar we all are with figurative language. Only as writers do we have to analyze just how both similes and metaphors work and how they are a special type of comparison. The marginal comments are the type you might find helpful when studying poems.

1. From Barbara Howes' "The Bay at West Falmouth":

   Serenity of mind poises

   Like a gull swinging in air *simile*

2. From Robley Wilson's "On a Maine Beach":

   ...rocks are like worn change *simile*

3. From Linda Pastan's "Domestic Animals":

   ...into the green *metaphor*

   jungle of our sleep

4. From Chase Twichell's "Rhymes for Old Age":

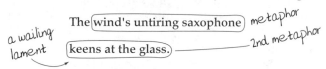

   The wind's untiring saxophone *metaphor*

   a wailing lament keens at the glass. ———— *2nd metaphor*

Notice that these examples of similes and metaphors are never simple comparisons. When we compare, for example, a starling with a grackle, we imply that *in most respects* the two objects are similar. But when Barbara Howes describes serenity as being like a gull, she certainly doesn't want us to picture the emotion as having a sharp bill and a raucous cry. Serenity is like a gull *only in certain respects*—in this case, the way it seems to float effortlessly in the air. As with most similes, the area of similarity is quite narrow. The impact of the figure of speech depends on how sharply it can make the reader see a new relationship.

A **metaphor** is often described as a simile that doesn't use *like* or *as*, but the real difference is much deeper than that. Similes are a special kind of comparison, but they are nonetheless phrased like comparisons. A metaphor, on the other hand, is a statement that is literally untrue. We understand its meaning only by implication.

It doesn't make literal sense, for example, to refer to a house as "lilting." Lilting is normally applied to melodies, not objects. You won't get far telling a builder to construct a lilting house. Yet this is the word Dylan Thomas uses in the second line of "Fern Hill" (see page 21). We understand his meaning through the context of the poem.

The best way to analyze how a metaphor works is to convert it to a simile. The result may be awkward, but it is a good technique to use with your own work as well as with published poems. In the case of Thomas' metaphor, the conversion comes out something like this: "A house as cheerful and merry as a lilting tune."

Notice how compressed the metaphor is compared with the corresponding simile. This is a case where a metaphor is far more than just a simile with *as* left out. Its compression makes it a kind of shorthand that provides greater impact. More than that, it's a true transformation. Because it is literally untrue, the reader has to make a jump to make the connection. This gives the figure of speech greater impact.

There are two terms that are extremely helpful in analyzing any figure of speech—including those in your own work. The critic I. A. Richards has suggested **tenor** to describe the poet's actual concern (often an abstraction) and **vehicle** as the image associated with it. Take, for example, the simile in this line from "Fern Hill": "Happy as the grass was green." The tenor or true subject here is the abstraction "happy," and "green grass" is the vehicle— with overtones of spring growth, vividness, intensity.

One advantage of being familiar with these terms is that they can help you identify and get rid of mixed metaphors. A **mixed metaphor** is one with two contradictory vehicles. Here is an *invented* example with marginal comments:

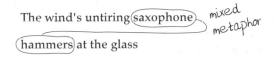

The wind, the tenor, here is described as being *like* the sound of a saxophone. Since *like* has been deleted, the phrase becomes a metaphor. The second metaphor is intended to suggest that the wind is also like a hammer pounding at the glass—not as fresh but usable. Joined together, however, they are "mixed" badly since saxophones are rarely used as hammers.

Here is the harmonious and effective version we saw in Chase Twichell's "Rhymes for Old Age":

> The wind's untiring saxophone
> keens at the glass.

This version also uses a double metaphor (that is, two vehicles applied to one tenor), but the vehicles are harmonious. A saxophone often produces a wailing sound, and the verb *to keen* means to wail for the dead. The two vehicles work together. In addition, that wail is appropriate to the theme of the poem, a lament for a woman close to death.

Other Figures of Speech

The term **figurative language** is used primarily to describe similes and metaphors. Most other figures of speech are specialized forms of the metaphor and are of more concern to critics analyzing literature than to writers in the process of composition. Three, however, concern us here. They are techniques you may wish to use.

Hyperbole is extreme exaggeration used for effect. Not all examples of exaggeration are hyperboles. People exaggerate simply to boast or to get a laugh. Hyperbole, however, is a true figure of speech because we as readers understand that, first, it is not meant to be taken literally and, second, it has an implied meaning. If you look closely at examples of hyperbole, you will see that they can, like metaphors, be converted to similes. Shakespeare, for example, in "Sonnet 3" writes: "Thou doest beguile the world." Obviously he doesn't mean that she literally charms everyone in the world; it is *as if* she had that power. And in "Sonnet 9" he writes in a darker mood, "The world will wail thee."

More recently, Lucille Clifton in "What the Mirror Said" (page 20) has her narrator look at her reflection and cry, "listen,/ you a wonder/ you a city / of a woman." This cheerful bit of self-affirmation is not just a casual exaggeration such as we might use in conversation; it is a figure of speech. Converting it to a simile, we end up with something like, "You're so complex and interesting, you're like an entire city."

The **pun** is one of the least appreciated figures of speech. In conversation it is greeted with groans rather than laughter, but poets from Shakespeare to the present have treated it like a metaphor. Dylan Thomas makes serious use of the pun in a poem that is a lament for a girl killed in a bombing raid of World War II, "A Refusal to Mourn . . .":

> I shall not murder
> The mankind of her going with a grave truth

The word "grave" here has both a literal meaning, "a serious truth," and a figurative use that implies the opposite: the traditional and often empty oration such as those given at the graveside. (Incidentally, the phrase "murder / The mankind" is a hyperbole that could be rephrased as "injure humanity.")

He uses an equally serious pun in "Do Not Go Gentle Into That Good Night" with the line, "Grave men, near death, who see with blinding sight. . . ." The simile buried in this pun could be rephrased as "men so near death they are almost in the grave."

As these examples show, the pun can occasionally be used for serious effect, but it is a risky device. If not handled with great skill, it will spoil the line (or even the poem as a whole) with what appears to be a comic note.

Synecdoche is the third of these helpful terms. It is a figure of speech in which a part is used for the whole. When we say "bread for the starving," we're not just appealing to baking companies. "Bread" represents food in general. Sometimes an individual is used for a group. When we say "the plight of the blue-collar worker," it's understood that we are referring to a whole class, not just an individual wearing a blue work shirt.

These examples are taken from common speech; poetic use of synecdoche is fresher, more original, and so has more impact. Compare the prosaic phrase "All day long" with Dylan Thomas' version, "All the sun long." The sun is only one aspect of the day, but by allowing it to stand for the day he is able to catch the overtones of summer warmth and, in this context, childhood.

Figures of speech are important to poetry because they help to increase the degree of compression. That is, they suggest more without being wordy. Be careful, though, not to "dress up" a poem by using figures of speech merely for adornment. Sometimes straightforward language is more appropriate.

The Cliché: A Dying Simile

We have all been warned against using clichés since grade school. Yet they remain a temptation—particularly when we are tired or careless. It is important to understand what a cliché is and why it is so damaging to any kind of writing, especially a poem.

In common usage we call any overused phrase a cliché. "Neat as a pin," "clean as a whistle," "a drug on the market," "strong as an ox," "dead as a doornail" are all familiar to us. Notice, however, that these are either similes or metaphors. The cliché, as George Orwell points out in his essay "Politics and the English Language," is actually a dying metaphor—that is, an expression that was once fresh enough to create a clear picture in the reader's mind but has lost its vitality through constant use.

Technically, most clichés are similes. The normal function of both metaphors and similes is to clarify an abstract word (*serenity*, for example) by linking it with a concrete one (like *gull*). But when the same image is used over and over, it loses visual impact. Often, we have forgotten what the original image was. As Orwell points out, "to toe the line" (literally to place one's toe on the starting line in a race) has strayed so far from the original metaphor that it is now often seen in print as "to *tow* the line." As for "a drug on the market," how many are aware that the original use of *drug* included dyes and valued foodstuffs such as chocolate and tea. When the ships brought too great a supply, the product became a drug on the market. But the cliché takes five words when *worthless* would probably do.

When a metaphor or simile "dies," it often becomes a part of the language as a single word that no longer appeals to a visual comparison. For example, we use the word *badger* to mean "harass," oblivious of the fact that the poor badger was originally the victim, not the tormentor. There's no harm in these **dead metaphors** because they have been converted to useful verbs or nouns. What does the damage to poetry are those phrases that are both wordy and too familiar to provide a mental picture. They're excess baggage.

There are three different ways of dealing with clichés that appear in an early draft. First, you can work hard to find a fresh simile or metaphor that will allow the reader to see (hear, taste, and so on) the tenor you have in mind. Second, you can drop the figurative language completely and deal with the subject directly. Finally, one can twist the cliché around so that it is revitalized in some slightly altered form.

For example, if you discover that you have allowed "blood red" to slide into your verse, you can avoid this ancient cliché with such alternatives as "balloon red," "hot red," or "screaming red," depending on the overtones you wish to establish. If none of these will do, go back to just "red."

A good way to improve your skill in dealing with clichés is to apply these techniques to phrases like "mother nature," "strong as an ox," "wise as an owl," and "where there's smoke, there's fire."

Hackneyed language is a related but broader term. It includes phrases that have simply been overused. They may not be true clichés, but they lack impact because of overuse. Certain subjects tend to generate hackneyed language. Sunsets, for example: the "dying day" is a true cliché, but perfectly respectable words like *golden, resplendent,* and *magnificent* become hackneyed in this context simply from excessive use. It's not the word itself that should be avoided—one cannot make lists; it is the particular combination that is limp from overuse.

In the same way, smiles are too often "radiant," "infectious," or "glowing." Trees, as we have seen, tend to have "arms" and "reach heavenward." The seasons are particularly dangerous: spring is "young" or "youthful," suggesting virginity, vitality, or both; summer is "full blown"; and with autumn some poets slide into a "September Song" with only slight variations of the popular lyrics. Winter is too easily used to suggest sterility and death.

Our judgment of what is hackneyed depends somewhat on the age in which we live. What was fresh and vivid in an earlier period may have become shopworn for us. "Any port in a storm" was probably fresh in the 18th century when it was first used as a proverb, and "blind as a bat" in the 16th century, but they're tattered from overuse today.

Surprisingly, many hackneyed phrases were stale hundreds of years ago and still won't die. They keep sprouting like tenacious weeds in mass-market poetry. In "Sonnet 130," Shakespeare pokes fun at conventional descriptions of beauty that were stale even in his time.

> My mistress' eyes are nothing like the sun;
> Coral is far more red than her lips' red. . . .
> And in some perfumes is there more delight
> Than in the breath that from my mistress reeks.

His mistress, we hope, realized that the poem was directed not at her but at the hack poets of the day who were content to use phrasing that even then was thoroughly stale. Yet more than 300 years later poetry is produced (more often by the greeting-card industry and pop-music writers than by students) in which eyes "sparkle like the sun," lips are either "ruby" or "coral red," and breath is either "honeyed" or "perfumed."

Your task as a poet is to find fresh insights. If you are dealing with the pleasures of being young, don't trot out the old springtime metaphors. Dylan Thomas, you remember, draws on the season indirectly with the line "I was green and carefree." T. S. Eliot uses spring in an entirely different way with the famous line from "The Waste Land": "April is the cruelest month." He counters the clichéd associations with April by observing how winter snow protects plants and the spring thaw exposes them. Then he compares the snow with forgetfulness and the loss of it with recollections we would rather leave buried. His metaphor tips our conventional notion of spring upside down.

The Image as Symbol

A **symbol** also adds density of meaning to a poem, but the way it functions is the opposite of a figure of speech. As we have seen, a figure of speech introduces an image simply for comparison. A **symbol**, on the other hand, uses an image that exists as a part of the poem and informs the reader that it has a greater range of meaning. If that strikes you as confusing in the abstract, consider these examples.

First, here is a simile (in italics) describing an older woman.

> My mother is almost weightless now,
> *Light as some fly* left to die on the window sill.

Here is the same image handled as a metaphor:

> My mother is almost weightless now,
> *a fly* left to die on the window sill.

In both cases, the woman exists in the poem, but the fly is introduced merely to make the comparison.

Now take a look at Elizabeth Holden's use of flies as a symbol in "As the Cold Deepens" (page 215).

> I think of flies
> how they live in a weightless armor
> tough, resistant, like a fingernail.
>
> My mother is almost weightless now

The flies here are the actual insects that the speaker and her mother used to sweep up from the windowsills when they opened their summer house. The narrator recalls those flies and then describes her mother. How do we know that the flies are being used as a symbol? The poet links the two with the word "weightless." The flies are not just a figure of speech; they exist in the poem and they also amplify some of the characteristics of a frail woman close to death.

Here is one more example: In "On a Maine Beach" (page 28), Robley Wilson uses a simile in the very first line. Again, the italics are mine:

> Look, in these pools how rocks *are like worn change.*

There is no pile of coins in this poem. "Worn change" is introduced figuratively just to help us see a particular aspect of the rocks.

The rock pool itself, on the other hand, really exists in the poem. And after a careful reading we realize that he isn't just describing a pretty aspect of nature. Through a series of hints, he informs us that such rock pools with their cycles of tides take on characteristics similar to our own life cycles. When he describes those snails "spending slow / Round lifetimes half awake," he isn't speaking merely as a naturalist. He has charged this scene with a broader meaning. He is commenting on an aspect of the human condition.

In distinguishing metaphors from symbols, it helps to use the terms **tenor**, the actual subject, and **vehicle**, the words used to describe that tenor. Ask this simple question, Should I take this vehicle literally? If not (like the "worn change" in the Wilson poem), it is a figure of speech. If the tenor is literally there (like the flies in the Holden poem or the rock pool in the Wilson poem), ask yourself whether it is serving as a symbol to suggest some broader concern (our mortality in each of those otherwise quite different poems).

At first, this may seem too analytical to be helpful—especially if you are just starting to write poetry. But as you begin to analyze your own work and that of others, these distinctions will be as important and useful to you as the distinction between the major and minor keys is for a musician.

For some, diagrams are anathema. If you are one of them, skip over the schematic drawing presented here. Others, however, find the pictorial approach more helpful than any description in words. This chart is meant for them.

In this diagram I have given examples from "Fern Hill," but the diagram will be more helpful if you select an image in another poem or perhaps from your own work and determine whether it is a figure of speech or a symbol.

Use of the image in comparisons, similes, metaphors, and symbols.

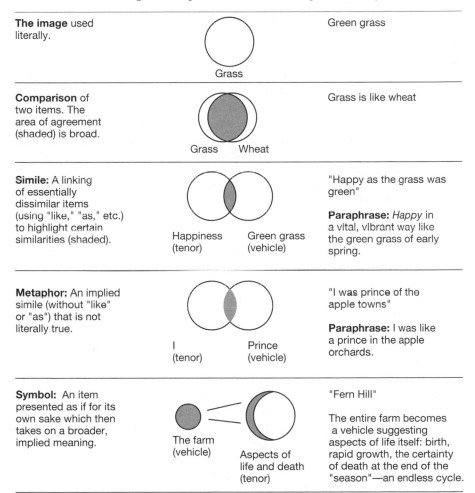

The term **public symbol** refers to symbols that are widely recognized and are almost a part of the language. The flag, for example, represents the country, the cross stands for the Christian church, the dove suggests peace, a shrouded figure holding a scythe is recognized as a symbol of death. These are so common that they can be used in cartoons.

Because public symbols are so overused, they are considered hackneyed. Poets generally avoid them and construct their own **private symbols** instead. Devised for a particular poem, a private or unique symbol has to be introduced in such a way that its meaning is made clear through the context of the poem.

Often the symbolic suggestion in a poem will come relatively late in the creative process. Suppose you are working on a poem that contrasts the way a house looked in its early construction and its appearance five years later, nestled into the neighborhood with lawns and plantings. This transformation of an ugly work site with its piles of lumber and concrete blocks into a finished home may be enough for a successful poem.

Now suppose that after the fourth draft you see a parallel between that process and, say, the transformation of the owner from a young, rather sloppy newcomer to a distinguished member of the community. This symbolic suggestion may add a new dimension to the poem, give it more resonance. Or it may not. It's up to you to weigh carefully whether developing that symbol will have those benefits, or whether it will simply clutter up a poem that was strong enough without an additional layer of suggestion.

Important as symbols often are, don't feel that they are essential. Donald Hall's "Naming of Horses" (page 37) is a moving tribute to farm horses who served patiently over the years. The poem may remind some readers of loyal servants, and others may think of long-time workers in a factory, but there is nothing in the poem to suggest that the horses were intended to be symbols. It's a mistake for a reader to force a symbolic suggestion onto a published poem without evidence, just as it is a mistake for a writer to impose a symbol on his or her own work just to make it seem deep.

As you write, examine your subject carefully and determine what it has meant to you. If a symbol comes to mind, let it develop naturally. Revise the poem so that your reader can share the symbolic suggestion. A private symbol that remains a secret is worth nothing, and making readers guess your intent without providing guideposts is a mean-spirited game. On the other hand, you have to be careful not to make it so obvious that the literary intent becomes obtrusive. When symbols are shaped with restraint and subtlety, they will be an organic part of the poem.

Building Image Clusters

Regardless of whether images are used figuratively, symbolically, or simply as enriching details, they are often more effective if presented in clusters. That is, a group of images that have the same source (a farm, a beach) or are linked visually (a series of circles) gain strength and impact as compared with unrelated images that are used once and then dropped.

When you read a new poem, look for such **image clusters** or groups of related details even before you are entirely clear about the theme. If you own the book, take the time to circle these clusters and identify them. Or you can photocopy the poem and mark the copy. This kind of visual analysis is not only helpful in the process of understanding new work, it will help you to adopt the same techniques in your own writing.

Here is an annotated copy of "On a Maine Beach" by Robley Wilson, which you first read on page 28. Look this over and then use it as a model to analyze a poem filled with related images, such as "Fern Hill" on page 21. Not until you do an analysis on your own will you fully appreciate the technique and be able to apply it to your own work.

money images   Look, in these pools, how rocks are like worn change

Keeping the ocean's mint-mark; barnacles

Miser on them; societies of snails

circle images   Hunch on their rims and think small thoughts whose strange

Salt logics rust like a mainspring, small dreams

Pinwheeling to a point and going dumb,

Small equations whose euphemistic sum

cycles of the tide   Stands for mortality. A thousand times

Tides swallow up such pools, shellfish and stone

Show green and yellow shade in groves of weed;

Rocks shrink, barnacles drink, snails think they bleed

In their trapped world. Here, when the sea is gone,

We find old coins glowing under the sky,

Barnacles counting them, snails spending slow

circles and cycles   Round lifetimes half-awake. Beach rhythms flow   *a return to money images*

In circles. Perfections teach us to die.

The first of these image clusters is coins. The second has to do with circles and spirals. As the last line suggests, watching these cycles of living and dying within the rock pool helps us to see our own mortality in perspective.

Playing Games with Images

When you first start working with similes and metaphors and their components, tenors and vehicles, the subject is apt to seem rather forbidding. It's hard to imagine playing games with them. But remember that although writing poetry is ultimately a serious and complex art, practicing in your own journal can be not only valuable but just plain fun.

Here for a start is a list of sentences that deal with abstractions or abstract qualities. The first is enhanced with a simile. See if you can do the same with the other four. Use images that are fresh and effective. Be careful to avoid clichés like "bright as a penny."

1. Her spirits rose *like a rocket*.
2. She was as bright as . . .
3. He felt fear like . . .
4. The desert was as desolate as . . .
5. A sad old dog like . . .

Now look over your list of similes and see if you can convert them to metaphors. In some cases you can simply delete "like" or "as," but often you will have to recast the sentence. It doesn't make sense, for example, to say, "Her spirits rose a rocket." But you could revise it as "Her spirits rocketed."

Now reverse the process. Here is a list of six images. Three of them are visual, one olfactory, one auditory, and one tactile. The first, italicized, has been used to create a metaphor. See if you can create similes or metaphors using each of the other five.

1. As a linebacker, he was *a charging bull*.
2. A tree bending in the wind
3. Broken glass
4. The smell of incense on a summer night
5. A child's shriek
6. The feel of rough concrete

Having trouble? Consider people, animals, songs, your mood on certain occasions. Recall moments when you were particularly contented, discontented, anguished, anxious, or joyful.

Games like these are for poets what finger exercises are for pianists. They are warming-up exercises, to use another metaphor. You are thinking in images, the language of poetry.

From Games to Serious Work

Poets never stop playing with language. But there is a difference between random experimentation in a journal and the concentrated effort required for a poem you take seriously. Journal writing is for your own benefit, an audience of one; but a poem that has been developed with care invites a wider readership. Unless you explain that it is still an early draft, your readers will assume that it deserves careful attention. There is something dishonest in passing off a carelessly or hastily composed poem as finished work and hoping that your readers will somehow make sense of it. Even if you are just starting to write, a finished poem is a revised poem, your best effort.

The more poetry you read, the more time you will spend revising your own work. I will have more to say about this at the end of the poetry section, but for now consider this: a textbook like this one can suggest what to look for in a poem, but it cannot be a substitute for careful reading of specific examples. This chapter has focused on various types of images and the ways in which they can serve to create similes, metaphors, and symbols. Before you go on to the next chapter, take some time to review the poems in Chapter 2 and perhaps others from an anthology. Circle the images you consider effective and determine for yourself whether they are used directly or as vehicles for similes or metaphors. Pick out image clusters. Identify details that have symbolic overtones. No good poem is ever spoiled by analysis.

As you turn from reading to writing, what you have learned from other poets will show you what a wide range of options you have. It will also help you to achieve an objective view of your own work. Have you made the best possible use of images? Will they suggest to your readers what you had in mind? No matter how sincerely felt your theme may be, the success of your poem will depend heavily on the effectiveness of your images.

5

THE SOUND OF WORDS

The oral tradition in poetry. Nonrhyming devices of sound: alliteration, assonance, consonance, and onomatopoeia. Rhymes, true and slant. Achieving subtlety in sound. Sound as meaning. Training your ear.

Poetry was recited aloud long before it was written down to be read from the page. We are fortunate today to have an enormous body of work available in print, but the genre has never lost its roots in the oral tradition. The growing popularity of poetry readings, both live and on videocassettes, is a good indication of how poetry, far more than prose, continues to appeal to the ear.

There are three ways in which spoken words can be linked to each other by sound. The first is to use words that begin with identical or similar sounds such as *big, black bear*. The second is to link sounds within two or more words as in d*eep* sl*eep*. The third, rhyme, is an identity of concluding sounds such as anx*iety* and soc*iety*. In addition, words can be linked in sound with the object or action they describe as in *hiss, babble,* and *chickadee*.

When we read for pleasure, we don't usually notice these linkages—at least not consciously. We may just have the vague sense that the work sounds melodic. But when we read as writers, that won't do. We have to identify the various techniques so we can discuss them accurately and eventually make use of them. To do this requires a certain critical vocabulary. The analysis of poetry necessarily uses more terms than that of prose, but I have limited them in this text to those terms really needed to discuss poems precisely.

Nonrhyming Devices of Sound

Nonrhyming linkages in sound are found both in rhymed and unrhymed poems. Because they are the least technical, they are a good introduction to the element of sound in language.

Significantly, these devices can be found in prose and oratory as well. The following passage, for example, is actually prose in spite of its **lyrical**, or musical, quality. It comes from Dylan Thomas' "August Bank Holiday" and describes a summer day at the beach not through plot but, in the manner of poetry, through a succession of vivid images. The first paragraph is typical. I have circled some of the linking sounds.

> August Bank Holiday.—A tune on an ice-cream cornet. A
>
> slap of sea and a tickle of sand. A fanfare of sunshades opening.
>
> A wince and whinny of bathers dancing into deceptive water. A
>
> tuck of dresses. A rolling of trousers. A compromise of
>
> paddlers. A sunburn of girls and a lark of boys. A silent
>
> hullabaloo of balloons.

What makes this prose passage sound "poetic"? Primarily it is all those linkages of sounds—some occurring at the beginning of words and others within words. Notice also how some words themselves echo the action or evoke the object or sensation they describe.

Anyone interested in the sound of poetry should be familiar with the following four nonrhyming techniques. If they are new to you, make an effort to use them in discussions so that they become a part of your active vocabulary.

• **Alliteration** is the repetition of initial sounds (often consonants) in two or more words. Needless to say, they have to be close enough for the reader to sense the linkage. There are three groups of these in the Thomas paragraph:

> slap—sea—sand
> wince—whinny (a similarity, not an identity of sound)
> dancing—deceptive

• **Assonance** is the repetition of similar **vowel** sounds regardless of where they are located in the word. (For those who are unsure about what vowels are and are ashamed to ask, they are the open-mouth sounds *a, e, i, o, u,* and sometimes *y*; all other letters are consonants.) Some good examples in the passage are:

> wince—whinny
> sunburn—girls (similarity of sound, not spelling)
> hullabaloo—balloons

• **Consonance** is the repetition of consonantal sounds. Whereas *alliteration* is used to describe similarities in initial sounds, *consonance* usually refers to sounds within the words. Often the two are used in conjunction. There are three sets of consonance in this passage:

> wince—whinny (both assonance and consonance here)
> girls—lark
> silent—hullabaloo—balloons

• **Onomatopoeia** is often defined as a word that sounds like the object or action it describes, but actually most onomatopoetic words suggest a sound only to those who already know what the meaning is. We are not dealing with language that mimics life directly; it is usually just an echo. There are three good examples in Thomas' paragraph of poetic prose:

> slap of sea (the sound of a wave on the beach)
> whinny (an echo of a horse's cry)
> hullabaloo (derived from "hullo" and "hello" with an echo of the clearly ono-matopoetic "babble")

Analyses like these tend to remain abstract and theoretical until one tries the technique in actual composition. Stop now and think of a scene, a friend, or a piece of music that comes to you with the soft, gentle contours you associated with the Oona figure in Chapter 3 (page 52). Now try a paragraph of descriptive prose in which you make use of as many sound devices as possible. Remember that this is prose, so there is no need to worry about rhythm or a rhyme scheme. It might help to circle the linkages in sound. The point of this exercise is merely to help you find and use sound clusters.

Now, by way of contrast, think of a place, a person, or a piece of music that more closely resembles the sharp characteristics of the Kepick figure (same page). Again, work out one or two prose paragraphs. This exercise is to poetry what preliminary sketches are to a finished painting.

Rhymes, True and Slant

True rhyme matches the sound at the ends of words. It can be defined in three short sentences: (1) It is an *identity* in sound in accented syllables. (2) The identity must begin with the accented **vowel** and *continue to the end*. (3) The sounds preceding the accented vowel must be *unlike*.

A distilled definition like this is about as off-putting as reading the rules of chess for the first time. The best approach is to move on to the examples that follow, returning to the three rules only when puzzled.

Here are four sets of true rhymes with the accented sounds in italics:

c*all*
t*all*
enthr*all*
(*all* is the identical sound; the preceding sounds are *c*, *t*, and *r*)

insp*ire*
adm*ire*
to h*ire*
(*ire* is the identical sound; the preceding sounds are *p*, *m*, and *h*)

h*eater*
m*eet her*
gr*eet her*

Notice that *true rhyme* requires an *identity* in sound. Thus "r*un*" and "c*ome*" are not true rhymes because of the subtle difference in sound. Nor are "s*een*" and "cr*eam*." These are called **slant rhymes** which I will turn to shortly.

Since we are dealing with sound, words with different spelling often rhyme. This is fortunate for those of us writing in English. "Girl" and "furl" rhyme in spite of spelling. The same for "through," "chew," "glue," "flu," "ewe," "PDQ," and "Tyler too." *Oo* sounds in English get the international prize for bizarre spelling, but they all rhyme.

Conversely, words with similar spellings but different pronunciation like "to read" and "having read" do not rhyme. These are known as **eye rhymes**. Look out for words in which the sound that comes before the rhyming sound is also identical. "Night" and "knight" are not true rhymes, for example, because the *n* is the same. Such pairs are technically known as *identities*.

These, then, are the fundamentals of rhyme. Now take a look at the table on page 76. To test yourself, cover all but the left column with your hand and decide which are true rhymes and which are not. Remember to start with the accented **vowel** and sound out the rhyming portion. Trust your ear.

Achieving Subtlety in Sound

When the sound of language becomes obvious and draws attention to itself, it dominates the entire poem. This is no problem with nursery rhymes where, as in the case of the Dr. Seuss books, rhyme and rhythm are half the fun. Nor is it a liability with mass-appeal poems like Kilmer's "Trees" in which, as we have seen, the goal is to soothe with familiar rhythms and well-known truisms. And **occasional verse**—light pieces written for special occasions like

RELATED WORDS	ACCENTED VOWEL SOUND	ACTUAL RELATIONSHIP AND EXPLANATION
1. night/fight	*i*	True rhyme (meets all three requirements)
2. night/knight	*i*	An identity (preceding consonant sounds are identical)
3. ocean/motion	*o*	True rhyme (*cean* and *tion* sound the same); also known as *double* or *feminine rhyme* (two syllables)
4. warring/wearing	*or* and *air*	Consonance or slant rhyme (accented vowel sounds do not match)
5. track to me back to me	*a*	True rhyme (a triple rhyme)
6. dies/remedies	*i* and *em*	Eye rhyme (*dies* is similar only in spelling)
7. then you see us; when you flee us	*e*	Quadruple rhyme—true rhyme (rare and usually appears forced— often comic)

anniversaries or birthdays—is frequently written with a pronounced rhyme, often for comic effect. But if you are working with a serious and complex set of themes, obtrusive rhymes can reduce all your efforts to a jingle. It's like trying to play a subtle Mozart quartet with a oompah-pah brass band.

There are several ways to mute the impact of rhyme, and the most frequently used is **enjambment**, or run-on lines. An enjambed line is one in which the grammatical construction or the meaning continues into the next line. It is distinguished from **end-stopped** lines, which usually close with a period or semicolon. Rhyme is less noticeable when the reader is drawn without a pause to the next line.

An excellent example of this technique is Maxine Kumin's "Morning Swim," which you read on page 32. This poem is written in rhyming couplets (two-line **stanzas**), a form rarely used today because in unskilled hands the rhyme can easily become monotonous and obtrusive. If you review that poem, however, you will see that ten of the twelve stanzas are enjambed. Some are fully enjambed like this one:

> Invaded and invader, I   No pause here
> went overhand on that flat sky.

There is no way you can stop or even pause at the end of that first line. Other lines are partially enjambed, like this couplet:

that fed the lake that met my sea || ⟩ *slight pause*

in which I sang *Abide with Me.*

You could stop at "sea" without being confused, but the sentence does continue into the second line.

Only two of the twelve stanzas are truly end-stopped. Here is one:

Fish twitched beneath me, quick and tame.|| *Full pause*

In their green zone they sang my name

As I mentioned, end-stopped lines usually conclude with a period or a semicolon, but not always. The deciding factor is whether the reader must continue to the next line to make grammatical sense. If you read this poem aloud, you will see how the lines blend, placing those rhymes in the background.

Kumin also uses another way of softening the impact of rhymes that is so subtle that it is easily missed. Instead of starting each line with a capital letter, as is done in a majority of poems, she capitalizes each sentence instead. It may seem odd that this would have any effect on the impact of the rhyme, but it changes the way we read the work. It highlights the sentence and downplays the line, encouraging us to read it more like prose. As a result, the rhyme endings are less noticeable.

The third method of muting the rhyme is far more common. It is simply separating the rhyming lines. The **rhyme scheme** in rhyming couplets is described as *aa bb cc dd* and so forth. If you have a three-line stanza you can elect to rhyme it *aba, bcb, cdc,* or even to leave the middle line unrhymed. A four-line stanza gives you even more choices.

If you take a close look at the rhyme scheme in Anthony Hecht's poem "Lizards and Snakes" (page 33), you will see that it is written as if in four-line stanzas even though the spacing suggests a longer unit. Here are the first two stanzas with a rhyme that occurs on alternate lines, a pattern that can be described as *abab, cdcd,* and so forth.

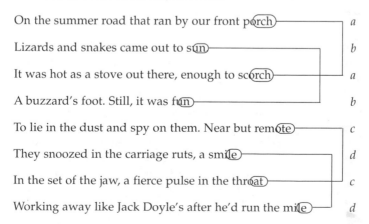

On the summer road that ran by our front porch   *a*

Lizards and snakes came out to sun   *b*

It was hot as a stove out there, enough to scorch   *a*

A buzzard's foot. Still, it was fun   *b*

To lie in the dust and spy on them. Near but remote   *c*

They snoozed in the carriage ruts, a smile   *d*

In the set of the jaw, a fierce pulse in the throat   *c*

Working away like Jack Doyle's after he'd run the mile   *d*

Notice that every rhyme in this stanza is true. In fact, in the entire poem there are only two slant rhymes. (If you look for them, be sure to identify the accented syllable.) Jack Doyle, by the way, was a famous runner whose specialty, the mile, is a convenient rhyme with "smile."

This poem also illustrates a fourth method of muting rhyme: the use of an informal or as-if-spoken **tone**. It's as if we were listening to someone tell about a childhood experience. This informality is deceptive in that it disguises the careful rhyme scheme. It is a device often used by Robert Frost in his longer as-if-narrated poems.

The fifth and final way of muting rhyme is by using **slant rhymes**, also known as **off rhymes**. In many cases these are a form of **assonance**, a similarity but not an identity of sound as in *account* and *about*.

Slant rhymes are frequently used in combination with other muting techniques. To hear the difference, read the following two passages aloud. The first is a wooden revision of the second stanza of Richard Wilbur's "The Pardon." Keep in mind that this is *not* how Wilbur wrote it; it is my shameless reworking to make a point:

> I went in close to where the poor dog was.
> I heard the flies' intolerable buzz.
> The air was heavy with honeysuckle-smell.
> It was twined with another whose source I could not tell.

Notice that not only does every line end with a true rhyme, the rhymes are highlighted by placing them next to each other in the form of couplets, *aa, bb*. In addition, each line is end-stopped with a period. The rhyme rings out like a gong: *was—buzz smell—tell*. It's verse like this that gave rhyming couplets a bad name.

Here, then, is how Richard Wilbur really wrote it.

> [I] Went only close enough to where he was
> To sniff the heavy honeysuckle-smell
> Twined with another odour heavier still
> And hear the flies' intolerable buzz.

You can hear the difference even from a casual reading of these two versions, but you have to know what you're looking for to see how the subtlety in Wilbur's version is achieved. The rhyme is there, but *smell* and *still* are slant rhymes. In addition, the scheme is, like the rest of the poem, *abba*. No line in this stanza is a complete sentence ending with a period, so there is no tendency to place a heavy emphasis on the rhyming words.

Wilbur uses slant rhymes sparingly—only three pairs out of twelve in the entire poem—and he distributes them through the poem. If you find that your slant rhymes are bunched toward the end, it probably means you were sleepy and quit too soon!

Many poets avoid rhyme altogether, but that does not mean that they necessarily ignore the sound of language. Dylan Thomas in "Fern Hill" (page 21), for example, relies almost entirely on alliteration, assonance, and consonance in much the same way he did in the prose passage at the beginning of this chapter. The only trace of rhyme is seen (if you look hard) linking the third and the eighth lines in all but one stanza. These are slant rhymes, and the gap is far too great to hear on first reading, but when they are added to the heavy use of other sound devices, they contribute to what we sense as the "musical tone" of the poem as a whole.

Some contemporary poets rely more heavily on images than on the sound of language. Donald Hall's "Names of Horses" (page 37), for example, not only is unrhymed but contains very few examples of assonance or consonance. The effect he achieves comes through a succession of highly visual, fresh, and memorable images presented in lines that are so long that they seem to resemble the plodding of the horses he is honoring.

The choice of whether to use rhyme or not will eventually be up to you, but many introductory courses in creative writing require the writing of one or more poems that make use of a regular rhyme scheme using true rhymes in a subtle manner. There is a good reason for this. As in music, painting, and many sports, reading about a technique is not the same as mastering it. Mastery comes by actually doing it. Often repeatedly. Only then do you have a true choice of whether to make further use of it.

Sound as Meaning

When working with rhyme, guard against the tendency to treat it as decoration or, worse, as a mechanical game, filling in the appropriate blanks. Sound devices are most effective when they become a part of the meaning. The best rhymes are those that draw together two images and produce a heightened or expanded meaning.

It is not possible to do this consistently, of course, but the meaningful linkage between rhymed words is more effective when it appears in concluding lines. W. S. Merwin makes use of the technique in the concluding stanza of "River Sound Remembered" (page 20). In that poem, you recall, he describes how the roaring of a river at flood time will remain with him longer than the petty sounds generated by our daily lives. As he puts it in the final stanza,

> . . . having listened absently but for so long
> It will be the seethe and drag of the river
> That I will hear longer than any mortal song.

The word "long" is linked by rhyme to the concluding phrase, "mortal song." In this way, the sound of nature is contrasted with social chatter.

Even though separated, the rhyming words highlight the theme of the poem.

Linking key words or phrases with rhyme is a particularly common device in the concluding lines of the **sonnet**. We will take a closer look at that form in Chapter 7, but our concern here is specifically on the ability of rhymed words to emphasize key concepts or images almost as if they were underlined. The concluding couplet in Shakespeare's "Sonnet 29" (page 18) is a good example. He has described his mood as truly depressed ("When in disgrace with fortune and men's eyes") until he thinks of his love. Then everything bursts into joy. Here is the concluding couplet with the key images italicized:

> For thy sweet love remembered *such wealth brings,*
> That then I scorn to change my state *with kings.*

Had he attempted to describe his joy with two unrelated images, the conclusion of that poem would have been weakened. Linking "wealth" and "kings" in the rhyming couplet draws those two lines together to highlight his sense of elation.

For a third example of meaning enhanced through rhyme review Maxine Kumin's "Morning Swim" on page 32. In that poem she links the act of swimming with that of singing a hymn of praise:

> and in the rhythm of the swim
> I hummed a two-four-time slow hymn.

This is more than a casual link of "swim" and "hymn." The rhythmical pattern of four stresses in each line echoes the musical "two-four-time" of the hymn the narrator is singing, and the two types of rhythm are joined by the rhyme of the two key words, "swim" and "hymn." Sound and sense are fused.

Nonrhyming sound devices like **assonance** and **consonance** are less noticeable than rhyme because they are often buried within the line, but they can also be used to link key images. Robley Wilson's "On a Maine Beach" (page 28) has a very loose rhyme scheme with as many slant rhymes as those that are true. But frequently he links key images with assonance. If you look closely at his simile "*rocks* like w*orn* change" you will see that visual association is enhanced with those round *o* sounds (italicized). They help to fuse the **vehicle** ("rocks") and the tenor ("worn change").

As you might expect, Dylan Thomas in "Fern Hill" (page 21) uses both assonance and consonance to link key images. Take, for example, the auditory metaphor "the *sabbath* r*a*ng *s*lowly." The *s* sounds and the repeated *a* sounds (all italicized here) and the pacing of those three stressed words all add to the illusion of church bells ringing. In the same poem his vision of fields marked with "rivers of the windfall light" is almost more auditory than it is visual as those *i,i,l,l* sounds reverberate in the reader's ear. The effect is best if you read those lines aloud. In that connection, what finer way is there to bid farewell to childhood than through an image fused by **alliteration** in "the *f*arm *f*orever *f*led *f*rom the childless land"?

If you are tempted to believe that these connections in sound are too subtle to affect the way we as readers respond to a poem, remember how dramatically our associations were altered by mere sound in nonsense words like Kepick and Oona back in Chapter 3. Casual readers don't usually notice how the sound of language affects meaning, but perceptive readers can, and poets learn by being perceptive readers.

Training Your Ear

It is hard to imagine a musical composer who doesn't spend a good deal of time listening to music. Yet some beginning poets are reluctant to read too much poetry for fear of being influenced. Actually there is no danger of becoming imitative if one reads a wide variety of works. Only by reading— preferably aloud—can one begin to appreciate the ways in which poetry is written for the ear.

So far in this chapter we have examined a variety of ways in which one can utilize the sound of language in poetry. But as I have pointed out before (and will again), passively reading about these techniques is like studying a book on how to play the violin. The learning process doesn't really start until you begin working on your own.

Now that you know what to look and listen for in poetry, turn once again to Robley Wilson's "On a Maine Beach" on page 28. First read it through without stopping—preferably aloud. Then go through it again, carefully marking as many of the rhyme endings and the nonrhyming sound devices as you can find. Now read the poem aloud once again for pleasure. This sequence of reading, analyzing, and then reading again is a good way to alternate an overall appreciation of the poem as a whole with close analytical study from the point of view of a fellow poet.

Next, turn to Chase Twichell's "Rhymes for Old Age" on page 36. We haven't worked as much on this poem, so most of the analysis of sound will be up to you. It is similar to the Wilson poem in that it has a rhyme scheme so muted you may have difficulty sorting it out. The basic pattern for each stanza is *aba cdc*. Look closely and sound out the linked words. You can teach yourself how to identify the sounds in this poem by using the same sequence that you used with the Wilson poem: read for pleasure, read line by line for analysis, then read nonstop again.

In training your ear to hear the sound of language, be careful not to stress rhyme at the expense of other devices. **Alliteration, assonance, consonance**, and **onomatopoeia** are equally important. For many poets like Dylan Thomas and E. E. Cummings, they are even more important.

Another method of training your ear is to listen to recordings of poets reading their own work. Most libraries have collections of audiotapes and videocassettes. Dylan Thomas' reading are particularly effective. Consider buying tapes for your own personal use. If your local bookstore caters to bestsellers and how-to books, use the Internet. Repeated listening is enormously valuable as well as pleasurable.

Remember, though, that to analyze techniques the way we have done in this chapter requires a close study of the written text. Whenever possible, listen with a copy of the poem in front of you. Make marginal comments and then play the tape again. You will actually hear more as you become increasingly familiar with the work.

Finally, write lines in your journal using these various techniques in sound. Don't limit yourself to lines that might develop into finished poems. Let yourself go. Experiment with assonance, with alliterative runs, with light verse in rhyme. Try a few imitations of poets with distinctive styles like Dylan Thomas or Richard Wilbur.

Sound in poetry is partly a matter of knowing what you are doing—technique. But it is also a matter of hearing what you are writing—a sensitivity to spoken language. Good poetry requires both.

6

TRADITIONAL RHYTHMS

Rhythms in daily life. The rhythm of stressed words. Syllabics: the counting of syllables. From syllabics to meter. The importance of line length. Keeping meter subtle.

Rhythmical patterns are embedded in every aspect of our lives. We celebrate the passage of each millennium, century, year, and birth date, and our calendars mark the passage of weeks and days in tune with the passages of the sun and moon. Our clocks chime the hours and tick the seconds. Internally a hundred biological clocks keep track of our age, our sleep–wake schedule, the regular functioning of our glands, our breathing, heartbeat, and brain waves.

It's no wonder that people in every culture feel the need to echo those cycles with ritual, song, and dance. Childhood chants heard today have been traced back to the 14th century, passed down not by parents or teachers but by older to younger children. They cross lines of class, nationality, and ethnic background.

The rhythms of poetry, then, are not mere adornment. They are not frills to be added for decoration. The rhythms of poetry are echoes of what goes on around us and within us. They echo the rhythms of life.

If you look again at the previous paragraph, you will see two overlapping prose rhythms repeated: *not . . . not; rhythms . . . rhythms.* Prose rhythms are simple compared with what one finds in poetry, and their effect is often subliminal. But this example illustrates how even prose rhythms can become a part of the meaning—in this case by emphasizing two key words as effectively as if I had underlined them.

Because poets control the length of the line, they have many more opportunities than prose writers to establish rhythmical patterns. In this respect, poetry is like music. One can sing poems or read song lyrics as if they were poetry. And it seems natural to use the word **verse** to designate both poetry in general and lyrics to be sung. A line of poetry is like a measure in music

There are two different approaches to creating rhythm in poetry. Although they overlap, it is helpful to examine them separately.

Traditional rhythms, the subject of this chapter, are recurring patterns that have been shared by poets for centuries. Although each poet uses a traditional pattern in a slightly different way, part of the pleasure for the reader (and the poet too) is the interplay between the familiar beat and the variations developed in a specific work.

Such work is usually based on a **stanza** of fixed length, and the rhythmical pattern is repeated—usually with variations—in each line throughout the poem. That is, the rhythm we detect in the first line becomes the model for the entire work. There are many such patterns, some based on stressed words and many more on stressed syllables.

Free-form rhythms, on the other hand, vary from line to line. The pattern is irregular, tailor-made for that poem. Although the technique is associated with what in the early 1900s became known as **free verse**, free-form rhythms go back to biblical verse. Creating unique rhythms is the subject of Chapter 8.

Rhythm of Stressed Words

The simplest traditional rhythm is based on the fact that when we speak we naturally place greater emphasis on some words than on others. We may not be consciously aware of doing this, but it is a part of how we use the language and is especially important in English. Take, for example, this straightforward sentence:

> I went to town to buy some bread.

Written on the page, it looks like eight one-syllable words of even weight. But imagine how the same sentence might sound to someone who doesn't understand English:

> i-*WENT* t'*TOWN* t'*BUY* s'm*BREAD*

The stressed words have muscled out the unstressed. No one teaches you to do this; you pick it up by listening to others speaking. It is easy enough for the poet to construct lines in which there are, say, four stressed words—especially in English, which has always relied heavily on stress. This is the system used in *Beowulf*, the Old English epic.

Here is a passage (translated into modern English) in which Beowulf, the hero, pursues a sea monster (metaphorically called the "brine-wolf") to her underwater lair. Read the selection a couple of times and underline the stressed words.

> Then bore this brine-wolf, when bottom she touched,
> the lord of rings to the lair she haunted,
> whiles vainly he strove, though his valor held,
> weapon to wield against wondrous monster
> that sore beset him; sea-beasts many
> tried with fierce tusks to tear his mail

Poets working in this tradition were concerned primarily with having four stresses in each line. They didn't count the unstressed syllables. Between each pair of stressed words is a pause known as a **caesura**. The beat is so simple and pronounced that one can pound on the table while chanting or singing it—which is probably just what the ancients did in the mead halls over a thousand years ago.

Such poems also make frequent use of **alliteration**—similar initial sounds (as we examined in the previous chapter). For this reason, *Beowulf* and many poems of this sort are referred to as **alliterative verse**.

This version is a translation of a manuscript that dates from the eighth century, so one might think that its rhythmical system would be of interest only to scholars. But poets can and do recycle anything that seems appropriate. In some respects rap music draws on that tradition today, whether the musicians know it or not. Boom boxes echo the mead-hall recitations from more than a thousand years ago.

More deliberately, in the 1970s the poet and playwright George Keithley wrote a book-length account of the ill-fated Donner party, a group of pioneers most of whom perished trying to cross the Sierra Nevada range in the 1840s. Like *Beowulf,* this is a dramatic story dealing with heroic effort, violence, and death. He adapted the same system of stresses, often using two in each line or, as in the following example, two pairs of stressed words. Here is a brief sample from *The Donner Party,* one of the few book-length **narrative poems** to reach a national audience and become a Book of the Month Club selection:

> The tongues of our flames licked at the dark.
> In time, our talking floated up like smoke
> and mingled with the chatter of the leaves.
> But the night unnerved us even as we spoke.

Syllabics: The Counting of Syllables

Rhythm that relies merely on stressed words in each line lends itself to long narrative poems, especially those with echoes of the spoken language. But the weakness of rhythm by stress is monotony. In unskilled hands, the work tends to sound like a drinking song. A more sophisticated approach is to count all the syllables in the line rather than just the stressed words.

Syllabic verse establishes a pattern based on the number of syllables in each line. One short but often subtle example of this is the **haiku**. The English version of this ancient Japanese form has just three lines. The first line has five syllables, the second has seven, and the third has five.

The haiku is called a **fixed form** since the rhythmical pattern has been established by tradition. But the form is more than just counting syllables. Unlike most fixed forms, the tradition includes aspects of the subject matter as well. Haiku almost always contain images from nature, and they also either state or imply a season. In addition, most suggest a striking similarity or even an apparent identity between two seemingly different objects. Here is a haiku from Chapter 2. Written by the Japanese poet Chora, it makes use of all three characteristics.

> After spring sunset
> Mist rises from the river
> Spreading like a flood.

As you can see, the syllable count in this translation follows the 5-7-5 pattern exactly. The poem also identifies the season, spring, and compares the gentle, harmless movement of spreading mist to that of a potentially devastating flood.

Centuries later, Etheridge Knight, an African American, taught himself to write haiku in prison and composed many that make full use of the same tradition both in structure and in content. Here is one you read in Chapter 2:

> A bare pecan tree
> slips a pencil shadow down
> a moonlit snow slope.

In this winter scene (the tree is bare) a moonlight shadow is seen as a pencil line on a white sheet of paper, an echo of the poet in the act of writing his poem. Though separated by centuries and distinctly different cultural traditions, these two poets share a type of vision through this fixed form.

Knight, in commenting on his development as a poet, described his indebtedness to the haiku. He found that the requirements of the form helped him to give up abstractions and search instead for simple but striking images. Other examples of his haiku are on page 19.

Another approach to syllabics is to have the same number of syllables in each line. This may not be noticed on first reading, but it gives a subtle sense of structure to the poem.

Syllabics can also take more complex forms in poems of two or more **stanzas**. Dylan Thomas' six-stanza poem "Fern Hill" (page 21) is a fine example. The lines are greatly varied in length, and it appears at first that there is no particular pattern. In fact, you can read the poem many times (as I did) without realizing that it is meticulously composed in syllabics. Instead of using a set number of syllables for all the lines, Thomas matches the number of syllables in each line with the corresponding line in the other five stanzas. To be specific, the first and second lines of every stanza have 14 syllables. The third line of every stanza has nine syllables. The fourth line regularly has six syllables, and the fifth always has nine. Up to this point the system is absolutely regular.

Now follow this: the sixth line has 14 syllables in every stanza except the first (which has 15); the seventh line also has 14 in every stanza except—you guessed it—the last (which again has 15). The eighth lines are either seven or nine syllables, and the final lines are either nine or six. Even Thomas' variations take on a certain order.

This is an astonishingly complex system of syllabics. Why on earth should he bother when a great majority of his readers will enjoy the poem as if it were an essentially free-verse work? The simplest answer is that Thomas, like many other poets, enjoyed working with ingenious systems many of which are apparent only to the most careful readers. As an accomplished poet, he was aware that such devices often have at least an unconscious effect on the casual reader.

In this particular case, however, there may have been a more precise motivation as well. Take a close look at that final line, "I sang in my chains like the sea." The first five stanzas are like a song about a wonderfully free-spirited childhood, but in the final stanza the "singer" (the narrator) as an adult is sadly aware that he is bound ultimately to his mortality. Life and death are as structured as the rising and falling of the tides. In the same way, the poem itself appears to be free and structureless, but in fact it is rigidly bound by an all-but-hidden form. He sings, but every line is bound by a precise rhythm.

Don't be intimidated by such ingenuity. The point here is simply this: syllabics, like all rhythmical systems, can contribute both to the pleasure and the meaning of a poem.

From Syllabics to Meter

Syllabic poetry has been particularly popular in France since the French language makes less use of stress. In English, for example, we pronounce *animal* with a heavy accent on the first syllable, but the French pronounce *l'animal* with equal stress on each syllable. These natural stresses in English are like a rhythmical system waiting for development. The **alliterative verse** in *Beowulf* and other Old English works of the 12th century and earlier were relatively crude. The next step was to establish identifiable patterns of stressed and unstressed syllables. This became the basis of **meter**.

One of the most helpful introductions to meter is "The Waking" by Theodore Roethke (page 29). Here is the first stanza in which he introduces the notion of entering into life ("I wake") while being aware that he will eventually die ("sleep").

> I wake to sleep and take my waking slow.
> I feel my fate in what I cannot fear.
> I learn by going where I have to go.

Now read the three lines placing exaggerated emphasis on the stressed syllables and whispering those that are not. The first line comes out like this:

I *WAKE* to *SLEEP* and *TAKE* my *WAK*ing *SLOW*

Notice that we are dealing with syllables here, so "waking" becomes a stressed and unstressed unit. To get the feel of it, write out the next two lines underlining the stressed syllables. The pattern is a perfectly regular series that we can describe as ta-*TUM*, ta-*TUM*, ta-*TUM*. Now with a little revision work (and apologies to Roethke) we can reverse that pattern so that it sounds like *TUM*-ta, *TUM*-ta, *TUM*-ta:

Waking, sleeping: take it slowly
(*WAK*ing, *SLEEP*ing: *TAKE* it *SLOW*ly)

If you do the same with the next two lines, you won't have to take my word for it that the mechanical conversion is relatively easy, even if it does do damage to Roethke's original version. What we have done is to start each line with a stressed syllable, making sure that the rest of the line follows the same pattern. All of this, by the way, is something poets can do and prose writers cannot because of the fact that the poet controls the length of the line.

Since it gets cumbersome and a bit silly to talk about how ta-*TUM* differs from *TUM*-ta, it's worth a few moments to learn some standard terminology. I will include here only those terms that are essential for discussing metered poetry. If you don't start using these terms accurately, discussions tend to get vague and unhelpful.

First, units of stressed and unstressed syllables are called *feet*. The **foot** we have been describing as ta-*TUM* is an **iamb**. The iambic foot is by far the most common in English. One reason for the popularity of the iambic foot is that so many two-syllable words fall naturally into this pattern: ex*cept*, al*low*, dis*rupt*, a*dore*, and the like. In addition there is a natural tendency for sentences to begin with an unstressed syllable like *a, the, but, he, she, I*.

There are three other types of feet that are also used as the basis for metered poems, and two that serve as useful **substitutions**, a technique I'll explain shortly.

The **trochee (trochaic foot)** is the reverse pattern we described as *TUM*-ta in the line "*WAK*ing, *SLEEP*ing: *TAKE* it *SLOW*ly." Although trochees can be used as the basic foot for an entire poem, they are more often used as substitutions for an iambic foot in an iambic poem. As we will see, this shift can give a special emphasis to a word or phrase, particularly if it is placed at the beginning of a line.

The **anapest (anapestic foot)** consists of three syllables—two unstressed followed by one stressed: ta-ta-*TUM*. We see it in words like *interdict* and *reimburse*, but it is far more common with phrases like *in the air* and *on the* *deck.* If I take the liberty to do one more revision of the first line of Theodore Roethke's poem in anapests, it might come out like this:

> ŭ ŭ ′ | ŭ ŭ ′ | ŭ ŭ ′ | ŭ ŭ ′
> In a lurch | I awake | but I learn | to relax

This tends to be a lively, cheerful beat, as in this anonymous couplet:

> ŭ ŭ ′ | ŭ ŭ ′ | ŭ ′ | ŭ ŭ ′
> With a swoop | and a glide | the swift | in delight,
>
> ŭ ′ | ŭ ŭ ′ | ŭ ŭ ′ | ŭ ŭ ′
> Arous|es our en|vy, our long|ing for flight.

Each line here has three anapests and one iamb. Notice how naturally the two iambic substitutions blend in and mute what might have been a singsong effect. Conversely, anapests serve well as substitutions in poems that are basically iambic. The anapest is not used as the basic meter in many poems, but it has real potential for work that is light and **lyrical**.

The **dactyl** is the reverse of the anapest: *TUM*-ta-ta as in *"HEAV*ier," *"FOL*lowing," and *"TALK* to me." It's a weighty foot.

Most metered poems in English use one of these four feet as a basic pattern, and more than half are iambic. There are, however, two more feet that are useful when you **scan** a poem—that is, analyze it metrically. You will find yourself using these two feet as substitutions as well.

The **spondee** consists of two heavy stresses, as in the words "spondee" itself and "heartbreak." The **pyrrhic** is two equally unstressed syllables, as in "in the" or "and the."

The following table will help to introduce you to these terms, but if you start using them in discussions you won't need the table for long.

FOOT	ADJECTIVE	STRESS PATTERN	EXAMPLES
iamb	iambic	ta-TUM	except; the deer
trochee	trochaic	TUM-ta	asking; lost it
anapest	anapestic	ta-ta-TUM	understand; in delight
dactyl	dactylic	TUM-ta-ta	heavily; talk to me
spondee	spondaic	TUM-TUM	heartbreak; campsite
pyrrhic	pyrrhic	ta-ta	in the; on a

The Importance of Line Length

In most metered poetry, both the basic type of foot and the number of feet in each line are constant throughout the poem. That is, the pattern you see in the first line is the pattern you get in the poem as a whole. This is not a matter of rules, but shifting the meter would be like writing a song that starts as a waltz and then switches abruptly to a polka.

One of the most popular lengths in English is five feet. This is called **pentameter**, a word that comes from the Greek *penta* for "five," as in *pentagon*. It has been a favorite metrical scheme in English for 400 years. You can see it in Shakespeare's "Sonnet 29" (page 18) and also in several contemporary examples such as "The Waking" by Theodore Roethke (page 29), "Design" by Robert Frost (page 15), and "The Pardon" by Richard Wilbur (page 34). The Roethke poem is the best introduction because it is unusually regular.

The four-footed line, **tetrameter**, is a close second in popularity. **Trimeter**, three feet to a line, is slightly less common, but it is also used widely. Lines that are longer than pentameter and shorter than trimeter are used far less frequently, but for the purpose of clarity, here is a list. Don't let these traditional terms put you off. You will find them helpful both when reading metered verse and when composing your own work. The more you use these terms, the quicker they will become a part of your active vocabulary.

Two feet to each line (rare and usually comic)	*dimeter*
Three feet to each line (fairly common)	*trimeter*
Four feet (sometimes combined with trimeter)	*tetrameter* ⎫
Five feet (most common in English)	*pentameter* ⎬ most common
Six feet (less used in this century)	*hexameter* ⎭
Seven feet (rare)	*heptameter*
Eight feet (a heavy, very rare line)	*octometer*

At this point, it would be helpful to try writing three lines of iambic tetrameter. Take some simple topic as if you were about to write a haiku and follow the iambic pattern: ta-*TUM*, ta-*TUM*, and so on. Don't worry about rhyme, and don't feel you have to be profound. This exercise is just to help you to feel the rhythm—and to assure you that it is easier than you might think.

Now try shifting your lines so that they are trochaic: *TUM*-ta, *TUM*-ta, and so on. Avoid articles like *a* and *the* at the beginning of the line since they are unstressed. Once you find a good, solid first syllable, the rest of the line should follow more easily.

Next, shift the topic to something lighter and try a few lines of anapests: ta-ta-*TUM*. For example, "In a leap and a bound, the gazelle in delight welcomes spring!"

Keeping Meter Subtle

Until now, we have been working with **scansion**—the analysis of meter. It is to metrical poetry what grammar is to prose. It is quite true that you probably learned to write prose without knowing much grammar simply by reading and listening to prose sentences since infancy. It is also true that you could write iambic pentameter simply by ear if you had started reading and listening to poetry every day from the time you were three. But you didn't. In some ways, discovering poetry seriously at this late stage is like taking up a new language. But mercifully the transition between learning the mechanics and developing the art is far more rapid.

When you first begin writing metered lines, it is natural to make it as perfect and obvious as possible. You are like a beginning ballroom dancer who still counts out each step. Once you feel at home with the mechanics, try to mute your meter just as you did with rhyme. This doesn't mean being careless; it means studying and adopting the methods of poets you admire.

There are four useful ways of keeping your metrical rhythm from taking over a poem, and often you will find it helpful to use several of them in a single work.

1. One of the most commonly used methods is to make sure that at least some of your words bridge two metrical feet. It is such a simple technique that you may not have noticed it in the poems you have read. Here is a line refashioned from the last stanza of Richard Wilbur's "The Pardon" (page 34). I have rewritten it so that every foot is made up of two one-syllable words:

$$\breve{\text{But if}} \mid \breve{\text{my dream}} \mid \breve{\text{was false}} \mid \breve{\text{or true}}$$

Here, in contrast, is the line as Wilbur wrote it. Notice that three out of the four feet bridge two words and there is an extra unstressed syllable at the end, a fairly common practice:

$$\breve{\text{But wheth}}\mid\text{er this}\mid\text{was false}\mid\text{or hon}\mid\text{est dream}\mid\text{ing}$$

There is nothing technically wrong with the first version, but the second avoids the regularity and monotony of a too-blatant metrical line.

2. An equally common method of softening the wooden effect of unvaried meter is called **substitution**. The poet occasionally substitutes a different foot from the one that has been adopted for the poem as a whole.

We have already looked at Wilbur's "The Pardon" (page 34) for examples of how to mute the sound of rhyme. The poem also serves to illustrate how to keep iambic pentameter from becoming monotonous. Here, for instance, is how he uses a trochaic substitution with the phrase "twined with."

To sniff | the heavly hon|eysuck|le-smell|

Twined wi th | anoth|er o|dour heav|ier still|

The substitution not only offers variation, it also highlights the metaphor that links the way smells mix and the way vines twist about each other. The substitution, then, is neither arbitrary nor careless. It adds to the emotional impact of the line.

Later in the poem there is a line that has two substitutions, an anapest and a trochee. I have left it unmarked so that you can **scan** it yourself.

In the carnal sun, clothed in a hymn of flies.

One way you can give special emphasis to the initial word in a line that is essentially iambic is to start the line with a trochaic substitution. In "Sonnet 29" (page 18) Shakespeare not only does this but, in addition, signals the dramatic shift from his dark mood in the first nine lines (". . . my self almost despising") to his elation when thinking of his love:

Haply I think on thee, and then my state,
Like to the lark at break of day arising

Robley Wilson in "On a Maine Beach" (page 28) also uses iambic pentameter, but the first four lines start with trochees. It's as if he is grabbing your arm and saying, "Hey, look at this!"

How many substitutions can a poem absorb and still be called metered? Anthony Hecht's "Lizards and Snakes" (page 33) is essentially iambic, but the lines alternate in length and some have as many as three out of five feet that are not iambs.

With so many variations, why do we call the poem iambic? Because *most* of the lines are primarily iambic with no more than one or occasionally two substitutions. When we come to a line that has more substitutions than that, we retain the memory of that iambic beat and assume that the poem will return to it—as indeed this poem does.

The process is very much like listening to a work of jazz in which there are extensive improvisations. If we are familiar with the original melody, we retain the memory of it. With poetry, however, there comes a point when the variations are so extensive that we can no longer hear the original pattern. In such cases we must conclude that the work is unmetered, no matter what the poet claims. Effective use of meter, after all, depends on the ear of the informed reader, not merely on the intention of the poet.

   3. A third method of muting meter is **enjambment**, also known as the **run-on-line**. An enjambed line, you remember, is one in which both the grammatical construction and the sense are continued into the next line. It is opposed to the **end-stopped line**, which is followed by a natural pause— usually concluded with a period, semicolon, or at least a comma. As I pointed out in the previous chapter, it is an effective way of softening the impact of rhyme; it also serves to keep your meter from sounding like a marching band.

Poems vary as to how frequently they use enjambment. Theodore Roethke's "The Waking" (page 29), for example, is unusual in that only one line in 19 is truly enjambed. All the rest come to a full stop or, in one case, a pause with a comma. In Richard Wilbur's "The Pardon" (page 34), on the other hand, all but five lines out of 24 are enjambed, giving the poem a conversational tone.

4. The fourth technique of softening the impact of meter is rare but well illustrated in Anthony Hecht's "Lizards and Snakes" (page 33). He changes his line length, alternating pentameter and tetrameter. That is, his first line has five feet and the second four, establishing a fairly consistent pattern that runs through the poem. A few of his lines even have six feet.

This is a risky approach, since readers tend to expect greater regularity. It's like climbing stairs of alternating height. One reason it works here is that it is a pattern many readers are used to in ballads, a stanza form I'll come to in the next chapter. In addition, the folksy, as-if-told tone lends itself to a looser structure.

5. Finally, remember that metered poetry doesn't have to be rhymed at all. Because a regular rhyme scheme intensifies the effect of the metrical beat, eliminating it softens the rhythm. The most popular line length for metered but unrhymed poetry is pentameter. Unrhymed iambic pentameter is called **blank verse**. Shakespeare used it frequently, and so have many contemporary poets.

Keep these five approaches in mind whenever you write metered verse. They will help you to maintain a metrical rhythm without having it take over. Only you can tell how pronounced to make your meter and how to mute it, but the more poetry you read the more unconscious those decisions will become. Review the metered work of such poets as Robert Frost, Anthony Hecht, Theodore Roethke, Timothy Steele, Richard Wilbur, and Maxine Kumin, all of whom are represented in Chapter 2. If you are drawn to one or two of these poets, take the time to find their collected work in your library. The difference between knowing the mechanics of meter and being able to incorporate it subtly in your own work will depend on how much metered poetry you have read.

7

FROM LINES TO STANZAS

Stanzas defined. Rhyming couplets: uses and risks. Triplets, rhyming and not. Quatrains and the ballad tradition. Rhyme royal. Sonnets, Elizabethan and Italian. The rondeau. The pantoum. The villanelle. The appeal of metrical forms.

In some ways, the stanza is like the paragraph in prose. Like the paragraph, the stanza can be used to unify a particular thought or feeling. In most cases it is also set off by an extra space.

In **syllabic** and **metered** poetry, however, the stanza serves an additional function not possible in prose. It takes on greater prominence by having a consistent number of lines—usually from two to eight. And if there is a rhyme scheme the pattern is repeated within this unit. In rhyming couplets, for example, each pair of lines rhymes; in four-line stanzas a common pattern is to rhyme alternate lines. In this chapter we will examine the most popular stanza types as well as four verse forms that make more varied use of stanzas.

Rhyming Couplets: Uses and Risks

The great asset of rhyming **couplets** is that each pair of lines becomes a tight little unit linked by sound and often by content as well. In the 17th and 18th centuries, poets like Alexander Pope (1688–1744) and Oliver Goldsmith (1730–1774) used them to deal with subjects we would now handle in prose as essays.

At that time, the couplets were often **end-stopped** (concluded with a comma or a period). Occasionally, they were complete on their own, a two-line poem expressing a pithy saying known as an **epigram**. For example, in speaking of how a nation can become prey to "hastening ills," Goldsmith wrote:

> Ill fares the land, to hastening ills a prey,
> Where wealth accumulates, and men decay.

The great liability of couplets, as I pointed out earlier, is monotony. In unskilled hands, it can become a boring beat and an obtrusive rhyme. As a result, the couplet has fallen on hard times, often reduced to jingles, greeting cards, and **occasional verse.** Even if you are working with a serious, sophisticated topic, your efforts may seem trivial by association with these simple verse forms.

If you are on guard against these risks, however, the form lends itself to highly sophisticated contemporary verse. It is particularly effective with **narrative poems**—those that tell a story.

As we have already seen, Maxine Kumin's "Morning Swim" (page 32) is an excellent example of how to mute the rhythmical impact of iambic tetrameter as well as the potential monotony of rhyming couplets.

Gwendolyn Brooks employs a strikingly original treatment of couplets in "The Pool Players" (page 24). Here, as a reminder, are the first two of four stanzas:

> We real cool. We
> Left school. We
>
> Lurk late. We
> Strike straight. We

If you tried to scan this, you were probably puzzled. But if you move the word "we" from the end of each line to the beginning, the lines can be read as anapests (*ta*-ta-*TUM*), though the stress is almost equal on all three words. More important, the stanzas become conventional rhyming couplets:

> We real cool.
> We left school.
>
> We lurk late.
> We strike straight.

This version makes sense, but the regularity of the rhyming couplets gives it a singsong quality like a skip-rope chant. Notice that each line in this revised version is **end-stopped**. They magnify the rhyming sounds. Brooks' version ends each line with an **identity** that normally would be blatant, but the **enjambment** pitches you forward into the next line. What in my revised version is an obtrusive rhyme is now softened as a series of **internal rhymes.**

Rhyming couplets are easy and fun to write for comic and satiric verse, but if you plan to use them for a serious subject as Gwendolyn Brooks and Maxine Kumin do, be sure to review all the techniques available for muting both the meter and the rhyme.

Triplets, Rhyming and Not

Triplets (also called **tercets**) provide more variations in rhyme than do couplets. Because rhyming all three lines (described as *aaa*) tends to be highly obtrusive, most poets prefer to keep the second line unrhymed, *aba, cdc*.

The **terza rima** is a beautiful extension of the triplet and lends itself best to longer poems. The middle line of each triplet is made to rhyme with the first and last lines of the next triplet in this manner:

First stanza	a	(b)	a
Second stanza	(b)	(c)	b
Third stanza	(c)	(d)	c
Fourth stanza	(d)	e	d

In this way each stanza is subtly linked with the next, but the sound linkages blend into the fabric of the poem.

Quatrains and the Ballad Tradition

The four-line stanza, or **quatrain**, is probably the most popular of all fixed-verse forms. One advantage is that it allows for such a variety of possible rhyme schemes. High on the list is *abab*, unobtrusive yet never fully lost.

A variation of this rhymes the two central lines: *abba*. Richard Wilbur's "The Pardon" (page 34) is a good example of this, though you will notice that he uses **slant rhymes** in almost every stanza.

Less noticeable (and less demanding as well) is *abcb*, which leaves the first and third lines unrhymed.

Perhaps because quatrains are ideal for memorization, the four-line stanza has become the traditional form for **ballads**. The term includes works that are intended to be sung, recited, or read, but what they all have in common is a lively story line and in most cases a four-line stanza. Ballads in English are often iambic tetrameter, although the five-footed pentameter is also popular. The rhyme scheme varies in the ways described: either *abab* or the looser *abcb*.

Ballad meter is one of the few stanza forms in which the lines alternate in length regularly—usually between iambic tetrameter and iambic trimeter. Normally the rhyme scheme is *abcb*.

The term *folk ballad* refers most often to those thousands of Scottish and English works in ballad meter that were composed and sung by untrained, often illiterate balladeers from the fourteenth to the sixteenth centuries.

That tradition of relatively simple narrative poems dealing with love (often lost or betrayed like our contemporary blues lyrics), war (often laments), and the supernatural is alive today in the form of popular folk songs. In fact, the word *ballad* is still applied equally to poetry and song.

Literary ballads are merely a refinement of this same tradition. "The Rime of the Ancient Mariner," by Samuel Taylor Coleridge, is one of the best known. Although he allowed himself occasional variations in traditional ballad meter, here is a dramatic stanza that contains only one rather inconspicuous substitution.

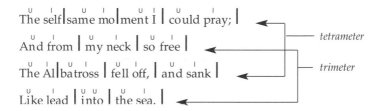

Anthony Hecht's "Lizards and Snakes" (page 33) adapts the ballad form to tell a story that is more complex than it appears on first reading. His stanzas look as if they are eight lines long, but if you draw a line after each fourth line and look at the rhyme scheme, you will see that it is really composed in quatrains like most ballads. He has increased the traditional line length by alternating iambic pentameter with iambic tetrameter. His rhyme scheme is *abab* throughout.

Hecht's variations on the basic ballad form show that there is nothing sacred about literary tradition. But notice that once he establishes his version of the ballad, he stays with it. A poem that begins with a traditional form and then deteriorates toward the end suggests that perhaps the poet was working late at night to meet an early morning deadline.

Rhyme Royal

If you like the sound of couplets but dislike their tendency to sound choppy and monotonous in spite of all your efforts, consider the solution introduced into English by Chaucer. The **rhyme royal** is a seven-line stanza in **iambic pentameter** with the following rhyme scheme: *ababbcc*.

The first three lines are linked with what is essentially a rhyming triplet, *aba*. Then there are what resemble two rhyming couplets. Don't forget that the first of those two couplets rhymes with the second line of the poem. Schematically, it looks like this

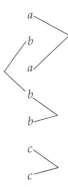

Whether you stop at seven lines or go on repeating the seven-line pattern is up to you. In an age of constant change, it's reassuring to know that something over 600 years old is as fresh and adaptable as it was for Chaucer.

Sonnets, English and Italian

While the ballad lends itself to storytelling, the **sonnet's** precise length is best suited for a single, well-defined theme or set of feelings. Occasionally sonnets are strung together as a sonnet series such as *The Golden Gate* by Vikram Seth, but these are rare.

There are two basic types of sonnets, the *English* (also called **Elizabethan**) and the *Italian* (also called **Petrarchan**). They are both 14 lines long, and both are traditionally written in iambic pentameter—five feet to the line. The primary difference between the two is the rhyme scheme.

The English sonnet, made famous by Shakespeare, can be thought of as three quatrains and a final rhyming couplet: *abab, cdcd, efef, gg.* The first eight lines are referred to as the **octave** and the last six as the **sestet**. Often there is some shift in mood at the beginning of the sestet, providing a contrast and what is called *poetic tension*. In these cases, the unity of the poem is established with the resolution in the final rhyming couplet.

Once you read a number of sonnets, you can identify the form in advance just from the basic 14-line shape. Occasionally English sonnets are printed as an unbroken block, but more often there is a space between the octave and a sestet. That concluding couplet is a distinguishing characteristic both in rhyme and, usually, in the way it draws together the theme of the poem.

The second basic type, the Italian sonnet, is also based on 14 lines of iambic pentameter, but it is usually arranged as two quatrains and two triplets: *abba, abba, cde, cde.* You can differentiate it from the Elizabethan sonnet immediately from the fact that it has no concluding couplet.

Sonnets are printed in various ways, but here is a schematic representation of the spacing and rhyme scheme often adopted:

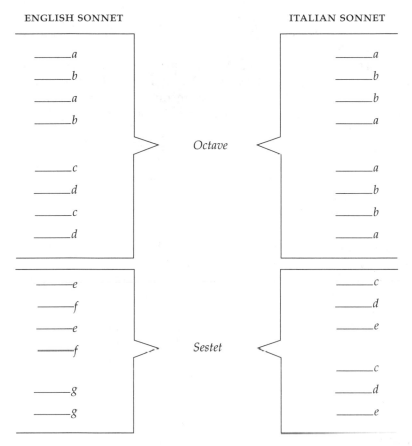

ENGLISH SONNET

_____a
_____b
_____a
_____b

Octave

_____c
_____d
_____c
_____d

_____e
_____f
_____e
_____f

Sestet

_____g
_____g

ITALIAN SONNET

_____a
_____b
_____b
_____a

_____a
_____b
_____b
_____a

_____c
_____d
_____e

_____c
_____d
_____e

To convert this diagram into actual poetry, keep one hand on this page and turn back to Shakespeare's "Sonnet 29" on page 18. If the book is your own copy, you may wish to draw a line between the octave and the sestet and then pencil in the rhyme scheme, *abab* and so forth. Notice that the sestet begins with "Yet in these thoughts"—just a hint of that change in mood. The real shift, though, comes in the next line with the trochaic "Haply."

Now do the same with Robert Frost's sonnet "Design" (page 15). It follows the Italian form faithfully, with one exception: he ends the poem with a rhyming couplet as if it were an English sonnet.

The Rondeau

There are many poetic forms that British and American poets have adapted from French and Italian models, but I would recommend the **rondeau** for those who are discovering new verse forms. It is relatively brief—usually just one line longer than the sonnet—and it is written in syllabics, the same number of syllables in each line. It is also a good introduction to the use of a refrain.

The most common pattern has three stanzas: a **cinquain** (five lines), a **quatrain** (four lines), and usually a concluding **sestet** (six lines). (Only an engineer would ask why.) There is a **refrain** that appears as an opening of the first line and is repeated at the end of the second and third stanza.

If we designate the refrain as *R*, the rhyme scheme is like this:

First stanza: *aabba*   (with refrain opening the first line)
Second stanza: *aabR*   (refrain as last line)
Third stanza: *aabbaR* (refrain as last line)

Now turn to James Bertram's tribute to Ernest Hemingway in "Is It Well-Lighted, Papa?" on page 31. Most of his lines have 10 syllables except for the two refrain lines, which have seven. Another fairly common variation is that his third stanza has four rather than five lines. As a result, the poem has 14 lines like a sonnet.

When you try this form, consider carefully just what your refrain will be. In Bertram's poem, "Papa" is the nickname for Ernest Hemingway and the refrain echoes the title of one of Hemingway's better known stories, "A Clean, Well-Lighted Place." Whatever you select should highlight the theme without being too bluntly analytical.

The Pantoum

The appeal of the **pantoum** (pronounced panTOOM) is the way in which the stanzas interlock with repeated lines. Originally a Malayan form, it was adopted by the French and the English. Written in quatrains, the form leaves the choice of meter and total length up to you. The traditional rhyme is *abab, bcbc, cdcd*. The unique aspect is the way the stanzas interlock through repetition: lines 2 and 4 of each stanza become lines 1 and 3 of the next.

The last stanza of the poem can take one of two patterns: either a couplet made up of lines 1 and 3 in reverse order (as in the example following) or a concluding quatrain using lines 1 and 3 of the first stanza as lines 4 and 2 respectively. Notice that both approaches reverse the repeated lines in the concluding stanza, ingeniously making the first line of the poem the same as the last.

You have already studied (I hope) "Always the One Who Loves His Father Most" by Clement Long, which appears in its entirety in Chapter 2. Here is an annotated version of the first two and last stanzas:

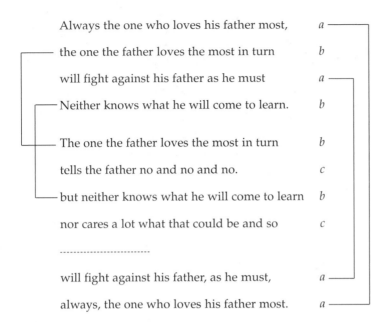

Always the one who loves his father most,   *a*

the one the father loves the most in turn   *b*

will fight against his father as he must   *a*

Neither knows what he will come to learn.   *b*

The one the father loves the most in turn   *b*

tells the father no and no and no.   *c*

but neither knows what he will come to learn   *b*

nor cares a lot what that could be and so   *c*

will fight against his father, as he must,   *a*

always, the one who loves his father most.   *a*

After studying the pattern here, go back and reread the poem in its entirety on page 23. Notice that this particular pantoum uses unusually regular iambic pentameter and maintains the rhyme scheme with just a few slant rhymes, as in "most" and "must."

As with many verse forms, the mechanics may seem like the main challenge at first. But this stage will soon pass. The next step is to find a topic that lends itself to that particular form. In this particular pantoum, for example, the theme focuses on the changing relationship between fathers and sons that is repeated generation after generation. The repetition of lines in the pantoum lends itself perfectly to the generational cycles the poem is describing.

The Villanelle

The **villanelle** may seem intimidating at first, but if you have tried writing a rondeau or a pantoum, you will find some of the same characteristics—the use of the refrain in particular. Once you flesh out the mechanical description with the example following, the form will become quite manageable. Far less complex than the rules of chess, a good villanelle can become musical like a melody intensified with repeated phrases.

Before we examine the mechanics of the villanelle, read once again Theodore Roethke's "The Waking" on page 29. We have used this poem in earlier chapters to illustrate aspects of meter and rhyme, but you may not have noticed that it is, in addition, a villanelle.

In reviewing the poem, note these three aspects: (1) It is made up of six stanzas of which the first five are tercets (three lines) and the last is a quatrain (four lines). (2) There are only two rhymes, *a* and *b*. (3) There are two refrains that recur in a regular sequence. Although Roethke has chosen to use unusually regular iambic pentameter lines, other meters are acceptable. Originally, sestinas were written in syllabic lines of equal length.

The following table shows the skeletal form. Don't try to memorize it. Instead, use it as you did with the diagrams of the sonnet and the rondeau. Keep your hand on this page for a guide and see how it is implemented in Roethke's poem. Again, you will understand the pattern best if you mark up the copy of the poem itself.

THE VILLANELLE

(1) 1. First refrain   *a*
　　　2. _____   *b*
　　　3. Second refrain   *a*

(2) 4. _____   *a*
　　　5. _____   *b*
　　　6. First refrain   *a*

(3) 7. _____   *a*
　　　8. _____   *b*
　　　9. Second refrain   *a*

(4) 10. _____   *a*
　　 11. _____   *b*
　　 12. First refrain   *a*

(5) 13. _____   *a*
　　 14. _____   *b*
　　 15. Second refrain   *a*

(6) 16. _____   *a*
　　 17. _____   *b*
　　 18. First refrain   *a*
　　 19. Second refrain   *a*

The two refrains of a villanelle are particularly important. Since they are repeated so often, they should be central to the theme. But they should also be used in slightly different ways to keep the poem from being repetitious.

Roethke's first refrain begins with "I wake to sleep." This is a **paradox**—a statement that on one level is logically absurd, yet on another implies a deeper meaning. In this case he is describing the fact that we are born only to die eventually. This would be depressing if it weren't for the rest of the refrain, "and take my waking slow." He will make the most of his life.

The second refrain amplifies this with the assertion that he learns "by going where I have to go." He gains experience by doing what must be done.

As for varying the way he uses these refrains, notice how the first four stanzas are simply a statement of belief, but in the fifth stanza the same refrain becomes advice to someone else:

> "And, lovely, learn by going where to go."

Whether he is addressing his love or you the reader is up to you. In either case, the refrain shifts from being an assertion of belief to advice.

If you look carefully at the whole poem, you will notice that Roethke takes certain minor liberties with the form. Some of the rhymes, for example, are slant rhymes, and one of the refrains is subtly altered—though without giving up the pentameter. But he is essentially faithful to the form, and if you enjoy this kind of challenge you will want to match his fidelity.

The Appeal of Metrical Forms

Metered verse and its various stanza forms dominated British and American poetry for some 500 years. Starting in the early 1900s, however, varieties of **free verse** with its nonmetrical systems of rhythm became a firm part of our tradition. We will be examining free verse in the next chapter.

At the same time as free verse had its ascendancy, poets like Robert Frost, Theodore Roethke, Richard Wilbur, and many others continued to work with metrical forms. As I mentioned in the last chapter, the increased interest in metrics since the 1980s has come to be known as the **new formalism**. Although it is not truly a movement, it has generated fresh and innovative uses of meter.

When one is first introduced to metrical schemes and various stanza forms, they may seem mechanical and limiting. There are new terms to master, just as there are when one begins a new language. But poets who prefer to work metrically don't usually start out by selecting a meter as if it were a mold into which one could pour words. Instead, they are more likely to let a poem begin intuitively and see what kind of line develops. If you have been reading metered poetry, your initial lines may suggest a metrical pattern that seems natural and appropriate for your material.

Once you get beyond the introductory stage in metrics, terms like iambic pentameter and trochaic trimeter become a part of you, a dance step that no longer has to be counted out, a rhythm with infinite varieties. The metrical beat is internal, and the pleasure of writing comes in the interplay between that pattern and your improvisation.

Returning to the parallel with jazz, you will find yourself like a trumpet player alternately straying from the melody and returning to it. Stray too far and too often, and the memory of the melody is lost; stick too close, and you run the risk of monotony. Those who enjoy working with metrical forms find that it adds one more dimension to the genre.

There are two other rewards from writing in meter that its proponents often mention. One is that meeting the requirements of a particular form often encourages them to consider words and phrases that wouldn't have come to mind otherwise. The other is that metrics allows the poet to emphasize or highlight a word or phrase by substituting a different foot. We have seen how using the heavy initial beat of a trochaic foot in a basically iambic poem can add emphasis, and how the lilting quality of an anapest can give a lift to a line that is otherwise consistently iambic or trochaic. This provides a delicate control of language.

For others, however, verse forms still seem too restrictive. They would rather devise unique rhythms for each poem in ways we will consider in the next chapter. But keep in mind that there is no sharp division between the two approaches. Traditional forms can be altered to fit the needs of a particular poem, and even the most intuitive free-verse poem may benefit from techniques we associate with metered verse. The more poetry you read, the more options you will discover.

8

FREE-VERSE PATTERNS

Freedom from meter and stanza forms: assets and liabilities. Visual patterns: what you see on the page. Auditory patterns: what you hear in the reading. The line versus the sentence. The unmarked border with prose. Developing your own patterns.

Free verse does not use meter or a regular rhyme scheme. Line length is varied. If there are stanzas, they are usually irregular in length. The visual pattern designed for each poem is unique.

The term *free verse* came into vogue around 1900, but unmetered poetry without a regular rhyme scheme has had a long and distinguished history. It is rooted in a variety of ancient sources, both written and oral.

⌊What free verse does *not* abandon is equally important. Like metered poetry, it makes deliberate use of the line.⌉And it frequently uses stanzas, though usually varied in length. Free from regular rhyme schemes, free verse draws instead on a number of different auditory devices including **alliteration**, **assonance**, **consonance**, and repetition. It occasionally employs scattered rhymes. Most important, it almost always maintains some type of rhythm.

Freedom from Meter and Stanza Forms:
Assets and Liabilities

When working with free verse you are free to devise your own visual and auditory patterns—line length, spacing, and linkages in sound. There are no regular forms to serve as a guide. In early drafts, the writing may be highly intuitive. If you have been working with meter, it will seem as if anything is possible—a heady sensation.

On the other hand, you're on your own. It's up to you to create your own rhythms and auditory aspects. If you don't pay attention to these aspects, you'll end up writing prose in short lines. Some find that without traditional guidelines it is more difficult to determine what is really effective and what doesn't work. It's hard to be sure when the poem has reached its full potential.

Although free-verse techniques are not as distinct as those of metered poetry, they can be divided into two closely related categories. The first is **typography**, the arrangement of print on the page. This includes line length, indentations, and extra space between words. It also includes the grouping of lines into **stanzas**, usually of varied length.

The other aspect is *auditory*, what you hear when the poem is read. All poetry, of course, appeals to the ear, but free verse relies on somewhat different techniques. Alliteration and assonance, for example, are used more often than rhyme. And repetition of words and phrases is often used to create rhythm and influence the pace of reading.

It's useful to examine these two aspects separately for analysis, but keep in mind that they are closely interrelated. Now that poetry is almost always presented in printed form, the arrangement on the page influences the way we read a poem aloud. We respond to these visual cues both consciously and unconsciously. Conversely, what you as a poet want the poem to sound like when it is presented out loud will affect how you arrange the work on the page. Just as playwrights imagine how their lines will be delivered in a production, poets "hear" a poem as they write.

Visual Patterns: What You See on the Page

Typography is the arrangement of words on the page. Writers of prose, as I pointed out in the first chapter, have almost no control over the placement of their words. Since line length is left up to the printer, sentence follows sentence like a series of freight cars. The only typographical option for the prose writer is the indentation that indicates a new paragraph. Poets, on the other hand, have full control over the placement of every word and even every syllable.

The length of lines and their indentation are extremely important in most free-verse poems. Some poets spread their lines out with many different indentations, even leaving extra spaces within the line. Other poets mold their free verse into fairly uniform units that look very much like metered stanzas. The choice depends partly on the poet's general style and partly on the demands of an individual poem.

Here, for example, is the opening stanza of Denise Levertov's "Merritt Parkway." The entire poem appears on page 27, but this portion is enough to remind you how she adopts an extremely loose typography to suggest the flow of traffic on a busy freeway:

> As if it were
> forever that they move, that we

keep moving—
    Under a wan sky where
  as the lights went on a star
      pierced the haze & now
  follows steadily
     a constant
  above our six lanes
  the dreamlike continuum . . .

It would be an exaggeration to say that a reader not familiar with English could identify the subject simply through the arrangement of words on the page, but because we know what is being described from the outset, the shape of the lines becomes a part of the total meaning. Anyone who has driven on an interstate highway can feel the flow of traffic, almost unbroken yet undulating as the car shifts lanes.

The lines (of the poem, that is) are of different lengths and are shoved to the left and right. Some of this spacing seems arbitrary, like the motion of cars, but others highlight a particular word. In the first stanza, given above, "a constant" is isolated to the right. It emphasizes the fixed nature of the star above the moving cars. In the next stanza (turn back to page 28), the word "unsure" is isolated to the right in exactly the same way. This stanza focuses on us, "the humans from inside the / cars." In this way the fixed, "constant," position of the star is set off against the fluid, "unsure" state of those driving.

Compare Levertov's long, undulating lines with the short, compressed lines of free verse in Philip Appleman's "Desire." Typographically, it is at the other extreme. Here are the first two of four stanzas from the poem, which appears on page 43 in its entirety:

1

The body
tugged like a tide, a pull
stronger than
the attraction of stars.

2

Moons
circling their planets,
planets
rounding their suns.

Here the effect is strikingly different from the flowing quality of the Levertov poem. What you notice first is that every line is extremely short. Some have only one word.

Why the difference between these two poems? In some cases, a poet's decision about how to shape a free-verse work is intuitive, but in this case we can see a direct relationship between the subject matter and the form. "Merritt Parkway" describes a specific East Coast highway with its steady flow of traffic. It focuses on what it feels like to be gliding along in that "dreamlike continuum." Those long and varied lines can be described with the same phrase the poet uses to end the poem: "a slurred sound."

"Desire," on the other hand, is a delicate description of longing. The speaker is comparing his or her desire for someone who is, in the last stanza, "oceans away." The poem moves from image to image, and the brevity of each line and each stanza urges us to read the work deliberately as if walking on stepping-stones.

In addition to the treatment of line length, free-verse poems often make use of stanzas. Unlike those in metered poetry, free-verse stanzas often vary in length. They are known as **nonrecurrent stanzas**.

Some nonrecurrent stanzas are inconspicuous while others are designed as a dominant device. In "Merritt Parkway," for example, you may not have even noticed on first reading that there are actually four stanzas, each designated by a double space just as they are in metered verse. They are almost lost, however, in that scattering of lines.

These stanza divisions may seem at first to be arbitrary, but if you look closely you will see that the first is an objective view ("they move"), the second turns to the passengers ("the people—ourselves"), the third focuses on the roadside ("houses . . .trees"), and the final three-line stanza is a summary. There is an order here, but it is very subtle.

The stanzas in Appleman's "Desire," on the other hand, couldn't be more dominant. Each is brief, either four or three lines. Each ends with a period. In addition, he has numbered them almost as if they were separate units. Each begins with a noun that announces the theme of that stanza. These concise, short-line stanzas each have the compression and simplicity of haiku even though they do not follow that syllabic form.

These are extreme uses of typography, and like most extremes they have certain pitfalls for less experienced poets. If you are tempted by the long and suggestive lines used by Levertov, remember that obvious use of typography can be just as damaging to a free-verse poem as simple, obvious use of meter and rhyme can be in traditional work. Because typographical arrangements are so blatant, so immediately apparent, they have to be used with considerable subtlety. Every writing class has been subjected to some version of this:

And on that happy afternoon we
   all
      fell
         down
            laughing.

This is too easy, too obvious.

The short-line, short-stanza poem also has its risk. Compression is commendable, but if pushed too far it fades into obscurity. Remember that your work is intended for readers, and you have to give them enough, as Appleman does, to share your feelings.

What do you have to do to achieve real freshness and ingenuity in typography? E. E. Cummings' poem "Buffalo Bill's" (page 30) is an example of a relatively extreme use of spacing. Take, for example, these three lines:

and break onetwothreefourfive pigeonsjustlikethat
                                    Jesus
he was a handsome man

Those run-together phrases are a sample of compressed spacing. Cummings actually speeds up your reading with that technique. This may not occur on your first reading, of course, since it takes time to figure out lines that are printed without spaces. But once you are used to the poem, the lines seem to ripple by as if they were moving.

Notice, too, how the word "Jesus" is suspended on the right with space above and below. At first it seems to be an exclamation of admiration about his shooting ability. In prose it would be followed with an exclamation mark. But as you continue to read, it leaps forward as if tied to "he was a handsome man." Like an optical illusion, it flips back and forth, serving both functions, tricky as Buffalo Bill himself. Of course, something similar might be tried in metered verse, but the ability to custom-design the typography in free verse gives the poet greater flexibility.

You may not have noticed that Cummings uses a form of syllabics in addition to typography. His run-together phrase "onetwothreefourfive" has exactly the same number of syllables as "pigeonsjustlikethat"—linking the number of his rapid-fire shots and the series of clay pigeons on a skeet range. This is a good example of the fact that when working with the unique rhythms of free verse, you can combine several techniques.

When we analyze poems like those of Levertov, Appleman, and Cummings, it should become apparent that much of what appeared on first reading to be arbitrary placement is in fact carefully planned to create an effect. But don't expect to find a rational explanation for every typographical element. As with the brush strokes of a painter, many decisions that go into making a poem are intuitive. If it were not for this aspect, typographical rhythms would tend to seem contrived, even forced. This is why it is important to keep working on different versions of the same poem, writing out each and reading them aloud. Trust your ear as much as your mind.

One even more structured form of typography is called **shaped verse**. It molds the shape of the work into the object it is describing. This technique was popular in the 17th century and is well illustrated by Herbert's frequently anthologized "The Altar" and "Easter Wings," as well as by Herrick's "The Pillar of Flame," each of which resembles the object suggested in its title. More recently, contemporaries like Allen Ginsberg have published poems in the shape of atomic clouds and, with the aid of punctuation, rockets.

For unknown reasons, what has for centuries been called *shaped verse* and *pattern poetry* was renamed **concrete poetry** in the early 1960s and hailed as a new technique. It quickly became a fad, often reduced to mere tricks. As a poem begins to rely more and more on its shape, it generally makes less and less use of the sound of language, rhythms, or metaphor. Even the theme becomes simplified. Highly obtrusive visual effects tend to overpower all other aspects. One can, for example, repeat the word *death* all over the page in such a way as to resemble a skull. It takes time and a certain mindless patience to do this, but the result is more like a cartoon than a poem.

If you flip through the poems in Chapter 2 or any standard anthology, you will see that extreme forms of shaped poetry are rare. Used with restraint, however, typography offers a wealth of possibilities.

Auditory Patterns: What You Hear in the Reading

Until now, we have been looking at free verse as it appears on the page. Never forget, however, that poetry has its roots in recitation and song. As the printed word became more widely available, oral presentation became less necessary, but the genre still appeals to the ear.

Free verse does not use regular rhyme schemes, but it does occasionally employ scattered internal rhymes. They can be used to add stress or to link related words. More often, free verse employs **alliteration**, the repetition of similar initial sounds. Elizabeth Holden uses it in "As the Cold Deepens" (page 15). Here are the lines in which the speaker describes her aging mother. I have circled the alliterative use of *b* and *h*.

My mother is almost weightless now

her flesh shrinks back toward the bone,

Braced in her metal walker

she haunts the halls, prowls

the margin of her day . . ..

These harsh sounds are in sharp contrast with the sibilance Donald Hall uses in "Names of Horses" (page 37). He is describing the gentle patience of a farm horse with these lines:

. . . your neck rubbed the window sill

of the stall, smoothing the wood as the sea

smooths glass.

An even more conspicuous auditory device often associated with free verse is **anaphora**—the repetition of a word or phrase at the beginning of two or more lines or sentences. The effect is often strengthened by using a similar type of sentence such as a series of questions or pronouncements. This creates what is sometimes called **syntactical rhythms**. It is frequently employed in oratory as well.

Here is a sample of anaphora in poetry combined with syntactical rhythm. It is taken from Walt Whitman's "Passage to India" and refers to that nation then under British control. The anaphoral word is *who*, and the syntactical rhythm is created by a series of short questions.

Ah, who shall soothe these feverish children?
Who justify these restless explorations?
Who speak the secret of impassive earth?
Who bind it to us? what is this separate Nature so
    unnatural?
What is this earth to our affections? . . .

In prose we generally try to avoid redundancies, yet here is a string of them. They seem appropriate in poetry mainly because rhythm is a part of the genre and because this particular type of rhythm has long been associated with the oral tradition.

Allen Ginsberg wrote "Howl!" in 1959, 104 years after Whitman first published "Leaves of Grass," and Ginsberg's indebtedness is unmistakable. Here he describes "the best minds of my generation":

> who bared their brains to Heaven under the El
>   and saw Mohammedan angels staggering on
>   tenement roofs illuminated,
> who passed through universities with radiant cool
>   eyes hallucinating Arkansas and Blake-light
>   tragedy among the scholars of war,
> who were expelled from the academies for
>   crazy & publishing obscene odes on the
>   windows of the skull,
> who cowered in unshaven rooms in underwear,
>   burning their money in wastebaskets and
>   listening to the Terror through the wall, . . .

Ginsberg is clearly influenced by Whitman, but both of them drew on a still earlier source, the Bible. Although the version Whitman knew was in English (the King James translation), and Ginsberg's version was in the original Hebrew, both men were strongly influenced by the rhythmical patterns found there. Compare, for example, the selections just quoted with this passage from Job 38:34-37:

> Canst thou lift up thy voice to the clouds,
>   that abundance of waters may cover thee?
> Canst thou send lightnings, that they may go
>   and say unto thee, Here we are?
> Who hath put wisdom in the inward parts?
>   or who hath given understanding to the heart?
> Who can number the clouds in wisdom?
>   or who can pour out the bottles of heaven?

For full effect, read that out loud. Notice that here, like the selections from Whitman and Ginsberg, it is the entire syntactical unit that is repeated to achieve the rhythm. The anaphoral words are cues that signal the repeated form. If this pattern interests you, you can find many other examples in the Bible. The rest of the Book of Job, Genesis, and the Psalms all are rich in anaphora and repetitions in sentence structure. Studying these works makes one far more open to the rhythms not only of Whitman and Ginsberg but of Ferlinghetti, Gregory Corso, John Ashbery, Amiri Baraka, and many others writing today

In the examples we have been considering, anaphora is unmistakable because it is followed by a pronounced similarity of sentence structure. But often it is used alone. Lucille Clifton's poem "What the Mirror Said" (page 20) appears to be light, spontaneous, and conversational. But if you look at it carefully, you will see that in the first half it is structured through three anaphoral words: "listen," "you," and "somebody":

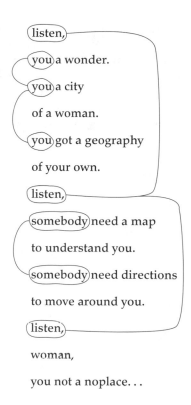

listen,

you a wonder.

you a city

of a woman.

you got a geography

of your own.

listen,

somebody need a map

to understand you.

somebody need directions

to move around you.

listen,

woman,

you not a noplace. . .

This rhythmical use of anaphora is not repeated toward the end of the poem, but Clifton does continue to use the one-word line to create a rhythm as emphatic as thumping one's hand on the table.

The Line versus Syntax: The Uses of Sentence Structure

When you read prose, you respond to the punctuation of the sentence even if you can't tell a compound sentence from a compound fracture. You pause at commas, come to a full stop at periods, and take a deep breath at the end of paragraphs.

When you read poetry, you tend to respond the same way to the ends of lines. Sometimes excessively. When schoolchildren recite poetry, they often have to be reminded not to pause unnecessarily at the conclusion of each line. As adults reading to ourselves, we unconsciously pause even when the context suggests that we should keep going.

When you write poetry, you have at your disposal both of these rhythmical devices—sentence structure and line length. Occasionally you will find a poem that emphasizes syntax to the point of ending each line with a period or a comma. Theodore Roethke's villanelle "The Waking" (page 29) is such a poem. Although metered, it is an unusual example of poetry stressing sentence structure. Out of 19 lines, all but one are end-stopped, concluding with a period, a comma, or a question mark. The syntactical rhythm—that generated by the sentence structure—matches almost perfectly the line length and in this case the meter as well. Such matching, however, is rare, especially in free verse.

In free verse, Philip Appleman's "Desire" (page 43) also stresses the syntax. As noted earlier, each of his four stanzas ends with a period and three of them are complete sentences.

Most poems, however, mute the impact of the sentence by employing enjambment. When a sentence runs on into the next line, it is less noticeable. As a result, we as readers pay more attention to the line break. Since sentences and lines each create their own rhythm, when they are combined neither becomes dominant and the rhythmical effect is kept from becoming monotonous.

Some poems, however, avoid all punctuation, relying exclusively on the line for rhythmical effect. This is a technique that lends itself to relatively short poems with short, syntactically simple lines. Haiku, for example, rarely use punctuation.

Nikki Giovanni's "Balances" (page 36) is one of the few longer poems in this volume that uses no punctuation at all. Notice how in these first five lines the lack of punctuation keeps the poem uncluttered. The effect is almost like someone walking step by step along a tightrope.

> in life
> one is always
> balancing
>
> like we juggle our mothers
> against our fathers

The great majority of poems use punctuation along with line length, the two working in subtle harmony or, in some cases, as counterpoint to each other.

Both metered and unmetered poetry, of course, give you the option of whether to highlight the syntactical rhythms with punctuation. The temptation to do without any punctuation seems great when you first plunge into the heady freedom of free verse. Remember, however, that your reader will unconsciously supply sentence structure through the context, whether you use punctuation or not. Most established poets find it helpful to use punctuation deliberately, as it provides one more source for rhythm.

The Unmarked Border with Prose

Between free-verse poetry and prose there is a misty, unmarked border. Some poets, for example, place little emphasis on the deliberate rhythmical systems we have been discussing, preferring instead to think in terms of **breath units**. On a literal level, that phrase suggests that a line is broken where the reader of the poem would naturally take a breath when reciting aloud. But different poets seem to have remarkably different lung capacities. In addition, the notion is complicated in poems that are presented through a **persona**, an implied speaker who may have cadences of his or her own.

In point of fact, lungs have less to do with poetic composition than does the poet's own sense of rhythm. It was not emphysema that caused Philip Appleman to describe his sense of longing and desire with these concluding lines:

> Undertow:
> I reach for you,
> oceans away.

Nor was it deep-breathing exercises that led Donald Hall to adopt lines like these in "Names of Horses" (page 37):

> For a hundred and fifty years, in the pasture of
>   dead horses,
> roots of pine trees pushed through the pale curves
>   of your ribs,

Both of these poets made deliberate choices, each selecting a line length he felt would create the tone he wanted to achieve.

Somewhere in that hazy, unmarked border between poetry and prose is a hybrid form called **prose poetry**. Although written in lines that look essentially like a prose paragraph, the writer usually maintains control over the line length. In most cases, though, the lines are long.

The form has its roots in folktales and parables, but many that are published today resemble **creative nonfiction**, relatively brief informal essays. Some of these works have less rhythm, fewer sound linkages, and less figurative language than the prose of, say, Dylan Thomas in "August Bank Holiday" (quoted in Chapter 5). In such cases, its primary function is to assure the reader that it should be read deliberately.

In other examples, the work is nudged toward poetry with the use of imagery and a greater concern for the sound of language. Some draw heavily on speech rhythms and develop some of the compression we associate with poetry. Such work might more accurately be described as *poetic prose*.

Developing Your Own Rhythms

When you begin composing a new poem, let the first few lines speak to you. Often they will suggest the kinds of rhythms that are appropriate for that particular poem. Your emotional involvement with the material, your personal preferences, and the nature of the subject matter will all influence what develops. And because so many factors are involved, the result will be unique.

As the poem develops, consider some of the techniques we have examined in this chapter: manipulation of the line on the page, nonrecurrent stanzas, and sound devices like alliteration and anaphora. Although we have analyzed them separately, they all are interrelated.

Keep in mind that any one of these devices if pushed to an extreme runs the risk of seeming tricky and obtrusive, dominating the entire poem. Strive to keep your rhythms subtle. Experiment with a number of different approaches and trust your feelings.

With this in mind, here is an exercise that will help you keep your options open. First, read the three prose sentences quoted in the next paragraph. Forget that they have been taken from a poem you have studied in Chapter 2. For purposes of this exercise, don't look back. Imagine that this is simply a prose passage that happens to be highly charged with visual and auditory images:

"The wind's untiring saxophone keens at the glass. The lamp sheds a monochrome of stainless steel and linens, the nurse in her snowy dress firm in her regimens. The form in the bed is a soul diminished to a fledgling, fed on the tentative balm of spring, sketch for an angel, half-finished, shoulder blades the stubs of wings."

After you have become familiar with the passage (you may want to look up a couple of words), convert it to two quite different poems using the same wording but breaking the lines in different ways. You may not be able to improve on the original version (printed on page 36), but you will come to understand how fluid this approach to rhythmical language is. You may also discover how deeply the rhythmical patterns affect the tone and even the statement of a poem.

Another helpful exercise is to take a descriptive prose passage from an article about nature or travel. This time, don't limit yourself to the wording of the original. Find your own language to add freshness and intensity to the passage and then, as before, devise two different rhythmical approaches. This is the kind of "sketching" that will make your poetry journal an effective part of your development.

In addition to exercises like these in your journal, spend some time each day examining the rhythms of published poetry. Since most poetry contains rhythmical patterns of some sort, every anthology and literary quarterly can serve as a source for study. By combining practice work in your journal and extensive, careful reading, you will soon find a way to express your own concerns in increasingly effective free verse.

9

INTERNAL ORDER

Internal order: the arrangement of a poem's content. Contrasts and comparisons. Shifts in attitude. Overt themes. Narrative patterns. Image clusters. Repetition and refrains. Combining types of organization.

In previous chapters we examined different ways of giving shape to a poem including stanza types for metered poetry and typographical techniques for free verse. These provide an external order. We now turn to internal order, the arrangement of the subject matter itself.

There is no need to concern yourself with internal organization as you begin a poem. It's a good idea to stay flexible in your early drafts, letting the ideas and images take shape freely. But at some point in the revision process, structure should become a major concern. If a poem rambles or lacks a sense of order, it will probably fail no matter how carefully you have worked on the external form.

After you have completed one or two drafts, stop and take a close, analytical look at what holds that poem together thematically. Why have you placed a particular line before another? Would a different order be more effective? Even if it was composed intuitively without much thought of organization, the poem probably has some type of structure that you have adopted without much thought. Now is the time to see if this is the most effective sequence.

There are many different ways of organizing the content of a poem. This chapter will deal with six of the most useful. Obviously not all of your work will fit one of these categories, but examining these patterns closely will give you the option of adopting them or devising some system of your own.

Contrasts and Comparisons

As a basic organizing strategy, the use of contrasts and comparisons is one of the most popular. In some cases the contrast may be directly stated, but in others it may be so subtle that it remains almost subliminal.

Philip Appleman's "Coast to Coast" (page 30) is a fine example of a contrast that dominates the entire poem. In the first stanza the poet describes how when we travel by jet we are oblivious to the scene below. As he puts it, we are "blind to milkweed, riverbanks, the wrecks / of elm trees" below us. The contrast is introduced in the second stanza when he describes crossing the country by car "on two-lane roads" from which one can see all those things that "make the busy continent worthwhile."

In the next two stanzas he gives us a series of highly visual, auditory, and tactile images depicting the kind of details we can respond to when driving:

> . . . the smell of woods and fields,
> the flash of finches and the scud of crows,
> the rub of asphalt underneath our wheels
> as tangible as sand between the toes.

The final stanza returns to jet travel: "Now, going home we're blind again."

Not only is this a contrast in modes of travel, it is also a contrast in the speaker's preference. Clearly, he misses the sights, sounds, and even the feel of auto travel. He regrets the fact that fewer and fewer people are singing the song of the "open road."

Linda Pastan works with a different type of contrast in "Domestic Animals" (page 16). During the day the friendly dog is "all sweet slobber" and the cat purrs with its deep "furred throat." But at night they have "dream claws and teeth" as they recall their origins. This contrast takes on broader implications with the phrase "the green / jungle of our sleep." The word *our* suggests that we too have our primal roots and perhaps a lingering "terrible hunger."

A third example is seen in a poem we have examined earlier for its use of syllabics: "Fern Hill" by Dylan Thomas (page 21). A careless reader might assume that the poem is simply a nostalgic set of memories from youth when the narrator was "young and easy under the apple boughs." Unlike the two poems described above, it doesn't reveal the significant contrast until the last of six fairly lengthy stanzas. It is then that the narrator wakes "to the farm forever fled from the childless land," leaving the narrator singing in his "chains like the sea." The boy in him still longs for those carefree days, but his adult self is aware that life is limited by mortality just as the restless sea is limited by the shoreline. Essentially, then, the poem is youthful innocence contrasted with adult realism, though most of the lines are devoted to the former.

Because comparisons, as opposed to contrasts, are made up of similar elements, you might think they would be less effective. But they often serve well. Poems that are dominated by a single figure of speech (known as a **controlling image**) are frequently based on a comparison. Remember, though, that the comparison doesn't become a basic organizational element unless it overshadows the poem as a whole.

Some of the best examples are seen in haiku which by tradition contain some kind of literal or metaphorical comparison. Etheridge Knight draws on this tradition in his haiku comparing convicts at the end of a workday with lizards in this brief but haunting picture:

> Eastern guard tower
> glints in sunset; convicts rest
> like lizards on rocks.

For a longer, more complex example of a comparison poem, review Barbara Howes' "The Bay at West Falmouth" (page 27). It starts off with a simile in the first two of twelve lines, and this comparison is a controlling image for the length of the poem:

> Serenity of mind poises
> Like a gull swinging in air,

Everything in the poem depends on and amplifies that initial comparison.

Shifts in Attitude

Poems based on some basic shift in attitude are closely related to those with contrasts. They focus, however, on inner perceptions and feelings rather than on external objects and events. One of the more famous of these is Shakespeare's "Sonnet 29," often referred to by its opening phrase, "When in Disgrace with Fortune" (page 18).

The entire **octave**—the first eight lines—is downbeat. The speaker describes feeling like an outcast; he is one who has cursed his fate, envying others. But in the **sestet**, just about at the point when we think he is indulging in excessive self-pity, the poem shifts with the word "yet."

> Yet in these thoughts my self almost despising,
> Haply I think on thee, and then my state,
> Like to the lark at break of day arising
> From sullen earth, sings hymns at heaven's gate,

The poem is a good example of how sonnets frequently adopt a new tone at the end of the octave. What concerns us here, though, is the fact that the organization of the poem is more than simply a matter of metrical form, it is generated by the content as well.

The shift of attitude in Mary Oliver's poem "The Black Snake" (page 26) is somewhat similar even though the motivating incident is entirely different. She spots a snake in the road that has been crushed by a truck. Here is her first reaction: "*death*, that is how it happens."

She stops the car and carries the snake to the bushes, seeing him

> . . . as beautiful and quiet
> as a dead brother.

She drives on, "thinking / about *death* . . . "But at the end of the fourth stanza the word "yet" signals an abrupt shift in attitude just as it does in Shakespeare's sonnet. In a dramatic reversal she thinks about the wonder of life, the power of which

> . . . sent the snake coiling and flowing forward
> happily all spring through the green leaves
> before he came to the road.

Dorothy Barresi's "Mystery" (page 39) has a somewhat similar shift in attitude, though the tone is entirely different. She uses bizarre exaggeration to create a dreamlike satire. Arguments between the couple erupt abruptly, dominating the entire house in such a wild and dreamlike fashion that the poem becomes grotesquely comic:

> Ashtrays and pillows begin to orbit the room
> Whatever furniture they have
> rears up on hind legs and howls.

But later in an astonishing reversal:

> . . . the couple kiss,
> Like guests on a television talk show,
> expecting nothing.
> Whatever they fought about is a mystery to them now.

Whereas Berresi deals satirically with what we take to be a repeated cycle, some contrast poems focus seriously on a single dramatic or even traumatic event. Theodore Deppe's "The Paradise of Wings" (page 42) is far darker and clearly a turning point in the relationship between two young people and their grandfather. First, the bond between the grandson and his grandfather is revealed through their sharing of a special place:

> My grandfather called it
> the Paradise of Wings, a clearing
> hidden in blue hills where thousands
> of geese gleaned stubbled corn
> beside a tapered lake. His favorite walk—
> shared with me as a secret—. . . .

But later, after his sister "stumbles from the house / panic in her face," they both come to fear the grandfather. As for that secret spot, it has become utterly transformed for them:

. . . my sister's hate
was the only living thing in paradise.

Overt Themes

Some poems are organized around a dominant theme that is clearly stated either at the beginning or the end of the poem. I hesitate to list this approach at all because it is fraught with danger. In fact, it is the cause of countless student failures and the distress of creative writing teachers everywhere. The perceptive reader, however, will discover two such poems in Chapter 2, so it seems prudent to discuss why they succeed and why so many imitators fail.

Stephen Dunn's "A Secret Life" (page 38) is one. We know exactly what the theme of this poem is going to be from the title and the opening four lines:

Why you need to have one
is not much more mysterious than
why you don't say what you think
at the birth of an ugly baby.

There it is: an overt statement of his theme. And he sticks with it through 27 lines. The same direct approach is used by Molly Peacock to present an opposing theme in "Anger Sweetened" (page 18). Her opening line is "What we don't forget is what we don't say."

There are two reasons these poems succeed in spite of the bluntly thematic opening. The first is that both are witty. We are assured from the opening lines that we are not dealing with a heavy-handed editorial. The second is that the themes they express are quirky. They run counter to conventional views.

The great risk of opening a poem with a strong thematic statement is that too often it turns into an editorial in verse. The result is even worse when the theme is a **truism**, a widely held belief, like the assertions that there shouldn't be so many poor people in a rich nation, that we shouldn't be cutting down the rain forests, or that battered women need greater protection. These are all good causes, but they won't be helped with bad verse. Nor will writing classes.

Poems organized around topics like these are unsuccessful mainly because they say nothing new, but on a deeper level they fail because they confuse poetry with editorials. An effective editorial presents an argument (ideally, an original one) in straight, logical prose. Its function is to inform or convince. A poem, on the other hand, is a literary art form that gives pleasure through its use of language and only secondarily describes some feeling or presents an insight.

The themes of these two poems are decidedly offbeat, and their treatment is fresh and clever. Dunn's defense of a secret life runs counter to the conventional belief that we should all be open and entirely honest. He starts off with two witty examples of the kind of secrets we actually keep. He goes on to develop ingenious metaphors. He describes what we write in our private journals late at night as being

> . . . like a small fire
> in a clearing, it's what
> radiates and what can hurt
> if you get too close to it.

We treasure our secrets, though at the same time we find them threatening. Dunn is defending what others have not. That's what I mean when I say that the theme is fresh and original.

In the same way, Molly Peacock dwells on what we don't like to admit: that what we don't say stays with us. She describes those memories of what we should have said as like "grasshoppers covered / by coagulating chocolate" which we must eventually eat, playing on the cliché "eat your words."

If you are tempted to start a poem calling for world peace or a defense of the beleaguered ozone layer, loosen up and read these two poems.

Generally speaking, you will be on solid ground if you avoid sweeping social statements altogether and focus on your own personal experience and your own feelings. Scenes, events, and personal relationships from your own life may well suggest broader concerns, but if these are rooted in what you personally know about and genuinely feel, they will maintain a sense of authenticity. And don't shy away from wit and irony. No matter what tone you use, remember that if it isn't more artful than prose in short lines, it isn't really a poem.

The Narrative Sequence

A **narrative** is a story, a sequence of events. It usually has a central figure called a **protagonist**. Narrative is as natural a structure for poetry as it is for prose. Although prose has come to be the preferred genre for lengthy fiction, poetry still draws on narrative as an organizing principle in shorter work.

Anthony Hecht's "Lizards and Snakes" (page 33) is a good example. As I pointed out in Chapter 7, Hecht has adapted the literary ballad by using a slightly longer line and by running his quatrains together to form eight-line stanzas. What concerns us here, however, is the way the story line is used as a basic method of organization.

The narrator, speaking in the first person, describes how he and his friend Joe used to study lizards and snakes that came out to sun on hot days. He reports that they used to slip lizards into his Aunt Martha's knitting box so that they would leap out and frighten her. But in the final stanza there is a high wind and they overhear her as she has a vision of the devil, an image that is close to the lizards they used to catch. They never played the trick again.

It is a relatively simple anecdote that starts with playful humor and ends on a more serious note. The reference to "carriage ruts" places the event back when belief in a literal devil was more common. The theme deals with the fact that what seems funny at one stage in your life changes as you grow up, but it is the story line that holds the poem together.

The narrative line in some poems is so underplayed that you hardly think of the work as telling a story, but the mere hint of a sequence of actions can provide an organizational structure. "The Pardon," by Richard Wilbur (page 34), is a good example. It begins, again in the first person, with the summer day on which the **persona**, a boy of ten, finds the body of his dog. It continues through to the burial. Then it jumps forward to when he has a nightmare about the experience. On waking, he begs "death's pardon." This is a highly sophisticated poem with a complex theme about reactions to death, yet it is organized and unified with a relatively simple story line.

In the same way, the story line in Maxine Kumin's "Morning Swim" (page 32) is minimal. The narrator simply goes swimming in the early morning and has a spiritual experience. That's barely a plot in fictional terms, but it is enough to unify the poem. It is a good reminder that a narrative sequence can be slight and still provide a structure for a poem.

You may not have recognized Dorothy Barresi's "Mystery" (page 39) as being narrative since it has no clearly defined narrator (it is in the third person), and the plot is even simpler than that of "Morning Swim." But the organization is clearly sequential: first the argument, then the bizarre and dreamlike transformation of the entire house, and finally the loving resolution. Structurally, it is a comic opera in three acts.

On the other hand, narratives can become so complex that you don't really think of the poem as telling a story at all. Donald Hall's "Names of Horses" (page 37) is such a case. Turn to it now and review it carefully. See if you can sort out three different narrative sequences that are woven together in that poem.

The first of these sequences is based on seasons of the year. It starts out "All winter" and moves in the second stanza to "April," turns to summer with "noon's heat" and finally to the fall with "one October" in the fifth stanza. This use of seasons is clear and fairly common as a device. But there is a second and longer sequence that is based on the stages of a single horse's life. The first four stanzas focus on the mature years when the horse can do heavy work; the fifth stanza starts when he is "old and lame" and is taken out to be shot, and the seventh stanza deals with the horse after death, when the roots of trees "pushed through the pale curves of your ribs."

The third cycle is the longest and most subtle. Far lengthier than the seasons of a single year, longer even than the story of one horse's life and death, it is that succession of horses moving through the same cycle "generation on generation." This generational sequence is the underlying narrative thread and the primary concern of the poem. We know that from the last line, a moving tribute to the long series of horses over the years: "O Roger, Mackerel, Riley, Ned, Nellie, Chester, Lady Ghost."

Just as a complex sound like a sustained note on a cello can be analyzed precisely as having sound waves of high, medium, and low frequency working together to produce a single note with rich overtones, so a poem can combine narratives of differing length to produce a single, unified effect. This is what we mean when we say that a poem has **resonance**.

Image Clusters

Images, as described in Chapter 4, can be used directly or as **figures of speech**. In either case, they are details that can be perceived with one of the five senses. They are at the heart of most poems. In the early drafts of writing a poem—particularly those drawing on some scene from nature—you will probably rely on a series of similar images. To rearrange these details effectively so that they form **image clusters** may take several different drafts. Still more work is needed if you plan to make those clusters the basic organizing principle of the poem.

Philip Appleman's four-stanza poem "Desire" (page 43) is a good example of how related images can be made to unify a poem. The first stanza focuses on "tide"; the second, on "moons," the cause of tides; and the final stanza highlights "undertow." Although his central concern, *desire*, is identified in the title, it is never mentioned in the body of the poem. He translates that abstraction into details we can see and feel. There are many images that might suggest desire, but he unifies the poem by selecting ones that are related to sea currents. These image clusters become the primary structure of the poem.

In Chapter 4 we examined how the images in Robley Wilson's "On a Maine Beach" are made more effective by being clustered. Actually they do more than that. If you turn back to page 69, you can review the linkages among "worn change," "mint-mark," "miser," "rims," "mainspring," "pinwheeling," "coins," "round lifetimes," "beach rhythms," and "circles." What we were examining there as a technique that links certain lines actually forms in a broader sense a unifying principle for the poem as a whole. The structure of image clusters is more subtle than, say, the sequence of events in a narrative poem, but it is equally effective.

One of the richest and most sustained sequences of image clusters appears in Anita Endrezze's "The Mapmaker's Daughter" (page 44). It is a poem about love, a risky subject because of all the simple and sentimental attempts on this topic. But her dreamlike, sensual treatment is fresh. Review it now before I provide a guided tour.

First, the fact that the central figure is a woman is established in the title, "The Mapmaker's Daughter." Her terrain ("geography") is love. While we normally live on terra firma, solid ground, the state of love is, she reminds us, "terra infirma."

We navigate this uncertain area in "a paper boat" decidedly fragile. The woman is at the helm, armed with "the map of longing." There is "rain that launches thirst" and "secret passages" all "far from shore," a reminder that this is "terra infirma." Ultimately, the couple discover "deep / territories we name / after ourselves."

The voyage is misty and dreamlike, but we are able to follow it thanks to Endrezze's "compass of . . . desire"—and her beautifully harmonious series of closely related images.

Repetitions and Refrains

When we write prose, we do our best to avoid repetitions. Repeated words are referred to as redundancies, and repetition of longer units are condemned as bad organization. Poets, however, love repetition. The genre is like music in that repetitions are often used for rhythm or for emphasis. When employed regularly through the length of a poem, they can serve as the organizing structure for the work as a whole.

The most blatant form of the **refrain** is the chorus, a repeated line or group of lines. It has long been a popular way to unify ballads. Whether sung, recited, or read silently, these repeated sections—often couplets or quatrains—help to hold a wandering narrative together.

As you remember, a refrain appears in each of the three stanzas of a **rondeau**. In the **villanelle** there are two one-line refrains that become an integral part of the organization. Each of the five tercets has one of two refrains, and the concluding stanza has both. Even if you don't spot this recurring pattern in a villanelle on first reading, it nonetheless provides a sense of order.

We have already examined the ways **anaphora**, the repetition of initial words or phrases, can serve as a rhythmical device. If it is used more or less consistently through the length of a poem, it can also serve as a basic organizational device. In "What the Mirror Said," by Lucille Clifton (page 20), for example, the word "listen" is repeated at the beginning of three lines. Although the repeated words are separated and seem as casual as informal speech, each introduces a new sentence. This is a subtle use of anaphora and provides a structure for a poem that on first reading may seem to be without design.

As you may remember, a poem can also be unified by the repetition of the final word in a majority of lines. The technique is rare, but Gwendolyn Brooks' "We Real Cool" (page 24) follows this pattern. It may be the only poem in existence in which seven out of eight lines end with "We," with the sentence concluded on the next line.

Combining Types of Organization

We have examined six of the most frequently used methods of establishing a sense of order in a poem. You will discover, however, that many poems combine two or more techniques. Multiple approaches are particularly common in poems based even slightly on a narrative sequence. Poems that merely tell a story may be entertaining, but they are almost always literarily simple. One of the most common methods of expanding the range of meaning in a narrative poem is to develop a contrast as well.

We have already seen how the narrative aspect of "Lizards and Snakes" by Anthony Hecht is given depth by adding a shift in attitude. This combination is similar to that in Dylan Thomas' "Fern Hill." In both poems the shift in outlook is as important as the story line in providing a sense of order.

In the case of Carole Oles' "The Gift" (page 17), the narrative is pronounced, telling the life story of a young woman from infancy through marriage with a dreamlike, detached tone like that of a **parable**. But unlike "Fern Hill" the contrast is made clear at the beginning of the poem and runs through to the end. As soon as the girl is referred to as "it" in the second line, we know that this is going to be not only a grim narrative but also a bitter contrast between the status of women as Barbie-Doll objects and men as owners of toys.

The combination of story line and theme in "The Gift" is dramatic, but in other poems the suggestion behind the narrative may be so subtle that it is easily missed. Such is the case in Maurya Simon's "The Dolphin" (page 25). On first reading, one might assume that this is a simple narrative describing how moving a news account about a dolphin losing its sense of direction and eventually dying can be. But take a close look at the fourth and fifth stanzas:

> Was it toxins spewed in the ocean
> that sent its brain to spinning,
> or do dolphins, just like humans,
> go off the deep end either with
>
> or without reason?

"Just like humans" is a key phrase. Here the simple narrative ends not with a contrast but with a haunting comparison: perhaps we humans are also subject to random, inexplicable ailments that send us turning in circles and eventually killing us "without reason." No wonder the image of that circling dolphin keeps spinning in the narrator's mind!

To what degree should a poem be given a clear sense of order? That's up to you and to the nature of each poem. Before deciding that a poem is finished, however, read it several times as objectively as you can. If the content seems a bit aimless or scattered to you, it will be even more confusing for your readers. In most cases there will be a contrast, a shift in perception, or some type of theme that shaped your early drafts even if they didn't come through on the page. See if you can clarify them. Or there may be the potential for image clusters or repetitions that occurred almost by chance. Again, consider developing them. It is not enough to have an order that is apparent only to you; your job is to structure your work so it appears orderly to your readers.

10

VARIETIES OF TONE

How meaning depends on tone. Serious tones: reflective, melancholy, critical, loving. Comic tones. The uses of irony. The cutting edge of satire. You and your persona. Keeping the tone honest.

"I want that."

This looks like a clear, unambiguous statement. How could we mistake its meaning? Easily. In fact, we can't even respond until we identify the speaker and the tone of voice. Here are three different situations, each with its own tone. Notice how the meaning changes even though the words do not:

1. A stranger on a dark street says this, pointing to your wallet.
2. A friend says this with a laugh as you both gaze longingly at an elegant BMW.
3. A woman says this with a sarcastic sneer about an unexpected tax bill.

The literal statement, the **denotation**, is the same in each case. But the implied meaning, the **connotation**, in each case is entirely different. The first is a threat, the second is a joke, and the third means exactly the opposite of the literal statement. Clearly, tone in everyday speech is not just an adornment to language; it is often a fundamental part of meaning.

Tone is equally important in poetry, but instead of being determined by the external situation, it is implied within the work itself. Because tone reveals the poet's attitude toward his or her subject, it becomes part of the meaning even more frequently than it does in common speech.

When we refer to the tone of a poem, we use such words as *reflective, melancholy, critical, loving, wry, comic*, and the like. Keep in mind, however, that there are really as many different shadings of tone as there are different tones of voice and that there are no sharp divisions between them. Like the names of colors, the terms we use are convenient segments of a spectrum.

Here is a sampling of the many different tones reflected in the poems in Chapter 2. We can think of them as grouped under the headings of "serious" and "comic," but this too is merely a convenient division. Poems often combine aspects of both.

Serious Tones

A reflective tone is widely used. There are three particularly good examples in Chapter 2, each focused on an aspect of nature: Robert Frost in "Design" (page 15) examines the extraordinary coincidence of finding a white spider holding a white moth while perched on a white flower. It is one of those rare events that makes one say, "Hey, look at that!"

It is similar to the tone in Robley Wilson's "On a Maine Beach" (page 28) in which he studies the details in a rock pool and, like Frost, draws conclusions from it. Wilson takes no stand, proposes no argument; he merely invites the reader to examine the details of the scene and reflect on its implications.

The same is true of Maurya Simon's "The Dolphin" (page 25) in which the persona describes a disoriented dolphin circling until he dies. This raises uneasy speculations about how we humans occasionally "go off the deep end," sometimes without reason. These three are thoughtful poems that expand our perception of the world about us.

A melancholy tone is natural when dealing with those who are ill or face other misfortunes. It is also the tone identified with the **elegy**, a poem mourning the dead. It is the tone in Chase Twichell's description of a bedridden woman in "Rhymes for Old Age" (page 36), Elizabeth Holden's memories of her mother in "As the Cold Deepens" (page 15), and James Bertram's elegy for Ernest Hemingway in "Is It Well-Lighted, Papa?" (page 31).

Although these three poems share a melancholy or somber tone, they differ subtly in how close they are to their subject. This aspect is called **distance**. When the subject matter is treated with detachment or objectivity, the poem is said to have greater distance as contrasted with those that are more subjective and personal. Twichell, for example, is careful to stay clear of sentimentality by using starkly clinical details. She maintains greater distance between her narrator and the woman in bed by not naming the patient or identifying her relationship with the speaker.

> The form in the bed
> is a soul diminished
> to a fledgling

The poem is no less compassionate than the others, but it is less intimate.

Holden, on the other hand, reduces the distance and makes the poem more personal by identifying the subject:

> My mother is almost weightless now,
> Her flesh shrinks back toward bone

Bertram reduces the distance still further by shifting from the third person to direct address:

> Is it well-lighted, Papa—this place
> where you have gone. . . ?

Melancholy tones in the form of self-pity are unfortunately common in student work. While many are sincere, others may be motivated by a hope that self-pity will protect them from harsh criticism. Keep in mind, though, that there is a difference between genuine melancholy and whining. A mature writer can express lament without playing the violin.

A critical tone covers an enormous span from disapproval to indignation and rage. It differs from the types we have examined so far in that it is essentially an argument: "behave like this" or "don't behave like that."

Because most of us don't like to be told what we should or should not do, poets often disguise their message in a number of different ways. Gwendolyn Brooks, for example, is careful not to sound as if she is giving a sermon against quitting school and leading a delinquent life in "We Real Cool" (page 24). But that's what her message is. She avoids a preaching tone by speaking in the first person through a **persona**, one of the pool players at the Golden Shovel. In addition, she has him adopt the insistent beat and the rhyming couplets that we now associate with rap music. The tone of the first three of those four couplets is that of a braggart. It is not until the last line that the true message of the poem snaps into focus: "We / Die soon."

Dick Allen adopts a different tactic in "The Narrow Mind" (page 24). You might think from the title that the poem would become a lecture urging us to be tolerant, broad-minded, open to new ideas. But he knows that if he took that route you would never read beyond the third line unless assured that it was going to be on the exam. Instead, the entire poem adopts the deceptive objectivity of a naturalist describing a frog. But this is no ordinary frog. This is a creature who

> . . . lives in a small backwater, and it doesn't know
> Much more than dragonflies and darning needles,

Further, we learn that

> It feeds on what's been whispered to it
> In secret meetings at dusk.

At no point in this poem is the tone openly critical. Its attack on narrow-minded people is unrelenting, but it is presented entirely through implication.

Incidentally, Allen safeguards himself against the charge of being narrow-mindedly opposed to narrow-minded people with his gentle conclusion. He advises us on how to deal with such an individual:

> You either must row around it or overwhelm it
> With goodness and mercy and bribes.

When poems with a critical theme are driven by a sense of rage, they become protest poems. Carole Oles' "The Gift" (page 17) is a good example. Her concern is the status of women—specifically how they are so often raised to become perfect, subservient wives. Like Dick Allen, however, she knows that her subject has been handled in countless articles and books. A head-on attack would no longer be fresh enough to have impact. So she turns instead to **satire** and adopts one of the oldest literary forms, the **parable**. The parable is a short allegorical story designed to instruct, so adapting it for poetic protest is most appropriate.

Oles does not reveal her satiric tone at the opening. In fact, the first few lines may seem almost sweet:

> Thinking she was the gift
> they began to package it early.

But within a few lines we realize that their gift is not *for* the girl, it *is* the girl! Referring to this poor female as *it* gives you an idea of how she is being raised as a product. After they have straightened her teeth and curled her hair and taught her to speak in honeyed tones, she is given to a man who puts her on exhibit as a trophy. Her ultimate function is to provide him with a son.

These three poems illustrate how often tone is made up of different elements. Although each maintains a critical tone, each uses a different tactic to disguise its true intent. Your own work will gain in impact if you select topics about which you feel strongly, but be careful not to present social issues as if writing an editorial in verse. If you are going to have an impact on your readers, you will have to find a fresh approach, possibly working by indirection rather than a head-on attack.

A loving tone is one of the most popular forms in verse as it is in song lyrics. For this reason, it is also one of the riskiest. Our heads are awash with the **clichés** of love pumped into us from every quarter—television, radio, recordings, films. If you approach the subject in the abstract, it will be hard to avoid hackneyed phrasing. Try instead to find an extended metaphor that is truly fresh, or focus on someone you know.

We have already examined the way Philip Appleman describes an aspect of love through **image clusters** drawn from the sea in his poem "Desire" (page 43). That brief poem moves from the pull of the tides to the gravitation of the moon to undertow. It ends, remember, on a warm and personal note:

> I reach for you
> oceans away.

Although the object of the speaker's love is not identified, we have the feeling that the poem is addressed to a real person, just as we do with

Shakespeare's "Sonnet 29" (page 18). Whether there was actually such an individual is not important; what counts is that the poem creates a sense of authenticity.

Anita Endrezze's poem "The Mapmaker's Daughter" (page 44) also relies on an extended series of closely related metaphors just as Appleman's does, but her treatment is far more extensive and elaborate. She populates the boat with mates, a woman at the helm, a "rain that launches thirst," and "a secret passage into the interior." While these two poems are good examples of a loving tone, they illustrate two quite different stylistic approaches. Appleman's treatment is what can be called *sparse*, or *highly economical*, while Endrezze's is *dense* or even *rococo* in the sense of being elaborate.

Comic Tones

A wry tone bridges the serious and the comic. It evokes a smile if not a laugh. Introducing even mild humor provides a kind of objectivity, what I have described as **distance**. It can serve as an antidote to self-pity.

Theodore Roethke's "The Waking" (page 29) is a good example of a wry tone. He is talking about the brutal fact that we are mortal. If he had started with "We're born without hope, doomed to die," most of us would quickly move on to another poem. Whining is not a pleasant tone. Instead, Roethke begins with "I wake to sleep, and take my waking slow." The metaphor of "sleep" refers to death, but the tone is light, almost whimsical, and his determination to make the most of life while it lasts provides a wry acceptance of our mortality. In the final stanza, he is even more aware of what is to come:

> This shaking keeps me steady. I should know.
> What falls away is always. And is near.

But even recognizing the eternal quality of death ("What falls away is always") and his advancing age ("And is near"), he maintains his light, wry tone and ends with the assurance that he will be learning, growing, until the very end. (Which, incidentally, he did.)

Employing even a slightly comic tone is too often avoided by beginning poets for fear of not being taken seriously. There is an unfortunate confusion in the English language between *serious* as a furrow-browed emotion and *serious* meaning complex or insightful. Roethke's wry approach to death should reassure you that it is quite possible to express serious themes with some degree of humor.

Humor also allows a poet to turn what some might think as a liability into an affirmation. Lucille Clifton's "What the Mirror Said" (page 20) does just this. The speaker looks in the mirror and glories in her size:

you a wonder,
you a city
of a woman.

She is so complex that someone would have to have a map to understand
her. We smile. It's a comic use of **hyperbole**, an exaggeration used for effect.
Notice, however, that we smile *with* the speaker, not at her. It is not a ridiculing poem; it is affirming.

As in Roethke's poem, Clifton's humor doesn't obscure the underlying
suggestions. This is clearly a woman's statement, and even if you were being
introduced to Gwendolyn Brooks for the first time, the as-if-spoken cadences
would suggest that the speaker is black. The poem is an assertion of self-
worth on both counts. The true theme of the poem is rooted in two major
social issues: black pride and female self-esteem.

Dorothy Barresi also uses an even stronger comic tone in her poem
"Mystery" (page 39) in spite of the fact that she is dealing with domestic
discord. She starts out with a pun in the second line, comparing the accusa-
tions flung by husband and wife at each other as "little earrings"—both hard
little gems and shouts that make the ears ring. Soon "Ashtrays and pillows
begin to orbit the room" and the furniture "rears up on hind legs and howls."
We smile at the exaggeration, another example of hyperbole, which in this
case is almost on the level of a cartoon. By the end of the poem the battle has
ended and peace returns. But take a second look at the last two lines:

the calm rising all around the house
like a blood pressure.

That's no happy and contented calm. That's an armed truce which is omi-
nously building toward another outbreak of hostilities. The tone is comic on
the surface, but the marriage being described is an ongoing nightmare.

The Uses of Irony

Both serious and comic poems can and often do make use of **irony**. All forms
of irony are based on a reversal of some sort. **Verbal irony** (also called **conscious irony**) is the type often used in daily conversation. On its simplest
level it takes the form of saying the opposite of what we mean, such as
responding to a hurricane with the statement, "Great day for a picnic." We
know the speaker isn't crazy because we are so used to this kind of irony in
daily speech. When it takes this form, we refer to it as sarcasm.

In poetry, however, irony is usually subtler and may not be at all sarcastic. It is often achieved by bringing together elements we normally consider incongruous. There are several examples in these lines from Richard
Wilbur's "The Pardon" (page 34). The scene, you will remember, is the one

in which the person dreams he sees the ghost of his dog. In the following quotation, I have indicated with arrows how the overtones of certain words are in sharp and *ironic* contrast with those of other words in the same line.

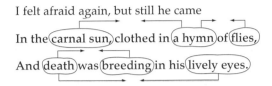

I felt afraid again, but still he came

In the carnal sun clothed in a hymn of flies,

And death was breeding in his lively eyes.

It is ironic to have a hymn associated with a "carnal sun" and a swarm of flies. It is equally ironic to think of death as "breeding." And there is a grim irony in those "lively eyes" of a dog that died some time ago.

There is another sample of irony in Chase Twichell's "Rhymes for Old Age" that you may have spotted in earlier readings of that poem. She describes the process of dying this way:

> One slips into it undressed,
>   as into first love . . .

When an ironic contrast is phrased in a way that makes it sound like a complete contradiction, it is called a **paradox**. John Donne, for example, in his sonnet "Death Be Not Proud," ends with these lines:

> One short sleep past, we wake eternally,
> And death shall be no more; Death, thou shalt die.

On one level it is illogical to say that death shall die, but as a description of eternal life, it makes sense metaphorically.

All these examples are contained in specific phrases. There are also broader ironic contrasts that are in some cases at the very heart of a poem as a whole. As we have already seen, Dylan Thomas' "Fern Hill" (page 21) appears to describe unending youth and apparent immortality; yet all that time the speaker is both "green and dying."

This type of irony is called *verbal* because it is formed with words, not from events in life; it is also called *conscious* irony because the writer is intentionally linking the incongruous items.

There are two other uses of the word *irony* that, though not directly connected with poetry, should be mentioned here to avoid confusion. **Cosmic irony** refers to reversals of expectation. The Olympic swimmer who drowns in the bathtub, the fire chief who becomes an arsonist, the drought-stricken farmers who finally receive rain only to be flooded. The other type is **dramatic irony**, in which characters on the stage speak lines that the audience knows have an entirely different significance. In the Greek play *Oedipus*

Rex, for example, a messenger says, "I bring good news" and the well-read audience shudders, knowing that disaster is at hand. More about that in the drama section of this volume.

The Cutting Edge of Satire

Satire criticizes or ridicules through some form of exaggeration. In mild satire the exaggeration may be only a matter of selecting some characteristics and neglecting others; the tone may be a gentle kidding. At the other extreme, satire may be wildly exaggerated and the tone vitriolic.

Satire and irony can be used independently from each other. All the examples of irony discussed are nonsatiric, and the first example of satire below does not use irony. But ridicule is particularly effective when it is presented "with a straight face." That is, the cutting edge of satire is sharpest when the poet gives the illusion of presenting an unbiased view. It is the tension between the poet's apparent honesty and the actual intent that makes satire almost invariably ironic. In fact, when satire is presented without irony, the result often appears rather crude. Such is the case with Kingsley Amis' "A Tribute to the Founder." In this first of four stanzas, the intent to ridicule is clear, but because the material is presented directly rather than ironically the attack lacks subtlety:

> By bluster, graft, and doing people down
> Sam Baines got rich, but mellowing at last,
> Felt that by giving something to the town
> He might undo the evils of his past.

There is, of course, irony in the title, since "tribute" is not intended literally. But the first line destroys all chance of sustaining subtlety. As soon as we see the words "bluster, graft, and doing people down," we know exactly where the poet stands, which is no sin in itself unless one asks more of poetry than one does of a good newspaper editorial.

William Jay Smith describes essentially the same sort of individual in his poem "American Primitive," and he also is satiric. But notice how different the effect is when irony is sustained:

> Look at him there in his stovepipe hat,
> His high-top shoes, and his handsome collar;
> Only my Daddy could look like that,
> And I love my Daddy like he loves his Dollar.

The lines flow like the ripple that runs silently down the length of a bullwhip; and with his final word comes the "snap," which is sharp enough to make the most sophisticated reader jump. This is still fairly light verse, but the satire, sharpened with irony, draws blood. The tension here lies in the contrast between the apparent tone of sentimental tribute and the actual tone of cutting protest.

Satire almost always has two elements: ridicule and exaggeration. Both Dick Allen's "The Narrow Mind" and Carole Oles' "The Gift," which we examined as examples of a critical tone, are also satires. And they both use irony, the calm, matter-of-fact tone played against the highly critical theme. But the comic tone of Lucille Clifton in "What the Mirror Said" is not at all satiric because, as I pointed out earlier, it does not ridicule, it affirms.

Satire on television and in magazines such as *Mad* and *National Lampoon* tends to be relatively simple. Like cartoons, it is designed as one-shot entertainment. Satire in sophisticated poetry, however, usually has more intricacies, more nuances. It draws us back for repeated readings.

You and Your Persona

When we discuss a poem, we never know for sure whether the speaker in the poem represents the poet or an imagined character. We have no biographical assurance that Robert Frost actually saw a white spider on a white flower holding a white moth or whether Richard Wilbur as a child had a dog; but there is an implied character in these poems who did. Occasionally we may say "Frost questions. . ." or "Wilbur feels that. . .," but in most cases it is better to refer to "the persona," "the speaker," or "the narrator."

As a poet you have a choice. You can create the illusion of writing about your own experience, drawing on your own life; or you can filter your material through a character distinctly unlike yourself. This is a matter of establishing **distance**. Oddly, whether you use the first person, *I*, or the third person is only one of several factors. Robley Wilson does not use *I* in "On a Maine Beach," nor does Chase Twichell in her description of an unnamed patient in "Rhymes for Old Age." But both *seem* more personal than Anthony Hecht's "Lizards and Snakes" which, though told in the first person, has some of the distanced feeling of a Norman Rockwell illustration.

Because contemporary poetry is often personal, there is a special appeal for using the first person. This is reflected in many of the poems you read in Chapter 2. Dylan Thomas' "Fern Hill," Judy Kronenfeld's "Chrysalis," Elizabeth Holden's "As the Cold Deepens," and Theodore Deppe's "The Paradise of Wings" all use *I* and have the strong illusion of personal experience. Still, we owe it to the poets not to make assumptions, so no matter how strongly the poem *appears* to be the poet's own experience, it is appropriate to refer to the speaker as the persona.

Distance is increased when a poem is presented through the eyes of a character clearly not the poet. This can be done either in the first or third person. As we have seen, Gwendolyn Brooks in "We Real Cool" (page 24) uses a persona who is one of the pool players at the Golden Shovel. The narrator reveals himself (we assume "he" perhaps unfairly) and his future without quite realizing how much he is saying. The approach, called a **dramatic monologue**, establishes considerable distance no matter how strong the theme may be.

Keeping the Tone Honest

Tone is not usually your first concern when you begin a new poem. In fact, you may not even be sure what your attitude toward your subject is when you start a new poem. You can be drawn toward an occurrence, an experience, a relationship, a setting, without knowing why. It may take one or two drafts before you realize that what attracts you to the material is a sense of love or perhaps anger or a feeling of nostalgia. The very act of translating experience into lines of verse occasionally opens up veins of emotions you hadn't expected—some stratum of love for someone you thought you hated, a hidden fear of a situation you thought you enjoyed, anxiety in an area where you thought you were secure.

At some point in the revision process you should stop and ask this crucial question: Is this what I *really* feel? Does the poem, for example, merely echo conventional sentiments (mothers and nature are wonderful; war and poverty are terrible), or does it honestly explore the complexity of what you feel?

More subtly, have you been softening the implications of your poem through psychic modesty? That is, have you been reluctant to reveal your private feelings? If so, the poem will probably lack a sense of power and authenticity.

Surprisingly, this reluctance to reveal very personal feelings or experiences is the primary cause of obscurity. Hiding one's true feeling behind an impenetrable haze is an understandable but unfortunate weakness in many poems. When the **theme** or a central **image** has two or more possible meanings, the result is **ambiguity**. *Intentional* ambiguity can be used effectively to suggest that two or more meanings are equally true or that they combine to suggest a third, broader conclusion. *Unintentional* ambiguity, on the other hand, places a barrier between the poem and the reader. When this happens, ask yourself if you are hiding your true feelings behind a smoke screen.

Expressing your inner feelings and revealing uncomfortable experiences often take considerable courage. If you are still uneasy about dealing with those personal details, consider presenting the material through an invented character. This may provide some sense of objectivity while still being true to the subject matter.

Modesty isn't always the problem. Exaggerating a personal agony or a painful experience can sometimes result in **sentimentality**. Intentional sentimentality is a form of dishonesty because it cheapens genuine feelings. It is contaminated with details selected primarily for their capacity to stimulate the tear ducts. It's a trick rather than a sharing of true emotions. But what about *unintentional* sentimentality? That is far more common. Occasionally you may honestly feel that you are the most miserable, most misunderstood person on earth or, on a happier note, that your grandmother really is unbelievably perfect. Remember, though, that if the poem sounds sentimental to others, it *is* sentimental. Perhaps a wry, slightly distanced tone would help to provide perspective and hold your readers.

In the same way, if you overdramatize a conflict or protest, going beyond your real feelings, your poem may lose some of its dramatic impact and may come across as **melodramatic**. When readers have the feeling that emotions like indignation or rage have been inflated just to attract attention, the poem will loose credibility. Consider some form of irony. Take another look at Dick Allen's "The Narrow Mind" (page 24) or Carole Oles' "The Gift" (page 17). As a general rule, the most appropriate tone to adopt is an honest reflection of how you feel about your subject.

When you are sure that you have come to terms with your feelings on that deepest level, take a close look at your tone on a more craftsmanlike level: How successful have I been in communicating my tone to my readers? Once you are satisfied, let others read it. Never mind explaining what you had hoped would come through. Remember that any literary work should reach readers on its own without your explanations. If it's ready to share, it's ready to stand on its own.

Learn from your readers how they have responded to the overtones of every word and phrase. Let them tell you when a soft word or phrase has weakened the impact of a protest poem, or a harsh detail sent an unwanted jolt through a gently contemplative poem.

Make sure, also, that the poem's tonal signals don't all repeat the same note. Poems that do this can lose effectiveness, just like a musical piece that strikes the same chord too often. This problem is relatively easy to correct if you can find a way to lighten the tone in some way. A note of humor can often provide a sense of balance. Or you may be able to reveal some type of ambivalence.

Keep in mind the point I made at the beginning of this chapter: tone is a part of meaning. The revision process is not complete until you have established just the right tone.

11

POETRY:

From Craft To Art

Craft versus art: Why development in creative art takes time. Reading regularly and critically. Writing regularly. Exploring new themes. Trying new approaches. Revise! Revise! Finding support groups.

Mechanical skills, craft, can be learned quickly. Developing a true artistic facility takes much longer. The effort can be frustrating, but the rewards are worth it.

Every literary **genre** has a body of techniques going back hundreds of years. It's called *craft*. The craft of writing poetry includes the effective use of images, the ways we create sound and rhythm with language, the ways we structure and order our material. Since reinventing all this from scratch would take another thousand years, it makes sense to draw on what others have done. Books like this, extensive reading, and courses in creative writing speed the process.

But craft is only a tool. It's an enabler. It's what empowers you to go on to the next step: developing the art of poetry in your own voice. Whether you plan to write poetry for pleasure or commit yourself to creativity as a vocation, you will find that the process of discovery and growth has no end. There is no retirement age.

As with any other art form, proficiency won't sweep over you like a magic spell. You have to take control, take time, and stick with it. What follows in this chapter is not a formula for success. It is a description of how serious writers move beyond craft and develop the art of writing poetry with depth, freshness, and resonance.

Reading Regularly and Critically

As I pointed out in Chapter 2, poets read the work of other poets. Serious poets read poetry seriously, that is, critically. This does not mean that they are necessarily critical in the negative sense. After all, admiration, wonder, and sheer envy all have their place. But it does mean that poets read analytically.

Is there a risk that you will become imitative? Not if you read widely. If you don't read other poets, you will end up imitating yourself, a sterile route. Besides, occasional imitation of poetry you admire is an effective form of study. Such work normally ends up in your journal, but the process will bring you close to the model. When you return to your own original work, you will draw on what you have learned.

When students tell me that they are "very serious" about poetry, I don't ask how much they have written; I ask what was the last volume of poetry they read through to the end and what poetry journal they subscribe to. This isn't intended as a put-down. It is merely based on what I have observed: developing poets are regular readers even when they are not taking courses.

How do you find out what to read? If you are in school, take literature courses as well as writing seminars. Don't shun poetry from earlier periods. It all has a bearing on your own work. If you are not taking classes, buy anthologies or find them in your library. And read poetry journals. Find out which poets speak to you. Then order collections of their work. Expensive? No more so than dinner for two. No poetry section in your mass-market bookstore? Use the Internet.

Reading critically requires more concentration than passive reading. It means applying what you have drawn from this and other analytical texts to what you are reading. It means marking up your own copy or photocopies of work printed in library books. It means commenting on these poems in your journal—not just likes and dislikes, but analytical aspects.

One word of warning. There are book clubs that will offer you an endless number of how-to books on craft with promises. Most, however, focus on commercial verse, not sophisticated poetry. If that is your goal, fine. But if you are concerned with writing work that is insightful and sophisticated, concentrate on the real thing, poetry itself.

When you read a poem critically, you adopt that poet as your teacher. He or she is your private tutor. For free! You will enjoy the works of some poets more than others, but you will learn from them all if you respond as a fellow poet.

And don't forget the auditory aspect. If you are near a college or library that offers poetry readings, make an effort to attend. An increasing number of bookstores and coffee shops also offer readings and book-signing events. Meeting and talking with poets helps to personalize their work, but your growth and development will come from the poetry itself, not with chitchat.

Even if you live miles from the nearest library and commute to a mindless job in a cultural desert, there is a solution for you: buy an inexpensive portable cassette player and record two new poems each evening, reading aloud from a collection, and then play them as you drive to work.

Writing Regularly

Poets write regularly. Even when they have full-time jobs, they write regularly. Even when they have children or are splitting up with their partners or considering bankruptcy, they write. I have met poets who get up at 5:00 a.m. to write before going to work, and others who reserve the late hours of the night for composition. But they write. Regularly.

True, a busy schedule does not allow for long blocks of time. But one of the blessings of poetry is that it doesn't require lengthy work sessions. A poet, unlike a novelist, can often recapture the mood of an unfinished poem in minutes and make good use of a spare half-hour a day. Thirty minutes a day may be frustratingly brief, but for most it is more productive than having a whole day for work once a week. Poems are relatively short, intense works, and they can take root in the chinks that remain in a tight schedule.

For most poets, short but regular work sessions are ultimately more productive than waiting for a summer vacation. It is regularity that generates new work. Waiting for ideal working time generates nothing.

Exploring New Themes

The third essential for growth is exploring new themes. True, familiar topics are valuable because you know the details. Look at what Dylan Thomas does with the farm of his youth, and Robley Wilson with a beach in Maine. But these two poets were careful not to repeat themselves too often. You should also. Compare what you are writing with your earlier poems. Make sure you haven't begun to repeat yourself. If you have, you may find your work losing its freshness and vigor. As any farmer knows, it is best to rotate your crops.

Thematic redundancy is a special risk for those who have been through a taxing or traumatic experience such as a breakup of a relationship, illness, or the death of someone close. It is natural and often fruitful to work with the situation, drawing on the intensity of feeling. But only you can tell when you have begun to repeat yourself. There is a subtle difference between poetry that draws on intense personal experience and therapy writing. With the former, the quality of the poem remains the poet's highest priority; with therapy writing, emotional recovery becomes the primary concern and quality suffers. Such work is not without value, but it may belong in your journal.

If you need to consider different subjects, look over this list and review the works suggested. They may help you explore different areas.

City living: Levertov, "Merritt Parkway" (page 27); Brooks, "We Real Cool" (page 24)

Country living: Thomas, "Fern Hill (page 21); Hayden, "Those Winter Sundays" (page 35)

Aspects of nature: Merwin, "River Sound Remembered" (page 20); Wilson, "On a Maine Beach" (page 28); Frost, "Design" (page 15)

Old age: Twichell, "Rhymes for Old Age" (page 36); Holden, "As the Cold Deepens" (page 15)

Animals: Pastan, "Domestic Animals" (page 16); Hall, "Names of Horses" (page 17); Wilbur, "The Pardon" (page 34); Simon, "The Dolphin" (page 25)

Death: Kronenfeld, "Chrysalis" (page 41); Bertram, "Is It Well-Lighted, Papa?" (page 31)

The status of women: Oles, "The Gift" (page 17); Clifton, "What the Mirror Said" (page 20)

Childhood experiences: Wilbur, "The Pardon" (page 34); Hecht, "Lizards and Snakes" (page 33); Deppe, "The Paradise of Wings" (page 42)

Love: Endrezze, "The Map Makers Daughter" (page 44); Appleman, "Desire" (page 43); Giovanni "Balances" (page 36); Shakespeare, "Sonnet 29" (page 18)

Generations: Allen, Paula Gunn, "Grandmother" (page 40); Long, "Always the One. . . " (page 23)

Trying Different Forms

Perhaps you are one of those who feel more at home working with free verse. If you have not written very much, it may be too soon for you to restrict yourself to one approach. You can expand your abilities by trying some metrical verse—a couple of **quatrains** of **iambic tetrameter,** for example, or the repeated lines of a **pantoum.**

If, on the other hand, you enjoy the structure of traditional stanzas, you may want to stretch yourself by experimenting with unmetered short lines or with long lines and with typography, both restrained and radical.

Browsing for models may help you to get you started, but you won't really learn from a poem until you stop to study it carefully. When you first read the poems in Chapter 2, you may not have known exactly what to look for. Now, however, you will be able to draw more from each work. You will get the most from your reexamination if you mark up your copy, making legible marginal comments about technique.

Another approach is to write in imitation of a particular poem using a different theme but emulating the style. If you share such work with others, be sure to give credit; but even if it remains in your journal you will gain a true understanding of what makes that poet's style distinctive.

Here are some specific techniques in metered verse illustrated by poems in this volume.

Iambic pentameter quatrains: Wilbur, "The Pardon" (page 34); Roethke, "The Waking" (page 29)

The sonnet: Frost, "Design" (page 15); Shakespeare, "Sonnet 29" (page 18)

The ballad: Hecht, "Lizards and Snakes" (page 33)

The pantoum: Bertram, "Is It Well-Lighted, Papa?" (page 31)

The villanelle: Roethke, "The Waking" (page 29)

And here are techniques in free-verse poetry well worth reviewing.

Long-line free verse: Hall, "Names of Horses" (page 37); Ginsberg, "Howl" (fragment) (page 112)

Short-line free verse: Appleman, "Desire" (page 43); Giovanni, "Balances" (page 36)

Anaphora: Clifton, "What the Mirror Said" (page 20); Ginsberg, "Howl" (fragment) (page 112)

Syntactical rhythms: selection from the Bible (page 112); Ginsberg, "Howl" (fragment) (page 112)

Scattered typography: Levertov, "Merritt Parkway" (page 28); Cummings, "Buffalo Bill's" (page 30)

Revise! Revise!

We have all seen movies in which the musician or poet is suddenly seized with inspiration and after a few glorious minutes whips out what will become a world-renowned work of art. It's a myth, a total fabrication.

Understanding how essential revision is in the creative process comes slowly for most. At first, one is unsure just what needs more work. The initial draft may seem perfectly fine. This is particularly true for those who have not read much poetry. The more one comes to understand the genre, however, the less satisfied one is with that first draft. Experienced poets normally spend far more time revising than they do with their initial draft.

Don't confuse *revision* with *tinkering*. Close, word-by-word reexamination normally comes last, not first. Instead, start with big questions: Exactly what are you trying to say? Is it worth saying, or is it a truism accepted by everyone? Have you made this theme available for a conscientious reader? Are you relying on fresh images, or are you falling back on abstractions like an editorial?

Second, what kind of rhythmical devices have you used? For metered poetry, this is a matter of scanning. Is it monotonous or, at the other extreme, so filled with substitutions that the original meter becomes lost? With free verse, ask yourself whether there is some purpose to the typography, or is it arbitrary? In either type of verse, have you made use of the sound of language?

Next, is there a sense of order? Would it help to shift the sequence of lines? Is the ending a real conclusion, or does the poem seem chopped off?

All this may require successive drafts. When you are satisfied with the larger questions, it's time for tinkering. Think of it as fine-tuning. Are your images effective? Examine each word and phrase. Use your dictionary.

All this takes time, but it can be a pleasurable effort. Keep in mind that creativity is less inspiration than it is a process. Don't rush it.

The Importance of Support Groups

The clichéd image of the writer living alone in a garret may seem ideal if your life is harried with many conflicting responsibilities, but it's not the way writers generally develop. Yes, you need time to read and to write, but you also need people who know what you are trying to do and will react in helpful ways.

For many, the answer is creative writing classes. The best of them are not in the form of lectures, they are workshop support groups. The instructor will share his or her experience and will keep the sessions focused on writing, but much of the benefit comes from the reactions of the seminar as a whole. This group response becomes increasingly valuable in advanced classes because your peers will be increasingly perceptive.

Don't make the mistake of defending every line you write. Listen carefully. Some comments will be of no benefit; just ignore them. If you become defensive you will discourage others from saying anything, cutting you off from suggestions that may be very helpful.

What comes after graduation? For many, it's life in the wilderness. You may discover that the kindly but vacuous responses of parents and lovers are, no matter how sweet, no more nourishing than cotton candy. Even good friends often don't know what questions to ask or how to advise. As a result, they tend to respond subjectively: "I like it—sort of," or "It doesn't do much for me," or "Why don't you write about something cheerful?" Reactions like these will tell you more about the speaker than about your poem.

You may have the feeling that there is no one who shares your interests. Rest assured that there are in this country thousands of people who read and write poetry regularly. Anyone who has judged a national poetry contest can tell you that the number of poets in this country is astonishing. The problem is not numbers, it is distribution. They are scattered across a great expanse.

If you are serious about developing as a poet, you will have to make an effort to find or create a support group. Put up a notice or place an ad in a local paper. One person who knows what you are doing is better than none. Two are better than one. Seven is an ideal number. Groups of twenty or more tend to become adulterated with individuals who would rather chat than work.

There are two great dangers to watch out for in any support group. The first is excessive assertiveness on the part of one or more members. Honesty is good, but harsh or insensitive comments will either turn the sessions into ego battles or will inhibit an open sharing of views. The other danger is allowing the discussion to turn into a bull session. Whenever the group strays off to personal preferences, personal experiences, or what they have read recently, the poem under discussion is no longer the subject. Someone in the group has to be the navigator, keeping the discussion on course.

The kind of criticism that will be most helpful to you as a practicing poet will be highly specific—even if it deals more with the craft of poetry than the art. It will focus on phrasing, on imagery, on rhythm. What you as a writer need to find out is precisely what came through to the reader. In the process you may learn what didn't come through as well.

A helpful critic might say something like this: "Your three opening images are really dramatic and got me into the poem, but I lost track of them later." Or "Perhaps you could develop this stanza." Or "It seems heavier than the subject justifies."

You may be tempted to use the well-worn defense, "That's the way I intended it," but resist that impulse! Make a note of the suggestion and decide later whether to act on it. Some comments may be quirky or based on personal preferences, but pay particular attention to those views that are shared by several members of the group.

Your development in the art of poetry will depend on your reading, your commitment to writing regularly, your willingness to explore new approaches, and your openness to criticism. These are the essentials. A good textbook should help you to get started, but it won't do the work for you. Growth in this or any creative art requires sustained effort.

12

FACT AND FICTION

Three types of prose writing: factual, creative, and creative nonfiction. Fusing fact and fancy. Simple versus sophisticated fiction. The forms of fiction. Three motives for writing fiction: personal, commercial, and literary.

We start telling stories almost as soon as we can put sentences together. At first, we may make no sharp distinction between what is make-believe and what really happened. But as we get older, most of us learn that this can get us into trouble. That's when we discover that fiction is one way to make things up without being called a liar.

This distinction between factual and creative writing becomes more serious in the adult world. In fact, it is the source of frequent lawsuits. In essence, there are three types of prose, each with its distinct set of priorities.

The first type is **factual writing**. It includes research papers, news reports, scientific papers, government reports, and political and economic analyses. Most of the writing we do in school and college is factual. Even when such writing deals with characters and a plot, as in historical accounts and biography, the writer's primary obligation is to events as they occurred. We may offer opinions or even present an argument, but first we must get the facts right.

Creative writing is profoundly different. Fiction, poetry, and drama are all *creative* or *imaginative* in the sense that they are created from the author's imagination. As writers of fiction, we often draw on our experiences and on details from the world about us, but we reshape them. Our first loyalty and primary obligation is to the artistic object we are creating. If we use characters, places, and episodes from life, they are simply raw material to be artfully recycled. Familiar places can be divided, mixed, and altered. Even our best friends can be transformed by age, sex, or temperament. We select what we need and invent the rest. Our sole commitment as fiction writers is to the creation of an artistic work, whether a story or a novel.

Creative or **literary nonfiction** is a third approach that is highly popular. The phrase is awkward, but it describes what used to be called the informal essay. Creative nonfiction is factual writing in which there is a heightened concern for language and, usually, a more personal, informal **tone**. The following table gives an overview of all three approaches to prose writing:

FACTUAL WRITING	CREATIVE WRITING	CREATIVE OR LITERARY NONFICTION
(First priority: factual accuracy and objectivity)	(First priority: artistic merit)	(Factual writing with heightened attention to language, style, and tone)
News reports	Fiction	Personal experience
Scientific research	Poetry	Biographical sketches
Government reports	Drama	Travel
Literary criticism		History with imaginative details
		Personal opinion

Fusing Fact and Fancy

Fiction tells an untrue story in prose. It is "untrue" in the sense that it is partly made up. It is an artistic creation in that it stands on its own no matter how much it may make use of characters, events, and settings from life. Like playwrights and poets, writers of fiction are free to assume the existence of ghosts, unicorns, or Hobbits. We can use material close to us—parents or friends, for example—without being accurate. As writers of fiction, we are free to present our material through the eyes of a **persona**, someone who may be quite unlike us. A story or novel cannot be criticized for being "untrue"; it is judged on whether it *seems* true.

One of the best ways to achieve this sense of authenticity is to draw heavily on the world you know best—your own life. Some beginning writers feel that their lives have been too ordinary, but everyone has had complex relationships with parents or foster parents, everyone has had to deal with people their own age, everyone has had defeats, successes, and learning experiences. And every experience is unique.

This does not mean that unrevised experience makes good fiction. Our lives are a jumble of unconnected events and repetitious activities. There is nothing as dull as a step-by-step account of what has happened to you over the length of an average day. No one wants to know what you had for breakfast. The bits and pieces of experience have to serve some literary purpose and almost always have to be revised or shaped to make them serve that purpose. Even a lengthy and dramatic episode from your life that might make an entertaining **anecdote** in conversation almost always needs to be reshaped and revised before it becomes a successful story.

Unrelated details have to be cut and new material has to be added. These changes may be minor, but often they involve creating new characters and new scenes. Sometimes the actual experience was too mild or, conversely, too melodramatic for fiction. Only through careful revision can we achieve the *tone* we have in mind. Keep reminding yourself that fiction is not a diary entry even if it is written to resemble one; fiction is an artistic creation with its own sense of unity and significance.

Often we edit our account unconsciously when we tell a friend about something that happened to us. A husband's version of a trip abroad will differ in tone and selection of detail from his wife's no matter how dedicated each is to "the truth." As long as we are describing our experiences, however, the basic facts have to be accurate. If not, someone is apt to say, "Hey, that's not what happened!"

As fiction writers, however, we are totally liberated from the experience as it happened. In fact there are good reasons for making sure a new story is not an exact replica of what happened. Heady as this freedom is, we take on a new obligation: to create "a good story," one with unity, theme, and credible characterization.

Suppose, for example, you want to base a story on an intense argument between a man and a woman you overheard in a restaurant. You may decide to use much of their exact phrasing (pure fact) but make them brother and sister (invention) and put them in your uncle's house (factual memory), telling the story from the point of view of a six-year-old daughter listening to them (invention) during a terrible rainstorm (factual memory from another occasion). If you do this right, no one will be able to separate what was drawn from life and what was created from your imagination. The two have become fused into a single, credible story.

Simple versus Sophisticated Fiction

As soon as we talk about the merit or worth of an artistic work, we enter the slippery area of what is good and what is bad. It is so difficult to defend the worth of a story that some people duck the issue entirely by saying, "I only know what I like." Personal preference, of course, is everyone's privilege. Some like gentle stories, some want heavy drama; some prefer stories about women, others like to read about men. Arguing seriously about our preferences is as pointless as debating whether dogs are better than cats.

There is, however, one distinction about which we can reach agreement: some stories, like some poems and plays, are relatively **simple** while others are significantly more **sophisticated**. These terms are enormously helpful for writers and underlie all of the analysis in this book.

Essentially, sophisticated works "do" more in the sense that they suggest more, imply a greater range of possibilities, and develop more subtle shadings of meaning than simple works do. This text is concerned with sophisticated writing, but that focus does not imply that such work is "better." It is simply "other" in the sense that the biologically simple crayfish is different from the far more sophisticated porpoise.

The span between the simplest fiction and relatively sophisticated fiction is enormous. Compare a comic strip about adolescents such as *Luann* or *Zits* with a novel about adolescents like John Knowles' *A Separate Peace* or J. D. Salinger's *Catcher in the Rye*. The cartoons and the novels are similar in that they all are samples of fiction. That is, they all tell untrue stories in prose. Further, they all have plots, characters, settings, and themes. Also they share certain basic fictional techniques: dialogue, thoughts, and action. They even draw on the same age bracket—that highly charged transition period between childhood and adulthood. Before we brand comics as "childish," remember that many intelligent adults read them with pleasure each morning. Conversely, while a majority believe that *Catcher in the Rye* is an excellent example of literary fiction, a few find it immoral and therefore "bad."

So what is the difference? To start with, the fictional protagonist in *Zits*, for example, is relatively uncomplicated. The plots tend to be brief and limited in scope. Comic-strip characters rarely deal with such issues as teen pregnancy or drugs. The portrayal of Holden Caulfield, the protagonist of *Catcher in the Rye*, on the other hand, is sophisticated in that he is shown dealing with fairly complex moral issues and inner doubts. He struggles with the uncertainties that are often associated with adolescence.

The enjoyment many take in reading a comic strip is an escape from the challenges of daily living, and we all need occasional periods of retreat. But in general, we read such episodes once and then forget them. They may give pleasure, but they are throw-away entertainment. In contrast, the pleasure derived from reading *Catcher in the Rye* comes from a greater understanding of the world about us. We can return to it and draw more from it in another reading. In short, each type of fiction serves a different need.

It is important here to distinguish this literary use of *sophisticated* from its popular use, which describes a person who is socially suave and urbane. The *portrayal* of a character, characterization, can be sophisticated even if the character is not. Literary sophistication refers to the degree to which the work develops characters (and themes too) with complexity, depth, and range of insight. Mark Twain's Huck Finn, for example, and Carson McCullers' Frankie in *Member of the Wedding* are certainly presented as unsophisticated individuals, but the subtlety and insightfulness with which these authors present their characters and the novels as a whole are literarily sophisticated.

As with poetry, there are an infinite number of gradations between the simplest forms of fiction and the most sophisticated. Juveniles—stories and novels written for adolescents—are far more intricate in characterization and theme than comic strips. Gothic novels, for all their repetition of plot and setting, have a certain sophistication of vocabulary, but they are not intended to be as subtle or insightful as literary novels. In fact, a standard, mass-market gothic novel manuscript may well be turned down by a publisher if it departs too far from the familiar and relatively simple pattern. In the case of murder mysteries, most of the sophistication takes the form of ingenious plots, but thematically they tend to be fairly simple. The fact that murderers often make a simple but crucial error is not exactly a fresh insight. Such novels are for most enthusiasts "a quick read."

There are essentially three large-circulation magazines that publish sophisticated short stories today—*The New Yorker, Harpers,* and *The Atlantic;* but there are literally hundreds of literary journals and quarterlies, like *Glimmer Train, Story Quarterly,* (both all-fiction), *The North American Review,* and *The Virginia Quarterly Review.* (A longer list appears in Appendix B.) These publications usually vary their offerings from relatively accessible pieces to works that, like sophisticated poetry, may require some effort on the part of the reader. Those who are seriously interested in writing sophisticated fiction should spend fully as much time reading as they do writing.

As a writer, how high should you aim? It would be a mistake to start out by attempting an extremely complex plot and an intricate theme. If you have one or two interesting characters and a single, insightful event, you can write a story that is fresh and rewarding.

As you gain experience and get in the habit of reading new work regularly, you will want to examine what makes some works more sophisticated than others. Take a close look at the four basic elements of the story: plot, characters, setting, and theme.

Plot, whether simple or sophisticated, consists of a sequence of actions. Simple fiction, however, not only reduces the complexity of plot, it usually avoids originality as well. Plots such as those recurring in television programs tend to be based on well-used **conventions** known as **formulas**. Plots like the good-cop-with-good-wife-is-tempted-by-drug-money are, for all the noise and profanity, tranquilizers derived from familiarity and repetition.

Sophistication of plot does not necessarily mean complexity. What one aims for is a sequence of events that are fresh and provide new insights. The determining factor is not how many twists and turns the plot may take but how much it reveals about the characters and the theme of the story.

Characterization, the portrayal of fictitious characters, is also significantly different in simple and sophisticated works. In simple fiction, the characters may do a lot (the restlessness of a James Bond), but you never get to know him or her the way you might come to understand someone in life. What you see is a repetition of the same traits and attitudes. The good stay good, and the bad stay bad. It's not likely you'll see Tarzan become addicted and sell the rain forest to finance his habit.

Characters in sophisticated fiction that are developed fully often reveal mixed emotions. Sharply contrasted feelings take the form of **ambivalence**, a simultaneous blending of opposite feelings such as love and hate for another person or a mix of courage and panic. Motivation may include both honorable and selfish elements. Behavior may reveal both maturity and childishness on different occasions, contrasts similar to those you may have seen in a close friend.

Setting in simple fiction often relies on geographic clichés that are repeated over and over. Students in New York are described as living in Greenwich Village, even though that area has not been a low-rent bargain for over 50 years; businessmen have their offices on Madison Avenue; San Francisco lawyers work "in the shadow of the Golden Gate"; artists in Paris have studios looking out on the Eiffel Tower. "Originality" often takes the form of the exotic—a ski resort high in the Andes, a spy headquarters 400 feet below the Houses of Parliament, a royal palace constructed entirely in glowing Lucite on the planet Octo. Bizarre settings often serve no purpose other than visual appeal. They tend to dominate rather than contribute to characterization and theme.

The setting in sophisticated fiction, on the other hand, generally avoids both the clichés and the bizarre. It may be based on a place known to the author or largely invented, but the details are fresh, not borrowed, and they are not obtrusive. Ideally, the setting helps to develop the theme.

Theme is another aspect of fiction that varies with the degree of sophistication. The theme is the portion that reveals some aspect of the human condition. Simple themes repeat what we already know. Many themes are borrowed from television. So-called action thrillers on television (successors to the once-popular detective stories in magazines) endlessly repeat the theme, "Crime doesn't pay, but it's exciting to try." Situation comedies repeat the notion that misunderstandings regularly lead to absurd confusions all of which are finally resolved in minutes without doing damage to anyone. Injustices are terrible but corrected in the end. These thematic patterns are so simple and repeated so often that we call them **hackneyed**. It takes both skill and practice to produce such work, but the goal is quick entertainment, not memorable themes.

Sophisticated fiction, in contrast, tends to develop themes that have depth and insight. Dishonest acts usually have a variety of consequences, some of them surprising. Misunderstandings frequently result in lasting damage. Outrageous injustice may endure or take another form. We learn something from such thematic suggestions. Our view of the world is altered, even if only slightly.

Whenever you read fiction, you evaluate the level of sophistication on the basis of elements like these, either consciously or unconsciously. When you write you must stay on guard against the easy and the glib; you should constantly strive for freshness and insight.

Another way to evaluate the degree of sophistication in your own work is to take a close look at what is called the five **narrative modes** of fiction: dialogue, thought, action, description, and exposition. These are the basic tools of the genre.

Dialogue and *thought* are two effective ways of suggesting character. In simple fiction they fit a familiar mold and reveal familiar types known as **stock characters**. Heroes speak heroically, and cowards snivel. In sophisticated fiction dialogue and thoughts reveal the subtle nuances of character—the variations that we detect only in those we know well. Often dialogue and thoughts are played against each other so as to reveal a contrast between the inner and the outer person.

Action is the dominant mode for simple fiction, particularly in adventure stories. As we will see in the examples in this text, sophisticated fiction depends on action too, but one never has the feeling that action is there for its own sake. It is a means of developing both character and theme, not an end in itself.

Description can be important even though it tends to slow the forward motion of a story. Descriptive details are justified when they are relevant. That is, they should have some purpose and should have a sense of authenticity.

Exposition is perhaps the most dangerous of the five narrative modes. It refers to those explanatory passages that give background information or commentary directly. It is risky because in simple (and inept) fiction it is often used to explain character and, worse, present the theme directly. "Old Mack looked tough but had a heart of gold" labels an aspect of character that in fiction would be better revealed through action and dialogue. "Thus we see that money isn't everything" is not only a **hackneyed** phrase, it is an attempt to state what should have been shown.

You're on safe ground if you limit exposition to peripheral or incidental information: "He had just turned 40" or "She had never been in Chicago." Sophisticated fiction reveals the rest through action and dialogue.

The reason for limiting the use of exposition is that the success of literarily sophisticated fiction depends in part on the degree to which readers have the feeling that they themselves have come to know the characters and discern the thematic suggestions in a story on their own. The process is similar to the way we make judgments about people and situations in actual life. We listen to what people say and watch what they do, and then we come to conclusions. In fiction, of course, the dialogue and action are carefully selected by the author, but when we read, we like the illusion of discovering significance on our own.

The Forms of Fiction

Fiction is commonly classified as falling into four categories: the short-short story, the story, the novella, and the novel. These terms are handy, but they are far from precise. There is no sharp line between one length and the next.

Short-short stories are usually defined as being between 500 and 2,000 words long. Since a typed, double-spaced manuscript (see Appendix B for details) comes to about 250 words a page, a short-short is from two to six pages. Contests for short-shorts are normally limited to 1,500 words, or about six pages. For contests, be sure to determine your word count accurately

Because of their brevity, most short-shorts have no more than one or two characters presented in one or two scenes in a brief time span. There is a temptation to indulge in trick endings, but with restraint you can generate real insight into character, feeling, and human relations.

Short stories generally run from 2,000 words (8 pages) to 6,000 words (24 pages). Some are longer, but these become increasingly difficult to place, since the greater length will force a magazine editor to reduce the total number of works in an issue. The great advantage of this length over the short-short is that it allows one to deal with more characters, have a more intricate plot, and make greater use of setting. But the short story is still a relatively tight art form.

Novellas generally run between 50 and 150 typed pages, halfway between a story and a novel. From time to time magazines will include one novella or will devote a special issue to several, but novellas are more often seen in published collections along with short stories by the same author.

Novels are more than just stories that have been expanded beyond 250 pages—or at least they should be. The length allows an author to do interesting things with the plot and to develop subplots. One can introduce more characters than in a story or novella, and some of them can change and develop over the course of time. The theme or themes of such a work can be broader and more intricate than in the shorter forms.

When you start writing, the short-short story is a good form to work with. In developing your creative abilities, it is important to try a number of different approaches—first person, third person, light tone, serious tone, close to experience, far removed from experience. You can achieve new skills and find your own voice better through a series of short-short stories than by locking yourself into a longer work too soon.

Three Motives for Writing Fiction

Whenever you become involved in creative work, it is worth asking yourself just what aspect of the activity is motivating you. Doing this may help you to determine in what direction you want to move right from the start.

There are many reasons for writing fiction, but they tend to fall into three broad groups. Since each involves a different approach and different goals, it is important to examine them separately.

First, there is the *private motive*. This is expressed in writing that is mainly for personal pleasure. It is intended for an audience of one—yourself. Often it takes the form of journal entries. Spontaneous and usually unrevised, journal writing requires no special training. Entries may be valuable for recording or clarifying your own feelings or as a way of sketching out possible scenes in fiction, or they may be just good fun as a release; but they shouldn't be passed off as finished work.

The second is the *commercial motive*. In its pure form, **commercial fiction** is the opposite of private writing since it is motivated largely by outer rather than inner demands. It is writing for others. Commercial writers usually define their work as a craft rather than an art, and their primary goal is monetary reward. They produce entertainment. Many spend more of their time writing nonfiction than they do fiction because the demand is greater.

The fiction produced by commercial writers tends to follow certain familiar conventions—the love story, high adventure, war, crime—because there is a large market for that kind of writing. As with businesspeople, their goal is to supply what the market wants. Although there is a tendency for literarily minded individuals to look down on commercial writing, it is an honest profession that fills a need.

The third is the *literary motive*. Although it is a primary factor in the creation of most literature down through the ages, it is perhaps the most misunderstood. Writers in this area are like painters, sculptors, and composers who value the quality of the work they produce. Having an audience is obviously important, and being paid for one's efforts seems only fair; but making money is not the principal drive. Because of this they do not generally tailor their work to meet the whims of the public, nor do they cater to commercial markets. They measure their efforts against what they consider to be the best fiction they have read.

Because literary writers require readers who have relatively sophisticated taste and experience, they must often (though not always) be content with a relatively small audience. Their novels may not be best-sellers, and their short stories frequently appear in "little magazines" that have small circulations and cannot pay their contributors lavishly. Writers in this area usually have to supplement their income—often by teaching. Many continue writing even when they receive nothing for their work. But when they publish they have a special satisfaction in knowing that they are reaching readers who will spend time with their work and will react to it with some sensitivity. In addition, they are working in one of the few areas where they do not have to compromise. For many, this is very important.

The literary motive is sometimes difficult for nonwriters to understand, especially in a society that tends to judge worth on the basis of economic reward. It helps, though, to compare the literary writer with the opera singer who knows that rock singers earn ten times as much. Opera continues not because its performers like being paid less but because this is what they do best and enjoy most.

The emphasis in most creative writing courses is on sophisticated rather than simple work. The same is true of this text. This does not mean that personal entries in a journal are without value. Nor does it mean that commercial writing, which by definition is aimed at a wide audience, is to be scorned. What it does mean is that because sophisticated or literary writing requires careful study and a lot of practice, many people find writing courses and a text like this helpful. Selecting the kind of writing you want to do depends entirely on what motivates you.

These motives for writing are not exclusive. Every writer, like every artist in the broadest sense, is driven by a combination of all three. Those who are concerned primarily with sophisticated writing, however, share a respect for literature as something of value in itself. With this as a base, there is no end of possibilities for fresh creativity.

13

WHERE STORIES COME FROM

The search for fresh material. The "seven deadly sins" of fiction. The authenticity of personal experience: family relationships, friends and acquaintances, moments of growth and discovery. Transformation: shifting from fact to fiction. Literary transformation: decisions about plot, characters, and theme.

Sophisticated fiction depends on fresh material. One source that is guaranteed to be fresh is your own life. When you draw on your experiences honestly, you can be sure that you are being original. Your life experiences, after all, are unique.

But as I pointed out in the previous chapter, creative writing is almost always a blend of what we know well and what we invent. Where does the new material come from? Ideally, it springs from our imagination, stimulated by what we have read, seen, and heard about. Unfortunately, this storehouse of secondhand material also contains a clutter of old plots, characters, and settings picked up from television and movies. It is all too easy to use bits and pieces from these shopworn sources unintentionally. When facing a writing deadline, you may even be tempted to use one intentionally. But if you do, you may contaminate the rest of your work.

Familiar **plot** patterns and **stock characters** are **clichés** on a big scale. When commercial writers of fiction and scriptwriters adopt these **conventions** purposely, it is politely called **formula writing**. Like fast food, formula writing serves a wide market and often earns top dollars, but it usually sacrifices subtlety and insight. When these conventions show up in sophisticated fiction, they are the tattered remains of material that often wasn't fresh even in the hands of professionals. As soon as readers recognize one of these familiar patterns, they are apt to slip into the glazed half-attention with which they frequently watch a standard television drama or listen to background music at a restaurant. Imagination is essential in creative writing, but what comes from the imagination must be original.

The "Seven Deadly Sins" of Fiction

How can one tell what is stale material? Essentially by reading a lot. Here, though, are seven danger areas to watch out for. They may not be deadly in a literal sense, but for serious writers they are sins because of the way they damage the quality of fiction.

The popularity of particular stock plots and character types shifts from year to year, but these seven are especially prevalent today. I list them not to discourage invention but to save you from spending valuable time on a story idea that may well be doomed from the start.

• **The High-Tech Melodrama.** A **melodrama** is any piece of fiction or drama that is overloaded with dramatic suspense. Unlike true drama, it is overdone. Television's relentless drive for more viewers tempts many scriptwriters to step over the line between drama and melodrama.

Everyone has a slightly different opinion of just where that line should be drawn, but regardless of labels, so-called suspense thrillers tend to have certain standard ingredients. Whether the protagonist is a solo detective, a cop, or a vice squad member, the props usually include both guns and late-model cars, and the plot turns out to be, at the mildest, some version of search-and-capture. More often, it's search-and-kill. The high-speed chase is repeated as regularly as was the shootout in Westerns of the 1950s. Replacing the magnum with a laser and moving the chase to another galaxy may be a challenge for the special-effects department, but the plot is remarkably similar, and the characters seem to speak the same lines.

It is not guns and uniforms by themselves that present the problem. If you have gone hunting, served on a police force, or been in the military, you could explore those experiences and find ways of sharing them with your readers. But serious problems arise when you start to borrow material from scriptwriters who themselves are borrowing from earlier scripts. Watch out for characters—male or female—who always maintain their cool in times of stress and reveal nothing of themselves. Guard against that too-easy dichotomy between the good and the bad. Keep asking yourself: Where did I get this stuff? Is it used property?

• **The Adolescent Tragedy.** The adolescent period is an excellent one for sophisticated fiction as long as you keep your material genuine and fresh in detail. But there are three pitfalls: lack of perspective, sentimentality, and melodrama.

Lack of perspective occurs when the experience is too recent and the author is more concerned with his or her feelings than the work as fiction. The result may end up like an extended diary entry. There are two warning signs: when you find yourself calling your fictional characters by the names of their nonfictional counterparts and when you feel you shouldn't change the plot because "that's not the way it happened."

To avoid this lack of objectivity, make sure that enough time has elapsed between the event and your attempt to convert it into fiction. The more emotional the experience, the more time will be required to gain some measure of detachment.

Sentimentality is a fictional virus often caught while watching television. The first symptom is the distant sound of violins. The difference between the sentimental story and one that is genuinely moving is a matter of sophistication. Sentimental stories sacrifice in-depth characterization and subtle themes in order to evoke tears.

Watch out for that miserable but blameless little boy and his totally evil father, the blind girl whose only friend is a blind puppy, or the terminally ill patient who finds love in the hospital. You don't have to be a cynic to spot these as tricks to trigger the emotions.

But what if you really were brutalized by a vicious father or found love in a hospital? Your job would be to develop characters with depth and find ambivalences that will break the mold and convince the reader that this is a genuine experience. In some cases you may have to alter the situation radically to avoid even the appearance of sentimentality. Saying, "But that's the way it happened" is never an excuse for bad writing.

Melodrama is tonally the opposite. In musical terms, sentimentality is played with plaintive violins while melodrama pounds on the drums. Here is one sample in essence: good kid is drawn into gang membership, is soon forced to test his manhood by shooting his brother, and is then knifed by a rival gang. How can this be melodramatic when events this violent happen every day on the street? Because it has been worked over too often; because it would take a full novel to develop; because we can spot the ending from reading the first paragraph; because it sounds like another high school instructional film on the evil of gangs. Those telltale signs will kill the story faster than a magnum.

Again, what if it almost happened to you? Find some corner of the experience that only you know about. Avoid the big, familiar pattern. Show us an aspect the rest of us never thought about before.

• **The Twilight Zone Rerun.** Like the fiction of Edgar Allan Poe, the scripts of the television program *The Twilight Zone* are characterized by the strange and the bizarre. They usually depend on a gimmick. A **gimmick** is a tricky idea worked into fiction or a script, one that surprises and entertains. In one episode, for example, a nearsighted book lover who is the sole survivor of World War III discovers an undamaged library for his private use. As he reaches for a treasured book, he—you guessed it—drops and breaks his glasses. Entertaining, yes, but it is **simple** entertainment. The trick becomes more important than the development of character or subtlety of theme. Like the anecdote or well-told joke, it depends on a punch line. Once read, there is little reason for going back to it.

- **Vampires Resurrected.** Count (and Countess) Dracula have, in their golden years, managed to upstage werewolves, though just barely. The resurrection seems to have originated not in Transylvania but in Hollywood. It was once good dream stuff, but the convention has been repeated so often that it has sunk to the level of comic strips and Halloween masks. Even professional scriptwriters, experts in recycling previously recycled works, are reduced to treating it as self-satire. There is little likelihood that a beginning writer can in eight pages breathe life into either the once-proud count or his recently liberated countess.

- **The Baby-Boomer Gone Wrong.** This is one of the most common patterns in college writing courses. The protagonist is a young, upwardly mobile individual who has put career and love of material objects ahead of personal relationships and spiritual values. He drives a Porsche, has a Jacuzzi, and lives in Silicon Valley or some mythical place with the same climate. In the end, he pays for his sins and succumbs to drink, drugs, or a bullet—sometimes all three.

These are morality tales with their roots in the Faust legend—medieval tales portraying a hero who sells his soul to the devil in exchange for knowledge and possessions. It has been redone in opera and countless films. The devil usually gets the best lines.

It would be nice to think that such plots were inspired by Goethe's play, the operas of Berlioz and Gounod, Theodore Dreiser's novel, *An American Tragedy*, or stories like F. Scott Fitzgerald's "Winter Dreams," all of which build convincing characters who echo the Faust myth. But it seems more likely that the source is television dramas and films, many of which do no more than dress the characters in different costumes.

In keeping with the times, the Faust plot is occasionally refashioned with a young woman as unhappy protagonist. But sex reversal alone does not create insight into character and theme. True, such individuals exist in significant numbers, but it takes real skill to avoid the time-worn ruts of imitations that are based on imitation.

Suppose, however, you knew a hard-driving individual who really did own a Porsche and tragically did commit suicide? It still would be a risky incident for fiction. Suicide is generally too big and complex a subject to handle convincingly in a short-short story. You may have to substitute some subtler indication of a character's sense of defeat and despair. As for the other details, sometimes you have to revise life's events to keep them from echoing the too familiar conventions of fiction and theater.

- **The Temptations of Ernest Goodwriter.** The protagonist walks up and down the beach, planning a great novel. He is tempted by invitations of fun-loving but superficial friends and an offer to join a major advertising firm.

After a tedious period of agonizing indecision, he returns to his typewriter or computer and his high literary principles.

Or perhaps he is in New York and will not change a word of a novel he has already written. Or he is in Los Angeles and is torn between trying to write a great novel that may or may not find a publisher and being paid a fortune to write formula scripts.

Hack writers have recycled this plot by giving the lead to a woman, shifting the setting, and trying other art forms (jazz musicians and painters mostly), but the plot and theme fit the same mold.

The sad fact is that morality tales make poor fiction. They are unconvincing because the characters have been upstaged by abstract ideas: good pitted against evil with no complexity or insight into the way people really live. In some cases the hero is so wooden you can't help hoping he or she will "go Hollywood," make a fortune, and live happily ever after.

- **My Weird Dream.** Recording your own dreams can be interesting and valuable—for your analyst. But for the rest of us, the aimless plot and shifting scenes are tedious at best. Only a conscientious writing instructor will actually get to the end.

Dream stories do have a history of sorts. In the 1920s they were called **automatic writing**. Writers simply typed whatever came into their heads for three hours and called the final fifteen pages a "story." Occasionally, segments were published (mostly in a magazine called *Broom*) but no one has republished them—for good reason.

There was another flurry of interest in the late 1960s, when this kind of writing was defended as "literary tripping," a hallucinogenic voyage on paper. Again, the writing was more fun than the reading.

The passing fad of aimless composition should not be confused with **stream-of-consciousness** writing. This technique, made famous by James Joyce, is designed to give the illusion of entering the mind of a fictional character. It is used as a part of story, usually as the thoughts of a character we have already come to know through more conventional writing. As such, it is a literary device with a purpose. A dream without a context belongs in your journal.

These, then, are seven of the most common causes for failure in short stories. Keep them in mind when you are planning a new story because time spent on shopworn material is time wasted.

But don't be intimidated! Remember that creativity is by nature a positive process, an unfolding of new material. When you draw on the many fruitful sources for fiction, you will find that the planning and the writing itself generate insights about yourself and your world, and what you create is bound to be fresh and original.

The Authenticity of Personal Experience

You know your own life better than anyone else does. When you write about your own experiences, your family, your friends, your neighborhood, your own feelings, you have inside information. If you select fresh details, you can draw your reader into the world you create.

Sometimes beginning writers avoid using their own experiences because they feel that their lives are too uneventful. But short fiction does not require high drama. Your life is filled with problem solving, minor achievements, betrayals, reversals, and discoveries. You know more about the details than anyone else. And the people you grew up with—friends and relatives—have revealed themselves in interesting ways from time to time. If you learn how to draw on material like this and how to reshape it, you will have discovered the essence of writing fiction.

A standard legal disclaimer states that "any similarity to actual persons or places is purely coincidental," but no one who writes fiction takes that seriously. A more honest statement would be that similarities to persons and places are frequent, intentional, and occasionally brazen, but generally fragmentary, inconsistent, and disguised with fanciful invention.

Using personal experience selectively and honestly is one of your best safeguards against work that is unconvincing. This is particularly true for those who are just beginning to write fiction. As you gain experience, you will learn how to keep one foot in the circle of familiarity while reaching out with the other. Memories of a summer job on a construction crew, for example, might allow you to explore what it would be like to be foreman or, pushed further, a civil engineer in conflict with the foreman. Some of the more demanding moments of baby-sitting might serve as the basis for a story dealing with the life of a single parent. At the outset, it is wise to stay relatively close to the original experience.

Finding a good incident with which to work may come easily, but often it will not. Even experienced writers have dry periods. Since "waiting for inspiration" is just a romantic way of describing procrastination, it is important to learn how to look for material in a constructive way. Here are some areas that are worth exploring.

Family relationships are natural subjects for fiction. Everyone has had either parents or foster parents; everyone has experienced in some proportion the mixture of love and resentment that is a natural part of most relationships. That instable balance is normally in constant flux.

The relationship one has with parents not only shifts day by day, it changes in more general ways over the years. Often it progresses from idealization through disillusionment to a new acceptance, usually based on a fairly realistic evaluation. But every family is different. Your job as writer is to find an incident that is unique to your own experience.

Big is not necessarily better. A major or traumatic shift in a relationship may prove too large in scope to be handled in a short-short story. Without the chance to develop the situation fully, you may unintentionally cause the work to sound melodramatic. Often the best material is more subtle and manageable.

In addition to child-parent relationships, there are a variety of other intrafamily attitudes that also keep changing: brother and sister, two sisters and a maiden aunt, two brothers and their cousin, a daughter dealing with a stepfather, the reactions of three brothers to their uncle. Relationships like these fluctuate in real life, and the shifts are remembered because something was done (action) or said (dialogue) in such a way as to reveal and dramatize the change. To some degree you can use such relationships directly, but often you will have to transform experience into something related but different—a process I will explain shortly.

Love relationships have been used a great deal in fiction, so certain patterns have become **hackneyed** from overuse. But don't let this put you off. Genuine emotions are always fresh. You can avoid the conventions of commercial fiction by asking these two related questions: What were my *real* feelings? Were there any **ambivalent** emotions?

On very rare occasions you may find that even the most honest development of an experience will seem on paper to resemble a scene from a second-rate movie. It's most unlikely, but perhaps you really did patch up a relationship while standing on the shore of Lake Concord under a full moon in June as violin music played in the background. As a writer of fiction you will simply have to break the mold. Douse the moon, change the name of the lake, get rid of the violin, and give the characters some uneasiness about that reconciliation. The truth is no excuse for bad fiction.

Some of the best relationships to examine are those with individuals who are much younger or older. Your first impulse will be to present the material through the eyes of the character who is closest to your own age. But try writing a page or two from the point of view of the other character. Even if you don't use that version, it may help you to see more aspects of the relationship.

For an overview of your resources, the following chart may help you to explore the complex relationships you have with those about you. At the top are some of those older than you and at the bottom those who are younger. You as author are at the center.

Charts and diagrams, of course, don't write fiction. The function of this one is merely to stimulate your memory and to suggest where to look for good material. To make full use of this diagram, jot down the names of individuals you know whose relationship with you has the potential for fiction.

great aunts and great uncles	grandmothers and grandfathers	friends of grandparents
aunts and uncles friends of parents	parents or stepparents	an employer a teacher a stranger
brothers and sisters half siblings	YOU AS AUTHOR	close friends other contemporaries (liked and disliked)
cousins		teammates
nieces and nephews	younger sibling or your own child	the kid next door

After you have selected two or three individuals from your own life, ask yourself how your relationship with them had an impact on you or on them. Did you learn anything from them, or they from you? Did the friendship itself improve in some interesting or dramatic way? Or was it shattered by events? Did the relationship lead to a surprising discovery about yourself, the other person, or a third person? Did any of these individuals change your attitude in a positive and growing way or, conversely, a negative way that created bitterness or resentment? Did it affect your development for the better or worse?

While examining these possibilities, take notes and use the actual names of people and places. Since you are exploring aspects of your own life, the notes you take are private. Keep them in your journal.

While you are exploring these personal relationships and experiences, don't neglect places that have stayed in your memory. Someone else's home, perhaps, or a shopping plaza, or a vacant lot where you used to play, a view from a car window, or a kitchen seen only once may have lingered in your memory with extraordinary sharpness. If so, they have remained for a reason. These places may have nothing to do with the people you are recalling, but they could end up serving as the setting when you begin to put this material together as fiction.

Once you have characters, a situation, and a setting to work with, you are like a carpenter who has gathered the materials needed for construction. It may be that the outline of a story will come to you at this point. If so, you're in luck. But creative writing tends to be much sloppier than building a house. Don't worry if you don't have a clear plot plan and theme in mind. All you need is more material than you can ever use and the faith that somehow your story will begin to take shape. With these you are at last ready to start writing fiction.

Transformation: From Facts to Fiction

Recalling the people, places, and experiences of your life is a natural first step in the creative process, but this material is a collection of facts, not fiction. Some published stories may seem like camcorder re-creations from the author's life, but they almost never are. All that raw material has to go through a process of transformation.

Transformation refers to basic alterations of events, characters, viewpoints, or settings occasionally all four. It is so fundamental and so primary that it is sometimes referred to as a process of **metamorphosis**, a complete change in structure and appearance.

Unconscious transformation often alters our memories even before we begin to plan a story. Without being aware of doing so, we block certain events and highlight others. We alter chronological sequences, forget that certain characters were present, shift scenes. For evidence of this phenomenon, listen to two people describe the same vacation trip. In a more serious vein, read the sworn testimony of different witnesses to the same crime.

We restructure memory to protect our own egos, maintain modesty, get a laugh, clarify, or dramatize an incident. Indeed, in conversation we are often *expected* to alter events. "Come on," someone says when we take too long telling a story, "get to the point."

Unconscious transformation of memory can occasionally work against us. We may be censoring an experience by making a fictional character kinder, wiser, or more moral than the model on which she or he is based. That kind of unconscious transformation can sanitize an experience or a character, making the story too bland or too vague.

We all tend to be shy when we contemplate writing about our friends and relatives. We are apt to have feelings about them that we don't want to advertise. Even if we feel very close to a parent, friend, or lover, we also see aspects in him or her that are less than perfect. Occasionally we may even spot aspects of ourselves that are less than perfect. Most of us can recall a number of incidents we would never reveal to a friend, much less to total strangers. How can we put these on paper for everyone to read?

More serious, unconscious censorship may prevent us from getting started at all. What is described as *writer's block* is frequently a reluctance to deal with material that is still too close and personal.

The solution to all these problems is *conscious transformation*. Don't confuse this with *revision*, a more subtle process that doesn't start until you have completed the first draft. Transformation is the first step in converting those bits and pieces of factual data floating around in your memory into a coherent narrative known as fiction. It involves restructuring, reordering, and a good deal of fabrication.

Transformation should come early in the creative process because it is your primary method of objectifying your subject matter. Unless you have some degree of objectivity, you will be hopelessly bound to the events and to the characters in your memory. Until you feel free to shape your material, you will not be writing fiction.

To begin, change the names of your characters. This is essential if you are going to give them fictional identities of their own. Fictional names will also help to free you from the events as they occurred. As a general rule, fictional names are more memorable if they are slightly unusual and varied in length. Leave Dick, Jane, and their dog Spot for the younger generation.

If you still feel overly influenced by the people you have selected as models, change the physical appearance of their fictional counterparts. If the person you have in mind is fat in reality, consider making the fictional version thin; if his wife is actually tall, you might make her short. More radical, consider changing the sex of a character. This may seem impossible at first, but sometimes it is easier than you might think—especially with children. One note of caution: when refashioning characters, be careful not to picture them as flawlessly beautiful or handsome. Such absolutes are what gave Hollywood a bad name.

Sometimes the events also have to be transformed. Highly personal episodes may have to be refashioned to release you from an understandable reticence. Consider presenting the story through the eyes of a character not based on yourself. Painful childhood memories, for example, can occasionally be made manageable by telling the story through the eyes of a parent.

Changing the setting is another possibility. Moving the story to another locale is a basic transformation that in some cases creates a fresh vision.

How much transformation is necessary? Sometimes very little. But there are two warning signs that are clear indications that more alterations are needed. First, if you find yourself referring to your **protagonist** as "I" and to your other characters by the names of their actual models, you are still thinking of the piece as factual writing. Second, if you catch yourself saying, "I can't have them do that; it just didn't happen that way," you're in trouble. There is no clearer indication that your first loyalty is still to the events as they occurred. You have not yet begun to write fiction. As I pointed out in Chapter 12, a fiction writer's only loyalty is to the literary work.

Literary Transformations

The first purpose of transformation, then, is psychological. It frees you from experience and starts you thinking in terms of fiction. But once that has occurred, further transformation is needed to give your work a literary shape. This is when you make some basic decisions about the plot, the characters, and the theme.

Fictional plots may resemble what goes on in daily life, but that is an illusion. Real life is a jumble of experience, much of it routine. If you reported everything that happened to you during a 24-hour period, you would on most days end up with 100 pages of utterly boring material. Not even your best friend would read it. This does not mean that your life is boring, but it does mean that we all spend a good deal of time doing routine things. Significant and interesting developments occur from time to time, but they are almost always embedded in unrelated events.

Fragments of personal experience left in a story for no good literary reason are essentially junk details. Readers of fiction are not deeply concerned with what a character had for breakfast the day he discovered that his kid brother had been arrested unless, implausibly, the two events are significantly connected. At best, such details are mere clutter; at worst, they can mislead the reader by appearing to give importance to something that contributes nothing to the story. What you leave in should have a purpose even if it is subtle.

To achieve this, you may have to shift or consolidate scenes and invent action and dialogue not because that's the way the event occurred but because that's what the story needs.

Characters also may have to be radically altered from the individuals you originally had in mind. Some will have to be toned down to keep them from dominating a story. More often, fictional characters have to be "toned up" in the sense of highlighting certain characteristics. The more you write fiction, the more you will be able to fuse two people you know into a single fictional character. There may be times when you come to know one of your fictional characters so well you forget who the original model was.

While the theme or themes of a story may take shape without much thought at least initially, remember that the same experience can be viewed in radically different ways. You can save yourself a good deal of revision work if you ask yourself just what aspect of the episode you plan to highlight. To achieve this clarity of purpose, you may have to transform much of the original experience.

Suppose, for example, a couple and their two adolescent children plan to drive to the beach some distance away on a hot August day, only to have the car break down on a city street miles from home. Such an incident has the feel of a short story because it is vivid and has the potential for both conflict and the resolution of conflict. But what aspect will serve as the best thematic center? Best for whom? Let's assume that this is an unusually literary family and that a week after the incident they decide that each of them should write a story based on the experience. Predictably, each will focus on a different theme:

1. The father writes about a married man who over the years has taken his wife rather for granted but discovers to his chagrin that she handles a crisis like this better than he. Even the children notice this. He loses his temper, but his rage, the story suggests, is less directed against the car as it is against her for being so competent.

2. The mother's version is kinder. Hers is a story about a mother and her normally rebellious adolescent daughter. The story version gets rid of the father by having him go in search of a garage and drops the son altogether. Mother and daughter start to bicker, but the shared heat and boredom actually bring them together in a new though slightly grudging acceptance of the other.

3. The son's story starts by satirizing a totally incompetent father and a domineering mother. He leaves the family and hitchhikes back on his own. He makes it home late that night but only after being mugged. Broke and humiliated, he expects punishment, but instead is greeted with tears of concern. Astonished, he realizes his parents aren't as awful as he used to think.

4. In the girl's version there are no parents. She is 18 and her brother becomes a 24-year-old boyfriend. The car breaks down, and he tries unsuccessfully to repair it. She discovers a burned-out fuse and replaces it. He appears to be impressed, but then sulks all the way home. She does her best to cheer him up and finally succeeds, but as he drops her off at her house she is disgusted at the compliant role she has played and tells him she'll never see him again.

These four stories all sprang from the same experience, but each went through a series of transformations even before being committed to paper. Each author placed the focus on a different character and highlighted a different thematic concern.

There may be times, of course, when such basic restructuring will make you feel that the entire story is crumbling before your very eyes. Too much choice can be a problem. In that case, try to reestablish what it was that drew you to the incident in the first place. That is, rediscover the personal connection.

As these examples show, good fiction almost never starts with an abstract idea. It is launched with a situation involving characters interacting with each other. It is energized with some type of conflict. Once you have these elements, the transformations begin, first to free you from experience and then to shape the story. At that point the variations open to you are limitless.

14

A STORY

by Stephen Minot

Sausage and Beer

I kept quiet for most of the trip. It was too cold for talk. The car was getting old and the heater hadn't worked for as long as I could remember. My father said he couldn't afford to get it repaired, but he bought us a camping blanket which was supposed to be just as good. I knew from experience, though, that no matter how carefully I tucked it around me the cold would seep through the door cracks and, starting with a dull ache in my ankles, would work up my legs. There was nothing to do but sit still and wonder what Uncle Theodore would be like.

"Is it very far?" I asked at last. My words puffed vapor.

"We're about halfway now," he said.

That was all. Not enough, of course, but I hadn't expected much more. My father kept to his own world, and he didn't invite children to share it. Nor did he impose himself on us. My twin sister and I were allowed to live our own lives, and our parents led theirs, and there was a mutual respect for the border. In fact, when we were younger Tina and I had assumed that we would eventually marry each other, and while those plans were soon revised, the family continued to exist as two distinct couples.

But this particular January day was different because Tina hadn't been invited—nor had Mother. I was twelve that winter, and I believe it was the first time I had ever gone anywhere alone with my father.

The whole business of visiting Uncle Theodore had come up in the most unconvincingly offhand manner.

"Thought I'd visit your Uncle Theodore," he had said that day after Sunday dinner. "Wondered if you'd like to meet him."

He spoke with his eyes on a crack in the ceiling as if the idea had just popped into his head, but that didn't fool me. It was quite obvious that he had waited until both Tina and my mother were in the kitchen washing the dishes, that he had rehearsed it, and that I wasn't really being given a choice.

"Is Tina going?" I asked.

"No, she isn't feeling well."

I knew what that meant. But I also knew that my father was just using it as an excuse. So I got my coat.

The name Uncle Theodore had a familiar ring, but it was just a name. And I had learned early that you just do not ask about relatives who don't come up in adult conversation naturally. At least, you didn't in my family. You can never tell—like my Uncle Harry. He was another one of my father's brothers. My parents never said anything about Uncle Harry, but some of my best friends at school told me he'd taken a big nail, a spike really, and driven it into his heart with a ball peen hammer. I didn't believe it, so they took me to the library and we found the article on the front page of the *Herald* for the previous Saturday, so it must have been true.

But no one at school told me about Uncle Theodore because they didn't know he existed. Even I hadn't any real proof until that day. I knew that my father had a brother named Theodore in the same way I knew the earth was round without anyone ever taking me to the library to prove it. But then, there were many brothers I had never met—like Freddie, who had joined a Theosophist colony somewhere in California and wore robes like a priest, and Uncle Herb, who was once in jail for leading a strike in New York.

We were well out in the New England countryside now, passing dark, snow-patched farm fields and scrubby woodlands where saplings choked and stunted each other. I tried to visualize this Uncle Theodore as a farmer: blue overalls, straw hat, chewing a long stem of alfalfa, and misquoting the Bible. But it was a highly unsatisfactory picture. Next I tried to conjure up a mystic living in—didn't St. Francis live in a cave? But it wasn't the sort of question I could ask my father. All I had to go on was what he had told me, which was nothing. And I knew without thinking that he didn't want me to ask him directly.

After a while I indulged in my old trick of fixing my eyes on the white lines down the middle of the road: dash-dash-dash, steady, dash-dash again. If you do that long enough, it will lull you nicely and pass the time. It had just begun to take effect when I felt the car slow down and turn abruptly. Two great gates flashed by, and we were inside a kind of walled city.

Prison, I thought. That's it. That's why they kept him quiet. A murderer, maybe. "My Uncle Theodore," I rehearsed silently, "he's the cop killer."

The place went on forever, row after row of identical buildings, four stories, brick, slate roofs, narrow windows with wire mesh. There wasn't a bright color anywhere. The brick had aged to gray, and so had the snow patches along the road. We passed a group of three old men lethargically shoveling ice and crusted snow into a truck.

"This is a kind of hospital," my father said flatly as we drove between the staring brick fronts. I had to take my father's word for it, but the place still had the feel of a prison.

"It's big," I said.

"It's enormous," he said, and then turned his whole attention to studying the numbers over each door. There was something in his tone that suggested the he didn't like the place either, and that did a lot to sustain me.

Uncle Theodore's building was 13-M, but aside from the number, it resembled the others. The door had been painted a dark green for many years, and the layers of paint over chipped and blistered paint gave it a mottled look. We had to wait quite a while before someone responded to the push bell.

A man let us in, not a nurse. And the man was clearly no doctor either. He wore a gray shirt which was clean but unpressed, and dark-green work pants with a huge ring of keys hanging from his belt.

"Hello there, Mr. Bates," he said in a round Irish voice to match his round face. "You brought the boy?"

"I brought the boy." My father's voice was reedy by comparison. "How's Ted?"

"Same as when you called. A little gloomy, maybe, but calm. Those boils have just about gone."

"Good," my father said.

"Funny about those boils. I don't remember a year but what he's had trouble. Funny."

My father agreed it was funny, and then we went into the visiting room to await Uncle Theodore.

The room was large, and it seemed even larger for the lack of furniture. There were benches around all four walls, and in the middle there was a long table flanked with two more benches. The rest was space. And through that space old men shuffled, younger men wheeled carts of linen, a woman visitor walked slowly up and down with her restless husband—or brother, or uncle. Or was *she* the patient? I couldn't decide which might be the face of illness, his troubled and shifting eyes or her deadened look. Beyond, a bleak couple counseled an ancient patient. I strained to hear, wanting to know the language of the place, but I could only make out mumbles.

The smell was oddly familiar. I cast about; this was no home smell. And then I remembered trips with my mother to a place called the Refuge, where the lucky brought old clothes, old furniture, old magazines, and old kitchenware to be bought by the unlucky. My training in Christian charity was to bring my chipped and dented toys and dump them into a great bin, where they were pored over by dead-faced mothers and children.

"Smells like the Refuge," I said very softly, not wanting to hurt anyone's feelings. My father nodded with an almost smile.

We went over to the corner where the benches met, though there was space to sit almost anywhere. And there we waited.

A couple of times I glanced cautiously at my father's face, hoping for some sort of guide. He could have been waiting for a train or listening to a sermon, and I felt a surge of respect. He had a long face with a nose so straight it looked as if it had been leveled with a rule. I guess he would have been handsome if he hadn't seemed so sad or tired much of the time. He worked for a paint wholesaler which had big, dusty offices in a commercial section of Dorchester. When I was younger I used to think the dirt of that place had rubbed off on him permanently.

I began to study the patients with the hope of preparing myself for Uncle Theodore. The old man beside us was stretched out on the bench full length, feet toward us, one arm over his eyes, as if he were lying on the beach, the other resting over his crotch. He had a kind of squeak to his snore. Another patient was persistently scratching his back on the dark-varnished door frame. Anywhere else this would have seemed perfectly normal.

Then my father stood up, and when I did too, I could see that what must be Uncle Theodore was being led in by a pock-marked attendant. They stopped some distance from us and the attendant pointed us out to Uncle Theodore. Then he set him free with a little nudge as if they were playing pin-the-tail-on-the-donkey.

Surprisingly, Uncle Theodore was heavy. I don't mean fat, because he wasn't solid. He was a great, sagging man. His jowls hung loose, his shoulders were massive but rounded like a dome, his hands were attached like brass weights on the ends of swinging pendulums. He wore a clean white shirt open at the neck and blue serge suit pants hung on suspenders that had been patched with a length of twine. It looked as if his pants had once been five sizes too large and that somehow, with the infinite patience of the infirm, he had managed to stretch the lower half of his stomach to fill them.

I would have assumed that he was far older than my father from his stance and his shuffling walk (he wore scuffs, which he slid across the floor without once lifting them), but his face was a baby pink, which made him look adolescent.

"Hello, Ted," my father said, "How have you been?"

Uncle Theodore just said "Hello," without a touch of enthusiasm, or even gratitude for our coming to see him. We stood there, the three of us, for an awkward moment.

Then: "I brought the boy."

"Who?"

"My boy, Will."

Uncle Theodore looked down at me with red-rimmed, blue eyes. Then he looked at my father, puzzled. "But *you're* Will."

"Right, but we've named our boy William too. Tried to call him Billy, but he insists on Will. Very confusing."

Uncle Theodore smiled for the first time. The smile made everything much easier; I relaxed. He was going to be like any other relative on a Sunday afternoon visit.

"Well, now," he said in an almost jovial manner, "there's one on me. I'd forgotten we even *had* a boy."

My face tingled the way it does when you open the furnace door. Somehow he had joined himself with my father as a married couple, and done it with a smile. No instruction could have prepared me for this quiet sound of madness.

But my father had, it seemed, learned how to handle it. He simply asked Uncle Theodore if he had enjoyed the magazines he had brought last time. We subscribed to *Life*, the news magazine, and apparently my father had been bringing him back copies from time to time. It worked, shifting the subject like that, because Uncle Theodore promptly forgot about who had produced what child and told us about how all his copies of *Life* had been stolen. He even pointed out the thief.

"The little one with the hook nose there," he said with irritation but no rage. "Stuffs them in his pants to make him look bigger. He's a problem, he is."

"I'll send you more," my father said. "Perhaps the attendant will keep them for you."

"Hennessy? He's a good one. Plays checkers like a pro."

"I'll bet he has a hard time beating you."

"Hasn't yet. Not once."

"I'm not surprised. You were always the winner." I winced, but neither of them seemed to think this was a strange thing to say. My father turned to me: "We used to play in the attic where it was quiet."

This jolted me. It hadn't occurred to me that the two of them had spent a childhood together. I even let some of their conversation slip by thinking of how they had grown up in the same old rambling house before my sister and I were born, had perhaps planned their future while sitting up there in that attic room the way my sister and I had, actually had gone to school together, and then at some point . . . But when? And how would it have happened? It was as impossible for me to look back and imagine that as it must have been for them as kids to look forward, to see what was in store for them.

"So they started banging on their plates," Uncle Theodore was saying, "and shouting for more heat. Those metal plates sure make a racket, I can tell you."

"That's no way to get heat," Father said, sounding paternal.

"Guess not. They put Schwartz and Cooper in the pit. That's what Hennessy said. And there's a bunch of them that's gone to different levels. They send them down when they act like that, you know. The doctors, they take a vote and send the troublemakers down." And then this voice lowered. Instinctively we both bent toward him for some confidence." And I've found out—that one of these nights they're going to shut down the heat *all the way. Freeze us!*"

There was a touch of panic in this which coursed through me. I could feel just how it would be, this great room black as midnight, the whine of wind outside, and then all those hissing radiators turning silent, and the aching cold seeping through the door cracks—

"Nonsense," my father said quietly, and I knew at once that it was nonsense. "They wouldn't do that. Hennessy's a friend of mine. I'll speak to him before I go."

"You do that," Uncle Theodore said with genuine gratitude, putting his hand on my father's knee. "You do that for us. I don't believe there would be a soul of us"—he swept his hand about expansively—"not a soul of us alive if it weren't for your influence."

My father nodded and then turned the conversation to milder topics. He talked about how the sills were rotting under the house, how a neighborhood gang had broken two windows one night, how Imperial Paint, where my father worked, had laid off a number of workers. My father wasn't usually so gloomy, but I got the feeling that he was somehow embarrassed at being on the outside, was trying to make his life appear less enviable. But Uncle Theodore didn't seem very concerned one way or the other. He was much more bothered about how a man named Altman was losing his eyesight because of the steam heat and how stern and unfair Hennessy was. At one point he moved back in time to describe a fishing trip by canoe through the Rangeley Lakes. It was like opening a great window, flooding the place with light and color and the smells of summer.

"Nothing finer," he said, his eyes half shut," than frying those trout at the end of the day with the water so still you'd think you could walk on it."

He was interrupted by the sleeper on the bench beside us, who woke, stood, and stared down at us. Uncle Theodore told him to "Go blow," and when he had gone so were the Rangeley Lakes.

"Rangeley?" he asked, when my father tried to open that window again by suggestion. "He must be one of our cousins. Can't keep 'em straight."

And we were back to Mr. Altman's deafness and how seriously it hindered him and how the doctors paid no attention.

It was with relief that I smelled sauerkraut. That plus attendants gliding through with carts of food in dented steel containers seemed to suggest supper, and supper promised that the end was near.

"About suppertime," my father said after a particularly long silence.

Uncle Theodore took in a long, deep breath. He held it for a moment. Then he let it go with the slowest, saddest sigh I have ever heard.

"About suppertime," he said at the end of it.

There were mumbled farewells and nods of agreement. We were thanked for copies of *Life* which we hadn't brought; he was told he was looking fine, just fine.

We were only inches from escape when Uncle Theodore suddenly discovered me again.

"Tell me son," he said, bending down with a smile which on anyone else would have been friendly, "what d' you think of your Uncle Ted?"

I was overwhelmed. I stood there looking up at him, waiting for my father to save me. But he said nothing.

"It's been very nice meeting you," I said to the frozen pink smile, dredging the phrase up from my sparse catechism of social responses, assuming that what would do for maiden aunts would do for Uncle Theodore.

But it did not. He laughed. It was a loud and bitter laugh, derisive, and perfectly sane. He had seen my statement for the lie it was, had caught sight of himself, of all of us.

"Well," he said when the laugh withered, "say hi to Dad for me. Tell him to drop by."

Father said he would—though my grandfather had died before I was born. As we left, I felt oddly grateful that the moment of sanity had been so brief.

It was dark when we got back to the car, and it was just beginning to snow. I nestled into the seat and pulled the blanket around me.

We had been on the road about a half hour and were approaching our neighborhood by an odd route. My father finally broke the silence. "I could do with a drink."

This was a jolt because my parents never had liquor in the house. I knew about bars but had never been in one. I wondered if perhaps drinking was something men did—a kind of ritual.

"Sure," I said, trying to sound offhand. "It's fine with me."

"You like sausage?" he asked.

"I love sausage." Actually I'd never tasted it. My mother said you couldn't tell what they put in it.

"A little sausage and a cool beer is what we need." And after a pause, "It's a place I go from time to time. Been there since God knows when. Ted and I had some good times there back then. But . . ." He took a deep breath and then let it out slowly. "It might be best if you told your mother we went to a Howard Johnson for a hamburger, O.K.?"

"Sure, Dad."

We were on city streets I had never seen before. He finally parked in what looked like a dark, threatening neighborhood and headed for a place with neon signs in the window. I had to trot to keep up. As soon as we entered, we were plunged into a warm, humming, soothing, smoky world. The sound of music blended with voices and laughter. There was a bar to our right, marble tables ahead, booths beyond. My father nodded at a waiter he seemed to know and said hi to a group at a table; then he headed toward the booths with a sure step.

We hadn't got halfway before a fat man in a double-breasted suit came steaming up to us, furious.

"Whatcha doing," he said even before he reached us," corruptin' the youth?"

I held my breath. But when the big man reached my father they broke out in easy laughter.

"So this is the boy?" he said. "Will, Junior—right?" We nodded. "Well, there's a good part of you in the boy, I can see that—it's in the eyes. Now, there's a girl too, isn't there? Younger?"

"She's my twin," I said. "Not identical."

The men laughed. Then the fat one said, "Jesus, twins sure run in your family, don't they!"

This surprised me. I knew of no other twins except some cousins from Maine. I looked up at my father, puzzled.

"Me and Ted," he said to me. "We're twins. Nonidentical."

We were ushered to a booth, and the fat man hovered over us, waiting for the order.

"Got sausage tonight?" my father asked.

"Sure. American or some nice hot Italian?"

"Italian."

"Drinks?"

"Well—" My father turned to me. "I guess you rate beer," he said. And then, to the fat man, "Two beers."

The man relayed the order to a passing waiter. Then he asked my father, "Been out to see Ted?"

"You guessed it."

"I figured." He paused, his smile gone. "You too?" he asked me.

"Yes," I said. "It was my first time."

"Oh," he said, with a series of silent nods which assured me that somehow he knew exactly what my afternoon had been like. "Ted was quite a boy. A great tackle. A pleasure to watch him. But no dope either. Used to win meals here playing chess. Never saw him lose. Why, he sat right over there."

He pointed out to the corner booth, which had a round table. All three of us looked; a waiter with a tray full of dirty glasses stopped, turned, and also looked at the empty booth as if an apparition had just been sighted.

"And you know why he's locked up?"

"No," I whispered, appalled at the question.

"It's just the number he drew. Simple as that. Your Dad, me, you—any of us could draw the wrong number tomorrow. There's something to think about."

I nodded. All three of us nodded. Then the waiter brought a tray with the order, and the fat man left us with a quick, benedictory smile. We ate and drank quietly, lost in a kind of communion.

15

THE MAKING OF A STORY:

A Case History

Difficulty in tracing the development of published stories. Origins of "Sausage and Beer." Transformations: evasion and discovery. Revision, an unending process. The melding of memory and invention.

One of the best ways to learn how to write effective stories is to examine published work. In most cases, however, what we study is limited to the final, published version. This is particularly true of work written since the advent of the computer. While in the past many authors left copies of early drafts revealing how a manuscript developed, the computer leaves no such paper trail. One draft now merges with the next, obliterating earlier versions, and the student is increasingly dependent on what is normally the last stage of a long process. We have to guess about where the material came from and what kinds of transformations and revisions went into the work before it appeared in print.

To make matters more difficult, many writers are reluctant to discuss those long hours of effort because they like to maintain the illusion of the story as a complete and seamless work. Revealing all the uncertainty, frustration, rethinking, and revision that goes into most stories makes the process seem less like an inspired burst of talent and more like what it really is, a lengthy and often demanding effort.

The following case history of "Sausage and Beer" is not conjecture. It's a record that only an author can provide about his own work. The many stages this story went through are not unusual. If you are taking a workshop course in writing, you may not have time for this much reworking, but one of the ironies of fiction writing is that the more proficient you get, the less satisfied you become with early drafts. Though this chapter focuses on a single story, its primary purpose is to illustrate a process of development that applies to all fiction.

Origins of "Sausage and Beer"

The story began with a determination to write something closer to my own life. Childhood trips to a mental hospital to visit my uncle were vivid in my memory. Those were the days before drug therapy. Large numbers of the insane were housed and fed, though the treatment was no more sophisticated than it had been in the asylums of the previous century.

The subject matter seemed promising partly because my feelings were an odd mix of fascination, revulsion, and fear. A combination of emotions has more potential for fiction than a single response. In addition, the setting appealed to me—at least as a writer. It was dramatically different from the familiar middle-class home in a nondescript neighborhood. Strange and disturbing, the setting was something I could share with readers who had never been there.

Another purely factual element that drew me was the language of the insane. I don't think I could have invented that if I hadn't listened not only to my uncle on numerous occasions but also to other inmates. It was far from gibberish (although there was some of that too), but it was not consistently rational either. What I found particularly interesting was the way the mind can move from lucidity to delusion without missing a beat.

My selection of that experience suggests a general pattern in fiction writing. As I have pointed out, fiction rarely begins with an abstract idea. If I had wanted to explore the life of the insane, I would have done some research and written a factual essay. I could have personalized it, developing some of my reactions, presenting the material as **creative nonfiction.** If I had shifted my central concern from the insane to the role of chance in our lives, those two genres would still have been the best choices.

What started this story—and most stories—was not an abstract concept but an experience. The experience seemed promising because it involved a complex relationship between three people, an unusual setting, and my contradictory set of emotions. It is rare indeed for a story to take shape without the benefit of interaction between at least two characters. That relationship can be warm, chilly, antagonistic, or distant and uncertain like the one in this story, but whatever the form it provides an energy that is essential in fiction.

Finding a situation with fictional potential is partly luck, but as I explained in Chapter 13, it helps to know where to look. In some ways the process is like prospectors searching for uranium with a Geiger counter. They listen for the hot spots and then start digging.

Transformations: Evasion and Discovery

These, then, were the factual memories that initiated the creative impulse. They were the memories I wanted to write about. But right from the start the developing story was being shaped by what I did *not* want to write about as well.

Those visits to the asylum were made with my mother, not my father. The patient was her brother, not my father's. That might have made an interesting story, but for me it was too close to some highly charged emotions. Fifteen years later I wrote a story about an adolescent and his mother called "Home," but at the time "Sausage and Beer" was written, the subject was too radioactive to handle.

Shifting an actual mother-son relationship to a fictional father-son relationship was an easy jump at first. It took the pressure off. But even that proved to be uncomfortable. So my real-life father, a short, overweight, outspoken man, became a tall, gaunt, reticent fictional father. Where did he come from? A distant relative of my father's generation who I barely remembered.

Major transformations of that sort can have consequences no writer can predict. What I had planned was a fairly simple initiation story: boy faces the reality of insanity and ends up more mature. But I was still in the planning stage when I found myself with a father I never had. This guy was distant but approachable, basically kind, even vulnerable. What a delicious discovery it was to allow my protagonist to have a moment of sharing and understanding with his father, a bonding I never experienced in life.

The next question was what to do with the fictional Uncle Theodore. In reality, he was lean and gaunt, physical characteristics I had already assigned to the fictional father. In spite of the fact that I had made them twins, I wanted to differentiate them. So Theodore ended up "a great, sagging man" whose stomach "had managed to stretch" until it filled his too-large pants. His hands were "attached like brass weights on the ends of swinging pendulums." Where did all that come from? I once saw a man in the lobby of a seedy hotel who looked just like this. I saw him only once and never spoke to him, but he got tucked away in my memory like those unsorted photos you shove into shoe boxes and store in the attic.

The bar scene at the end of the story comes from another shoe box. My real father never would have taken me to a bar, partly because he found children an annoyance and partly because he died when I was ten. The bar came to mind because I wanted to highlight the bonding that resulted from fictional father and son having shared this ordeal. A clap on the shoulder in the parking lot just wasn't enough. The bar had a slightly illicit overtone that seemed right.

At the time, I thought I was inventing the place, but as I look back I now realize that it was an echo of an actual experience. On my thirteenth birthday I put at the head of my list of birthday wishes a trip to a real nightclub. Since I was then fatherless, a much older half brother volunteered. It was an act of kindness on his part, a low-key version of the bonding that went on in the story.

As I suggested in Chapter 13, transformation of details in the initial stages of planning can lead anywhere. In this case, by choosing to alter certain facts radically I inadvertently opened up new veins with real potential.

Revision, an Unending Process

The transformations just described occurred before I started writing. If they hadn't, I would have wasted a great deal of time producing fundamentally different versions. By the time I started typing, I had a fairly clear notion of where to go with the story. And once the first draft was completed, the revision process began.

Those who are new to fiction writing sometimes think of "revision" as consisting of one-word changes. As you begin to acquire a more demanding sense of what is necessary, however, you will find yourself adding or deleting whole paragraphs—sometimes pages. Revising usually takes far more time than writing the original draft.

Much of the bar scene, for example, was added in successive drafts. As I remember it, there was an early version in which the father merely suggested that they have a drink together. That was intended to suggest the newly formed bond between them. But that version didn't seem strong enough. The bar and the bartender began to take shape. The bartender's pronouncement on the role of chance in our lives ("It's just the number he drew") came very late and suggests a secondary theme that never occurred to me when I started the story.

A far more significant revision was made after the story had been accepted for publication by *The Atlantic*. Conscientious editors used to take the time to make helpful suggestions on stories that had been accepted for publication. It was understood that these could be acted upon or ignored. (Sadly, this personal involvement on the part of editors is becoming less common.) What I submitted was about the sixth draft and, to my mind, perfect. This is a common delusion with writers. That version had about two additional pages at the beginning about the narrator and his sister, Tina. My purpose was to highlight the twin pattern, linking the bond between the two younger people and that between the father and his brother Theodore. In each case, a warm and somewhat naive relationship is broken by the harshness of reality: the boy can never marry his twin sister, and the father can never reclaim the easy friendship he had with his twin brother.

The editor's point, however, was that so much emphasis on the sister early in the story would suggest to the reader that she would become a significant part of the plot. But she never appears again. The essentially needless material would have created a false lead. Stories make implied promises, and this promise was unfulfilled. Besides, all that background material made the opening sluggish. The story didn't really start until father and son were on the road. It was one of those suggestions that is so good it makes a writer feel stupid for not having seen it. So the story now begins with "I kept quiet for most of the trip."

Cutting blocks of material can be a painful act at any stage of your career. One way to ease the agony is to set the pages aside if you are typing or to establish a "LostGems" file if you are working on a computer. In two weeks you will wonder why you saved it.

Since stories are printed on paper, not etched on tablets, they can be revised at any stage. F. Scott Fitzgerald, for example, wrote a second version of his novel *Tender Is the Night* long after the first version had been published. I hope I never feel obliged to do that, but revisions to this story continued years after its original publication. An author has a chance to revise every time a story is reprinted in an anthology, collection, or textbook, and many take advantage of that opportunity.

The first printed version of the story was set back in the late 1920s, previous to my own memory. I did this so I could make that bar a speakeasy, one of those illegal nightclubs that flourished during Prohibition. To establish the historical setting, I identified the car in the third sentence as a 1929 Dodge and reinforced the historical period with a reference to a "bearskin robe," which many cars had before there were heaters, and a hand-operated windshield wiper toward the end of the story

The advantage of this historical setting was that the illicit aspect of the speakeasy intensified the bond between father and son. It also dramatized that aspect of the story that suggests a coming of age. Speakeasies were common but illegal. Those who have access to the second edition of this text can compare that original version with the present one.

The disadvantage was that the story became a period piece. Fixing the date that far back seemed to suggest some thematic significance when, in fact, all I wanted was to use the overtones of the speakeasy, a minor detail. Besides, the number of readers who could even identify the bar as a speakeasy from my subtle hints and could respond to the overtones was dwindling with every passing year.

So I made another revision. When preparing the fourth edition of this textbook I deleted the historical period from the story simply by removing the date, the bearskin rug, and the manual windshield wiper. With those three minor changes I wiped out 40 years of history!

The Melding of Memory and Invention

Every story has a different ratio of memory to invention. Many, however, share the same pattern: a specific memory serves as the starting point, and it is restructured with radical transformations that are often decided upon before the actual writing begins. These transformations sometimes draw on memories unrelated to the original experience and frequently need invention to make them fit. Once into the writing, more memories are spliced in and more imaginative aspects are added. Face it, fiction writers are as unscrupulous as magpies, borrowing and stealing whatever suits their fancy.

Here is a rough breakdown of the thefts, borrowings, and inventions that went into "Sausage and Beer."

THE INITIAL MEMORY

Visits to the mental hospital (consolidated into a first trip)
The narrator and his feelings
The setting, both outside and inside the hospital

BORROWED MEMORIES FROM OTHER SOURCES

The father's appearance (based on a distant relative)
Uncle Theodore's appearance (based on a stranger)
Uncle Theodore's dialogue (a composite of his and others')
The bar (borrowed from a later experience)
The twin sister, Tina (based on an older sister, the name taken from a cousin)

PURE INVENTION

The father's withdrawn personality
The mother
The twin motif (no twins in my family)
The hospital attendant
The bartender
The father-son bonding

As you can see from this outline, ascertaining whether a story or a novel was truly "based on personal experience" is about as difficult as determining whether an automobile is "American-made."

Before you declare a story finished, make sure that all those fragments of remembered and invented details have become melded into a single, unified work. Read it over with a cool, objective eye. Be particularly careful to check the following three areas for continuity and consistency.

Transitions: When two fictional scenes were originally based on two quite different experiences, make sure that there are no inconsistencies. If, for example, your characters live in a ranch-style house, make sure they don't go up the stairs in the next scene. If they have a dog in one scene, don't let it become a cat in the next.

Internal consistency: Guard against contradictions and omissions within each scene. If you have three characters arguing, don't lose one of them. If he or she falls silent, say so. Characters not accounted for at least briefly may seem to disappear. Try to visualize who is "on stage" in each scene. And pay attention to the passage of time. Don't end a lunch scene with a character saying "goodnight."

Characterization: On the simplest level, make sure bearded characters stay bearded and a character on crutches doesn't run to answer the phone. More subtle problems arise when you base a fictional character on two different acquaintances. Make sure that your fictional portrayal is a new creation, so consistent that he or she seems real.

To achieve these goals you have to keep going over your work from start to finish, seeing it as a whole. Imagine yourself as someone else reading it for the first time. In addition, if it is at all possible, have someone else give you some honest critical responses. Remember that no matter how many different memory-based and invented elements were used to get your story started, the finished version must be a seamless work of art.

16

A STORY

by Deborah Joy Corey

Three Hearts

The morning after the big snowstorm Mama is real sick. Her hair has twisted itself into tight knots like spikes all over her head and she is so weak that her words are puffy and low. We are all up, listening to the radio that sits on top of the fridge to see if there will be any school. Bucky and I sit at the wooden table that wobbles on the crooked floor and wait with our elbows pressed like seams into the plastic tablecloth. Mama is lying on the kitchen couch, wrapped in a red robe, rolling her head from side to side, sighing.

Her eyes are like faded jeans and she sounds scared, so I go over and stand by her head. I take one of Daddy's newspapers from under the couch and fan her a bit. The newspaper leaves black on my finger and I rub it onto my soft corduroys. Mama has *nerves* and when my other brother, Eddie, drinks they get worse. She says that nothing could make her more weak than the fact that she has a fifteen-year-old child with a drinking problem.

Eddie has an angry streak like steel running through his heart. He quit school last year and now he sleeps all morning and stays out all night. He drinks with a man called Cake who lives on welfare and drives a big car. Mama and Daddy can't manage Eddie. They tried to make him go back to school, but whenever they brought it up his temper would roll, and he would slam himself at the walls. I remember Mama telling Daddy that maybe Eddie shouldn't go to school, that maybe his whole problem was that the teacher picked on him. But Daddy told her right up quick that Eddie had drinking in his blood just like Daddy's whole family did. Daddy used to drink on weekends. He'd go to the Legion every Friday night after supper and sometimes not come home until Sunday. The last time I saw my Daddy drunk, his lip was broken wide open and purple.

"Who did that to you?" Mama said.

"My old man." Daddy made the words sound like they were the last ones left in him. They echoed like a bobcat snarl.

Mama wrinkled here forehead. "Why?"

One of Daddy's eyes went wet. "Because he was drunk, too."

Mama blames herself for everything. When I smile at Mama, she always says, "Poor girl, she's got her Mother's crooked teeth," but I always say, "Mama, I grew these teeth, not you."

"I'm so warm," Mama says, and I think of calling Daddy at the County Garage to see what to do with her, but I figure he's sure to be out plowing the roads with all this snow. Mama is sicker than usual because Eddie didn't come home and she sat up all night waiting for him. In the night I could hear the rocking chair in Eddie's room moving back and forth like a song and I knew Mama had her face wrapped in her cool hands. I stroke Mama's hair and she says to the air: "You wonder if he's dead or alive."

The radio is playing "O happy day, when Jesus washed, my sins away," and I wonder how they get all those singers in the radio station so early in the morning. Bucky is still waiting at the table.

"I wish they'd say school's cancelled," he says.

"It is," I guess, and stand on the chair and press my face against the top part of the window so I can see out over the snow. In the shiny glass I can see my ghost looking back at me and I blow steam on the window and make three little hearts that Mama will complain about later. Big cutout flakes are still coming down and the veranda is a lake of snow, swirling up and around the railing and window in waves. I think of my feet sinking deep into the new snow—O happy day—and then I think of Eddie frozen in a snowbank.

"Upper Valley Elementary," Bucky yells. "We're closed. No school." He jumps up from the table and does a little circle. "Mama, where are my snow pants? Mama?"

He rubs Mama's face like he is polishing an apple and a smile sneaks out from under her half-moon lips.

When Eddie comes home, Bucky and I are in the hallway putting bread bags over our wool socks so our feet won't get wet. He comes through the door all dressed in black and loose and he looks like a puppet. A cigarette is burning at the side of his mouth and he steps over us as if we are stones.

"Eddie," Mama sits up. "Where have you been? I'm sick from waiting. What do you do all night?"

Eddie doesn't answer Mama. He gives her one of those stares that Daddy says could freeze hell and Mama stands up in front of him.

"Eddie," she begs and he uses his long blue hand to push Mama back down on the couch. Mama chokes back her air and cries like a baby that's got its feelings hurt. Eddie throws his cigarette in the sink and goes up the back stairs to his room and I know he is drunk by the way he smells. I twist a hole through the bread bag and listen for Mama to stop being sad. Bucky is all ready to go. Mama wipes at her face and pulls herself up. She ties her robe tight like a package and takes her pills from her pocket. She shakes them and reads the label.

"I need some sleep," she says to the bottle. Mama comes into the hall-way and steps over the water spots that Eddie left. Her feet are pink and crusty. "Will you be warm enough?" She ties a green scarf around my neck and looks down at my face.

"Stop painting your lips with Mercurochrome," she says and she rubs my lips until they burn. "Double up on your mittens, Bucky."

Mama leans on the doorframe and watches us march out the door. "Have fun," she says, "your Mama's going to lie down."

The snow is white and heavy flour. Bucky pushes the wooden storm door closed behind us and we fall on our knees, piling the snow up at the door like we want to bury it.

"Now Mama can rest," Bucky says and he packs the cracks with lots of snow.

I love Bucky's face. It is pointed and always looks to smile like a dolphin's, and even though he is thirteen months younger than me, he seems older. We wade out to the yard and the snow is so deep and heavy that we just stop for a long time and look at things. The white cover is perfect except for Eddie's footprints in from the road. The tiny wind smells brand new and the telephone wires have so much snow on them that they are almost invisible. The snowflakes try to get in our eyes and we squint at one another.

"Catch it on your tongue," Bucky says. We tilt our heads back and stretch our tongues on our chins. Bucky's tongue is watermelon color.

We pull our scarves up over our noses and my breath is warm and wet on the wool. I look back at the house and in the fuzzy snow it looks like a big blank face. The windows are as dark as molasses and nothing moves in them. I think of Eddie hidden in a stack of pillows with his mouth open, while the wind whispers around his window. I think how Daddy will pull him out of bed when he comes home. "I told you to look for work today," he'll say, and Eddie will squirm out of Daddy's hands like he always does.

"Let's make angels," Bucky says.

We look at the yard which is as smooth as a statue and we begin to drop down on our backs and slide our arms like we are trying to fly. We make so many angels that there is no untouched snow left and I tell Bucky if the birds were out, they'd think it was an angel graveyard. We wade around the house and look at all the high drifts. There is a huge drift in front of the shed that is connected to our house so we go around where there is a wooden ladder and climb up on the shed's roof. The roof is slippery, but we know if we fall we will just land in the soft snow and laugh. We slide down the roof into the drift and the snow comes up to our hips. Bucky almost can't get out of the snow and he pretends he is in white quicksand. He waves his arms and screams: "Help, I'm drownin', help me."

"Kick your knees," I say half-mad, and he pushes himself free, tee-heeing.

We're lined up on the roof like pigeons when we hear the snowplow coming. We push off together and land just in time to see Daddy going by. He honks and we rush out of the snow so we can run and see him. Swish, swish, swish, our legs are fat and noisy in our snow pants. When we get there, there is nothing but a swirl of white dust and the low growl of Daddy's machine going over the far side of the dirt road. After, everything is soft and still.

We scuff our boots through the snow and blank out five whole angels. There's a big bank of snow by the road and we make foot holes and climb up to the top. The snow is all packed hard and the top is as flat as a stage. As soon as I get up, Bucky pushes me off. That's what Eddie used to do when he played with us, that's exactly what he did. I slide down over the bank and land on my back.

"I'm the king of the castle and you're the dirty rascal," he sings and I don't move. I let the snow whip around my face and I stay perfectly still until the ends of my fingers go stiff.

"Sis," Bucky says, "Sissy, get up. C'mon, let's play. Come back up."

He climbs down beside me. "You're not dead," he says and kicks a pile of snow in my face.

Bucky starts to build a tunnel in the side of the bank. We dig and round it out like an igloo. It's real warm on the inside and when we are finished Bucky leans back against the hard wall and sucks the snow from his mitten.

"Bucky, don't eat snow, it's got worms in it."

"It does not." He wipes his nose with the back of his jacket sleeve.

"Mama says it does," I say.

"It's not snow, it's blubber," he says and just the thought of it makes me laugh.

"Get some icicles," he says.

The icicles are always my job. Bucky says Eskimo women do all the stuff like that. "Anything they can do without their husband's help, they do. They're brave," he told me once.

I climb up on the railing along the veranda and grab one big icicle to knock the rest down. The icicles tick off as I move across the railing and they fall like darts in the snow. I dig them out and carry them back as if they are kindling. We use the tips of the icicles to draw on the walls of the igloo. I always draw a trailer park because that is where I would like to live when I grow up, but Bucky does different things. Today, he draws Eddie with a huge set of drums. Eddie likes the Beatles. He combs his black hair down over his forehead and seals it with Dippity-Do so he looks like Ringo. Sometimes when Bucky and I come home from school, Eddie is sitting in Daddy's brown recliner beating the arms of the chair with two wooden spoons. His timing is even and his blue eyes are storm clouds when he plays. "Get away from me," he always says.

We get tired and pile the icicles in the middle for firewood then lie on our backs and study the white walls. We never make any rules, but both Bucky and I know that whenever we build an igloo, he's the husband and I'm the wife. After a while, he leans over and kisses my cheek with his wet lips and then lies back down. We both close our eyes.

When our pretend night is over, Bucky sits up, rubbing himself all over because he is freezing. "Get up," he says. "We need more firewood."

My head is still empty from my rest when I poke it out of the tunnel. The air is thick and cold and the flakes have turned into small white dots. I run through the snow to the veranda and climb up to get the icicles. In the distance, I can hear Daddy's plow. I turn and brace my feet holding two big sticks of ice in my hands like swords. I wave them crossways when I see Daddy coming. I think of the people on *Gilligan's Island* waving to airplanes. Snow flies up from the road and Daddy gives a big toot when he goes by and it looks like the plow is empty, like it is driving itself.

I carry the firewood back to the tunnel and I start to feel dizzy when I can't find the igloo's hole. I carry the icicles along the bank thinking maybe I've lost my place and slowly the whiteness is all I can see. I dump the ice and start to crawl through the heavy snow on my knees, and I say, "Bucky, Bucky."

I look back along the bank for a piece of Bucky and I dig at a dark spot hoping it is his mitten, but it's just dirt or a shadow. I stop and listen for him and the weather squeezes in around me. When I get to the veranda, I don't remember running there. The door is piled high with snow and I pull at the handle but the door won't move. I brush the snow back from it with both hands. I get it open just a tiny crack, but I still can't get inside. I jerk the handle back and forth and bang the door hard. "Eddie, Eddie," I holler after each bang.

I get so tired from banging that the ghost in me takes over and I begin to dream. I am dreaming while my body bangs the door. I am all grown up with breasts like Mama and I am standing in front of the house screaming for Eddie to wake up. His window is black and empty. I'm screaming "Eddie, help me. Bucky's suffocating. Eddie, help." I scream until my voice leaves me.

I dream that I climb up the side of the house toward the window. Splinters peel off the house and stick to my fingers until the tips turn purple and begin to bleed. The blood makes the wooden siding slippery and I start to slip back down to the ground. I leave long thin red strips like scratches on the house.

I am staring down, rubbing my frozen fingers together like I have just discovered them when Mama opens the door. Her face is foggy and I tell her fast what has happened.

"Go," she yells, pushing me out into the yard. "Show me."

I point at the flat side of the bank where I think the hole is and I'm scared that I am wrong and that Jesus won't wash my sins away. Mama's red robe works its way open in the front and her flowered nightie looks strange in the snow. I watch the soles of her feet right below me that are staring up with all their cracks and dryness and something about the way they twist and cuddle looks like two baby pigs. I wonder if they feel cold or if Mama has forgotten everything but Bucky. She is breathing with the wind.

"What happened?" She turns her eyes to me for the shortest second and I don't know what to say.

I remember how the plow shook the windowpanes in our house when it rumbled by. It reminded me of thunder.

"What happened?" she says again.

"The plow," I say, "The plow came by," and then I wished I'd blamed myself. That's what Mama would have done.

She has both arms in the snow and she is talking to herself like she is praying, like the bank is her altar. I look back at the house and wonder why Eddie hasn't heard us. Why he hasn't come to help? I am almost ready to let my tears out when Mama reaches way in with her head and all.

"Oh, my land," she says, her words just a whisper.

She pushes her shoulders in and she gets ahold of something and pulls two or three times. I can tell she is getting tired and I am afraid she will give up. She reaches one more time and hauls Bucky out by the arm. His body is limp and one double mitten falls to the white ground. He's flat on his back. Mama stares at his face which looks tired and sleepy and she shakes him.

"Bucky, Bucky, Bucky," she says quick, like his name is a rhyme. She puts her ear on his mouth and listens. She opens her thin lips and puts them on his in a circle. Specks of snow fall down and land on her hair. Bucky opens one eye and squints at the flakes.

"Bucky," Mama says soft and pushes her face against his cheeks, first one side, then the other. She holds his head on both sides. Bucky reaches his hand up and Mama pulls him to her chest and he snuggles into her flowered nightie. Mama's lips are shaking and her eyes are watery blue.

"It's all my fault," she says. She lifts Bucky up on his feet and keeps her hands under his arms. His face is red and full and I touch his bare fingers that hang in the wind like leaves.

"Come, baby," Mama says.

Bucky walks on his own, but Mama holds him tight. Mama's robe flies in the wind behind them and the way it swirls and prances makes me think she is dancing.

I fall back and let my bottom make a snug chair in the snow. I am jerky on the inside and my stomach feels small and hard. I thought Bucky would be dead and that his face would be caved in from the heavy snow. I pick up his mitten and try to forget the melted look that I thought he would have when Mama pulled him out. I take the mitten apart. The inside one is blue. The outside one is an old mitten of Eddie's and it is grey and full of holes. Each hole has a string of wool in it and I pull on the yarn to make the hole bigger, but the hole puckers together in a kiss. I fix every hole this way and the mitten rumples itself into a little ball.

I look at the house. Orange light comes from the kitchen and shadows move past the window in slow motion. I bet Mama is rubbing Bucky's chest with Vicks VapoRub. I think of his round chest that juts out in the middle and my throat goes all full and tight. I listen and everything is big and quiet and I wonder if Daddy will come home soon. I stuff Eddie's grey mitten inside of Bucky's and waddle myself free from the snow.

17
VIEWPOINT:
Who's Seeing This?

Viewpoint (means of perception): the character through whose eyes we see the action. The advantages of a single means of perception. Multiple viewpoints. Testing alternative viewpoints. First or third person? The focus. Reviewing your options.

Fiction, unlike drama or film, is presented through the eyes of a specific character. What we see and hear are what that character sees and hears. We enter his or her mind, but we can only guess what the other characters are thinking.

Take, for example, this simple fictional sentence: "The boy looked at his grandfather, wondering if the old man had understood." Here the **viewpoint** is that of the boy. We know what he is wondering and so we are "in his head." We don't know what the grandfather is thinking, and if the story continues with a single point of view, as most do, we readers, like the boy, will not find out what went on in the grandfather's head until the old man reveals his thoughts either through what he says or through his actions.

The terms **viewpoint**, **point of view**, and **means of perception** are synonymous, so I will use them interchangeably. But don't confuse the literary use of *point of view* with its other use referring to *attitude*, as in "from the British point of view." Remember that when applied to fiction, *point of view* is a precise literary concept—and an important one.

The Advantages of a Single Means of Perception

A great majority of short stories and many novels as well limit the means of perception to a single character. The character who is the means of perception at the opening of such stories remains so to the end.

The logic of this is clear in the case of stories written in the first person. Using "I" gives the reader the sense of a character telling about his experiences. To go back to our example, let's assume the story began in the first person: "I looked at my grandfather, wondering if he understood." We as readers wonder too, and because we tend to identify with the narrator it seems natural to maintain that illusion. We are willing to wait until the narrator finds out.

The same is true with stories in the third person, using "he" or "she." In either case it would be possible for the next sentence to read, "Actually the old man was thinking about supper and hadn't heard a word the boy had said." Possible, but few stories take that route. The single means of perception has been the dominant approach in short stories since the 19th century. There are exceptions—especially in novels—which I will describe shortly, but they are rare.

This apparent restriction bothers some beginning writers because it seems limiting. There are, however, two good reasons for its popularity. First, it increases the readers' sense of identification with the fictional character, drawing them into the story. This natural tendency for readers to enter into a fictional work, "the willing suspension of disbelief," is not necessarily bound to feelings of sympathy, respect, or even approval. It is the illusion of being someone else for a short period of time.

The second advantage to limiting the means of perception to a single character is that it helps to maintain suspense. Suppose in our fictional example the grandfather was pretending not to understand because he was planning to steal the boy's winning lottery ticket. Revealing this by entering his mind might well undermine the climax of the story. In fiction, what we as authors withhold from the reader is fully as important as what we reveal.

In "Sausage and Beer," for example, the boy's curiosity about who Uncle Theodore is and what he will be like becomes the reader's puzzlement as well. There is no rule against beginning that story with a clear, explanatory introduction, but it would reduce the reader's sense of curiosity. Here is an opening that tells too much:

> When I was twelve my father invited me to visit my
> Uncle Theodore, a patient in a large mental
> hospital. They were twins, but their lives had
> taken dramatically different routes.

If, after an introduction like that, I had then gone on with the boy's speculations about whether the uncle was a farmer, a solitary mystic, or possibly a murderer in prison, it might have sounded patronizing or condescending, as if the author is saying, "But we know better." The reader is apt to smile at the protagonist rather than sharing the uncertainty with him.

The same applies to the boy's reaction of alarm when the man in the bar shouts, " 'Whatcha doing . . . corruptin' the youth?' " It is only a small moment of reader anxiety, but compare the effect with this version in which I have italicized the information that comes from the author.

> I was alarmed when the headwaiter came out and, *pretending to be angry*, said. . .

Deliberate withholding of information through a single means of perception is just as important in "Three Hearts." That story, like "Sausage and Beer," was written in the first person, and much depends on our sharing the experience step by step.

Multiple Viewpoints

Multiple viewpoints are more common in novels. Because novels are longer, the psychological jolt that occurs when the means of perception shifts from one character to another is less obtrusive. Even in a novel, however, that break has some of the same effect as a shift of scenes in a play. For this reason, most novelists select only two or three characters to serve as the means of perception. In addition, entire chapters are often presented through the eyes of one character rather than shifting frequently.

Only occasionally is the same technique used in short stories. One example is Ernest Hemingway's much-anthologized story "The Short Happy Life of Francis Macomber." The story is unusual in that not only does the point of view shift from character to character, but at one point it even enters the mind of a wounded lion. Another highly popular experiment is Shirley Jackson's "The Lottery." She does not enter the minds of her characters at all, maintaining a journalist's objective style. The situation she is dealing with is so terrible that presenting it in a cool, detached manner keeps the story from spilling over into melodrama.

Another form of a divided means of perception is when the author steps in and presents information not known to the characters. This is called **author's intrusion**. The term doesn't include those minor bits of exposition that simply fill in background or provide a transition to a new scene. "His sister had joined the police force three years earlier," for example, provides information that, if it is something the protagonist knows, merely saves time. The same for "They discussed their alternatives for several hours" or "For the next 24 hours, the storm grew steadily worse." True author's intrusion provides information the implied narrator doesn't know: "He never suspected that for three years she had secretly been a CIA agent." Here the author has become the means of perception at least briefly.

The greatest temptation to use author's intrusion occurs at the opening and closing of stories. Here, with apologies to Deborah Corey, is how "Three

Hearts" might have begun had she been tempted to open her story with a heavy-handed paragraph from the author's point of view:

> Sissy's mother looked frail and spent much of her time on the couch, groggy with tranquilizers, but before the day was out she would prove that deep within her lay maternal strengths strong enough to save her son Bucky from almost certain death.

You probably spotted this as an unsuccessful opening, but why? Because the author has stepped in and not only predicted the outcome of the story but stated the **theme** rather than letting the story unfold through action and dialogue.

The reason we are tempted to step in at the beginning of stories is that often we are still thinking about what the theme of the story will be. The introductory paragraph is too often a note written by the author to the author. It is also an echo of essay writing in which the theme of the work is often stated in condensed form in the first paragraph. But fiction, as you know, is not factual writing. The reader of fiction discovers thematic patterns indirectly through the length of the story. So put that bit of author's intrusion in your journal and let the story develop on its own as it should, through action and dialogue.

The temptation to explain rears its head again at the end of stories when we are unsure whether we have really revealed what we set out to show. Author's intrusion in that final paragraph is in most cases a reflection of author's insecurity. Notice how both "Sausage and Beer" and "Three Hearts" end not with a summary by the author but a **symbol**. My story uses "a kind of communion" and Corey's "I stuff Eddie's grey mitten inside of Bucky's," two symbols that I will discuss further in Chapter 27. Other approaches are to end with a line of dialogue or simple action that suggest the theme rather than stating it as one might in an essay.

Author's intrusion was popular in the 18th and 19th centuries partly because fiction writers often adopted the stance of stories told out loud. It was not at all unusual to have detailed commentary on a character ("He was a dour gentleman with a military man's high regard for order") or generalized observations ("Such behavior is rarely rewarded these days"). This approach has become less popular today because the trend is away from the impression of listening to a narrated story and toward the illusion of entering a story directly—possibly an influence of film. But the voice of the author is still being used, particularly in novels by authors such as John Fowles, Margaret Drabble, and Milan Kundera. Because author's intrusion has been out of fashion for so long, it now seems fresh and innovative when employed skillfully. You will see an unusual and effective example in the opening paragraph of "Obst Vw," the story that appears as Chapter 23. Look for it.

As we write, we are **omniscient** because we are (or ought to be) all-knowing. We know all about our characters and what will become of them. Because we choose what we will reveal at each stage of the story, the approach is often referred to as *limited omniscience.* Remember, though, that the choice of what to reveal is up to you as author.

Testing Alternative Viewpoints

When you start a new story, there is a tendency to stay with the viewpoint that first occurred to you. Nine times out of ten, that will be the right route. Still you can't be sure whether you're missing an even more effective approach unless you visualize your material with alternative viewpoints. Even if you stay with your original conception, the very act of imagining the material through different viewpoints often generates new insights.

What, for example, would happen if we shifted the point of view in "Sausage and Beer"? Set aside the question of whether a transformation might be less effective. Simply consider how a particular change would affect the story.

First, imagine that story told from the father's point of view. Almost necessarily the story would highlight his attitude toward his son and probably toward children in general. Perhaps he entered into parenthood late and finds it difficult to relate to children. What impelled him to bring his son along for this visit and not his daughter? What might he recall about his own childhood growing up with Theodore? What kind of a relationship does he have with his wife? What does *she* think of Theodore? These questions are not developed in the published version, but they would all be important in a story told from his point of view.

How about the story with Theodore as the means of perception? Fiction from the point of view of an insane patient is surprisingly popular with beginning writers, but too often such stories take the form of an apparently mild-mannered murderer. This plot is so frequently repeated it might be nominated as the eighth "deadly sin" of fiction! Using an insane character in fiction is risky unless you have listened a good deal to mental patients or have been one.

Still, it is worth visualizing a story presented through the eyes of someone whose mind slides without warning from one decade to another and whose perceptions are frequently distorted by anxiety and by erratic but genuine fears. Imagining myself in Theodore's world helped me to present him sympathetically even though I was never tempted to write the story from his point of view.

"Three Hearts" offers even more possibilities since there are more characters who could be given a central position. The mother comes to mind as a natural choice. One would lose most of the children's imaginative play in the igloo, but some of that material might be revealed through some other game she might overhear indoors. Less would be seen of Sissy and her brother Bucky, but more might be developed about the father and the agonizing task of raising Eddie. A version like that would probably be more explicit about the past since the mother would be able to recall more of it than Sissy. The mother's memories presented in the first person might be interestingly blurred because of her medication.

A story told through Bucky's eyes would be similar to the published version, though the climactic scene would be far more dreamlike and necessarily less focused on the mother. Writing the story through Eddie's eyes, on the other hand, would be entirely different. His view of his parents would be distorted with resentment and possibly suppressed guilt. Such a story would hardly mention Sissy and Bucky, but it might make much more of "a man called Cake who lives on welfare and drives a big car," a character mentioned only once in the published version.

Clearly there are advantages and disadvantages to each approach. Even though you may have no intention of transforming your story, consider the alternatives early in your planning. Doing so will provide fresh insights into your characters and the thematic potential of the story.

First or Third Person?

It does make a difference whether you cast a story in the first **person**, using "I," or present it in the third person, referring to your protagonist as "he" or "she." But the difference is more subtle than you might imagine. Oddly, it is sometimes difficult to remember whether a story you read the day before used the first or third person.

Here to test you are two versions of each of the two stories you have read so far. Can you spot which approach was used in the actual story?

A. He kept quiet for most of the trip. It was too cold to talk. The car was getting old and the heater hadn't worked for as long as he could remember. His father said he couldn't afford to get it repaired. . .

B. I kept quiet for most of the trip. It was too cold for talk. The car was getting old and the heater hadn't worked for as long as I could remember. My father said he couldn't afford to get it repaired. . .

A. The morning after the big snowstorm, her mother is real sick. . . They are all lined up, listening to the radio that sits on top of the fridge to see if there will be any school.

B. The morning after the big snowstorm Mama is real sick. . . We are all lined up, listening to the radio that sits on top of the fridge to see if there will be any school.

These stories could have been written either way. Even if you identified the second as being the author's choice in each case, recasting these stories in the third person would not have been a major transformation. Shifting from first to third person is far less radical than changing the means of perception.

Still, it is worth reading the first page of a new story in both ways. Your initial choice may be the right one, but there are advantages to each that are worth considering.

One good reason for using the first person is that you may want to maintain the naiveté or innocence of a young protagonist. "Sausage and Beer" deals with a boy who is going through a new and strange experience. Using the first person was a natural way to suggest a **narrator** and to share his feelings with the reader without commentary. "Three Hearts" deals with a girl who witnesses an emergency. It is different in that through her experience we learn something significant about the mother; but again, maintaining the naive voice of a child narrator is easier in the first person.

A closely related advantage of the first person is that you can adopt the tone of a story being narrated out loud. Such stories occasionally identify a listener, but more often they do not. The illusion is usually created by word choice and phrasing. Very few authors indulge in phonetic spellings like "goin' " for "going" and " 'em" for "them," because spelling changes easily become obtrusive. But you can suggest a regional or foreign accent through phrasing without altering the spelling of a single word.

Corey often uses phrasing that is both vivid and childlike: The mother's speech is described as "puffy and low"; her eyes are "like faded jeans"; Eddie's "blue eyes are storm clouds"; and after Bucky's near-suffocation she feels "jerky on the inside." It would be possible to use some of those phrases if the story had been in the third person, but too often the author would have had to introduce them with "to her it seemed like . . " or "to her it looked like. . . " Although the story is not fully "as-if-spoken" with a listener identified, the fact that it is in the first person allows the author to use colloquial phrasing in her narration.

The first person is also useful when the primary point of the story is to ridicule or satirize the narrator. You can achieve an effective irony when characters try to justify or defend themselves in ways that actually damn them in the reader's eyes.

Oddly, the first person may not be the right choice for a story based on an event that is recent and is recalled with highly charged feelings. To put this more positively, the third person is an excellent way of holding material at arm's length. If you have just broken up with someone who was important to you, or if you are trying to deal with a recent death, try transforming the event by selecting the third person. And if doing that doesn't work, shift the protagonist to someone else.

The greatest advantage of the third person is flexibility. The writer can use the protagonist as the primary means of perception, using "he" or "she," while occasionally drawing on a more objective view for incidental or background information.

The popular notion that the first person provides a sense of immediacy or realism that cannot be achieved in the third person is not justified. Readers enter a story using "he" or "she" just as easily as they do one that begins with "I." But the decision of which to use should not be made carelessly. Your first inclination may be entirely justified, but do consider the alternative. If in doubt, convert a sample paragraph from first person to third or the reverse fairly early in the writing.

The Focus of the Story

The **focus** of a story refers to the character who is the central concern. Don't confuse focus with **viewpoint**. In many cases, the character through whose eyes you are seeing the events is also the focus of the story, but not always.

"Three Hearts" is an excellent example of a story in which the character who is the means of perception is not the true focus of the story. Sissy is our only means of seeing the action, so she clearly is the viewpoint character. But if you look at the story thematically, you will see that it is primarily about a dysfunctional mother, an invalid both physically and emotionally, who in spite of her disabilities responds to an emergency with astonishing energy and courage. The daughter is the narrator, but the mother is the true subject of the story.

How is this focus established when so much of the story has to do with Sissy and her brother? The opening scene places the spotlight on the mother, and the highly dramatic climax is dominated by her heroic action. The games the children play in the igloo are significant in the way they keep returning to the subject of death and the relationship between men and women, but the true theme has to do with the competence of the mother as opposed to the incompetence of the men who for three generations have been debilitated by alcoholism.

Focus is closely tied to theme, an aspect I'll return to in Chapter 27. The important point here, however, is that the character who is the means of perception is not necessarily the one on center stage. A story can be told through the eyes of a relatively innocent observer.

Reviewing Your Options

When a story idea first comes to you, it will probably be a mix of personal experience and invention. Let it run through your head like a daydream. Don't concern yourself at this early stage about the means of perception, person, and focus. If you analyze too much too soon, you may lose the feel of the story.

There will come a point, however, when it seems as if you have enough to work with. This is when some writers like to make a few notes about plot and characters so they won't lose the original concept. This is also when you should consider alternative strategies of presentation. Transforming a story by altering the point of view or the focus is a lot easier when it is still in your head than it is when a draft is down on paper or on your computer screen.

When examining the means of perception at this early stage, try to resist the temptation to play tricks with point of view: the first-person account of a disaster at sea in which all are drowned turns out to be a note in a bottle; the third-person story picturing the terrible life of an oversupervised little girl turns out to be about a happy little dog; a brother-sister story turns out in the last sentence to have concerned two robots. All these have been done (even before *The Twilight Zone* scripts), but they and stories like them all depend on a simple twist in the means of perception. Any story that relies on a one-shot trick or **gimmick** will be forgotten as quickly as a standup comedian's joke. Viewpoint is an important aspect of sophisticated fiction, but when it is used as the whole point of a story, the result becomes trivial entertainment.

Shifting a story from third person to first or the reverse is not as radical a transformation as changing the means of perception. But as we have seen, it involves more than changing "I" to "he" or "she". If you have any doubts about which approach is most appropriate for a particular story, take the time to write a paragraph each way. To a large degree, this is an intuitive choice.

Focus, on the other hand, is fundamental. It involves the theme or central concern of the story. Make every effort to get this right at the start. Have you turned the spotlight on the right character? Do you really know what the story is suggesting? Sometimes you may be inclined to forge ahead with the first draft without being sure, and there are writers who recommend doing this. But hiking without maps or compass has its risks. Whatever you do, develop a clear focus before you ask others to spend valuable time reading the draft. Claiming that it should mean whatever readers want it to mean is simply asking them to do your work.

One final note of reassurance: there will be times when in spite of your most careful efforts you will discover late in the development of a story that the means of perception really should be changed. Or, worse, you may realize that the character you had thought was the focus of a developing story is not the true subject. All your efforts may seem to crumble. It's panic time!

If this happens to you, here are four first-aid steps that may make the difference of life or death for the story:

1. Don't tear up the draft. Hollywood movies show frustrated writers ripping pages from the typewriter and crumpling them. Don't. The draft may look better in the morning.

2. With regard to the means of perception, simply rewrite the first page with the viewpoint changed. You can tell far better from writing an actual sample than you can by trying to analyze the situation in the abstract. See if your sample page *feels* better. Trust your instinct.

3. If changing from first to third person is what is bothering you, write a sample page each way. Again, trust your instinct. This is a nonproblem.

4. Focus, on the other hand, can be a real problem. If you have doubts in this area, look carefully at the first and last pages. Sometimes you can successfully change the focus of a story without staying up all night simply by rewriting the opening and the closing. Try setting the manuscript aside and writing the first and last pages from memory. A new opening and closing may be just the transformation you need. Review once again how neatly focus is established in the first half page and the conclusion of "Three Hearts."

When you start writing fiction, finding the right subject matter seems like the primary challenge. As you gain experience, however, you will find that questions of viewpoint are even more important.

18
STRUCTURE:
From Scenes to Plot

Clock time distinguished from psychological time. Scene construction in two stories. Varieties of plot patterns: chronological, flashbacks, frame stories. Crucial paragraphs: openings and closings. Controlling the pace. Scene awareness.

Clock time moves at a steady rate. And in one sense, so do our lives. Awake or asleep, our allotted time flows from birth to death minute by minute at a steady pace.

Psychological time, however, does not. Take a moment to review what you did yesterday from waking up to sleeping again. As soon as you begin putting the events into words, that smooth chronology turns into a list of separate segments: getting dressed, eating breakfast, and, for students, attending classes, taking a coffee break with friends in the cafeteria, holding a conversation in the hall, and eating lunch.

For nonstudents, the activities will be different, but no matter what the content, the memory of the day has quite unconsciously become structured. While the *clock* has been moving without a break, our *life* as we look back is recalled as a sequence of episodes.

In daily conversation, this process of shaping the memory goes on with very little conscious thought. But the episodes we recall have certain recurring characteristics that every writer of fiction should consider. First, we often identify them by where they occurred—the **setting**. Second, we recall who was there—the *characters*. Third, such episodes remain clear long after we have forgotten what came just before and just afterward. The dull periods of time that merely link one episode with the next (driving, waiting, reading, watching television) tend to blend together and blur quickly. In conversation we may fill in long blocks of time with a simple phrase like "After waiting three hours for the rain to stop. . . . "

Finally, we don't always remember these events in the order in which they occurred. Students complaining about bad teachers they have had are not necessarily going to start with kindergarten; football fans recounting dramatic games they have watched are not going to begin with the first one they attended; and someone recalling her love for a friend is not necessarily going to begin with the day they met.

Fiction tends to imitate these patterns. What we call *episodes* in life become **scenes** in fiction. These are the basic units. And their arrangement is what we call **plot**.

Scene Construction in Two Stories

Scenes in fiction are not as clearly defined as they are in drama, but they are similar in their formation as well as their purpose. A new scene is signaled most clearly when the setting changes, but often all it takes is a character arriving or leaving. No double space is required to show these divisions; readers are used to fiction being segmented at least roughly into a series of scenes.

If you recall the plot of "Sausage and Beer" without looking back, you will probably think of it as taking the form of three major blocks: the trip to the hospital, the actual visit, and the bar scene. They stand out because each has a distinctly different setting. But if you examine that story with a writer's analytical eye, you will see that there are actually six scenes.

1. The narrator is being driven by his father to see the boy's uncle. (Includes a brief **flashback**—a scene within a scene—in which the father invites his son to visit his Uncle Theodore.)
2. A short scene outside the hospital building. This is set off by a description of the hospital and grounds.
3. The waiting room. Father and son wait for Uncle Theodore to appear.
4. The visit with Uncle Theodore. This begins with Theodore's arrival and ends with the conclusion of visiting hours. Notice that the setting hasn't changed, but there is a psychological break when Uncle Theodore appears.
5. A short scene in the car.
6. The scene in the bar. Notice that this is not only a different setting, it is a different climate as well. The bar is warm and friendly.

Why six scenes? There is no formula. These are the segments that seemed appropriate for what turned out to be the final draft. The same flexible approach is probably the best for your own work: plunge into an initial draft and see how many scenes naturally develop. But once the first draft is down on paper, take a close and critical look at the number and length of your scenes. Occasionally you will have to add a new scene. But more often you will find that you can cut. As I described earlier, a two-page flashback was cut from what I had originally submitted for publication.

When a story appears to be too long, there is sometimes a tendency to nibble at it word by word. After an hour of such work, you may find that you have cut less than a paragraph. It is far more effective to look at the scenes and weigh the possibility of eliminating one entirely.

There comes a point, of course, when a story cannot be cut further without doing damage. In terms of plot alone, this story could be reduced to a single scene—the one at the hospital. But too much would be lost. The earlier scenes establish the relationship between father and son while also providing suspense, and the concluding scenes shift the story from a simple initiation (the boy introduced to the disturbing reality of mental illness) to a kind of first communion in which a young man is welcomed into the fellowship of adult life with all its distressing ironies.

The scene construction in "Three Hearts" is slightly more diffuse. If you rely on your memory, you may recall it as essentially two major blocks: the first in the house with the mother and the other outside in the snow. But it has to be more complicated than that since Sissy is not with her brother when he is buried in the snow. If you look closer, you can find seven scenes. Although the divisions are sometimes fuzzy, here is one way to describe the pattern:

1. The kitchen. Narrator, Bucky, and their mother listen to the radio. (Includes a flashback with dialogue between the parents.)
2. The hallway. Eddie comes home.
3. Outside in the yard. Sissy and Bucky play in the snow.
4. In their "igloo."
5. Backyard again. Sissy gathers "firewood" (icicles). When she returns she can't find the tunnel.
6. Back to the house. Tries to wake Eddie. Can't, tells her mother what has happened.
7. The yard again. The mother saves Bucky. Sissy lingers there.

These scenes are all necessary. It's important to have at least a quick glimpse of Eddie since he illustrates how dysfunctional the male members of this family are. Playing in the snow provides several important references to death, and playing house in the igloo subtly reveals early attitudes toward sex roles ("Eskimo women do all the stuff like that"). There has to be a scene that gets Sissy out of the igloo when it is knocked down (significantly by the father). And the high-drama scene is the one in which we see that this is really a story about the mother. The end of the final scene, when Sissy is alone, may seem at first reading to be expendable. The symbol of Eddie's mitten, which is "full of holes," is poignant, however, and gives the story a depth of suggestion that it would not have had if it had ended with action alone, like another Disney adventure tale.

Varieties of Plot Patterns

The two stories you have read so far move **chronologically** from scene to scene. A majority of stories do, particularly those that are relatively short. But even in those cases, the writer is not bound to move relentlessly forward in time. The author, like the scriptwriter, is free to include glimpses of past action.

The **flashback** is a simple method of inserting an episode that occurred before the main flow (or **base time**) of the **plot**. The term *flashback*, first used by film writers, describes more than a simple reference to the past seen through a character's thoughts or dialogue. A true flashback consists of a whole scene that took place before the main action of the story and is presented with setting and often with dialogue.

Take, for example, the flashback that occurs in the opening scene of "Sausage and Beer." The father and son, you remember, are driving in silence, and an earlier incident is dropped in almost as if in brackets:

> The whole business of visiting Uncle Theodore had come up in the most unconvincingly offhand manner.
>
> "Thought I'd visit your Uncle Theodore," he had said that day after Sunday dinner. "Wondered if you'd like to meet him."
>
> He spoke with his eyes on a crack in the ceiling as if the idea had just popped into his head, but that didn't fool me.

Notice that the reader is informed of the fact that the story is moving back to an earlier time by the brief use of the past perfect: "*had* come up" and "he *had* said that day." This is a standard method of entering a flashback in past-tense stories, even though many readers are not consciously aware that they are being signaled by a shift in tense. In fact, many writers have used the technique without knowing that the *had* form is called the past perfect. Never mind the terminology; *had* is the cue for your reader. After one or two sentences, shift back to the simple past.

How do you come out of a flashback? The most obvious way is to identify the transition directly: "But that was hours ago" or "But that was when he was much younger." More often, authors simply make sure that the new paragraph starts with a bit of action or a line of dialogue that clearly indicates to the reader that the story has returned to *base time*, the events and setting of the primary plot line. In this particular flashback the reader should be set straight by the paragraph that begins: "We were well out in the New England countryside now."

The same kind of cues are used when you are writing in the present tense. The shift in these cases is from the present to the simple past tense. There is a good example in the opening scene of "Three Hearts":

> The last time I saw my Daddy drunk, his lip was broken wide open and purple.
>
> "Who did that to you?" Mama said.
>
> "My old man."

We know that we are out of the flashback as soon as the author returns to the present tense: "Mama blames herself for everything."

In many cases, you can make the return to base time clear simply by starting a new paragraph and shifting the tense. But be sure that the setting is clearly different. If your story is set in, say, a restaurant, avoid having your flashback in a similar restaurant. There's no point in needlessly confusing your reader.

Oddly, even careless readers follow cues like these, often without having the slightest idea of how they work. Writers, on the other hand, have to be acutely aware of the technique.

Flash-forwards are rare, but they do have a particular use. There is an excellent example in Sharon Solwitz's story "Obst Vw," which appears in Chapter 23. In a daring stylistic tactic, she opens the story with an event that will not occur until a year after the story that follows:

> Next year, writing his personal experience essay to convince admissions at Penn he's Ivy League material despite uneven grades, he'll describe in amusing detail the one baseball game his father took him to, and get in on a scholarship despite his father's explicit pessimism.

She closes the flash-forward within the same paragraph:

> But now on Rachel's bed, unraveling a hole in the knee of her jeans while her parents yell at each other downstairs, he cannot join in her raillery. "Let's go," he says.

Flash-forwards have an interesting effect on the **tone** of a story. They almost invariably increase the **distance** between the reader and the material. When we as readers are given information not yet known to the characters, we, in effect, rise above the story, looking down on the action. For those who feel that immediacy and emotional impact should be primary goals in fiction, this may seem like a poor tactic. But remember that when the emotional element is pushed too far in fiction it becomes sentimental or melodramatic. When you read Solwitz's story, notice how that flash-forward helps us to keep those characters and their very real distress in perspective. Their suffering is genuine, but it is not high tragedy.

Multiple flashbacks are sometimes used when the author wants to suggest a complicated set of clues leading to a symbolic or a literal trial.

Joseph Conrad's *Lord Jim* is in this form; so is William Faulkner's well-known "A Rose for Emily." Such an approach tends to fragment the story line, of course, and it may be for this reason that it is usually found in longer works and those that have a type of mystery or trial to maintain the story's unity and the reader's interest.

The **frame story** traditionally refers to fiction in which a narrator relates events that occurred previously. In a sense, the entire work is one long flashback. Sometimes this is presented in the third person; but more often the narrator speaks in the first person, recalling one or more incidents that happened some time in the past.

"Sausage and Beer," for example, could have opened with the narrator looking back like this:

> As I stood with my wife waiting for the funeral to begin, I realized how little I had really seen of my father. It was as if he were a stranger until I was twelve. The turning point came one day when he took me to visit my Uncle Theodore.
>
> As I remember it, I had kept quiet for most of the trip. It was too cold for talk.

Notice the traditional use of the past perfect for a single sentence and then the simple past. And if the story were to have a complete frame, the ending might be rounded out with a return to the opening scene.

> Sitting there in the chapel, listening to the service intended to honor my father, I couldn't help feeling that he and I had experienced a more meaningful ritual there in that most secular bar years ago.

Such an ending seems wooden and a bit too obvious. But it does indicate how any story can be surrounded in a frame. As a variation of this device, the frame can be left incomplete simply by not returning to the narrator at the end. This avoids the risk of a needless summing up.

Think twice before you consider the frame pattern for a **short-short story**. It tends to clutter a work of that length. But the frame is well justified with a slightly longer work, especially when you plan to contrast the present and past attitudes of the narrator.

Crucial Paragraphs: Openings and Closings

When you have finished your first draft, take a close, critical look at your opening paragraph. If it is a long and rambling description of the setting or the characters, it may reflect your own effort to get in the mood. Sometimes it can be cut entirely. Remember too that those leisurely starts seem dated, echoes from the 19th century. Because the form is so short, the tendency now is to jump in quickly.

How quickly? Ask yourself this key question: At what point do we enter the mind of the character who will be the means of perception? This is the moment when the reader is able to identify with a character. This is when the story really begins. If an entire paragraph precedes this point, it may well be exposition from the author's point of view, a prelude. Your reader will be impatiently waiting. Consider cutting the whole paragraph or even the entire first page. The information it provided can be broken up and inserted at various points later.

One way to study openings intensively is to go through an anthology and read nothing but first paragraphs. Which draw you and which do not? Exactly where is the means of perception established? How quickly is the situation established? Take some notes and compare different approaches.

Endings are equally crucial. The challenge is to reveal or expand the theme indirectly rather than stating it as one does in an essay. Once again, that familiar bit of advice applies: show, don't tell. Let the reader discover the aspects you consider important rather than laying them out in exposition.

You can prepare for such an ending if you provide somewhat earlier what James Joyce called an **epiphany**. Although he used the term in a somewhat more limited sense, it has come to mean an important moment of recognition or discovery. It may be an insight that the reader and the protagonist discover at the same time, or it may be something only the reader perceives.

In "Sausage and Beer" there are, I believe, two such moments. The first is given through the fat man at the bar who, in a serious moment almost at the end of the story, poses the question of why one of two brothers lived a normal life while the other ended up in a mental hospital. His answer is that it's "just the number he drew." We are all, he suggests, subject to random chance. The boy and the reader come to realize this simultaneously.

The suggestion in the final sentence of the story, however, is too complex for the boy to understand at this stage in his life. The father and son are now sharing something like a communion—not a religious experience but a partaking of life itself.

As I have urged before, guard against the temptation to step in as author at the very end and explain the story. If you have already revealed what you had in mind, an explanation is as tedious as a guest who won't leave. But if you haven't revealed the theme or themes by then, that's your cue to go back and revise the story once more no matter how late the hour.

Endings don't have to be dramatic. Often they consist of some small, apparently insignificant piece of action that may highlight the theme rather than announcing it with trumpets. Occasionally a line of dialogue may serve the same purpose. In "Sausage and Beer," the father and son "ate and drank quietly, lost in a kind of communion." In "Three Hearts," Sissy fixes the holes in Eddie's mitten and stuffs it "inside of Bucky's." Without knowing it (and also without the author telling us), she has tried—perhaps ineffectually—to mend the terrible gaps in that family.

You can study endings the same way you examine openings. Compare ten in an anthology even if you haven't read the stories themselves. Determine whether the conclusion was dramatized with a line of dialogue or thoughts, some significant action, or, in rare cases, amplified through exposition. Even without understanding what that last paragraph refers to, you can learn a good deal about the range of techniques.

Controlling the Pace of Plot

Every reader can sense when some sections in a story drag while others move quickly. A writer, however, has to know why this has happened.

In part, the **pace** of fiction is controlled by the style—particularly the length and complexity of the sentence structure. Long sentences slow the pace. This is discussed further in Chapter 29. By far the greatest factor, however, is the **rate of revelation**. That is, a story seems to move rapidly when a great deal is being revealed to the reader; conversely, it slows down when the work turns to digression, speculation, description, or any type of exposition.

The pace is up to you as author. You can, if you wish, maintain a high rate of revelation simply by developing what reviewers like to call an "action-packed plot." This is how many best-selling suspense novels and adventure stories maintain the pace. Extreme examples are seen on television every night. Unfortunately, among the victims of high-speed car crashes and catastrophic explosions are subtlety of theme and richness of characterization.

When you write sophisticated fiction, you have to be on guard against both ends of the spectrum: an unrelentingly high rate of revelation may maintain interest for a while, but then it runs the risk of boring readers for lack of significance. The work will seem superficial. But if you dwell too long on descriptive passages or background information, the forward motion of the story will come to a dead stop. The best way to avoid these two risks is to vary the pace throughout the work.

Openings are frequently given a high rate of revelation. It helps to plunge into an ongoing situation that will arouse the reader's interest. "Sausage and Beer," you remember, begins with the narrator driving with his father and wondering what his Uncle Theodore will be like.

In "Three Hearts," the opening rate of revelation is even higher. The very first sentence informs us that there has been a heavy snowstorm and the mother is sick. By the end of that paragraph we meet three members of the family and share with them the question of whether school will be canceled. In the very next paragraph we are introduced to Sissy's father and Eddie with his drinking problems. With a dysfunctional family like that, anything can happen.

Both of these stories jump into a situation that arouses the curiosity of the reader. Once you as writer have overcome the reader's reluctance to get started, you can afford to fill in the setting and provide background.

As a story develops, it is a good idea to continue alternating between the vitality of fresh plot development and the richness of description and exposition. In this way the pace of fiction often resembles that of a skater: the forward thrust is followed by a glide. If the glide is too long, the story, like the skater, will lose momentum.

The best time to review the pacing is when you have completed the first draft. Read the work without stopping and notice where it seems to slow down. If your low-key sections are brief, you have no problem. But if even you find it slow, consider adding new developments.

On the other hand, if your story strikes you as "full of sound and fury" without serious significance, ask yourself just what theme you want to suggest and then consider moderating the dramatic action. The short-short story is a relatively delicate form, and it is all too easy to drown out thematic concerns with a thundering drumbeat of action. A story ending with a fatal shooting can be revised to seem less like a routine television scene if you replace the death with an injury; a story capped by a suicide (often a too-easy ending) may be more convincing if the protagonist shows his or her despair in a more subtle way.

When determining the pace of a story, consider the length. A short-short of three to six manuscript pages may be based on a single scene and may move at essentially the same pace from beginning to end. The longer a story, the more natural it is to have multiple scenes. As soon as you do, the pacing becomes increasingly important. "Three Hearts," for example, seems like a relatively short story when printed, but it would come to slightly more than 14 double-spaced pages in manuscript. A story of this length can afford the relatively slow-paced scenes of the children playing in the snow and in their igloo. But look at the rush of activity toward the end as Sissy leaves the tunnel, goes back to the house, returns to the tunnel, discovers it has collapsed, races back to the house a second time, then returns with her mother to find Bucky. That breathless quality is not caused by the emergency alone; it is enhanced by short, action-charged scenes.

It is sometimes difficult to judge the pacing of a story you have just written because you are still so close to the material. If possible, set the manuscript aside for a day or two and then read it nonstop as if for the first time. Also try to find others to read it. Even if they are not writers, they will be able to identify scenes that seem to drag.

Scene Awareness

When you read for pleasure, you don't have to pay attention to scenes. But when you turn to writing fiction, they become a prime concern. You can increase your awareness of scenes by analyzing them in published fiction or story manuscripts. Block out the material in your own mind. From time to time, mark the scene divisions in a couple of stories. Like an architect learning from the work of others, analyze the structure.

There may be times when a story you are writing flows so effortlessly that you won't want to get analytical as you write. Go with it! But after that heady rush is over and the first draft is complete, return to your calmer, critical self and take a close look at the scene construction. Would flashbacks help? Will the opening arouse the reader's interest? Is the conclusion subtle enough? Are there scenes that are too long or too slow or both?

Scenes form the structure of a story. If they are sound, the story will also be sound.

19

A STORY

by Ann Hood

Escapes

What I do with my niece Jennifer is this. I ride the cable cars again and again, paying four dollars each time. She is fourteen and gets a thrill hanging off the side of the car as it plunges down San Francisco's steep hills. She says it is like flying, and indeed the wind does pick up her Esprit scarf, the one decorated with purple and yellow palm trees, and tosses it stiffly backward in the same way that Charles Lindbergh's scarves appear in old flying photos of him.

I take her to Candlestick Park for the Giants' last game of the season and sit shivering under an old blanket I bought in Mexico long ago. Jennifer does not understand baseball, but I try to explain it to her. Three outs to an inning, nine innings to a game, the importance of a good shortstop. But she does not get it. When Chris Sabo of the Reds strikes out she says, "Caryn, why is it still their turn? You said three outs to an inning."

"But three strikes," I tell her, "is just one out." Jennifer shakes her head and closes her eyes for the rest of the game. Even when I shake her and say, "Look! A home run!" she keeps her eyes closed, does not move.

We spend an entire day at the Esprit factory outlet. Jennifer fills a shopping cart with bargains. She is tall, like her father, my brother, was. She is fourteen and already almost six feet, and so thin that her hip bones poke out from her faded blue jeans. She does not have to wear a bra. She keeps her hair long, so that it flies around her head like a golden cloud. One of the saleswomen asks Jennifer if she is a model. "Me?" Jennifer says, confused, embarrassed. She slouches even more than usual and shakes her yellow hair. Then she walks away. But when we go into the dressing room and she sees that there is no privacy, no curtains or doors, that everyone is standing half-naked in front of mirrors, Jennifer leaves her shopping cart and walks out of the store without trying on a thing.

What I do not do is mention Jennifer's arms. Tiny uneven scars creep up her wrists like a child's sloppy cross-stitch. She wears long-sleeved blouses, and dozens of tiny bracelets, but still the scars peek through. I pretend that Jennifer's wrists are as smooth as the rest of her. That the scars are not even there. I don't ask her any questions about it. Instead, I take her to the Top of the Mark at sunset. I bring her to Seal Rock where we stare through telescopes at the sea lions sunning themselves.

Right before Jennifer came to stay with me, my boyfriend, Luke, left. He said he needed to try his luck in New York. Maybe, he said, he'd become really famous there. Like Laurence Olivier. That was in August and I haven't heard from him since.

Sherry, Jennifer's mother, called me on a Saturday morning in late September and said, "You've got to take her. She's been kicked out of school. Sell her. Adopt her. I don't care. Just take her. I'm going nuts." I looked out my window at the California sky, a bluer, higher sky than anywhere else in the world. Since Luke left, I hadn't done much of anything except swim two miles a day, go to work at the tiny magazine office on Polk Street where I'm a copy editor and dream of where to escape to next. Sometimes, I rented old movies, ones with Barbara Stanwyk and Joan Crawford in them. Ones that forced me to cry.

While I looked at the sky I thought about my life as a flat straight line like a dead person's heart on a monitor. Sherry told me that Jennifer was really out of hand now. "And I have my studies to worry about," Sherry added. She was in travel-agent school. On weekends, she got to take junkets to Puerto Vallarta and New Orleans.

I had not seen Jennifer in almost two years when Sherry called me that day. My brother Daniel had been dead for almost ten years. So I'm still not sure what made me say yes, I'll take her for a while. Except for maybe the thought of sharing that ultrablue sky with someone seemed so appealing, and the thought of a few bleeps and peaks in my life seemed like a good idea.

Before she hung up, Sherry said, "Don't feel compelled to talk about her cutting her wrists or anything. She wants to put that behind her."

"What?" I said. Had I missed something here? I thought. Jennifer had cut her wrists? They say suicide is contagious and Daniel had done it, hung himself in his jail cell where he was serving time for dealing drugs. "I thought you weren't going to tell her," I told Sherry. We had invented a story when it happened to Daniel. He was in a car accident, we'd decided. He fell asleep at the wheel.

"I didn't," she said. "It must run in your family or something."

"It does not," I said, wishing I had not agreed to take Jennifer. What did I know about teenagers? Or suicide? Or anything at all?

On Fisherman's Wharf, Jennifer buys more bracelets. They are copper or gold, with tiny beads in the center or chunks of stones, turquoise and amethyst. I wait, bored, gazing at the Golden Gate Bridge while she chooses them from the street vendors that line the sidewalks. She has been with me for two weeks and shows no signs of leaving. Yesterday, she got a postcard from Sherry in Acapulco, written entirely in Spanish. She read it, her face a blank, then tossed it in the trash. "I didn't know you could read Spanish," I told her.

"I can't," Jennifer said.

Jennifer loves all the tourist trap things around the wharf. She spends hours in the souvenir shops and pushing her way through the crowds. She does not smile much, but here her face softens and I almost expect her to break into a grin. Daniel was a great smiler. And so was Sherry. But their daughter's face is set and hard. A mask.

"What's that?" she asks me as we eat our crab cocktails at the crowded food stall. We are crushed against a family of tourists wearing identical pink-and-blue striped sweatshirts, all fresh-faced and blond.

I look at where she is pointing, across the bay.

"Alcatraz," I tell her.

She frowns. "Alcatraz."

"It was a maximum-security prison."

"Can we go there?" she asks me. Her eyes are topaz. They remind me of a tiger's.

"Maybe next week," I sigh, tired of sight-seeing.

"Okay," Jennifer says, fixing her eyes on the hunk of rock in the water. Around her neck, a charm on a chain catches in the sun. A cable car.

"That's pretty," I say. "When did you buy it?"

She looks at me now. "You can have it if you want," she says. She slips the chain over her head and holds it out to me.

"No, that's okay," I tell her.

But she is putting it on me even as I protest. The little gold cable car settles against my collarbone. I feel guilty for not wanting to take her to see Alcatraz and I promise myself we'll definitely go next week. If she hasn't gone home to Miami by then.

I get a letter from Luke in New York. It is written on paper with his initials on the top, and sounds like it is from a stranger. He tells me about the weather there, and how difficult it is to figure out the subway system. He signs the letter "Sincerely, Luke."

"Who's Luke?" Jennifer asks me.

I did not show her the letter, so I figure she has been looking through my things. Somehow, this does not even make me angry. My tiny apartment on Fourth Avenue has been so lonely that the idea of sharing it and everything in it makes me almost happy. For a while, Luke's shirts were crammed into my one closet, his deodorant and toothbrush and comb cluttered my bathroom. Now, Jennifer's things are mingling with mine. When I turn off the bathroom light, her toothbrush glows orange. Her multitude of bracelets are everywhere I look, as if they are actually reproducing.

So I tell her who Luke is without mentioning that she really shouldn't be reading my letters.

"Did you love him?" she asks me.

I only shrug. "Who knows?" I say.

"Did my mother love my father?" she asks then, suddenly.

I answer, "Yes," immediately, but then I wonder about my answer. To me, Sherry and Daniel were like Bonnie and Clyde. They were always doing something illegal. Their apartment was filled with an air of danger. Once, in a kitchen drawer, I saw dozens of stolen credit cards. Their cars disappeared mysteriously. They kept scales and spoons and plastic bags where other people kept pots and pans. How do I know that they loved each other? But Jennifer seems satisfied with my easy answer.

Jennifer says, "Some things don't make sense to me. Like why was my father in a car in Pennsylvania when we lived in Miami? And why aren't there any pictures of us all together?"

"I don't know," I tell her. "I was away at the time." I don't fill in the details, that I was living in St. Thomas, serving tropical drinks and soaking up the sun until my skin turned very brown.

She studies my face for a long time, searching for something that I can't give her.

When Sherry calls I ask her when she will take Jennifer back. "She should go to school," I tell her.

"She'll be expelled again anyway. She steals from kids' lockers, takes whatever she wants. Can you believe it?"

I feel like both Jennifer and Sherry are hiding things from me, giving me little bits and pieces but keeping the big parts to themselves. I try to imagine Sherry in the small pink house she and Jennifer live in. Jennifer has told me that they have orange trees in their backyard, and a plastic pink flamingo on their lawn. I can see Sherry there, in her high-heeled sandals and platinum hair. I used to think she looked exactly like my old Barbie doll, all pointy breasts and tiny waist. Her hair is blond like Jennifer's, but bleached and molded into a tight bubble. That is how I imagine her as she talks to me now, a Barbie doll in her Florida toy house, surrounded by bougainvillea and orange blossoms, staring blankly at a plastic lawn ornament.

"She is nothing but trouble," Sherry is telling me. "Stealing and cheating on tests. She actually copied a *Time* magazine article about Houdini and handed it in as her report on a famous person. Like the teacher wouldn't know someone else wrote it."

Jennifer is stretched out on my couch, lazily flipping through a magazine. She does not seem to be listening to the conversation.

"Well," I ask Sherry, "what's the problem?"

"Who knows? I'm trying to make a better life for us. Travel agents get discount tickets and hotels. We could see the whole world if we wanted to."

Over the years, Sherry has learned many skills. She was a licensed electrologist, removing women's mustaches and shaping their eyebrows. She booked bands for a nightclub and tried her hand at calligraphy. None of it worked as well as her days with Daniel breaking the law.

"I would think she'd want to travel," I say. It was all that I used to want, my way of getting out of tough spots, of leaving men and looking for new ones.

Sherry laughs. "All she wants is to make trouble. But you say she's being good there, so let her stay for a bit more."

I want to explain that I am tired of Jennifer being here. That she is not really helping me decide what to do next. That I have an urge, once more, to pick up and go. To L.A., maybe. Or even Hawaii. Luke signed his letter "Sincerely" and I want to run.

But I say none of these things. I just stare at Jennifer and wonder how she could have actually done it to herself. How she felt when it didn't work. From Miami, Sherry makes excuses for having to hang up. She doesn't ask to speak to her daughter, and I don't offer.

"Wow," Jennifer says when I take her to my tiny, cramped office. "Look at all of these places." She touches the photographs that line my desk and walls and shelves. Pictures of Peru and British Columbia, of people climbing a frozen waterfall and of seals in the Galápagos Islands.

From my window, I can see hookers on the corner, a man drinking something from a paper bag. They call this area of the city the Tenderloin. That sounds gentle to me. Tender loins. This is not a gentle place.

"Have you been to all these places?" Jennifer asks me. She holds out a picture of a dense jungle. She has on a new ring, a thin gold one with two hearts dangling from it.

"No," I tell her. "I just put them in the magazine."

"If I could," she says, still clutching at the jungle photograph, "I would go everywhere. Around the world. I'd even volunteer to go on the space shuttle."

I frown, thinking about Sherry. "When your mother finishes travel-agent school—"

Jennifer laughs. "She'll never finish. She never finishes anything."

"She told me you were expelled from school," I say softly.

Now Jennifer sighs. "I was. I'd rather stow away on a ship than go to school every day. There's nothing there."

"She told me—"

"Whatever she told you is true," Jennifer says firmly.

"Oh."

My eyes drift to her wrists, to her bracelets and beneath them, to her scars.

"Caryn," Jennifer says, "what was he doing in Pennsylvania? What was his job?"

I hesitate. His job was dealing drugs, I say in my mind.

Jennifer laughs again. "My mother says I'm a wild thing. She says I'm like my father." She leans out the open window, too far out. My heart seems to slow down, to freeze. I think, she is jumping from this fifth-floor window but I can't reach out in time to grab her. Then she pulls herself back in, and looks at me as if she didn't just dangle five stories.

"I like looking out," she says. And then she smiles. A smile that makes her face look like it hurts.

Somewhere, I have a map of Hawaii. I will find it, I decide, and study it. I will make plans for a new life in the shadow of a volcano. I've served drinks before at seaside resorts. I can do it again. The names of the islands are magical. Maui and Kauai. For days, the fog here in San Francisco has been thick as mashed potatoes and it is starting to depress me. Every morning, Jennifer is staring at me, waiting for answers. It's time, I think, to move.

I search my drawers, but the map is gone. What I find instead are handfuls of jewelry: the bracelets Jennifer likes to wear, and thick ropes of rose quartz and yellow jade, and earrings made of dangling crystals and rings in all sizes. There is no way that Jennifer could have bought all of this jewelry. Where would she get the money? I lay everything out across my bed, and it sparkles and winks at me in the late-afternoon light. Then I put it all away.

The fog is still thick on the day we go to Alcatraz. We wait in line, then crowd onto the ferry. I have paid an extra dollar for us to get the recorded tour, which comes from a bright-yellow Walkman and clunky headphones that make us look like Martians. Jennifer is wearing a Cal Berkeley sweatshirt and a boy asks her if she goes there.

"I'm in ninth grade," she tells him.

The boy walks away.

On the island, we walk through the steps that the tour instructs us to take. Stop at the sign that says DINING HALL, we are told. Take a right on Michigan Avenue. Stand under the clock. Look at the pictures on the wall. We do whatever the voice tells us, like robots. Jennifer's tape is two steps ahead of mine, and every time I approach her it seems she has to walk on to somewhere else.

The recorded voice tells us how on New Year's Eve, the prisoners could hear music and laughter from a yacht club across the bay.

We step inside a cell and pretend we are in solitary confinement. All around us, families snap pictures of each other behind bars. I stand in my cell in the dark and close my eyes. The voice tells me about the cold, damp air here. About all the tricks inmates used to help them get through solitary. Throw a button on the floor and try to find it in the dark. Imagine entire movies.

I can feel Jennifer come and stand beside me, I can smell the perfume she wears all the time. She takes my hand in hers.

"Imagine being locked in here and knowing that San Francisco is right across the bay," she says. "Hearing people at a party."

I open my eyes. "But we can walk out," I tell her. "We're not in solitary."

"I know," she says. "But imagine."

We are way behind on our tapes now. And we have to fast forward to catch up. Quickly, Jennifer and I go through the prison, poking our heads into cells and rooms, until we find the rest of the tour. We are at the end, listening to a description of escapes from Alcatraz.

There were many that failed, the voice croons in my ears, and only one that perhaps was successful. I listen to the details of that escape, of how the men collected hair from the barber shop floor to use on papier-mâché masks of their faces. How they dug for months to get through the prison walls to an air shaft. They were never found, the tape tells me.

Jennifer and I stand on the top of Alcatraz, looking out. Her hair is blowing wildly in the cold breeze, but she does not try to control it, to hold it down.

"I know you took all that jewelry," I tell her. "I know you stole it."

She doesn't answer me. I cannot see her face under her blowing hair.

Finally, she says, "I like to think they made it."

"Who?"

"Those three men who tried to escape. Maybe one of them didn't drown. Maybe at least one of them is free."

I gaze down the rock to the water pounding the shore. I don't agree with her. I think they must have all died down there.

"About that jewelry," I say.

She turns to me. "Here," she says. "Take it." She unclasps each bracelet, letting them drop into my hands.

"I don't want them," I tell her. "That's not the point."

But she keeps taking them off, until finally she has bare arms, and all of her crooked scars are revealed. She is standing before me, arms turned upward, naked of all the turquoise and amethyst and copper.

I take her wrists in my hands, lightly. There are so many questions I could ask her. So many things I want to know. But what I realize, standing there, feeling the bumps of her skin under my hands, is that there really is no escaping. Not for Sherry, not for Jennifer, not for me. The only thing left to do is to stick it out.

Jennifer's eyes are set right on me. She says, "If I really wanted to do it, I would have made the cuts deeper. And up and down instead of across. No one understands that I knew the real way. The right way. But I just wanted to see what would happen, to faint or go away for a little while."

"It's not worth it," I say. "Sooner or later you have to come back."

She nods. There are tears in her eyes, but they could be from the stinging salty air, like mine. The ferry is chugging toward us, and still holding on to each other we slowly make our way down that rock.

We stand in the line, waiting for the ferry to take us back.

Suddenly I turn to Jennifer. "Your father did it," I say. "He hung himself."

Her expression doesn't change at all.

"He was in prison," I continue. "For drugs. And he killed himself."

"I know," she says. "I found the death certificate last year when we moved. I wanted my mother to tell me the truth."

I say, "That's the truth."

The ferry arrives, and we move forward, toward it. Its steps are steep, and we have to link arms for the climb.

20

CREATING TENSION

Tension as a driving force. Conflict: struggling against adversaries. Inner conflicts. Stressful relationships. The dynamic opening. Dramatic questions. How much is too much? Energizing a slack story.

"Well, it's a pleasant little story." If you hear that about a piece you've just written, don't smile. It may sound like a compliment, but it isn't.

Creative writing classes and editors as well receive too many "pleasant little stories," and often the authors remain oblivious to what is wrong with them. A dull story is like a dull meal at a restaurant: patrons don't complain, but they don't come back. The sad aspect is that the chef, hearing no specific complaints, never improves.

What those pleasant little stories lack is **tension**. Tension in fiction is what gives it energy and vitality. It's what keeps the reader reading. Without tension, a story goes limp. And unread.

There are many different ways of creating tension, but they all consist of pitting one element against another. Conflict is the most easily identified. It can take the form of one on one, an individual against a group, or a struggle against nature. A more subtle form of tension is internal, a character struggling with two opposed impulses.

In addition to conflict, there are two other ways of creating tension. One is the anxiety that is formed in an uneasy relationship. The two may not be adversaries, but mutual suspicion or mistrust can generate an electric charge. This is closely connected with what is probably the most used device for creating tension: withholding information from the reader.

Although we will be examining these as separate devices, they are almost always used in conjunction with each other. Together they have the power to turn a slack story into one that is dynamic.

Conflict: Struggling against Adversaries

There is something elemental about pitting one individual against another. In its basic form, the **protagonist** or **hero** takes on an enemy. We're used to that in plays, narrative poetry (particularly ballads), and most often in film.

In simple work, **conflict** is heightened at the expense of character development and subtlety of theme. Adventure stories from Edgar Rice Burroughs' *Tarzan* series to most television thrillers pit characters against each other with great regularity. The conflict in such work is fairly straightforward: the good guys are good and their opponents are unmistakably bad. Few if any are bothered by inner doubts. The pattern is essentially the same when an individual faces a group such as a gang, mob, or enemy troops. Occasionally, the hero must outsmart not only the evil bunch but law enforcers as well, a good example of how mere complexity of plot doesn't necessarily create subtlety.

With associations like these, it is no wonder that beginning writers sometimes avoid all forms of conflict and keep their characters passive or isolated. But there is no need to avoid conflict in even the most sensitive fiction. It will add essential vitality to your fiction as long as you make sure that it doesn't take over and become the dominant effect.

"Three Hearts" is a good example. There are several different conflicts in that story. The father and his father were hostile to the point of physical fighting. Eddie is set against the entire family. His alienation almost results in the death of Bucky. Notice, however, that none of these conflicts is allowed to dominate the story. They dramatize the dysfunctional nature of the family, but they are kept in check.

At the climax of that story, the conflict shifts from person to person to a struggle with nature. But tense as that is, the conflict does not become an end in itself. Its primary function is to reveal a hidden strength in the mother, a revelation of character. Through her actions we come to see how a sickly, emotionally drained, and apparently tranquilized mother can still find inner strength when a member of her family is threatened.

Struggles with nature can be used as the major dramatic device in a story. The variety of threats is endless—storms, a mountain, floods, fires. When planning a story, however, ask yourself from the start whether the conflict you have in mind has the potential to reveal some aspect of character or to develop a thematic concern more insightful than the simple desire to succeed.

Inner Conflict

One of the characteristics of simple fiction is that conflict is rarely muddied by inner conflict. Superman does not question his almost neurotic fascination with crime; Spider-Man is never seriously tempted to take a bribe. But look at the inner uncertainties of the mother in "Three Hearts": she would clearly like to retreat from responsibilities and stay in bed, wrapped in that red robe, "rolling her head from side to side, sighing." Yet she is the one who plunges into the snow to save her son. She is clearly being pulled in two directions, but ultimately it is her mature and loving side that wins.

Caryn, the protagonist in "Escapes," is reluctant to care for her 14-year-old niece right from the start. "I'll take her for a while," she says. When she hears that the girl had tried to commit suicide, her resistance increases:

> . . . wishing I had not agreed to take Jennifer. What did I know about teenagers? Or suicide? Or anything at all?

But on the other side is the fact that the girl is the daughter of Caryn's dead brother and, more subtle and perhaps more of a factor, Caryn's life is in stasis. All she does is swim, work at a dead-end copy-editing job, go to the movies alone, and "dream of where to escape next." This may not be the best argument for taking on the responsibilities of a substitute mom, but it's enough for her to agree at least temporarily.

That highly **ambivalent** relationship might, in a simple story written for a high-circulation magazine, resolve itself with laughter, tears, and a hug. But life is rarely that simple, nor is this story. Halfway through, Caryn talks with her sister-in-law and reveals, to the reader at least, that she is still torn in her feelings.

> I want to explain that I am tired of Jennifer being here. That she is not really helping me decide what to do next. That I have an urge, once more, to pick up and go. To L.A. maybe. Or even Hawaii.

But she doesn't say any of this to her sister-in-law. She just stares at Jennifer and wonders how the girl could have messed up her life so. There is just enough concern there to keep her from giving up.

Is it resolved? Never fully. Certainly not with hugs, kisses, and tears. But they end up together, and the wording of the concluding sentences is positive. The ferry has arrived and the two of them "move forward." The path is not going to be easy: "Its steps are steep, and we have to link arms for the climb."

This is a story that is dominated by inner conflicts in both characters. Those charged feelings run all the way through the story. Even though they never fully disappear, they become manageable.

It is useful to analyze types of conflict so that in your own work you can either intensify or modify what develops. But as I have pointed out before, it is not generally a good idea to start with an abstract notion like conflict. Cast about for characters who are in an ongoing relationship, and chances are you will discover some form of conflict already present. At that point you can sharpen or refine the lines of conflict.

One final suggestion regarding internal conflict: be careful not to rely too heavily on your protagonist's thoughts. Long passages in which characters debate with themselves begin to sound like explanatory essays. Even too much analytical dialogue may sound like author intrusion. As much as possible, reveal conflicting attitudes through the way your characters act and talk. Caryn's feelings are occasionally expressed through thoughts, but we also hear them reflected in her conversations with her sister-in-law and with Jennifer herself. And we see them reflected in her behavior.

The inner conflict experienced by the mother in "Three Hearts" is even less articulated. This is partly because the story is not told from her point of view, eliminating the possibility of providing her thoughts directly. In addition, she is by nature reticent. She doesn't analyze her feelings even to herself the way Caryn does in "Escapes." Here is how "Three Hearts" might read if it were presented from the mother's point of view and she examined her inner conflicts directly the way Caryn does.

> But no, I must rouse myself to save Bucky, I must find inner strength. I must!

Instead, her conflict is shown through her actions, letting us contrast her behavior at the end with the picture we had of her in the opening scene.

Stressful Relationships

Conflict in its various forms is not the only way to create tension in fiction. Some relationships contain none of the aggression or even the hostility we associate with conflict, yet they keep the characters on edge, apprehensive, or even fearful. Such feelings are passed on to readers, fueling their sense of concern and involvement.

In "Sausage and Beer" the boy and his uncle are not in conflict. There isn't even a hint of hostility between them. But the boy is uneasy about what is in store, and his sense of apprehension is, I hope, shared by the reader.

Ann Hood makes full use of a stressful relationship in "Escapes." Occasionally Jennifer, the girl, acts in ways that might be construed as hostile (the refusal to open her eyes at the baseball game, the minor thefts), but she and Caryn are not true antagonists. They behave like two cats circling each other in edgy mistrust.

The more we as readers discover about Jennifer's history the more likely it appears that something will go terribly wrong. First we learn about her suicide attempts, then her history of stealing and cheating. This uncertainty sustains itself until aunt and niece finally achieve that cautious truce and unspoken need for mutual support at the end of the story.

The Dynamic Opening

Most contemporary stories create tension at the very start. A situation is described that arouses the reader's curiosity, but the details are initially withheld. The reader's desire to know what is going on is countered by the author's refusal to reveal too much too soon. This dynamic tension depends on both the freshness of the initial circumstances and the rate at which the details are revealed.

One reason that leisurely, chatty openings are increasingly being replaced by a more dramatic approach is that contemporary readers, perhaps influenced by the media, tend to be impatient. Increasingly, they expect their curiosity to be aroused right away.

In commercial writing, the technique of grabbing the reader's attention at the outset is far from subtle. The "bait" is called the **hook**. Often it takes the form of a quick jolt: "She was the third showgirl to be murdered that week"; " 'In precisely seven minutes,' the Captain announced calmly, 'we'll be blown sky high' "; "When the plague was finally over, Dr. Nighthawk found he was the last surviving human on the planet Esto." For some, flagrant hooks like these are appealing; for others, they are signals that the work will be plot-dominated and obvious.

The openings of sophisticated stories also generate curiosity, but they don't draw attention to themselves. Frequently they promise something interesting about character and situation rather than pure plot. Take a close look at the type of curiosity generated at the start of the three stories you have read so far. Try to recall your initial response.

In "Sausage and Beer" we wonder where are we going and who is this mysterious uncle Theodore? In "Three Hearts" the mother is the source of curiosity: Why is she so weak? Why is she "rolling her head from side to side, sighing"? The mother's emotional state and the unmanageable brother named Eddie are withheld until the third paragraph. In "Escapes" the girl Jennifer seems normal enough at first, but why does she shut her eyes at a baseball game and flee the dressing room with no explanation? Her scars are described in the fifth paragraph.

Not one of these stories starts with the narrator waking up, yawning, wondering what the day will bring. Not one starts with a lengthy physical description or character sketch. Not one gives a paragraph of explanation as to what led up to that opening scene. All three begin with ongoing action *in medias res*—in the middle of things.

These openings are dynamic but they are not blatant appeals for attention. You don't have to have a body slump to the floor or a bridge collapse into raging water to interest a discerning reader. What you do need is an actual, ongoing situation that tweaks the reader's curiosity. It may be as mild as the appearance of a perfect stranger standing at the front door with his suitcase, two six-year-old children getting off the bus in a small town with no one to meet them, or a husband and wife arguing about whether to have a child. Situations like these are openings waiting for a story.

Dramatic Questions

Arousing initial curiosity will get you started, but then what? Without sustaining some form of tension, the story will die. That stranger at the door isn't going to hold the reader very long if he turns out to be dull Uncle Harry who stays one night and is not mentioned again. As soon as the opening situation has been established, there have to be new questions to hold the reader's interest.

Think of these as **dramatic questions**. As soon as the stranger's identity is clarified (a notorious Uncle Harry from Australia, for example), we can raise another: Is he really an uncle? Can we trust him? Will he ask for money? And overlapping that: How long will he stay? As you can see from the stories you have read so far, there is usually a succession of dramatic questions. As soon as one is answered, another is introduced.

In "Sausage and Beer," for example, once the identity of Uncle Theodore is established, we wonder what he will be like in person. How irrational will he be? After that scene there is the anxiety about the bar. Doubt and uncertainty continue to provide new tensions until the final moment of harmony.

The other two stories develop similar sequences. In "Three Hearts" there is a lull when the children play in their igloo, but soon Sissy's inability to find the tunnel generates a surge of tension followed by the question of whether Bucky will live or die.

In "Escapes" the dramatic questions are more modulated but also more frequent. Notice how deliberately the author supplies bits of crucial information: the suicide attempt, the suicide of Jennifer's father, his prison record, Jennifer's stealing. Interestingly, the narrator describes her own sense of frustration in a statement that also applies to the pattern used by the author in the story itself:

> I feel like both Jennifer and Sherry are hiding things from me, giving me bits and pieces but keeping the big parts to themselves.

The author, of course, is not trying to frustrate the reader. She is maintaining interest by doling out information in "bits and pieces," keeping careful track of what I have described as the **rate of revelation**. Revealing too much too soon would have made the second half of the story boring, and failing to account for questions posed earlier would have left the reader puzzled and unsatisfied.

How Much Is Too Much?

Tension generates interest, and increasing the tension creates **suspense**. Reviewers of novels sometimes use *suspense* as high praise, so it is a temptation for some short-story writers to pack as much conflict as possible into a story. Unfortunately, there comes a point when blatant suspense will turn your work into a *melodrama*.

Melodrama is a form of simple writing where everything has been sacrificed to achieve an exciting plot. Intense, unrelenting action tends to destroy depth of characterization and originality. Many melodramas are populated with **stock characters**—good guys and bad guys in their various guises. An excessively suspenseful plot also has a way of simplifying the theme, sometimes reducing it to a matter of victory or defeat.

This does not mean that all suspenseful novels are melodramas. Some are able to combine high tension with subtlety of characterization and complexity in theme. But it does mean that packing too much suspenseful drama into a short story is risky. The shorter the form, the more delicate it is. Trying to supercharge a short-short story is like sending 400 volts through a thin wire.

With apologies to Deborah Joy Corey, take a look at what would have become of "Three Hearts" if that final scene had been allowed to dominate the entire work and make it melodramatic. The revised version might describe in detail the snowplow coming closer and the brute of a father at the wheel with the radio turned up too high to hear warning cries of his daughter. Then the story would describe poor Bucky buried beneath tons of snow, sobbing, then going silent. Next comes the frantic calls by the mother and help from neighbors. When at last Bucky is found, there are cheers and tears. The mother's role in this version would be reduced to that of a heroic family dog. ("Oh Lassie, you found him!") The rescue story would give the reader a quick but entirely forgettable rush of pleasure.

If you suspect that you may have stepped over the line from drama to melodrama, there are five aspects of your work you might consider. First, look closely at the length of your work. Highly dramatic conflicts leading to violence such as bloody fights, rape, or murder require a lot of preparation. Is your story long enough to make it credible, or have you packed too much into a short space? If so, consider muting the action a bit. Fights can be made less lengthy and less bloody, rape can be suggested symbolically through other acts of sexual hostility, and murder can be downsized to injury.

Second, make sure that the ending is not predictable. This is a recurring problem with survival stories and those that depend heavily on the outcome of a fight or a sports event. In such cases you may be offering the reader a simple choice of two endings—winning or losing.

You can avoid this kind of predictability by making sure that the simple alternative of winning or losing is not the story's only concern. Revise the struggle so that it reveals some fresh insight about a character or human nature generally as it does in "Three Hearts."

Third, take a close look at where your original idea came from. Is it close enough to your own experience so that you can make it convincing? If the topic is entirely strange to you—a fishing dispute off the coast of Japan you read about, or labor violence in India—you may have trouble dealing with anything but raw plot. Search for a situation close enough to home so that you can populate it with convincing characters, not cardboard cutouts.

Fourth, look closely at the characters. Are some too good to be credible and others entirely evil? Do they lack inner conflict or even uncertainty? If so, they may have been simplified to generate a suspenseful plot.

Finally, don't forget the power of wit and humor to counter a melodramatic tone. Something as slight as that scene in "Three Hearts" when the two children play husband and wife in an igloo can lend a light touch that helps counter the heavy drama of the next scene.

The essential point to remember is that while tension is necessary to keep your work energized and moving forward, it should not be pushed to the point where it becomes the most memorable aspect. Each of the stories you have read so far develops a variety of tensions, but none of them steps over the line into melodrama. Uncle Theodore does not attack his brother and nephew with a knife; Bucky does not die in the arms of a sobbing mother; Jennifer does not kill herself. The conflicts are there, but none of them does damage to characterization or subtlety of theme.

Recharging a Slack Story

This chapter began with a discussion of stories at the opposite end of the spectrum from melodrama: bland fiction. Even if you are fully aware of the various ways to energize fiction with different types of tension, a final draft may still appear to you to be slack. If so, don't give up. Even if you have completed a couple of drafts, you may well find aspects of the work that contain the seeds for greater tension. It helps, though, to know where to look.

The areas most likely to need revision are relationships between characters. Pick out minor differences of opinion or attitude and see if you can intensify them. Often such revisions will be enough to generate the tension you need.

If this doesn't work, you may have to subject the characters to a **transformation**, as described in Chapter 13. You don't have to destroy the more harmonious aspects, but you can alter one or both characters enough so that you can charge the relationship with some **ambivalence**. This should help you generate some tension.

Finally, make sure that you haven't explained too much of the theme or aspects of your characters, eliminating the chance to withhold information. If you have whole paragraphs of exposition, see if they are really necessary. Help your readers to make discoveries on their own through action and dialogue rather than explaining too much.

Remember that the degree of tension is entirely up to you as author. In most cases, it is a mistake to blame the situation you have chosen as being inherently melodramatic on the one hand or without dramatic potential on the other. Use your creative imagination to adjust the degree of tension. Your goal is to hold interest without sacrificing characterization and thematic insight.

21

SETTING:

Where Are We?

Where am I?—introducing a setting. How much detail?—major versus minor emphasis. Real places versus invented settings. Time as setting: hour and season. Historical periods. Major transformations. Revising the details.

When readers plunge into a new story, the first thing they want to identify is the **means of perception**. The second is where they are. **Setting**, or **orientation**, is what fixes a work of fiction not only in place but in time as well. There is a strangely abstract tone to stories that do not establish the setting fairly early. If you delay (and some stories do), it should be for a good reason.

We naturally think of setting in terms of place, but it also involves time—the hour of the day or night, the season, and occasionally the historical period.

Some stories, of course, make scant use of setting, but even the most dreamlike fantasies, like dreams themselves, usually provide details that help readers to imagine themselves in a specific place. As writers, we have to judge which aspects of the setting are important for a particular story and how we can present them convincingly.

Where Am I? Introducing a Setting

"Where am I?" is the common cry of those regaining consciousness. It is also the instinctive question of readers who have just begun a new story or novel. This is why most stories establish the immediate setting early. Like a stage set, the surroundings help to place readers in the story. A particular house, a room in that house, a field, a beach, a factory assembly line—these and countless other settings not only help to start a story and make the opening scene come alive, but they may contribute to characterization and theme as well.

Watch out, however, for the opening paragraph that is a solid block of descriptive details. Get your situation launched; give your protagonist a brief thought or line of dialogue to establish the viewpoint first. Then work in where this is taking place. In most stories the setting is established briefly within the first page. More details are filled in later. This is the pattern in the three stories you have read so far:

1. "Sausage and Beer": The opening establishes the fact that we are in a car that is cold (brief setting) and are on a trip (the situation). Not until the second page are there more details about where they are:

    We were well out in the New England countryside now, passing dark, snow-patched farm fields and scrubby woodlands where saplings choked and stunted each other.

2. "Three Hearts": First comes the fact that there has been a big snowstorm and that "Mama is real sick" (the situation). Then within the same paragraph comes the setting:

    Bucky and I sit at the wooden table. . . .Mama is lying on the kitchen couch, wrapped in a red robe. . . .

    From the first sentence you learn that the season is winter, and by the end of the first paragraph you have a picture of the kitchen and who is present

3. "Escapes": Like the others, this story plunges into an ongoing situation, but unlike them it identifies a real city where this is taking place:

    I ride the cable cars again and again, paying four dollars each time. She is fourteen and gets a thrill hanging off the side of the car as it plunges down San Francisco's steep hills.

    In the next paragraph the scene shifts to a baseball park, an actual place. And in the fourth paragraph the scene is set at "the Esprit factory outlet," an actual store known to many readers.

As you can see from these three examples, settings in literary short stories are usually specific and frequently memorable as well. Contrast this concern for freshness with the all-too-familiar set used repeatedly in television shows and even some plays, a layout known as "the sitcom living room." The details are etched in our memories: couch in the middle, coffee table centered, upholstered chairs on either side, front door to the left and stairs to the right. Everything is neat, new, and middle class. If you use that in fiction, you will invite glazed inattention.

Instead, work hard to find vivid and convincing details that will be remembered. The qualities to keep in mind are summed up in two words: *distinctive* and *specific*. Just as poems depend on the freshness of images, fictional settings depend on precise, carefully selected visual details.

Details often make the difference between settings that contribute to a story and those that are hardly noticed. Compare the following two descriptive passages

A. It was a large, sparsely furnished room. A number of people wandered about, but it was hard to tell whether they were patients or visitors.

B. The room was large, and it seemed even larger for the lack of furniture. There were benches around all four walls, and in the middle there was a long table flanked with two more benches. The rest was space. And through that space old men shuffled, younger men wheeled carts of linen, a woman visitor walked slowly up and down with her restless husband. . . Or was *she* the patient?

Passage A is brief and clear but provides few details. There would be nothing wrong with such a description if the setting were not going to serve any significant purpose. But in "Sausage and Beer" that room is used to create a mood and help the reader share the boy's reactions. The details in passage B, quoted from the story, serve a special purpose.

To be specific, although "large" is used in both versions, it is emphasized and given a more personal tone in the second version by adding the boy's reaction: ". . . seemed even larger for the lack of furniture." And the sparseness is highlighted by identifying those "benches around all four walls."

The simple assertion that it was hard to tell which were the patients is fleshed out in the second version by describing a particular couple. This is not merely a matter of adding words; it is a selection of details and impressions that re-create what a boy might notice and, at the same time, help the reader to share the experience.

Although the hospital setting in "Sausage and Beer" is described in a single paragraph for impact, many descriptions are spaced out in fragments so as to make them less obtrusive. The kitchen in "Three Hearts," for example, comes to us in a series of separate details scattered through the opening scene: the room has a "radio that sits on top of the fridge" and a "wooden table that wobbles on the crooked floor." The table is covered with a "plastic tablecloth." There is also a "kitchen couch" on which the mother lies; and when Sissy wants to fan her mother, she uses "one of Daddy's newspapers from under the couch." Unmistakably not your sitcom kitchen set!

One way to highlight the setting and make it memorable is to move the action outdoors on occasion. Notice that all three of these stories do that. As we will see, shifts in setting not only enliven each of these stories, they contribute to the themes in each case.

How Much Detail? Major versus Minor Emphasis

Not all settings are used as fully as the ones in these three stories. Some are intended merely to orient the reader and provide a sense of authenticity. They give substance to a story and contribute to what we think of as realism. At a minimum, they may simply imply that the story is taking place in some unnamed city or rural area.

More often, however, literary short stories use the setting as these three have, to highlight some aspect of their themes. To do this, they must include more detail, and frequently they contrast the setting of one scene with that of another.

In "Sausage and Beer," for example, that chilly automobile ride and the hospital visiting room in which we hear about Theodore's fear that they will turn off the heat are played against the "warm, humming, soothing" world of the bar at the end. That contrast helps to emphasize the difference between the boy's anxiety in the face of a strange and vaguely threatening experience and his relief at the end.

In "Three Hearts" it may seem at first that the igloo scene is merely an amusing interlude, but in fact it reveals some of the attitudes the children have picked up about the role of women ("brave" but also relegated, in Bucky's eyes, to gathering firewood) and death (the yard begins to look like "an angel graveyard"). In an ironic reversal, the harmony of their make-believe domestic life makes that igloo warm.

I'll examine these symbolic details in greater length in Chapter 27, but for now simply review those settings for their subtle contribution to theme.

"Escapes" is a particularly good example of how a setting can be prepared for briefly and then reintroduced in more detail later. As you remember, it opens with that scene riding the cable cars in which Jennifer seems free and happy. Later there is a brief reference to Alcatraz. The author is very careful to let the reader know through dialogue that it was once a maximum-security prison situated on an island across the bay. This much is established a third of the way into the story and then dropped for a while.

When Alcatraz appears again in the last third of the story, it is already familiar to the reader. There is a double-space break emphasizing the shift in scene. The new setting is vividly established with: "The fog is still thick on the day we go to Alcatraz." We know by now that Jennifer is not the happy kid she appeared to be in that first scene, and the foggy view of that prison highlights the shift in our perception.

The two of them listen to the recording and "do whatever the voice tells us, like robots." Already they are acting like the prisoners who were once held there. Significantly, their surroundings lead them to talk about the three prisoners who tried to escape (echoing the title), Jennifer's stolen jewelry, and finally about suicide. Far from incidental, the prison setting gives the author a way of revealing how the two of them establish a bond and manage to escape the mistrust that has kept them at odds.

When you select details that will make a setting vivid, it is natural to think of the visual aspect first, but don't forget smells, sounds, and temperature. We have already seen how cold and warmth play a part in "Sausage and Beer," the chill of snow contributes to "Three Hearts," and "the cold damp air" adds to the prison scene in "Escapes." The range of smells is limitless: musty cellars, kitchens in which liver and onions are being fried, oily-smelling filling stations, the trace of cigar smoke in a car. As for sounds, some houses are dominated by the roar of traffic while others are located near a jetport. Characters have to yell in an auto-body shop or a disco, reducing dialogue to short phrases. Desert winds can dominate one environment and pounding surf another. All these can increase the impact of your setting.

Real Places versus Invented Settings

Some stories name an actual city or state as the setting, while others create one entirely from imagination. The majority take a midcourse, suggesting a geographic region without using known place-names. Each approach has its advantages and potential problems.

Of the three stories you have read, "Three Hearts" is the least specific in terms of geography. The snow scenes indicate a cold climate, but there is no hint as to whether the family lives in northern United States or Canada.

"Sausage and Beer" is somewhat more specific. There is a single reference to "the New England countryside." The fact that the source for the fictional hospital is in Danvers, Massachusetts, is not important to the story and so is not mentioned. The general area is identified simply to echo the rather stiff and austere character of the father.

Of the three stories, "Escapes" is the only one that makes precise use of an actual place—not only the city of San Francisco but more specifically Alcatraz Island. Keep in mind, however, that when we say "actual place" with reference to fiction, we are still dealing with illusion. Fictional settings are imaginary, and if three writers set works in the same city, each version will reflect his or her imagination.

Your true choice, then, is not, "Shall I set this story in a real city?" but "Shall I use the name and certain details of an actual city in the exercise of my imagination?"

There are two advantages to drawing on a known city and naming it, as is done in "Escapes." First, it can serve as a geographic shorthand for the reader. There are features of our larger cities that are known even by those who have not been there. In addition, using a real city can be a convenience for you as a writer if you know the area well. It will save you the trouble of making up your own map.

But there are a couple of risks, too. Unless you are really familiar with the city you are using, you may begin to depend on scenes and details you have unconsciously absorbed from other stories and from television. Students who have never been to New York, for example, may fall back on such standard conventions as jazz clubs on 52nd Street (long since gone), artists in Greenwich Village (driven out by rising rents), and muggings in Central Park (sadly still there, but overused in fiction).

The same is true for Paris. If in blind ignorance the author spices a story with shots of the Eiffel Tower, cancan dancers, and prostitutes with hearts of gold, the fiction is bound to reflect the musical comedies from which this material was taken.

To avoid these weaknesses, make sure you know what you are writing about. And even when you are familiar with the city, avoid its most obvious aspects. Focus instead on districts and details that will seem authentic to your readers.

Another problem with using a specific place is that you may find it frustrating to be locked in by the physical details. Sometimes this is a mechanical problem: moving your characters around in an environment that cannot be radically altered. If you set a story in Chicago, you can't have your protagonist leave his downtown office on his lunch hour and take a walk in the countryside. But more frequently the risk is a psychological limitation. You may feel bound by a particular neighborhood. This is a particularly common problem when the plot has been adapted from recent or intense experience.

Perhaps for this reason, fictitious place-names are frequently used even when the setting is closely tied in the writer's mind to an actual place. Invented place-names liberate the imagination in the same way that inventing the names of characters does. It gives the author flexibility while still preserving the sense of authenticity that one can achieve with details from an actual place.

John Updike describes this relationship between a real place and fictional settings in his foreword to *Olinger Stories*:

> The name Olinger is audibly a shadow of "Shillington," the real name of my home town, yet the two towns, however similar, are not at all the same. Shillington is a place on the map and belongs to the world; Olinger is a state of mind, of my mind, and belongs entirely to me.

In this spirit, Updike has used Olinger, Pennsylvania, in eleven short stories. The names and ages of the protagonists vary, but essentially they are the same boy. The approach is similar to that of Sherwood Anderson in

Winesburg, Ohio. On a broader scale, William Faulkner blended historical and fictional elements in this way in his stories and novels set in his imaginary Yoknapatawpha County, Mississippi.

There is a long tradition of fiction that makes much more direct use of specific regions than any of these stories. Known as **regionalism**, or, formerly, **local color** writing, it became particularly popular toward the end of the 19th century. Mark Twain, Bret Harte, and Sarah Orne Jewett were the best-known practitioners. A number of lesser-known writers, however, gave the term a bad reputation by concentrating on regional dialects and customs in a patronizing manner.

Regionalism in the best sense is flourishing today. Every area of the country is producing short fiction that draws heavily on local attitudes, values, and culture, and several anthologies of short fiction reflect these concerns. Writers with distinctly regional or ethnic backgrounds should consider drawing on those traditions.

Good regional writing depends on two elements: personal familiarity and respect. You really have to know what you are writing about if you are going to do justice to the people of a specific region or culture. It is important to write from the inside, not as an outside observer. And even though you may see their weaknesses and vulnerabilities, you have to have a basic respect for them if you are going to avoid a patronizing tone. This is the true distinction between local color writing in its worst sense and genuine regionalism. If you spend some time in New Mexico as a tourist, for example, you may gather some excellent material for a story about tourists in New Mexico, and you certainly will be able to draw on the physical characteristics of the area, but that doesn't mean that you are equipped to depict the life of a Navajo on the reservation. Leave that to those who have lived there.

Time as Setting: Hour and Season

The time of day or night is often important in a story. When a character is hurrying to catch a plane or get to a wedding, you can add to the suspense by identifying the time precisely, sometimes more than once. Whether it is morning (as in "Three Hearts") or afternoon approaching suppertime (as in "Sausage and Beer"), specifying the time may help to give shape to specific scenes.

Watch out, however, for a pattern that has become so common it has turned into a cliché: the wake-up opening. It takes many forms, such as a ringing alarm clock, the flicker of a fading dream, the smell of coffee, a pounding headache. But they all draw on the too-neat link between the start of the day and the start of a story.

Fewer stories, but still too many, conclude with a version of the old film ending: watching the sun go down and "looking forward to another day." Try something new.

Even if you are not making specific use of the time of day, keep track of it in your own mind. Doing this will help you to avoid careless errors such as having a character take a morning coffee break, engage in dialogue, and without a transition head home for supper. All it takes is a simple phrase: "At the end of the day she. . . ."

Carelessness in time sense can also lead to an error that is subtler but almost as damaging: a character goes to his friend's apartment to see if he can borrow her car for the weekend. She lets him in and they sit down. He says, "Hey, can I borrow your car?" and she says "Sure." He leaves. The plot has advanced, but credibility is lost. People don't sit down as if for a conversation and then say one sentence. What's missing is some reference to the rest of what went on. It doesn't have to be in dialogue form; use exposition to allow for the requisite small talk and the passage of time. Again, a simple transition sentence will do: "He explained in detail how his car had broken down again" or "She was reluctant but finally agreed."

The time of year is another aspect of time that may prove to be helpful. If the season has no real significance in a story, you can ignore it without the reader even noticing. Such is the case in "Escapes." Contrary to reputation, San Francisco really does have seasons, but the author doesn't use them.

In "Sausage and Beer," on the other hand, the season is a important part of the setting. The story starts with the fact that "it was too cold for talk." And at the hospital Uncle Theodore tells about his nightmarish theory that some night the hospital will shut off the heat and freeze the patients to death. At the end of the story that pattern of cold is broken as they enter the bar. The room is "a warm, humming, soothing, smoky world" with the "sound of music blended with voices and laughter." Nonsmokers will wince at "smoky" being used in a positive way, but there was a day in which smoking was, sadly, a part of sociability. As we have seen, the warmth of the bar scene highlights the newfound relationship between father and son.

The winter scene in "Three Hearts" is even more important. It's hard to imagine that story without deep snow. It establishes the drama of the opening and then gives the children a chance to make angel patterns in the snow, looking to Sissy like "an angel graveyard." Then it provides that igloo as a chilly make-believe home for the children. The whole plot depends on snow in the setting; and on a more subtle level the cold of the season adds to our sense of the characters' chilly separation from one another, an important part of the theme.

Historical Periods

Most short stories are set in the same historical period as the one in which they are written. This is partly because it takes time to establish the atmosphere of an earlier period, time that one can't easily spare in so short a form. In addition, if you move back to the 19th century, it is difficult to avoid having your stories resemble Westerns, historical romances, or so-called costume gothics with their standard plots and stereotyped characters.

There are, however, two ways of using an earlier historical period effectively without running the risk of echoing formulaic fiction. In both approaches the writer maintains some personal link with the earlier time. First, it is sometimes possible to develop good fiction from extensive conversations with elderly people such as grandparents. Thanks in part to lightweight tape recorders and camcorders, there has been a growing interest in oral history of the immediate past. If your subject is willing to provide it, material gathered in this manner can become the basis of fiction that has the true ring of authenticity.

You do have to pick your subject carefully. Some people are more articulate than others. Some enjoy recalling their past, but others do not—occasionally for understandable reasons. If your informant is agreeable, however, let him or her do plenty of talking. Occasionally you will have to ask questions in order to clarify certain facts, but try not to be too directive. Let your informant determine the direction of the conversation.

The most effective interviews are with those whose childhoods were significantly different from our lives today—those who came from Europe or Asia, those who endured the hardships of farming or factory work. Be very careful, however, not to sound patronizing or, even with the best intentions, sentimentally admiring. Since you are using borrowed material, your safest route is to maintain a fairly neutral tone. Let the story and its characters speak for themselves.

Be careful, too, not to turn your story into a simple **anecdote**. Anecdotes depend primarily on a turn of events, a clever little plot. This may be entertaining in conversation, but if you use it as the basis of a story you run the risk of trivializing your subject. To guard against this, concentrate on characterization. If you pay careful attention to the ambivalent feelings of your informant, you will add depth that anecdotes usually lack.

The other use of the past applies only to those writers who are themselves old enough to remember when life was different. The accumulation of memory is one of the compensating benefits of age, and that layering of experience is an excellent source for fiction. One word of caution, however: be careful not to place undue emphasis on the differences between the period being described and the present day. If you draw too much attention to how inexpensive things were, for example, the reader may begin to view the material as quaint. Try instead to draw readers into that period; help them to share it.

Major Transformations

When a new story has its origin in an actual event, you naturally recall it in the original setting. This may be a fine choice for fiction. If it seems right, plunge into the writing and postpone revisions until you finish the first draft. On the other hand, the setting may present problems. If that is the case, consider the technique of **transformation**.

Transformation, you remember, is more than revision. It is a fundamental alteration. Applying it to the setting may seem at first far too drastic, but remember that you are free to re-create any aspect of a story idea.

If you are considering such a radical change, it's a good idea to do it early—even before you start writing the first draft. The further you get into the actual writing the more difficult it will be revise the setting.

The most common reason for altering the setting that comes to you ready-made from experience is reticence. If you find yourself staring at a blank page or computer screen, it may be that the setting brings back memories that are too close to you, too emotionally charged. We examined how this can happen with plots taken from experience, but sometimes just the setting will stop you dead. In such cases the setting may need to be fundamentally transformed before you can work with the material with some degree of objectivity.

If, for example, a highly personal experience occurred on the bank of a river, consider moving the story to a beach or possibly a city park. If it was originally a city scene, consider moving it to a small town. Even changing the season will sometimes free you. An episode that occurred in the heat of midsummer can sometimes be shifted to January merely to remove it from the confines of experience.

If you take that route, be careful to guard against the clichés of season. A first love that opens with a paragraph about the spring buds on the apple tree might be, if highlighted, as hackneyed as the story about an old couple that ends with the fallen leaves of November. Seasons can be enormously valuable, but only when they are used with subtlety and originality.

A second reason for transforming your original setting is when it simply has no relevance to the theme. In life there is no guarantee that events should happen in settings that are in some way related, but in fiction everything is connected. As we have seen in the stories you have read, the most effective settings are those that contribute to the theme. Good plots can be moved to areas that have the potential to contribute at least to the mood of the story or, better yet, to the meaning.

Revising the Details

Once you have decided on an appropriate setting, you are ready to start writing. Move ahead with confidence, knowing that if details have to be revised, those changes can be done later.

It may be that the setting will not be a major aspect of the story as it develops. No problem. Many stories keep the surroundings at a minimum.

But if you plan to draw on the setting in a major way, imagine yourself in that place and start providing not only the visual details but the smells and feel of the place.

As you write, let the story speak to you. Don't be so rigid that you hold to your original course, blind to possible changes. Details that seemed unimportant to you in the first draft may suggest new meaning that can be developed.

Once you have completed your first draft, take a close look at what you have done with the setting. There are four questions you can ask yourself:

First, are there details already there that you might highlight? If a sense of place is important in this story, see which details are likely to draw your reader into the setting. Do any need more emphasis? Remember that long descriptive passages can slow the pace of a story, but it is easy enough to spread out the visual aspects. Review how the look of the snow is touched on several times in "Three Hearts" and the feel of the prison is spaced out in "Escapes."

The setting in your first draft may have been selected without much thought. Now is the time to determine whether it is the best possible choice. Suppose your story takes place on a hot day mainly because that's when the original experience occurred. Is there some way to use that heat (muggy? dry? windy? breathless?) to augment the theme. Or would it be more effective to use cold as a vehicle?

The second question is just the opposite: Are there aspects of the setting that need to be muted? Have you, for example, quite unconsciously borrowed part of your setting from well-known sources? The kinds of clichés that damage fiction have already been described, but I should stress here that even experienced writers occasionally borrow overused details. Our experiences sometimes echo a fictional cliché, and either the plot or the setting has to be changed to maintain credibility. Breaking the familiar setting may require moving the story to another setting, changing night to day, or trying a different season.

In addition, guard against those settings that, though far from hackneyed, echo well-known literary conventions. Stories about migrant workers tend to sound like John Steinbeck; hitchhiking stories often pick up the smells and sounds of Jack Kerouac's *On the Road* or motorcycle films; scenes involving city gangs tend to use darkened streets from television dramas. One often has to mute these details and stress elements that the reader will see as if for the first time.

Avoid any detail in your setting that the reader is likely to associate with the work of another author, a film, or song lyric. Muting those details and highlighting other elements will be necessary, and usually you can do this without losing your original conception.

Finally, take a hard look at those details that don't seem to serve a purpose. They may be nothing more than fragments from your memory. The fact that they are vivid in your mind doesn't mean that they necessarily belong in the story. A novel can afford a few nonessential details, but a short story doesn't have that much momentum; it is easily dragged down by excess baggage. In some cases you can amend those details so that they contribute to the theme or at least to the mood of your story. If that doesn't work, they probably should be cut.

Should your setting have symbolic details? Not necessarily. Many stories use settings that merely provide a vivid sense of place. If you do see some aspect of the setting that has symbolic potential, however, be sure that it is subtle enough to blend in with the story. When reading "Three Hearts," for example, you may not have been consciously aware of how the icicles that the children pretend are firewood reflect their longing for warmth and domestic harmony, but the detail added to your almost subliminal sense of what was missing in their lives. I'll return to the use of symbols in Chapter 27, but remember that when a symbolic detail in the setting jumps out at the reader, it looks artificial and contrived. If one occurs to you, be sure to keep it subtle.

When working with the setting, always keep this essential fact in mind: place and time are not adornments to a story. They are a part of what you see and feel as you write. Even more important, they are the primary means by which your readers are going to enter your story and experience it as if they were physically present. It is this sense of being there that makes fiction an "as-if-real" experience.

22
DIALOGUE AND THOUGHTS

Dialogue as "the sound of fiction." The conventions of writing dialogue. Paraphrasing: indirect quotations. The illusion of thoughts. The illusion of a foreign language. Pacing: maintaining forward motion. Speech patterns: character and mood.

Dialogue is the sound of fiction. True, it's the *illusion* of sound, but all fiction is illusion. You can write a story without dialogue, but successful examples are about as rare as silent films.

There are good reasons for this. If you don't let your characters reveal themselves and unfold the plot through what they say, you will find yourself depending more on **exposition**. That is, you will have to explain more as author and show less. This makes it more difficult for readers to enter the story. What started as fiction begins to take on the characteristics of the informal essay.

While the primary function of dialogue is to reveal character, the subject of Chapter 24, dialogue also serves to advance the plot without the heavy hand of the author telling the reader what is going on. For dialogue to work, however, it must be convincing. That's the subject of this chapter.

The first step in learning how to write good dialogue is to listen to how people really talk. By *listen*, I mean analyze. It is difficult to do this when you yourself are engaged in conversation because you are trying to keep up your end. You are responding more to the content than the manner of speech. Far better to eavesdrop. Restaurants and cafeterias are good places. Listen for contemporary phrasing, the incomplete sentences, the frequency of interruptions, the patterns of dominance. Even the pauses are worth noting.

Having said that, I cannot stress enough that successful dialogue in fiction is not a tape recording of what you hear in the cafeteria. Talk is cheap, and we squander it daily in chitchat that, though pleasurable, is largely uninformative and directionless. It is filled with empty phrasing and redundancies. *Phatic* is a little-used word that describes speech used for sociability rather than exchanging information. Much of what we call "small talk" is phatic. Dialogue uses small samples for flavor, but re-creating large blocks of it will sink a story with boredom.

Dialogue in fiction creates the *illusion* of characters speaking, and thoughts give the *illusion* of a character thinking. The first step in learning how to create these illusions is to examine the **conventions** of fictional dialogue and thoughts. These are the cues readers are familiar with and respond to easily. Then we can consider the various tactics available to make the words and thoughts of characters both convincing and revealing.

The Conventions of Dialogue and Thoughts

Conventions are not rules; they are simply identifiable patterns that are widely used. The conventions of writing dialogue and thoughts in fiction are mechanical cues that are so familiar to readers that they are hardly noticed. Most writers follow these conventions because they want dialogue to blend with the work as a whole. The dialogue itself has to be fresh and true to character, but the mechanical form should be so familiar that it is not noticed. This is one of those cases where art should conceal technique. That is, the creative aspect of your work should conceal the mechanical aspects.

First, most (but not all) stories use quotation marks around words spoken out loud but not around thoughts. This is a helpful distinction that readers are used to. Single quotation marks (like apostrophes) are used to set off quotations within quotations. Here is an example that includes thoughts, quoted material, and a speaker quoting someone else.

> If only, she thought, the rest of the committee had heard how enthusiastic the client had been over her proposal.
> "He really liked the design," she said to her husband that evening. " 'It's the best we've seen so far,' he told me. Those were his exact words."

If one speaker's words continue for more than one paragraph without a **dialogue tag** ("he said" or "she said"), use quotation marks at the beginning of each paragraph but not the ends until the close of the quoted material. This may seem odd, but it's a convention.

Second, most writers indent the first line of speech of each new speaker. Doing this may appear to waste paper, but readers are used to it both in fiction and in drama. One advantage of regular indentation is that in lengthy exchanges between two characters, the reader does not have to be told each time which one spoke. Just use tags as reminders from time to time.

Third, don't hesitate to use "said" repeatedly. Readers respond to tags like "she said," "he said," and "I said" the way they do to punctuation marks. Because of this, most writers since the 1930s repeat them freely. For years you have been told to avoid redundancies, and that's good advice in nonfiction. But dialogue tags are an exception. It sounds amateurish to keep using substitutions like "she retorted," "he sneered," "she questioned," "he hissed." Repeated alternatives become obtrusive.

In this connection, guard against adding modifiers to "said." There is usually no reason to write "said angrily" or "said shyly," since almost always the tone is clear from the dialogue itself. The same is almost always true of exclamation marks. If you really have to reverse the reader's first assumption, it may be more effective to use a separate phrase as in,

> "Boy, are you dumb!" she said, rolling her eyes, her tone still loving.

Fourth, contemporary writers rarely try to imitate spoken language by using phonetic spelling. You can find examples in 19th century writing (Mark Twain's *The Adventures of Huckleberry Finn*, for example), but most contemporary writers find that, because it slows the pace seriously and draws attention to itself, phonetic spelling defeats the goal of realism. Revising the spelling on the printed page is so noticeable that it exaggerates the effect one is trying to create. As a result, it also poses a risk of sounding patronizing.

For all these reasons, most authors prefer to catch the flavor of a regional or foreign accent through word choice and characteristic phrasing rather than tinkering with conventional spelling.

Paraphrasing: Indirect Quotations

When our friends talk, we have to listen to every sentence. Even when they repeat themselves. Even when they bore us. That's a mark of friendship. But your readers have no such contract with your characters. When readers are bored, they quit. They may not even tell you.

When dialogue stops advancing the plot or expanding an understanding of the speaker, it's time for a paraphrase. Grammatically it is known as indirect quotation, but it is not really a quotation at all. It describes what was said in condensed form without quotation marks. It's simplest use is to avoid quoting routine or uninteresting conversation by substituting a summary like this:

> She told him that she had missed the flight but had switched airlines and asked him to meet her at midnight.

Indirect quotations can also be used to paraphrase much lengthier and more general exchanges. It's not a good tactic to portray a long, dull conversation with a long, dull block of dialogue. Paraphrasing may be your best solution, as in these two samples:

1. The conversation at the funeral parlor touched on the weather (remarkably warm), the traffic on Elm Street (growing worse), and what auto mechanics are charging these days (shocking).
2. She thought he would be pleased to see her after all these years, but instead he spent the entire dinner telling her about his miserable dog's long succession of ailments and eventual demise.

In addition to summarizing dull dialogue, paraphrasing is sometimes used to dramatize events that, though lively, don't justify the space it would take to handle in dialogue. This often applies in scenes that are not central to the story.

> When she finally came home he met her at the door and in a rush spelled out the domestic disasters of the day: kitchen sink plugged, the twins' refusal to nap, the computer meltdown, and the cat giving birth in the linen closet.

Often indirect quotations are used in conjunction with direct quotes. In "Sausage and Beer," for example, much of the conversation with Uncle Theodore is summarized with periodic switches into spoken lines:

> At one point he moved back in time to describe a fishing trip by canoe through the Rangely Lakes....
> "Nothing finer," he said, his eyes half shut, "than frying those trout at the end of the day."

There is a somewhat similar example from "Escapes" in the brief scene at the ballpark. The author condenses Caryn's explanation of baseball and then follows it with Jennifer's query directly quoted:

> Jennifer does not understand baseball, but I try to explain it to her. Three outs to an inning, nine innings to a game, the importance of a good shortstop. But ... when Chris Sabo ... strikes out she says, "Caryn, why is it still their turn?"

The Illusion of Thoughts

To a certain degree, dialogue in a story is an echo of what we actually hear when people talk. What, then, do thoughts echo? Nothing, really, but our imagination. We write out thoughts as if they were spoken dialogue without using quotation marks, but what goes on in our heads only rarely is formed in sentences or even words.

True, we occasionally force order on our thoughts to generate something close to speech:

> Wait a minute, he told himself. First I should buy the flowers, then the wine. If I can't afford a cab, there's still time to walk.

The phrase "he told himself" shows how close it is to spoken dialogue. It is the kind of deliberate thinking that we may even mutter out loud.

A great majority of what goes on in our heads, however, is far less structured. Some thoughts may come in flashes, essentially without words. For this reason, thoughts are often described in ways that are less precise than dialogue. In "Three Hearts," for example, much of what is going on in Sissy's mind is implied by what she describes, as in this passage:

> ...the snow is so deep and heavy that we just stop for a long time and look at things. The white cover is perfect except for Eddie's footprints in from the road. The tiny wind smells brand new and the telephone wires have so much snow on them that they are almost invisible.

Technically, this is a descriptive passage, but the language is hardly objective. The details are so distinctively her view, and the phrasing is so unmistakably hers, that we read the passage as thoughts. The author doesn't have to say, "I got to thinking how beautiful everything was."

Caryn, the narrator in "Escapes," is an adult and more verbal, so her thoughts are closer to what she might say aloud. But even in that story there aren't blocks of thought starting out with "I began to think that.... " Instead, they are brief passages woven into the story unobtrusively as in this case:

> While I looked at the sky I thought about my life as a flat straight line like a dead person's heart on monitor.

And later in that same section:

> So I am still not sure what made me say yes, I'll take her for a while. Except for maybe the thought of sharing that ultrablue sky with someone seemed so appealing, and the thought of a few bleeps and peaks in my life seemed like a good idea.

Notice how in that rather indirect description of what is going on in her head there is a line that in dialogue would be considered a direct quote and placed in quotation marks: ". . . yes, I'll take her for a while." Here it is blended in with the grammatical jumble of a mind at work.

When composing the thoughts of a fictional character, stay on guard against a common weakness. Don't use thoughts simply to present background facts to the reader, particularly if they are well known to the character. It is not at all convincing to have a character think, "I am 23 years old, tall, handsome, and from Omaha." For material like that to be credible as thought it would have to be motivated ("They wouldn't treat me like that back in Omaha, he thought"). Or it can be slid into dialogue, again in the context of what is going on ("Just because he's handsome doesn't mean that . . ."). Or as a last resort it can be stated as exposition ("He was 23 that spring but still lonely for Omaha").

People don't review their past for no reason, so when fictional characters are allowed to do it, readers spot those "thoughts" as a writer's clumsy attempt to avoid author's intrusion. Thoughts, like dialogue, have to be motivated by the situation, not simply by the author's need to insert background facts.

One excellent way to explore the various ways thoughts are revealed in fiction is to go through stories you have already read and circle passages that give the reader a vista into the mind of a particular character. You will discover that they are significantly different from dialogue. The boundaries are less distinct. Sometimes it is hard to distinguish thoughts from description or from exposition. But this is how it should be. Thoughts, after all, are slippery and elusive.

The Illusion of a Foreign Language

Creating the illusion of a character speaking in a foreign language has always been a challenge. And with the United States becoming an increasingly multicultural nation, it grows in importance.

There are many approaches. About the only agreement among writers is that the traditional Hollywood film solution of having characters speak English with a foreign accent is an almost comic failure.

The purest solution is simply to use the other language. This is entirely logical and effective if the fiction is intended for the small but growing number of periodicals that cater to a bilingual readership. If the fiction is intended for a general audience, however, it has a serious drawback: it walls out those who do not know that particular foreign language. Unfortunately, that will be a majority of readers. If the dialogue in a foreign language is extensive, you not only make the story confusing for most readers, you run the risk of irritating them to the point of not finishing the story.

For this reason, using the foreign language directly is usually done only if the phrases are brief. Occasionally the English translation is added either after a dash or in parentheses.

The most generally adopted approach is to use English and to identify the language being spoken in the tag: " 'How well do you know him?' she asked in Spanish." Or, "Speaking French he asked, 'How well do you know her?' " You can avoid the direct quotation altogether if you use indirect speech: "She asked in Spanish how long he had known her."

If you are using this approach with longer passages, consider adopting some of the word order that is characteristic of that language. Further, it sometimes helps to translate a few foreign idioms directly into English, as Hemingway occasionally did with his Spanish-speaking characters. This can add the flavor of a foreign language without making the characters sound as if they were speaking English with an accent.

Pacing: Maintaining Forward Motion

Long blocks of dialogue tend to slow the forward motion of a story. It's not the dialogue itself that does this; it's the lack of action. There are stories written entirely as a **monologue**, one character talking. But if you look at these stories closely you will see that they maintain interest in one of two ways: by reporting a lively event or by revealing a great deal about the narrator, often aspects he or she is not aware of. In general, though, dialogue is broken up with action and occasional exposition.

A series of short, fragmentary exchanges of dialogue can do wonders to enliven a scene that has become bogged down in description or low-key action. But if sustained for too long, an unrelieved exchange between two characters can have the reverse effect. If the alternating lines of dialogue are about the same length, they will create a ping-pong effect, and all that talk will deprive the scene of action just as a long monologue would.

The best way to study different ways of balancing dialogue and other modes is to thumb through several stories without actually reading them. Look for the indentations and the quotation marks. You can see how often dialogue is used and the length of quoted passages simply from the typography. You will see that in most cases the author has consciously or unconsciously avoided entire pages without dialogue and, at the other extreme, entire pages made up of one long monologue. Again, this is not a rule; it is simply a pattern that most authors find effective.

Determining the frequency of passages in dialogue is not something that should concern you when writing the first draft. Let the story develop naturally. But when you are into the revision process, take a close look at your pacing. If the story seems to drag at some point as you are reading it aloud to yourself, determine if the fault rests with a too-lengthy block of dialogue. Or if in looking it over you see a couple of pages with no dialogue, ask yourself if perhaps having your characters talk more might provide the sense of vitality that dialogue often provides.

Speech Patterns: Character and Mood

If you listen analytically to people you know, you will discover that many have distinctive rhythms. Fast talkers sometimes trip over themselves, leaping from one idea to the next. In extreme cases, they will fail to use complete sentences in their cascade of speech. At the other extreme are the slow talkers. Their distinctive pattern may be more than deliberate pacing; it may be combined with long sentences and a more extensive vocabulary than average.

Then there are those who use irritating little phrases like "You know?" or "Right?" as needless punctuation. They have no more linguistic purpose than a nervous "err" or "ah," but these tics become a characteristic aspect of their speech.

Students have an advantage when it comes to analyzing speech patterns because they can listen to instructors without having to respond. If you take notes on the recurring characteristics, you may also get credit for appearing to be fascinated with the lecturer's subject.

Two words of caution, however. First, people with consistently distinctive speech patterns are in a minority. The same is true in fiction. In many cases, what will concern you is simply making sure that the diction and phrasing of your characters conform with what they are like. Make sure your older characters don't use teenager slang; don't let your street gang characters pontificate.

Second, keep in mind that any hint of an identifiable speech pattern is twice as noticeable on the page than it is when listening to someone speak. Variations from the norm leap out at the reader. Anything close to a tape-recorded rendition will make your character seem absurd, even comic. If you use distinctive speech patterns at all, use them very sparingly.

Speech patterns also define the mood of the speaker. This is as true in fiction as it is in life. Dogs, after all, can detect human moods through voice and most can't even understand English.

Calm, reflective moods are often characterized by longer sentences and greater attention to grammatical conventions like completing sentences with a subject and a verb. But with moments of crisis, dialogue often becomes fragmentary, abrupt, and frequently redundant. Dialogue and thoughts become mixed. Here is the section from "Three Hearts" when Sissy's mother is first told about Bucky:

> "What happened?" She turns her eyes to me for the shortest second and I don't know what to say. I remember how the plow shook the windowpanes in our house when it rumbled by. It reminded me of thunder.
> "What happened?" she says again.
> "The plow," I say. "The plow came by."

Notice how the spoken dialogue is broken up into brief fragments while thoughts are given whole sentences. The thoughts are describing what is racing through her head while the spoken dialogue literally quotes what she says, and what we say in crises tends to be in short phrases or single words. Notice, also, the redundancy of "What happened" and "the plow." All these become cues for the reader, the syntax itself heightening the drama of the moment.

We have focused on the techniques that help to make the writing of dialogue and thoughts more convincing, but ultimately you will have to rely on your ear. For this reason, keep reading your work aloud. Those with acting experience have an advantage here. Also consider asking a friend to read sections of your dialogue aloud. Listen to the opinion of others—even if they are not writers. They can help you spot unconvincing passages even if they can't advise you how to correct them. Both dialogue and thoughts in fiction are illusions, but your job as a writer is to make them seem genuine.

23

A STORY

by Sharon Solwitz

Obst Vw

Next year, writing his personal experience essay to convince admissions at Penn he's Ivy League material despite uneven grades, he'll describe in amusing detail the one baseball game his father took him to, and get in on a scholarship despite his father's explicit pessimism. And he'll do well, though he's not as brilliant as his father, just a pretty smart kid who's used to working hard. But now on Rachel's bed, unraveling a hole in the knee of her jeans while her parents yell at each other downstairs, he cannot join in her raillery. "Let's go," he says.

"Wait. This is the part about who was the first unfaithful one!"

"Let's go!" he says. He has a curfew, a job to get up for tomorrow. Then there's the air outside the house, the smell of new grass mixing with the smell of Rachel when she lets him touch her under her T-shirt.

"Dame, please. It's funny, really. It's high comedy."

But she doesn't protest as he takes her hand and leads her down and outside.

Rachel is seventeen, a year older than Demian, though in the same grade. She lost a year when she went, as she says, loony, and spent several months in the bin getting her spirit broken to the point where she'd attend school and respond, numbly, to teacher and test questions. Still, her grades are better than his. Sometimes it seems to him he can't stand her, half an inch taller than he is, the way when she's not thinking about it she arcs down into herself like a long-necked bird, the way tall girls aren't supposed to. He used to love to play baseball, it was all he wanted to do—if not on the field then in a symbolic version with cards and dice in his room—and when this feeling of loathing comes over him, it brings on a desire for baseball, for playing shortstop, to be specific, standing between second and third with his knees bent, whispering in the direction of the batter—hit it to me, I dare you.

He remembers his two best friends from then, brothers a year apart, Tom and John Frank, the clean, sharp edge of the way they bad-mouthed each other after the game. And then the queasiness comes, because something he has done with Rachel or is about to do has rendered him unfit for baseball.

He walks quickly now, a step ahead of her, over to the playground behind the local preschool, where they've gone the past months to talk and kiss and perform all but the final technical act of sexual intercourse. The ground is laid in gravel through which sharp, hard weeds poke up, but the chain-link fence is low enough to climb over, the large wooden sandbox lies half in the shadow of the building, the sand is cool and dry and molds after a while to one or the other's back.

Tonight, though, they do not embrace. Rachel sits down on the dark side of the sandbox. At first she seems to have disappeared. Then he sees in the dark the lesser darkness of her face, the pale stretch of her shoulders, too wide for a girl. She smells sour and sweet like strawberries. He is moved by something in Rachel, her craziness, her cynicism, facets of personality he dimly perceives he may have to own some day. He remembers a school assembly where she danced on center stage with the other dancers weaving around her, her turns and leaps bolder than theirs, more complete. "Rachel," he says, "I really like you."

She doesn't respond, but the prickle of the skin of his arms tells him he said the wrong thing. He tries again. "You're a really good dancer." He elaborates on the performance he saw, comparing her dancing to the way he used to feel about baseball. Still feels sometimes. She doesn't help him out. Her silence is a hole he walks around and around.

"Rachel," he says in despair, "I feel bad for you." He doesn't mention her parents. Really, he doesn't want to talk about them. Their dads by some fluke knew each other in college, and Rachel's sometimes asks him how his father's doing, a show of interest or courtesy his father doesn't return. Demian himself can barely manage to speak to her father, who makes more money than his father and calls him the Old Hippie. "Ask him about Woodstock," Mr. Geller once said, and Demian said, "Why don't you ask him yourself," knowing his father hadn't gone to Woodstock, as Mr. Geller also knew. Mr. Geller is soft-looking and bottom-heavy like an old pear. Demian can't stand Mr. Geller, has only broached the subject as a gift for Rachel.

She says, "They're not my real parents."

He laughs, though she has said that before.

"I'm going to divorce them," she says. "There's a new law, in Vermont."

"In Massachusetts, I think."

She shrugs, irritated with his quibble. He talks quickly to assuage her. "Then you can marry *my* parents."

"Who wants your parents?"

"What's wrong with my parents?"

"Your father has a mean streak."

"No he doesn't!"

His eyes have adjusted to the light. He can see the parts of her face that jut out, eyebrows, cheekbones, slope of nose. She seems too sharply constructed, a witch woman, though she's sitting cross-legged like a child, pouring handfuls of dry sand over her thighs. "He won't let you do stuff for no reason," she says. "For spite."

Demian knows that in similar words he has complained to her about his father, who gave him a curfew earlier than that of his friends' younger brothers, frequently refused him permission to attend parties, and who wasn't planning—he'd warned him—to let him get his driver's license till he was eighteen years old. Teenagers have glop for brains, he'd said. Though as a teenager himself—his mother had told him—he'd dropped out of college and done a lot of the drugs teenagers were supposed to say no to these days. Demian hasn't really spoken to this father since the day he refused to sign the learner's permit. But now Demian says, "He has his own ideas. He does what he thinks is right and not what everybody else does!"

She claps her hands.

"What is that supposed to mean?"

"You are so *canned.*"

He's about to stand up, leave, maybe. But she takes his arm. "Demian, I love you."

"So you can say anything you want to me?"

She puts her arms around him, thrusts her tongue into his mouth. He keeps up his end of the bargain. Soon he is urgent, panting. She is, too. His fingers are wet with her. As usual he tries to pull off her shorts. As usual she pushes away from him. Once he questioned her, learned that her non-compliance had to do with something apologetic she detected in his attitude toward sex. Since then, his efforts have been mild, ritualized. She is his first real girlfriend. He is pleased to be kissing and touching her even at the level of intimacy she has ordained. She hurls herself at his hand, trembling.

He has to be home by 10:30 and it's 11:35 by the oven clock as he tiptoes across the kitchen. He has never missed curfew before, but the evening is still warm on his skin, he fells invulnerable. And his father is surely asleep.

He takes his shoes off in the living room. His father is *inactive,* his mother says. The understatement of the year, Demian thinks. Tired from working in the bookstore, which doesn't bring in enough for him to hire a manager, his father often falls asleep on the couch in the front of the ten o'clock news, and Demian and his mother have to prod him up to bed.

But he's up now, standing in his PJs at the top of the stairs. His long, thin, still young-looking face is blank; not even his lips seem to move as he says, "You're grounded." His lips are pressed close together, a tuck in the long swatch of his face, but the words linger in the air well after his lanky body has vanished behind the master bedroom door.

In bed Demian is stiff with fury. There is no recourse; the only question is how long. And even worse than not seeing Rachel is seeing her with the weight of his father's edict on his shoulders, making him smaller than he is, unworthy of her.

Four years from now Demian will fly home from school in time to watch his father breathe in comatose sleep, then cease breathing—feeling nothing, because from now on nothing he does for good or ill will have any impact on his father. Later he'll rage at his father for dying before he was ready for him to die, and later still he may decide that if his father wasn't ideal he did the best he could. But now Demian has hopes for what he can be to his father and what his father can be to him.

Demian is up early, hours before he has to leave for Bi-Rite's, rehearsing the speech he'll give his father at the breakfast table. He has it outlined in his head like a five-paragraph essay, and now with the sun turning the sky pink, then blue, he sits at the kitchen table while his mother, who has to leave soon to teach summer school, performs five or six brisk cleaning and cooking acts. His father sips coffee. His father butters a piece of rye toast, as slowly as an old man, though his hair is still thick, his face unlined; people sometimes think he's Demian's older brother. Demian says casually into the space between bites, "I want you to reconsider."

His father looks to the left, the right, all around the room. "Who's talking? Is somebody talking to me?"

Demian's ears feel hot. This is the first direct statement he's made to his father in several months. "Dad, I'm never late. I shouldn't be punished the first time I mess up. Give me a second chance."

"Look, you." His father's voice is quiet, but it takes up the room. "If some dude walks into my store with a gun, and I say hey now just wait a minute, do I get a second chance?"

Demian sees the illogic of his father's argument, but his father stands up, leaning forward as if about to fall on him. "If you get sick, kiddo. If your heart hurts, air sticks in your throat, you say with your last feeble breath, God, Jesus, Krishna, whoever—please, what did I do, could you please, please give me a second chance, what's He going to say to you? Tell me, Demian."

Demian wants to ask his father what makes him think he's God, but the air or something is stuck in his throat.

"Let's say you get your girlfriend pregnant, Demian. Let's say for the sake of argument you knock up your young lady. But you aren't ready to be Papa yet. You want to walk across Turkey in your stocking feet. You want to climb Mt. Tamalpais and keep on going."

His father has just said more, it seems, than he has ever said to Demian before. His hands are waving, his face is white, and Demian's mother pats his back, leads him back to the table. She gets him more coffee, hovers over him, though she's running late, till his face warms up. He kisses her good-bye a beat longer than he has to. Says nothing to Demian. Demian feels sick, choking on the words he can't speak to his father. "Mom," he whispers after door is shut, "is he mean, or what?"

"Demian," she says, "you've got to give him some slack. The business isn't going well."

"Who cares?" Demian's voice rises. Every once in a while he's allowed to sneer in front of his mother. It's his one respite, acting like his father in front of his mother. "Mine isn't going well, either." He watches her face, prepared to shut down at the first sign of her disapproval.

"Demian," she says, "he may have to declare bankruptcy. Don't say anything to him, please. Eat your breakfast."

Her lips look blue, like the lips of little kids who have been in the water too long. Demian eats his cereal, a piece of toast, then, absentmindedly, the rest of his father's toast. It's not even eight o'clock, he has plenty of time. He eats while his mother says nice things about his father. How good he is to her. How well his friends like him, even the rich, much-respected ones. Demian is aware that people listen when his father speaks. Demian would like his own friends to treat him as his father's friends treat his father. Sometimes he quiets his voice, thins it out a little, to see if that's the trick.

"He's way too smart for what he does," His mother is saying. "He did well in college without studying. He could remember everything he'd ever read. He was a great talker, there was nothing he couldn't have done if he'd wanted to—do you know how high his IQ is?"

"Higher than mine," Demian says.

His mother doesn't protest, just shakes her head as if in wonder. "He never got time to sit and figure things out. He was too young to have a child."

"Mom," Demian says, "he was twenty-six when I was born. He's forty-two."

"He was too young," she says firmly, gathering up her books. "But he loves you like crazy, you ought to know that."

Pedaling to work Demian thinks about his father's IQ how many points it might be higher than this own, and tries to see him as the Disappointed Man in his mother's fiction. He says *bankrupt* under his breath, trying to diminish his father enough to forgive him. It doesn't work. He tries to feel his father's love for him, remembering a ballgame his father took him to on his tenth birthday—him and his best friend, John Frank, and John Frank's father. He remembers sitting next to John in the back of their old Rabbit with his baseball glove in his lap for catching foul balls. Remembers listening to his father up front talking with John's father, John's father laughing at his father's jokes, though John's father drove a Volvo and everyone called him Dr. Frank. Demian was proud of his father. It was clear even then that although his father talked less than his friend's father, it was his father's words that thickened in the air. His father had given him and John their own tickets to hold, and jouncing along on the back seat, they squinted at the blue and white cardboard oblongs, discussing the numbers and letters that stood for what they were about to experience. SAT AUG 1:20 PM. AISLE 518 ROW 5 SEAT 242. GAME #52 CHICAGO CUBS VS. NEW YORK METS. ADMIT ONE SUBJECT TO CONDITIONS ON BACK NO REFUND NO EXCHANGE. There was one set of letters he couldn't fathom: OBST VW. He showed the ticket to John. "Obstetrician?" John asks.

"Its a beer ad. Obst Blue Ribbon!"

"That's *Pabst* Blue Ribbon!"

"I know, fart head."

Only when they got to the park and sat down in seats behind a pillar that let him see half the field if he craned to the right, did he realize the letters stood for Obstructed View. At first he didn't mind. He'd never been to a major-league game before. The smell of hot dogs and popcorn filled his mouth and nose, the stands were cool and dim like a naptime bedroom, the playing field bright green under the sun. He put his glove on, waiting for his father to sit down next to him, not necessarily to talk to him, since of course he had more to say to Dr. Frank, but just to be there so Demian could ask him questions or may be just sit quietly beside him, watching him watch the game. But when Demian had finished taking in the brightness and darkness, and located his favorite Cub, Shawon Dunston, who could hurl the ball like the end of a whip, his father was still standing in the aisle. "We'll get you guys after the game," he called to them, holding out a five-dollar bill. "Don't eat too much." Demian took the bill, folded and folded it again as his father and Dr. Frank descended the steep steps, vanishing toward seats Demian knew had an unencumbered view of the field. Still, he wasn't sure what to make of the turnaround. It wasn't exactly what he'd pictured when he'd asked on his tenth, his double-digit birthday, not for something to ride or look at or hold in his hand, but for an event to experience with his father. The man who took his father's seat told him stories about the ballplayers' personal lives. It was lots of fun sitting with John, leaning hard one way around the pillar to watch the ball come off the bat, then the other way to see where the ball ended up. Shawon Dunston threw the ball into the dugout, and the Cubs still won. But although he and John wore their gloves all nine innings, the foul balls went to seats below them in the sun. And although he and John kept good track of the game, marking the P.O.'s, F.O.'s, K's, H's on their scorecards with their short yellow ballpark pencils, some of the balls fell where neither of them could see. The man in his father's seat said Shawon Dunston would never learn to take a walk because he was mentally retarded. When Demian's father returned for them after the game, the skin of his arms looked dark gold in the sun, and it was clear to Demian that the game he'd seen was not as good a game.

Demian leans back in his chair at the Geller breakfast table, puts his feet on a second chair, takes the cup of coffee Rachel has poured him. He's never had coffee before, and he gulps it like milk, burns his throat, swallows his grimace. Rachel doesn't ask him why he isn't at Bi-Rite's this morning. She talks rapidly, of nothing he has to respond to. She's barefoot, in a long, wrinkled shirt she must have slept in. He imagines what's under the shirt; his face burns. Her brown hair looks white blond on the side where the sun hits.

She runs into the kitchen, returns with a plate of kiwi and nectarines, and two dark blue cloth napkins. But on the gray tile of the kitchen floor she has left patches of red. She is limping. He watches, frozen, as blood wells out of her foot. She sits down, crosses her leg over her knee, eats a nectarine, while her blood drip-drips onto the gray tile. He thinks, Why doesn't she wipe it up? Should he wipe it up? Someone should wipe it up. It gives him the creeps, these bright red splashes, but the cloth napkin she presents him seems too fine for this use. He's looking around for paper when she throws a piece of broken china onto the table in front of him. "Parental carnage," she says.

It's the source of her injury, picked up from the kitchen floor—a white shard, triangular in shape, a thin gold line around the part that had been rim. The broken edge is red. "*Carnage,*" she says, accenting and softening the last syllable like a French word. This morning her father had relieved some of his anger by throwing a cup at the refrigerator. Her mother relieved hers by refusing to sweep. "They need to *see* this," she says, placing the broken piece of china on the blue cloth napkin in the middle of the breakfast table. She seems thrilled almost, as if the bloody shard is the final piece of the puzzle of her life. She arranges a kiwi on the napkin, a bud vase alongside. "It's our new centerpiece! A still life! What'll we call it, *Terror at Teatime?*" She speaks with a British accent, biting off her words with her teeth. "No, something simple: *Daddy.* That's it—*Daddy!*"

He starts laughing. "That's terrific. It's really funny." He laughs more, in loud bursts. He has never laughed like this before. He tells her the story of the one baseball game his father took him to, exaggerating his hopes so that their obstruction by the pillar seems purely comic. She takes his hand, squeezing hard, and he elaborates, this time stressing his naïve reverence for his father, his father's indifference. What had his father called out, descending the stairs? Demian doesn't remember now, makes it up: "Try and have fun, kiddo!" "We'll be thinking of you, suckers!" "Look, you—you're lucky you weren't offed in utero!" It doesn't sound like his father but makes him laugh hysterically.

She starts laughing, too. "He slapped me this morning. I told him what I thought of people who can't control themselves, and he held me by the hair and slapped my face. Like this." She grabs a hunk of her hair, yanks her head to one side, giggles. "He said, 'I'll show you how I control myself.' "

He smooths her hair where she yanked. He has begun shaking a little, though he doesn't feel sad or scared. "Sometimes in the room with him I feel like I don't exist. I don't have a body. I don't know how to talk, even." He's shaking harder, down to the soles of his feet. He has never spoken like this. "He'd slap me, too, if he thought I was important enough. The truth is, I bore him. Poor Dad, bored by his son." He replays what he said, awed by what seems to be the utter truth of it. It seems reckless and marvelous saying these things about his father. He's an explorer, charting ground never before seen by mortal eyes. "I really don't need him. If he died tomorrow it wouldn't make the least difference in my life. It might improve things."

Later, with his father's blood leaking into his brain, he'll remember what he said, and even though over the years his father had grown no more interested in him, he'll think for a moment of all the things his father wanted to do that he couldn't do, couldn't ever do now, and he'll sit down in a chair by the bed, for a moment unable to breathe.

But now he's on his knees before Rachel's chair. She puts her arms around his shoulders, presses her face to the top of his head. He hears her heart beating through her T-shirt. His teeth are chattering, and to stop them he starts kissing her through her shirt—her shoulder, the two round bones at the top of her chest, the long swell of breast. In the past he has treated this part of her body reverently, but now he sucks as if he were drinking, wetting the cloth of her shirt till it feels to his lips like rough, wet skin. He has stopped trembling. "I hate him," he murmurs, almost lovingly.

"Has he ever knocked your mother down? Called her a slut? Said he could smell it on her? I'm in the same room, here at this very table eating my cantaloupe."

He can't tell if she likes what his mouth is doing, but she has made no objection. He raises her shirt, observes her body in the daylight; thinks, *There is so much of her.* He says, "He made me sit behind a pole. He traded in his ticket and sat with a buddy. The only baseball game he ever took me to."

It doesn't sound quite awful enough. He looks at her for confirmation, but she seems not to have heard him. "Has he ever come home drunk and gotten in bed with you? And when you screamed he put his hand over your mouth? And when you bit his hand he told lies to your mother? Who still thinks you're a slut though she doesn't say so?"

"Is that true, Rachel?"

She shakes her head no. "Another example of my sick imagination."

Her voice is light but he can't shake off the terrible picture. "If it were true I'd kill him."

"Me, too."

Her last comment comes without inflection. He tries to read her face, but it doesn't help. He hugs her hard. She returns it with a slight time lag, mechanically stroking the back of his head. She seems uncharacteristically passive. He feels sure that if he were to take off his pants, she'd sigh once, then let him have her. The thought terrifies him. "Rachel, where are you?"

She looks at him, smiling with the corners of her mouth only. He wants to be gone from here, to be riding back to Bi-Rite's, whose manager is a friend of his dad's and might not question the excuse he'll make up on the way. But Rachel is sitting so still in her chair, she seems to take up no space. He imagines that if he left her, he'd never find her again. When he called, her mother would say, *She's traveling in Europe.* Her mother would say, *There's no one here by that name.*

"Rachel," he whispers. He touches her face, the curves of her arm, side of her knee, arch of her wounded foot, softly so as not to miss her faintest whispered response. Her foot feels cold, and he warms it between his hand and his face. Then he puts his lips to the injured spot, cleaning off the dried blood with his tongue, smoothing down the flap of the torn skin.

24

CHARACTERIZATION:

Creating Credible People

How we learn about people. How we learn about fictional characters. Characterization through dialogue and thoughts. Characters revealed through action. Multiple cues: getting to know Demian. Onion skin disclosure: Jennifer revealed. Three goals of effective characterization: consistency, complexity, and individuality.

No, writers don't actually create people. They create fictional characters. But art is an illusion, and in this case the illusion is one of actually getting to know people. If the characters are fully drawn so that we can see different facets, we call them **"round" characters**. If they are not developed and serve merely to advance the plot, they are "flat." These terms were suggested by the novelist E. M. Forster not as precise categories but as useful generalizations. A fully developed fictional character will remain in the memory of a reader as vividly as an old friend.

How We Learn about People

Before we turn to the art of creating as-if-real characters in fiction, consider for a moment how we get to know people in daily life. We meet strangers frequently. Some we will never see again: friends of friends, store clerks, the TV repair person. With others, however, we make an effort to find out what they are really like. Rightly or wrongly, we often start with a quick visual assessment. We all know how risky and unreliable this process is, but still we do it. We form quick and notoriously unreliable classifications such as "wimpy-looking," "assertive," "cool," "elegant" on the basis of physical characteristics, dress, makeup, and the like.

Next, we start the conversation ritual. Talking with strangers is a form of exploration: we ask what they do for a living, what films they have seen lately, how long have they've lived in the neighborhood. With students the questions tend to focus on courses taken, music, and whether you have mutual friends. These seem on the surface like bland queries, but they're ways of finding out what the other person takes seriously and what he or she is like as an individual. Deeper questions such as political loyalties and religious beliefs are usually postponed until later meetings, and the approach is apt to be more cautious and indirect. If we move too fast, we're considered nosy, so we tend to be evasive. This is why we spend so much time talking.

Talk, however, is not enough by itself. In order to get to know someone really well, we need to see him or her in action. When we say, "But I don't really know him," we usually mean that we've talked a lot but haven't done much together. Activities such as dancing, bicycling, hiking, or participating in some social club give us a chance to see whether their behavior matches what we thought we learned from conversation. No one likes being caught in a thunderstorm while on a long hike or staying up all night in rehearsals for an amateur dramatic performance, but we do learn more about people when we share stressful experiences.

These various stages in the process of getting to know someone well have one aspect in common: they provide a great clutter of specific details from which we draw certain conclusions. Many details are of no value, some have created impressions we aren't consciously aware of, and some are clearly informative. The process is inefficient and slow, but trying to bypass it can lead to trouble.

How We Learn about Fictional Characters

Learning about characters in fiction *seems* to be similar, but that's an illusion. Fiction, especially the short story, can't afford to be that leisurely. So while getting to know a character in fiction appears to use the same methods, the process we call **characterization** is enormously compressed and ingeniously hidden. What might take months in life can be compressed into 15 minutes of reading. In order to maintain the reader's sense of personal discovery, the writer of fiction has to supply a series of little hints, and they have to be slipped in stealthily.

There will be times when you as a writer will tire of all this indirection and will be tempted to bypass it with a solid block of character description. After all, such descriptions were popular in 18th- and 19th-century novels. But describing the inner workings of a character in exposition is avoided today because readers like the sense of getting to know characters on their own. This means avoiding exposition that seems to be **author's intrusion**. Many (but not all) authors feel that describing a character directly is rather like having a playwright step on stage and comment on his or her characters.

Another disadvantage of describing a character's personality at length is that it slows the pace. The same is true of extended physical descriptions. Like all exposition, such passages are static. The reader must wait for the story to get moving again. The best way to maintain forward motion is to rely on dialogue, action, and thoughts.

This is not to say that you can never comment on a character. In "Three Hearts," for example, we are told through the narrator that "Mama and Daddy can't manage Eddie." That says a lot about the character of Eddie and is close to exposition, but it is far from author's intrusion because it is presented through a narrator. In addition, it is brief and describes a minor character.

In "Obst Vw," you doubtless noticed the unusual and unmistakable example of author's intrusion at the very outset. Solwitz as author provides information that won't occur until a year after this story ends. This is a **flash-forward**. Since this is information the characters don't yet know, the point of view, as with most flash-forwards, is the author's. In addition, the author states that her protagonist is "not as brilliant as his father, just a pretty smart kid who's used to working hard."

The justification for this has to do with **tone**. Whenever an author steps in like that, the intrusion establishes at least briefly a sense of **distance**, a pulling back from the story. In this case it assures the reader that while these two characters often speak **melodramatically**, their anguish, though real, will pass in time.

The flash-forward is rarely used because with most stories there is no need for this distancing. Normally the goal is just the opposite: to maintain a high degree of reader involvement. The best way to achieve this is to follow the mantra of every writing class: "show, don't tell." You can create a full and revealing portrait through what a character says, thinks, and does.

Characterization through Dialogue and Thoughts

Much of what you learn about a person in daily life is through dialogue. Even if people don't tell you exactly what is going on in their heads, they reveal themselves indirectly through what they say. The same is true in fiction.

In "Obst Vw," for example, it is clear that Demian's mother has an over-riding sense of loyalty to her husband despite his dark moods and occasional irascibility. How do we come to know this? Not by the author telling us but through this exchange:

> "He's way too smart for what he does," his
> mother is saying. "He did well in college without
> studying. . . . He never got time to sit and figure
> things out. He was too young to have a child."

> "Mom," Demian says, "he was twenty-six when I was born. He's forty-two. . . .
> "He was too young," she says firmly, gathering up her books.

This dialogue contributes to our understanding of her by revealing not only her unquestioning defense of her husband but a certain stubbornness even in the face of contrary evidence. In addition, it gives us further insight into Demian's inner torment. The father's failures can't logically be blamed on having had a child at twenty-six, but if that excuse has become a family myth, the accusation is the sort that can lay a heavy guilt trip on a son.

The father also reveals a good deal about himself in an angry outburst that is so illogical it is almost funny.

Demian has been grounded and has asked his father for a second chance. The father scoffs, asking if God would give him "a second chance" if he were dying. Then, groping for still another wild analogy, he says:

> "Let's say you get your girlfriend pregnant. . . . But you aren't ready to be Papa yet. You want to walk across Turkey in your stocking feet. You want to climb Mt. Tamalpais and keep on going."

This is an absurd exaggeration, but it reveals more about the father than he realizes. At forty-two he still has the longing for freedom and adventure that apparently he himself missed. Through this outburst we see in the father an unstable mix of authoritarian rigidity and childish romanticism. This is a fairly complex insight considering that he is only a secondary character.

As you can see from examples like these, dialogue is a particularly effective device for revealing not just outward characteristics but internal conflicts as well. We also see internal conflict and inconsistency in Rachel's dialogue. The most dramatic example is when toward the end she describes what seems to have been a sexual assault by her father. Horrified, Demian asks if that is really true.

> She shakes her head no. "Another example of my sick imagination."

This quick switch of attitude reflects a pattern of vacillations in Rachel. Sometimes she is stoic about her parents' violent hostilities, joking about their fights. But on other occasions she exaggerates the extent of their depravity, describing her father in melodramatic terms. Then, as in this case, she switches back, making a joke about herself. What we see in Rachel is someone desperately trying to cope with an impossible home life, veering from one approach to another.

Characterization through Action

In simple fiction like thrillers and mass-market historical novels, action often serves as the primary method of revealing character. Fighting others or some aspect of nature is a fairly blunt literary tool. It's good entertainment, though, and serves to distinguish good guys from bad. But the downside is that it tends to blot out subtle aspects of character. For this reason action tends to be restrained in sophisticated fiction.

"Escapes" is a good example. There is action, but it is not highlighted. They ride the cable cars, go shopping, and visit a former prison, but no one is shot. There isn't even a physical fight. True, an attempted suicide and an earlier successful one play major roles in revealing the turmoil going on in Jennifer, but those traumatic events occur offstage. We learn about them through dialogue.

"Obst Vw" also relies heavily on dialogue and thoughts, but there are two uses of action that provide important insights into the emotional state of the two central characters. For Demian, it is that baseball game in which his father leaves his son in the seat with obstructed vision rather than sitting with him. It's far from child abuse in the traditional sense, but we can see by the way Demian keeps returning to that event how deeply it affected him. Representing an accumulation of disappointments, it becomes a kind of emblem of his relationship with his father.

As for Rachel, she is revealed in significant ways by the incident in which she cuts her foot on a broken cup and refuses to bandage the injury. She lets the blood drip on the floor, trying to make a joke out of it. Her self-pity is mixed with her rage against her parents. "They need to *see* this," she says.

The breaking of the mug also gives us a vista into the daily life of her parents: the father venting his anger by throwing the cup against the refrigerator, and the mother making her statement by refusing to sweep it up.

Of the three stories, "Three Hearts" makes the most extensive use of action as a means of revealing character. In our first view of the mother she is "lying on the kitchen couch . . . rolling her head from side to side, sighing." This is obviously not just a case of lethargy. She is ill and, we suspect, overmedicated. Since the story is not told from her point of view, we don't have access to her thoughts, and her condition limits what she is able or willing to say. Our view of her apparent incompetence is based almost entirely on what we see in that opening scene.

At the end of the story we see her digging in the snow in a frenzy. She, not her husband or her dissolute son, is the one who saves Bucky. Without crossing over into **melodrama**, the story reveals her hidden strength through action.

The problem brother, Eddie, is not developed fully, but the fact that he has been out all night is a significant bit of action, and there is a brief detail when he comes home in the morning that helps us to place him. The younger children are putting on their boots and Eddie comes in "all dressed in black and loose and he looks like a puppet." He then "steps over us as if we are stones." It's a minor detail, but it contributes to our understanding of his state and his alienation from the family, an alienation that contributes to the near-death at the end of the story.

Multiple Sources: Getting to Know Demian

We've been looking at the ways dialogue, thoughts, and action can reveal a fictional character as if they were quite separate. In actual practice they are used together, sometimes even within a single sentence. If you look closely at the way we come to know Demian in "Obst Vw," you will see that the reader is picking up multiple cues throughout the entire story.

This in-depth examination of character and feelings is particularly important in this story because the theme deals with the ways people misunderstand each other. As you have probably noticed, the title (pronounced "obst view") refers not only to the obstructed-view seat Demian was given at the baseball game but also to the obstructed vision the two young adults have of their parents and, equally, the limited view the parents have of their offspring. In fact, almost all the relationships in that story are badly damaged by limited and distorted views of each other. But the reader's view is in no way restricted. We are given many ways of perceiving the inner life of both Demian and Rachel through their dialogue, actions, and thoughts in combination. When the author steps in, it is only to give us some perspective, not to analyze the characters directly. Here is a partial list of what we learn about Demian, along with the various ways the author has informed us.

1. *He loves Rachel deeply.* We learn this (a) *Through dialogue*: Awkwardly trying to avoid clichéd expressions of love, he tries, "I really like you" and "I feel bad for you." (b) *Through actions*: We see both his strong physical attraction for her and his concern for her as well. At the end of the story we see him symbolically trying ease her psychological injuries by treating her physical wound, putting "his lips to the injured spot. . . smoothing down the flap of torn skin."

2. *He has mixed feelings about Rachel and about sex.* We see this (a) *Through thoughts*: As they sit in the sandbox she seems to him "too sharply constructed, a witch woman. . . . " Toward the end of the story it seems to him that she would "let him have her," but "the thought terrifies him." (b) *Through past dialogue* referred to without quoting: In response to a question she had said she found "something apologetic. . . in his attitude toward sex." He was, we gather, of two minds.

3. *A part of him hates his father.* We learn this (a) *Through action*: He doesn't speak to his father "for several months" after his father refused to sign the learner's permit for driving. (b) *Through thoughts*: When his father grounds

him for returning home late, he feels "stiff with rage." He tries to feel sympathy when his mother tells him that his father is facing possible bankruptcy, but "it doesn't work." (c) *Through dialogue*: Later he is able to tell Rachel, "If he died tomorrow it wouldn't make the least difference in my life. It might improve things."

4. *Another part of him admires and even loves his father.* We come to see this (a) *Through thoughts*: When they are driving to the baseball game and he hears his father talking with Dr. Frank, Demian feels "proud of his father." At the game he wishes his father would stay with him "just to be there so Demian could ask him questions or just sit there quietly beside him, watching him watch the game." And years later when his father is dying, "he'll think for a moment of all the things his father wanted to do that he couldn't do. . . and he'll sit down in a chair for a moment unable to breathe." (b) *Through dialogue*: When Rachel says his father "has a mean streak," he denies it. And later, " 'I hate him' he murmurs, almost lovingly."

5. *He is conscientious.* This is revealed (a) *Through action*: He conscientiously holds the after-school job, and (b) *Through dialogue*: He argues calmly with his father about being grounded yet finally accepts his father's strict curfew.

6. *He is also rebellious.* We see this (a) *Through action*: He visits with Rachel when he should be at work and considers "excuses he'll make up. . . . " (b) *Through thoughts*: He feels like "an explorer" charting new ground when (c) *Through dialogue*: We hear him say to Rachel that his father's death would mean nothing to him.

7. *He is unconsciously competing with Rachel for the title of who has been the most damaged by their parents.* We learn this (a) *Through dialogue*: He tells her the story of his father taking him to the baseball game and (b) *Through thoughts*: "It doesn't sound quite awful enough" in comparison with her situation.

This is a relatively short story, yet we come to know Demian far better than we do a new friend even after hours of talk. All the author's exposition has done is to assure us that in spite of these tormented emotions, he will eventually "do well." As readers we have the feeling we have come to know him on own, but in fact we have responded to a variety of carefully inserted cues in the form of action, dialogue, and thoughts.

This analysis, of course, is not how one goes about writing a story. We have been examining a final draft. The creative process is far more intuitive in inception and messier in development. You write a first draft with a rough outline of a plot in mind and an idea of what your characters will be like. You keep adding and revising the dialogue and the action to reveal what you want about your characters, and at the same time you weed out details that don't contribute. If you stay flexible, you will discover more about your characters with each new draft.

Onion Skin Disclosure: Jennifer Revealed

The onion is often used as a metaphor to describe stories that unfold characters layer by layer. "Escapes" is an excellent example. While "Obst Vw" opens with a slightly detached view, assuring us with that flash-forward that we're not dealing with a suicidal protagonist and then proceeding immediately to give us intense insights, "Escapes" opens with a picture of the protagonist as she might look to a stranger and proceeds to reveal layer by layer her true self.

Our first view of Jennifer, you remember, is of an apparently exuberant 14-year-old girl riding the cable cars of San Francisco. Like many kids, she "gets a thrill hanging off the side of the car," her scarf flying. It's not a dishonest picture since she really is having a good time, but it gives no hint of the turmoil within her.

In the third paragraph we have the first hint that something is going on with her below the surface. Confused by a baseball game, she "closes her eyes for the rest of the game." Another hint comes at the clothing store where she fills her cart, selecting items with apparent enthusiasm but, when facing a dressing room with no privacy, "walks out of the store without trying on a thing."

The next layer of the onion comes in the following paragraph when we see Jennifer's arms. "Tiny uneven scars creep up her wrists like a child's sloppy cross-stitch." We've already come a long way from that initial picture of the apparently joyful teenager, but we keep wanting to know more. The process is similar to what I described as "dramatic questions" in the building of plot, but here plot and character development go hand in hand.

In quick succession we learn that (a) Jennifer has been "kicked out of school," (b) she has tried to commit suicide, and (c) her father had successfully committed suicide "in his jail cell where he was serving time for dealing drugs."

The story then shifts the focus to the narrator and her own problems. Returning to Jennifer as they visit Alcatraz, the story reveals (a) that she has been a compulsive shoplifter specializing, significantly, in bracelets, (b) that she has a softer, dependent side we haven't seen before ("She takes my hand in hers"), and (c) that she is aware that stealing is wrong (she takes off her bracelets, revealing her scars). At last, (d) she is willing to face the reality of her suicide attempt (" 'If I really wanted to do it, I could have made the cuts deeper' "). And (e) we learn that Jennifer has known about her father's suicide all along, and, (f) most important, what she has longed for is honesty and trust ("I wanted my mother to tell me the truth") The story ends with Jennifer and Caryn linking their arms "for the climb."

The unfolding of the layers of Jennifer's character progresses from that defensive pose characteristic of those deeply disturbed to the beginnings of trust and honesty. But the author is careful not to be unrealistically optimistic at the end. A simple "feel-good" story written for a mass-market magazine might end with a hug, tears, and laughter, implying that their problems have all been solved. Ann Hood, however, guards against that with the final sentence: "Its steps are steep, and we have to link arms for the climb."

The onion approach to character revelation is made much easier when there is a narrator who is, like the reader, unaware of the facts in the beginning. This can be an **antagonist**, one pitted against the **protagonist**, but it is more likely to be a companion such as a friend, parent, spouse, or, as in this case, a reluctant guardian.

Although we have focused on the unfolding of Jennifer's character, don't forget that to a slightly lesser degree Caryn, the narrator, is being revealed as well. Although she is not presented in that step-by-step manner, we come to understand her own needs through the fact that her boyfriend had left her "right before Jennifer came to stay with me." Later she reflects, "My tiny apartment on Fourth Avenue has been so lonely that the idea of sharing it and everything in it makes me almost happy."

In addition, her sister-in-law, Sherry, is revealed through her phone conversations as restless, impatient, unsympathetic, and selfish—all that without a bit of exposition. It is unusual to come to know three characters this well in a story of this length, but it is important that they all be included since the dominant theme applies to them all: "What I realize . . . is that there really is no escaping. Not for Sherry, not for Jennifer, not for me. The only thing left to do is to stick it out." Notice, incidentally, that this bit of reflection comes too close to exposition to provide an effective ending. Instead, it is slid in unobtrusively. The actual conclusion comes in the form of significant action: linking their arms "for the climb."

One word of warning about the onion approach to character revelation: don't confuse this potentially subtle approach with the trick ending. That simple but entertaining type of story as seen in O. Henry's work and countless murder mysteries depends on cues that are false. Misleading information is carefully planted in order to intensify the surprise at the end. The onion approach, in contrast, is not a trick. It reveals aspects of the truth gradually and in stages.

Three Goals of Effective Characterization

If you look closely at fully developed characters in published fiction, you will notice that most fulfill these three characteristics: they are consistent in what they say and do, they are complex, and they are highly individualized. These qualities are goals to aim for.

Consistency is the dominant characteristic of minor characters. The heavyset owner of the bar in "Sausage and Beer" has some important lines, but he is a flat character, one who is there merely to serve a function and so is not developed. But even complex, round characters have a basic consistency. The father in "Sausage and Beer" is consistently reserved. The mother in "Three Hearts" acts in a way that is surprising, but her love for her children is a constant. What surprises us is the sudden surge of clarity and strength at the end, not a reversal of attitude. Demian and Rachel react in different ways to different types of parental insensitivity, but each is consistent. Not one of these characters acts in a way that is left inexplicable at the end of the story, and that is the key to consistency.

Complexity is what differentiates fully developed or "round" characters from those that serve only one function. To achieve complex characterization, you have to reveal more than one aspect of a character. You can do this by establishing a pattern, countering it in some way, and showing how both elements are a part of the whole character. Caryn, in "Escapes," for example, appears at first to be an independent type. Her boyfriend has left her and there is no mention of other friends. But in subtle ways the author lets us know that she is lonely and without a sense of direction. It is not surprising at the end of that story when she reaches out for companionship.

In "Obst Vw" both characters try to laugh at what hurts them the most. Rachel insists that the sound of her parents shouting at each other is "funny, really. It's high comedy." And when she jokes about the cut on her foot, calling it " 'parental carnage,' " Demian starts laughing. " 'That's terrific,' " he says, " 'It's really funny.' " But in the end his sense of compassion for her is revealed in his actions. Rage, bitter humor, and love have alternated throughout that story.

To achieve complexity in characterization, provide some type of fresh insight, something not revealed early in the story. This may be an aspect that the reader shares with the character, as in the stories already discussed, or something only the reader fully appreciates, as you will see in the story that appears in the next chapter. If the change is too subtle or obscure, readers will feel that the story lacks **closure**, that sense of being fully completed. "I'm not sure what the point is," your readers are apt to say. If the change is too great or unconvincing, on the other hand, readers will feel that the character lacks consistency. "I just don't believe she would behave like that," they might say, and the story has failed. Shifts in attitude must be credible.

Individuality is what makes a character memorable. Characters have to be interesting in some way, and it helps if they are introduced through an original plot and vivid setting.

A story about Tom and Mary who attend a typical university and spend the afternoon in a typical student cafeteria complaining to each other about their typically awful parents is not going to hold the attention of even your most admiring reader.

An uncle in a mental hospital is more memorable than a pleasant but bland relative who joins the family for dinner. A mother who lives in a twilight zone of painkillers and tranquilizers who draws on inner strength to save her son in a snowbank is far more striking than a competent mother who faces the same crisis. What individualizes Demian and Rachel is the sequence of abrupt shifts in mood I referred to above. In addition, they are made more memorable by the contrasting settings: the sexually charged scene in the preschool sandbox, the ballpark scene with its obscured view, and Rachel's family kitchen with shards of a broken cup on the floor.

Be careful, however, not to overdo the attempt to be different. There comes a point when distinctiveness turns artificial and unconvincing. An inconsequential tale about two bickering college roommates is not going to be improved by being transformed into an inconsequential tale about two bickering mutants living in a burned-out fun house amid the rubble of World War III. Individuality for its own sake becomes a **gimmick**, a contrived and superficial attention-getter.

As you can see from the stories you have read, well-developed characters should be consistent enough so that at least by the end of the story we understand why they said and did what they did; they have to be complex enough to seem real, not just types; and they have to have enough individuality to make them interesting and memorable. If this seems like a tall order, remember that these qualities do not snap into place in the first draft. They are the goals you keep in mind as you move through successive versions.

25

A STORY

by Donald Barthelme

The Balloon

The balloon, beginning at a point on Fourteenth Street, the exact location of which I cannot reveal, expanded northward all one night, while people were sleeping, until it reached the Park. There I stopped it. At dawn the northernmost edges lay over the Plaza; the free-hanging motion was frivolous and gentle. But experiencing a faint irritation at stopping, even to protect the trees, and seeing no reason the balloon should not be allowed to expand upward, over the parts of the city it was already covering into the "air space" to be found there, I asked the engineers to see to it. This expansion took place throughout the morning, a soft imperceptible sighing of gas through the valves. The balloon then covered forty-five blocks north-south and an irregular area east-west, as many as six crosstown blocks on either side of the Avenue in some places. That was the situation, then.

But it is wrong to speak of "situations," implying sets of circumstances leading to some resolution, some escape of tension; there were no situations, simply the balloon hanging there—muted heavy grays and browns for the most part, contrasting with walnut and soft yellows. A deliberate lack of finish, enhanced by skillful installation, gave the surface a rough, forgotten quality; sliding weights on the inside, carefully adjusted, anchored the great, varishaped mass at a number of points. Now, we have had a flood of original ideas in all media, works of singular beauty as well as significant milestones in the history of inflation, but at that moment there was only *this balloon*, concrete particular, hanging there.

There were reactions. Some people found the balloon "interesting." As a response this seemed inadequate to the immensity of the balloon, the suddenness of its appearance over the city; on the other hand, in the absence of hysteria or other societally-induced anxiety, it must be judged a calm, "mature" one. There was a certain amount of initial argumentation about the "meaning" of the balloon; this subsided, because we have learned not to insist on meanings, and they are rarely even looked for now, except in cases involving the simplest, safest phenomena. It was agreed that since the meaning of the balloon could never be known absolutely, extended discussion was pointless, or at least less meaningful than the activities of those who, for example, hung green and blue paper lanterns from the warm gray underside, in certain streets, or seized the occasion to write messages on the surface, announcing their availability for the performance of unnatural acts, or the availability of acquaintances.

Daring children jumped, especially at those points where the balloon hovered close to a building, so that the gap between balloon and building was a matter of a few inches, or points where the balloon actually made contact, exerting an ever-so-slight pressure against the side of a building, so that balloon and building seemed a unity. The upper surface was so structured that a "landscape" was presented, small valleys as well as slight knolls, or mounds; once atop the balloon, a stroll was possible, or even a trip, from one place to another. There was pleasure in being able to run down an incline, then up the opposing slope, both gently graded, or in making a leap from one side to the other. Bouncing was possible, because of the pneumaticity of the surface, and even falling, if that was your wish. That all these varied motions, as well as others, were within one's possibilities, in experiencing the "up" side of the balloon, was extremely exciting for children, accustomed to the city's flat, hard skin. But the purpose of the balloon was not to amuse children.

Too, the number of people, children and adults, who took advantage of the opportunities described was not so large as it might have been: a certain timidity, lack of trust in the balloon, was seen. There was, furthermore, some hostility. Because we had hidden the pumps, which fed helium to the interior, and because the surface was so vast that the authorities could not determine the point of entry—that is, the point at which the gas was injected—a degree of frustration was evidenced by those city officers into whose province such manifestations normally fell. The apparent purposelessness of the balloon was vexing (as was the fact that it was "there" at all). Had we painted, in great letters, "LABORATORY TESTS PROVE" or "18% MORE EFFECTIVE" on the sides of the balloon, this difficulty would have been circumvented, but I could not bear to do so. On the whole, these officers were remarkably tolerant, considering the dimensions of the anomaly, this tolerance being the result of, first, secret tests conducted by night that convinced them that little or nothing could be done in the way of removing or destroying the balloon, and, secondly, a public warmth that arose (not uncolored by touches of the aforementioned hostility) toward the balloon, from ordinary citizens.

As a single balloon must stand for a lifetime of thinking about balloons, so each citizen expressed, in the attitude he chose, a complex of attitudes. One man might consider that the balloon had to do with the notion *sullied*, as in the sentence *The big balloon sullied the otherwise clear and radiant Manhattan sky.* That is, the balloon was, in this man's view, an imposture, something inferior to the sky that had formerly been there, something interposed between the people and their "sky." But in fact it was January, the sky was dark and ugly; it was not a sky you could look up into, lying on your back in the street, with pleasure, unless pleasure, for you, proceeded from having been threatened, from having been misused. And the underside of the balloon, by contrast, was a pleasure to look up into—we had seen to that. Muted grays and browns for the most part, contrasted with walnut and soft, forgotten yellows. And so, while this man was thinking *sullied,* still there was an admixture of pleasurable cognition in his thinking, struggling with the original perception.

Another man, on the other hand, might view the balloon as if it were part of a system of unanticipated rewards, as when one's employer walks in and says, "Here, Henry, take this package of money I have wrapped for you, because we have been doing so well in the business here, and I admire the way you bruise the tulips, without which bruising your department would not be a success, or at least not the success that it is." For this man the balloon might be a brilliantly heroic "muscle and pluck" experience, even if an experience poorly understood.

Another man might say, "Without the example of————, it is doubtful that————would exist today in its present form," and find many to agree with him, or to argue with him. Ideas of "bloat" and "float" were introduced, as well as concepts of dream and responsibility. Others engaged in remarkably detailed fantasies having to do with a wish either to lose themselves in the balloon, or to engorge it. The private character of these wishes, of their origins, deeply buried and unknown, was such that they were not much spoken of; yet there is evidence that they were widespread. It was also argued that what was important was what you felt when you stood under the balloon; some people claimed that they felt sheltered, warmed, as never before, while enemies of the balloon felt, or reported feeling, constrained, a "heavy" feeling.

Critical opinion was divided:

"monstrous pourings"

"harp"

XXXXXXX "certain contrasts with darker portions"

"inner joy"

"large, square corners"

"conservative eclecticism that has so far governed modern balloon design"

:::::::"abnormal vigor"

"warm, soft, lazy passages"

"Has unity been sacrificed for a sprawling quality?"

"Quelle catastrophe!"

"munching"

People began, in a curious way, to locate themselves in relation to aspects of the balloon: "I'll be at that place where it dips down into Forty-seventh Street almost to the sidewalk, near the Alamo Chile House," or "Why don't we go stand on top, and take the air, and maybe walk about a bit, where it forms a tight, curving line with the façade of the Gallery of Modern Art—" Marginal intersections offered entrances within a given time duration, as well as "warm, soft, lazy passages" in which . . . But it is wrong to speak of "marginal intersections." Each intersection was crucial, none could be ignored (as if, walking there, you might not find someone capable of turning your attention, in a flash, from old exercises to new exercises). Each intersection was crucial, meeting of balloon and building, meeting of balloon and man, meeting of balloon and balloon.

It was suggested that what was admired about the balloon was finally this: that it was not limited, or defined. Sometimes a bulge, blister, or sub-section would carry all the way east to the river on its own initiative, in the manner of an army's movements on a map, as seen in a headquarters remote from the fighting. Then that part would be, as it were, thrown back again, or would withdraw into new dispositions; the next morning, that part would have made another sortie, or disappeared altogether. This ability on the part of the balloon to shift its shape, to change, was very pleasing, especially to people whose lives were rather rigidly patterned, persons to whom change, although desired, was not available. The balloon, for the twenty-two days of its existence, offered the possibility, in its randomness, of getting lost, of losing oneself, in contradistinction to the grid of precise, rectangular pathways under our feet. The amount of specialized training currently needed, and the consequent desirability of long-term commitments, has been occasioned by the steadily growing importance of complex machinery, in virtually all kinds of operations; as this tendency increases, more and more people will turn, in bewildered inadequacy, to solutions for which the balloon may stand as a prototype, or "rough draft."

I met you under the balloon, on the occasion of your return from Norway. You asked if it was mine; I said it was. The balloon, I said, is a spontaneous autobiographical disclosure, having to do with the unease I felt at your absence, and with sexual deprivation, but now that your visit to Bergen has been terminated, it is no longer necessary or appropriate. Removal of the balloon was easy; trailer trucks carried away the depleted fabric, which is now stored in West Virginia, awaiting some other time of unhappiness, sometime, perhaps, when we are angry with one another.

written 1966

26

LIBERATING THE IMAGINATION

Stretching the imagination. Building on a premise. Developing a fantasy.
Innovations in style. Three popular misconceptions. Does it work?

In Chapter 13, "Where Stories Come From," I stressed the fact that personal experience is a rich source of material for new fiction. If you have been writing stories, you probably have been transforming episodes from your own life by altering the **point of view**, rearranging events, and changing the **setting**. You are getting used to the process of creating fictional characters by using aspects of people you have known or briefly met. These are the steps most writers take when creating carefully developed, realistic stories.

But what about those flights of fancy that suddenly sweep in like a sudden squall? They may spring from some absurd and unrealistic notion. Like the tornado in *The Wizard of Oz*, they have the power to propel us into a fantasy world. Some may be distortions of the world we know; others may be dreamlike. They may lack "essential" elements such as well-developed characters or a setting. Or they may exaggerate some aspect of style, pushing language beyond the conventional range.

How can we draw on such explosions of imagination? And if we manage to get them down on paper, how are we to judge whether they are merely journal entries or concepts worth developing into a story to be read by others? This chapter deals with innovative flights and what to do with them.

Stretching the Imagination

You can't force yourself to be creatively innovative any more than you can will yourself to be funny. But you can explore fanciful plots, fantasies, and experiments in style and see what develops. If your imagination is quirky, new ideas may come easily. Most will remain as entries in your journal. But there is always the chance that one of them will have promise and will warrant the time and effort to develop into a story.

Keep in mind that the appeal for innovative fiction varies with every writer. Some find its emphasis on novelty too close to the tricky, too far removed from the richness of characterization. Others are drawn to experimental work almost from the beginning. To some degree your preferences in reading will shape your preferences in writing. But every writer can benefit from an introduction to work that pushes beyond the conventional such as Donald Barthelme's, "The Balloon."

One of the best ways to explore new directions is to keep a literary journal. A journal can be handwritten, typed in a loose-leaf notebook, or recorded as a special file on a computer. Journal writing frees you from the sense of commitment you feel (or should feel) when writing what you hope will be a fully developed story. Because it is private, it releases you from the concern for how others will respond. Journal writing liberates your imagination.

Many prefer late-night writing on the computer. Others like the portability of a handwritten journal in a bound notebook they can use on their lunch hour or while waiting in the dentist's office. In any case, don't confuse a literary journal with a diary. Your journal is the place for dialogue fragments, reactions to fiction you have read, story ideas, fantasies. Assume from the start that most if not all of this material is for your own use and enjoyment. This is for you what a sketch book is for painters. Anything goes. If by chance an entry shows promise of being developed, set your journal aside and shift gears. Work intended for readers requires a different mind-set.

For those who are not already at home with journal writing, here are four possible directions to get you started. Consider them warm-up exercises.

1. *The "what-if" game*: What if your sister developed the ability to fly? Would you be jealous or proud? How would you explain her to friends? Or what if all the dogs of the world rebelled against their masters on the same day? What if a blind man had the ability to hear the thoughts of those around him? What if an accomplished flutist found that she could not play without attracting swarms of monarch butterflies?

2. *Turning "like" into "is"*: We all use **similes** and **metaphors** in daily conversation almost without thinking. Turning routine **figurative language** into literal situations often has bizarre results. If a good friend's laugh is *like* a sheep bleating, what if he *became* a sheep at awkward moments? Would others pretend not to notice? Could he maintain old friendships? Would friends try to avoid references to lamb chops? What about his marriage? Or if a sleepless night is *like* a video of all the day's problems, what if a character goes to the movies and finds the film *is* all his day's problems with himself playing the lead role? But what if his wife, sitting beside him, has

apparently seen a film with herself as the lead? How does he find out what she has been watching? Will they go back the following night? Will they bring the children?

3. *The undirected fantasy:* Let yourself go. Write fast and without plan. Borrow from fairy tales, dreams, or daydreams. It might be boring for others to read, but it has its function in the privacy of your journal. The dreamlike plots and bizarre characters may surprise you. You can look at them as vistas into your unconscious or, if you dislike psychological analysis, as possible material for fiction. Entertain yourself. See where your imagination will lead you.

4. *Stylistic games:* Describe an automobile accident entirely through the dialogue of three characters. Avoid all exposition and description. Use what they say to reveal what they are like as characters and how they differ from one another. Or write a short scene involving action using "you" rather than "he" or "she." If you need a starter, begin with "You're waiting in a restaurant for your best friend to join you when you see your brother cross the room with a policeman."

Write two versions of the same scene, one with the longest sentences you can construct without sounding absurd, and the other in the shortest possible sentences.

Experimentation has no limit in journal entries. As soon as you decide that you are working on something you hope to share with others, however, your goals and your approach should shift. Without losing your original vision, you should examine the nature of the fiction and explore ways of shaping it.

Building on a Premise

Many innovative works of fiction are based on a **premise**, a single, identifiable distortion of the world as we know it.

The **fable**, for example, is one of the oldest forms of premise fiction. Aesop wrote his fables more than 2,500 years ago, but they are still a part of our culture. Some contemporary writers adopt the same approach. The premise in most fables is simply that animals can talk, think, and behave like people. Quite often, fables also suggest a moral of some type—either serious or satiric.

When the fable form is extended so that each character is consistently a symbol for some abstraction, the result is an **allegory**. In John Bunyan's *Pilgrim's Progress* the premise is that abstractions like "glib" and "deceitful" can be seen as characters with names like Mr. Worldly-Wiseman and the smooth-talking Mr. Legality. *Pilgrim's Progress* was written in the 17th century and for more than a hundred years was almost as popular as the Bible. In 1945 George Orwell employed the allegory for his political satire, *Animal Farm*.

A premise can take many different forms. The as-if element may be that a king can be blessed (and cursed) with the ability to turn everything he touches to gold. King Midas has become a part of our culture. In Lewis Carroll's *Through the Looking Glass* the reader accepts the notion that there is a parallel world that exists behind mirrors.

Many of Franz Kafka's stories and novels are based on an initial premise. Everyone knows that adolescents sometimes feel like an insect and are treated as such, but Kafka took this one step farther. In "The Metamorphosis" a young man actually becomes a six-foot cockroach. (If you haven't read it, look it up.) When we suffer from a sense of guilt and worthlessness, we may feel that life is like a trial, but in Kafka's novel *The Trial* the protagonist finds himself actually immersed in a dreamlike, unending court case. If you take this fictional route, be careful not to rewrite Kafka.

"The Balloon," by Donald Barthelme, is also a premise story, but unlike "The Metamorphosis" the key to the premise is not revealed until the end. We are given a great deal of physical description of the balloon at the beginning, arousing our curiosity without providing a hint of what the thematic suggestion may be. We learn its precise location, its size, its color, its strength. Public reaction matches that of the reader—puzzlement. Some describe the balloon with the same word frequently used by polite people to describe fiction they don't understand, "interesting." Some feel the balloon "sullied the otherwise clear and radiant Manhattan sky." As the narrator reports, "Critical opinion was divided."

At last the narrator's lover returns from Norway. Once they are reunited, the balloon "is no longer necessary or appropriate." It is stored away for possible use at a later date.

Essentially, this story is a development of the second of the exercises I suggested for journal writing: turning "like" into "is." Separation for the narrator was not just *like* living under a cloud, it *was* living under a cloudlike balloon. His gloom was such that it covered the entire city.

Notice how precise the details about the cloud are. Size, shape, color, composition are all included as well as the various opinions of the public. This is a characteristic of many premise stories. Once Kafka establishes the notion that a person can become a cockroach, the rest of that story is undistorted. This *appearance* of reality is referred to as **verisimilitude**.

The single premise is also used in some science fiction works, especially short stories. In longer works the number of premises increases, often creating an entire civilization. Such work may become a **fantasy**.

The line between the literary premise story and science fiction is hotly debated, but one difference is the emphasis that literary works often place on character and feelings. "The Metamorphosis" focuses on what it is like to be an adolescent in a rather rigid and traditional family, and "The Balloon" is concerned with the melancholy of separation. There are many exceptions, but science fiction tends to deal more with social issues.

Developing Fantasy

Whereas premise fiction deals with a single as-if exception to the world as we know it, **fantasy** creates an entirely new environment. This may be a futuristic or past society, or a world populated by beings other than humans. The highly popular Harry Potter series is a fantasy in which the protagonist and others are given unusual powers. The environment is like our world in some respects but quite different in others, in the tradition of some fairy tales. J. R. R. Tolkien created a world of Hobbits in his trilogy, *The Lord of the Rings*. The world he pictures is further from reality than in the Harry Potter series. In *Watership Down*, Richard Adams deals with a society of rabbits.

You will notice, however, that these examples are long works—either novels or even a series of novels. This is partly because it takes time to create a new universe. Short stories tend to draw on a single premise or on innovations in style.

Innovations in Style

Innovative use of style is limitless. One approach is to find ways of suggesting our thoughts by abandoning normal syntax and punctuation. In the famous **stream-of-consciousness** section in James Joyce's *Ulysses*, Molly Bloom's thoughts are presented without punctuation. The sequence of topics is not arranged logically but meanders by association.

A more recent example of innovative narration is seen in "Gotta Dance," by Jackson Jodie Daviss, a story that appears in Chapter 28. The protagonist is a young street dancer striking out on her own. Her narration is not unusual until she begins dancing. At that point, it explodes in a burst of enthusiasm. In this passage she describes the climax of her performance:

> Then I did my knock-down, drag-out, could-you-just-die, great big Broadway-baby finish.
>
> Didn't they applaud, oh honey, didn't they yell, and didn't they throw money.

The phrasing here goes beyond the familiar impression of a character talking to the reader. Those questions without question marks are not questions at all, they are expressions of wonder and enthusiasm. The language has left the level of realism and echoes the spirit of the moment.

Another approach, suggested in the warm-up exercises at the beginning of this chapter is to avoid "he," "she," and "I," replacing them with "you," as in this anonymous description of a bipolar "high."

> Buoyed with the with mindless joy and confidence, you dazzle your friends and confound your enemies. You are filled with generosity and love, leaving $100 tips and giving your wallet to a homeless man. You phone friends and strangers, giving them advice for hours at a time. It is not your fault that your speech comes too fast for others to understand. It is not your concern when they insist you can't buy two new beautiful cars with no money in the bank. You've left them all behind. You're spinning too fast for the world to catch up.

The defense of the "you" is that it thrusts the reader directly into the situation; the risk is that in longer stories it can become tiresome.

Some authors have created almost a new language, mixing English with a jargon or, in other cases, **dialect**. In novels, the author has the time to teach the reader how to respond to a new vocabulary. This is what Anthony Burgess does in his novel *Clockwork Orange*. Most readers find it confusing at first, but those with patience gradually learn how to respond to it. The same is true in *Far Tartuga*, by Peter Matthiessen, in which a Caribbean dialect is used so directly that the reader has to make some effort to master it. This particular approach lends itself to the novel more easily than the short story because of the time it takes for the reader to master it.

Another stylistic innovation is seen in **postmodern fiction**. This places such a strong emphasis on ingenuity of language itself that characterization and plot all but disappear. In some cases reader interest is maintained, if at all, with wit and verbal ingenuity.

Metafiction is a relatively recent approach in which characterization is also downplayed. Instead, the story is designed to illustrate the craft of writing itself. In John Barth's highly readable story "Lost in the Funhouse," for example, the boy in the funhouse is also the author in the process of writing. Barth stops the action periodically to comment on how the story is or is not progressing. The funhouse becomes fiction with all its tricks, special effects, and distortions. At the end, the protagonist is described as one who will go on to "construct funhouses for others . . . though he would rather be among the lovers for whom funhouses are designed."

Other experiments in style make extreme use of dialogue. In Virginia Woolf's novel *The Waves*, for example, each unnumbered chapter begins with a page or so of highly poetic prose describing the sun and the changing landscape. The remainder of each chapter is presented in the form of unbroken dialogue shifting among six characters. Since there are no references to action and no exposition whatever, the reader comes to know these six characters from childhood to old age entirely through their reminiscences and their reactions to each other and the world about them. The novel has to be read at the deliberate pace we use for poetry.

Three Popular Misconceptions

One serious misconception about nonrealistic fiction is that what was fun to write must necessarily be fun to read. Journal writing often provides a delicious sense of release from the demands of writing fiction, but the result is not necessarily going to make sense for your reader. Most of such formless writing should remain in your journal. When an entry does seem to have literary potential, it will probably require some basic transformations and careful revisions. Never confuse private writing with serious work intended for readers.

A second and closely related misconception is the hidden-meaning theory. It holds that an aimless work written from the heart must necessarily have some secret meaning that, though unknown to the author, can be ferreted out by a conscientious reader. Overworked writing instructors and editors waste countless hours patiently trying to interpret works that do not contain anything to interpret.

Some beginning writers submit essentially meaningless work not out of malice but because they have heard teachers provide explanations of published works that seemed unintelligible on first reading. They conclude that if an instructor can draw meaning from difficult literary passages, he or she can do the same with carelessly composed student work. Not even a well-read and well-trained teacher, however, can draw meaning from random and thoughtless writing. It's a disservice to ask others to spend time on work you yourself don't understand.

The most serious misconception is the claim that a work of fiction should mean all things to all people. True, a group of readers will see and respond to different aspects of any work. But there is almost always a core of agreement. In "The Balloon," for example, some may focus on the serious sense of melancholy described through that symbolic balloon, while others see it as a satire of how the public responds to fiction it doesn't understand. Still others may see it as a comical fantasy in which the reader is tricked until the end. Those are three views of the same work. But no one is going to propose that the story is a satire of militarism, a criticism of the medical profession, or a protest against illegal drugs. The story obviously does not mean all things to all people. When novice writers defend their work with that claim, they are admitting that it has no discernible meaning.

Does It Work?

The more innovative a work is, the more difficult it is to evaluate. Because the familiar elements of traditional fiction have been altered or even abandoned, writers have trouble describing what succeeds and what doesn't, and so do their readers.

The first question to be faced is the degree of obscurity. Innovative work often has to be read more carefully than traditional fiction, but excessive obscurity simply means that the story has failed. Think of architecture: innovation is admired, but if the structure collapses, the rubble is worth nothing. Back to the drawing board. Determining the degree of obscurity is a special problem for writers who are trying to evaluate their own work without the benefit of a group. One's own intent often seems crystal clear, even brilliant. It takes a special effort to read what one has written with objectivity.

If there is any question as to what will make sense to a conscientious reader, try to find two or three individuals who are familiar with experimental fiction. Ask them for their reactions. Don't be content with those initial kindly comments friends feel obliged to give; ask them to describe exactly what they drew from your work. If their answers become evasive ("Well, I don't really know what you're doing, but I liked reading it"), ask yourself what you hoped they would see. You may be able to meet your readers halfway. If, however, you were just writing off the top of your head, stick the effort in a file called "scraps."

Those in writing classes or discussion groups are luckier. But even there one can face problems. Groups are sometimes hesitant to be open and honest when discussing a complex and experimental work. No one wants to appear dumb, so sometimes unsuccessful works are treated too gently and described as "interesting."

To get the most from a class, don't start out by explaining a story. As a serious writer you want to find out what the story has communicated on its own. If their response is disappointing, try not to be defensive. Remember that they are your allies, not the enemy. Work with them. It may be necessary to ask bluntly what came through and what remains unclear. See if you can devise revisions that will draw readers into the work without abandoning your original conception.

To be more specific, if there is a premise involved, is it eventually revealed? It may be established at the start, as in Kafka's "The Metamorphosis," or it may be revealed at the end, as in "The Balloon." But if it remains murky, the story will end up like a photo that is out of focus.

Second, if innovative style is employed, is it consistent? And does it have some purpose? What would the story be like if the language were more conventional? It might lose a great deal, but on the other hand, it might reach a wider readership. In short, is the style an asset or a hindrance?

Third, look at the **tone**. Some experimental stories start out so stridently that there is no way to sustain the emotion. This is particularly true of works that take a strong social, political, or ethical stand. Hitting the same chord too loudly and too often can reduce the impact. This also applies to obscenities and profanities. Repetition becomes boring.

The tone may benefit from a little wit and humor. Some experimental stories are so heavy they seem like bread baked without yeast. Take a look at the tone Barthelme adopts in "The Balloon." He's not dealing with a deadly plague that settles on New York, he is describing through a whimsical symbol the sense of melancholy that comes from separation. The absurd nature of the premise and the cool, controlled tone keep the story from wallowing in self-pity. Never underestimate the power of comedy to convey serious emotions.

Fourth, is the story memorable? That is, will some readers want to read it again? Or is it simply a clever idea that gives a moment of pleasure like a well-told joke? Have you provided enough richness, enough suggestibility? Notice that in "The Balloon" Barthelme suggests more than simply the melancholy of separation. His characters echo the phrases some readers use to describe odd and unfamiliar fiction (some found it "interesting"). Other characters look for "meaning." "The apparent purposelessness of the balloon was vexing. . . . " The children are much less concerned with interpretation than they are with the pleasure of playing with it. The function of the balloon continues even after the couple are reunited. It is carried away to "West Virginia, awaiting some other time of unhappiness." The more you read this story, the more ramifications you can find.

There is one more factor in determining whether an innovative story is successful: Does it give pleasure? That is, are there elements in plotting, style, or theme that are really fresh and striking? One of the goals of innovative work is to dazzle the reader with techniques that are unique. Sometimes it is language, but in other works the language is neutral (as in "The Balloon") and the originality is in the concept. Remember that an innovative story usually takes a little extra effort to read. In return for that exertion, you owe the reader some special pleasure. If you are going to be innovative, be fresh and entertaining.

Nonrealistic fiction provides many possibilities, but like **free verse** it is not anarchy. It is not scribbling. A piece may begin spontaneously with little or no plan, but before it is ready for others to read it has to be shaped and given purpose. There are many different traditions that you can draw on and learn from. It is important to familiarize yourself with them so that you can distinguish an informal journal entry from a story with literary merit.

27

HEIGHTENED MEANING:

Metaphor, Symbol, and Theme

Converting abstractions into images. How similes and metaphors work. Vehicles and tenors. The impact of a symbol. Theme: the portion of a story that comments on the human condition. When themes need revision.

Nonfiction tends to use **abstractions** like "self-consciousness" and "excitement." Fiction often translates these into **images** that we can see or feel. Compare, for example, the two versions of these three statements:

ABSTRACT STATEMENT	VISUAL VERSION
Sometimes she is self-conscious about her height.	She arcs down into herself like a long-neck bird.
He feels excited at being able to say things he has never said before.	He's an explorer, charting ground never seen by mortal eyes.
Hostilities between parents often do damage to their children.	She is limping . . . blood wells out of her foot.

The second choice in each pair provides a visual impression that is both more vivid and more memorable than the corresponding abstract statement. Similar as these three examples are in this respect, each one represents a slightly different technique. The first is a **simile,** the second is a **metaphor,** and the third is a **symbol**. Casual readers don't have to know the difference; a general sense of vitality is enough. But practicing writers can't always rely on impressions. It is hard to discuss any work of fiction, our own or someone else's, unless we define what we are talking about. To do this we have to use basic analytical terms precisely.

How Similes and Metaphors Work

First, some quick definitions. A **simile** is a comparison in which we state that one item (often an **abstraction**) is like something **concrete.** Frequently this is a visual image, but it may be anything we can respond to with one of the five senses. Thus "She fought like a lion" implies strength and courage. Notice, however, that it is not a simple comparison as in "Lemons are like oranges." We are not suggesting that this woman used claws or bit her opponent. We are saying only that the way she fought brings to mind the ferocity of a lion. It's impossible to see abstractions like ferocity, determination, or courage, but we can easily visualize a lion in action.

A **metaphor** serves the same function, but it makes the comparison without "like" or "as." This distinction is more significant than one might think because a metaphorical statement is literally untrue. It is only **figuratively** true. In this case we might have, "She is a lion when fighting for civil rights." *Is* a lion? Well, is *like* a lion. When we analyze metaphors, it is helpful to convert them into similes.

Similes and metaphors are both called **figurative language** or **figures of speech** because they use words in a nonliteral way. A **symbol,** incidentally, is not a figure of speech for reasons I will explain shortly.

Some authors use figurative language more than do others. It is possible to write a highly effective story without using a single figure of speech or a symbol. Most authors do, however. In this collection, all the stories contain both figures of speech and symbols.

In some cases similes and metaphors are used together so naturally that one hardly notices the difference. In "Obst Vw," for example, Demian makes this statement about his relationship with his father:

> "Sometimes in the room with him I feel like I don't exist. I don't have a body."

This is such a familiar feeling that we hardly think of it as figurative language. But to feel "like I don't exist" is a simile, since to feel *like* that is literally true. The next statement, "I don't have a body," is a metaphor since it is literally untrue. Notice how much more impact it has than it would have as a simile: "as if I don't have a body."

Figurative language is not a literary embellishment added to make one's style sound elegant. It is natural to common speech. Many of the examples we hear in daily life are so common that they have become **clichés**—similes and metaphors that have lost all impact from overuse. Stockbrokers aren't visualizing an animal when they refer to a "bull market," parents have no picture in mind when they ask children to make their rooms "neat as a pin," and none of us is sure why a whip is "smart." Similes and metaphors that heighten the meaning, make it vivid and intense, have to be fresh and original. If they are harmonious with the vocabulary and speech patterns of a character, they will blend into dialogue or narration just as naturally as into exposition.

Deborah Corey's "Three Hearts" contains many good examples. It is written, you remember, in the first person from the point of view of a young girl, Sissy. She frequently uses similes and metaphors that echo the way she might talk. She describes her mother's eyes, for example, as being "like faded jeans." This suggests more than just the color; there are overtones of being worn out as well. The author is more aware of the overtones than a girl Sissy's age would be, but the phrase blends in as a natural part of her narration.

In the same way, Sissy describes her brother Eddie as having "an angry streak like steel running through his heart." The phrase "angry streak" alone is technically a metaphor, but it is so familiar that we don't picture the streak. Having a "streak like steel running through his heart" is both visually arresting and at the same time natural to a young girl's language. In another simile, Sissy describes not only an action but an attitude behind the action. Eddie, returning after a night on the town, "steps over us as if we are stones." The frequency and vividness of these metaphors don't make the narrator sound precocious because they are the sort we often hear from children.

When figurative language is used as a part of dialogue or, as in this case, narration, it must be harmonious with that character's natural vocabulary and speech pattern. But even if it appears in exposition, it should blend in. When similes and metaphors are exaggerated for effect or to seem clever, they make a work of fiction seem affected or "literary" in the worst sense. Their function is to enrich the story without being conspicuous.

Vehicles and Tenors

The terms **vehicle** and **tenor** were originally suggested by the critic I. A. Richards, and they are used frequently by writers and poets because there is no better way to analyze precisely why one figure of speech is effective and another fails. As in poetry, the terms are also essential for an understanding of how similes and metaphors differ fundamentally from symbols.

The **vehicle** of a simile or metaphor is the image itself—usually a concrete object, something we can see or at least hear or feel. The **tenor** is the implied subject. If these terms are new to you, think of the **vehicle** as the transporter, carrying a message to the reader. As for the **tenor,** think of intention, since it is the intended meaning, often an abstraction.

In the example from "Three Hearts" describing how the brother "steps over us as if we were stones," the vehicle is the picture of someone stepping over stones in a field. The tenor is the total indifference with which Eddie treats his younger brother and sister. It might take a paragraph to spell out Eddie's attitude in exposition, but the vehicle gives us a mental picture in a single phrase.

The same is true of Demian's mix of exhilaration and anxiety when he begins to express hostile feelings about his father. For one who has longed for his father's respect and companionship, it is a terrible thing to be saying, "If he died tomorrow it wouldn't make the least difference in my life." How is the author to describe his emotions? She begins with a sentence of exposition: "It seems reckless and marvelous saying these things about his father." But then she shifts to the metaphor I quoted earlier: "He's an explorer, charting ground never before seen by mortal eyes." The explorer is the vehicle, but it would take a paragraph to describe the tenor in detail. Briefly, there are overtones of adventure, risk, pride in his courage, even bravado, fear. The best metaphors have tenors that are complex and often charged with mixed emotions.

The Impact of a Symbol

We are all familiar with **symbols** when they appear in political cartoons. The American flag, Uncle Sam, the cross, the Star of David, the Russian bear—all are built into the culture as representing abstractions such as a country or a religion.

Literarily simple novels particularly historical romances and gothic tales—have their fairly obvious and often-used symbolic images: the drinking of a toast by two evil plotters in which the wine spills, assuring us that they will fail; howling dogs on the moors signaling once again that someone is in torment. These are sometimes referred to as **public symbols** because they are widely known.

Sophisticated fiction, on the other hand, uses fresh images. The term **private symbol** is occasionally used but is rather misleading. *Original symbol* would be a far more accurate term. Such symbols are devised for a particular literary work rather than borrowed from the warehouse of well-known symbols. The meaning of an original symbol is revealed through the context of the story or novel. As a result, those who have not read extensively sometimes have difficulty in identifying them.

To see how a symbol differs from a metaphor, let's go back to our original example of a metaphor: "She was a lion in battle." The image of the lion is introduced simply for the purpose of comparison. There is no actual lion in the story. That's why we call it a *figure of speech*. Contrast this, however, with a story set in Africa that deals with a real lion. If the story is intended to contrast the cowardice of a hunter with true courage, it might be possible to describe the lion in ways that suggest the quality of courage. If this is done carefully, the lion could be made into a symbol for those qualities.

The difference between this symbolic use of the lion and the figurative use is clear once you see that in the case of a metaphor the vehicle (the lion) is not a literal part of the fiction. With a symbol, on the other hand, the vehicle is physically present in the story—all 400 pounds of him. The symbolic meaning, the tenor, is suggested through implication.

The difference between metaphors and symbols is made clear when they are used together in the same scene. At the end of "Sausage and Beer," for example, the waiter brings the order and then leaves "with a quick, benedictory smile." Translating that metaphor back to a simile: "with a smile as if it were the expression of a clergyman at the conclusion of a service." Father and son are then "lost in a kind of communion"—not a literal one. They are not, after all, in a church. In contrast, the sausage and beer that the waiter brings are real, not figures of speech, and a careful reader will see that together they are a symbol for the bread and wine of certain religious services. How can we be sure? Not just because the author says so but because the reader has been prepared by those two previous metaphors. In addition, the significance of the image is highlighted by its use as the title.

Sometimes complex symbols are found in a first-person story narrated by a character who is far too young to be aware of them. "Three Hearts," for example, ends with a symbolic detail that the narrator, Sissy, does not perceive. Bucky has almost died because their brother Eddie would not get out of bed to help. Bucky has survived only because the sickly mother has dug into the snow, found him, and performed mouth-to-mouth resuscitation. After their mother takes Bucky inside, the narrator picks up Bucky's mitten and the one that belongs to Eddie. (This action was prepared for early in the story when Mama tells Bucky, "Double up on your mittens. . . ." Details like this require a great deal of rewriting.)

Eddie's mitten is "grey and full of holes." She pulls on the yarn, "but the hole puckers together in a kiss." She then does this with every hole, and the mitten finally "rumples itself into a little ball."

The story, you remember, informs us in the third paragraph that Eddie has been a continual problem, a dropout who stays out drinking all night and sleeps during the day. The family members, especially the mother, treat him gently, even with love. In exactly the same way, Sissy ineffectively tries to mend Eddie's mitten: the hole puckers "in a kiss" and eventually "rumples itself into a little ball," just as Eddie himself sleeps inside, as useless as the little ball of yarn.

The mitten is real—not a figure of speech—and so becomes a symbol for Eddie's damaged and hopeless state. The question to ask when distinguishing a metaphor from a symbol is simply this: Is the vehicle a figure of speech (like that metaphorical kiss), or does it, like the mitten, exist in the story?

"Obst Vw" is a highly symmetrical story dealing with two characters almost equally. Their problems are revealed through two separate symbols, each of which is given a prominent emphasis. They become central to the story.

Before I go on, stop for a minute and see if you can identify on your own the primary symbol for each of these characters. Remember that occasionally titles serve to highlight a symbolic detail, as in "Sausage and Beer."

For Demian, that ticket with the abbreviation "obst vw" is a clear and tangible symbol. It suggests the obstructed vision Demian has of his father as well as his father's view of him. In addition, it comments on the relationships Rachel's parents have with each other and that Rachel has with them. In a minor but significant way, it also applies to the absurdly inaccurate view Rachel's father has of Demian's father, calling him "the Old Hippie" for no logical reason. In fact, every relationship in that story, with the possible exception of Demian and Rachel, is damaged by an obscured or distorted view.

The central symbol characterizing Rachel's emotional state is appropriately more dramatic. It is a broken cup. The father has thrown it against the refrigerator in his rage, and the mother has shown her disdain by refusing to sweep it up. It is the daughter who is injured—a rather basic symbol reaffirming the well-known fact that children are damaged when parents fight.

The real subtlety of that broken cup and the injury lies in Rachel's attitude toward it. Instead of bandaging the cut, she flaunts it, sitting there "while her blood drip-drips onto the gray tile." It's her statement to them. "They need to *see* this," she says. The gesture is partly a longing for sympathy and partly hostility. It may also be an unconscious appeal for Demian's sympathy. At the end of that story, you remember, Demian kisses the injured spot, "smoothing down the flap of torn skin," a sincere but possibly futile attempt to heal her wounds, both physical and emotional.

Notice that the vehicles of these two symbols—the ticket marked OBST-VW and the broken cup—have both been expanded into **scenes**, each with its own **setting**. The entire episode at the ballpark and the scene in the kitchen become symbolic. If you read those scenes over you will see how many details refer in different ways to the tenor. Notice too that they are not just dropped into the story like meteors from outer space, they are planned for and used extensively. They are, to use a slightly shop-worn metaphor, woven into the fabric of the story.

There is a central symbol in "Escapes" too, though it is a place rather than an object. Alcatraz is not just a vivid setting, it is a prison. And the author makes sure that you won't miss its symbolic importance. Caryn and Jennifer enter a cell and they pretend that they "are in solitary confinement." Jennifer speaks:

> "Imagine being locked in here and knowing that San Francisco is right across the bay. . . . Hearing people at a party."

This is also a description of their own state of isolation. They have no friends there other than each other. Like the prisoners, they can hear the sounds of San Francisco but are not a part of it.

Caryn points out that they can walk out of the prison, but later she reflects on this.

> I realize, standing there. . .that there is really no escaping. Not for Sherry, not for Jennifer, not for me. The only thing left to do is to stick it out.

That prison has become a symbol for their state. Physically they can leave, but in a deeper sense they—indeed, all of us—will always be in solitary. Like the prisoners, we devise tricks to help us deal with this isolation, but the best we can do is "to stick it out." With this in mind they "link arms for the climb."

Incidentally, many readers study that story without noticing that the narrator's name is also symbolic. Caryn is revealed as one who is *caring*. One note of warning, however: symbolic names are risky indeed. Chris is too often bearded and saintly, Victor is predictably one who wins or, ironically, loses, and Adam is a firstborn who eventually gets thrown out of his Edenic home. Only a few names, like Willy Loman (low-man), in *Death of a Salesman*, are unobtrusive. If you are going to select a symbolic name, make it original and its significance close to subliminal.

For some readers, picking out figurative language and symbols seems like a literary game that detracts from the pleasure of a story. As a result, some student writers avoid any symbolic suggestion for fear of sounding artificial or self-consciously literary. Keep in mind, however, that reading as recreation is different from reading analytically as a writer. The only way to create subtle symbolic suggestions in your own writing is to study how others have done it.

A few reassurances may help. First, symbols are not a necessary ingredient in fiction. Excellent stories and novels—sophisticated in the best sense—are written without even the hint of a symbolic detail.

Second, neither figures of speech nor symbols are the invention of teachers. They are a part of common speech. We use figurative language without much conscious thought, just as the narrator does in "Three Hearts." We dream in symbols. Fantasies tend to be symbolic. They have been a special concern of writers in every age because the visual element often provides a far greater range of suggestion than can be achieved through straightforward, literal language.

Finally, very few stories are ruined for a reader if he or she does not see symbolic elements at first. This may have been true for you after your first reading of any of these stories. Few works depend on them as fully as does "The Balloon."

Turning now to your own work, here is a cardinal rule to remember: keep it subtle. Far better that some of your readers miss your symbolic suggestions than to be overwhelmed by them. When readers recognize a blatant symbol, your effort as author becomes apparent. The illusion of reality breaks and the story seems contrived.

In the interest of subtlety, think twice before you let a serious story depend utterly on a symbol. Barthelme's "The Balloon" is an exception because the **tone** is light and whimsical. Trying to guess what the balloon represents is part of the fun. But unless you're in a joking mood, works that place excessive emphasis on a central symbol often sacrifice credibility, overwhelmed by that central abstract idea. Picture what "Escapes" would be like if the entire story were set in that prison or if "Obst Vw" were limited to the kitchen, Rachel's foot dripping from start to finish. The best approach is to move cautiously and let the story suggest to you what might be made symbolic. Whenever possible, develop your symbolic material from the events, the setting, and the characters of the story itself. The goal is to have symbolic details serve the story, not dominate it.

The Importance of Theme

Journal entries don't usually have a theme. They record events or describe personal feelings often without any unifying concern. Sophisticated fiction, on the other hand, almost always implies an unstated central concern. Readers look for it. If you don't provide some kind of theme, readers are apt to ask, "What's the point?" or "What are you getting at?"

There are many ways to define **theme**, but I have found that this is the simplest and most useful for writers: *Theme is the portion of a work of fiction that comments on the human condition.* In most cases that comment is implied, not stated. If you think of theme in this way, you will never confuse it with **plot**. Plot is what happens. When we talk about plot, we name characters and describe events. When we talk about theme, we discuss in abstract terms the underlying suggestion of the story.

To describe the theme of a story, use a full sentence, not just a word. "Isolation" is not the theme of "Escapes." It is a topic. Even "Fear of isolation" is not yet a statement. You need a complete sentence, such as "Fear of isolation leads us to reach out and share our lives with another person."

Because the theme is almost always implied rather than stated, different readers will phrase it differently. Those variations reflect what aspect each person feels is most important. When discussing the theme of a story in a group, the goal is not to agree on one specific wording but, rather, to uncover aspects of the story that passive readers might easily miss. When the work being discussed is your own, make a real effort to remain silent, at least at first. This is the only way to find out what aspects reached your readers and which did not.

Put in simplest terms, the **plot** of "Three Hearts" can be summed up this way: "a boy is saved from suffocating by a mother who in spite of disabilities summons inner strength." The **theme**, on the other hand, might be described as "The weakest member of a family occasionally turns out to be the strongest in a real emergency." Or, if we wish to emphasize the role of women, "No matter how debilitated a mother may be, she can call on inner strength when her children are threatened." There may be readers who will want to highlight Eddie as described in that final image of the balled-up mitten: "No matter how sympathetic a family is toward a dysfunctional member, he or she may end up beyond repair." The first two thematic statements are like describing a glass as being half full, and the third describes it as half empty, but each applies to the same story. Each describes an aspect of the human condition.

All thematic statements are necessarily simplifications. They are abstract distillations of meaning. As you can see, most sophisticated stories have a cluster of related themes. Often there is a dominant concern that provides thematic focus and then a cluster of related themes. For this reason, some critics and writers prefer the phrase **central concern** rather than *theme*. The two terms are used in the same way.

Turning to "Obst Vw," there are several different statements we could use to describe the central concern, but they all deal with the relationship between adolescents and their parents. Remember that *theme* doesn't describe the plot or even mention the characters by name. One statement might stress the harm done to young people this way: "Parental indifference can be as damaging to an adolescent as actual violence." Another might focus on how the effects differed: "Parents who act out their rage against their children do more serious and lasting damage than those who are merely distant and insensitive." Others might prefer to highlight a more positive aspect: "When young people feel cut off from parental affection, they sometimes can find solace with someone their own age."

As you analyze the themes in published stories, it may seem as if authors somehow hold all those threads in their heads from the start. Not so. What you read in print is a final draft, and rarely do authors have all those intellectual concerns in mind when they begin a new story. Developing thematic concerns is an evolving process.

Here, then, is an important aspect of the creative process that can't be taught: a complex story speaks to its author through successive drafts. The story itself develops certain characters, highlights certain scenes. Most important, it often informs the writer about new thematic possibilities. Each suggestion, of course, requires more rewriting. The author who quits after the first draft can never hear the story suggesting new implications that might be developed. Although the notion of a dialogue between the story and the author is a metaphor, it is often a fundamental part of the creative process.

When Themes Need Revision

If you come to the conclusion that there is something wrong with the theme of the story you are working on, you may be tempted to abandon the work. The situation is indeed serious, but it may not be fatal. Here are some correctable problems.

A recurring weakness in student fiction is settling for a theme that is a **truism.** That is, the theme is nothing more than a widely accepted and obvious assertion. Who wants to read a story that does little but remind us that you should say "no" to drugs, that you shouldn't drink and drive, that people who don't express their emotions get into trouble. These are all reasonable statements, and they may serve as part of a theme, but if that is all a story suggests, it is going to seem as dull as one of those newspaper editorials you don't finish reading.

At the beginning of the fiction section I warned against seven "deadly sins," plot patterns that have become clichés. Thematic clichés are subtler because they can be disguised, but they are equally serious. If you take the time to compose a thematic statement that describes your story and all you can come up with is one of those trite slogans, you know you're in trouble.

But all is not lost. Often you can salvage such a story. One way is to look closer at the characters you are working with. A banal theme is usually a sign that you have started with an idea rather than a character or a situation. You may not have to scrap the whole story if you can develop greater subtlety in characterization. "Obst Vw," for example, could be described as having a simple theme, like "Bad marriages produce unhappy children," but as we have seen from composing various thematic statements for that story, it has a far greater range of concerns.

A second weakness is excessive reiteration of a theme. Avoid having every scene bluntly repeat the macho quality of the protagonist or the dishonesty of a corrupt businessman or some fundamental contrast in character between a husband and a wife. When the author's intent becomes obvious, the story loses credibility.

The solution, once again, is to look more closely at the characters. If they were conceived as a type such as a typical homeless man, a typical lawyer, a typical firefighter, replace him or her with a disguised version of a person you know. Then explore that person's individuality. Look for ironic contrasts, mixed feelings, strengths and weaknesses. Remember that materialists aren't always grasping, spiritual types aren't always motivated by pure thoughts, dishonest people are occasionally capable of kindness and even love. Demain's father, for example, is rigid and often insensitive to the feelings of others, but not unrelentingly so. Look at the pressure he is under at work and the frustrations left over from his own adolescence.

Don't be afraid to develop the odd twists in human relationships. As you develop a credibly complex character, the story will no longer strike the same note repeatedly. And in the process you may find that the theme becomes richer, more original.

Themes that are obscure present a third problem that calls for careful revision. I've already warned against a plot that is baffling, but a clear plot with an obscure theme can be just as dissatisfying. In some cases you may find that you can't describe the theme of your own story in a single sentence. That should tell you something. Or the theme may be obvious to you but not to others. If three or more readers are puzzled, making comments like, "What are you getting at?" don't assume they are all dumb. Having this kind of input available is the advantage of working in a writing class or with a group of fellow writers.

If the theme needs clarification, resist the temptation to add a line of exposition at the end explaining the story. See if you can find ways of dramatizing the theme through action, dialogue, or thoughts earlier in the story. You might also consider a concluding action that will bring the story into focus. If you review the endings of a number of stories you have read, you will see how many ways there are to highlight a theme in the final paragraph without explaining everything to the reader in the form of an analytical statement.

"Escapes" is a good example. The theme is revealed in three stages. First, both characters imagine what it would be like to be held in solitary confinement. The dialogue reminds us how isolated each of them has been. Second, Caryn through her thoughts expresses the idea that none of us can escape the sense of being in isolation. We can only "stick it out." Finally, in the form of action they "link arms for the climb." The theme of that story is unfolded throughout the work, but notice how these three key passages take the form of dialogue, thoughts, and finally action.

Theme is only one aspect of a story. The freshest and most insightful theme won't make a story succeed if the characters are not convincing and the action implausible. But without originality and complexity of theme, a story becomes nothing more than a simple piece of passing entertainment. A truly sophisticated work of fiction appeals to the mind as well as to the emotions.

28

A STORY

by Jackson Jodie Daviss

Gotta Dance

Maybe I shouldn't have mentioned it to anyone. Before I knew it, it was all through the family, and they'd all made it their business to challenge me. I wouldn't tell them my plans, other than to say I was leaving, but that was enough to set them off. Uncle Mike called from Oregon to say, "Katie, don't do it," and I wouldn't have hung up on him except that he added, "Haven't you caused enough disappointment?" That did it. Nine people had already told me no, and Uncle Mike lit the fire under me when he made it ten. Nine-eight-seven-six-five-four-three-two-one. Kaboom.

On my way to the bus station, I stopped by the old house. I still had my key and I knew no one was home. After ducking my head into each room, including my old one, just to be sure I was alone, I went into my brother's room and set my duffel bag and myself on his bed.

The blinds were shut so the room was dim, but I looked around at all the things I knew by heart and welcomed the softening effect of the low light. I sat there a very long time in the silence until I began to think I might never rise from that bed or come out of that gray light, so I pushed myself to my feet. I eased off my sneakers and edged the rug aside so I could have some polished floor, then I pushed the door shut.

Anyone passing in the hall outside might've heard a soft sound, a gentle sweeping sound, maybe a creak of the floor, but not much more as I danced a very soft shoe in my stocking feet. Arms outstretched but loose and swaying, head laid back and to one side, like falling asleep, eyes very nearly closed in that room like twilight, I danced to the beat of my heart.

After a while, I straightened the rug, opened the blinds to the bright day and walked out of what was now just another room without him in it. He was the only one I said good-bye to, and the only one I asked to come with me, if he could.

At the bus station, I asked the guy for a ticket to the nearest city of some size. Most of them are far apart in the Midwest and I liked the idea of those long rides with time to think. I like buses—the long-haul kind, anyway—because they're so public that they're private. I also like the pace, easing you out of one place before easing you into the next, no big jolts to your system.

My bus had very few people on it and the long ride was uneventful, except when the little boy threw his hat out the window. The mother got upset, but the kid was happy. He clearly hated that hat; I'd seen him come close to launching it twice before he finally let fly. The thing sailed in a beautiful arc, then settled on a fence post, a ringer, just the way you never can do it when you try. The woman asked the driver if he'd mind going back for the hat. He said he'd mind. So the woman stayed upset and the kid stayed happy. I liked her well enough, but the boy was maybe the most annoying kid I've come across, so I didn't offer him the money to buy a hat he and his mother could agree on. Money would have been no problem. Money has never been my problem.

There are some who say money is precisely my problem, in that I give it so little thought. I don't own much. I lose things all the time. I'm told I dress lousy. I'm told, too, that I have no appreciation of money because I've never had to do without it. That may be true. But even if it is, it's not all there is to say about a person.

There is one thing I do well, and money didn't buy it, couldn't have bought it for me. I am one fine dancer. I can dance like nobody you've ever seen. Heck, I can dance like everybody you've ever seen. I didn't take lessons, not the usual kind, because I'm a natural, but I've worn out a few sets of tapes and a VCR. I'd watch Gene Kelly and practice until I had his steps. Watch Fred Astaire, practice, get his steps. I practice all the time. Bill Robinson. Eleanor Powell. Donald O'Connor. Ginger Rogers. You know, movie dancers. I'm a movie dancer. I don't dance in the movies, though. Never have. Who does, anymore? I dance where and when I can.

My many and vocal relatives don't think much, have never thought much, of my dancing—largely, I believe, because they are not dancers themselves. To be honest, they don't think much of anything I do, not since I left the path they'd set for me, and that's been most of my twenty-three years. These people, critical of achievement they don't understand, without praise for talent or dreams or the elegant risk, are terrified of being left behind but haven't the grace to come along in spirit.

Mutts and I talked a lot about that. He was a family exception, as I am, and he thought whatever I did was more than fine. He was my brother, and I backed everything he did, too. He played blues harmonica. He told bad jokes. We did have plans. His name was Ronald, but everyone's called him Mutts since he was a baby. No one remembers why. He never got his chance to fly, and I figure if I don't do this now, I maybe never will. I need to do it for both of us.

The bus depot was crowded and crummy, like most city depots seem to be. I stored my bag in a locker, bought a paper and headed for where the bright lights would be. I carried my tap shoes and tape player.

When I reached the area I wanted it was still early, so I looked for a place to wait. I found a clean diner, with a big front window where I could read the paper and watch for the lines to form. I told the waitress I wanted a long cup of coffee before ordering. After a half hour or so, she brought another refill and asked if I was ready. She was kind and patient and I wondered what she was doing in the job. It seems like nothing takes it out of you like waitress work. She was young; maybe that was it. I asked her what was good and she recommended the baked chicken special, said it was what she'd had on her break. That's what I had, and she was right, but I only picked at it. I wanted something for energy, but I didn't want to court a side ache, so the only thing I really ate was the salad. She brought an extra dinner roll and stayed just as pleasant the whole time I was there, which was the better part of two hours, so I put down a good tip when I left.

While I was in the diner, a truly gaunt young man came in. He ordered only soup, but he ate it like he'd been hungry a long time. He asked politely for extra crackers and the waitress gave them to him. When he left, he was full of baked chicken special with an extra dinner roll. He wouldn't take a loan. Pride, maybe, or maybe he didn't believe I could spare it, and I didn't want to be sitting in a public place pushing the idea that I had plenty of money. Maybe I don't know the value of money, but I know what discretion is worth. The guy was reluctant even to take the chicken dinner, but I convinced him if he didn't eat it, nobody would. He reminded me of Mutts, except that Mutts had never been hungry like that.

When the lines were forming I started on over. While I waited, I watched the people. There were some kids on the street, dressed a lot like me in my worn jeans, faded turtleneck, and jersey warm-up jacket. They were working the crowd like their hopes amounted to spare change. The theater patrons waiting in line were dressed to the nines, as they say. There is something that makes the well-dressed not look at the shabby. Maybe it's guilt. Maybe it's embarrassment because, relatively, they're overdressed. I don't know. I do know it makes it easy to study them in detail. Probably makes them easy marks for pickpockets, too. The smell of them was rich: warm wool, sweet spice and alcohol, leather, peppermint and shoe polish. I thought I saw Mutts at the other edge of the crowd, just for a moment, but I remembered he couldn't be.

I was wearing my sneakers, carrying my taps. They're slickery black shoes that answer me back. They're among the few things I've bought for myself and I keep them shiny. I sat on the curb and changed shoes. I tied the sneakers together by the laces and draped them around my shoulders.

I turned on my tape player and the first of my favorite show tunes began as I got to my feet. I waited a few beats, but no one paid attention until I started to dance. My first taps rang off the concrete clear and clean, measured, a telegraphed message: *Takka-takka-takka-tak! Takka-takka-takka-tak! Takka-takka-takka-tak-tak-tak!* I paused; everybody turned.

I tapped an oh-so-easy, wait-a-minute time-step while I lifted the sneakers from around my neck. I gripped the laces in my right hand and gave the shoes a couple of overhead, bola-style swings, tossing them to land beside the tape player, neat as you please. I didn't miss a beat. The audience liked it; I knew they would. Then I let the rhythm take me and I started to fly. Everything came together. I had no weight, no worries, just the sweet, solid beat. Feets, do your stuff.

Didn't I *dance*. And wasn't I *smooth*. Quick taps and slow rolling, jazz it, swing it, on the beat, off the beat, out of one tune right into the next and the next and I never took one break. It was a chill of a night, but didn't I sweat, didn't that jacket just have to come off. Didn't I feel the solid jar to the backbone from the heavy heel steps, and the pump of my heart on the beat on the beat on the beat.

Time passed. I danced. A sandy-haired man came out of the theater. He looked confused. He said, "Ladies and gentlemen, curtain in five minutes." I'm sure that's what he said. Didn't I dance, and didn't they all stay. The sandyhaired man, he was tall and slim and he looked like a dancer, and didn't he stay, too.

Every move I knew, I made, every step I'd learned, I took, until the tape had run on out, until they set my rhythm with the clap of their hands, until the sweet sound of the overture drifted out, until I knew for certain they had held the curtain for want of an audience. Then I did my knock-down, dragout, could-you-just-die, great big Broadway-baby finish.

Didn't they applaud, oh honey, didn't they yell, and didn't they throw money. I dug coins from my own pockets and dropped them, too, leaving it all for the street kids. Wasn't the slender man with sandy hair saying, "See me after the show." I'm almost sure that's what he said as I gripped my tape player, grabbed my sneakers, my jacket, and ran away, ran with a plan and a purpose, farther with each step from my beginnings and into the world, truly heading home.

The blood that drummed in my ears set the rhythm as I ran, ran easy, taps ringing off the pavement, on the beat on the beat on the beat. Everything was pounding, but I had to make the next bus, that I knew, catch that bus and get on to the next town, and the next, and the next and the next. Funeral tomorrow, but Mutts will not be there, no, and neither will I. I'm on tour.

29

STYLE AND TONE

Style: from inconspicuous to conspicuous. Diction (word choice). Syntax (sentence structure). Density (figurative and symbolic language). The balance of narrative modes. Tense: present and past. Person: first and third. Tone, the attitude of the author or the persona. Irony and satire.

Style is the manner in which a work is written. All fiction has style. You can't compose without it any more than you can write your name without revealing your handwriting.

Varieties of style run all the way from inconspicuous to conspicuous. Inconspicuous styles may have identifiable characteristics, but the average reader is not aware of them. The fact that such work does actually have a style becomes clear if you compare a contemporary story or novel with one written in 1900 or earlier. The style we use is shaped by the age in which we live, our unconscious inclinations, and our conscious choices as individual writers.

Conspicuous styles are readily apparent. They may be devised for particular works, especially those that are first-person narratives. Or they may apply to all of that author's work so consistently that you can identify the author from a sample page just as easily as you can recognize the voice of a friend on the telephone. The fiction of Ernest Hemingway, for example, tends to have short, relatively simple sentences, while that of Henry James is distinctive for its lengthy, complex sentences and its extensive vocabulary that frequently sends a conscientious reader to the dictionary.

The term **voice** has come into prominence since the 1980s. In its broadest and least helpful sense it is used as an unneeded synonym for **style**. A more precise and useful use of the word is limited to styles that are distinctive, especially those presented through a **persona** or first-person narrator. As-if-narrated fiction often has the sound of spoken language.

"Escapes" employs an essentially inconspicuous style. Like all fiction, it does have a style, but it is subtle and the casual reader is not consciously aware of it. The style in "Gotta Dance," on the other hand, is conspicuous. The voice of the persona, Katie, is very much in evidence. Even on first reading it is clear that the language is close to how she might speak. The voice used in that story contributes to our understanding of the narrator.

To see the contrast, here are two passages that are similar in that they each describe a moment in which the narrator makes a very important decision. The first is from "Escapes" and the second from "Gotta Dance":

> I had not seen Jennifer in almost two years when Sherry called me that day. . . So I'm still not sure what made me say yes, I'll take her for a while. Except for maybe the thought of sharing that ultrablue sky with someone seemed so appealing.

> Uncle Mike called from Oregon to say, "Katie, don't do it," and I wouldn't have hung up on him except that he added, "haven't you caused enough disappointment?" That did it. Nine people had already told me no, and Uncle Mike lit the fire under me when he made it ten. Nine-eight-seven-six-five-four-three-two-one. Kaboom.

With that comic echo from a rocket launching, the reader is assured that this story will do lively things with style. As it turns out, the innovations become pronounced as soon as Katie begins to dance. That entire scene is an excellent example of a distinctive **voice**

Because there is no end to the number of stylistic effects you can achieve, the analysis of style can become confusing. Surprisingly, however, style is determined by just six factors:

1. **Diction**, the choice of words
2. **Syntax**, sentence structure (short, long; simple, complex)
3. **Density**, the presence or absence of figurative and symbolic language
4. **Narrative modes**, the relative emphasis on dialogue, thoughts, action, and exposition
5. **Tense** past or present
6. **Person**, first ("I"), third ("she/he"), and very occasionally "you" and "they"

Don't think of these as a checklist to be considered before you start a new story. Trust your inclinations and get that first draft down on paper. These basic elements of style, however, are enormously important when you begin revising. In addition, they have two other functions: they will help guide any discussion group by keeping the analysis precise and helpful. And, equally important, they will help you to read published work with greater understanding. If you understand the importance of these six aspects, you will find yourself reading actively like a writer.

Diction

Those of us who write in English have one real advantage: we have far more words at our disposal than do those using any other European language. We have one set of words from our Norse-Germanic heritage and another from Greek and Latin sources filtered through French. In addition, we have borrowed from the Chinese ("gong," "tong"), Hindi and Tamil from India ("khaki" "curry"), Eskimo ("kayak," "igloo"), and a great many other languages. English, to the dismay of foreign students, has been a hospitable language for centuries, adopting whatever is useful as its own.

This makes for a great deal of duplication. Many of our words with Anglo-Saxon or Old Norse origin have a corresponding word with a Greek or Latin source. Although they have essentially the same meaning, they almost always have different **overtones**. In general, Anglo-Saxon words (on the left below) are considered more informal. Some, not listed here, are viewed as obscene. Those with Greek or Latin roots (on the right) strike us as elevated or formal.

sweating	perspiring
grabbed	embraced
boat	vessel
got in	entered
hate	detest
the sea	the ocean

Then there are words that have distinctly different overtones regardless of derivation. A *car* seems less expensive than *automobile*, but *motor car* is reserved for the truly luxurious. Real estate agents deal with *houses, homes, properties,* and *estates;* and though dictionaries don't rank them, we unconsciously view the terms on a scale from modest to expensive.

How does all this affect us when we write fiction? Word choice is a major factor in characterization, and it can reveal aspects of theme as well. The impact of diction is most evident in stories that are presented in the first person through a narrator. Works like "The Balloon" and "Gotta Dance," among others, give the illusion of a story being told out loud even though no audience is identified.

Often, much is revealed about such characters by the words they use. For example, the cool, rather formal narrator in "The Balloon" uses words like "pneumaticity" and phrases like "an admixture of pleasurable cognition." The volatile narrator in "Gotta Dance," on the other hand, uses slang, as in "Kaboom" and "Feets, do your stuff." She also uses one-syllable words that create a lively rhythm like "and the pump of my heart on the beat on the beat on the beat." Both narrators are responding to serious emotions—the absence of a dear friend in one case and the death of a brother in the other.

Yet the contrast in diction is unmistakable. Imagine Katie in "Gotta Dance" saying "a spontaneous autobiographical disclosure"!

While diction is particularly important when the story is told in the first person, it also has a major impact on third-person fiction. The words characters use in dialogue shape our view of them as well.

In reviewing the dialogue of your characters, consider age, education, and personality. Each will use a slightly different **level of usage**, ranging from formal to slang. Background may also be a factor. A city cab driver, for example, will have a different vocabulary from, say, a dairy farmer. Just a few words that seem "out of character" will spoil the sense of realism.

Fiction, of course, is not written word by word. When the writing is going well, let it flow. The time to take a close look at your diction is when you read over the completed first draft. Decide what effect you want to achieve, and revise accordingly.

Syntax

Syntax means sentence structure, and occasionally it has as much to do with the stylistic effect as diction. There is a subtle but significant difference in syntax in "Obst Vw." Both Demian and Rachel tend to use short, simple phrases as in this sample:

> "Who wants your parents?"
> "What's wrong with my parents?"
> "Your father has a mean streak."
> "No he doesn't."

Demian's parents, on the other hand, often use somewhat longer sentences. In the chapter on characterization we examined how the mother's dialogue reveals her loyalty to her husband. Now take a look at how the syntax subtly reveals the intensity of her feeling.

> "He's way too smart for what he does. . . . He did well in college without studying. He could remember everything he'd ever read. He was a great talker, there was nothing he couldn't have done if he'd wanted to—do you know how high his IQ is?"

Notice how the grammatical structure breaks down as she becomes more emotionally concerned. The fourth sentence runs on with a comma instead of a period (what was called a *comma splice* when grammar was taught) and then is continued after a dash which in formal English would have been a period. This is not careless writing. Grammatical rules are often bent in fiction to reveal the mood of the speaker.

The same lengthy and altered syntax is used by Demian's father. The content is an absurdly exaggerated response to Demian's simple request for a second chance, but what concerns us here is how the fractured syntax underscores his simmering rage and frustration:

> "If you get sick, kiddo. If your heart hurts, the air sticks in your throat, you say with your last feeble breath, God, Jesus, Krishna, whoever—please, what did I do, could you please, please, give me a second chance, what's He going to say to you?"

As a general rule, long sentences tend to slow the pace of a story. This applies to "The Balloon," which has a measured, almost stately pace in spite of being a love story of sorts. But as you can see from the way Demian's father occasionally talks, broken syntax can move quickly and suggest high emotions. In this case the man's frustrations about his own life are reflected in his fragmented outburst.

On a happier note, Katie's manic mood in "Gotta Dance" is echoed in her long but unconventional sentences:

> Quick taps and slow rolling, jazz it, swing it, on the beat, off the beat, out of one tune right into the next and I never took one break. It was a chill of a night, but didn't I sweat, didn't that jacket just have to come off. Didn't I feel the solid jar to the backbone from the heavy heel steps, and the pump of my heart on the beat on the beat on the beat.

In formal nonfiction a passage like this would be criticized for having *run-on sentences*. But this is innovative fiction. The rhythm of those long sentences with their repetitions echo the unbroken rhythm of her dancing. You can almost hear her taps with "on the beat on the beat on the beat."

As you can see from these examples, long sentences don't necessarily slow the pace. It depends on the rhythm, the diction, and the context. Since there is no firm rule to describe the effect of sentence structure, the best approach is to read your work out loud. If you hope to achieve a special effect, you should treat syntax like music.

One note of caution, however: most fiction is written with relatively standard syntax. That means using sentences with subjects and verbs and varying the length for variety. It also means selecting diction that is appropriate and accessible. If you try to impress your readers with long, complex sentences and words you found in a synonym dictionary, you will be indulging in what is known as **overwriting** or, worse, **purple**

prose. The writing will seem artificial or affected. When style draws attention to itself, readers are apt to focus on technique rather than the story as an integrated whole.

Density

A **dense style** is achieved when a great deal is implied about characterization and theme. With such work we often draw more from the second reading than we did the first time through.

Low density doesn't necessarily mean a story was badly written. We may refer to it as "fun," "entertaining," or "clever." With novels the phrase is "a quick read." The implication is that entertaining as it may be, we are unlikely to read it a second time.

Density is achieved when a story develops one or more characters in some detail, when the theme has complexity and insight, and when figurative language and symbolic suggestion are used. "Obst Vw" is a good example of dense style. As we have already seen in Chapter 24, it explores the subtleties of not just one but two central characters. And although Demian's parents are secondary, they too are revealed with some complexity. There are several themes dealing with parents and their children as well as the relationship between adolescents. And as we have seen, both characterization and themes are presented through symbolic details like the "obst vw" baseball ticket and the broken cup that cuts Rachel. In short, there is a lot going on in that story.

None of the stories included in this text really lack density, but "The Balloon" provides a good contrast with "Obst Vw." The character of the narrator is never fully developed and the person he misses is not even named. The enjoyment of the story rests almost entirely on the development of the central symbol, the balloon that suggests the dark but bearable sadness of separation. The story also pokes fun at how the reading public often responds to unusual fiction. It would be fair to say that it stresses theme and humor at the expense of characterization. Whether this is more enjoyable as fiction is entirely a personal decision, but we can agree that there is less density and as a result the style is lighter.

Returning now to your own writing, there may be times when you feel that the style of a story you are working on is too light, too insubstantial. In such cases you may want to develop a character's **ambivalent** feelings or reveal more about a second character. Sometimes a single theme can be expanded so that it becomes a cluster of themes.

Occasionally, though less often, you may find that you have taken on too many threads so that the story begins to seem cluttered and confused. This is not true density. In such cases, you may want to back off and focus on a single aspect. Or consider developing a humorous aspect. This is a matter of **tone** which I will turn to shortly.

In short, lack of density makes fiction seem slight; excessive density can make it turgid or, worse, confusing. Determine the level of density that is appropriate to your material.

The Balance of Narrative Modes

The third method of influencing your style in fiction is the balance of **narrative modes**. I am using *mode* in the special sense introduced at the beginning of the fiction section: dialogue, thoughts, action, description, and exposition.

Stories like "Escapes" or "Gotta Dance" that appear to be presented through a first-person narrator are in a sense all dialogue. But the approach is only an echo of actual speech, so work like this is not usually placed in quotation marks.

In spite of sounding like narration, such stories make use of the same five narrative modes as are found in third-person work. They may, however, stress a single mode at the expense of the others. Barthelme's "The Balloon" is at one extreme. Although it is presented in the first person, the fact that it is as if narrated is all but forgotten. What the reader responds to is almost entirely description with some explanatory exposition. Actual dialogue in quotation marks has been reduced to just a few scattered samples. In terms of style, the work resembles **creative nonfiction**. It is still fiction, however, because in spite of its lack of characterization and action, it has a plot that is clearly fanciful.

Another approach, not represented here, is to emphasize **dialogue** to the extent that almost all of the work becomes an exchange between two or more characters. This often has the effect of increasing the pace, but at a cost: it becomes much more difficult to present visual details such as the setting and the characters.

Description, one of our five modes, is important in some stories and not in others. In "Escapes," for example, Jennifer is described as "almost six feet, and so thin that her hip bones poke out from her faded blue jeans." In "Gotta Dance," on the other hand, we are given no details about Katie, the protagonist, except for her clothing. The emphasis in that story is on action, especially when she is dancing.

As we have seen, description is the dominant mode in "The Balloon," but in most stories it is kept in balance even when it is important. In "Sausage and Beer" much depends on the contrast between the austere hospital and the warm, friendly bar at the end of the story, and in "Escapes" the physical details about Alcatraz are given symbolic significance. But neither story allows description to be the dominant mode.

This does not mean that you should strive for an even balance of the five narrative modes in every story. It does suggest, however, that you should be aware of how that balance can affect the overall stylistic effect. If an early draft of a story seems heavy and slow, consider adding dialogue. Giving your characters a chance to talk often adds energy to an otherwise leaden story. On the other hand, if your story seems superficial or trivial, it may be that you have relied too much on insignificant dialogue and not enough on thoughts and description.

The two modes that give the most trouble are thoughts and **exposition**. Thoughts, like description, slow the pace. If that seems to be the trouble, get your protagonist moving and talking. Look at the way Katie's action in "Gotta Dance" keeps that story alive even though the motive for that action is a deep melancholy over the death of her brother. More dialogue may also help to enliven a story that has become bogged down with introspection.

Too much **exposition** is even more dangerous. Not only does it slow the pace, it may also explain too much. As I have pointed out before, fiction normally depends on action and dialogue to maintain the reader's sense of discovery. Exposition, even when filtered through a narrator, nudges a story in the direction of the essay. "The Balloon" runs that risk, but for most readers that essay-like tone is lightened by wit and satire.

While action can enliven your style, remember that too much may make the story superficial. If most of the story is devoted to what happens, there may be scant attention to characterization and theme.

The balance of modes shouldn't be a major concern when working on your first draft. The time to examine it is when you start revising. There is no inherent harm in favoring one mode over the others in a particular story, but try to judge as objectively as you can how this approach has affected your style. A few revisions at this early stage may make a major difference in the overall effect.

Tense

The matter of **tense** has become a controversy of sorts in the past decade. Traditionally, most short stories and novels were written in the past tense. Starting in the early 1980s, however, an increasing number of authors began using the present tense. Some readers, including some editors, dislike the practice on principle, but the number of present-tense stories in print continues to increase.

The effect of the present tense on style is highly subjective and difficult to judge. For some, it seems illogical and therefore disruptive to imply that events are occurring at the time of the telling. The counterargument is that readers really don't respond to present-tense stories as if they were diary entries. Readers lose themselves in the action, and after the first paragraph the matter of tense is largely forgotten. Can you, for example, recall which three of the six stories in this volume are written in the past tense?

Present-tense enthusiasts often claim that fiction is livelier and more immediate in that tense. If this were so, however, past-tense fiction would not have dominated fiction for over a century

There is one good technical reason for adopting the present tense. If a story in the past tense contains a number of **flashbacks**, the author normally cues the reader with the past perfect each time: "She had been an excellent lawyer in her 30s," for example. Then the flashback itself, you remember, reverts to simple past tense. If the main part of the story is written in the present tense, however, the author can signal the start of those flashbacks simply by shifting to the past tense and staying there. Sharon Solwitz, for example, one of the three in this book writing in the present tense, is able to slide into that flashback about going to the ball game simply by shifting from the present tense to the past.

As you remember, that story is unusual for its use of the future tense to indicate **flash-forwards**. This technique is extremely rare because it breaks the reader's connection with the ongoing action and places him or her outside the story. As I pointed out, it is justified in this particular case as a device to keep the story from becoming melodramatic, but used carelessly flash-forwards can spoil the illusion of reality.

It is odd that while the overall choice of present versus past tense is often hotly debated, its effect on fiction is almost negligible. If you are uncertain which to use with a particular story, try an opening half page first in past tense and then in present. One will seem better than the other, and you can invent a good explanation later.

Varieties of Tone

Whereas **style** has to do with the manner in which a work is written, a distinctly literary element, **tone** deals with the emotional element. In general usage, it can refer either to the emotion generated by the work itself or to the author's attitude toward that work.

The **tone** of a work itself can be described with adjectives like "comic," "amusing," "dark," "exciting," "sad," "merry," "eerie," or "depressing." When **tone** is applied to the author's attitude toward his or her material, it can be described as "close," as in works that seem autobiographical, or "distant," as in Barthelme's comic but detached style in "The Balloon." The author's tone can also be critical or disapproving of characters or institutions. It is important when discussing tone to make it clear whether you are talking about the story itself or the author's attitude toward the material.

"Gotta Dance" is a particularly interesting example because the tone of the story is not the same as the author's tone toward the subject matter. As we begin reading the story, the tone appears to be lighthearted. Katie is about to do something all her relatives urge her not to, and we assume that this will be a comic story of rebellion. The tone becomes slightly more serious in the scene when she returns to her home. That's when we learn by implication that her brother has died. Still, the story has a basically cheerful feel to it. When she arrives in a strange city and begins to dance, the tone becomes truly manic. "Feets, do your stuff" she exclaims to herself and goes into a whirlwind performance. But at the very end it becomes clear that the attitude of the author toward her work is unmistakably serious.

> I had to make the next bus, that I knew, catch that bus and get on to the next town, and the next, and the next and the next. Funeral tomorrow, but Mutts will not be there, no, and neither will I. I'm on tour.

At that point we realize that the apparently lighthearted tone of Katie as narrator is a front. She is sustaining her own courage and determination to pay honor to her dead brother. Not until the end do we realize that the author's tone is fundamentally serious. The author, in commenting on that story, has pointed out that in spite of the humor, her subject is grief.

> Some of us deny it, others wallow in it, and many simply limp along with it. . . . The people who seem to me to deal most successfully with grief are those who accept it and use the very intensity of it to transform the unbearable into something that can be borne with grace.

What tone should you adopt? Your first inclination may be the best, but not always. If you are writing a story that is at least partially based on personal experience, it will seem natural to present it with the tone you still feel. Remember, though, that what you are writing is fiction, not a diary entry. If the episode you are using might strike readers as a bit melodramatic or sentimental, it may be wise to lighten up a bit.

This is exactly what Solwitz does from time to time in "Obst Vw." Her protagonist is seriously alienated from his father, but the author is careful not to let the story sound like a soap opera in which the son is driven to suicide by an insensitive father. That flash-forward at the very beginning in which we as readers learn that Demian will in a year's time look back on the trip to the baseball game with amusement assures us that the incident won't utterly destroy him. It provides a touch of objectivity, and objectivity is the best guard against melodrama.

Even in that agonizing scene when Rachel has cut herself on the broken cup, there is something wryly comic about her act of letting the blood drip on the floor, a sad, futile, but offbeat attempt to make contact with her parents.

These two stories provide an interesting contrast in tone. "Gotta Dance" sustains a lighthearted tone in spite of the fact that the author's approach to the subject is serious. In "Obst Vw," on the other hand, the characters are darkly depressed about their parents and adopt a somber, almost melodramatic tone, but the author reminds us in different ways that theirs is not a life-and-death situation. The author's tone is one of genuine concern tempered with gentle amusement.

Irony and Satire

There are several types of **irony**, but they all involve a reversal of either meaning or of expectations.

Verbal irony is achieved when characters or authors say something that is intentionally different from what they really mean. In casual conversation we often call this **sarcasm**, although sarcasm is generally hostile and critical. Irony can take the form of simple understatement, as when someone describes a hurricane as "quite a blow." Stronger irony can be a full reversal of meaning, as when the same character, while watching a house being washed away in the storm, says, "Great day for a sail." We don't call him crazy, because we know he is speaking ironically rather than literally.

Verbal irony in fiction occurs most often in dialogue. It suggests a character who is wry and given to understatement. As such, it is one more way dialogue can help define character. We see it in Rachel's dialogue as the two teenagers are listening to her parents shout at each other at the beginning of "Obst Vw":

> "Wait. This is the part about who was the first unfaithful one!. . . It's funny, really. It's high comedy."

Verbal irony isn't limited to dialogue. Here is a passage in which Donald Barthelme chides the reading public with a flash of sarcasm:

> There was a certain amount of initial argumentation about the "meaning" of the balloon; this subsided because we have learned not to insist on meanings . . . and they are rarely even looked for now, except in cases involving the simplest, safest phenomena. It was agreed that . . . extended discussion was pointless.

Since the work as a whole deals with complex themes under a comic surface, the apparent indifference to "meaning" in this passage is ironic.

Dramatic irony is similar except that the character making the statement does not understand the true significance of what he or she is saying. It is called "dramatic" because it often is used in plays, especially those that make use of mistaken identifies. It would be dramatic irony, for example, if in a play a swindler enthusiastically outlined his latest scheme to someone known to the audience as the very person he plans to cheat.

In fiction, dramatic irony is often used in first-person stories in which narrators reveal more about themselves than they realize.

There is a good example of dramatic irony in "Three Hearts." While the two children are playing in the igloo, Bucky tells her sister to get some icicles. Sissy, the narrator, comments:

> The icicles are always my job. Bucky says Eskimo women do all the stuff like that. "Anything they can do without their husband's help, they do. They're brave," he told me once.

Neither of them, or course, is aware that this description of Eskimo women will apply to their mother. The statement turns out be ironic because it is prophetic without their awareness.

Cosmic irony, or *irony of fate*, also involves a reversal, but in this case the reversal is in events rather than words. It refers to any outcome that is the opposite of normal expectations. One often hears it used in a careless way to describe anything that is unexpected. True irony is stronger than that. It is ironic for a composer like Beethoven to lose his hearing or for an Olympic swimmer to drown in his own bathtub.

Historical events occasionally provide ironic twists that are too blatant for fiction. Bad enough that America's first major toxic waste disaster should occur in a place called the Love Canal, but what story writer would have dared call the polluter the Hooker Chemical Corporation?

Ironic reversals in fiction tend to be more muted so that they don't become obtrusive. One occurs in "Sausage and Beer" in the visit with Uncle Theodore. Although one might expect that bizarre behavior would be the most disturbing aspect of meeting someone who is mentally ill, it is actually Theodore's one moment of lucidity that jolts the boy.

In "Three Hearts" it is ironic that while the mother appears at first to be the weakest and least functional of all the characters, she ends up to be the only strong one.

Satire is best defined as exaggeration for the purpose of ridicule. It is almost always rooted in irony, but as you can see from the above examples, irony doesn't necessarily involve ridicule.

Most satire adopts a serious or even solemn **tone** while making fun of the topic through exaggeration. Occasionally the technique is reversed and a serious subject is treated as if it were high comedy. Either way, there is always a charged contrast between the apparent tone and the true intent.

Many readers are introduced to simple satire through magazines such as *Mad* and *National Lampoon* and films such as those produced by the Monty Python group and Woody Allen. Neither these nor the satiric sketches often seen on television are very subtle. In fiction there is a greater range and greater subtlety.

While "The Balloon," for example, is primarily concerned with the way we feel when separated from someone we love, it also satirizes how the public and some literary critics respond to experimental fiction such as "The

Balloon." Barthelme subtly ridicules those who feel that the only way we should judge a work of art is to describe our subjective reactions:

> It was also argued that what was important was what you felt when you stood under the balloon; some people claimed that they felt sheltered, warmed, as never before, while enemies of the balloon felt, or reported feeling, constrained, a "heavy feeling."
> Critical opinion was divided: . . .

If you replace the phrase "when you stood under the balloon" with "when you read this story," what follows makes more sense. He goes on to list other samples of "critical opinion," wildly inconsistent and subjective reactions such as "inner joy," "abnormal vigor," and "warm, soft, lazy passages." He presents them in fragments that resemble the almost meaningless quotations from critical reviews and used by publishers in their ads.

Barthelme's tone is relatively light, softened with wit. But satire can also serve as the voice of protest. As such, it can become bitter and hostile. When satire loses its sense of humor, it also tends to sacrifice subtlety in order to stress the message. In a sense, strong satiric pieces are to mainstream literature what political posters are to paintings.

If this approach interests you, keep in mind that there are two dangers in the writing of satire. The first is lack of focus. Decide in advance just what kind of person, institution, or attitude you wish to ridicule. Keep your satiric attack precise and detailed even if, like Barthelme's, it is complex.

The other danger is a matter of excess. If your exaggeration becomes extreme, you might find the piece turning into slapstick. Such work may, like cartoons, be very funny but, also like cartoons, be quickly forgotten. If you want to study (and enjoy) some examples of light but durable satire, read some of the novels by J. P. Marquand or Peter DeVries. For heavier, more biting satire, try George Orwell's *Animal Farm*, a comic but ultimately savage attack on Soviet communism of the 1930s, or Joseph Heller's *Catch-22*, a funny yet bitter view of war.

Style and tone are enormously important, but don't let them distract you when you are starting a new work. You can suffer a serious case of writer's block if you stare at a blank piece of paper or computer screen worrying about your stylistic options. As I have urged before, let the story develop. Have faith in your original vision. Once you have a rough draft safely down on paper or on the computer screen, then turn critic and examine these literary aspects.

Remember, too, that this chapter is largely a distillation of abstract concepts. For a real appreciation of what you can do with style and tone, you have to read a lot of fiction. This chapter will help you identify and evaluate the elements of style, but your growth and development over the years will come from fiction itself.

30

THREE KEYS TO DEVELOPMENT

Reading, Writing, Revising

Writing on your own. Why writers read. A regimen for writing. Rewriting and more rewriting. Seven critical questions. Setting priorities.

Those who discuss works of fiction without having studied the genre are limited to personal responses—the characters they liked or disliked, how they would have acted if they had been in that situation, people they know who are like those in the story. Such comments are generally sincere, but they don't deal with the story. They are chitchat.

Studying a textbook gives you a language for discussing fiction. It helps you to examine the work objectively. Your preferences are still important, but your discussion will focus on the work itself. It will be precise and helpful.

This applies whether you are examining a published work, the manuscript of a friend, or your own work. Even if you are working alone, you will start by asking the right questions.

Taking a course speeds this process. It develops your critical skills as well as the all-important capacity to accept criticism without cringing. And while no one enjoys deadlines, courses do generate an impressive output.

But what happens when you finish the textbook and leave the stimulus of class discussions and deadlines? How can you continue to develop? For most writers, it's difficult at first to shift from the structure of a class to self-motivation. Whether you are still in college or facing the complexities of a nonacademic life, there are three essential keys to continued development: regular reading, a schedule for writing, and tireless revision. Each is essential if you are going to expand your abilities. Each deserves close consideration.

Why Writers Read

Here is a humbling question for all those who take creative writing courses and for those who teach them: How did literature flourish in all those centuries before creative writing courses were introduced in the 1940s? The answer is simple: Writers spent more time reading than writing. They learned from studying other writers. And they still do.

Courses and textbooks speed up the process, but they are no substitute for reading a lot of good fiction. Student writers who have read extensively before attending college have a distinct advantage. And graduates who continue the reading habit in spite of other demands will continue to have an edge over those who don't.

The first essential for those who want to develop as writers is to spend at least as much time reading as they do writing. Preferably more. Surprising as it may seem, there are many who do not. As a result, they don't expand their abilities because they have cut themselves off from the greatest resource a writer has: published fiction.

It is a mistake to limit one's reading to contemporary work. Fictional styles change, but one learns from every period. The experiments in language of James Joyce and Virginia Woolf seem contemporary because they have influenced our age. The plot structure of a Charles Dickens novel or the use of **voice** in a Joseph Conrad novel will open up new possibilities you would not have considered on your own. Think of these authors as your mentors.

As I have mentioned before, *reading* refers to two quite different activities. Passive or recreational reading is the sort we do when we want to turn off and be entertained. It is a relatively inexpensive, legal pastime and has no dangerous side effects. We all need to do it from time to time, but we do so more for pleasure than for growth. Active reading, on the other hand, is what writers do. It is an analytical activity. When we read actively, we are not only making value judgments ("terrible character development," "slow pacing," "skillful irony," and the like), we are examining the work for unusual techniques ("a flashback within a flashback—does it work?" "that house is being treated like a character"). And we may be responding competitively ("I could do that scene better"; "that character is more fully developed than any of mine, damn it!").

Active reading may require finishing works you do not enjoy. You can't judge them accurately until you do. In such cases, the pleasure you derive is analytical. If you find the work unsuccessful, figure out why. Sometimes you can learn as much from fiction you dislike as from works you enjoy.

For some, active reading means keeping a pencil and paper handy for notes—not just on plot development and names of characters but on interesting techniques. If you keep a literary journal (strongly recommended), it's worth jotting down your reactions there. Make your comments full enough and legible enough so that later they will bring the work back into focus the way a photo album helps you recall past experiences. In the case of stories published in magazines, be sure to note where they appeared so you can refer to them later.

At first you may have a problem knowing where to find good fiction. Try anthologies. They will introduce you to new authors. Some anthologies cover the past few decades. Recent short stories can be found in two annual collections: *The Best American Short Stories* and *Prize Stories, the O. Henry Awards*. These are in almost every library and can be ordered through a bookstore. It is decidedly preferable to own your own copies so you can make marginal comments.

As for magazines, there are two large-circulation publications that include fiction in every issue: *The New Yorker* (usually one story every week) and *The Atlantic*, a monthly. There are also about 100 little magazines, many of them quarterlies, which publish stories along with poems, articles, and reviews. Some, like *Story Quarterly* (actually a sizable annual of excellent contemporary work), publish nothing but fiction. So does *Glimmer Train*. Others, like *The North American Review*, and *The Virginia Quarterly Review*, regularly include several stories along with poetry. More titles are listed in Appendix C.

How do you find these publications? Chain bookstores and, shockingly, many college stores as well ignore them. But don't let that intimidate you. Start by reading whichever magazines are available in your public or school library. Then select one or two and subscribe. A year's subscription costs less than a couple of CDs or a single rock concert. When you have your own copy of the magazine, you will be sure to read it, will feel free to mark it up, and will have it for future reference.

Writers of fiction are even more isolated than poets. They do not give readings as often, and they have difficulty finding individuals who are willing to spend the time it takes to read a story carefully and give helpful criticism. Quarterlies and little magazines provide the best way for writers to stay in touch with others in their field.

If you want to develop your ability as a writer, don't isolate yourself. Make sure you invest at least as much time in reading what others have written as you do writing. If you value fiction, you will not find the cost of books and subscriptions excessive. Your growth as a writer will depend in large measure on how active and perceptive you are as a reader.

A Regimen for Writing

One great advantage of taking a creative writing course is that it provides a regimen of regular deadlines. Those due dates serve an important function: the writing gets done. Sometimes the work is good, sometimes it is rushed and not very good, and we often feel harried; but that kind of pressure is surprisingly effective in maintaining output and improving abilities.

It is almost impossible to maintain that pace in college if you are not taking a writing course. Some students rise early and try to put time in before turning to regular assignments; others reserve the late-night hours for creative work. Still, it takes considerable effort to keep the writing time from getting squeezed—particularly toward the end of the semester.

One way to counter this problem is to form your own support group. If you meet with three or four other writers, you can give each other encouragement as well as deadlines.

Once you graduate, you face an even greater challenge. Everyone knows that when it comes to weight loss or body building, a regular program is necessary, but some don't realize that the same applies to writing. Those who wait for the perfect fictional idea to spring from the heavens forget that much of our progress as writers of fiction is a matter of trial and error. To put it bluntly, we learn nothing about writing when we write nothing. Busy people can't wait for spare time to occur; they create it.

Under these circumstances it is all the more important to join a writers' group or start one of your own. All it takes is three individuals who are serious about their work. Five is ideal, and eight is about maximum. There is solid benefit from receiving criticism of your own work, and the deadlines serve as great motivation.

Be careful, however, to consider whether the other members are working with material that is like yours in intent if not in style. Some so-called writers' clubs are more social than literary. Or they may have more commercial writers than you find helpful. The best way to judge is to attend one or two meetings on a provisional basis before committing yourself.

If you can't find or form a group, you may have to impose a schedule on yourself, such as a completed story every two weeks. Those who are at the stage of submitting work for publication often use contest dates to prod them into intense activity. Due dates are listed in *Poets and Writers*, a highly useful publication. The addresses of this and other helpful journals are listed in Appendix C, "Resources for Writers."

Fiction writers need longer blocks of time than do poets. Professional obligations—teaching or any other—make that difficult. But active fiction writers share one thing with active poets: somehow they find time for creative work. It may be early morning or late at night, or it may require giving up full-time work for part-time. But the writing gets done. It's a matter of priorities.

Rewriting and More Rewriting

As I have pointed out, those who have just started to write fiction usually spend very little time on revisions. It is not that they are so sure of themselves, it is simply a matter of not knowing how to evaluate what they have done. What is there on the page seems fine.

One of the functions of this textbook is to make such writers less satisfied with their first or even second draft. With practice, the time spent on revisions usually becomes greater and greater. Unfortunately, extensive revisions are not always possible when one is taking a course. An academic term is relatively short, and the effectiveness of a course requires a high output of new material. Revision work cannot in most cases be given as much credit as new writing receives.

When you are finished with your writing courses, however, you can and should double the time you spend revising. Most professional writers spend from four to five times as much time on the revisions than on the first draft.

A new draft is not just tinkering. First read your manuscript through to the end with as much objectivity as you can. Those who work with a computer sometimes prefer to do this review on a printed copy to avoid spending time making one-word changes at this stage. Mark in the margins which paragraphs need expanding or cutting. Decide where you need new material. Then follow though on all the notations. The result constitutes a "new draft." It may take several such drafts spaced out over a period of days or even weeks before a story is ready for fine tuning. Those little revisions in phrasing should be postponed until you have what you consider the best possible draft.

Seven Critical Questions

To make effective revisions, you have to know what you are looking for. The following seven critical questions can be used after you have reread a draft of your own story or of someone else's work. They can also be used to stimulate discussion in a class or informal writers' group. Although they echo the topics raised in previous chapters, the questions are arranged in an order that is most conducive to group discussion. Characterization is a good starting point, and more abstract concerns like theme and style are best reserved until later.

Not every question will be appropriate for every story, but as a whole these seven represent the kind of concerns every writer should consider about a work in progress. If you review the major headings often, they will become internalized. They will not only help you pick out what needs to be revised in your own work, they will encourage you to read published work critically rather than passively.

Feel free to reproduce this list without written permission as long as credit is given and copies are not sold for profit.

1. *Are the primary characters convincing or, in the case of satire, effective?* If the story develops characters fully, do you have the sense of having actually met them? How much do you know about them? If the story is satiric, the characters are probably not intended to be realistic in the same way, but are they effective?

When discussing a fictional character in a class or an informal group, be careful not to go off into personal preferences as if this were a real person. Keep the focus on characterization—the ways in which character is presented in the story. How much do you find out about this character, and how do you learn it?

2. *Is the viewpoint effective?* Is it consistent? Would the work be improved if it were presented through the eyes of a different character?

3. *Is the structure effective?* Just how many scenes does it have? Are additional scenes needed? Or is it cluttered? If so, can certain scenes be cut or combined? Are the transitions effective? If there are flashbacks, is it clear where they begin and end? Are there scenes that seem to drag?

4. *Is there enough tension to keep the story moving?* If not, is it because there is not enough interaction between characters? Does it need more action? If, on the other hand, it is "action-packed," does all that drama bury subtlety of theme and characterization?

5. *Is the setting effective?* Is it interesting? Does it contribute to the theme of the story? If there is only one setting, would a second one help to provide variety and contrast?

6. *Is the theme fresh and insightful?* What exactly is the story suggesting? How would you sum it up in a single, complete sentence? Is it a truism or an insight you hadn't considered in quite this way before?

7. *Is the style effective?* Is it too elaborate or formal for the material? Or is it so sparse that it is tiresome to read? Would variation in sentence length help? Is there an effective balance of modes? Is it either too talky or too packed with action? Or does too much exposition or description slow it down? Is it melodramatic or sentimental? If so, is poor characterization at fault? If it is a satire, is it clear as to what is being satirized?

I have presented reading, writing, and revising as three keys to development as if they were separate concerns, but actually they are intertwined. Everyone can enjoy reading as a personal pleasure, but those who want to continue developing as fiction writers have to combine critical reading with a regimen of regular writing that includes long hours of revision. It's not easy to sustain this program of activity when one's life becomes cluttered with other responsibilities, but we all set priorities either consciously or unconsciously. A writer is one who has placed creative work at the head of the list.

31

DRAMA:

A Live Performance

The appeal of a live performance. Six unique aspects of drama: dramatic impact, visual appeal, auditory aspects, physical production, continuous action, a spectator art. Getting started: selecting a concept, primary characters, a plot outline.

The transition from writing fiction to writing plays is not as great as one might think. Both depend heavily on **plot**. Both reveal **character** through action and **dialogue**. Both are presented with a distinctive **tone** and are unified with some kind of **theme**. If you have written short stories, you will find these aspects familiar.

There is, however, one fundamental difference that sets drama apart as a unique genre: a play is a live performance. It is a physical presentation in which actors, male or female, perform and speak their lines for an audience. Although most of us have read more plays than we have seen performances, it is important to remember that a script is only a portion of a finished dramatic work. It is a skeleton. The written script provides the lines to be spoken and brief notes about the action, but the play itself is a cooperative effort shared by actors, a director, set designers, stage crews, lighting crews, and many others. A good playwright never forgets this. As a result, the writing of a play script is dramatically different from composing a poem or a work of fiction.

The physical aspect of a theatrical performance is drama's greatest asset and explains why it is flourishing today in spite of competition with film and television. Ever since the first "talking movie," critics have predicted the end of **legitimate theater**—live performance on a stage. But not even the competition of television and then video and DVD have stopped the constant growth of new theaters. Most major and many middle-sized cities have resident companies, and these are augmented with university theaters offering both student and professional productions.

Legitimate theater continues to be popular in part *because* of television, not in spite of it. The cost of mass-audience television programs requires that they appeal to the widest possible audience. Sponsors demand it. As a result, there is a certain uniformity in sitcom and action-drama scripts. Plotting, characterization, and theme are frequently reduced to the simplest level and repeated with ritualistic regularity. Those who prefer subtlety and originality remain hungry for legitimate theater.

Every **genre** has its special attributes—qualities that distinguish it fundamentally from other forms of writing. It is a mistake to think of a play as fiction acted out on the stage or as a poem performed or as a low-budget version of film. It is none of these things. Before you begin writing your first play script, consider carefully the true assets of this genre.

The Unique Aspects of Drama

There are six characteristics of drama that distinguish it from the other genres. You will be able to find plays that do not contain all six just as you can find some poems that make little use of rhythm and some stories without dialogue. But they are rare. Most playwrights value all six as the prime assets of the genre.

• First, **drama** is by definition a *dramatic art*. That is, it generally has an emotional impact or force. In the case of comedy, we call it vitality. This is not just a tradition; it is a necessity in an art form that requires an audience to give its undivided attention for two-and-a-half to three hours.

This impact is often established early in a play with a **dramatic question** that seizes the attention of the audience long before the **theme** becomes evident. Dramatic questions are usually blunt and simple: Is this stranger a threat? For whom are they waiting? Why do these characters hate each other? Often these initial questions develop into specific conflicts and generate **tension.** Although the need for tension is not as strong in very short plays and in comedies, it remains a common characteristic in all drama.

As in fiction, **irony** and **satire** often add to the dramatic impact of a play. This is particularly true in comedy. Still another device is the use of surprise. Unusual or unexpected developments are effective in holding the attention of an audience.

Dramatic impact, however, is hard to sustain. If maintained relentlessly, the audience will become numb. For this reason, most plays work up to a series of peaks, allowing the emotions of the audience to relax in between. This system of rising and falling action does not follow any prescribed pattern and is often intuitive on the part of the playwright, just as it is in the writing of short stories. But the need for such structure tends to make drama more sharply divided into scenes and acts—divisions that help to control the dramatic impact.

- Second, drama is a *visual art*. Plays thrive on action. The way characters move about and interact physically is often as important as the lines are. This concern for the visual extends beyond the characters. The set itself can be an important part of the production. Sophisticated lighting boards can convert the set from a static backdrop to a dynamic factor in developing the tone of each scene. The quest for visual impact has led some playwrights to experiment with mixed media by adding projected images.

- Third, drama is an *auditory art*. It appeals to the ear. Except for brief stage directions, every word in the script is **dialogue** and is intended to be spoken out loud. Even thoughts. The sound of those lines becomes very important. In some respects, this element brings playwrights closer to poets than to writers of fiction. Repetition, for example, is a technique found in both drama and poetry. For this reason, playwrights often read their lines out loud or have others read them, listening to the composition rather than studying it on the page.

  This special attention to the sound of language applies as much to plays that are in the tradition of realism as to works that develop the dreamlike distortions of nonrealistic drama. Not only are the sounds important, silence can be used dramatically. Sometimes it has as much dramatic impact as a shout.

- Fourth, drama is a *physically produced art*. This is sometimes difficult to remember for those who have been writing fiction. Since sets have to be constructed with wood and nails, there is not the freedom to shift from scene to scene the way one can in a short story—or film. Scriptwriters should keep in mind just what kinds of demands they are placing on set designers and stage crews.

  At first this requirement may seem like a limitation, but there are compensating assets. Playwrights have an intense, almost personal contact with their audiences that is entirely different from the detached connection fiction writers have with their readers. Also, the constraints of the stage often stimulate the imagination. For many playwrights these aspects outweigh any disadvantage.

- Fifth, drama is a *continuous art*. Members of the audience, unlike readers of fiction or poetry, must receive the play at whatever pace the playwright sets. They can't linger on a sage observation or a moving episode. They can't turn back a page or review an earlier scene. Those who shift from writing fiction to drama find that they can present their themes more directly. Some playwrights, as we will see, highlight aspects of their themes or specific feelings through repeated phrases like the refrains one finds in poetry.

  As you become involved in play writing, you will find that the flow of drama is an aspect you can utilize. There is a momentum to a play that you can control. With practice, you can make one portion of a scene seem to move rapidly and another more slowly. Fiction writers can't maintain quite this kind of control over their material.

• Finally, and closely connected, drama is a *spectator art*. Even more than with spectator sports, audience reaction is important. Poets are relatively far removed from readers of their work. It is rare indeed for poets to change lines of their verse because of a critical review or poor public response. Novelists are slightly more susceptible to "audience" reaction. Their circle of readers is potentially larger than a poet's, and for some fiction writers wide circulation is more important. Many novelists will make revisions on the basis of their editors' suggestions. Once the book is in print, however, the revision process almost always ends.

Not so with plays. Playwrights often revise when their work is in rehearsal, after the opening-night reviews, and even later. They frequently base their revisions on audience reaction—those awful moments when it laughs at the wrong moment or squirms with boredom.

This does not mean that dramatists are slaves to the reactions of audiences and critics. In most cases playwrights have a basic conception of the work that remains unalterable. But there is a direct and dynamic relationship between playwrights and their audiences. For many, this is one of the real pleasures in writing for the legitimate stage.

Getting Started

Poems frequently begin with an image; stories usually begin with a character in a situation. Plays more often begin with what is called a **concept.**

A dramatic concept includes basic situation, some type of conflict or struggle, and an outcome, all in capsule form. A clear, useful concept can be expressed in two or three complete sentences. You can, of course, start a play as tentatively as you might begin a story, hoping to shape and develop the plot as you work through the first draft. But such an approach is generally not as successful in play writing because so much depends on the whole dramatic structure.

Plays, like stories, often evolve from personal experience, but the need to create a dramatic situation with conflict or struggle between two or more people often requires transformations of the original episode from the start. Although there are many fine exceptions, plays are less likely to be based directly on personal experience than are stories. Feel free to explore newspaper stories and accounts told to you about individuals you have not met, as long as the situation is familiar enough for you to make it appear authentic.

If you keep a literary journal, jot down a number of possible concepts. If one seems to take shape in your mind, add the names and a brief description of one or two characters. Actually giving these characters names at the outset will help stimulate your imagination.

Next, write a sample of dialogue. Try to "hear" your characters interacting. See if you can create a little scene that at least roughly contributes to the concept you have in mind. Read the lines out loud. Imagine actors (male or female) saying those lines. Close your eyes and visualize the scene.

If you have done all this and you still feel that the concept has potential, begin to block out the action. That is, develop an outline in which each brief sequence of events is described in a telegraphic phrase or sentence. Such an outline might start this way:

1. Morning: Tammy and Max are in a frenzy to clean up the apartment, urging each other to hurry. Tension in the air.
2. Doorbell rings. Mrs. Colton enters. Looks around, disapproving. Tammy and Max apologize for remaining mess.
3. Tammy excuses herself. She must go to work. Exits.
4. Mrs. Colton launches a tirade against Tammy. Her attitude toward Max, however, is distinctly friendly. Max continues to pick up the place, defending Tammy as best he can.

Since this is for your own benefit, adopt whatever form seems natural to you. Most playwrights, however, find some kind of outline helpful because drama, much more than fiction, is constructed in specific **scenes**.

Even if you are writing a one-act play with a single set—a good pattern to start with—you will want to think in terms of **scenes**. I will have more to say about this in the chapter on plot (Chapter 33), but from a playwright's point of view a scene is not one of those major divisions of an act that may be printed in the script. It is a far shorter unit marked by a character entering or leaving the stage. The little outline presented here, for example, contains four such scenes.

Some short plays have been written without these subtle yet important divisions, but they are rare. *Hello Out There,* which is presented as the next chapter, uses eight such scenes. After your initial reading, go over the script and mark these divisions. You will see how they provide structure for the play.

As for the form of the script, follow the pattern used by the plays included in this volume. At first it may seem monotonous to repeat the name of each speaker, but it is the customary practice, one that actors depend on in rehearsal. If you are working with a computer, you may be able to program the name of each major character as a macro so that it will appear on the left margin with a simple two-stroke command.

Stage directions are written in italics. Italics in manuscript are still indicated by underlining even if your computer is capable of producing special type. Underlining is a traditional signal to the printer. Place directions in parentheses when they are short. It is helpful to list the names of your characters after the title, arranging them in order of appearance.

There are three complete plays in this section. The first is serious, **realistic,** and highly dramatic. The second is dreamlike, initially comic, but serious in theme. The third is a **farcical, satiric fantasy**. These three short works are markedly different in tone and treatment and are a good indication of what an enormous latitude you have in tone and treatment.

To get started, then, begin with a good concept—not just an idea but a situation with potential conflict between two or more characters. Describe it in two or three complete sentences. Then develop your characters, fleshing them out with notes about their backgrounds and personalities. These notes are for your own benefit. (Rarely do playwrights describe more than basic physical characteristics in the script.) Next, block out the action by outlining a plot scene by scene.

As you write, keep in mind that your script is more than something to be read silently on the page. Visualize what is going on, scene by scene. Where are your actors sitting or standing? Have you given them enough to do? Read their lines out loud. Imagine the impact of each scene on your audience. Even if you have never worked with drama, remember that your script is the first step in the creation of what you hope will be a live performance before a live audience.

32

A PLAY

by William Saroyan

Hello Out There

for George Bernard Shaw

Characters

A Young man
A Girl
A Man
Two Other Men
A Woman

Scene

There is a fellow in a small-town prison cell, tapping slowly on the floor with a spoon. After tapping a minute, as if he were trying to telegraph words, he gets up and begins walking around the cell. At last he stops, stands at the center of the cell, and doesn't move for a long time. He feels his head, as if it were wounded. Then he looks around. Then he calls out dramatically, kidding the world.

YOUNG MAN: Hello—out there! *(Pause.)* Hello—out there! Hello—out there! *(Long pause.)* Nobody out there. *(Still more dramatically, but more comically, too.)* Hello—out there! Hello—out there!

A GIRL'S VOICE is heard, very sweet and soft.

THE VOICE: Hello.
YOUNG MAN: Hello—out there.
THE VOICE: Hello.
YOUNG MAN: Is that you, Katey?
THE VOICE: No—this here is Emily.

YOUNG MAN: Who? *(Swiftly.)* Hello out there.

THE VOICE: Emily.

YOUNG MAN: Emily who? I don't know anybody named Emily. Are you that girl I met at Sam's in Salinas about three years ago?

THE VOICE: No—I'm the girl who cooks here. I'm the cook. I've never been in Salinas. I don't even know where it is.

YOUNG MAN: Hello out there. You say you cook here?

THE VOICE: Yes.

YOUNG MAN: Well, why don't you study up and learn to cook? How come I don't get no jello or anything good?

THE VOICE: I just cook what they tell me to. *(Pause.)* You lonesome?

YOUNG MAN: Lonesome as a coyote. Hear me hollering? Hello out there!

THE VOICE: Who you hollering to?

YOUNG MAN: Well—nobody, I guess. I been trying to think of somebody to write a letter to, but I can't think of anybody.

THE VOICE: What about Katey?

YOUNG MAN: I don't know anybody named Katey.

THE VOICE: Then why did you say, Is that you Katey?

YOUNG MAN: Katey's a good name. I always did like a name like Katey. I never *knew* anybody named Katey, though.

THE VOICE: *I* did.

YOUNG MAN: Yeah? What was she like? Tall girl, or little one?

THE VOICE: Kind of medium.

YOUNG MAN: Hello out there. What sort of a looking girl are *you*?

THE VOICE: Oh, I don't know.

YOUNG MAN: Didn't anybody ever tell you? Didn't anybody ever talk to you that way?

THE VOICE: What way?

YOUNG MAN: You know. Didn't they?

THE VOICE: No, they didn't.

YOUNG MAN: Ah, the fools—they should have. I can tell from your voice you're O.K.

THE VOICE: Maybe I am and maybe I ain't.

YOUNG MAN: I never missed yet.

THE VOICE: Yeah, I know. That's why you're in jail.

YOUNG MAN: The whole thing was a mistake.

THE VOICE: They claim it was rape.

YOUNG MAN: No—it wasn't.

THE VOICE: That's what they claim it was.

YOUNG MAN: They're a lot of fools.

THE VOICE: Well, you sure are in trouble. Are you scared?

YOUNG MAN: Scared to death. *(Suddenly.)* Hello out there!

THE VOICE: What do you keep saying that for all the time?

YOUNG MAN: I'm lonesome. I'm as lonesome as a coyote. *(A long one.)* Hello—out there!

THE GIRL appears, over to one side. She is a plain girl in plain clothes.

THE GIRL: I'm kind of lonesome, too.

YOUNG MAN *(turning and looking at her)*: Hey—No fooling? Are you?

THE GIRL: Yeah—I'm almost as lonesome as a coyote myself.

YOUNG MAN: Who *you* lonesome for?

THE GIRL: I don't know.

YOUNG MAN: It's the same with me. The minute they put you in a place like this you remember all the girls you ever knew, and all the girls you didn't get to know, and it sure gets lonesome.

THE GIRL: I bet it does.

YOUNG MAN: Ah, it's awful. *(Pause.)* You're a pretty kid, you know that?

THE GIRL: You're just talking.

YOUNG MAN: No, I'm not just talking—you *are* pretty. Any fool could see that. You're just about the prettiest kid in the whole world.

THE GIRL: I'm not—and you know it.

YOUNG MAN: No—you are. I never saw anyone prettier in all my born days, in all my travels. I knew Texas would bring me luck.

THE GIRL: Luck? You're in jail, aren't you? You've got a whole gang of people all worked up, haven't you?

YOUNG MAN: Ah, that's nothing. I'll get out of this.

THE GIRL: Maybe.

YOUNG MAN: No, I'll be all right—*now.*

THE GIRL: What do you mean—now?

YOUNG MAN: I mean after seeing you. I got something now. You know for a while there I didn't care one way or another Tired. *(Pause.)* Tired of trying for the best all the time and never getting it.*(Suddenly.)* Hello out there!

THE GIRL: Who you calling now?

YOUNG MAN: You.

THE GIRL: Why, I'm right here.

YOUNG MAN: I know. *(Calling.)* Hello out there!

THE GIRL: Hello.

YOUNG MAN: Ah, you're sweet. *(Pause.)* I'm going to marry *you.* I'm going away with *you.* I'm going to take you to San Francisco or some place like that. I *am,* now. I'm going to win myself some real money, too. I'm going to study 'em real careful and pick myself some winners, and we're going to have a lot of money.

THE GIRL: Yeah?

YOUNG MAN: Yeah. Tell me your name and all that stuff.

THE GIRL: Emily.

YOUNG MAN: I know that. What's the rest of it? Where were you born? Come on, tell me the whole thing.

THE GIRL: Emily Smith.

YOUNG MAN: Honest to God?

THE GIRL: Honest. That's my name—Emily Smith.

YOUNG MAN: Ah, you're the sweetest girl in the whole world.

THE GIRL: Why?

YOUNG MAN: I don't know why, but you are, that's all. Where were you born?

THE GIRL: Matador, Texas.

YOUNG MAN: Where's that?

THE GIRL: Right here.

YOUNG MAN: Is this Matador, Texas?

THE GIRL: Yeah, it's Matador. They brought you here from Wheeling.

YOUNG MAN: Is that where I was—Wheeling?

THE GIRL: Didn't you even know what town you were in?

YOUNG MAN: All towns are alike. You don't go up and ask somebody what town you're in. It doesn't make any difference. How far away is Wheeling?

THE GIRL: Sixteen or seventeen miles. Didn't you know they moved you?

YOUNG MAN: How could I know, when I was out—cold? Somebody hit me over the head with a lead pipe or something. What'd they hit me for?

THE GIRL: Rape—that's what they *said*.

YOUNG MAN: Ah, that's a lie. (*Amazed, almost to himself.*) She wanted me to give her money.

THE GIRL: Money?

YOUNG MAN: Yeah, if I'd have known she was a woman like that—well, by God, I'd have gone on down the street and stretched out in a park somewhere and gone to sleep.

THE GIRL: Is that what she wanted—money?

YOUNG MAN: Yeah. A fellow like me hopping freights all over the country, trying to break his bad luck, going from one poor little town to another, trying to get in on something good somewhere, and she asks for money. I thought she was lonesome. She *said* she was.

THE GIRL: Maybe she was.

YOUNG MAN: She was *something*.

THE GIRL: I guess I'd never see you, if it didn't happen, though.

YOUNG MAN: Oh, I don't know—maybe I'd just mosey along this way and see you in this town somewhere. I'd recognize you, too.

THE GIRL: Recognize me?

YOUNG MAN: Sure, I'd recognize you the minute I laid eyes on you.

THE GIRL: Well, who would I be?

YOUNG MAN: Mine, that's who.

THE GIRL: Honest?

YOUNG MAN: Honest to God.

THE GIRL: You just say that because you're in jail.

YOUNG MAN: No, I mean it. You just pack up and wait for me. We'll high-roll the hell out of here to Frisco.

THE GIRL: You're just lonesome.

YOUNG MAN: I been lonesome all my life—there's no cure for that—but you and me—we can have a lot of fun hanging around together. You'll bring me luck. I know it.

THE GIRL: What are you looking for luck for all the time?

YOUNG MAN: I'm a gambler. I don't work. I've *got* to have luck, or I'm a bum. I haven't had any decent luck in years. Two whole years now—one place to another. Bad luck all the time. That's why I got in trouble back there in Wheeling too. That was no accident. That was my bad luck following me around. So here I am, with my head half busted. I guess it was her old man that did it.

THE GIRL: You mean her father?

YOUNG MAN: No, her husband. If I had an old lady like that, I'd throw her out.

THE GIRL: Do you think you'll have better luck, if I go with you?

YOUNG MAN: It's a cinch. I'm a good handicapper. All I need is somebody good like you with me. It's no good always walking around in the streets for anything that might be there at the time. You got to have somebody staying with you all the time—through winters when it's cold, and springtime when it's pretty, and summertime when it's nice and hot and you can go swimming—through *all* the times—rain and snow and all the different kinds of weather a man's got to go through before he dies. You got to have somebody who's right. Somebody who knows you, from away back. You got to have somebody who even knows you're wrong but likes you just the same. I know I'm wrong, but I just don't want anything the hard way, working like a dog, or the *easy* way, working like a dog—working's the hard way and the easy way both. All I got to do is beat the price, always—and then, I don't feel lousy and don't hate anybody. If you go along with me, I'll be the finest guy anybody ever saw. I won't be wrong any more. You know when you get enough of that money, you *can't* be wrong any more—you're right because the money says so. I'll have a lot of money and you'll be just about the prettiest, most wonderful kid in the whole world. I'll be proud walking around Frisco with you on my arm and people turning around to look at us.

THE GIRL: Do you think they will?

YOUNG MAN: Sure they will. When I get back in some decent clothes, and you're on my arm—well, Katey, they'll turn around and look, and they'll see something, too.

THE GIRL: Katey?

YOUNG MAN: Yeah—that's your name from now on. You're the first girl I ever called Katey. I've been saving it for you O.K.?

THE GIRL: O.K.

YOUNG MAN: How long have I been here?

THE GIRL: Since last night. You didn't wake up until late this morning, though.

YOUNG MAN: What time is it now? About nine?

THE GIRL: About ten.

YOUNG MAN: Have you got the key to this lousy cell?

THE GIRL: No. They don't let me fool with any keys.

YOUNG MAN: Well, can you get it?

THE GIRL: No.

YOUNG MAN: Can you *try*?

THE GIRL: They wouldn't let me get near any keys. I cook for this jail, when they've got somebody in it. I clean up and things like that.

YOUNG MAN: Well, I want to get out of here. Don't you know the guy that runs this joint?

THE GIRL: I know him, but he wouldn't let you out. They were talking of taking you to another jail in another town.

YOUNG MAN: Yeah? Why?

THE GIRL: Because they're afraid.

YOUNG MAN: What are they afraid of?

THE GIRL: They're afraid these people from Wheeling will come over in the middle of the night and break in.

YOUNG MAN: Yeah? What do they want to do that for?

THE GIRL: Don't *you* know what they want to do it for?

YOUNG MAN: Yeah, I know all right.

THE GIRL: Are you scared?

YOUNG MAN: Sure I'm scared. Nothing scares a man more than ignorance. You can argue with people who ain't fools, but you can't argue with fools— they just go to work and do what they're set on doing. Get me out of here.

THE GIRL: How?

YOUNG MAN: Well, go get the guy with the key, and let me talk to him.

THE GIRL: He's gone home. Everybody's gone home.

YOUNG MAN: You mean I'm in this little jail all alone?

THE GIRL: Well—yeah—except me.

YOUNG MAN: Well, what's the big idea—doesn't anybody stay here all the time?

THE GIRL: No, they go home every night. I clean up and then I go, too. I hung around tonight.

YOUNG MAN: What made you do that?

THE GIRL: I wanted to talk to you.

YOUNG MAN: Honest? What did you want to talk about?

THE GIRL: Oh, I don't know. I took care of you last night. You were talking in your sleep. You liked me, too. I didn't think you'd like me when you woke up, though.

YOUNG MAN: Yeah? Why not?

THE GIRL: I don't know.

YOUNG MAN: Yeah? Well, you're wonderful, see?

THE GIRL: Nobody ever talked to me that way. All the fellows in town—
  (Pause.)

YOUNG MAN: What about 'em?
  (Pause.)
 Well, what about 'em? Come on—tell me.

THE GIRL: They laugh at me.

YOUNG MAN: Laugh at *you*? They're fools. What do they know about anything? You go get your things and come back here. I'll take you with me
  to Frisco. How old are you?

THE GIRL: Oh, I'm of age.

YOUNG MAN: How old are you?—Don't lie to me! Sixteen?

THE GIRL: I'm seventeen.

YOUNG MAN: Well, bring your father and mother. We'll get married before we go.

THE GIRL: They wouldn't let me go.

YOUNG MAN: Why not?

THE GIRL: I don't know, but they wouldn't. I know they wouldn't.

YOUNG MAN: You go tell your father not to be a fool, see? What is he, a
  farmer?

THE GIRL: No—nothing. He gets a little relief from the government because
  he's supposed to be hurt or something—his side hurts, he says. I don't
  know what it is.

YOUNG MAN: Ah, he's a liar. Well, I'm taking you with me, see?

THE GIRL: He takes the money I earn, too.

YOUNG MAN: He's got no right to do that.

THE GIRL: I know it, but he does it.

YOUNG MAN *(almost to himself)*: This world stinks. You shouldn't have been
  born in this town, anyway, and you shouldn't have had a man like that
  for a father, either.

THE GIRL: Sometimes I feel sorry for him.

YOUNG MAN: Never mind feeling sorry for him. *(Pointing a finger.)* I'm going
  to talk to your father some day. I've got a few things to tell that guy.

THE GIRL: I know you have.

YOUNG MAN *(suddenly)*: Hello—out there! See if you can get that fellow with
  the keys to come down and let me out.

THE GIRL: Oh, I couldn't.

YOUNG MAN: Why not?

THE GIRL: I'm nobody here—they give me fifty cents every day I work.

YOUNG MAN: How much?

THE GIRL: Fifty cents.

YOUNG MAN *(to the world)*: You see? They ought to pay money to *look* at you.
  To breathe the *air* you breathe. I don't know. Sometimes I figure it never

is going to make sense. Hello—out there! I'm scared. You try to get me out of here. I'm scared them fools are going to come here from Wheeling and go crazy, thinking they're heroes. Get me out of here, Katey.

THE GIRL: I don't know what to do. Maybe I could break the door down.

YOUNG MAN: No, you couldn't do that. Is there a hammer out there or anything?

THE GIRL: Only a broom. Maybe they've locked the broom up, too.

YOUNG MAN: Go see if you can find anything.

THE GIRL: All right. *(She goes.)*

YOUNG MAN: Hello—out there! Hello—out there! *(Pause.)* Hello—out there! Hello—out there! *(Pause.)* Putting me in jail. *(With contempt.)* Rape! Rape? *They* rape everything good that was ever born. His side hurts. They laugh at her. Fifty cents a day. Little punk people. Hurting the only good thing that ever came their way.*(Suddenly.)* Hello—out there!

THE GIRL *(returning)*: There isn't a thing out there. They've locked everything up for the night.

YOUNG MAN: Any cigarettes?

THE GIRL: Everything's locked up—all the drawers of the desk, all the closet doors—everything.

YOUNG MAN: I ought to have a cigarette.

THE GIRL: I could get you a package maybe, somewhere. I guess the drug store's open. It's about a mile.

YOUNG MAN: A mile? I don't want to be alone that long.

THE GIRL: I could run all the way, and all the way back.

YOUNG MAN: You're the sweetest girl that ever lived.

THE GIRL: What kind do you want?

YOUNG MAN: Oh, any kind—Chesterfields or Camels or Lucky Strikes—any kind at all.

THE GIRL: I'll go get a package. *(She turns to go.)*

YOUNG MAN: What about the money?

THE GIRL: I've got some money. I've got a quarter I been saving. I'll run all the way. *(She is about to go.)*

YOUNG MAN: Come here.

THE GIRL *(going to him)*: What?

YOUNG MAN: Give me your hand. *(He takes her hand and looks at it, smiling. He lifts it and kisses it.)* I'm scared to death.

THE GIRL: I am, too.

YOUNG MAN: I'm not lying—I don't care what happens to me, but I'm scared nobody will ever come out here to this Godforsaken broken-down town and find you. I'm scared you'll get used to it and not mind. I'm scared you'll never get to Frisco and have 'em all turning around to look at you. Listen—go get me a gun, because if they come, I'll kill 'em! They don't understand. Get me a gun!

THE GIRL: I could get my father's gun. I know where he hides it.

YOUNG MAN: Go get it. Never mind the cigarettes. Run all the way.
(*Pause, smiling but seriously.*) Hello, Katey.

THE GIRL: Hello. What's *your* name?

YOUNG MAN: Photo-Finish is what they *call* me. My races are always photo-finish races. You don't know what that means, but it means they're very close. So close the only way they can tell which horse wins is to look at a photograph after the race is over. Well, every race I bet turns out to be a photo-finish race, and my horse never wins. It's my bad luck, all the time. That's why they call me Photo-Finish. Say it before you go.

THE GIRL: Photo-Finish.

YOUNG MAN: Come here. (*THE GIRL moves close and he kisses her.*) Now, hurry. Run all the way.

THE GIRL: I'll run. (*THE GIRL turns and runs. The YOUNG MAN stands at the center of the cell a long time. THE GIRL comes running back in. Almost crying.*) I'm afraid. I'm afraid I won't see you again. If I come back and you're not here, I—

YOUNG MAN: Hello—out there!

THE GIRL: It's so lonely in this town. Nothing here but the lonesome wind all the time, lifting the dirt and blowing out to the prairie. I'll stay *here*. I won't *let* them take you away.

YOUNG MAN: Listen, Katey. Do what I tell you. Go get that gun and come back. Maybe they won't come tonight. Maybe they won't come at all. I'll hide the gun. When they let me out you can take it back and put it where you found it. And then we'll go away. But if they come, I'll kill 'em! Now, hurry—

THE GIRL: All right. (*Pause.*) I want to tell you something.

YOUNG MAN: O.K.

THE GIRL (*very softly*): If you're not here when I come back, well, I'll have the gun and I'll know what to do with it.

YOUNG MAN: You know how to handle a gun?

THE GIRL: I know how.

YOUNG MAN: Don't be a fool. (*Takes off his shoe, brings out some currency.*) Don't be a fool, see? Here's some money. Eighty dollars. Take it and go to Frisco. Look around and find somebody. Find somebody alive and halfway human, see? Promise me—if I'm not here when you come back, just throw the gun away and get the hell to Frisco. Look around and find somebody.

THE GIRL: I don't *want* to find anybody.

YOUNG MAN (*swiftly, desperately*): Listen, if I'm not here when you come back, how do you know I haven't gotten away? Now, do what I tell you. I'll meet you in Frisco. I've got a couple of dollars in my other shoe. I'll see you in San Francisco.

THE GIRL (*with wonder*): San Francisco?

YOUNG MAN: That's right—San Francisco. That's where you and me belong.

THE GIRL: I've always wanted to go to *some* place like San Francisco—but how could I go alone?

YOUNG MAN: Well, you're not alone any more, see?

THE GIRL: Tell me a little what it's like.

YOUNG MAN (*very swiftly, almost impatiently at first, but gradually slower and with remembrance, smiling, and* THE GIRL *moving closer to him as he speaks*): Well, it's on the Pacific to begin with—ocean water all around. Cool fog and seagulls. Ships from all over the world. It's got seven hills. The little streets go up and down, around and all over. Every night the foghorns bawl. But they won't be bawling for you and me.

THE GIRL: What else?

YOUNG MAN: That's about all, I guess.

THE GIRL: Are people different in San Francisco?

YOUNG MAN: People are the same everywhere. They're different only when they love somebody. That's the only thing that makes 'em different. More people in Frisco love somebody, that's all.

THE GIRL: Nobody anywhere loves anybody as much as I love you.

YOUNG MAN (*shouting, as if to the world*): You see? Hearing you say that, a man could die and still be ahead of the game. Now, hurry. And don't forget, if I'm not here when you come back, get the hell to San Francisco where you'll have a chance. Do you hear me?

THE GIRL stands a moment looking at him, then backs away, turns and runs. The YOUNG MAN stares after her, troubled and smiling. Then he turns away from the image of her and walks about like a lion in a cage. After a while he sits down suddenly and buries his head in his hands. From a distance the sound of several automobiles approaching is heard. He listens a moment, then ignores the implications of the sound, whatever they may be. Several automobile doors are slammed. He ignores this also. A wooden door is opened with a key and closed, and footsteps are heard in a hall. Walking easily, almost casually and yet arrogantly, a MAN comes in.

YOUNG MAN (*jumps up suddenly and shouts at* THE MAN, *almost scaring him*): What the hell kind of jailkeeper are you, anyway? Why don't you attend to your business? You get paid for it, don't you? Now, get me out of here.

THE MAN: But I'm not the jailkeeper.

YOUNG MAN: Yeah? Well, who are you, then?

THE MAN: I'm the husband.

YOUNG MAN: What husband you talking about?

THE MAN: You know what husband.

YOUNG MAN: Hey! (*Pause, looking at* THE MAN.) Are you the guy that hit me over the head last night?

THE MAN: I am.

YOUNG MAN (*with righteous indignation*): What do you mean going around hitting people over the head?

THE MAN: Oh, I don't know. What do you *mean* going around—the way you do?

YOUNG MAN (*rubbing his head*): You hurt my head. You got no right to hit anybody over the head.

THE MAN (*suddenly angry, shouting*): Answer my question! What do you mean?

YOUNG MAN: Listen, you—don't be hollering at me just because I'm locked up.

THE MAN (*with contempt, slowly*): You're a dog!

YOUNG MAN: Yeah, well let me tell you something. You *think* you're the husband. You're the husband of nothing. (*Slowly.*) What's more, your wife—if you want to call her that—is a tramp. Why don't you throw her out in the street where she belongs?

THE MAN (*draws a pistol*): Shut up!

YOUNG MAN: Yeah? Go ahead, shoot—(*Softly.*) and spoil the fun. What'll your pals think? They'll be disappointed, won't they. What's the fun hanging a man who's already dead? (*THE MAN puts the gun away*). That's right, because now you can have some fun yourself, telling me what you're going to do. That's what you came here for, isn't it? Well, you don't need to tell me. I *know* what you're going to do. I've read the papers and I know. They have fun. A mob of 'em fall on one man and beat him, don't they? They tear off his clothes and kick him, don't they? And women and little children stand around watching, don't they? Well, before you go on *this* picnic, I'm going to tell you a few things. Not that that's going to send you home with your pals—the other heroes. No. You've been outraged. A stranger has come to town and violated your women. Your pure, innocent, virtuous women. You fellows have got to set this thing right. You're men, not mice. You're homemakers, and you beat your children. (*Suddenly.*) Listen, you—I didn't know she was your wife. I didn't know she was anybody's wife.

THE MAN: You're a liar!

YOUNG MAN: Sometimes—when it'll do somebody some good—but not this time. Do you want to hear about it? (*THE MAN doesn't answer.*) All right, I'll tell you. I met her at a lunch counter. She came in and sat next to me. There was plenty of room, but she sat next to me. Somebody had put a nickel in the phonograph and a fellow was singing *New San Antonio Rose.* Well, she got to talking about the song. I thought she was talking to the waiter, but *he* didn't answer her, so after a while *I* answered her. That's how I met her. I didn't think anything of it. We left the place together and started walking. The first thing I knew she said, This is where I live.

THE MAN: You're a dirty liar!

YOUNG MAN: Do you want to hear it? Or not? (*THE MAN does not answer.*) O.K. She asked me to come in. Maybe she had something in mind, maybe she didn't. Didn't make any difference to me, one way or the other. If she was lonely, all right. If not, all right.

THE MAN: You're telling a lot of dirty lies!

YOUNG MAN: I'm telling the truth. Maybe your wife's out there with your pals. Well, call her in. I got nothing against her, or you—or any of you. Call her in, and ask her a few questions. Are you in love with her? (*THE MAN doesn't answer.*) Well, that's too bad.

THE MAN: What do you mean, too bad?

YOUNG MAN: I mean this may not be the first time something like this has happened.

THE MAN (*swiftly*): Shut up!

YOUNG MAN: Oh, you know it. You've always known it. You're afraid of your pals, that's all. She asked me for money. That's all she wanted. I wouldn't be here now if I had given her the money.

THE MAN (*slowly*): How much did she ask for?

YOUNG MAN: I didn't ask her how much. I told her I'd made a mistake. She said she would make trouble if I didn't give her money. Well, I don't like bargaining, and I don't like being threatened, either. I told her to get the hell away from me. The next thing I knew she'd run out of the house and was hollering. (*Pause.*) Now, why don't you go out there and tell 'em they took me to another jail—go home and pack up and leave her. You're a pretty good guy, you're just afraid of your pals.

THE MAN draws his gun again. He is very frightened. He moves a step toward the YOUNG MAN, then fires three times. The YOUNG MAN falls to his knees. THE MAN turns and runs, horrified.

YOUNG MAN: Hello—out there! (*He is bent forward.*)

THE GIRL comes running in, and halts suddenly, looking at him.

THE GIRL: There were some people in the street, men and women and kids— so I came in through the back, through a window. I couldn't find the gun. I looked all over but I couldn't find it. What's the matter?

YOUNG MAN: Nothing—nothing. Everything's all right. Listen. Listen, kid. Get the hell out of here. Go out the same way you came in and run—run like hell—run all night. Get to another town and get on a train. Do you hear me?

THE GIRL: What's happened?

YOUNG MAN: Get away—just get away from here. Take any train that's going—you can get to Frisco later.

THE GIRL (*almost sobbing*): I don't want to go any place without you.

YOUNG MAN: I can't go. Something's happened. *(He looks at her.)* But I'll be with you always—God damn it. Always!

He falls forward. THE GIRL stands near him, then begins to sob softly, walking away. She stands over to one side, stops sobbing, and stares out. The excitement of the mob outside increases. THE MAN, with two of his pals, comes running in. THE GIRL watches, unseen.

THE MAN: Here's the son of a bitch!
ANOTHER MAN: O.K. Open the cell, Harry.

The THIRD MAN goes to the cell door, unlocks it, and swings it open. A WOMAN comes running in.

THE WOMAN: Where is he? I want to see him. Is he dead? *(Looking down at him, as the MEN pick him up.)* There he is. *(Pause.)* Yeah, that's him.

Her husband looks at her with contempt, then at the dead man.

THE MAN (trying to laugh): All right—let's get it over with.
THIRD MAN: Right you are, George. Give me a hand, Harry.

They lift the body.

THE GIRL (suddenly, fiercely): Put him down!
THE MAN: What's this?
SECOND MAN: What are you doing here? Why aren't you out in the street?
THE GIRL: Put him down and go away.

She runs toward the MEN
THE WOMAN grabs her.

THE WOMAN: Here—where do you think *you're* going?
THE GIRL: Let me go. You've no right to take him away.
THE WOMAN: Well, listen to her, will you? *(She slaps THE GIRL and pushes her to the floor.)* Listen to the little slut, will you?

They all go, carrying the YOUNG MAN's body. THE GIRL gets up slowly, no longer sobbing. She looks around at everything, then looks straight out, and whispers.

THE GIRL: Hello—out—there! Hello—out there!
CURTAIN

33

THE DRAMATIC PLOT

The importance of concept. The scene as the basic unit of drama. Providing dramatic questions throughout the play. Controlling the pace through rising and falling action. The value of subplots.

A good dramatic plot starts with a good concept. As I explained in Chapter 31, a **concept** is a very brief description that includes a basic situation, some type of conflict or struggle, and an outcome.

A concept is not the same as a theme. **Themes**, which we will examine in Chapter 41, are the abstract ideas implied by a play. They are the portion of a play that comments on the human condition. Since thematic statements are abstract, they do not include events or names of characters. The *concept*, on the other hand, is a compressed plot statement, from one to three complete sentences, about what happens to whom. There is nothing intellectual about a concept. Think of it as a sales pitch.

Crass as concept statements may seem, they are important because they keep you on track. Many concept statements are too vague to be helpful. Here are some concepts that are distinctly unpromising, and ways they could be improved:

- "It's a play about jealousy."

Too general. Who is jealous of whom? Why? And what is the outcome? A better version: "Because Estelle could never forget her unfaithful father, she couldn't trust her husband until she confronted her past."

- "War is hell."

This is a **truism** that has been repeated so often it no longer has impact. To become meaningful, it would have to give some notion of the plot and the primary characters. Here is one possibility: "For years the family revered the memory of Frank, who had been killed in the Vietnam War, but only belatedly did they realize how seriously his younger brother had been psychologically damaged in the same war."

- "A college student's first summer job."

Yawn! We need specifics and some assurance that this is going to be a fresh treatment of a frequently used situation. For example: "Kathleen is delighted to be hired as a mechanic at an auto repair shop but faces a moral dilemma when she discovers that her new friends are reconditioning stolen cars."

These revised concepts briefly describe who is involved (the primary characters) and what happens to them. They don't, of course, do justice to the complexities and insights that good plays provide, but composing such statements is a good way to test whether you have a situation that is dramatic enough to keep your audience in the theater. The concept is the starting point, whereas the theme, the intellectual component of a play, often takes shape in the writing and is highlighted in subsequent drafts.

We can be fairly certain, for example, that the starting point of William Saroyan's *Hello Out There* was not an abstract theme about dangers of hypocrisy in society and the fundamental need for individuals to make genuine contact with one another. Plays, like stories, rarely spring from abstract principles. It's more likely that he began with a vision of a well-meaning drifter held in a small-town jail on a false rape charge and a young woman trapped in the same town, a prisoner in a different way. These two join forces, trying to break free, only to be overwhelmed in the end. A concept like that describes specific people in a particular dramatic situation and an outcome. Once you have a clear, interesting concept, you are ready to block out a plot.

The Scene as Basic Unit

As I explained earlier, the word *scene* is often used to describe subdivisions of acts in longer plays. They may be written into the program notes and involve a lapse of time or even a change of setting. In some cases they replace acts altogether.

For dramatists and actors, however, the word *scene* also refers to each unit of action that begins with an entrance or an exit and ends with the next shift of characters on the stage. To avoid confusion, think of these as *secondary scenes*. They are the essential and basic units of action for the playwright, the actors, and the director as well.

Occasionally, a secondary scene may have a dramatic unity in itself. That is, it may build to a **climax** and then be punctuated by the departure of one or more characters. For greater impact, it may conclude with an **exit line**, a memorable, startling, or dramatically revealing statement. More often, the unity is subtler. It establishes the almost unnoticed rise and fall of action that distinguishes the play that is "dramatic" from one that seems "flat" or "dull."

Hello Out There is an excellent example of careful scene construction. It is a one-act play presented in one primary scene. There is one stage set and one apparently uninterrupted flow of action. But from a playwright's point of view, the work is divided into eight secondary scenes. Each of these is marked by an exit or entrance, and each has an influence on the rise and fall of dramatic impact.

Here are the scenes listed in the kind of outline some playwrights find helpful when planning a new play. The word *girl* is used rather than the more contemporary phrase *young woman* simply to conform with Saroyan's script.

1. Man alone on stage; talks to girl offstage
2. Girl enters; they get to know each other
3. Girl exits; man gives a brief monologue
4. Girl returns; they make a pact
5. Girl exits; husband enters, argues, shoots
6. Husband exits, girl returns
7. Husband and pals return, drag body out
8. Girl alone on stage; repeats the refrain

This sparse outline demonstrates how many separate units will be involved, but it doesn't indicate which are major scenes and which are minor, which are highly dramatic and which merely develop relationships. Each of these secondary scenes deserves a closer look.

Although the opening scene has only one actor on the stage, it is far from static. Notice that the man is not musing philosophically to himself or addressing the audience. His first lines call out for contact with someone else, and then almost at once he is interacting with the young woman even before she is on stage. This is no prologue. Psychologically, the play begins as soon as these two characters are in voice contact.

The second scene begins when the young woman actually appears. If one merely reads the script on the page as if it were fiction, her entrance may not seem significant. But a playwright always keeps the visual aspect in mind, imagining the action from the audience's point of view. In production, her arrival on stage is the psychological start of a new scene.

This second scene is the longest in the play. Saroyan has to fill in a great deal of background and, in addition, draw these two strangers together convincingly. It would have been possible to have Emily on stage from the start, but postponing her entrance helps to keep that lengthy second scene from becoming even longer.

The third scene is very brief. She goes out to look for tools, and he is left on the stage alone. But it is important because it allows him to lash out vehemently against what he sees as injustice. The fact that he is alone on the stage indicates to the audience that he is speaking his inner convictions, his true feelings expressed out loud. Were it not for this little scene, we might suspect that he was cynically lying to the girl simply to save himself.

The fourth scene is one in which Emily and Photo-Finish make the pact to meet in San Francisco. Notice that their relationship has grown with surprising speed. In fiction one might be tempted to spread the action out over the course of a day or more; but in plays the dramatic development tends to be compressed.

Emily leaves, ending the fourth scene, and there is only a moment of sound effects before a new character suddenly appears on the stage. The tension mounts as we learn that this is the angered husband. An argument pushes the dramatic impact to new levels, and the husband draws his gun. The scene culminates with three shots.

In the sixth scene the husband has fled and Emily returns. The dying **hero** and heroine are alone on the stage. If this were opera, it would be the point where the final duet is sung. As realistic drama, it is a brief, terse, yet tender moment.

But a problem arises here. How is the playwright going to maintain dramatic interest in that brief yet important section which follows the death of the protagonist? Once again, a new secondary scene is prepared for—the seventh. First, the audience hears activity building offstage. Saroyan is careful to include this in his stage directions: "The excitement of the mob outside increases." The husband, two friends, and then the wife all burst on the stage. Emily demands that they put the body down—in what we can assume is the first dramatically assertive act of her life. She is slapped and pushed to the floor.

The last of these secondary scenes is so brief that it consists of only one line. But to understand just how powerful the device is, imagine the girl delivering that last line with the other characters still on stage, struggling to drag the body off. Emily would be literally upstaged. Her line would be a mere continuation of the preceding dialogue. Having her alone on the stage, probably with a single beam of light on her, isolates the final words. Her plight—now matching that of Photo-Finish at the very beginning of the play—becomes the focal point of the play.

When one first reads a play like this, it is easy to assume that it is one continual flow of action. True, many of these scenes could be combined by eliminating all the exits and entrances up to the point of the husband's arrival. But that long, unbroken scene would lose much of its energy. It might well seem to drag. Exits and entrances in this play provide the basic organizational structure with which the dramatic impact is heightened and lowered and then heightened again in regular succession, holding the audience from beginning to end.

At the other extreme, too many very short scenes can make the play seem choppy and insubstantial. Because most of us have seen more films than plays, it is easy to be influenced by the rapid pace of cinema scenes. The camera not only can blend extremely brief units of action into an apparently smooth flow, it can shift setting without a break. Changing the set on the stage, however, is time-consuming and tends to break the illusion of reality. For this reason, many full-length plays and almost all one-act plays maintain a single set. There is a tendency, also, to use plots that cover a single time span. Although there are excellent exceptions, skipping a year or more lends itself better to longer plays.

In judging the length of your secondary scenes, keep imagining the effect on your audience. Too many very short scenes reduce the chance to develop character and relationships; lengthy scenes may create monotony and slow the pace. You can make these decisions more easily if you have a chance to hear your script read aloud or, best of all, to see it in production.

Providing Dramatic Questions

How are you going to hold your audience in their seats? When you write fiction, this is less of a problem. A story or novel can be read in installments. But when you produce a play, you are asking an audience to give it their uninterrupted attention—often while sitting on uncomfortable seats.

Because of this, most plays are energized with a series of **dramatic questions.** These are like lures to hold the interest of the audience. We have already seen how fiction also makes use of dramatic questions (Where are we going? What will this stranger be like?), but plays depend on them to a far greater degree.

Looking at the full range of drama from Sophocles to our own decade, there are certain dramatic questions that recur frequently. This recurrence does not make the plays redundant; one hardly notices the similarity. But their widespread use does suggest just how valuable dramatic questions are.

1. *Will he come?* Shakespeare charged the first act of *Hamlet* with this question, applying it to the ghost. More recently, it has been broadened to cover the full length of plays. Clifford Odets' *Waiting for Lefty*, written in the thirties, Samuel Beckett's *Waiting for Godot*, and Harold Pinter's *The Dumb Waiter* all rely heavily on anticipation of a character who never appears. And to some degree, the question is a factor in *Hello Out There* as soon as the threat of a lynching is raised.

2. *Who did it?* This is, of course, the literary version of "Whodunit?" We find it running the full length of drama from *Oedipus Rex* to Tennessee Williams's *Suddenly Last Summer*. The trial scenes in *The Caine Mutiny Court Martial* and, in a loose sense, *Tea and Sympathy* and *The Crucible* are simply variations of this question. In some cases the audience knows who is guilty; the dramatic question arises out of the attempt on the part of the *characters* to find out. It is a highly variable device, though the trial scene has become overused.

3. *Will he or she succeed?* This is by far the most used of all dramatic questions. It has been applied to noble and evil characters alike. The answer is rarely a simple "yes" or "no" since this is too close to predictable. The audience has visualized these alternatives from the start. More often, the conclusion is qualified: the protagonist wins in some significant way but at a price or, conversely, loses the struggle but gains in a way not previously anticipated by the audience.

In Saroyan's play, Photo-Finish faces overwhelming odds and loses his life, but Emily, though still trapped, achieves for the first time a moment of assertiveness.

4. *Will he or she discover what we know?* The classic example is Sophocles' play *Oedipus Rex*, in which the attention of the audience is held by a character gradually discovering terrible truths about himself. It is also a factor in *Othello*. And it has been adapted in plays of psychological self-discovery such as Arthur Miller's *Death of a Salesman*.

5. *Will a compromise be found?* This question has held audiences in such varied plays as Sophocles' *Antigone* (the answer is "no") and John Galsworthy's *Strife* (the answer is "yes" but with terrible consequences for both sides). Both of these plays, by the way, carefully avoid the temptation to pit blameless individuals or groups against opponents who are totally evil. Such plays end up being **melodramas** no matter how well intended.

6. *Will this episode end in violence?* This question is frequently used in contemporary drama. In fact, it is one of the final questions in *Hello Out There*. Even though almost every indication points to a tragic ending, we keep hoping otherwise until those shots are fired. There is high drama in violence, but relying on it excessively drags the work down to the level of the least imaginative television thriller.

7. *What's happening?* This is the question most frequently asked of plays in the **absurdist** tradition. Like dream fiction, these works plunge the audience into a confusing, often inexplicable environment. Playwrights like Pinter, Beckett, Ionesco, and occasionally Albee utilize ambiguity as a dramatic question. This is, however, a risky device for the novice. Like free verse, it seems easy at first but can all too easily slide into meaninglessness. It requires genuine wit or intellectual ingenuity to keep the play alive. In short, a dull play is not improved by being made an obscurely dull play.

The opening dramatic question is often referred to as the **hook**. It arouses interest from the start. But most plays move from one dramatic question to the next so that the audience is kept wondering about immediate problems as well as about what the ultimate resolution will be. *Hello Out There* is a good example of how the playwright can create a new question just as an old one has been resolved.

The opening scene poses the question, "What is happening?" We begin to receive answers from Emily, but we are now concerned with "Will they succeed?" When it appears that they won't, we wonder "Will there be violence?"

Playwrights, of course, don't start with such questions; they start by shaping a plot. Early in the revision process, however, they examine just how successfully the play will hold an audience. If a scene seems to drag, it may be due to a lack of action or excessive length, but more often it simply needs a better dramatic question.

Controlling the Pace

Pace is all-important in a play. Scenes that seem slow continue to be revised well into production. Although one rarely hears about a play in which the pace is too rapid, it is possible to race too quickly through scenes that should unfold character or clarify aspects of the plot. And too much dramatic voltage at the beginning of a play can create a slump later on. These are all matters of pacing.

Traditional terms are helpful if we remember that they apply mainly to the plots of traditional plays. **Rising action,** for example, accurately describes the mounting complications with which many plays from all historical periods are begun. In full-length dramas, problems may be compounded with **subplots** involving secondary characters acting as **foils** to highlight or set off the major characters. The **crisis** is not the very end but the turning point at which the protagonist's fortunes begin to fail. From there on we have **falling action,** which in tragedies results in a **catastrophe** or **denouement**—often the death of the hero.

Sound old-fashioned? True, Aristotle described drama in those terms. True, they apply to Greek and Elizabethan tragedies. But they also apply to many modern works by such playwrights as Eugene O'Neill, Arthur Miller, and Tennessee Williams. In condensed form, they can be seen in William Saroyan's *Hello Out There* as well.

The rising action involves the young man meeting an ally and planning an escape. The crisis occurs when the enraged husband returns. From there on it is falling action through to the death of the protagonist. Although the play is brief and in one act, the plot structure is similar to that of a traditional three-act play or a Shakespearean tragedy of five acts.

This plot pattern continues to be popular not because playwrights who use it are imitative but because it is good theater. It lends itself to a variety of situations and it holds audiences.

There are, in addition, other effective ways to handle the pacing of a dramatic plot. One focuses on characterization and is sometime referred to as the *onion approach:* A series of scenes exposes the inner life of a character or a couple like peeling the layers of an onion. Eugene O'Neill's *The Iceman Cometh* reveals a single character this way; Edward Albee's *Who's Afraid of Virginia Woolf?* exposes the illusions of a couple with equal intensity.

Another type of loose structure is sometimes called the *Grand Hotel* pattern. The title refers to a film based on a novel by Vicki Baum. The plot brings together a number of different characters to portray European society in the 1920s. This approach weaves together many parallel plots. It is particularly effective in longer plays. A good contemporary example is *The Hot l Baltimore* by Lanford Wilson. Once again a hotel (this one not so grand) is used to link characters, and the plot is episodic. Arthur Miller's relatively short *A Memory of Two Mondays* deals with the men who work in the shipping room of an auto-parts warehouse. It is concerned almost equally with all the characters.

The pace in loosely structured plays like this is controlled not by the rise and fall of a protagonist but by a series of dramatic questions arising from the problems faced by a number of different characters.

With **satiric** works, which I will examine in more detail in Chapter 40, pace can also be controlled by posing and then answering dramatic questions. In addition, one can increase the level of exaggeration. Many such plays intentionally start on a low key. This avoids the risk of establishing a pace in the opening you can't sustain. When you read the two satiric plays included later in this volume, notice how each begins with a deceptively mild opening scene and builds from there.

Clearly there are no firm rules about how to construct a good plot. Whether you are writing a serious play or a comedy, you are free to draw on certain traditional patterns or experiment with new approaches. This is not to say, however, that anything will work. You must maintain forward movement in some way. If you don't create dramatic questions and don't make use of rising and falling action, you will have to find some other method of keeping your production alive. If you ignore pacing and let your play go slack, your audience will be quick to let you know.

The Resonance of Subplots

A **subplot**, is a sequence of actions involving secondary characters that runs parallel to the main plot. It is difficult to use in short plays because of the time required to introduce secondary characters in any detail, but as soon as you start working with a longer play, the technique is well worth considering.

In most cases a subplot either echoes the main plot or provides a contrast. If, for example, the main plot deals with a couple's serious marital conflict, the subplot might introduce another couple with similar but less serious problems. Or the subplot might contrast the challenges faced by a woman as single parent with those faced by a man in similar circumstances.

Often the subplot is lighter than the primary plot, thereby establishing a tonal contrast, a kind of counterpoint. It can even provide comic relief, a technique of easing tension that I will discuss in more detail in Chapter 40.

The problems generated in the subplot are usually resolved before the conclusion of the main plot so as not to interfere. Be careful not to allow the subplot to dominate the play. If it begins to do so, the play will seem to lack a focus. The only exception to this principle is the "Grand Hotel pattern," in which there are many equally important plots. These are not, however, true subplots since there is no central and dominant story line.

After you have written several short plays, you will want to expand your horizons with a full-length work. Much will depend on how much drama you have read and seen in production. Earlier in this chapter I referred to many well-known plays. If you are serious about play writing, you will want to read as many of these as you can. They will give you a good sense of how to plot a longer work, including those with subplots.

Plot is found in narrative poetry; it is even more important in fiction; but it is central in most dramas. Although there are plays that take the form of an extended monologue, those few that succeed depend on highly sophisticated wit and verbal ingenuity. They are risky models.

The long history of drama is dominated by visual activity and the lure of an unfolding plot. Fiction can afford to suspend the flow of action for passages of reflection or description, but a play must be nonstop and relentless.

Maintaining this momentum is a challenge, but for many it is well worth the effort. A dramatic plot gives you as writer an opportunity to seize and hold the attention of an audience with a sustained intensity rarely given the written page. This direct and charged contact between artist and viewer is one of the special rewards for the playwright.

34

CONFLICT:

The Driving Force of Drama

Conflict as the prime energizing force. Avoiding melodrama. Person against person. Triangular conflicts. Inner conflicts and how to reveal them. Comic conflicts. Creating a network of conflicts.

Almost all plays over the course of the past 2,500 years are conflict-driven. This is not just a matter of tradition. It is a natural response to the fact that plays are performances that require uninterrupted attention.

When we say that a work is "dramatic" or "powerful," we are implying that conflict of some type has been used convincingly. Dramatic questions, described in the previous chapter, arouse curiosity. Conflict is stronger and frequently is maintained throughout the work. In serious drama it evokes fear, excitement, anger, commitment. It pumps adrenaline. In comedy it evokes laughter.

Conflict comes in many forms, some more subtle than others. But before we can examine them, it is important to understand the greatest danger present in all serious plays: **melodrama.**

Avoiding Melodrama

Anyone who has watched television dramas or action thrillers in film has been bomborded by simple dramas known as **melodrama.** Such work is usually based on a simple struggle between good and bad. The loyalty of the audience is fixed from start to finish. It's our team versus theirs, our country versus theirs, our law enforcers against lawbreakers, good people (or animals) against aggressors. Seeing this pattern so often in popular film and television dramas makes it easy to forget that conflict doesn't have to be melodramatic. It can also be the mainspring of complex and sophisticated drama.

There is nothing wrong with melodrama as entertainment. It is to sophisticated drama what a simple adventure story is to literary fiction. Even Abraham Lincoln enjoyed a good melodrama as a way to forget the burden of his office, just as many intelligent people today find pleasure in a James Bond film. But if you want to write a play that offers more than escape, you will want to guard against melodrama.

There are two basic elements in any melodramatic play. First, the conflict has blotted out subtle characterization. Second, it has done away with all themes except who will ultimately win. In short, the conflict has become an end in itself.

Hello Out There is a good example of a play with a strong set of conflicts that do not spill over into melodrama. Take a look at the characterization. In a melodrama the hero would be blameless and the villain pure evil. While Saroyan is far from impartial, he is careful to develop Photo-Finish's weaknesses—his perilous lifestyle and his habit of taking risks, his reliance on luck for survival. As for the **antagonist,** the husband, he is not a cold-blooded murderer. He is frightened, unsure about his wife, and intimidated by his pals.

The theme also has its subtleties. It is more than a simple matter of life versus death. There is, for example, a parallel between being a prisoner in a cell and being trapped in a small, mean-spirited community. Another theme focuses on the degree to which violence is motivated by attempts to "save face." A third theme develops the way loneliness can affect both men and women. Although the conflict between Photo-Finish and the husband is central, it is a means of developing a number of related themes rather than being an end in itself.

The shorter the play, the more likely it is that a violent conflict between central characters will overpower both characterization and a variety of themes. There simply isn't time to develop other concerns.

Novice playwrights are sometimes tempted to push conflict to the point of murder or suicide simply to keep a lackluster script lively. Before you go to this extreme, make sure that your characters and themes are strong enough to keep from being overpowered by the action.

Fortunately, you have the ability as playwright to adjust the level of conflict almost as easily as you turn the volume up or down on a radio. And you can do this without changing the structure of the play. Murder can be moderated to a fight, and a fight downgraded to a verbal attack. Suicide can be downsized to poignant expressions of despair.

Your judgment as to how much intensity is appropriate to dramatize a conflict depends on your ability to spot at what point you have pushed your drama into melodrama. Review for a moment that final scene in *Hello Out There* in which Emily, alone on the stage, repeats in a whisper, "Hello—out—there!" Now picture a revised ending in which Emily stabs herself in the heart, letting her lifeless body drop on top of her newfound friend, fake blood trickling across the stage. That's true melodrama. Why? Because the play has already been charged with as much violence as the situation can absorb. One step farther and the audience will no longer take the scene seriously. What the playwright had hoped would be moving might well produce only snickers.

Person against Person

A majority of plays pit a **protagonist** against an **antagonist** in one way or another. (The word *hero* is often avoided since it implies greatness. *Protagonist* is both morally neutral and gender-free.) In many cases, however, the opponent represents a group or some aspect of society. The husband in Saroyan's play pulls the trigger, but he acts in response to his buddies, and they in turn reflect a brutal and mindless portion of society.

This aspect of the conflict gives Saroyan an opportunity to comment on society as a whole. He unmistakably takes sides. On the one hand, the individual characters are treated with some compassion, even the worst of them. Society, on the other hand, is pictured as the real culprit. Photo-Finish, musing to himself, says, "This world stinks." Later, outraged at the charge of rape and also at how the town has treated Emily, he says, "Rape? *They* rape everything good that was ever born." When there is still hope of escape, she asks, "Are people different in San Francisco?" He replies:

> People are the same everywhere. They're different only when they love somebody. More people in Frisco love somebody, that's all.

In the conflict between the individual and society as a whole, Saroyan clearly sides with the individual.

Society for Saroyan is a fairly general concept, but others have portrayed it in much more specific terms. Some playwrights see society as the rich and powerful. Their work takes a political stance. For many black playwrights, society is the white world. I will have more to say about socially conscious drama and themes of protest in Chapter 41, "Dramatic Themes." What concerns us here is the way in which conflict between individuals is often used as a commentary on opposing forces in society.

The dramatic impact that can be generated by a plot that pits an individual against society is enormous. If you take that route, however, be careful not to let your play turn into a sermon. Sermons have their place, but they make poor drama—except for those who already agree. The most successful plays dealing with society are the ones that can translate those relatively abstract convictions into person-to-person conflict. Even when social statement is the primary concern of the playwright, it is personal conflict between credible characters that generates the most effective impact.

Triangular Conflicts

Three-way conflicts have certain advantages over those limited to two opponents. Triangles add more than just an additional character. They compound
the possibilities of character development.

The first pattern that comes to mind is the love triangle, the relationship
of two individuals threatened by a third. It has an venerable history. A wife's
betrayal by a husband who fell in love with another woman has been told
and retold from Euripides' tragedy, *Medea*, around 440 B.C., to Robinson
Jeffers' moden verse play with the same name. The same pattern of betrayal
and revenge is repeated endlessly in contemporary play and film scripts on
both serious and comic levels.

If you plan to use a love triangle as the basis of conflict in a one-act play,
you will have to work hard to achieve originality. The sexy baby-sitter or an
obliging secretary are **stereotypes**, too familiar for use. But triangles do continue to exist in life, and in some cases the unique circumstances of an actual
case will suggest a fresh dramatic situation.

Triangles don't necessarily have to involve love relationships. Three
individuals vying for a job, a promotion, or an award become a triangle. Two
parents and a child often become a triangle in conflict. Two senior workers
who find themselves having to take orders from a newly promoted younger
associate can be an explosive triangle.

The third member of a triangle doesn't even have to be a person. In
contemporary dramas, both husbands and wives have been seduced by
professional commitments that become the third member of a triangle. A
married person's involvement with a political cause or a religious faith
can also have the impact of an infidelity. Watch out, once again, for versions that have been overdone. The marriage that is threatened by a
husband's preoccupation with his business can, if not done in a fresh
manner, become as hackneyed in drama as in fiction. Merely reversing the
sexes doesn't add much if the characters are still cardboard. And there
should be a moratorium on drama plots based on painters and writers
who wreck their marriages for the sake of art. But even setting these aside,
there are enough triangulations left to serve future dramatists for some
time to come.

Inner Conflicts and How to Reveal Them

Presenting inner conflicts is one of the best ways to achieve subtlety in characterization. The very phrases with which we describe such indecision
suggest dramatic tension: a character is "of two minds," "struggling with
himself," or even "at war with herself." Such individuals are torn between
love and fear, courage and timidity, anger and affection. Or they may be

attracted to two different people, two opposing ethical positions, two sexual identities. Inner conflict is a part of the human condition.

But how is one to reveal what goes on in the mind of a character in a genre that depends almost entirely on dialogue and actions? If you have been writing fiction, your first inclination may be to consider **monologues.** After all, Shakespeare used them. The soliloquies of Hamlet and Lady Macbeth are among the most quoted dramatic lines in the language. But remember that those monologues were embedded in five-act plays. If we hadn't heard those famous passages so often and studied them so carefully out of context, they would blend into the work as a whole. In addition, Elizabethan drama accepted the convention of major characters expressing their inner conflicts eloquently in **blank verse.** Most contemporary, realistic plays are intended to reflect more closely the behavior and speech of daily life. Inner debate expressed through a monologue often seems artificial.

When monologues are used in realistic drama today, they are usually brief. Saroyan's first scene begins with a short sequence, and he repeats the device by having Photo-Finish alone on the stage in that abbreviated third scene. This second monologue is particularly important because it is the only hard evidence the audience has that Photo-Finish really is fond of Emily and is not just using her for escape. Although Emily's two-sentence monologue at the very end of the play takes only a moment, it effectively reveals her inner lament.

During the 1960s and 1970s there was a certain vogue for long monologues among playwrights in the **absurdist** school. Their plays were often dreamlike, philosophical, and talky. The best of them maintained interest through flashes of insight and wit, but the approach was short-lived. It takes remarkable skill on the part of both playwright and actor to hold the attention of an audience with thoughts alone.

A far more effective way to reveal inner conflict is to provide your protagonist with a *confidant*, a personal friend who is not quite central to the action. If you are working with two couples, the wives or the husbands can sometimes reveal inner conflict when talking with each other, private feelings that they are reluctant to share with their partners. In longer plays, the confidant may be a **foil,** a minor character who serves primarily to set off a primary character by contrast. The foil is often a relatively comic character in an otherwise serious play.

Another approach is to use action. People often reveal their inner conflicts unconsciously through the way they behave. It is not difficult to have your characters do the same. There is a small example in *Hello Out There* which, though easily missed, represents a well-used device. Emily is torn between the desire to do whatever Photo-Finish asks and her fear of leaving him for a minute. When he asks her to go and look for cigarettes, she does leave, but almost at once she comes running back. Alternating behavior like this can be used in more significant scenes as well. A character starts to do one thing, then abruptly does another. Often no lines are needed to spell out the inner conflict.

Sometimes inner conflict takes the form of indecision; in other cases it is true **ambivalence,** two opposing desires that exist simultaneously. In either case, it is an excellent way to humanize a character and make him or her credible.

As you examine these different types of conflict, keep in mind that although they are enormously important, they don't make a good starting point for a play. You don't begin by deciding to write about a triangle or a battle with society and then fill in the blanks. As I have pointed out before (and will again), plays begin with a concept—specific characters in a dramatic situation. Once you have that in place, you will be able to see where the major conflicts lie and start revising the script so as to make the best use of them.

Comic Conflicts

Comedies also use conflict. Although we will be exploring comic drama in detail later, it is worth noting here that comedy without some form of conflict becomes a simple skit.

To some degree, the varieties of conflict in comedy are the same as in serious drama. There are, however, two differences. The first is that melodrama is no longer a threat. Melodrama does damage to serious work because the audience no longer takes either the characters or the themes seriously. But in comedy this can be used to advantage.

When a comedy is a satire (as many are), pushing the plot into absurdly exaggerated extremes and turning characters into **stereotypes** is an excellent way of ridiculing people, institutions, or attitudes. This is particularly true of **farcical** comedy, that which is highly exaggerated. You will see how effective this can be when you read *The Cowboy, the Indian and the Fervent Feminist*, which appears in Chapter 39. It is essentially a comic melodrama.

The other major difference between comic conflict and that found in serious drama may surprise you. Comedy tends to stress conflict of ideas. In this respect, comedy above the level of **slapstick** is often more intellectual than serious drama. Remember that the impact of conflict in serious drama is rooted in the fact that we take the characters seriously. The audience feels an emotional identification. With comedy, however, that sense of compassion is largely lost. The audience tends to remain outside the characters, laughing at their foibles. Satire ridicules people, institutions, and attitudes, and comic conflicts exploit these. Whether kindly or biting, satire deals with ideas.

Creating a Network of Conflicts

Until now, we have been examining various types of conflict as if they were separate and distinct. A well-developed drama, however, contains a network of conflicts that reinforce each other.

One of the reasons *Hello Out There* serves as such a good model for short, realistic plays is that it generates just such a network of conflicts. Primarily, of course, it is a struggle between Photo-Finish and his antagonist, the outraged husband. In a simple melodrama, that conflict would stand alone as the prime and perhaps only concern of the work. Saroyan has made sure, however, that it is only one of many interrelated conflicts.

When the play opens, no antagonist is in sight. The first major conflict to be introduced is a prisoner against a hostile town. The enemy is "them," a vague notion of forces outside that jail. This conflict of man against society is highlighted when we learn that the name of the town is Matador. If the town is the bullfighter, he is the bull in the pen, waiting for the deadly sport to begin.

Next we learn that Emily is also pitted against this town. Her life is not threatened, but her spirit is. She is not just lonesome, she is alienated. The men in town, she reports, laugh at her. Her father takes what little money she earns. She is willing to take great risks to escape.

Their conflict with this oppressive town is soon overshadowed by the direct confrontation between Photo-Finish and the husband. But the man is not acting alone. The town remains an antagonist right through to the end of the play.

Although the husband is the enemy, he has his own conflicts. First, it is clear that he and his wife are antagonists. He actually puts his gun away when Photo-Finish starts revealing the truth. The man keeps calling Photo-Finish a liar, but he continues to listen. And when he is asked whether he is in love with his wife, he doesn't answer. Pathetically, when he is told that his wife asked for money, he responds with, "How much did she ask for?" Clearly this is a tormented relationship.

We see still more conflicts when it is revealed that he is being driven by pressures from his wife and friends. As Photo-Finish puts it, "You're a pretty good guy, you're just afraid of your pals." Saroyan has him repeat this line for emphasis. As with so many acts of violence, the perpetrator is motivated in part by fear of his own peer group. This doesn't excuse his actions, but it does humanize him. When you look closely at what drives these characters, it is clear that this play is far from the simple television plot of man against the mob. The tragic killing is a result of a network of conflicts. In the end, Emily is also a victim and in conflict with the town, though now she has money and a new assertiveness.

At first, it may seem almost impossible to generate so many different conflicts in the limited time frame of a relatively short one-act play. But if you get to know your characters well, you will see that none of them is purely good or purely bad. They are all driven by different and conflicting forces and needs. Once you understand this, developing and dramatizing a variety of conflicts will become a natural part of the revision process through successive drafts.

The play that follows as the next chapter is different from *Hello Out There* in many respects. First, it is **nonrealistic;** it creates its own world. Second, it is much shorter. Third, it is a comedy. Read it through once for pleasure; then read it again for analysis. Ask yourself what the play is suggesting about the relationship between writers and the individuals they use to create a literary work.

In addition, examine the different conflicts that run though this play. Even though the work is short and essentially comic, it is the various conflicts that give the play a sense of dramatic energy.

35

A PLAY

by Glenn Alterman

Coulda, Woulda, Shoulda

Characters

CY

YETTA

MARTY

Scene

A small, simply decorated kitchen. It is about 11: 30 A.M. Yetta is seated at the kitchen table finishing her coffee. Cy is rushing around, getting dressed.

CY: You're kidding? He said that?

YETTA: That's what he said.

CY: When?

YETTA: This morning when I gave him his bath.

CY: What a kid.

YETTA: Could you bust?

CY: (*looking around*): Where's my belt?

YETTA: On the chair (*He gets it, puts it on.*) Stood up in the tub, put his hand on my shoulder and said, "Ma, I want to be a rabbi."

CY: A rabbi? You're kidding? Every morning it's something else.

YETTA: At first, first, I thought he said "a rabbit."

CY: (*stops for a moment*): What?

YETTA: Yeah, thought he said "I want to be a rabbit, Ma." Almost dropped the sponge I laughed so hard. I mean can you imagine? But then he looked at me, seemed so serious. You know those eyes of his. Said it again, loud and clear, black and white. Looked like a little Moses in the tub waiting for the waters to part. (*Slowly, very strong.*) "Ma, I want to be a rabbi. A rabbi, you understand?" I stopped, smiled, what could I . . . ? Said, "Sure, okay honey, if that's what you want." Washed the soap off, towel-dried him, baby powder, kissed him on the head and gave him a big hug. Well he gave me a look, got upset, started to cry.

CY: Cry? Why?

YETTA: I don't know. I asked him, wouldn't answer. Looked at me like I was the worst mother in the world. Like I'd just stabbed him in the heart or something. Ran to his room, slammed the door, locked it shut. Wouldn't let me in. Couldn't get him out. Been in there all morning.

CY: All morning?

YETTA: All morning long!

CY: You're kidding? Where's my shoes?

YETTA: By the sink. (*He gets the shoes, starts putting them on.*) I've been sitting here, waiting for you to get up. We've got a problem, Cy.

CY: I'll say, our son—Marty! I'm taking that lock off his door first thing when I get home tonight. Enough of this shit!

YETTA: What are you talking about? You've got to go talk to him.

CY: Me? About what? I didn't have no fight with him.

YETTA: What fight? Who fought? A misunderstanding, that's all.

CY: I don't got time for this now. He'll come out when he's good and ready. And stop giving him so many baths for Christ's sake!

YETTA: Talk to him.

CY: Didn't you hear me?

YETTA: He's your son!

CY: I'm late. I'll talk to my son—later.

YETTA: When, at four in the morning when you get home?

CY: (*grabbing his coat, starting to go*): Whenever!

YETTA: (*blocking the door*): The drunks of the world can wait!

CY: Hey, the drunks of the world put food on this table and don't you forget it. You should thank God we got that bar. (*Then, looking through his coat pocket.*) Where's my keys?

YETTA: (*ignoring him, looking toward the bedroom, calling sweetly*): Marty, come on out. Daddy's leaving for work, come say good bye.

CY: (*looking around*): Where the hell's. . .?

YETTA: (*sweetly, calling to the bedroom*): Marty.

CY: Where the hell are they?

YETTA: On the bureau, where you left them!

CY: (*as he storms off, calling to the bedroom*): Marty, come on out. I don't got all day. (*Yetta looks anxiously toward the bedroom. Loud banging.*) Martin get out of there! You hear me? Out!

(*It's quiet for a moment. Then returning, carrying the keys, under his breath*):

He doesn't want to come out.

YETTA: So you're just gonna leave?

CY: What do you want me to do, break the door down?

YETTA: (*turning away, upset*): Go 'head, go. GO!

CY: (*He starts to leave, but then returning, upset*): Why's it always gotta be this way? Huh, why? Why do I got to leave here almost every day with you crying and me with a knot in my stomach? Why, huh, I'm asking you?

YETTA: (*tensely, looking straight at him*): I am not crying!

CY: Can't I leave here just once, JUST ONCE YETTA, a pleasant goodbye, kiss on the cheek? Why's it always got to be Marty's been bad, or Marty's. . .? Always something!

YETTA: (*furiously*): The drunks of the world are waiting. Go ahead, go!

MARTY (*from the bedroom, yelling*): Stop it! Stop it already, both of you!

(*A light change. They both turn toward the bedroom. A door slams. Marty enters. He's in his forties, wearing large children's pajamas, a pair of glasses and a black hat. He's carrying a pen and pad.*)

YETTA: What? What's wrong?

MARTY: I can't concentrate! This constant arguing, bickering back and forth!

YETTA: You don't have to yell.

MARTY: Why, did anybody ever just talk here?

CY: Told you he'd come out when he was good and ready.

YETTA: Marty, take your hat off in the house.

MARTY: Ma, I'm trying to finish this scene, please!

YETTA: So what's stopping you? We were just . . .

MARTY: Please, I've got a whole play ahead of me.

YETTA: (*very cool*): Sorry, Mister Playwright.

MARTY: All right, let's just go back a bit. You were standing here, Ma, I'm still in the bedroom, and he's about to leave.

YETTA: But you're here now, just say goodbye. What's the big. . .?

MARTY: Ma, please, don't tell me how to write my play. I'm still a kid in this scene. There's a scene later on when he leaves us that's the big goodbye scene.

YETTA: He leaves us?

MARTY: Yeah, but it's not for years. There's still five scenes before . . .

YETTA: What happens then?

MARTY: Ma!

YETTA: What? After he leaves, what happens then? Tell me.

MARTY: You divorce. He runs around, starts drinking, becomes a drunk. Finally, burnt out, broke, he has to move back in with his mother, gets diabetes, loses both his legs. There's a big father-son hospital scene. And then when I leave, he dies.

CY: I die? Alone?

MARTY: Yeah, but it's not till late in the second act.

YETTA: What happens to me?

MARTY: You . . . never remarry, Ma. End up bitter, alone, miserable in Miami.

YETTA: That's it?

CY: This is a comedy?

YETTA: Was that all true? Is that what really happens?

MARTY: It's a play, Ma, make-believe.

CY: So you made all that up, right? It's not really . . . ?

MARTY: Let's see, where were we? Ma, you were just about to cry. Dad . . .

YETTA: Does he really leave us?

MARTY: How do I know? I'm not God.

CY: Of course not Yetta! I'd never leave, I swear!

MARTY: You liar! You leave when I'm eleven years old.

CY: But you just said . . . !

MARTY: I make it up as I go along.

CY: What are you tryin' to pull here, huh?

MARTY: Nothing.

CY: Got to start trouble again, don't you?

MARTY: What?

CY: Some things never change!

MARTY: What are you talking about?

CY: You, Mister Playwright! It's just like when you were a kid, little mister in-between.

YETTA: Why are you blaming him?

CY: How she cooed and pampered you—her little Lord Fauntleroy.

MARTY: I hated . . . That's why I always ran to my room. Dad, you've got it all wrong!

CY: Yeah, wrong, right! You sucked up all her. . .! Nothing left for me. No room left at the inn!

MARTY (*throwing his pad and pen down*): That's bullshit!

YETTA: What's going on here?

MARTY: You were too busy fooling around with all your girlfriends! Never home with us. Couldn't wait to. . .!

YETTA: What's all this blame? Blaming!

CY: Only reason I fooled around was because your mother wouldn't . . .!

YETTA: The play, Marty! Your play! WHAT THE HELL'S GOING ON HERE?

(*Marty and Cy look at her. It's quiet in the room for a moment, then*)

MARTY: Nothing, Ma, nothing. This is part of the play. A dramatic moment. Dad and me were rehearsing the big father-son confrontation scene, top of the second act.

YETTA: So much anger, hostility? Can't you fix it? Make it funny?

MARTY: Ma, this isn't "It's a Wonderful Life." You can't always make things better. Now let's see, where were we?

CY: (*putting his arm around Marty's shoulders*): Marty, you gotta change that ending. Please, me dying all alone like that, it's just too sad.

MARTY: Everybody's a critic.

CY: Please?! Couldn't you just . . . ?

MARTY (*walking away from him*): I'm sorry, I can't.

YETTA: You've made me the villain here, you realize that?

MARTY: No I didn't.

YETTA: Couldn't you just . . .

MARTY: Coulda-woulda-shoulda! What happened, happens. It all stays in the play!

CY: (*upset, starting to leave, going toward the bedroom*): Well then it happens without me!

MARTY: Dad, you don't leave yet! We've still got . . .

CY: (*as he leaves*): No? Just watch me! (*He leaves, goes to the bedroom, slams the door.*)

MARTY (*calling to him*): Dad, that's my room! (*Marty turns to Yetta. She looks at him for a moment, then starts to leave.*)

MARTY: Where are you going?

YETTA: I'm sorry, Marty.

MARTY: But Ma, you don't leave.

YETTA: No? You still haven't finished the play yet, remember? And what happens, happens. (*She leaves, goes to Marty's bedroom.*)

MARTY (*calling to her*): Ma. Ma!

(We hear the bedroom door slam and lock. A light change. Marty slowly looks around the kitchen. He picks up the pen and pad off the floor, writes something.)

"Marty slowly looks around the kitchen. He picks up the pen and pad off the floor, writes something."

(*He sits down, takes his hat off and puts it on the table.*)

"He sits down, takes his hat off and puts it on the table."

(*Suddenly he turns toward his bedroom.*)

"Suddenly he turns toward his bedroom and calls out . . ."

(*Just as Marty opens his mouth . . .
Blackout*)

CURTAIN

36

THE NONREALISTIC PLAY

Realistic and nonrealistic drama distinguished. Distortion of time. Distortions of character. Dreamscape settings. Risks in the nonrealistic approach. Learning from nonrealistic plays. Making choices.

Until now, we have been dealing with **realistic drama.** It creates an illusion that reflects and conforms with the world about us. Events may be surprising, but they are believable. It avoids the **deus ex machina,** the improbable event used to solve a problem. The passage of time is generally chronological. If the plot skips ahead a week or a year, the jump is made clear. There is no imprecise blurring of past and present or of different centuries. Settings are clearly defined (a living room, a jail cell, a forest), borrowed from the world as we know it. Characters are mortal and limited in the same way we are. They can't fly like birds or turn into frogs.

The term *realism* also applies to a period in literary history, but I will use the term in its nonhistorical, purely descriptive sense. These plays mimic life.

Nonrealistic drama, on the other hand, is an illusion that in some ways resembles a dream. Such plays often *seem* real just as dreams usually do, but the plot may be an illogical sequence of events in which time is distorted or ignored, characters may behave in ways that lack motivation, and the setting may be strange or a satiric exaggeration.

Nonrealistic drama is a broad term that covers a variety of approaches, all of which depart from what we think of as the natural order. It includes fantasies, dream plays, and cartoon-like satires. Like free verse, these plays don't abandon all form; they merely replace the familiar conventions of realism with a world designed for that particular play.

At first glance, realistic and nonrealistic drama appear to be entirely different. Actually they have much in common and frequently borrow techniques from each other. I will begin by describing their differences, but keep in mind that there is no sharp line between them.

Distortions of Time

Realistic drama keeps track of time. If there is a gap, it is often made clear in the program notes: "Next week," the audience is told, or "A year later." Nonrealistic plays tend to ignore or twist time.

Samuel Beckett's *Waiting for Godot* has become a popular prototype for **theater-of-the-absurd** plays and illustrates the way time can be ignored. There is nothing in the script that indicates a historical period. You can think of it as a contemporary or a medieval drama—take your pick. And although there are references to times of the day, there is also a sense that this has been going forever. The play is like a long and rather hazy dream with no distinct beginning or end. This indifference to both historical time and clock time is common in nonrealistic plays.

Another approach to time is to warp it. Time warps are popular in science fiction, but they are often given some kind of rational explanation. In nonrealistic drama, time frequently slides without explanation.

Time in *Coulda, Woulda, Shoulda* is particularly inventive. As the play opens, we see a young married couple with a child of about four or five. The familiar kitchen setting and the two parents seem to suggest that this is going to be a realistic play. Our assumption, however, is shattered when Marty the son enters. The stage directions tell us that he is "in his forties, wearing large children's pajamas, a pair of glasses and a black hat. He's carrying a pen and pad."

What's going on? In one sense, the time has leaped forward 35 years. Marty has grown up. You could show this in a realistic play by starting a new scene without the parents or with them grown old, thereby accounting for the passage of time "logically." But in this play the parents remain just as they were, and Marty appears as an adult—a blend of the 40-year-old playwright and the child he was, still in his pajamas.

Later he confirms this fusing of time periods by saying, "I'm still a kid in this scene." On one level he is referring to the script he, Marty, is writing in which the character based on himself is still a child, but in another sense the line refers to the scene in the play we are watching. He is *both* the 40-year-old playwright and the child in the same scene. Is this logical? Not literally. But think for a moment what it would be like to be writing a play that includes a character based on yourself at four or five. As you write, aren't you both the playwright and the child? The distortion of time then becomes a metaphor: the situation is *like* being a writer and a child at the same moment.

Alterman doesn't stop there with his time tricks. Marty as playwright begins to tell his parents what will become of them in the future. His father will become a drunk, go broke, get diabetes, lose both his legs. As for his mother, she will end up "bitter, alone, miserable in Miami."

Is the playwright, Glenn Alterman, saying that this is what will really happen to the parents, or is Marty, the playwright in the play, making this up? We laugh, but to Cy this is no joke.

The distortion of time becomes a commentary on the illusion of theater in this exchange:

> YETTA: Was that all true? Is that what really happens?
> MARTY: It's a play, Ma, make-believe.

She has believed his story enough to be alarmed at the future that seems to be in store for her and her husband. We smile at how quickly she has been taken in by something that is "only a play." But what about us in the audience? Aren't we accepting the illusion that these people on the stage are going through a real crisis?

Toward the end of the play, there is one more time shift. First Marty's father leaves and then his mother. But notice that they don't go outside. Instead, they go into Marty's room and slam the door. Where are they really? In Marty the playwright's mind. The bedroom, after all, is the room for memory and for dreams.

If you look closely at what this play does with time, you will see that there are three scenes. The first, with the parents alone, is unmistakably the past. It is Marty's childhood presented realistically. The second is a dream-like blend with the parents as they once were and the son grown, an "unrealistic" mix of two periods. We accept the absurdity of it just as we accept similar distortions in dreams. The final scene begins as soon as both parents are offstage. Marty, alone, is writing a play about Marty the playwright. And what will happen when this fictional playwright calls out to his parents after the last line of the play? We can't say for sure, but isn't it logical that the three of them will go through this again? Anyone who has written about people who were once close to them will remember how often one goes through these confrontations.

The distortion of time in that play occurs within the life of the protagonist. We can call this type *biographical time warps*. Another way to bend time is to slide historical periods together, creating *historical time warps*. Characters from history can appear in contemporary time periods; characters from the present can slide back. When those shifts are made in fairly simple drama and films designed for mass audiences, they are usually introduced with a so-called scientific explanation involving some kind of time machine. The concept was not entirely new even when H. G. Wells popularized it in *The Time Machine* in 1895, and it has been repeated in plays, films, and novels regularly ever since. When historical time warps are used in more sophisticated contemporary works, however, that halfhearted attempt to provide a mechanical explanation is usually dropped. The result is looser, more dreamlike.

I have focused on time here because it is one of the most visible distortions in many (though not all) nonrealistic dramas. In a broader sense, however, it constitutes a different approach to plot itself. The realistic plot seems logical because it conforms to our daily lives. The nonrealistic plot seems logical because it echoes our dreams. After all, our dreams have the power to evoke pleasure, fear, laughter, and tears. The same is true of drama.

Distortion of Character

Characters in realistic drama, as in realistic fiction, are a mix of consistency and variation. The variations are what give a character individuality, but they have to be explained at some point. If a normally kind father strikes his child apparently without cause, the audience expects to find out what drove him to it before the play ends.

Characterization in nonrealistic drama may be confusing in literal terms, but usually there is a symbolic explanation. Marty in *Coulda* is a good example. In the central portion of the play he is both a child in pajamas and an adult "in his 40s." His parents treat him as a child ("Marty, take your hat off in the house") and also as an adult playwright ("Sorry, Mister Playwright"). He also has a third role, that of a seer or oracle who can literally see into the future. His mother asks, "After he leaves, what happens then?" And when Cy learns what is in store for him, he says, "I die? Alone?" They're not talking about a play being written, they've come to believe that this is their future.

So in a single character we have a child, an adult playwright, and an oracle of future events. Alterman the playwright is doing in dramatic terms what Pablo Picasso did in art when he drew figures portraying simultaneously both frontal and profile views. There is a logic there, but it is a symbolic logic, not a literal representation.

The parents too are treated symbolically, though with less distortion. In the opening scene they appear to be highly realistic. They are fond and concerned parents. The father's growing irascibility in no way violates what we would expect in a realistic play. But as soon as their son appears as a grown man, they are seen in a different light. They become credulous individuals, prepared to believe that their son can predict the future. At the end of the play, they serve a different function. By entering Marty's room, they become mere memories rather than flesh-and-blood characters. The implication is that they may be recalled by Marty the playwright at any time.

Coulda is an inventive mix of realistic and nonrealistic elements. In other plays, we are in a nonrealistic dream world from start to finish. In a bitter and brutal play called *The Lesson* by Eugene Ionesco, a raving professor berates his young students in a manner that by realistic standards we would classify as child abuse. Eventually he kills them for no apparent reason. If we made the mistake of viewing this play as an attempt at realism, we would find it an appalling act of violence without credible motivation. The arbitrary nature of the killing would lead us to judge the play to be a failure. "That's just not believable," we would say. But the playwright is not concerned with psychological motivation or even characterization. His theme has to do with the nature of authority and the abuses of absolute power. He has, in effect, drawn a savage cartoon to illustrate his point. Cartoons have the power to argue, even shock, but they deal with ideas, not people as people.

When characters in nonrealistic plays are satiric representations of abstractions like the professor in *The Lesson,* they are usually "flat." They don't have much background. They seem to spring fully formed from nowhere. But this doesn't mean that such characters are more easily created. You have to make sure that the audience understands your intent. If you are too obvious, the play may turn into a simple skit, but if you are not clear enough, the audience will be too baffled to applaud.

When historical figures are used in nonrealistic plays, characterization is often comically different or even the opposite from the generally accepted view of that individual. It's easy enough to do this in an adolescent way just to get laughs—as simple and forgettable as drawing a mustache on a photo of the Mona Lisa. But when it is done with skillful wit, distortion of a historical or public figure can become memorable satire.

One of the most successful examples of this approach is *Picasso at the Lapin Agile* by Steve Martin, the comedian. It is a full-length play in which the artist Picasso meets and argues with Einstein and Lenin. Far more than slapstick, the play explores aesthetic and political values with wit and ingenuity.

Dreamscape Settings

Many nonrealistic plays call for realistic sets. *Coulda* takes place in a realistic kitchen. But in some plays the set itself is nonrealistic. Often the distortions are symbolic. Elmer Rice's *The Adding Machine* deals with a protagonist who is a cipher in a highly mechanical and stratified society in which his associates go by numbers rather than names. Appropriately, he is named Mr. Zero. His apartment is covered with numbers—on the walls, the furniture, and even the lampshades. The set amplifies the symbolic imagination that dominates the play.

Sometimes a dreamlike set is so striking and so fanciful that it remains in the memory long after the characters have been forgotten. The set in Ionesco's play *The Chairs,* for example, is a castle in the middle of the sea. The semicircular room is very sparse but has a total of ten doors—all of which are used. The script calls for the realistic sound of boats moving through the water as guests arrive, but we have no idea where they are coming from. The audience does not ask itself where this might be; it accepts this dreamlike setting just as it accepts the time warps in *Coulda*.

Risks in the Nonrealistic Approach

Since there are no clear guidelines in nonrealistic drama, it is easy to start with an unpromising concept. Here are three approaches that are likely to get you off to a bad start.

The first is the too-familiar **allegory.** No matter what you do with characters who resemble Adam and Eve, they will still seem like all the cartoons we have seen over the years. The same applies to Christ-like figures, no matter how sincere your intent. And the last-couple-on-earth plot is as tired in drama as it is in fiction. You run against terrible odds if the audience's reaction is, "Oh, not another one of those" at the very outset.

Another type to guard against is the humorless sermon. It seems to be a particularly great temptation in nonrealistic plays because they tend to be what is known as thesis-driven rather than character-driven. That is, nonrealistic plays are often dominated by an idea rather than rooted in character. For this very reason, the thesis shows through more blatantly. Your message may reflect your deepest convictions, but you're not going to win converts by having a character shout, "Don't you realize that violence generates more violence?" or "The trouble with you rich slobs is . . ." or "Under the skin we're all the same." A good rule to follow is: Don't have your protagonist state the theme of the play directly. Let him or her reveal it through action or some indirect reference. It doesn't matter how noble your convictions may be, sermons are box-office turkeys.

This doesn't mean that your plays should be bland. Nor should they be without convictions. Look at how Saroyan slides in his strongly felt beliefs. It does mean that you have to present your case obliquely. Have your characters talk about specifics, not broad moral statements. Another approach is to use comic lines. When Marty the protagonist in *Coulda* tells his parents that his mother will "end up bitter, alone, miserable in Miami," his father says, "This is a comedy?" It's a laugh line, but in an almost subliminal way it contributes to the theme as well. It asks a larger question: Just what is comedy? Where is the division between comedy and serious drama? In this case, Marty, the playwright in the play, is writing what seems like a serious and possibly humorless script, but the playwright Alterman is a witty writer with a flare for comedy. We laugh at aspects of the play we are watching, but hidden just below the surface is a serious statement about how difficult it is to write a play based on people who still have a strong emotional hold on you. That valuable insight sneaks up on you after the curtain drops.

The third and most serious danger for beginning playwrights will sound familiar to you because I described a version of it in the fiction section: the hopelessly obscure nonrealistic play. If your audience can't see any coherent pattern, it will simply walk out. You can't depend on novelty value alone. And you can't draw on the emotional appeal of characterization the way realistic drama often does because your approach is necessarily idea-oriented.

Make sure that the ideas you are working with hold together and make a statement that is both logical and compelling. Martin Esslin puts it this way in *The Theatre of the Absurd*:

> Mere combinations of incongruities produce mere banality. Anyone attempting to work in this medium simply by writing down what comes into his mind will find that the supposed flights of spontaneous invention have never left the ground, that they consist of incoherent fragments of reality that have not been transposed into a valid imaginative whole.[1]

As often as this wise warning is repeated, obscure and confused plays continue to be the bane of drama workshops. When they get into production, they are an agony to watch. Some are unintelligible because the playwright has not read his or her script from the audience's point of view. Private references known only to the playwright, personal visions from waking or sleeping dreams, and symbols too elusive to be grasped even after a careful reading all contribute to the unintentionally obscure play.

Worse, some plays are knowingly obscure. The motive may be a misguided notion that sounding deep will win a following. Or it may be a simple disdain for the audience. It should (but doesn't) go without saying that drama is one of the most public arts. It involves not only the writer but producers, directors, actors, and, ultimately, audiences. It should never be treated as a private indulgence.

Learning from Nonrealistic Plays

When one first approaches nonrealistic drama, it sometimes seems like literary anarchy without limits or traditions. Actually it has a significant history from which one can learn a good deal. Although the focus of this text is on the process of writing, not literary history, a brief introduction to the two major schools of nonrealistic drama is important. Studying what has been done in this area is one of the best ways of discovering new directions for your own work.

[1] *The Theatre of the Absurd*, Martin Esslin, Penguin Books.

The first of these two schools is **expressionism.** This movement, closely associated with painting but also including fiction and poetry, began around 1900 and continued through the 1920s. Early examples in drama are seen in the plays of August Strindberg, a Swedish playwright. Plays like *The Dance of Death* and *The Dream Play* are readily available in translation and provide vivid contrasts to the realistic drama of the time. Strindberg's plots were dreamlike, his characters symbolic rather than psychologically comprehensible, and his tone often dark and pessimistic.

Another excellent example of early expressionism is the work of the Czech dramatist Karel Capek. His nightmarish vision of the future, *R.U.R.*, is an early sample of science fiction complete with robots who revolt against their masters. More thematically comprehensible than many of Strindberg's dense works, *R.U.R.* has a strong and clear element of social protest. This contemporary-sounding play was written in 1920.

For a good example of American expressionism, I would recommend Elmer Rice's *The Adding Machine*, a play I described earlier with regard to the highly symbolic and dreamlike set. Costumes, set, action, and dialogue are all distorted, as they are in dreams, but also as in dreams there is an internal consistency that allows us to make sense of it all. We know what it means to be treated like a number, and most of us have on occasion been made to feel like a zero. What we see and hear in this play is distorted, but what we feel is sadly familiar and real.

In the 1950s and 1960s there was a new surge of interest in nonrealistic drama. This movement became known as **theater of the absurd** because many of the playwrights shared the existential notion that life is absurd in the sense of being without ultimate meaning. Oddly, few of them recognized the other important aspect of existential thought: that we create meaning and values by the way we act. As a result, absurdist plays tend to be pessimistic and often cynical.

This school is best represented by the works of Eugene Ionesco, whose plays *The Lesson* and *The Chairs* I have already described. Other such playwrights include Samuel Beckett, Harold Pinter, and occasionally Edward Albee.

Making Choices

As I have pointed out, there are very real risks in the nonrealistic approach. In spite of these dangers however, there are distinct assets as well. It is a particularly tempting approach if your theme is more important to you than your characters. You can cut through to the heart of your statement in a bold and imaginative manner without having to create credible characters or to construct a plausible plot. You are working with a medium that, like the political cartoon and the poster, lends itself to strong statements.

As for form, you can let your imagination take flight. Like free verse, nonrealistic drama offers freedoms and also the obligation to find new and effective structures.

You may already have a strong preference for one approach over the other. Many playwrights do. But in deciding which basic route to take, keep an open mind. Consider the special nature of your projected play. If you are deeply concerned with the complexities of character, it may be best to work in a realistic manner. If, however, the concept you have in mind is charged with a strong idea or has come to you in a satiric vein, you may want to consider the freedom of the nonrealistic play. Your final decision will be based partly on what type of drama you enjoy and partly on the nature of the work at hand.

37

DRAMATIC CHARACTERIZATION

Making characters memorable. Using dialogue to reveal character. Action that reveals feelings. Creating depth of character. Characters in flux: "character change" and shifts in audience perception. The function of minor characters.

Characters in plays are often more intense than they are in life. Actions and passions may be slightly exaggerated. Much of this is due to the nature of the genre. Playwrights don't have the leisure of story writers; they must create memorable characters in a rush—the length of a single performance.

The challenge for playwrights is increased by the fact that characterization is essentially limited to dialogue and action. Fiction writers can reveal thoughts naturally and frequently without slowing the action; they can comment directly about characters through exposition. Not so for playwrights. While it is possible to enter the mind of characters through monologues, the technique is used sparingly and briefly today because of the way it interrupts the action. As for exposition, the playwright must resort to something like a chorus. While this is possible, having an outside observer not only slows the action, it also breaks the audience's illusion of entering into the play. As a result, characterization is normally handled through dialogue and action alone.

Using Dialogue to Reveal Character

When we first meet people, we listen to what they say and how they say it. We have the feeling that we are getting to know them. Later we may learn that the first impression was inaccurate. Their true character is quite different. In life this process of getting to know the true nature of someone may take months or even years. In a play, it has to happen in a matter of minutes.

For many seeing *Hello Out There* for the first time, the first impression of Photo-Finish is negative. He is in jail and accused of rape. Even if the charges are exaggerated, he seems untrustworthy. And when he turns his gambler's charm on a naive girl, we suspect that he may be lying to save his own skin.

At this point Saroyan as playwright is faced with a particularly difficult challenge. How can he induce an audience to look favorably and sympathetically at a small-time gambler and drifter who has been jailed for rape?

Saroyan begins by giving Photo-Finish lines that are hesitant, nonthreatening, appealing. They focus on loneliness and reach out for sympathy and companionship. Further, all that repetition has comic overtones. For many members of the audience, the tone of his lines is enough to create trust. The fact that at least part of the audience accepts his claim as quickly as Emily does is a dramatic illustration of how rapidly a good playwright can establish character through dialogue.

For a minority, however, there are lingering doubts about his actual feelings toward Emily. He is, after all, a gambler, a drifter, in a life-and-death situation, and Emily is no beauty. Does he really feel love for her? Or does he see her as the last chance for escape?

Saroyan clears up any lingering doubts by providing Photo-Finish with that brief monologue in which he describes his true feelings. As I pointed out before, this is as close as a playwright can get to quoting a character's thoughts. When he says to himself that she is "the only good thing that ever came their way," we have to take that as his honest feelings. Saroyan has preserved the integrity of his protagonist in two ways: first by the tone of those opening lines and, second, by the quick vista into Photo-Finish's thoughts.

Notice, incidentally, that the speed with which these two meet, fall in love, and face death might well seem absurd in fiction. A short-story writer probably would spread the action out over several days to make it credible, and a novelist might allow a month to pass. But what you read is a script, not fiction. A script, as I have pointed out before, is merely an outline of a play. Drama as a genre tends to compress its plots. Audiences seeing works in production are willing to accept a slightly stylized and compressed plot structure.

Although *Coulda, Woulda, Shoulda* is a comic play, much shorter, and nonrealistic, it also uses dialogue to reveal both the outer appearance of characters and something of their inner life as well. Although all three characters are revealed in some detail (rare in so short a play), the treatment of the father, Cy, is a particularly helpful example.

When we first see him he is hurrying to get to work as the owner of a bar. He makes it clear through dialogue that he doesn't want to spend time talking with his son who has locked himself in his room. "I don't got time for this now," he says. "He'll come out when he's good and ready."

Our first impression of Cy is negative: he seems like a stereotype of the work-oriented father. Later, however, we see a softer side. When he hears how his son has portrayed him in the play he is writing, Cy reveals his inner insecurity and his fears about death.

> Marty, you gotta change that ending. Please, me dying all alone like that, it's just too sad.

This is a comic shift, but one that reveals through dialogue a good deal about the character.

Action that Reveals Feelings

The visual aspect is so important in drama that the next chapter is devoted to it. But it is worth considering here the specific ways action can also be used to reveal character.

As I pointed out in the chapter on conflict, Emily's infatuation with Photo-Finish in *Hello Out There* is vividly revealed in a short scene that has no dialogue at all. While she wants to do whatever Photo-Finish asks, she is also terrified of leaving him for a minute. When he asks her to go and look for cigarettes, she does leave, but almost at once she comes running back.

Later Photo-Finish reveals the depth of his feelings toward her by giving her his last eighty dollars to escape her own imprisonment in that town and get to San Francisco on her own. It's a minor action, but it provides one more assurance that his love for her is genuine.

The opening of *Shoulda* makes dramatic use of action. While Cy's wife tries to talk with him, Cy is spending time looking for his clothes. First it's his belt. Later he is looking for his shoes. Then he grabs his coat but searches the pockets for his keys. In each case, his wife helps him to find what he needs. This man who appears to be macho and dominant is revealed through action to be dependent on his wife for the simple mechanics of daily living.

Creating Depth of Character

The central characters in serious, realistic drama are usually well rounded and carefully delineated. Achieving this effect in a short one-act play is a challenge, but it can be done. Saroyan, for example, manages to tell us a good deal about Photo-Finish in only a few minutes of playing time.

Consider how much we come to know about Photo-Finish: He is lonely but not a whiner. He has a whimsical sense of humor yet can be serious about both practical matters of survival and broader concerns such as what makes people so heartless. There is a merry quality to the way he treats Emily, but we know almost from the start that he is genuinely scared about his position. These contrasts provide a range of characteristics and attitudes, and it is this range that gives us a sense of knowing him as an individual.

Characterization in this play is particularly important because so much depends on the audience feeling sympathy for this unsuccessful gambler. Only if we take him seriously will we respond to one of the major themes of the play: the capacity of love to transform "little punk people" to someone with heart.

The goal in dramatic characterization is to balance consistency with variation. Consistency requires that the character never behave in a way that seems implausible. A line of dialogue or a particular action may seem surprising to the audience at first, but in realistic drama it must ultimately be explained.

On the other hand, excessive consistency makes the character overly predictable. In drama, predictable means dull. So every major character should have a variety of characteristics. Photo-Finish, for example, is neither a perfect hero nor an absolute villain. Such characters are unrealistically consistent, the type we associate with **melodrama**.

Saroyan provides depth of characterization through surprising but credible contrasts. Photo-Finish is both a small-time hustler who has been living precariously on the fringes of the racetrack world, but he also can see the good qualities in a young woman like Emily and can even appreciate the conflicts in the outraged husband. These insights and the sense of compassion are in sharp contrast to what we might expect.

That contrast is important, but equally important is the fact that for most viewers it has been made credible. Saroyan keeps the variations in character within bounds. If he had made Photo-Finish a convicted murderer and serial rapist on the run who ends up marrying Emily and going to medical school, the audience would head for the exits.

Notice, too, that there is nothing in the play to suggest that Emily is tall, beautiful, or sophisticated. Even her name, Emily Smith, suggests the ordinary. (My apologies to the Emily Smiths who may be reading this!) Yet she is elevated in stature at the very end, and we take her concluding cry of "Hello out there!" seriously.

Coulda, Woulda, Shoulda is half the length of *Hello Out There* and essentially a comedy, but even that play contains more depth of characterization than one would expect. We have a brief glimpse of Marty as a solemn child who wants to become a rabbi. This gives us an insight into what makes him such a serious and dedicated playwright as an adult. We see how close he has been to his mother (though he denies it) and how he resents his father's infidelities. The fact that Marty the character is not simply an echo of Alterman the playwright is made clear by the fact that Marty the character is writing what appears to be a heavy-handed and humorless melodrama while the play we are reading is a comedy packed with satirical details.

The father, too, has surprising complexity, considering the brevity of the play. As I pointed out earlier, he appears at first to be a workaholic whose only concern is his job. But later we learn that much of his time has been with other women, a charge he doesn't deny. Further, his rather harsh self-assurance in the opening scene turns to fear of "dying all alone like that."

None of these examples approaches the degree of complexity possible in longer plays, but they do suggest that when writing very short plays one doesn't have to settle for stereotypes.

One way to achieve depth of characterization, combining both consistency and some measure of contrast, is to take the time to write out a character sketch. Put down more than you will ever need: what their parents were like, whether they have sisters or brothers, where they went to school, what they are good at, and what their weaknesses are. Determine some aspects that suggest consistency ("gentle temperament; almost never loses her temper") and some contrasting trait ("can't stand messy people or a disorderly house"). You won't actually use more than a small portion of these details, but you will come to know your character as a person rather than just a type.

If you have trouble writing more than a few sentences, try basing your description on a friend or member of your family. But be inventive. Don't lock yourself into that particular individual. Make a point of transforming some aspects so you will begin to deal with a newly formed stage character. Alter a basic element such as age, sex, or appearance so that you don't lose friends or, worse, become inhibited out of respect for the person who served as model. Keep in mind that the process of creating a dramatic character is almost never pure invention; it is a transformation of what is familiar to you. The goal is to create new and interesting characters who are generally consistent and yet also reveal certain contrasting traits.

Characters in Flux

Drama by definition cannot be static, and this rule applies to the characters as well as the plot. Major characters in realistic drama usually go through some type of significant development, for good or for bad. They are not the same at the end of the play as they were at the beginning. This process is often referred to as *character change*.

Another way to achieve that all-important sense of change and discovery is to reverse the process: allow the character to remain the same but provide information that will dramatically shift the audience's perception of him or her. Oddly, this approach can generate just as much impact.

The phrase *character change* is often used informally to describe both patterns, but it is a bit misleading. Characters in plays rarely go through a fundamental personality change any more than people do in life. Only in comedies do villains finally see the light, go through a complete character transformation, and undo the damage they have done. Still, there is nothing wrong with using the term *character change* as long as you remember that what we are really talking about is a shift either in the character's attitude or in the audience's perception of that character.

Such shifts can be highly dramatic. In plays, as in life, characters are shaped by dramatic events and end up stricken with remorse, given new hope, shattered by a crisis, or strengthened by it. Friendships form between unlikely pairs, and "ideal" couples become alienated. Quite often a naive character is suddenly made aware of some harsh aspect of life; occasionally a sophisticated character is taught how to appreciate some simple truth. The impact of these shifts is similar to the jolt we feel when an apparently trustworthy character turns out to be dishonest or one we had assumed was incompetent has actually been in control. These are all the stuff of powerful drama.

Where does one find characters who have gone through such a shift in outlook? Start with your own life. Even if you feel that your development has been uneventful, it has in fact moved in stages, each one introduced by some fresh view of yourself or the world about you. Always keep in mind that you can transform a relatively mild personal experience so that it generates dramatic impact.

In addition, consider what you have heard about other members of your family, present and past. Almost every family has stories with dramatic potential. Don't be shy. Transformation can disguise anything. Also look for "cold material"—reports you have read in the newspaper or history texts, stories about strangers. If you take this route, consider grafting the events onto someone you have known. This association will help to make your characterization more convincing.

The farther you get from your own life and experience, the greater the danger that you will begin to borrow from something you have seen on television or in a movie. Sometimes this happens entirely unconsciously. Remember that in the dark recesses of your memory is a great trash heap of stock characters from fiction and film. If you put them in your play, they will be no more convincing than mannequins. You are on safer ground when you develop characters who are at least indirectly linked to people you know.

The other type of character change focuses on audience perception. As writer, you have to pay attention to what you withhold and what you reveal at every stage. You have probably seen this technique in murder mysteries in which the character who seems least likely to be the killer is revealed in the end to be just that. In such scripts characterization is often relatively simple, but the same approach lends itself to more sophisticated dramas.

One of the best-known examples of this technique in full-length plays is in *The Country Girl* by Clifford Odets. It concerns the efforts of an older actor to make a comeback. For much of the play the audience is convinced that he is doing his best to cope with a very difficult wife. But it turns out that he is an alcoholic and she has been heroically trying to cover for him. The audience has been misled, as have the other characters, and the revelation has genuine dramatic impact.

There are all kinds of deceits that can be created in this manner and then exposed dramatically. Some are the result of conscious scheming, as in the Odets play, but others develop from self-deception. If you are working with this type of reversal, drop small hints along the way so that when the correct view is revealed the audience will have that special sense of, "Oh, I should have seen it."

The Function of Minor Characters

E. M. Forster's distinction between **"round"** and **"flat"** characters in fiction applies just as well to drama. Although flat characters are seen in only one dimension, like cardboard cutouts, and they rarely change or develop, they can be essential elements of a play. In many comedies, for example, all of the characters are relatively flat. But there are different degrees of character development. As we have seen, *Coulda* has provided some depth to the two parents, especially the father. The closer a play comes to **slapstick**, broad and boisterous comedy written mainly for laughs, the flatter the characters. The satiric characters in the last play in this text (see Chapter 39) are essentially flat. Their function is to ridicule specific attitudes. But even they are provided with some history, some semblance of characterization.

Truly flat characters provide a single purpose. They may serve as **catalysts**—necessary elements for the advancement of plot or for the development of a major character without themselves changing. But we don't know their background or what they are like.

The two men who accompany the husband in *Hello Out There*, for example, are flat yet extremely important. Their presence just outside the jail room drives the husband to the point of murder. They are essential elements, but as individuals they are faceless, even interchangeable, and utterly consistent.

There is a tendency to become careless with minor characters, creating them to perform trivial tasks that are not truly essential—delivering pizza or mail. Anyone who has been active in professional theater companies can tell you that production costs place a premium on plays that can be presented with a minimum number of actors. Entirely aside from that practical consideration, there is an aesthetic factor. A play is apt to have more power if a lot is suggested by a few carefully developed characters rather than being cluttered by a variety of minor characters.

There are two questions to ask about any minor character: What significant function does this character serve, and exactly what would happen if we removed him or her? If we apply those questions to the pair of unnamed men in the Saroyan play, we can see that they serve the function of a mob; without them, the play would suggest that the husband was driven to murder by an unquestioning sense of revenge rather than in part by trying to look good in the eyes of other men.

Characterization in a realistic play is a continuing concern at every stage of writing. It takes time and many revisions to make major characters both vivid and credible. You have to consider both consistency and variation. Realistic drama is, among other things, the illusion of getting to know total strangers surprisingly well in a very short period of time.

38

VISUAL IMPACT

The impact of the familiar. Distortions that enhance realism. Symbolic sets. The bare stage. Lighting for effect. Costumes: realistic and symbolic. The visual impact of action: defining scenes, controlling the pace, revealing attitudes. Writing from the tenth row center.

There are many different things writers can do on a stage. They can read their poetry or fiction, present monologues, or read their play scripts. But only if the performance has a visual component, characters moving about on the stage, do we call it drama.

This visual aspect, what Aristotle called the **spectacle**, includes a variety of forms: the physical set, the lighting, the costumes, and, most important, the action of actors. Directors, set designers, and actors all contribute in this cooperative effort, but the script must allow for visual impact. This chapter has one urgent message that I will repeat several times: when you write any type of play script, maintain a mental picture of what your stage looks like scene by scene, moment by moment. In short, remember that a play is to be seen, not just heard.

The Realistic Set: The Impact of the Familiar

The term **set** includes everything the audience sees except the actors themselves. Although each set designer will approach a play differently, playwrights usually specify what the locale is and what the stage should look like. This brief introduction often identifies the set as falling into one of three loosely defined types: realistic, symbolic, or bare.

The **realistic set** is so common today that we tend to think of it as the traditional approach. Actually it is a fairly recent development—less than 200 years out of the 2,500-year-old tradition of Western drama. Truly realistic details on the stage had to wait until the introduction of electric lights. When Ibsen's plays were first produced in England in the late nineteenth century, audiences gasped with amazement at the sight of a perfectly reproduced living-room scene complete with real books in bookcases, portraits on the walls, and doors that opened and shut. Soon the stage directions for the plays of James M. Barrie and George Bernard Shaw began to reflect this new realism by including the most minute descriptions, even to the title of a book left "carelessly" on a coffee table.

We can no longer depend on that kind of naive wonder, of course. Film and television have made realism commonplace. But when a realistic set is constructed with skill and imagination, it still can create enormous impact. Even today, highly effective sets presented on traditional stages are occasionally greeted with applause even before the first character appears on stage. The audience is applauding the illusion of the familiar.

How much detail should a script include? There is no standard policy, but the tendency now is to be brief. One reason is that there is such a variety of stages today that playwrights can no longer be sure of just how their work will be presented.

The traditional stage has what is known as a **proscenium arch**, which forms a picture frame for the action and uses a curtain to open and close separate acts. But many stages now have no arch and no single picture effect because they are open on three sides. This design, called a **thrust stage**, allows more of the audience to sit close to the action. In such theaters, the lowering of a curtain is replaced by a dimming of the lights. **Theater in the round**, or **arena theater**, extends this concept further by having the audience encircle the playing area as it does in a circus tent. The playwright's description of the set in the script should be flexible enough to allow set designers to adapt to a wide variety of stages.

In *Hello Out There*, for example, Saroyan merely states that this is to be "a small-town prison cell." On a traditional stage, this might be handled realistically with walls and barred windows. But on a stage that is surrounded on all sides by the audience, the cell might be suggested by no more than a few bars suspended in dreamlike fashion. A good deal can be left to the imagination of the audience even in a realistic play.

Distortions That Enhance Realism

A realistic stage set always requires imagination. In fact, it is the distortions of reality that stimulate the imagination. A living room on the stage, for example, has no fourth wall. The audience imagines itself in that room even though in a literal sense we are looking at a half-dismantled house. In a play called *Period of Adjustment*, by Tennessee Williams, the focal object is a television set. Because it is often on, it is placed with its back to the audience upstage center. The set in the Broadway production was meticulously realistic, yet from a literal point of view the audience was impossibly wedged between the back of the television set and where the wall should be. In other plays, the audience finds itself behind fireplaces. Oddly, even the least imaginative theatergoers accept this kind of distortion and imagine themselves being in the room with the characters.

The significance of this impression for playwrights is that one can use a high degree of distortion to achieve a realistic effect. This is particularly helpful in plays that include both indoor and outdoor scenes. A yard may be separated from the interior of, say, a kitchen by a low board; a door may be used to suggest the division between two areas without adjoining walls. The same applies to the second story of a house suggested only by a flight of stairs. If the actors treat these divisions as real, the audience will perceive them this way too.

In Arthur Miller's *Death of a Salesman*, for example, the script calls for an upstairs room, two rooms downstairs, and a portion of the yard outside. It is realistic in that the entire set is treated as if it were a real house and yard, yet it requires an act of imagination to separate what is outside from what is inside. An actor in the kitchen can obviously see what another actor is doing outside; but it is soon made clear that a character must open the door in order to see. This setup is not as extraordinary as it seems when you recall that children at the beach can create the same sort of illusion playing house with various rooms merely marked in the sand. It's no accident that we call drama a play.

Another ingenious use of realistic design is seen in William Ritman's set for Harold Pinter's *The Collection*. Working closely with the director and the playwright, Ritman managed to present the illusion of three entirely unconnected separate yet realistic settings on the relatively small stage of the Cherry Lane Theatre in New York. It has been duplicated on larger stages since then. As the action shifts from one area to the next, the lights on the other two are dimmed. The illustrations (drawn by Richard Tuttle) appear on pages 376 and 377. Turn to them now and notice how the illusion of one's location shifts simply with a change in lighting.

The great advantage of a set like this is that the playwright does not have to stop the action for a change of set. As I have mentioned, dropping the curtain or even dimming the lights breaks the illusion and returns the audience to the theater itself. If in addition you ask a stage crew to scurry about in the dark and change a set, that break becomes even lengthier and more distracting. A set divided into different playing areas allows a playwright to maintain a steady flow of action.

A word of warning, however. If you, like most people, have watched more television and films than plays, you may unwittingly suggest an impossibly complex set. Remember that whatever you call for in the script will have to be built with wood and held together with nails. The set I described for *Death of a Salesman* is about as complex as you can get, even

The Collection, **showing emphasis on the modern apartment, with the other areas dark.**

The Collection, **showing emphasis on the telephone booth, which is, in the play, some distance from either home.**

Set design for Harold Printer's *The Collection* by William Ritman. Illustrations by Richard Tuttle. Reprinted by permission of William Ritman and Richard Tuttle.

The Collection, showing emphasis on the ornate apartment, with the other areas dark.

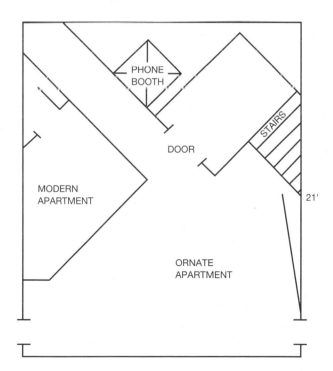

The Collection: a diagram of the stage, showing the technique of representing three entirely different scenes simply by shifts in lighting. Note how the unusual angles add both variety and depth even on a small stage.

on a big stage. It is a serious challenge in a small space. The three-part set for *The Collection* has the advantage of being essentially on one level, but on a small stage this is about the maximum number of playing areas that you can manage.

Fiction, film, and drama can all create the illusion of realism, but they do it in quite different ways. Fiction calls for the greatest use of imagination, translating words into as-if reality directly; film uses the least imagination, though it must convert a flat image into the illusion of reality. Drama has the advantage of live performers and three-dimensional sets, but it must use distortions creatively to develop a sense of actually being there.

The Symbolic Set

No matter how many distortions are used in a realistic set, the goal is to place the audience in an environment that is similar to the world in which we live. The goal of the *symbolic set* (see **set**) is in some ways just the opposite: it takes the audience out of this world. As in dreams, the surroundings may generate familiar sensations—fear, anxiety, confusion, or even childlike pleasure—but they don't resemble a familiar place.

Also like dreams, the symbolic set "makes sense" on a symbolic rather than a literal level. The undefined but dreary landscape of *Waiting for Godot* by Samuel Beckett, for example, does not bring to mind any specific place on earth, but it does seem to echo the dreary and uncertain lives of the characters who try without much success to make sense of life itself.

Other symbolic sets may be far more specific in detail. In Chapter 36 I pointed out how precise Ionesco is in describing the reception room of the castle in the middle of the sea in *The Chairs*, but you won't find that island in any atlas. Ionesco, like Elmer Rice, uses the set to suggest pictorially certain aspects of the human condition.

Some symbolic sets give delight through deception. The set of William Carlos Williams' play *Many Loves* is actually a series of tricks. As the audience enters the theater, the curtain is already raised and stagehands and electricians are still at work preparing the stage. One is on a ladder repairing a hanging lamp; another vacuums the floor. Members of the audience tend to check their watches and mumble about sloppy amateur productions. Only gradually do they realize—usually one at a time—that the play has already begun. The stage crew are in fact the characters. Then actors begin rehearsing a play, and the audience gradually becomes absorbed in that "reality."

Just as the play within a play appears to be a major concern, a director jumps up from the first row and objects. And so does the playwright—not Williams but the author of the play-within-a-play. Our attention turns to the relationship between these two men. The "many loves" of the title are as unstable as the audience's perception of the true setting of this play.

Nonrealistic plays like *Coulda* can be presented with realistic settings, and essentially realistic plays like Arthur Miller's *After the Fall* (based roughly on Marilyn Monroe) can employ dreamlike shifts that are themselves highly symbolic. The choice is yours as to whether you want a stage set that suggests an as-if-real place or one that is designed to mimic a mood or suggest a theme in a dreamlike fashion.

The Bare Stage

This third approach, the *bare stage* (**see set**), can be used in either realistic or nonrealistic plays. Thornton Wilder's *Our Town* is one of the most famous examples of an almost bare-stage play. The script calls for a couple of folding chairs, two stepladders, and a plank, which in certain scenes is laid between the ladders. The play is realistic and serious in tone; leaving the stage almost bare in no way reduces the illusion of reality.

When *Our Town* was first produced in 1938, presenting a major production without an elaborate set was considered innovative. Yet no one was confused. Like many daring experiments in theater, it was based on an old tradition. Elizabethan audiences were required to use their imaginations to visualize the rapid succession of scenes in Shakespearean plays. If this approach interests you, examine closely how Shakespeare ingeniously identifies the setting at the beginning of each new scene.

If you plan to call for such a set, be sure that you indicate through the dialogue and stage directions where the characters are and what the audience is being asked to imagine.

Here are some suggestions for making the best use of your set no matter what type:

- Don't assume that because your play is nonrealistic the set should be. And conversely, if your play is realistic, don't feel bound to call for an elaborately realistic set. Select a stage set that will be the most effective for your particular play.
- Consider ways in which the set can have an impact right from the start. Think twice before you call for the too-familiar sitcom living room—couch centered, two upholstered chairs on either side, front door to the left, kitchen door to the right, and stairs. We've been there too often.
- Be practical. Remember that some stages are small, budgets are tight, and there are limits to what one can build. Don't make impossible demands.
- Be brief. Let set designers adapt your basic description to the type of stage and budget they are working with.

- Above all, use the set. Keep it in mind as you write, and give your characters a chance to move about in the space you have provided.

Lighting for Effect

Lighting is the newest of all dramatic techniques. The Greeks depended on the sun, as did the Elizabethans. And from the time of the first enclosed theaters in the late sixteenth century until 1914, lighting consisted of a glare of footlights designed simply to illuminate actors.

In 1914 the first spotlights were hung on the balcony rail of Wallack's Theater in New York. That was a radical improvement. But the progress made in the past thirty years with modern lighting boards is a quantum leap forward for drama. Although some playwrights leave lighting cues entirely to the director, others see lighting as an integral part of the whole effect and write basic instructions into the script.

The most obvious use of lighting is to suggest the time of day. It is a simple matter to have the lights rise in the early morning or slowly dim as the sun sets. If the fading light also echoes an increasingly somber mood of the scene, the lighting will be even more effective.

On a more subtle level lights are used to reflect the tone of the scene, whether inside or out. Quiet, low-key, or intimate scenes are enhanced with lowered lights; and conversely, scenes that are lively or dramatic can be charged with brighter lights. Techniques like these can be effective with any type of drama, but they are more frequently associated with nonrealistic plays.

In addition to influencing the overall tone of a scene, lights can be used to highlight a particular portion of the set while leaving other areas dark. As you can see from the illustrations of the three-part setting for *The Collection*, lighting effectively directs the audience's attention from one portion of the stage to another. In effect, selective lighting has the power to change the set.

In Arthur Miller's *After the Fall*, a play that gives the illusion of a sequence of memories, lighting becomes essential to achieve the effect. Miller states in the script that his characters must "appear and disappear instantaneously, as in the mind; but it is not necessary that they walk off the stage." This effect is normally achieved through a complex series of lighting shifts. This technique is well worth considering if you have many scenes. It allows you to create virtual sets without the distracting break in illusion caused by conventional scene shifts.

Lighting can also place a special emphasis on a character or highlight a key speech the way music occasionally does in film. Although Saroyan doesn't provide light cues in *Hello Out There*, it would be dramatic to isolate

Emily at the very end with a single overhead spot in an otherwise darkened stage. This effect might repeat a similar one for Photo-Finish at the beginning of the play, drawing those two scenes together visually just as they are in dialogue.

Costumes: Realistic and Symbolic

Like the lighting, the costumes are a visual effect that in some cases is left to the costume designer. In other cases descriptions are written into the stage directions. In realistic plays with a contemporary setting there usually is no mention of costumes in the script. Plays set in an earlier historical period may call for some description, though the director has the option of using contemporary dress. Nonrealistic plays, however, may make special use of costume to achieve symbolic significance. In such cases, playwrights sometimes become very specific.

The script for Alterman's *Coulda, Woulda, Shoulda* initially makes no mention of costume, so most directors would use what would be natural for a bartender and his wife. But the costume of Marty, the son, is precisely described in the script. His entrance is a dramatic turning point. It is the moment when an apparently realistic play suddenly becomes nonrealistic. How is this change achieved? First with a simple but significant stage direction: "A light change." This signals that something important will happen. Then the door opens and the audience is jolted by the sight of an adult Marty "wearing large children's pajamas, a pair of glasses, and a black hat."

It is essential that the playwright be precise in the description of costume here, and it is equally essential that a director follow those directions. The fact that the character who has been described as a child is now standing there as a man "in his forties" is startling, but that alone doesn't communicate the symbol the playwright has in mind. Marty is not just a child grown up, he is simultaneously an adult playwright (he is carrying a pen and pad) and a child in his pajamas.

Why the black hat? Remember that as a little boy he had announced that he wanted to become a rabbi. He did not become a rabbi, but he wears the black hat that is frequently worn by rabbis, and in the tradition of prophets he seems to have the power to predict the future. In fact, he has to remind his mother. "I'm not God." But as any playwright knows, creating a good play is the next best thing.

In that absurd and comic costume, then, the character named Marty becomes part child, part playwright, and part prophet.

The concluding play, *The Cowboy, the Indian and the Fervent Feminist* (Chapter 39), is a comic satire in which costume contributes directly to the theme. The husband is "dressed in full cowboy regalia . . . all purchased second-hand or 'bruised' by Ralph Lauren." We know from the start that he is not a genuine working cowboy.

It is not necessary to specify costuming any more than it is required to give stage directions regarding the lighting. Normally, a sentence or two will suffice. If these visual details have some symbolic importance, however, or if they contribute to characterization, be sure to provide some basic details.

The Visual Impact of Action

Action gives shape to a play. As I described in the chapter on plot, most plays are divided into a number of secondary scenes. Those units are begun and ended by entrances and exits. On this basic level, then, the very structure of a play depends on action.

These entrances and exits have a significant effect on the pace and rhythm of a play. If you have too many of them, the work as a whole may seem choppy and disjointed. If you have too few—a more common weakness—the play may seem static no matter how absorbing the theme may be.

For this reason, most playwrights take the time to outline their plays scene by scene at an early stage of the writing. This is a particularly helpful technique if you are new to the genre. It can save a great deal of rewriting later.

If it appears from your outline that an individual scene will go on too long, that scene may slow the forward motion of the entire play. The solution may be to revitalize it by adding more action or simply to cut unnecessary lines. In some cases it can be broken into two scenes by means of another entrance or exit. Far easier to do this in the outline than revising a completed draft.

Take a close look at the action you provide within each scene. Up to a point a good director can enliven a static scene by adding **stage business**, minor activity such as crossing the room, opening a window, pacing up and down. But there are limits to this. And occasionally you may find that you have made matters even more difficult for the director by specifying that your characters sit while they talk.

In the opening scene of *Coulda* the two parents discuss their young son. In a series of unobtrusive stage directions, the script calls for constant action on the part of the father. At the very outset Cy is described as "rushing around, getting dressed." He interrupts his wife by asking, "Where's my belt?" She tells him and he puts it on. Next he asks, "Where's my shoes?" She tells him and he gets them, starts to put them on. Toward the end of that scene he grabs his coat and starts to go. His wife physically blocks the door, insisting that he talk with his son. As she continues to call to Marty, Cy discovers he doesn't have his car keys. Just before Marty's entrance, Cy finds the keys.

As I pointed out in the last chapter, these activities reveal that beneath his gruff and macho exterior, Cy is dependent on his wife. In addition, they keep what might have been a static scene charged with energy. Imagine that opening as it would be if the couple were sitting on the couch. Not even an inventive director could have devised enough casual **stage business** to keep that scene lively. By keeping the character in constant motion, the playwright contributes to the tension of the scene and keeps it dramatically charged even before the appearance of the son.

Notice, by the way, how brief those stage directions are. Unlike exposition in fiction, they never explain motivation such as "In his haste to get to work. . ." or "Anxious to avoid dealing with his son.. . . " Alterman's parenthetical stage directions are so terse that the casual reader might easily miss them. But no actor would. They provide the action that makes the difference between a static scene and one that has dramatic energy.

The play is divided into three scenes—short, long, short. The first, as I have pointed out, is energized by minor action. The second, the relatively long one, also has action, but the dominant concern is thematic. The audience is held by questions about the creative process and the relationship between art and life. The last scene, short as it is, has the most stage directions. There is a good reason for this. The playwright is facing the difficult situation of having a character alone on the stage, so every bit of action has to be spelled out to keep that scene not only alive but vivid. If you look at that work closely, you will see that the playwright has paid close attention to the dynamics of motion on the stage.

How does all this apply to your own work? In practice, the most common problem with early drafts of both serious and comic plays is that there is simply not enough action to keep the play moving. If your characters don't do something on stage, neither profound nor witty language is enough to hold an audience larger than your closest friends. One way to test whether your script is visually dull is to write a description of each scene without quoting any of the dialogue. If you can summarize certain scenes with bland statements like "They sit on the couch and blame each other for the state of their marriage," you may have some serious rewriting to do.

Writing from the Tenth Row Center

When you write fiction, you tend to enter the scene and imagine it through the eyes of a chosen character. To a large degree, you are within the work. Writing drama is different partly because there is no single point of view and also because you are writing for a live audience. As a result, when you work on a script a good portion of you remains outside the action. You are seeing and hearing each scene as if you were in the reputed best seat of the house— the tenth row center.

If you have been writing fiction and are turning to drama for the first time, it may take a while to maintain this objectivity. It's important, though, because drama is written not for readers but, ultimately, for live audiences. Part of the scriptwriter must also be a spectator.

Out there in the tenth row looking at your own work you will never confuse the script and the play. While scripts don't micromanage details about the set, the lighting, and costuming, they have to provide opportunities for set designers, directors, and actors.

As for pacing, remember that scripts can be read silently at five times the speed of a play in performance. The reader can skim over dreary, static scenes and get to the good parts. Not so with the audience of a production. They are trapped in their seats. One way for you as writer to share that experience is to read the entire play out loud. That way you will remain a spectator in the tenth row. If some scenes are tedious, you too will have to endure them. You will find out what it is to squirm in your seat and check the theater for exit signs.

You are not, however, a passive spectator. The other part of you is a playwright in control. It is up to you to judge whether a character has been long-winded or if everyone on stage has been glued to the floor like so many talking mannequins. It is up to you as playwright to determine when another character should come in with some fresh insight. It's up to you to devise ways of using the set or lighting. When you revise with an acute awareness of what the audience is seeing and hearing, you are not just writing a script, you are shaping a play designed for performance.

The play that follows is *The Cowboy, the Indian and the Fervent Feminist*, written by Murray Schisgal. A veteran playwright and nationally known scriptwriter, Schisgal has an impressive number of works to his credit. He is particularly well known for the stage and screen hit *Luv* and, more recently, for coauthoring the award-winning screenplay of *Tootsie*.

Cowboy is pure **satire**. Like all satires, it uses exaggeration to ridicule attitudes and institutions. Unlike short satiric skits, however, the characters in this play do change and develop—in bizarre and comic ways.

Read it once for pleasure. Enjoy it. Then go though it again, carefully listing the various attitudes and movements that are being derided. Notice how many little details are included and exaggerated for comic effect. Finally, ask yourself what you think the playwright's own feelings are. Does he take sides? Remember that while your first reading is for fun like a member of the audience, your second reading is analytical, examining it from a writer's point of view.

39

A PLAY

by Murray Schisgal

**The Cowboy, the Indian and
the Fervent Feminist**

Characters

ALICIA
STANFORD
BIBBERMAN

*Glendale, Long Island, a middle-class suburban community within fifty miles
of New York City.*

TIME: The Present: late autumn; early evening.

SOUND: A drum beating; softly.

*AT RISE: A symmetrically furnished contemporary dining-room: at rear right and
rear left, two long, narrow pine buffet tables. Center, downstage, a fairly large, rectangular, pine table with two ladder-back, pine chairs, cushioned, at either end. The
table is set for dinner: glasses, silverware, napkins, a bottle of mineral water; a small
vase of freshly-cut flowers. One is asked to imagine doors, windows and walls. A TV
set and stereo unit are in view. Alicia Gerard enters from left, carrying a tray on
which there are two bowls of chicken broth, an oval sourdough bread and condi-
ments. She hears the drum beat and is puzzled by it. What is that noise? A drum?
Who would be beating a drum? Is someone playing a radio too loudly?*

The drum beat fades to silence.

*Relieved, Alicia continues to the dining table; she transfers everything from the
tray to the table; puts empty tray on buffet table.*

It's apparent Alicia is under great stress. We see it in her behavior and facial expression. She's an attractive woman, in her late thirties, normally willful and self-confident. She wears a too short, too tight, black skirt; black stockings; black, mid-heeled shoes; a white, rayon, long-sleeved blouse. There's been an effort on her part to look "sexy."

She takes a beat or two to steel herself. Then she moves to rear, far right.

ALICIA. (*Calls to outside.*) Stanford? (*Clears her throat; a bit louder.*) Stanford, sweetheart, dinner is ready! Will you come in, please? (*Hesitates a beat.*) I . . . I don't want the soup getting cold. And I have a roast chicken with baked potatoes in the oven. I made everything myself. And. . . . And it wasn't my turn for cooking tonight . . . darling. (*Hesitates a beat.*) Please, Stanford. Do come in now. (*Evidently he is starting towards the entrance door. She quickly moves to sit at left end of dining table; pulls down her skirt, fluffs her hair, etc. Stanford Gerard enters. He is fifty-plus years of age, dressed in full cowboy regalia: boots, spurs, chaps, flannel shirt, bandana, leather vest with sack of Bull Durham tobacco visible in one of its pockets, Stetson, all purchased second-hand or "bruised" by Ralph Lauren. He slaps at his pants, raising puffs of dust around him. He gives the impression of having been on horse-back for several hours if not several days.*)

STANFORD. (*With Texas twang as he imagines it.*) Whew, Goddamn! It's like a dust bowl out there! You can't go ten feet without gettin' the breath knocked outta you! Whew, I was up on the north range, bringin' in this here stray heifer that got itself separated from the herd. I never seen anything like it. The sand was blowin' right up into my nostrils. (*He pulls out farmer's handkerchief from rear pants' pocket and blows his nose.*) Damn, it's more work than I bargained for. I been thinkin' a puttin' on another hired hand. Oh, I know your objection, girl: it's more outta pocket expense. But it's the only way we're gonna get that herd to market come spring.

ALICIA. (*Repressing her impulsive anger.*) Stanford, would you . . . would you like to wash before you sit down?

STANFORD. Can't be doin' that, girl. Ain't you heard? The water's frozen in the well. Thick as an iceberg down there. I'm gonna have to start chippin' at it in the mornin' to get us a couple a buckets a drinkin' water. (*He moves to buffet table, looks through tapes next to cassette player.*) I tell you, this winter's gonna be a real humdinger. We got a heap a preparation to be doin' if we're gonna survive the next couple a months.

ALICIA. (*Forcing a smile.*) The soup is getting cold . . . dear. Will you please sit down and . . .

STANFORD. I bought us some new-fangled tunes at the general store. I'd like you to be hearing one of 'em. It's a real amusin' piece a music. Now you jus' listen. See if it don't get your tootsies knockin' on the floor. (*He* pushes tape into cassette. We hear "I'm An Old Cowhand"* or some such Western song. Stanford mimes the lyrics, lips-syncing with the singer on the tape, moving and gesturing like a television cowboy. He sings the first full chorus, AABA. Stanford then shuts the cassette player. He moves to dining table, throws his leg over the back of the chair and sits down.) Hot-diggity-dog. Nothin' like country music to get your juices flowin'. What you be thinkin' a that, girl? Ain't she a humdinger? I'm gonna be rehearsin' it over an' over until I get it plum right. I'm hopin' to be doin' it for our New Year's Eve bash down at the Silver Dollar Saloon.

ALICIA. Stanford, today I saw . . .

STANFORD. (Raises hand.) Hold it. Hold it right there. You forgettin' what we do when we sit down at the dinner table?

ALICIA. (With effort.) I . . . I'm sorry. I apologize. (Stanford takes off his Stetson, presses it to his heart, staring downward. Alicia also stares downward, her hand, clasped on edge of table. She is very unhappy with all of this.)

STANFORD. Lord, we thank you for your blessings and for givin' us the strength to do our daily chores. I'm offerin' a special prayer this evenin' for my neighbor Ezra Slocum's wife, Annabelle Slocum, and ask you in your mercy to relieve her of child-bearin' fever. I also be offerin' a special prayer for my friend Bald Eagle who I hear was bit by a grizzly up on Mount Morgan. We do humbly thank you, dear Lord, for the bounty on our table. Amen, (He stares fixedly at Alicia.)

ALICIA. Amen.

STANFORD. Now we can eat. (He tears a handful of bread and bites into it.)

ALICIA. (Anxiously.) Stanford, I saw Doctor Bibberman today. We had a truly rewarding conversation. I asked him innumerable questions and he was very forthcoming and . . . (A breath.) I want to apologize to you, my sweetheart. I was so involved with what I was feeling that I was totally blind to what you were feeling. Doctor Bibberman pointed out that you've been under enormous stress and you have not been having an easy time of it since you were let go by our mutual employers. It was as if Doctor Bibberman had removed a blindfold from my eyes and I saw you, myself and our precious daughter in a new and healthier and more optimistic light. (Stanford picks up bowl of soup between his hands and drinks, not deliberately noisily, from it. Alicia swallows several spoonfuls of soup.) I admit, I admit, I was wrong, I was insensitive, I was cruel even. But not nearly as cruel and insensitive as Benton, Gerber and Pollock. And I say this knowing full well that I started working there myself as a lowly secretary, your secretary, my sweetheart, my darling. You gave me my first opportunity, my first chance, my first introduction into the fascinating world of advertising, and today I'm proud to say, I'm second in line for

*See Note on Songs and Recordings on copyright page.

Chief Merchandising Officer. But what they did to you, darling, discharging you so summarily after having served them faithfully for twenty-four years, half of that time as Executive Vice President of Creative Copy. . . . To discharge you without reprieve or redress during this awful recession we're having. . . . That was unforgivable of them. And even though I fought on your behalf, my darling, my dearest, fought with Ray Pollock until my own job was in imminent jeopardy . . . . I don't have to go into that. But I do want you to know how ashamed I am. I had no right these past few weeks, no right whatsoever to dispute or ridicule you about your desire to . . . to have a new life for yourself, whether that life be based in reality or fantasy. Doctor Bibberman pointed all that out to me today. He even brought up the subject of your deeply unhappy relationship with your father, how removed you were from each other, how your father never took you to a baseball game or on camping trips or passed on to you values that would help you achieve maturity. It may sound far-fetched but Doctor Bibberman also spoke of your childhood games of *Wagon Train* and *Gunsmoke* and how they affected your decision to become a cowboy after you suffered the trauma of sudden unemployment.

STANFORD. You jus' reminded me, girl. Did you chop the firewood like I tol' you?

ALICIA. (*With effort.*) No. No. But I will. Tomorrow. Do let me finish, please. (*Stanford tears off another handful of bread.*) When you left your first wife and your three young children to marry me, your secretary, an unsophisticated, callow, some-what slovenly woman seventeen years your junior, a woman without prospect or resources, and when you took on the burden of supporting two families, sending our own precious Lucinda and your three children from your former marriage to private schools and then on to universities at great expense and obligation on your part, you proved beyond a measure of a doubt that you were a man of rare principle and generosity. And now that you're practically penniless, my darling, my love, my dear, dear husband, now that you're getting on in years so that future employment is highly problematic for you, I want you to know that I will do *every, every, everything* humanly possible to make your burden lighter and less suffocatingly oppressive.

STANFORD. (*Stares at her a beat.*) You soap an' brush down the horses like I tol' you?

ALICIA. I will. Tomorrow. I promise, I'll finish my little speech to you by saying that it's my whole-hearted intention to love you, love you, love you to death, and be supportive of whatever dream it is that gets you through the day. Doctor Bibberman feels that with time and with your continued visits to his office, you'll eventually discard this . . . this fantasy of yours and return to a reality that we both can share and enjoy and build a happy, happy future on. In other words, my sweetheart, my dearest, you're not going to have any more quarrels or arguments with me, no matter what demands you make or how improbable your suggestions are. As an active feminist this is all very difficult for me, but my love for you is so complete, so enormous a part of my life that I will do whatever has to be done to make you healthy again, so help me God.

STANFORD. (*Stares at her a beat.*) You feed the hogs this mornin'?

ALICIA. I . . . I couldn't find the hogs.

STANFORD. They were in the barn! I seen 'em myself on the way out to pasture! Ten beautiful-lookin', prize-winnin' hogs! (*Rises.*) I best go an' find 'em. We can't be affordin' to lose . . .

ALICIA. No, no, no, don't. (*With effort.*) I . . . I forgot. I did see them. And I fed them. I did. I've been so busy, it slipped my mind.

STANFORD. Whew, you scared the bejeebers outta me. I'm plannin' to sell those hogs for us to be gettin' through the winter.

ALICIA. Stanford, I deposited a thousand dollars in our joint account. You're free to withdraw any of that money for whatever . . .

STANFORD. (*Leans across table.*) What I tell you, girl?

ALICIA. Tell me?

STANFORD. 'Bout callin' me Stanford. Didn't I tell you that when we came out to Tombstone the boys gave me the nickname a Sonny?

ALICIA. Sonny?

STANFORD. You heard right, girl.

ALICIA. (*Forcing it out.*) Yes. You did.

STANFORD. An' didn't I say I prefer bein' called Sonny over my Eastern name a Stanford?

ALICIA. Yes. You did.

STANFORD. You know why the boys come to call me the nickname a Sonny?

ALICIA. No. I don't.

STANFORD. They gave me the nickname a Sonny 'cause I got the disposition of a man much younger than my years. I can ride, I can shoot an' I can lasso like a nineteen year old. That's why they call me Sonny.

ALICIA. Then I will definitely call you Sonny. From now on. I promise. And darling . . . dearest . . . since you brought up the subject of names, would you be terribly offended if I asked you not to call me girl?

STANFORD. You don't like me callin' you girl?

ALICIA. (*Vehemently.*) I loooathe it! I find it so demeaning and . . . (*Controlling herself.*) Sonny, I . . . I would appreciate it, greatly, greatly, if you called me Alicia or Alish or Allie or even Al, but I beg you, from the bottom of my heart, do not call me girl.

STANFORD. I meant you no offense.

ALICIA. Oh, I know that, sweetheart.

STANFORD. I jus' figured my bein' seventeen years your senior it's only natural for me to be callin' you girl.

ALICIA. Forgive me but. . . . No, it's not natural. And it's not right. I am a woman . . . Sonny. A woman is not a girl. Would you like it if I called you boy?

STANFORD. I wouldn't be objectin'. I done ask the boys to call me Sonny-boy instead a jus' plain Sonny. But they kinda objected to it. Would you be again' me callin' you woman?

ALICIA. No, no, not at all. I like that. So long as it's done with respect.

STANFORD. (*Raises hand.*) Okay. We got us a deal, woman. Now how about that there roast chicken an' baked potatoes? My gut is jus' about ready to start in barkin'. (*He moves to cassette player as Alicia exits to kitchen.*) An' while you're doin' your chores, I'll be rehearsin' that there tune for the New Year's bash. I gotta be gettin' it right, if I'm not gonna be embarrassin' the Lazy Bones ranch. (*He presses start button. We hear "I'm An Old Cowhand"* or some such Western song. Stanford mimes the lyrics, lip-syncing with the singer on the tape, moving and gesturing like a television cowboy. He sings the second full chorus, AABA. During the above, Alicia enters with a platter of roast chicken and baked potatoes. She puts it at Stanford's end of the table so that he can carve the chicken. She then sits at her end of the table. He shuts cassette player.*) So whatta you be thinkin' a my performance? Gettin' any better?

ALICIA. (*With effort.*) You're doing . . . well. It's entertaining and. . . . You seem to enjoy it.

STANFORD. You again' me doin' it? (*Picks up carving utensils.*)

ALICIA. No, no, if that's what you want to do . . . Stan . . . Sonny, I want you to be happy. I want us both to be happy and have a full, productive, emotionally rich life together. I know you love me and you must know I love you and if we allow anything to separate us . . .

STANFORD. (*Points at chicken with knife.*) What's that on top there, woman?

ALICIA. (*Rises; leans over to look at chicken.*) On top of what, dear?

STANFORD. On top a that chicken! That brown stuff layin' on it!

ALICIA. Oh, I see, I see it. It burned a little. I can scrape it off . . .

STANFORD. (*On his feet; indignant.*) Scrape it off? Whatta we talkin' about here, woman! That's a roast chicken. That ain't a piece a linoleum. If you burn a chicken, you don't scrape it off 'cause that there burnin' goes straight to the middle a the chicken! An' I can't be eatin' no burn' chicken!

ALICIA. (*Rises.*) Stan . . . Sonny, I . . . I am sorry. It's unfortunate but . . . I have not had an easy time of it these past few weeks either. As I told you, tonight was not my night for cooking and yet I went ahead and tried to cook you a very special meal . . .

STANFORD. (*Knocks his chair to the floor.*) I don't wanna hear any more a that! Your night a cookin'! My night a cookin'! I been out there workin' my butt off since sunup woman! I been fixin' fences, herdin' strays, brandin' calves, helpin' Ezra Slocum nail down a new roof on his shed. Now I

---

*See Note on Songs and Recordings on copyright page.

been doin' all a this so come winter there'll be food on this here table and heat in this here house and maybe some pretty ribbons an' bows for Lucinda when she comes visitin' us for the holidays.

ALICIA. I don't want us to quarrel, darling. That's the last thing I want. But you have to realize that I work, too. I get up every morning at six A.M. and I travel over an hour to get to the . . .

STANFORD. (*Picks up chair.*) Now that's somethin' I been meanin' to talk to you about. Your goin' to town an clerkin' for Ray Pollock. That's got to come to an end.

ALICIA. (*Tightening.*) Are *you* suggesting that I quit my . . . ? (*Cools it; with effort.*) Darling . . . Dearest, I've worked very, very hard to get where I am in business. I can't throw all that away to . . . to cook and clean and bake and sweep. It's . . . retrograde. You're not asking me to do that, are you, sweetheart?

STANFORD. Yeup. That's what I be askin'.

ALICIA. But I . . . I can . . . I can bring in money to help you through the winter! I told you I deposited a thousand dollars. I'll deposit . . . five, ten, twenty thousand dollars! More if necessary! I can support you and the Lazy Bones ranch! We can buy all the hogs and horses and chickens you . . .

STANFORD. (*Knocks his chair to the floor.*) I don't wanna be hearin' that kinda talk, woman! How many times I tell you I got the responsibility a providin' for this here family! Don't you be takin' away *my* job! An' if none a this here suits you, you can jus' pack your bags an' take the next stage to your folks in Yuma county!

ALICIA. (*Moves away; wrings her hands; to herself.*) It's hard. It's so hard. Why is it so hard to live with . . . someone? (*Turns to him.*) Stan . . . Son. . . . Would you like me to call you Sonny-boy?

STANFORD. (*Picks up chair.*) I sure enough would. Sonny-boy was my choice but the boys wouldn't go for it.

ALICIA. (*A brave smile.*) Then Sonny-boy it is, darling. I made a promise to Doctor Bibberman and I will try with all my heart to keep my promise. Let me . . . think about giving up my job and staying home to be a . . . (*Swallows.*) . . . house-wife. But I would like you to know that in the old west there was a feminist movement, the suffragettes; they fought for women's rights a hundred years ago and today their descendants are still fighting for women's rights.

STANFORD. (*Sits in chair; puts potatoes on his plate.*) I don't recall seein' any of 'em in Tombstone.

ALICIA. (*Sits in chair; invents story she tells him.*) Don't you remember seeing Abigail Gibson carry that sign down Main Street?

STANFORD. (*Perplexed.*) What sign you talkin' about?

ALICIA. On it was printed, "Our bodies. Our choice." She walked right into the Silver Dollar saloon carrying that sign and spoke out clearly and powerfully for women's rights. Weren't you there that day, Sonny-boy? It was sometime last week, I believe.

STANFORD. (*Inventing his own story.*) Oh, yeah. You bet I was there. I was playin' poker with Ezra, Big Sam Cooper an' Doc Halaway. Abigail came in an' she made that there little speech a hers an' then Big Sam Cooper gets up, stands on his chair . . . (*Stands on his chair.*) . . . an' he says, "That there was a mighty pretty speech, Abigail, but I gotta be remindin' you that you can't be changin' the natural order a things. You go out to the barnyard an' you'll see the bull get up on top a the cow; you'll see the stallion get up on top a the mare; an' you'll see the rooster get up on top a the hen. That there be the natural order a things an' you can't be changin' God's work!"

ALICIA. Yes, yes. Big Sam Cooper did say that standin' on his chair, but then Abigail Gibson's sister, Felicity, she stood up on her chair . . . (*Stands on her chair.*) . . . and she said, "Big Sam, I hate contradicting you, but God's work is man and woman living together fruitfully, with mutual love and mutual respect. God's work is not confrontation, is not sexual aggression, is not who's on top and who's on bottom! Women will no longer tolerate second-class citizenship in politics, in business, or in the home! So you better change your ways, Big Sam, or consider yourself doomed to bachelorhood for the remaining days of your life!"

STANFORD. Yeup, I recall Felicity Gibson sayin' all a that 'cause it was right then an' there that I stood up on the table . . . (*Steps from chair to table.*) . . . an' in a thunderin' voice I said, "Ladies an' gentlemen a Tombstone, I regret to inform you that the institution a marriage is dead as a doorknob. For thousands a years it was the basis for Christian civilization. For thousands a years Pop went off to work in the fields six days a the week, an' Mom stayed home an', after sendin' the kids off to school, she'd be fillin' the kitchen with the smells a baked bread an' boilin' potatoes an' roast chicken that didn't get itself burned 'cause a inattention an' neglect. (*With reverence removes hat.*) An' then it'd be that on the seventh day a the week, there'd be no workin' the field, no washin' an' cookin', no sendin' the kids off to school. There'd be the Sabbath, a day put aside so's the family could go off to church, scrubbed an' polished an' filled with gratitude for the Lord's blessin's an' the Lord's bounty. (*Harshly; puts on hat.*) But all a that is gone now," I declared in a righteous voice. "It's gone 'cause the womenfolk were dissatisfied, like in the days a the Garden a Eden when they took from the Tree a Knowledge a crabapple an' condemned all a us to the aches an' pains a mortal life. This time the womenfolk were dissatisfied at the way the family was arranged an' they started in rearrangin' it. No more Pop goin' off to the fields, no more Mom fillin' the kitchen with smells a good cookin', nobody home anymore to see the kids off to school, that's iffen they're goin' off to school at all. (*Sadly.*) The womenfolk have won their battle, ladies an' gentlemen a Tombstone," I said. "Nowadays there's divorce an' there's separation an' broken homes an' broken hearts an' no more family to be speakin' of. We are all equal an' we are all livin' our separate lives, cold and lonely like Ol' Mount Morgan in the middle of a winter frost."

ALICIA. (*Embittered.*) Yes, you said all of that to the people in the Silver Dollar saloon, Sonny-boy. And that's when I decided to take things into my own hands. (*Steps from chair to table.*) "My dear friends, my dear neighbors," I began my speech in a firm, reverberating voice. "I do thank the Gibson sisters, Abigail and Felicity, for expressing their opinions to you, but it's time I spoke with my own tongue and my own mind. What my husband, Sonny-boy Gerard, failed to tell you is that family life as practiced since Biblical times is far from the rosy picture he painted for you. Physical and emotional abuse, sexual degradation and a life of servitude and exploitation were the inevitable consequences for a woman entering into the state of holy—forgive me for laughing—matrimony. Of necessity, out of pain and humiliation, women were forced to open their eyes, recognize the barrenness of their lives and cry out, 'Enough! Enough! I am no beast in the field! I am no rib, no handmaiden, no receptacle for a man's feeble excesses!' Women fought back, my friends, fought ferociously for their lives. And at last, at long last, in the second half of the twentieth century, women succeeded, women *were* victorious. And for the first time in all of recorded history, a woman could look a man straight in the face and shout out jubilantly, joyously, triumphantly. . . . !"

STANFORD. (*Interrupts; he's heard enough of her fantasy.*) You didn't say any a that, woman! You're makin' it up!

ALICIA. I did so say it! We were in the Silver Dollar saloon . . .

STANFORD. (*Gets down from table.*) You were in no Silver Dollar saloon! I was in there, playin' poker . . .

ALICIA. (*Gets down from table.*) I saw you! I know you were in there! Don't you remember we got into an argument, the two of us, about how men and women have changed over the years?

STANFORD. (*A chance to even the score.*) Oh, yeah. Ohhh, yeah. I remember us arguin'. I said to you, I said, "Ain't it strange how women ain't women anymore? You notice how they be changin', how their skin's gettin' all chapped an' rough, how their breasts are gettin' smaller an' how they're growin' whiskers on their chins?"

ALICIA. (*Grimly.*) Yes, you said that. And I said, I said, "You notice how men can't do a day's work anymore; how lazy they've become; you notice how they talk less and less, move less and less, and how in bed, at night, with their wives . . . "

STANFORD. I don't remember you sayin' any a that.

ALICIA. I did say it. You made me so angry that I . . . couldn't restrain myself. I told them everything.

STANFORD. (*Incredulously.*) You tol' my friends . . . ?

ALICIA. (*Nods.*) Everything. I told them about you losing your job back east, about your visits to Doctor Bibberman, about your . . . sexual . . . disabilities. (*Wow! That hurts. Taking a deep breath, pulling back his shoulders, Stanford walks with a deliberate swagger to the stereo, presses start button. And at once he mimes "I'm An Old Cowhand"* or some such Western song along with the tape, giving his best, upbeat performance. He sings the third full chorus, AABA. He then shuts the cassette player, moves to table, pleased with his performance. He sits in his chair and starts mashing the potatoes on his plate with his fork. He totally ignores Alicia. Alicia sits in her chair and watches him. She wishes she hadn't offended him. Sound: a drum beat; softly. Alicia leans forward in her chair to listen.*) Stan . . . Sonny-boy? (*No response from Stanford.*) Are those drums I'm hearing? (*No response from Stanford.*) It's . . . inordinately difficult for me to surrender, not to fight back when I'm assaulted. It goes against my nature. (*A short beat.*) If it's an apology you want, I . . . apologize. I didn't tell your friends or . . . anyone about . . . your problems. I wanted to hurt you, that's why I said all of that. I'm sorry. You must know that Doctor Bibberman believes your . . . impotence is a stage and it will pass and it's nothing for us to be overly concerned with. (*Irritatedly.*) Where are those noises coming from?

STANFORD. Injuns.

ALICIA. Are you trying to frighten me now?

STANFORD. (*Rises.*) Nope. There's been trouble between the Comanche an' the Sioux. Bald Eagle's callin' for a meetin'.

ALICIA. Darling, is there no hope for us? Can't you just stop it? Can't you come back to those who love you?

STANFORD. (*Moves to the buffet, right.*) I don't know what you're carryin' on about, woman. We might be havin' a war an' you're still talkin' nonsense. (*Sound: drums grow louder, more insistent.*)

ALICIA. Who is that? Who's making that noise? Why doesn't . . . ? (*"Someone stop them?"*)

STANFORD. Shhh! (*He listens. Sound: drums a bit softer now.*) The ranchers are gonna have to choose between joinin' the Comanche or the Sioux. Ezra an' Sam Cooper are votin' for the Sioux. I'm votin' for the Comanche 'cause a my friendship with Bald Eagle. (*He pulls a shotgun out of buffet drawer. He breaks it open to make certain it's loaded, then snaps it shut.*)

ALICIA. Where. . . . Where did you get that gun?

STANFORD. Don't be askin' silly questions. I advise you to keep your voice low an' when I say get down on the floor, you get down on the floor.

ALICIA. Did you . . . ?

---

*See Note on Songs and Recordings on copyright page.

STANFORD. Shhh. *(He moves to rear, crouched over; he peeks out of an imaginary window.)*

ALICIA. *(Whispers.)* Did you pay someone to beat a drum out there? Are you trying to deliberately frighten me?

STANFORD. *(Whispers.)* There's somebody near the barn. I don't see more 'an one. Douse some a the lights.

ALICIA. *(Moves to buffet, right; determined.)* I'm telephoning the police. This has gone far enough. I'm not playing any more of your games, Stanford. Where . . . ? Where is the phone? Did you take the phone?

STANFORD. *(Shuts a light or two; crouching low; he peeks out of "window.")* You gonna get us both killed if you don't stop your yappin' *(Moves to second "window;" peeks out.)* He's comin' closer. He's down by the gate now. *(Sound: along with the beating drum an Indian chant is heard.)*

ALICIA. *(Clutching chest; frightened.)* What is that, Stanford?

STANFORD. *(Waves her toward him; whispers.)* Come here. Over here. Stay down low. *(Crouched over, Alicia moves towards him. They both lean against an imaginary rear wall. The chanting and drum-beading fades to silence.)*

ALICIA. What is he doing now?

STANFORD. *(Peeks out.)* I . . . I can't see him. I don't know where he is.

ALICIA. Stanford, this isn't real! There's no one out there! You've arranged for someone to pretend . . . *(Suddenly an ear-splitting scream as an Indian flies into the room, after, presumably, smashing open the entrance door. In warrior paint and fairly authentic costume, with a single feather taped to his bald head, the Indian chants as he beats the drum and dances about in a circle. His knowledge of Indian culture is gleaned from television re-runs of old Westerns.)*

STANFORD. Bald Eagle!

ALICIA. Bald Eagle? That. . . . That's Doctor Bibberman! *(The Indian stops chanting and dancing.)*

BIBBERMAN. When sun high in sky, me Doctor Bibberman. When sun fall under sky, me Bald Eagle, Comanche chief!

ALICIA. *(To Stanford.)* What is this? What is he doing here? Has he gone crazy, too?

STANFORD. Don't you be interferin', woman. This here's man's work. *(To Bibberman.)* Did you get to speak to the Sioux?

BIBBERMAN. I speak to Chief Gray Wolf. I say, "Before brother kill brother, we talk. I bring ranchers. We all meet at campfire on banks of Iron Horse Creek." You come now. They wait.

STANFORD. Is Ezra Slocum . . . ?

BIBBERMAN. He be there. Sam Cooper be there. And I ask Senator Monahan to be there.

STANFORD. Good. *(Turns to Alicia.)* Woman, you lock that there door after we go an' you don't open it for anybody. It's gonna be a long night. *(Suddenly a bit shy.)* I . . . I think you should be knowin', if it ain't in the cards for me to be comin' back, I did the best for you an' Lucinda I could.

But you ladies had no use for a workin' cowpoke. Once you got yourselves a college education an' your equal rights an' your banks a frozen spermatozoa, you had no need for the likes a me. I bear you no animosity. It's been a rewardin' experience. *(To Bald Eagle.)* We better get movin'. *(He moves to rear, right.)*

BIBBERMAN. I watch your husband, Mrs. Gerard. You have promise of Bald Eagle. *(He moves to rear; turns to Alicia.)* And Doctor Bibberman, too. *(And he continues to rear, softly beating on drum, chanting. Stanford joins him in chant. They exit. We can still hear the chanting and drum-beat, faintly. Alicia moves D. She stares upwards, her fists clenched in front of her, in a fierce voice.)*

ALICIA. I swear by all that's sacred in this world, I will *never, never* trust a man again . . . as long as there's a breath of life in me . . . *so help me God.* *(A loud, insistent beating of the drum, a screeching chant from Stanford and Bibberman, and, simultaneously, silence, and . . . blackout.)*

40

THE VOICES OF COMEDY

Tonal choices: humor and wit. Satire: from subtle humor to farcical ridicule. Pacing: buildups and jolts. Comic relief in serious work. Five pitfalls of comedy. Developing a comic sense.

It may seem odd to analyze comedy. We think of it as springing from an intuitive ability. While it is true that a sense of humor can't be taught, almost no one is totally humorless. You don't have to be an accomplished comedian to capture a comic experience, exaggerate it, and turn it into a dramatic scene or an entire play.

It helps, though, if you know what you are doing. As with any art, one learns from the successes and failures of others. Some approaches will muddy an excellent concept; others will bring out the best. Matters of timing and tone can spell the difference between success and failure. Inserting a farcical scene, for example, into a play that is otherwise built around a gently humorous development of character can do real damage. A blockbuster opening may seem great in an early draft, but it's the wrong tactic if the play runs down from there on. You can avoid a great deal of rewriting if you determine what type of comedy is appropriate for your particular play before you even outline the plot.

Tonal Choices: Humor or Wit

Although there is no sharp line between the tonal effects of humor and of wit, and both are often found in the same work, they do refer to significantly different approaches. *Humor* tends to be gentle and supportive. It shares with an audience foibles that we have experienced or are familiar with, such as the awkwardness of young people in love, the tensions associated with rituals like a job interview or a wedding, the anxieties, frustrations, and misunderstandings that parents face dealing with children and, conversely, that children experience dealing with parents. We tend to smile or laugh *with* such characters, not *at* them.

Humor is often based on incongruities: the priest at a beer party, the gang member at an art opening, a man married to a woman half his age, or the reverse. Some of these situations have been overused in the endless stream of situation comedies for television, but fresh events occur in our daily lives and can be developed with greater insight than one often finds on the tube.

Wit, on the other hand, tends to be sharper than humor. It is often based less on the human condition than on verbal tricks: jokes, puns, plays on words. It often appears in the dialogue of characters who are themselves clever, even snide. But wit can also be used to ridicule characters who are serious, even witless. When wit is used to criticize characters, attitudes, or institutions through exaggeration, we call it **satire**, a form of comedy I will turn to shortly.

Tonally, wit tends to be sharp-edged and critical compared with the softer, more accepting approach of humor. Wit can get nasty. Members of the audience rarely feel the kind of empathy generated by humor. They remain outside the characters, laughing *at* them rather than *with* them. If you can imagine a graph that measures emotional response, humor would be shown by a gently undulating line while wit would produce spikes.

Gentle humor is the dominant tone in the opening scene of *Coulda, Woulda, Shoulda*. When the mother, Yetta, reports that their son in the bath announced solemnly that he wants to be a rabbi, the audience assumes, incorrectly, that this is going to be a mildly humorous, realistic play. When Marty actually enters, revealed as an adult in a child's pajamas, the humor is more intense, but it is still humor.

The play maintains this tonal vein in spite of the serious themes. But in addition there are also some samples of wit in the lines. After Marty has announced the terrible future in store for both his parents, his father asks, "This is a comedy?" There is an unintentional double meaning here. The play we are reading (or watching) is indeed a comedy, but Marty's play within a play appears from his description to be a dismally depressing melodrama. A similar kind of double meaning occurs after Yetta complains about "so much anger, hostility" in her son's play and begs him to "fix it," confusing art with life. Marty's response is, "This isn't 'A Wonderful Life,' " referring to an actual and popular play (and film) with an upbeat theme. The comment operates like a triple pun, applying to the play on the stage (with its serious themes), to Marty's play within a play (a depressing melodrama), and to what we see of their lives as well.

Wit, not humor, dominates *The Cowboy, the Indian and the Fervent Feminist*. It's not that the characters themselves are witty—all three are utterly humorless. We laugh because the play exaggerates the positions they hold, making them seem absurd. It's intentionally unkind. This is wit pushed to the point of farcical ridicule. It is a prime example of **satire**.

Satire: From Subtle Humor to Farcical Ridicule

Satire ridicules by comic exaggeration. Those two elements, ridicule and exaggeration, are fundamental in all satires. Good satire defines its target carefully, aiming not just for laughs (though that's an important element) but also for criticism. The tone of the criticism can vary enormously, running from the mildest sort of friendly spoof to the most vitriolic attack. Hostile satire can become so savage that one can hardly recognize it as comedy, but if the playwright's intention is to evoke laughter, the work is still satire.

Because of this comic element, one often misses the fact that every satire is also to some degree a moral statement. Even the silliest satiric skit on television attacks people (usually public figures), types (particularly the pompous and hypocritical), or institutions (the bigger the better). Since stage plays have the advantage of being aimed at smaller, more selective audiences, satires tend to be more sophisticated. Often they are more challenging and provocative. And there are fewer taboos. It is no accident that totalitarian regimes maintain tight control of theaters and playwrights. Satire is an effective weapon against injustice and oppression.

Gentle as Alterman's humor is in the opening scene, the play soon generates some formidable satire. The short-tempered and insensitive father whose first priority seems to be getting to work, the indulgent mother who actually believes her beloved son can see into the future, and most of all the angst-ridden, humorless playwright who is blind to the fact that his script is a way of unloading a lifetime of antagonism. (Never confuse Marty the character with Alterman the playwright.) In our laughter, we recognize familiar types. The satire in this play, however, is rooted in character and is softened with elements of compassion. The characters are all unhappy people, and to some degree we feel sorry for them.

The satire in *The Cowboy*, on the other hand, is so heavily exaggerated that we call it **farce**. The characters in farce are often cartoon-like in their simplicity. Since we do learn a bit about the backgrounds of Alicia and Stanford, some members of the audience may feel a twinge of sympathy for them; but most find them absurdly comic. No one in that play comes off well, yet still we laugh.

Some farcical satires strive so hard for the easy laugh that they lose focus. But not this one. There are two primary targets: the aggressive member of the women's movement and the deluded conservative male who follows an extreme version of what been called the men's movement. That much would make an easy skit on *Saturday Night Live*, but Schisgal does far more. The wife, for all her feminist views, is also one who believes fervently that psychiatrists are always right. She represses her feminist convictions in her willingness to play along with her husband's delusions simply because this is what the revered Dr. Bibberman has recommended.

Where did Dr. Bibberman's name come from? A *bibber* is a heavy drinker. And what does he suggest? A wild exaggeration of traditional male attitudes and the men's movement that sprang from that, complete with the beating of drums and man-to-man bonding rituals.

Irony is frequently found in satiric work. As I described in the fiction section of this text, all irony is based on a reversal of expectations. Verbal irony often takes the form of a statement that is the opposite or clearly different from the intended meaning, like a golfer saying "great shot" when his opening drive veers into the woods. Less often, it describes a statement that is unknowingly inaccurate, as when a character in a historical drama says of the young Abraham Lincoln, "He'll never amount to anything." In the play *Indian*, however, the irony is in behavior rather than spoken words.

It is ironic, for example, that the role of traditionally passive and submissive wife be displayed by a character who is at heart a fervent feminist. Conversely, behavior that resembles the Marlboro Man version of a hypermasculine cowboy is played by a man who was not only fired by his advertising firm but was replaced by his "lowly secretary," as his wife so modestly describes herself.

Further, it is a bizarre bit of irony to have someone in the highly regarded profession of psychiatry behave like a cartoon version of a Indian. In fact, discovering that the esteemed doctor by day turns into Bald Eagle, Comanche chief, at night is a comic jolt.

The satire, then, starts with an exaggeration of the women's movement (Alicia's rise to power), counters it with a delusionary male response, adds a contemporary guru, the psychiatrist, and ends with an explosive betrayal. Unfair? Politically incorrect three times over? Justified? High comedy? You be the judge.

Pacing: Buildups and Jolts

Most successful comedies progress from a simple situation to a complex one. The initial scene often poses a dispute or a problem, and the plot builds on that, increasing the degree of absurdity and, in the case of satires, the exaggeration.

This pattern is relatively easy in short comedies, but the longer the work the greater the challenge. Sustaining that buildup can be a problem. For this reason, many plays work up to an emotional jolt, something quite unexpected. This can either end the play or launch a new buildup. The pattern is similar to that in serious drama where, as we have seen, the interest of the audience is held with a **dramatic question** which is then answered and replaced by another.

Although the two comedies you have read are quite different, they both follow this pattern. *Coulda,* you remember, opens with a mild exchange between the mother and the father: She has an amusing anecdote to tell about their son, but her husband is much more interested in finding his clothes and getting to work. This erupts naturally into a debate about their child. Then the jolt: Marty enters "in his forties, wearing large children's pajamas." It's an absurd leap into fantasy.

The next buildup is based on Marty's increasing hostility toward his father, ending with the revelation that Cy has been an unfaithful husband. The jolt that follows this is more subtle: First one parent and then the other leaves the stage, entering Marty's room. We see them now as memories of the playwright, vivid yet insubstantial.

Is this even a comedy? That's what Cy asks, though he is referring to the somber play Marty is writing. Yes, *Coulda* is a comedy because it pokes fun at work-oriented fathers, indulgent mothers, and anguished playwrights. In spite of its brevity, it is a carefully paced comedy.

Pacing is even more important in *Cowboy* because it is more than twice the length. The longer a comedy the greater the chance that it will have a slow section. Notice that *Cowboy* does *not* start with the shouting match between Alicia and her husband. Instead, it opens on a gentle tone—even more low-key than the opening of *Coulda*. Alicia, alone on the stage, is bringing on the dinner that she has prepared. Although she is described as appearing to be "under great stress," nothing dramatic is going on. Not yet.

The buildup begins with the introduction of Stanford, increases when we learn about how Stanford was fired and about Dr. Bibberman. If you review the stage directions when they begin their serious argument, you will see how the playwright increases the absurdity through action: "Stands on his chair," "Stands on her chair," "Steps from chair to table."

How can Schisgal cap that? With the sound of Indians beating drums. In a bizarre fashion, Stanford behaves as if they are about to be attacked. Never mind that Alicia shouts, "Stanford, this isn't real! There's no one out there!"

It's time for the jolt. It comes with "an earsplitting scream as an Indian flies into the room." It is none other than Dr. Bibberman in his Indian chief mode. Pushing the macho man's position to comic extreme, the two of them go off together, saying of women, "Once you got yourselves a college education . . . you had no need for the likes a me." The battle between the sexes ends with alienation and separation. Described this way, it hardly sounds like a comedy, but the play in performance generates laughter from both sexes. The key is in the buildup of exaggeration and the calculated use of a jolt as a climax.

Comic Relief in Serious Work

To this point, we have been treating comedy as if it were totally distinct from serious drama. Actually, the two are frequently blended. In fact, one of the most common weaknesses in student-written plays is a failure to employ **comic relief** in plays that are weighed down with unrelieved drama. The result is like bread made without yeast. The play Marty is trying to write in *Coulda* appears to be just such a work.

Most of us were introduced to the technique of comic relief when we first read a Shakespearean tragedy or his history plays. Shakespeare had a talent for judging just how much the audience could take and how to relieve the pressure with some kind of wit or satire.

His clowns (as in *King Lear*) specialize in wit: jokes, puns, and clever phrasing. They often comment on the more serious aspects of the play in ironic terms. In the history plays such as *Henry IV: Parts I and II* and more briefly in *Henry V,* he employs satire of character in the form of Sir John Falstaff, a loudmouthed liar and reveler who because of his wit becomes engaging and memorable.

Contemporary drama almost always contains some form of comic relief. You may remember *Hello Out There* as unrelieved tragedy, but Photo-Finish as a character is given a whimsical sense of humor that bubbles unexpectedly until the crisis looms toward the end of the play. The constant repetition of "Hello out there" in the first two scenes usually receives gentle laughter in production. His calling her Katey and later saying that it is a name "I've been saving for you," is not a laugh line, but it provides a light touch in an otherwise dark play. The same is true of his description of San Francisco as different because "More people in Frisco love someone, that's all." Without these touches, the drama would have run a risk of become a **melodrama.**

In longer plays comic relief still takes the two forms Shakespeare found effective: a witty minor character who can comment on the action or even kid the protagonist without being centrally involved, or a more important character, a foil, who is presented in satiric form. They may appear only briefly and apparently casually, but there is nothing casual about *when* they appear. The playwright must decide when the audience will start squirming and must counter that restlessness by inserting comic relief.

Five Pitfalls of Comedy

Comedies are such fun to read and to watch that we forget they require just as much work as serious drama. No checklist is going to guard against all the potential problems, but there are five areas in which many student plays (and even a few produced plays) founder. Consider them carefully.

• *Poor pacing.* This heads the list. It is natural enough to let a first draft pour out as the ideas occur, but then it is time to take a close look at the buildup. We have already examined the incremental buildup in each of the two comedies you have read and the way in which a jolt is used to energize a scene. Use these two plays as models.

If you have opened your play with the liveliest action or the strongest satire, you have nowhere to go but down. As I have pointed out, you will probably do better starting on a low key and working up.

Longer plays, of course, can absorb a slow scene from time to time, but a one-act play of less than ten printed pages is like a hundred-yard dash—it's a mistake to pause along the way.

• *Fragmentation.* Sometimes writing a satire becomes such fun that one forgets what is supposed to hold the play together. Stop and ask yourself just what the target is. As in the case of *Coulda,* there may be a cluster of closely related themes (fathers, mothers, playwrights), but what unifies that play is not satirical at all. Its central concern is the dilemma faced by the playwright who uses autobiographical sources.

Comedies and especially satires that have no central focus may receive laughs just as the routine of a standup comic can, but they are less durable, less lasting than a carefully focused comedy.

• *Imitation.* No form of contemporary writing in any genre is more subject to being imitative than comic drama. The reason is that television writers pump an endless stream of popular comic dramas into the American consciousness 365 days a year. Traces of these plots and characters are apt to lie like sludge in the recesses of our memories. It is all too easy to dredge up segments of them.

Television is forever imitating television, recycling last year's sitcoms shamelessly. The writers know they are not working for the ages; like managers of fast-food chains, they are meeting a commercial demand. But when one writes for the stage, one hopes to create something a little more enduring. Check to make sure that both your characters and your plot are original.

• *Slapstick* is farce with little or no thematic content. The term comes from vaudeville and refers to the stick designed to make a loud "whack!" when actors hit each other. Vaudeville died, but the Three Stooges maintained the tradition in every detail except for sexual innuendo.

Slapstick comedy has no goals other than obtaining laughs. It has its appeal just as comic strips do, and there is no harm in it. But as we have seen, it is possible to write comic drama with a considerable degree of sophistication.

On first reading, *Cowboy* may seem like slapstick. The absurdity of the plot and the characters reach that point. But if you look at the attitudes that are being satirized, you will see that the core of the play has real substance. For the past several decades, the women's movement has been a major force in our society, and predictably there has been a countermovement on the part of men. Further, some psychiatrists have taken strong positions and achieved extraordinary influence. Every movement and every profession has its extremists, and these are natural subjects of satire.

Cowboy is pushed to the point of being a comic farce, but it is not slapstick. Most sophisticated comedies have serious implications. Don't be content to serve up just a succession of easy laughs; give your audience some substance as well.

- *Visually static comedy* is the final pitfall. There is a fundamental difference between the performance of a standup comic, no matter how clever, and a comic play. Adding a second standup comic provides more wordplay, but unless there is a plot—something going on—it is not drama.

The very word *actor* implies action, and drama without dramatic action is a contradiction in terms. A monologue, no matter how good, is a *performance*, not a play. Judging by recent contest submissions, clever but plotless scripts have in the past few years become one of the most serious pitfalls for aspiring dramatists.

Developing a Comic Sense

If you are interested in writing comedy, you need to engage in two essential activities: read as many comic plays as you have time for, and see as many as you can afford. Never mind what century—you can learn from the few samples of Greek comedies just as you can from the Elizabethan period and contemporary works.

One advantage to reading plays is that you can finish one in a single setting. The more you read, the better. Granted, Elizabethan English slows you down, but start with a play you have read before and you will see how much more rewarding the second experience is. To find contemporary dramas, turn to Appendix C, "Resources for Writers," in the back of this book and follow through by spending time in the nearest library.

Naturally, you will find some works that strike you as unsuccessful. Be careful, however, not to shrug them off. Often you can learn from the mistakes of others if you take the time to analyze exactly what you would have done differently.

Scripts are, you remember, only descriptions of plays in performance. Attending actual performances, professional or amateur, will give you a richer understanding of what goes into successful comedies. Whenever possible, read the script in advance and then attend a performance while the work is still fresh in your mind. Remember that you are not concerned primarily with entertainment; you are in a learning mode. Compare your response to the script with your experience seeing the play in performance. Every evening is different, surprising even the actors on occasion. But you will get a sense of what aspects of comedy work well on the stage if you remain critically alert.

In essence, the task is to immerse yourself in comedies of all sorts. The best playwrights have learned from other playwrights. Now it's your turn.

41

DRAMATIC THEMES

Theme and plot defined. Presenting themes through tragedy. Sliding themes into comedy. Hiding themes in farce. The thesis play: social and political issues. Finding your own themes.

The **theme** in drama is that portion of the work that comments on the human condition. It is similar to a theme in fiction except that in plays it is frequently presented in bolder and more vivid ways—that is, more dramatically.

Be careful not to confuse theme with plot. **Plot** is what happens. A plot outline includes names of characters and a brief description of the action. Theme, on the other hand, deals with abstract ideas, not events. It is a description of the concerns and insights suggested by the play.

The *plot* of Shakespeare's *Hamlet*, for example, might be described in highly condensed form like this: "A Danish prince named Hamlet has been urged by the ghost of his murdered father to avenge the father's death, but Hamlet delays taking action and eventually is killed along with his mother and his stepfather."

The *theme*, on the other hand, might be described this way: "The agonizing conflict between our instinct for vengeance and our ethical code of civilized restraint can lead an individual to inaction and disaster." Notice that the thematic statement does not name a particular character or identify exactly what happened. It focuses on the idea behind the play, not the events or characters.

A play can have more than one theme. But for the sake of clarity and accuracy, each should be described in a complete sentence. Referring to the theme of *Hamlet* simply as "revenge" or "indecision" is too vague to be helpful. Taking the time to describe in complete sentences one or two themes in an early draft of your own work often helps to clarify your intent. If you find it impossible to do so, it may mean that what you have is more of a **skit** than a play.

As in fiction, what appears at first to be a single theme is often made up of a number of different but closely related concerns. The longer and more intricate a play, the more thematic suggestions it may contain. But as we will see, even short plays can contain a variety of related concerns. For this reason, the phrase **central concern** is in some ways more accurate than *theme*. I will use the two terms synonymously, as I did in the fiction section.

Themes do not generally provide answers to the questions a play raises. *Hamlet* doesn't instruct you how to deal with unruly stepfathers, and *Hello Out There* is hardly good advice on how to earn a living at the racetrack or how to handle a lynch mob. Although there are plays that do take very specific positions on political and social issues, these are said to present **theses** rather than themes. A thesis is a specific argument. The function of a play with a thesis is to persuade or convert, not to explore. I will return to that approach later in this chapter.

The three plays in this volume are quite different in treatment: a tragedy, a comedy, and a farce. Yet each has a cluster of related themes. The plays are helpful models for your own work because they manage to suggest a good deal in a very short space. As we examine them, however, keep in mind that the complexity of thematic suggestion that you see in a published play is not usually what came to the playwright in the first draft. Themes often develop slowly as the writer moves through successive drafts.

Presenting Themes through Tragedy

Hello Out There is remembered by theatergoers mainly for its dramatic impact, but if it had nothing more to offer than that, it would be a melodrama. The terror of an individual facing a lynch mob has been repeated frequently in film and television dramas. What keeps Saroyan's play from becoming a simple thriller is partly the characterization; but to an even greater extent it is due to the complexity of themes. For all the tension and eventual violence, the play provides important insights about the human condition.

The playwright has woven several themes together. Your selection of which one you feel is *the* theme depends on which aspects of the play you found the most compelling. This is not to say that the play means whatever you want it to mean. Specific themes are clearly and intentionally stressed. Which one seems the most important, however, will vary with each individual.

Here are three thematic statements, each of which is suggested in the play through dialogue and action:

1. The world is full of genuinely lonely people whose efforts to make contact with others are frustrated at every turn.
2. Being poor and young in a small, mean-spirited town is very much like being a prisoner in a jail.
3. If you depend heavily on luck to survive, the time may come when the odds run against you.

This is not an exhaustive list; probably you could add to it. But they do represent a core, and we can support each not just with conjecture but with hard evidence from the play.

I put the one about lonely people first because Saroyan places such heavy emphasis on it. His main technique is repetition. "Hello out there" is clearly the cry of a lonely person. It is not only used in the title, it appears as the opening and closing lines. In between, it is repeated twenty-five times! Saroyan also repeats the word "lonesome" twelve times, six of them just before and just after Emily appears for the first time.

How does Saroyan get away with so much redundancy? In a conventional essay these repetitions would be considered serious errors in style. But a play is not an essay. A dramatic performance, remember, is a continuous art form in that it flows by the audience nonstop. Repeating a line of dialogue in a fast-moving play is an effective way of highlighting an important phrase and stressing the fact that it has thematic significance. Repetition like this is like a refrain in a poem or a repeated chorus in a ballad. It is a reminder of how drama often borrows from the techniques of poetry.

Photo-Finish is not the only character who is lonely and reaching out for contact with someone else. Emily is equally isolated. She repeats the word "lonesome" just as much as Photo-Finish does. She tells Photo-Finish that the men in town laugh at her, and her father takes what little she earns. She has hung around the jail just to be able to talk with this new prisoner. She describes her feelings directly:

> It's so lonely in this town. Nothing here but the lonesome wind all the time, lifting the dirt and blowing out to the prairie.

Even the woman who has accused Photo-Finish of rape is given the benefit of the doubt. She is pictured as a sad and lonely woman alienated from her husband.

As in many tragedies, there is a moment when it seems as if this yearning for companionship will be fulfilled by Photo-Finish and Emily, but then his luck runs out and she ends up being as lonely and isolated as he had been at the beginning of the play.

The second thematic statement shifts the emphasis to the parallel between Emily's life trapped in an isolated prairie town and someone held in jail. Those who have identified with her might see this as a primary theme. Clearly it is *a* theme even if it isn't the dominant one. The fact that the playwright has so carefully placed her in exactly the same position as Photo-Finish was at the beginning of the play and has given her the very same lines is ample evidence that this was one of his concerns.

The third thematic statement, the one suggesting that those who depend fully on luck will eventually fail, is supported partly through the action of the play but also from the young man's nickname. In explaining it to Emily, he tells her that he has earned that reputation because the horses he bets on always lose by a nose. The fact that he is a gambler stresses the theme of luck, and his bad track record adds an ominous note.

As a writer you have to be careful about significant names like Photo-Finish. If your choice is too obviously significant, you undermine the sense of realism. If Saroyan had named his protagonist *Hy Risk*, it would seem contrived. But *Photo-Finish* is explained as a nickname and so seems plausible—though hardly subtle.

As you may have noticed, Saroyan also uses names of towns to highlight certain thematic aspects. The town where the protagonist is about to meet his death like a bull in the arena is called "Matador." And the town from which the freewheeling, irresponsible men come is "Wheeling." Saroyan makes sure that the audience does not miss these names by repeating each one twice—a recognition of the fact that in drama significant details have to be repeated if they are to be remembered.

The various themes or concerns in *Hello Out There* are presented fairly directly, and if you work with the script closely they may seem too obvious. But remember that the audience watching a play in performance cannot dwell on technique. If they respond to details like the name "Matador," they will do so almost subliminally. It is possible to find names that are thematically suggestive without being so obvious that they seem contrived. Many people have read or seen Arthur Miller's *Death of a Salesman* without noticing that the protagonist, a man who is low in the social order, is appropriately named Willy Loman.

Sliding Themes into Comedy

In spite of serious themes, *Coulda, Woulda, Shoulda* is a comedy because the complications that arise early in the play are more or less resolved at the end. There is no catastrophe as there is in most tragedies. Also there are many details that are satiric and just plain funny.

But *Coulda* was not written merely to produce laughter. It is a play that, unlike most sitcoms, has themes worth examining and intricacies that call for a second look. In short, it has **resonance**.

Again, there is no one "correct" statement of the theme, but here are four that are clearly supported by evidence from the script:

1. Writing a play may seem like playing God, but a play is still just a play.
2. Writing a play about one's parents can become a vehicle for expressing old resentments.
3. Nonwriters often misunderstand the nature of the creative process.
4. Writing a play sometimes forces the playwright to look back to childhood and forward into the future at the same time.

The first statement goes to the heart of what is called the creative process. There is something godlike in creating people and places on the stage. Indeed, Quakers until fairly recently felt that the writing of both fiction and drama was too presumptuous to be encouraged in school. But as *Coulda* clearly demonstrates, the process is far from divine creation. "I'm not God," Marty assures his mother, but she still believes that he can change the future through his writing.

The second—the emotional difficulties encountered when one is writing about parents—is one that will be recognized by anyone who has tried to do so. There is something sadly comic about Marty's harsh dramatic treatment of his parents. He pictures his father getting a divorce, turning to drink, getting diabetes, losing his legs, and then dying. What a revenge! As for his mother, she ends up "bitter, alone, miserable in Miami." That takes care of her!

The theme suggested here is that it is all too easy to take out one's hostilities on individuals—especially parents—when writing drama. We see this through the kind of play Marty, the protagonist, is writing. It seems dark and heavy-handed, probably melodramatic. By poking fun at this temptation, Glenn Alterman presents the theme with a light, satiric tone.

The third thematic suggestion—that others don't understand what goes into a creative work—will also be familiar to those who write drama or fiction. Nonwriters often assume that what they see happen on the stage is what actually occurred in the playwright's life. And in this case the parents extend that misapprehension into the future, treating their son like some sort of prophet. "It's a play, Ma, make-believe," Marty tells her, but she doesn't accept that. When dramatists (and novelists too) dump on their parents, the general public often assumes that the work is true to life. It is difficult for nonwriters to understand how the creative process draws from both life and the imagination, mixing the two.

The fourth thematic concern turns the spotlight from the audience to the playwright. In the act of writing, one must look back to childhood—often to unpleasant episodes—but such writing also requires speculating about the future. What might become of this or that character? Where will he or she end up? The implications are not always rosy.

In addition to these major concerns, there is a thematic suggestion that adds depth to the characterization of father and son. The play touches on the fact that while some, like Cy, feel that their first loyalty is to earning a living even at the expense of being a caring, considerate parent, others, like Marty, are willing to risk financial insecurity to express themselves through art. This theme is not developed at length, but it provides a dramatic tension between father and son in this play.

These are all serious concerns, but rather than being thrust at the reader through repetition of key words and phrases as the themes in *Hello Out There* are, they are slid in almost unnoticed midst the laughter. That moment when

Marty enters is a perfect example. There he is, a man in his forties in kids' pajamas. The audience, having expected a child, laughs. When we are reading the script, and can pause long enough to reflect on what is being suggested thematically, it seems clear that the play is showing us both the writer as he is (the adult man with his pen and pad) and the child that is within him. But the audience watching the play in production isn't analyzing. It's laughing. The themes will be communicated almost unconsciously, and of course they will become clearer after the performance is over. Comedies can have just as many serious themes as tragedies, but they tend to be presented less directly, woven into the laughter.

Hiding Themes in Farce

Farce is usually so exaggerated, even bizarre, that serious themes are often buried even more than they are in a comedy. *The Cowboy, the Indian and the Fervent Feminist* is high satire throughout, but behind the laughter are social issues that have been with us for centuries and have become particularly intense in the past 40 years. Here are three of the most prominent:

1. The notion of male dominance can reach such extremes that it resembles a psychotic delusion.
2. Strong feminists are sometimes able to displace their bosses in the work place.
3. The traditional respect for psychiatrists can induce some people to behave contrary to their deepest beliefs.

Which of these three is the **central concern**? That depends on which aspect you want to stress. They are all, however, contemporary concerns with roots that run deep in our society. Just because they are presented with zany, madcap exaggeration in no way diminishes their importance.

If you read this list without having read or seen the play, you would have no idea whether the work was serious, a mild comedy, or a farce. Themes, remember, are abstract statements about the human condition. They do not describe the plot, the characters, or the tone. Think of them as the intellectual core of a work. Because satire exposes or denounces an attitude, an institution, or a person, it almost always has a serious target no matter how absurdly comic the action and the characters may be.

Murray Schisgal and William Saroyan are both concerned with social issues, but their plays could hardly be more different in tone. Alterman's themes differ from both those plays by focusing on the creative process and the relationship between life and art.

When you review the way these three playwrights present their themes, you will see how crucial it is to imply your themes indirectly. Furthermore, you have to do so in ways that are neither too subtle for an audience to grasp in a single viewing nor so obvious as to appear forced and artificial. In serious, realistic drama, you depend on the credibility of characterization and the dramatic power of the plot to keep the themes from being too obvious. In comedy, your themes have to be disguised by being a part of the humor. In highly exaggerated satire, the themes may be more blatant, but you have to be careful not to sound preachy. As in all comedy, it is the humor that keeps your thematic concerns just under the surface.

The Thesis Play: Social and Political Issues

Drama has always been associated with social statement and political protest. Medieval miracle plays were originally intended to teach biblical stories and doctrine to illiterate peasants. During the depression years of the 1930s vehement political protests were made through plays; and later, opposition to the Vietnam War became an equally strong topic.

Today, **black theater** is a dynamic force in socially concerned drama. Some plays develop themes of black identity, sharing the black experience with the whole society. Others present a specific thesis—a demand for political or social change or a call for reform.

The development of black theater is relatively recent. With a few rare exceptions, theater was a white art form until well into the 1960s. Black playwrights like Langston Hughes, Ossie Davis, and Lorraine Hansberry are known to most for one successful play each, but few white theatergoers can name the others they wrote. Langston Hughes alone turned out more than 20 plays. As a result, black playwrights, as well as black directors and actors, have been deprived of audiences and of the training that comes from regular production. This backlog of artistic frustration has amplified a deep sense of social injustice and has produced themes of bitter denunciation.

The harshest of these are written consciously and directly to a white audience. Plays like *The Toilet* by Amiri Baraka (LeRoi Jones) are intentionally designed to shock white, middle-class theatergoers. Rather than themes, these plays present **theses**—strong statements that often recommend specific social action.

Conscious appeal to a white audience is also found in plays that are thematic and less accusatory. In Charles Gordone's *No Place to Be Somebody*, for example, the plot of the play is stopped twice for lengthy monologues delivered like prose poems from the center of the stage. One of these is formally titled "There's More to Being Black than Meets the Eye." The other is a verse narrative of what it is like for a black to try living like a white suburbanite, suffering the scorn of both urban blacks and white neighbors.

Other plays address themselves more specifically to black audiences. The seven plays selected originally by the Free Southern Theater group for its pilot program are good examples: *Purlie Victorious* by Ossie Davis, and *Do You Want to Be Free?* by Langston Hughes among others. Another important play of the period is Martin Duberman's *In White America*. August Wilson has also achieved wide critical acclaim.

Women have also had a significant impact on drama in the past decade. As with black drama, plays by women vary from those that explore the woman's experience to those that make strong social or political statements. One of the more innovative playwrights is Ursule Molinaro, whose works vary from brief, nonrealistic plays in the absurdist tradition to full-length works. In one, *Breakfast Past Noon*, a mother and daughter have a series of arguments without ever addressing each other directly. They refer to each other consistently in the third person. The effect is like two antagonists who refuse to make eye contact. The play is a highly effective dramatization of a hopelessly alienated relationship.

This play and others by women have been collected in an anthology called *The New Women's Theater*, edited by Honor Moore. For a retrospective collection that gives historical perspective, I recommend *Plays by and about Women*, edited by Victoria Sullivan and James Hatch.

If you are committed to a social or political issue and hope to present it in the form of a thesis play, keep these two factors in mind. If the play is strongly confrontational, it may end up being read and seen mainly by those who already agree with you, sometimes called "preaching to the faithful." On the other hand, if the play has been softened in order to appeal to a wider audience, it may fail to make a strong enough statement to be effective. The best way to make a decision in this area is to read a number of thesis-oriented plays. I have mentioned many titles in this chapter. Use these as a basic list and you will be able to determine what audience you are writing for and how to present your convictions.

Finding Your Own Themes

When you start planning a new play, you will probably focus on the plot and the characters. Plays, like stories, usually begin with characters facing some type of conflict. But before you start outlining that plot, see if you can describe the theme in a single, complete sentence. If there are a number of themes (as there are in the plays you have read), use a complete sentence for each.

Take a close look at these thematic sentences. If they do not reflect your genuine feelings, the play will probably not ring true. Conventional concerns, or **truisms**, are often early warning signs that you have settled for **hackneyed** situations and **stock characters.** Plays that have vitality, whether they are serious or comic, usually have themes that are strongly felt by the dramatist.

But don't feel that to be dramatic you have to focus on a social cause. Look at *Coulda*. It doesn't deal with themes like injustice, inequality, or violence. Instead, it explores the nature of art and life. These are not trivial matters, and clearly the playwright takes them seriously in spite of the comic nature of the play. The fact that a play is comic doesn't mean that it has to be mindless.

Can you say the same about a farce? There are plenty of lively farces written for stage and screen that are designed simply for laughs, but they are simple in the literary sense, and as insubstantial as Saturday morning cartoons. Schisgal has a great sense of crazy humor and an ability to exaggerate a common conflict until it is almost dreamlike. But what gives *Cowboy* resonance, what makes it worth a careful second look on the page, are the thematic concerns we have been examining.

Keep in mind that themes are not a good starting point for drama. If you begin with an intellectual idea, the play is apt to end up being an illustrated lecture; if you start with a social slogan, your play may seem like propaganda. But if you begin with a situation that is emotionally charged and seems genuine to you, themes will emerge. Then they can be clarified and developed.

Where does one find supercharged situations that might develop into a drama? One area to explore is your own roots. If you have a distinctive racial or national background, there will be tensions and perhaps successes and defeats associated with it. If your own life has been relatively secure, what about your parents' lives?

Even if you feel that your life has been in the mainstream and essentially uneventful, it hasn't been entirely smooth. No one's is. Seek out those situations that made you mad or frustrated or challenged, and transform them until they are large enough and significant enough for the stage.

In some ways, finding good thematic material for a play is similar to the process in fiction. But there are these three differences: First, you need a situation or an incident that dramatizes genuine conflict. Fiction also thrives on conflict, but it can be subtle. Drama calls for a confrontation with real impact. Look at the three plays you have read. Each is driven by a fundamental conflict.

To find genuine conflicts with potential for meaningful themes, review those moments in your life or in the lives of those close to you when individuals or groups of individuals were pitted against each other. Ask yourself exactly what were the themes behind the conflict. A play in which two individuals compete for a job may have action with no thematic element. But a play in which a young woman is about to be fired from her job in an appliance store for a theft that in fact her father has committed—there is a play concept with a cluster of potential themes about ethics, family loyalty, love, and the status of women.

Second, you need a theme that can be handled on a physical stage in a limited period of time. Never mind dramatizing *War and Peace*. Focus your theme on one manageable incident. If your concern is racial justice, for example, let one specific situation stand for the general problem. If the events you have in mind include several different settings or occurred over a span of several years, see if you can transform them into a plot that can be handled with a single set and a single time period. Unity of place and time are far more important in drama than they are in fiction, especially if your play is short. Your themes will be easily lost if the plot is fragmented.

Finally, consider ways to reiterate your theme. Remember how all these thematic repetitions in *Hello Out There* seemed so blatant when examined on the page? They blend together in an actual performance just the way brush strokes in a Rembrandt portrait merge when viewed from a proper distance.

Regardless of whether you are working with tragedy, comedy, or farce, fresh and significant themes will add depth and a sense of resonance to your work.

42

DEVELOPING AS A DRAMATIST

Three ways to "see" your own play: silent reading, dramatic reading, public reading. Core questions that should be asked and honestly answered. Immersion in drama: reading, seeing, taking part. The world's largest free academy.

You have now read three quite different plays—a tragedy, a comedy, and a farce. You have begun to see drama as a succession of interrelated scenes. You have become conscious of the need for conflict, vivid characters, and action. And you have come to expect some significant themes, whether the play is serious or comic. That's a start.

Continued growth as a playwright, however, will depend on two additional factors that no textbook can give you. The first is the ability to act as your own severest critic. This is an art in itself. The second, for those who want to go still farther, is to plunge yourself into theater—reading plays, seeing plays, and taking part in productions.

Three Ways to "See" Your Own Work

It is unlikely that your initial efforts will be given a full production. There are, however, ways to "see" your work in imagination. This process is fundamentally different from evaluating your own poetry or fiction because of the fact that a script is not a play. A *script* is a manuscript, words on the page; a *play* is the production as it appears on a stage, a collaborative effort. In your mind, you have to translate what you are writing into a live performance. There are three ways of doing this.

Once you are finished with a rough but complete draft, give the script a silent, beginning-to-end reading. While you were writing you naturally read and reread sections; but a nonstop reading is different. Lock the door and turn off the phone. Read the play without interruption. Don't stop to make corrections, take notes, or get a cup of coffee. Give the reading your sustained and undivided attention.

As you read, picture all the action. Visualize where each actor is standing as she or he speaks. Supply the action in your mind's eye. You are now your own first audience.

When you are through and the imaginary curtain drops, switch roles. Now you are the director at the end of the first dress rehearsal. With clipboard in hand, write down everything that went wrong—scenes that were static, characters that sounded like alien creatures posing as humans, themes that echoed editorials you wouldn't bother to finish. Be tough, but compassionate. "You can do better," tell yourself.

After more revisions and a lapse of time (days, not weeks), take the second step: read it out loud. Again, isolate yourself from all distractions. One mechanical purpose for this is timing. The total playing time can be estimated fairly accurately if you allow for action that occurs without lines. If the play is divided into acts and scenes, it will be important to know how long each one is. You will need this information when deciding where to cut and when to expand. You will also want to record the total playing time. This information is often required when a play is submitted to a contest.

In addition to these mechanical concerns, the spoken reading is an effective way for you to judge the quality of your revised dialogue before anyone else hears it. Phrasing that seemed satisfactory on the page may sound awkward or not true to character when spoken. Long speeches that slid by smoothly when read silently may slow the forward motion of the play when read out loud. This will require cutting and more rewriting. Always that. Then you may be ready for the third method of "seeing" your play: a group reading.

Your readers will do a better job if they are familiar with the script. They don't have to memorize the lines, but they need to have some sense of the character they are playing. In addition to readers, you need a few listeners. Participants are concentrating on their lines and won't have time to think critically about the work. The listeners should be encouraged to take notes. It is also helpful to tape-record the reading for your own review.

In the discussion that follows the reading, make sure that it doesn't go soft with flattery (delicious as that is) or deteriorate into general conversations about the issues suggested by the play. Remind your critics that the subject is the play itself. To keep them focused, you may wish to photocopy the six "core questions" listed below (giving credit, of course) and use them as guidelines for the discussion.

While poets and writers of fiction usually turn to other writers for criticism, dramatists value *everyone's* reactions. Because drama is a spectator art intended for a wider, more general audience, the response of nonwriters becomes particularly valuable. Some writers, of course, may hesitate to include parents after reading *Coulda*, but for most, the more amateur critics the better. Members of this informal audience may not be able to provide solutions, but they can pick out dull scenes, faulty characterization, the plaintive note of sentimentality, or the drumbeat of melodrama. In the case of comic drama, their failure to crack a smile should tell you something. Conversely, the sound of laughter is sweet indeed.

Poets listen politely to comments from their listeners after a reading, but they rarely act on them. Playwrights, on the other hand—even highly successful ones—pay close attention to audience reaction and often make successive revisions during the run of a play.

Core Questions That Should Be Asked—and Answered

Here are six question you as playwright should ask yourself and then answer honestly. These questions will also help to keep friendly critics on track.

1. *Scenes: Are there any that drag?* If so, what's the problem? In many cases it is either lack of action or lack of development. Make sure that there are dramatic questions that hold the attention scene by scene. Focusing your attention on specific scenes is far more helpful than sweeping statements about the play as a whole.

2. *Conflict: Exactly what kind of conflict is there?* Who is pitted against whom? Or is a character struggling against some aspect of society? Is the conflict strong enough to hold an audience? Is it augmented by inner conflict? If the conflict is excessive, the play may be **melodramatic.** If it is too gentle, the work is probably nondramatic.

3. *Characterization: Are the characters convincing and/or memorable?* In the case of serious realistic drama, it is essential that at least the major characters be convincing. Their dialogue must seem appropriate and their actions comprehensible. Otherwise they may turn out to be stick figures representing some abstraction like courage or treachery. With comedy, farce, and nonrealistic plays, on the other hand, the goal may be simply to make the characters memorable. Often this is achieved by exaggeration. Remember that a character doesn't have to be likable to be memorable. You may not want to invite Photo-Finish to dinner or join Stanford on his imaginary ranch, but you won't forget either of them.

4. *Action: Is there enough?* Make sure the play is not just talk. Are *scenes* defined by characters appearing or leaving? And is there enough significant activity to keep the play visually stimulating? (*Hello Out There* is a particularly good example of how to handle action.) Does the visual aspect of your play contribute to the total effect?

5. *Themes: What themes are being explored, and how are they developed?* Just what themes actually reach the audience? As playwright, don't explain your intent and ask for confirmation. Let your critics tell you how they interpreted what they saw. Are the themes too blatant (preachy) or too familiar (truisms) or too obscure (fuzzy)?

6. *Tone: How would you describe the tone, and is it effective?* This is the most difficult question, because tone is an elusive concept. Major tonal problems: Is it **melodramatic**? Is it **sentimental**? Is it unjustifiably offensive? (Yes, there are thesis-driven plays that can be defended as justifiably offensive.) More subtle tonal concerns: Is it too bland, too saccharine, emotionally dissatisfying, needlessly negative, in need of **comic relief**?

There is one more question that all playwrights must ask of themselves: Am I listening to criticisms with an open mind, accepting those that seem justified, or am I taking a defensive attitude? Only by accepting and weighing criticism objectively can one grow and develop as a writer.

Immersion in Drama

Writing a play can be valuable even if you never do it again. You will learn a good deal about the medium, and your capacity to enjoy performances will be greatly enhanced. As with any sport, those who have done it at least briefly acquire a special understanding and appreciation.

If you want to go beyond the level of informed theatergoer, however, if you want to develop as a playwright on your own, you will have to immerse yourself in the medium.

The process starts with intensive reading. This is essential (as it is in poetry and fiction) if you are to acquire a broad view of the medium. Insufficient reading is a major cause of unsuccessful play scripts.

At the same time, supplement your reading by seeing performances. Take in whatever is available—student and amateur productions as well as those presented by professional companies. If cost is a factor, you may be able to get special rates just before opening night. Since it is the play itself that concerns you and not the level of performance, a missed line or two won't bother you.

Whenever possible, take part in a production. Even if acting is not your primary concern, a bit part will help you to understand the dynamics of putting on a play. Or you might consider volunteering for the stage crew. Working with hammer and saw gives you a respect for both the limits and the opportunities of a stage set. Being part of the crew also gives you a chance to see a production repeatedly. If you are not at a college or university, consider a summer stock company. The mechanics of producing a play should be a part of any playwright's education.

Where you live is also a factor for serious playwrights. Poets and writers of fiction have the option of living and writing in relative isolation. Books and magazines serve as their connection with other writers. Playwrights, on the other hand, thrive best by being where the action is. That usually means a city with an active drama scene. The actual writing of a script may be a relatively solitary act, but the production—the actual play—requires the physical and emotional cooperation of many. As I have pointed out before, drama is truly a collaborative art. It is important to join in this collaboration.

The World's Largest Free Academy

When you have completed a course in play writing, you may feel cut off from the stimulation and motivation of fellow writers. Don't panic, however. If you are serious about the genre, you can draw on a host of playwrights covering a span of 2,500 years. They are now your teachers, and through their published work they are willing to instruct without charging tuition. Think of them as the world's largest free academy.

Every library has collections of "best plays" for particular years, and these will give you a wide variety. If you read one play script each night five times a week, you will have read 260 plays in a year, and the chances are that not one of them was offered in production in your area during that period. When you find a playwright whose work you admire, try to find more by the same individual.

Don't limit yourself to recent work; you can learn a lot from the way Shakespeare presents a dramatic question early in his tragedies or sets the scene in a history play or balances heavy drama with comic relief. If you are interested in strong themes, the plays of George Bernard Shaw will show you ways of masking highly didactic notions with wit and satire. Reading plays from all periods will be far more profitable for you than any number of "how to" books on technique.

Some playwrights will help you more than others, but that is true of all teachers. Remember that they have faced the same problems you will, considered some of the same options you will. Let them be your guide. With their help, you will acquire the ability to develop your own individual vision and your particular voice for a play that is uniquely yours.

A

TROUBLESHOOTING GUIDE:

Topics for Quick Review

When your work seems weak in a particular area, consider reviewing the topic in this textbook. This Troubleshooting Guide is designed to help you. It is arranged by genre (poetry, fiction, and drama) with subheadings grouped alphabetically by topic for easy access.

This guide may also be useful for instructors in creative writing. Simply add "Please review pages . . ." in comments on student work. It will not only help students to revise effectively, it will suggest topics for discussion in conferences.

As the title implies, this list is limited to common problem areas. For a more complete and precise listing of specific terms and concepts, use the Glossary-Index at the end of this text. It lists alphabetically all the literary terms mentioned in this text along with brief definitions.

Poetry

DICTION (WORD CHOICE)

Fiction

Drama

Themes (same as central concern)

Thesis plays: social and political issues

Tone

B

SUBMITTING WORK FOR PUBLICATION

Myths about publishing. Judging whether one is ready to submit material. Mechanical considerations: the manuscript, keeping records. Computers. What to submit. Where to submit: listings, agents, small presses, double submissions. Marketing plays. A planned approach to publication.

Some novice writers submit material long before there is any chance of publication; an equal number are reluctant to submit even though they are ready. The sad fact is that even writers who have taken creative writing courses often know very little about marketing.

First, let's clear away a number of myths about publishing. One hears, for example, that nothing is published without "pull," that neither fiction nor drama can succeed without sex and violence, that poetry must be obscure to gain critical approval, that agents are unreliable, that book publishers are only interested in the bottom line, and that you have to live in New York to publish a play. Even more fanciful is the notion that if a piece of writing is really good it will be published without serious effort on the part of the writer.

Publication is no more fair than life itself. There will always be good works that are not accepted and incompetent material that is. But be assured that if talent, practice, and a practical system of submission are combined, one can alter the odds in one's favor.

There are two tests that will help you to decide whether you are ready to submit material. First, you should have written in that particular genre for some time. When you read that a story is an author's first publication, it doesn't mean that he or she is a novice. In most cases, the author has been writing for years. So-called "first novels" usually have been preceded by considerable practice in short stories and quite frequently by one or two unpublished novels as well.

The second test is whether you have been a regular reader. I have repeatedly stressed the need to read carefully and regularly in the genre of your choice. Writers who do not spend twice as much time reading as they do writing are at an enormous disadvantage. They risk settling into a rut, repeating themselves in style and content. Successful writers and poets are almost always perpetual students. Through reading they are not only discovering new approaches for their own work, they are getting to know individual magazines and book publishers.

If you have been writing for some time and have been an active, conscientious reader, you may be ready for the long and sometimes frustrating process of submitting material.

Mechanical Considerations

Almost all writers today use computers. Even if you are one of the few who own a typewriter, your final copy should be typed or printed on standard white paper. For fiction, everything but your name and address should be double spaced. Poetry can be single spaced. Use pica type, 10 characters to the inch (cpi), not elite or 12 cpi. If in doubt, check with a ruler.

Resist the strong temptation to use fancy type, italics, gothic, or script. These suggest that you are an eager amateur. With all manuscript submissions, underline the material that is to be printed in italics. (Don't use italic font unless you have been asked to submit a diskette.) Don't vary your type size, since editors like to estimate the word count if you haven't provided it.

In the case of stories and poems, don't use a separate title page. Instead, place your name and address on the left of the first page about two inches down from the top. Type "Fiction" or "A Poem" on the right. Some authors add the word count and social security number there, but this is not essential. Poets often give the number of lines.

The only exception to this is when you are submitting to a contest that is to be judged "blind." In those cases, you must include two title pages, one with the title, your address, and phone number, and the other with title only. In such cases, no indication of your name should appear after that initial sheet.

The title is usually centered, in capital letters (not underlined or placed in quotation marks) about a third of the way down the page. Your name and address are single spaced, and all fiction is double spaced. Here is how it looks:

```
Woody B. Grate                          Fiction
205 Main St.                            5,280 wds.
Middletown, IL 62666                    015-42-3642



                        LOOKING FORWARD
```

The story begins two double-space lines spaces below the title. Remember to double space the fiction and indent the first line of each new paragraph three or five spaces.

Separate title pages are used only with novels, collections of stories, or collections of poems. In the case of contest submission, be sure to send for guidelines or download them from the Internet. They will tell you whether the manuscript is to be submitted "blind" or not.

The pages (after the first) should be numbered in Arabic numerals along with your last name in the upper right corner: Smith 2, Smith 3, and so on.

Don't place a story in a folder or binder and do not staple it. A simple paper clip will do unless you are otherwise instructed. Novels are normally sent loose in a box. (Though some contests prefer big elastic bands.)

Covering letters are not necessary with poetry or fiction unless you have something specific to say. If the editor has added a kind word to a previous rejection slip or has actually written a letter, be sure to remind him or her. In any case, be brief and factual. Defending or even explaining one's work is a sure sign of an author's amateur status.

If all this seems rather restrictive, remember that freshness and originality belong in what you write, not the packaging.

Who should you send it to? If you don't know anyone on the staff, merely send the manuscript to the fiction or poetry editor at the address given in the magazine or a directory. But if you have met or corresponded with an editor or even a junior reader, send it to him or her. Be sure to read a current issue. Sending a manuscript to a dead or otherwise departed editor is not a promising start.

For mailing, the envelope should be large enough so that the manuscript need not be folded. If you buy $9\frac{1}{2}'' \times 12\frac{1}{2}''$ envelopes for sending, you can include a $9' \times 12''$ self-addressed, stamped envelope (SASE) for its return. If this is too complicated, merely fold the second $9'' \times 12''$ envelope so that it can be placed inside the first with the manuscript. In either case, be sure that your address and proper postage are on it. Failure to do so not only irritates the editor but increases your chances of never seeing it again.

Poems and stories are sent first class. Novels are wrapped or boxed and sent in padded mailers. "Media mail" is what they now call book rate and is slightly cheaper, but it is slow and unreliable. Priority mail is preferred. United Parcel Service rates vary by zone and may be cheaper in some cases, but some contests forbid its use for unknown reasons.

In awaiting a reply, allow about two months for poetry and short stories and an agonizing three months for novels. (The waiting period gets longer every year and is in some cases six months!) Resist the temptation to inquire about work sent until at least twice the expected time has passed.

Keeping records is extremely important. It is impossible to remember what went out when and to which magazine if you don't keep a submissions notebook. In addition, it is invaluable to record not only which editors had a kind word or two, but which magazines sent specifically worded rejection slips.

The lowest level of rejection slip is merely a printed statement saying that they appreciated receiving your work but were unable to use it. In addition, most magazines have one or two special slips with wording like "this was of particular interest to us" or "we hope to see more of your work." Take these seriously. Next on the scale is the penned comment on the bottom of the slip like "good dialogue" or "try us again." These are infuriatingly brief, but they are worth recording. Be careful, however, not to inundate a magazine with weekly submissions. An editor who has commented on one poem is not going to be impressed with a flood of inferior work. Treat such individuals as potential allies who deserve only your best efforts.

The highest point on this rejection scale is the *letter*. Even if brief, this is close to acceptance. If they suggest specific revisions that seem appropriate, revise and resubmit. If they don't, send your next really good piece. These are two situations in which you should definitely include a short covering letter.

Computers: For the Uninitiated

If you already work with a computer, skip this section. If you don't, read it carefully. Should you get one? If you spend four or more hours a week writing prose or poetry and can afford the investment, you are foolish not to buy a computer. In most undergraduate writing classes today, almost no one uses a typewriter.

A computer will not create a good writer any more than a new car will produce a good driver. But it will certainly aid in your process of development. The ease of revision will without question improve the quality of your work. You will find yourself going through many more revisions than when each one had to be retyped. Moving blocks of fiction or lines of poetry is done quickly and painlessly, and two versions of the same scene or stanza can be compared instantly by flipping from one document to the other. Best of all, what you see is always a neat, clear draft. You can read it at a steady pace, judging the flow accurately.

In addition, you can keep a record of everything you have done on diskettes with backup copies stored elsewhere. This is your best insurance against loss.

There are three disadvantages that no computer magazine will warn you about. First, your typing accuracy will deteriorate. Corrections are so easy to make that you become permanently careless. (It is for language what a calculator is for basic math.) The spell check will lull you into false confidence. It is no substitute for proofreading since it is illiterate when it comes to spotting fifth-grade errors like confusing *its* and *it's* or *to*, *two* and *too*.

Second, your computer *will* die with no warning at some point. It will plunge all your work into oblivion. I stress *will*, not *when*. In addition, even a three-second break in electrical power (increasingly common) will delete what you have not saved. Your only safeguard is making backup copies on diskettes and updating them at least daily. (I do this every hour.) This is hard to remember until you have an entire story or even a novel simply disappear permanently and (contrary to claims) irretrievably. It will take one major disaster before you start to update your backup copy regularly.

Finally, you will bore all your noncomputing friends. Conversationally, computers are as addictive as baseball.

What kind to buy? That's a big topic, but here are some basic guidelines:

- Talk with friends about their computer experiences. Often they will tell you more than you really want to hear. Ask them not only what computer they recommend but what software package they prefer. The software is like a language, and you will be investing time to master it.
- If your primary need is writing, don't spend extra money for capabilities required by business firms, chemical laboratories, and computer-game freaks. Encyclopedias that talk are of use only for illiterates. There is a real temptation to be swept into more capabilities than you will ever use.
- Watch out for the incredibly cheap computer price that is tied to an expensive three-year Internet contract. (For a while, computers were being given away free in return for such contracts!) No one will tell you that by accepting a limited number of hours a month on the Web can cut your monthly charge in half.
- If it is your first purchase, stick to major brands that offer a full-year guarantee, and make sure it is in writing. Unlike automobiles, computers are just as likely to have major breakdowns in the first year as in the third. To be specific, I had a nationally known, highly recommended computer that had to be junked in precisely 364 days of moderate use. It was replaced but would not have been the following Monday.
- Beware the Web! Yes, it has some educational value when used with specific goals in mind. But for some people, surfing becomes a black hole, sucking up all available free time. Serious writers are always short of time and have to be on guard against all types of addiction.

What to Submit

This decision must rest ultimately with you. Although the advice of other serious writers can be helpful, don't be swayed by friends who are not themselves serious writers. Classmates or neighbors who never read sophisticated fiction or poetry are not going to be very helpful as critics.

This does not hold for play scripts, however. Since such work is designed to reach larger audiences, the advice of nonwriters may be of real value.

Poets should select a group of three or four carefully revised poems to be submitted as a packet. Writers of fiction should limit each submission to one story. Once the choice is made, send the work out repeatedly. A single editorial rejection means absolutely nothing. A manuscript is not "dead" until it has been turned down by at least ten or fifteen magazines.

The best approach is to send the work out on the very day it is returned. Otherwise you are apt to lose courage. As a practical matter, just as many manuscripts are accepted after six or eight rejections as after only one. This is largely due to the fact that so many nonliterary factors go into selecting a work for publication, such as the number and kind of manuscripts on hand, the balance of a particular issue, and the personal preferences of the first reader. Once the decision is made to send a work out, stand by it until you have cumulative proof that the work is unpublishable.

Where to Submit

Don't submit "blind"—that is, to magazines you haven't read. Directories such as those listed in Appendix C can be helpful, but they won't tell you enough to make a judgment as to whether a particular magazine is your kind of publication. "Blind submissions" not only waste your time and money, they are a terrible burden for the editors, who frequently work for little or no salary.

As I have suggested in earlier chapters, the place to start studying publications is your nearest library. Pick out the literary quarterlies. Since there will be a confusing array of magazines, you may want to use the list of literary journals in Appendix C as a guide. Look these magazines over and make a list of those that print work like yours. Note approximately how many poems and how many stories they print, the poetry or fiction editor, and the address. Directories (including the one in Appendix C) cannot be perfectly current.

Mainstream novels—those aimed at a broad audience—should be circulated through a literary agent, a topic I will turn to shortly. You are on your own, however, with innovative or experimental novels, collections of stories, and book-length collections of poetry. Look over your own shelves and list the publishers who handle work that is somewhat similar to yours. Then do the same in a bookstore. Next, look up the addresses of the publishers in *The International Directory of Little Magazines and Small Presses*. Major presses are listed in *Literary Market Place* (known as *LMP*).

If you are circulating a book-length collection of stories, a novel, or a collections of poems, you will save a great deal of time, postage, and frustration by sending a query letter first. Small, independent presses are only able to publish a few titles a year, and you have to catch them the very month they are open to new submissions. A great majority of your letters will bring you a negative response, and a surprising number won't be answered at all, but this is far better than having your manuscript tied up for half a year. Query letters should be no longer than one page. Simply describe the work in positive (but not glowing) terms and enclose a bibliography. You can include sample poems, a story, or a chapter, but this is not necessary unless your list of previous publications is very scant.

Once you have decided to send out a book-length manuscript, keep submitting it until you have been rejected by at least 13 or 14 publishers. This will take about three years—time enough for you to complete the next novel or collection.

Circulating novels and book-length collections of short works raises four questions that are asked at every writers' conference. First, what about *vanity presses*? A vanity press is a for-profit publishing firm that charges the author for all publication costs. Distribution is largely or entirely up to the author. Many such organizations are perfectly honest, but some make promises about distribution and sales potential that are fanciful. Since all the costs plus their profit margin will be paid by you, be sure to read their proposed contract very carefully.

Cooperative presses are quite different. They are generally nonprofit and run by individuals who love books and are willing to live a marginal economic life to work with them. Such presses are used less for novels, but they are a growing outlet for collections of poems and stories. The author still has to pay, but because no one is making a profit, the investment is liable to be less. It is a shared venture.

Another question raised by those submitting book-length manuscripts is whether it is appropriate to make use of a personal contact at a publishing house. Yes, it most certainly is. Even if your acquaintance is not in the editorial department, submit through him or her. Using such a connection probably won't get a bad manuscript published, but it may bypass that first reader who has a great many manuscripts to review. In the case of rejections, the writer is apt to receive a lengthier comment if the reader has some personal interest. I can testify to the fact that such personal contact is not a prerequisite for having stories or novels accepted; but it is neither unethical nor a waste of time to make use of any interested reader or publisher.

Third, should you submit copies of the same work to different publishers at the same time? Not unless the publisher has specifically stated in a directory "multiple submissions accepted." An increasing number of magazine editors have adopted this policy and even a few small publishers, but most have not. You will read tantalizing reports about agents submitting a novel manuscript to a group of publishers simultaneously in what is called a "brokered offering," but that is only done for nationally known authors whose previous works have sold extremely well.

Generally speaking, book publishers assume that if they accept a novel, they are investing in an author. Standard contracts usually insist on a first refusal on whatever book-length manuscript you may submit next. This does not apply to individual stories or poems, but most editors assume that if they are going to spend time reading and evaluating a manuscript, they are the only ones considering it. Some authors do take a chance, however, and double submit. But remember that the publishing world is small and closely connected. Becoming known as one who double submits is like having a bad credit rating—it's hard to correct. If in doubt, send a query letter.

Finally, what about agents? Don't even consider using an agent if you write short stories intended primarily for little magazines or poetry of any sort. Placing material in literary quarterlies is an honor well worth struggling for, but they pay relatively little (or none at all), and an agent's 10 or 15 percent of relatively little (or nothing) is not enough to cover postage. Agents, unlike writers, cannot afford to work for love alone.

On the other hand, you *should* consider looking for an agent if you have completed a mainstream novel or if you have a group of five or six potentially publishable stories that might be considered by quality magazines (*The Atlantic The New Yorker,* or *Esquire* or the men's magazines (*Playboy, Penthouse*). Manuscripts submitted to such magazines through agencies usually receive more careful scrutiny by readers with more editorial authority. Many agents, however, no longer deal with short fiction at all.

Most reputable agents are now charging a flat 15 percent of all material sold through them and make no other charges whatever, regardless of how much postage or time they spend. In return, they expect to handle all your work. A few agents are now requiring a "reading fee" for unpublished writers. Don't confuse this with a "criticism fee," for which you will receive a critical report. Watch out for those who charge "overhead"— additional fees. Although this may become a growing trend, the basic 15 percent contract is still the standard.

If you are unpublished, it will be difficult but not impossible to find an agent. Some writers try to place their first book and then secure an agent to handle the contract when it is offered by a publisher. Others send query letters to many different agents (addresses in *LMP* and *Novel & Short Story Writer's Manual*, Writer's Digest Books) describing the completed manuscript they hope to place. It is perfectly all right to send out many query letters at the same time. Be sure to ask them to recommend another agent if they cannot take on your work themselves. Occasionally they will recommend a younger agent who is looking for new clients.

Marketing a play requires a somewhat different approach. There are four basic techniques that can be adopted separately or together:

- *Enter play contests.* The best listings are in the *Dramatists Sourcebook* (Theater Communications Group, 355 Lexington Ave., New York, NY 10017). This annual is fully revised each August. In addition, consider *Poets and Writers Magazine* (201 W. 54th St., New York, NY 10019).
- *Submit to theaters.* Again, use the *Dramatists Sourcebook.* Another listing appears in *Writer's Market* (Writer's Digest Books), but it is much shorter. Each theater has special needs, requirements, and deadlines, so read the fine print carefully.
- *Work with a theater group.* Any theater experience will be useful. In addition, you will meet people who will guide you. Even as a volunteer you will benefit.
- *Submit to publishers of plays.* The two major publishers are Baker's Plays and Samuel French (their addresses are in Appendix C). They accept many new plays (mostly mainstream) each year. If you are offered a contract, consider the terms carefully.

There is probably no other branch of the arts more committed to personal contact than drama. "Networking" is the polite word; more bluntly, "pull." If you know a producer, director, actor, or even a stagehand, write to him or her. This situation is not necessarily a matter of commercial corruption. The fact is that although book publishers come to know potential writers through little magazines (which they read with professional care), producers have no such resource. They may be completely unaware of a playwright whose work has appeared in small theaters in some other state. This situation will continue until there are more little magazines willing to specialize in original play scripts. Meanwhile, playwrights must struggle with the particularly difficult task of getting known through word of mouth.

Writers of fiction, poetry, and drama all have to adopt a realistic attitude toward publication. It is naive to assume that marketing your work is crass and demeaning. Publishers have no way of discovering you if you make no effort to circulate your work. On the other hand, a mania to publish at all costs can be damaging to the creative process. It often leads to imitative and conventional work and to feelings of hostility toward editors and publishers.

To avoid these most unrewarding extremes, begin with an honest evaluation of your own work. Then follow through with a planned, long-range program of submissions. There are, of course, writers who achieve wide recognition very suddenly; but this is rare and not always a blessing. Ideally, creative work is a way of life, and the effort to publish is an important though not a central portion of that life.

C

RESOURCES FOR WRITERS

General Reference Books

The following six reference books are annuals of particular interest to writers of fiction and poetry. They can be found in most libraries. A specialized directory and information book for dramatists is described in the drama section of this appendix.

- *The International Directory of Little Magazines & Small Presses*, Dustbooks. By far the most inclusive listing of little magazines, quarterlies, literary journals, and small presses. It devotes a paragraph to each magazine, describing what it publishes and listing names of editors, payment scale, and the like. It gives cross-listings by subject, genre, and region. It does not list large-circulation magazines or major publishers. There are no "how-to" articles. Strongly recommended.

- *Directory of Poetry Publishers*, Dustbooks. A specialized version of the above. It provides information on more than 2,000 book and magazine publishers of poetry.

- *Literary Marketplace*, R. R. Bowker Co. *LMP* does not list magazines, but it remains the most authoritative annual listing of mainstream book publishers, literary agents, writers' conferences, and addresses of those in publishing. It is entirely factual and does not contain articles on how to write or market your material. It costs over $200, but most libraries have it.

- *Novel & Short Story Writer's Market*, Writer's Digest Books. A representative listing of book publishers and periodicals with a paragraph on each. It is far more complete than *The Writer's Handbook* (listed below) but less complete (and slightly cheaper) than *The International Directory* from Dustbooks. A valuable source for fiction writers in spite of many commercial listings. [Note: Don't confuse this with *Writer's Market*, also from Writer's Digest. Although it has a helpful list of agents and theaters looking for plays, the volume is dominated by consumer magazines (aviation, sports, travel) and trade magazines (pest control, podiatry management).]

• *Poet's Market,* Writer's Digest Books. More complete than *The Writer's Handbook* (listed below) but less complete than *The International Directory* from Dustbooks. Valuable for poetry writers in spite of many commercial listings.

• *The Writer's Handbook,* The Writer, Inc. Much of this annual is devoted to brief and basic "how-to" articles on all aspects of writing. Most are written for the beginner with an emphasis on commercial markets. The list of literary magazines is less extensive than any of the volumes listed previously.

Informative Magazines

These magazines provide information and advice for writers, poets, and, to a lesser degree, dramatists. They do not generally publish fiction or poetry. Consult library copies for current subscription rates.

• *AWP Chronicle,* Tallwood House, Mail Stop 1E3, Fairfax, VA 22030-0079. Published by Associated Writing Programs; tabloid format; six times a year. Articles, interviews, criticism, and news items about writers, poets, creative writing programs, contest winners, and the teaching of writing. Circulation 13,000.

• *Poets and Writers Magazine,* 72 Spring St., New York, NY 10012. This non-profit publication is a must for anyone who writes poetry or fiction. It is published six times a year. Its articles deal with problems faced by all literary writers: how to find time to write when teaching, how to arrange readings, publishing translations, dealing with small presses. It is also the best source of contest and grant application deadlines, dates of conferences and readings, and winners of awards. Circulation: 58,000.

• *Publishers Weekly,* 205 E. 42nd St., New York, NY 10017. Of particular interest to those in the business end of publishing, this magazine covers which books are about to be released, who is doing what in the field, author profiles, and future trends.

• *The Writer,* 8 Arlington St., Boston, MA 02116. This monthly focuses more on mass markets than does *Poets and Writers Magazine.* Articles give advice on writing and marketing a great variety of material from gothic novels to "confessionals" and from poetry to greeting-card verse.

• *Writer's Digest,* 1507 Dana Ave., Cincinnati, OH 45207. Fiction and verse outlets. Similar in emphasis to its competitor, *The Writer* (above).

Large-Circulation Magazines: Fiction and Poetry

Although these four large-circulation magazines are primarily devoted to in-depth articles and reviews, they also publish one or two stories and a couple of poems in each issue. Even though beginners are not encouraged to submit, everyone interested in contemporary fiction and poetry (and social issues) will benefit from subscribing to at least one.

- *The Atlantic.* A distinguished monthly. Usually one story and one or two poems each issue.
- *Esquire.* Usually one story each issue. Published fortnightly.
- *Harpers.* A monthly. Usually one story and a poem along with articles, features, reviews.
- *The New Yorker.* A weekly except for one double issue. Normally one story each week; more in the annual fiction issue. Some find the magazine's drift toward the trendy disappointing, but it is still a major source for serious fiction and poetry as well as significant nonfiction.

Little Magazines: Poetry and Fiction

These magazines, also known as *literary journals* and *quarterlies* (though they may appear from one to six times a year), publish fiction, poetry, articles, and reviews in varying proportions. The following list, a small sampling of the many fine literary journals being published today, has been selected especially for writers of fiction and poetry. They should all be available in your public or university library. (If not, urge your librarian to add the missing titles.) Be sure to read at least one copy before submitting. Collectively, they offer a valuable picture of what is being written today. If you take creative writing seriously, subscribe to at least two. Subscription rates are generally less than one forgettable evening at a restaurant.

- *Agni*, Boston University, 236 Bay State Rd., Boston, MA 02215. Fiction, poetry, and excerpts from novels; two issues a year. Submit Oct. 1 to Apr. 30 only.
- *American Poetry Review*, 1721 Walnut St., Philadelphia, PA 19103. Mostly poetry and articles about poetry; some fiction, art, interviews. Six times a year in tabloid form; larger circulation than most little magazines.
- *Beloit Fiction Journal*, Box 11, Beloit College, Beloit, WI 53511. Fiction only. Accepts short-shorts. One issue a year.
- *Beloit Poetry Journal*, 24 Berry Cove Rd., Lamoine, ME ME 04605. All poetry; a quarterly established in 1950.
- *The Black Warrior Review*, P.O. Box 862936, University of Alabama, Tuscaloosa, AL 35486-0027. A balance of fiction poetry, art, interviews, reviews; two issues a year.

- *Field*, 10 N. Professor St., Oberlin College, Oberlin, OH 44074. Devoted to poetry (including long poems) and essays on poetry. Two issues a year.

- *The Georgia Review*, University of Georgia, Athens, GA 30602-9009. A balance of fiction, poetry, interviews, criticism, reviews. Highly competitive.

- *The Gettysburg Review*, Gettysburg College, Gettysburg, PA 17325. Fiction, poetry, articles, satire.

- *Glimmer Train*, 710 SW Madison St., Suite 504, Portland, OR 97205-2900. A quarterly. Fiction and an occasional interview. Send **SASE** for submission guidelines or download from www.glimmertrain.com.

- *Indiana Review*, Ballantine Hall 465, 1020 E. Kirkwood Ave., Bloomington, IN 47405. Fiction, poetry, literary essays.

- *The Missouri Review*, 1507 Hillcrest Hall, University of Missouri, Columbia, MO 65211. Fiction, poetry, articles, interviews, reviews. Three issues a year.

- *New England Review*, Middlebury College, Middlebury, VT 05753. Fiction, poetry, articles, longer poems, and parts of novels.

- *The North American Review*, University of Northern Iowa, Cedar Falls, IA 50614. Mostly fiction. No postmodern work. Some poetry and nonfiction. Founded in 1815, it is the nation's oldest quarterly yet thoroughly contemporary.

- *Paris Review*, 541 E. 72nd St., New York, NY 10021. Fiction primarily; also poetry, articles; famous for its interviews with authors and poets. Circulation 10,000. Allow a shocking eight months for a decision.

- *Ploughshares*, Emerson College, 120 Boylston St.. Boston, MA 02116. Poetry and fiction primarily; revolving editorship. Check current issue for future plans.

- *Poetry*, 60 West Walton St., Chicago, IL 60610. Poetry and reviews. Twelve issues a year. Informally known as "Poetry Chicago."

- *Poetry East*, Department of English, DePaul University, 802 W. Belden Ave., Chicago, IL 60614. Mainly poetry; also fiction, articles, interviews, criticism. Some issues limited to a particular topic.

- *The Poetry Miscellany*, English Department, University of Tennessee, Chattanooga, TN 37403. Mostly poetry with some interviews, criticism, reviews. An impressive list of contributors.

- *Prairie Schooner*, 201 Andrews Hall, University of Nebraska, Lincoln, NE 68588-0334. Fiction, poetry, articles, interviews.

- *Sewanee Review*, University of the South, 735 University Ave., Sewanee, TN 37383-1000. Articles, fiction, poetry in about that order.

- *StoryQuarterly*, 431 Sheridan Rd., Kenilworth, IL 60043-1220. A book-sized volume of stories published as an annual anthology. Recent issues contained over 40 titles each. Used in many creative writing courses.

- *TriQuarterly*, Northwestern University Press, 2020 Ridge, Evanston, IL 60208. Fiction, poetry, criticism. Tends to be innovative or experimental. Read first; then write for contributors' guidelines.

- *The Virginia Quarterly Review*, One West Range, Charlottesville, VA 22903. Several stories in each issue. Also poetry, articles, and reviews in about that order. Established in 1925.

Poetry Anthologies

Anthologies contain the works of many different writers. The following will introduce you to a wide variety of contemporary poets. *Collections*, on the other hand, are limited to the work of one author or poet. Use anthologies to browse and explore. Get to know those whose work you enjoy. Then consider collections of those writers you particularly admire. You can order them through your local (preferably independent) bookstore or through the Internet at www.barnesandnoble.com or www.amazon.com. If a title is out of print, check those two for used copies or try www.bookgarden.com.

Collections are often available (without shipping charges) at poetry readings as well. Owning your own copy will allow you to study the poet's work at leisure.

- *The Best American Poetry*, Scribner. An annual with different editors each year. An excellent survey of current work.
- *Contemporary American Poetry*, A. Poulin Jr., ed., Houghton Mifflin (paperback). This extensive paperback collection offers a good variety of poets. Women and black poets are well represented. It is frequently adopted for college courses.
- *The Harvard Book of Contemporary American Poetry*, Helen Vendler, ed., Harvard University Press. This is a solid collection compiled by a distinguished critic, but it is not available in paperback.
- *No More Masks! An Anthology of Twentieth-Century American Women Poets*, Florence Howe, ed., Anchor/Doubleday. Fortunately back in print as a new edition. More than 100 poets from Amy Lowell to Rita Dove.
- *Poems for the Millennium*, J. Rothenberg and P. Joris, eds., University of California Press. Highly experimental and innovative poetry from the modern and postmodern schools. No metered or rhymed poetry.
- *Strong Measures: Contemporary American Poetry in Traditional Forms*, P. Dacey and D. Jauss, eds. Harper and Row. This 492-page paperback is devoted to poetry in a great variety of metrical forms. There is no free verse. It includes a useful appendix with helpful definitions of metrical terms. The emphasis is in sharp contrast with *Poems for the Millennium* (above).
- *Vintage Book of Contemporary American Poetry*, J. D. McClatchy, ed. Each poet is represented by several poems, a valuable policy.

Poets Writing About Their Craft

By far the best way to learn from poets is to read their poetry itself; but after you have done that, it is often helpful to read what they have written in prose about their craft. Here is a brief sampling:

- *Letters to a Young Poet*, Rainer Maria Rilke; paperback editions of this classic still available from both Norton and New World Library.

- *On the Poet and His Craft: Selected Prose of Theodore Roethke*, Ralph J. Mills, ed., University of Washington Press. Out of print but still available on the Web.
- *Poetry and the Age*, Randall Jarrell, Echo Press.
- *The Triggering Town, Lectures and Essays on Poetry and Writing*, Richard Hugo, Norton.
- *Twentieth Century Pleasures: Prose on Poetry*, Robert Hass, Echo Press.

Listening to Poetry

There are two ways to hear poets read their own work. First, attend poetry readings. Most colleges and universities offer poetry readings that are open to the public. So do many libraries. Coffeehouses often have "open mike" evenings in which anyone may read. Poets also read at writers' conferences (listings in *LMP*; ads in *Poets and Writers*).

The second approach is through recordings. Most libraries have good audio- and videocassette collections. Compact discs and tapes may also be ordered through good music stores or the Internet. Recordings allow you to locate and then follow a printed version of each poem. You can also repeat a poem or a stanza as many times as you wish.

Fiction Anthologies

There are two widely read annual anthologies of short stories published in magazines during the previous year. While no two editors will agree on the "best" stories published in any year, these volumes provide a fine overview of good contemporary fiction.

- *The Best American Short Stories*, Houghton Mifflin. This volume has been published annually since 1915. Edited for 36 years by Martha Foley, the collection is still referred to informally as "the Foley collection." The editorship is now changed each year.
- *Prize Stories: The O. Henry Awards*, Larry Dark, ed., Doubleday. Better known as "the O. Henry collection," this is another view of the best fiction published during the previous year. It serves as an excellent companion work to *The Best American Short Stories*.

In addition to these two annuals, there are many short-story anthologies of recent work designed mainly for college use. They offer a broader yet still contemporary selection.

- *Look Who's Talking*, Bruce Weber, ed., Pocket Books. An inexpensive collection of American stories from the 1930s to the present, many with a strong sense of voice. Out of print, but used copies still available on the Web at last report.

- *Norton Anthology of Contemporary Fiction*, R. V. Cassill and J. C. Oates, eds. Norton. A solid collection of fairly recent fiction.
- *The Scribner Anthology of Contemporary Short Fiction*, Lex Williford, ed., Scribner. Fifty American stories since 1970 with emphasis on the 1980s and '90s.
- *Sudden Fiction*, R. Shapard and J. Thomas, eds., Gibbs Smith. All stories under 2,000 words. Uneven quality, but some excellent.
- *You've Got to Read This*, Ron Hansen and Jim Shepard, eds, Harper. A variety of stories, mostly 20*th* century, each with an introduction.
- *Vintage Book of Contemporary American Short Stories*, Tobias Wolff, ed., Vintage.

As with poetry anthologies, these volumes will introduce you to a variety of work. When you find an author you admire, see if he or she has published a collection of stories. In many cases you can find such volumes in your local library. If you wish to order your own copy, turn to the "Author" section of *Books in Print* in your library, or check one of the Web sites such as amazon.com or barnesandnoble.com.

A number of university presses publish collections of short stories by a single author in paperback. Among these are The Johns Hopkins University Press (Baltimore, MD 21218), the University of Pittsburgh Press (Pittsburgh, PA 15260), and the University of Tennessee Press (Knoxville, TN 37996-0325), among others. Write to these publishers for a list of their short-story collections and prices.

Outside the university, small publishers like the Permanent Press (Noyac Rd., Sag Harbor, NY 11963) and Sarabande Books (Dundee Rd., Suite 200, Louisville, KY 40205) publish new fiction and will provide you with catalogues.

Books about the Craft of Fiction

As in the case of poetry, there is no substitute for reading extensively in the genre itself, but as a supplement here are four works on fiction writing that will be useful:

- *The Art of Fiction: Notes on Craft for Young Writers*, John Gardner, Knopf. Sound advice.
- *Becoming a Writer*, Dorothea Brande, Tarcher. Classic advice regarding attitude and commitment, not specific technique.
- *Writing Down the Bones: Freeing the Writer Within*, Natalie Goldberg, Shambhala (distributed by Random House). Recommended for the hesitant and the inhibited.
- *Writing Fiction: A Guide to Narrative Craft*, Janet Burroway, Addison-Wesley.

Books for Playwrights

- *Best American Short Plays*, Applause Theater Book Publishers. This annual has been published for over half a century. Back issues can be found in many libraries.
- *Dramatists Sourcebook*, Theater Communications Group, 355 Lexington Ave., New York, NY 10017. This annual is fully revised each August. It contains a wealth of current information including submission policies of many theaters, contests, and the like. It is the basic source of information for any playwright.
- *One Act: 11 Short Plays of the Modern Theatre*, Samuel Moon, ed., Grove Atlantic and Econo-Clad Books. A good variety of twentieth-century short plays including some innovative work, but none more recent than the 1970s.
- *Take 10, New 10-Minute Plays*, Eric Lane, ed., David Mckay. Thirty-two short plays. Great variety.
- *Twenty-Four Favorite One-Act Plays*, Van Catmell and Bennett Cerf, eds., Doubleday. A paperback collection containing a variety of fairly traditional plays from the past 100 years.

Publishers of Play Scripts

This list includes publishers who buy, print, and sell play scripts or simply publish scripts. Most include both one-act and full-length works. Those that deal largely with schools and regional companies prefer traditional work. Check *Dramatists Sourcebook* for Web sites and E-mail addresses.

- *Baker's Plays*, P.O. Box 699222, Quincy, MA 02269. In business since 1845, Baker's Plays offers not only a great many light comedies and mysteries for younger audiences, but also a number of serious dramas that have had Broadway success. Their scripts are relatively inexpensive to buy and offer a good way to study plays not found in drama anthologies. They accept unsolicited manuscripts (those not sent through agents). Theatrical related material only.
- *Confrontation*, Martin Tucker, ed., English Department, C. W. Post College of Long Island University, Greenvale, NY 11548. Publishes one-acts for "literate" audiences.
- *Contemporary Drama Service*, Theodore Zapel, ed., Meriweather Publishing, Ltd., P.O. Box 7710, Colorado Springs, CO 80933 (E-mail: merpcds@aol.com). Publishes 50–60 plays a year, many short. Prefers comedies. Query with synopsis.
- *The Dramatic Publishing Co.*, P.O. Box 129, Woodstock, IL 60098. Established in 1885, this company prints 40 to 60 titles a year.
- *Poems & Plays*, Gaylord Brewer, ed., English Department, Middle Tennessee State University, Murfreesboro, TN 37132. Publishes one-acts and short plays and poetry. An annual. Accepts scripts Oct. 1 to Dec. 31 only.

- *Prism International*, Chris LaBonte and Andrea MacPherson, eds., Creative Writing Program, University of British Columbia, Burch E462-1866 Main Mall, Vancouver, BC, Canada V6T 1Z1. Publishes one-acts and excerpts from full-length plays up to 40 pages.
- *Samuel French, Inc.*, 45 W. 25th St., New York, NY 10010. The oldest (1830) of these three venerable publishing houses, Samuel French, has branches in England and Canada and publishes about 50 titles a year.

Although there are relatively few periodicals that publish plays, there are more than 100 theaters that read new scripts for possible production. They are listed in *Dramatists Sourcebook* (best list) and *Writers Market* (less complete), both previously described.

Remember, finally, that if your interest is in play writing, it is essential that you see as many productions as you can. Whenever possible, combine your study of the script with seeing the work performed. Each approach will provide insights the other cannot.

A Final Note

If you are in college, it will seem as if you have no time to do anything but complete your assignments. And if you are out of college, you may find yourself being swept along with the demands of daily life. We all like to believe that we "have no choice." But the fact is that the allocation of time is fundamentally a matter of personal choice. Consciously or unconsciously we set priorities. Serious writers allocate time not only to write but to expand their abilities and vision through these resources.

CREDITS

Allen, Dick, "The Narrow Mind" is reprinted from ODE TO THE COLD WAR: POEMS NEW AND SELECTED, published by Sarabande Books, Inc. © 1997 by Dick Allen. Reprinted by permission of Sarabande Books and the author.

Allen, Paula Gunn, LIFE IS A FATAL DISEASE. Albuquerque: West End Press, 1997.

Alterman, Glenn, "Coulda, Woulda, Shoulda." Copyright © 1996. Reprinted with permission of the playwright.

Amis, Kingsley, "A Tribute to the Founder" (fragment) from A LOOK ROUND THE ESTATE, Harcourt, Brace. Copyright © by Kingsley Amis 1962-1967. Reprinted by permission of the author.

Angelou, Maya, "This Winter Day" from OH PRAY MY WINGS ARE GONNA FIT ME WELL. Copyright © 1975 by Maya Angelou. Used by permission of Random House, Inc.

Appleman, Philip, "Desire"from LET THERE BE LIGHT published by HarperCollins. Copyright © by Philip Appleman 1991. Reprinted by permission of Philip Appleman. "Coast to Coast"from LET THERE BE LIGHT published by HarperCollins. Copyright © by Philip Appleman 1991. Reprinted by permission of Philip Appleman.

Barresi, Dorothy, "Mystery" from ALL OF THE ABOVE. Copyright © 1991 by Dorothy Barresi. Reprinted by permission of Beacon Press, Boston.

Barthelme, Donald, "The Balloon" from UNSPEAKABLE PRACTICES, UNNATURAL ACTS, Farrar, Straus and Giroux, 1966. Copyright © 1966 by Donald Barthelme, reprinted with the permission of The Wylie Agency, Inc.

Beilenson, Peter (trans.), "After Spring "(Chora) and "Even with Insects" (Issa) from CHERRY BLOSSOMS, JAPANESE HAIKU, SERIES III. © 1960 by Peter Pauper Press. Reprinted by permission of the publisher.

Bertram, James, "Is It Well Lighted Papa?" is reprinted by kind permission of the author.

Brooks, Gwendolyn, "We Real Cool," © 1991, from BLACKS, published by Third World Press, Chicago. Reprinted by permission of The Estate of Gwendolyn Brooks.

Clifton, Lucille, "What the Mirror Said" by Lucille Clifton. Copyright © 1980, 1987 by Lucille Clifton. First published in AMERICAN RAG, Fall 1978. Now appears in **good woman: poems and a memoir 1969-1980**, published by BOA Editions, Ltd., 1987. Reprinted by permission of Curtis Brown, Ltd.

Cory, Deborah Joy, "Three Hearts" from LOSING EDDIE by Deborah Joy Corey. Copyright © 1993 by the author. Reprinted by permission of Alqonguin Books of Chapel Hill, a division of Workman Publishing.

Cummings, E. E., "Buffalo Bill's." Copyright 1923, 1951, © 1991 by the Trustees for the E.E. Cummings Trust. Copyright © 1976 by George James Firmage, from COMPLETE POEMS: 1904-1962 by E. E. Cummings, edited by George J. Firmage. Used by permission of Liveright Publishing Corporation.

Daviss, Jackson Jodie, "Gotta Dance," by Jackson Jodie Daviss, first appeared in the Summer 1992 edition of STORY. Reprinted by permission of the author.

INDEX OF AUTHORS
AND TITLES

GLOSSARY-INDEX

This section lists alphabetically all literary terms used in this text as well as a few others. For a handy, more concise list of problem areas listed by genre, see the Troubleshooting Guide (Appendix A, page 421). In addition, an Index of Authors and Titles appears on page 451.

This Glossary-Index can be used both for a review of literary terms and as an index. The definitions are limited to the aspects discussed in the text. Numbers refer to pages. The abbreviation ff. indicates that the discussion continues on the following page(s). Words in small capitals indicate a cross-reference either in the same or a closely related form; for example, METERED may be found under Meter, RHYMING under Rhyme.

Abstraction, 3, 57, 280. A word or phrase that refers to a concept or state of being. It is at the opposite end of a scale from *concrete* words (see IMAGE), which refers to objects we can see and touch. *Peace* is an abstraction; *dove* is a concrete word.

Absurdist, 339, 347. See THEATER OF THE ABSURD.

Adjective, 58. A word that modifies (describes) a noun. Similar to *adverb*, a word that modifies a verb. In many cases, finding just the right noun eliminates the need for any modification.

Adverb. See ADJECTIVE.

Allegory, 273, 361. A work of FICTION, VERSE, or DRAMA in which characters, setting, and other details form an all-inclusive SYMBOLIC system. *Pilgrim's Progress* and George Orwell's *Animal Farm* are good examples.

Alliteration, 73, 85, 110. See SOUND DEVICES.

Alliterative verse, 85. A RHYTHMICAL system based on a regular pattern of stressed syllables in each line without regard to the unstressed syllables. It usually employs a CAESURA, a pause, in the middle of most lines. So-called because it traditionally makes regular use of *alliteration* (see SOUND DEVICES). Example: *Beowulf.*

Allusion. A reference, usually brief, to a familiar person or thing, often a detail from literature.

Ambiguity, 136. A THEME or IMAGE in literature that has two or more possible meanings. *Intentional ambiguity* can be used effectively to expand thematic suggestion or increase RESONANCE by suggesting that two or more meanings are equally true or that they combine to suggest a third, broader conclusion. *Unintentional ambiguity* is a weakness usually resulting in confusion of intent or damaging obscurity.

Ambivalence, 49, 149. Conflicting or contrasting emotions that are held at the same time. It may be expressed or implied by the writer or revealed in a character's attitude. Lack of ambivalence sometimes results in SIMPLE WRITING.

Analogy. See METAPHOR AND SIMILE.

Anapestic foot, 88. See METER.

Anaphora, 111ff. Repetition of a word or phrase at the beginning of two or more lines, sentences, or clauses. It is a common RHYTHMICAL technique in FREE VERSE and is also found in some PROSE, especially oratory.

Anecdote, 48, 146, 234. A clever, sometimes humorous account usually told in conversation rather than written. Anecdotal FICTION tends to be SIMPLE, depending more on a twist of events (PLOT) than on CHARACTERIZATION.

Antagonist, 264, 345. A character who opposes the PROTAGONIST in a NARRATIVE work.

Archaic diction, 53. Words that are primarily associated with an earlier period and are no longer in general use.

Arena stage, 374. See STAGE DESIGNS.

Assonance, 73. See SOUND DEVICES.

Author's intrusion, 191ff., 257. Any passage in FICTION written from the author's point of view (see MEANS OF PERCEPTION).

Automatic writing, 159. See STREAM OF CONSCIOUSNESS.

Ballad, 96. A NARRATIVE POEM often (but not always) written in *ballad meter:* quatrains (see STANZAS) of alternating iambic tetrameter and trimeter (see LINE) with a RHYME SCHEME of *abcb. Folk ballads* are often intended to be sung and are relatively SIMPLE. *Literary ballads* are, generally, a SOPHISTICATED use of the old form.

Ballad meter, 96. See BALLAD.

Base time, 202. See PLOT.

Black theater, 411. Plays written by African-Americans. Although playwrights like Langston Hughes and Ossie Davis wrote many works in the 1930s and '40s, the term often refers to those who have come into prominence since the 1960s, such as Amiri Baraka, Paul Carter Harrison, Lonne Elder III, Adrienne Kennedy, and August Wilson.

Black verse, 132. VERSE written by African-Americans such as Lucy Smith, David Henderson, Rita Dove, Lucille Clifton (page 20), Maya Angelou (page 25), Gwendolyn Brooks (page 24), and Nikki Giovanni (page 36).

Blank verse, 93. Unrhyming iambic pentameter (see VERSE and METER).

Breath units, 115. See RHYTHM.

Caesura, 85. A pause or complete break in the RHYTHM of a LINE of VERSE, frequently occurring in the middle. It is particularly noticeable in Old English ALLITERATIVE VERSE (see also SOUND DEVICES) such as *Beowulf*. It is also found in METERED VERSE.

Catalyst, 371. A seemingly minor event or line of dialogue in fiction or drama that nonetheless reveals some aspect of the THEME or advances the plot in some significant way. Sometimes a minor ("flat") character unwittingly serves as catalyst.

Catastrophe, 340. See PLOT.

Central concern, 288. See THEME.

Characterization, 149, 256ff. The technique of creating a fictional character in FICTION, DRAMA, or NARRATIVE POETRY. Basic elements: consistency, complexity, and individuality. SIMPLE characterization stresses consistency at the expense of complexity and often results in a STOCK CHARACTER or a *stereotype*, a form of SIMPLE WRITING. Fully developed characters are called "round" and those that are not are called "flat."

Chronology, 202. See PLOT.

Cinquain, 100. A five-line STANZA, sometimes called a quintet.

Cliché, 63ff., 281. A METAPHOR or simile that has become so familiar from overuse that the vehicle (see METAPHOR) no longer contributes any meaning whatever to the tenor. It provides neither the vividness of a fresh metaphor nor the strength of a single, unmodified word. "Good as gold" and "crystal clear" are clichés. The word is also used informally to describe overused but nonmetaphorical expressions such as "tried and true" and "each and every." See HACKNEYED LANGUAGE.

Climax, 335. See PLOT.

Closure, 265. The reader's sense that a story, novel, or poem has come to a natural or appropriate end. Lack of closure results in the reader's confusion or disbelief.

Comedy, 397ff. DRAMA that is light in TONE and ends happily. Such plays are usually characterized by humor, wit, and occasionally SATIRE. When comedy is used to lighten the TONE of a serious play, it is called *comic relief. Farce* is comedy in which CHARACTERIZATION and PLOT are highly exaggerated for comic effect. *Slapstick* is extremely SIMPLE skit designed only for laughs.

Comic relief, 401ff. See COMEDY.

Commercial fiction, 153. FICTION that is relatively SIMPLE and conforms to certain CONVENTIONS of PLOT and CHARACTER, usually for the sake of wide popularity. Short-story forms include the "pulps" (confessionals and romance periodicals) and the "slicks" (*Cosmo, Redbook, Ladies' Home Journal*). Novel types include "gothic," "romance," and "action thrillers" designed primarily for a mass market.

Conceit. A relatively elaborate or fanciful metaphor. The term is used both in a descriptive sense (as in the conceits of John Donne) or in a negative sense implying artificial complexity.

Concept, 334ff. A brief, factual description of a play (or film script) that describes very briefly the basic plot and characters. It is not to be confused with THEME, which describes in abstract terms the ideas suggested by the work, the portion that comments on the human condition.

Concrete poetry, 110. See SHAPED POETRY.

Concrete words, 57, 281. See ABSTRACTION.

Conflict, 218ff., 345ff. See TENSION.

Connotation, 6. An unstated suggestion implied by a word, phrase, passage, or other element in a LITERARY work. The term ranges from the emotional overtones or implications of a word or phrase to the symbolic significance of a character, setting, or sequence of actions. It is contrasted with *denotation*, the literal meaning.

Conscious irony, 132. See IRONY.

Consonance, 74. See SOUND DEVICES.

Consonant, 73. See VOWEL.

Controlling simile, 118. See METAPHOR.

Convention, 11, 149, 236ff. Any pattern or device in LITERATURE that is repeated in different works by a number of different writers. It is a broad term that includes basic devices like PLOT, DIALOGUE, the division of a play into acts and SCENES, and the FIXED FORMS of POETRY like the SONNET and BALLAD. It also refers to recurring patterns in subject matter. Such conventions can be subtle or HACKNEYED. The term includes everything that is not unique in a work of LITERATURE.

Cooperative press, 435. See VANITY PRESS.

Cosmic irony, 133, 306. See IRONY.

Couplet, 94ff. See STANZA.

Creative nonfiction, 115, 145ff. Factual PROSE in which there is a heightened concern for language and, usually, a degree of personal involvement on the part of the writer. It includes reminiscence, travel, nonacademic history, and informal biography. It is more personal and imaginative than journalism and formal essays and is distinguished from FICTION primarily because it is faithful to actual events, places, and people. Also called *literary nonfiction.*

Creative writing, 145ff. The writing of poetry (see VERSE), FICTION, DRAMA, and CREATIVE NONFICTION. Although all forms of writing require some degree of creativity, *creative writing* (also called *imaginative writing*) implies a high commitment to artistic merit, drawing on LITERARY techniques including STYLE, as opposed to more utilitarian *factual writing* such as analysis, description, and argumentation. Consequently, *creative writing* is used to describe college courses in the writing of these four GENRES and excludes courses in expository writing, assertive writing, journalism, and (usually) COMMERCIAL WRITING.

Crisis, 340. The turning point in a TRAGEDY when the PROTAGONIST's fortunes begin to fail.

Dactylic foot, 89. See METER.

Dead metaphor, 64. A METAPHOR (or by extension a simile) that has entered the language as a word without its former visual association. Unlike a CLICHÉ, it no longer is encumbered by a too-familiar metaphor and so has become built into the language as an independent word acceptable in general usage. Examples: a *current* of electricity, a *cliffhanger* election, *slapstick* comedy, a *seedy* hotel, a *deadline,* to be *stumped.*

Denotation, 6. See CONNOTATION.

Denouement, 340. See PLOT.

Density, 6ff., 300ff. The degree of compression in a poem, play, or work of fiction. High density means that a great deal is implied about character and/or THEME. The PACE may necessarily be slower. Low density reveals less but usually increases the pace.

Deus ex machina, 356. The use of an unexpected and improbable event to solve a problem in drama or fiction. Literally "a god out of a machine," it is an unconvincing turn of events. Occasionally it is used for comic effect.

Dialect, 276. DIALOGUE that echoes a regional or ethnic speech pattern. With some exceptions, it is achieved by word choice and word order rather than the obtrusive use of phonetic spelling.

Dialogue, 151, 238ff. Any word, phrase, or passage that quotes a character's speech directly. In FICTION it normally appears in quotation marks. *Monologue* is reserved for relatively lengthy and uninterrupted speeches. *Soliloquies* are monologues spoken in plays. *Interior monologues* are directly quoted thoughts in fiction or poetry, usually written without quotation marks. *Indirect dialogue* in FICTION (also called *indirect discourse*) echoes the phrasing of dialogue without actually quoting.

Dialogue tag, 239. The phrase that identifies the speaker in fiction such as "he said" or "she said." In 20th century fiction, the repeated use of "said" is preferred to finding alternatives such as "responded," "complained," "cried out," "expostulated."

Diction, 297. The choice of words in any piece of writing. Diction is a significant factor in determining STYLE.

Dimeter, 90. See LINE.

Distance, 128, 135, 203, 258. The aspect of TONE that suggests how close an author (or narrator) appears to be to his or her fictional material. Highly autobiographical and apparently personal work gives the illusion of having very little distance. TRANSFORMING the PROTAGONIST or the SETTING or adding an IRONIC or humorous TONE increases the distance.

Double rhyme, 76. See RHYME.

Drama, 315ff. A NARRATIVE acted by performers on a stage. Drama is generally a "dramatic art" (has emotional impact or force), a visual art, and an auditory art. In contrast to the written script, drama is presented physically on a stage, moves continuously, and is designed for spectators, not readers. A *script* is the written text itself, including the dialogue and brief notations on the action.

Dramatic irony, 133, 305. See IRONY.

Dramatic monologue, 136. A poem (see VERSE) that is presented in the first person as if it were speech or thoughts of a particular character or PERSONA. The speaker often unwittingly reveals aspects of his or her character or attitudes.

Dramatic question, 222ff., 316, 238ff. The emotional element in a play or work of FICTION that holds the attention of an audience or readers. An initial dramatic question is called a *hook*. Dramatic questions are relatively SIMPLE emotional appeals based on withheld information to generate curiosity or SUSPENSE. When dramatic questions are stressed at the expense of THEME or CHARACTERIZATION, the result is usually MELODRAMA.

Dramatic conflict, 345ff. See TENSION.

Elegy, 128. A poem written in a mournful TONE, especially one that is a lament for the dead. The adjective is *elegiac* (pronounced el-i-JI-uk).

Elizabethan sonnet, 98ff. See SONNET.

End-stopped line, 76. See ENJAMBMENT.

Enjambment, 76, 92. LINES in VERSE in which either the grammatical construction or the meaning or both are continued from the end of one line to the next. One function of this technique is to mute the rhythmical effect of METER and/or RHYME. It is contrasted with end-stopped LINES, which are usually terminated with a period or a semicolon.

Epic poem, 6. A long NARRATIVE POEM that deals with mythic, legendary, or historical events and is often FOCUSED on a HERO such as in the *Iliad* and *Beowulf*. Contemporary use has come to apply *epic* to lengthy novels and films often with historical concerns.

Epigram, 94. A brief and pithy saying in VERSE. It may appear as a portion of a longer poem (especially as a couplet) or as a short poem in itself. For example, Goldsmith's warning:

> Ill fares the land, to hastening ills a prey,
> Where wealth accumulates, and men decay.

Epiphany, 205. A moment of awakening or discovery on the part of a FICTIONAL character, the reader, or both. Originally suggested by James Joyce, this term is generally limited to FICTION.

Exit line, 355. In drama, a comic or strikingly dramatic line of DIALOGUE used to conclude a SCENE.

Exposition, 151, 302. Factual writing as in an essay or report. In fiction, it refers to passages that give background information or commentary directly, not through action or dialogue. It is one of the five NARRATIVE MODES.

Expressionism, 363. See REALISTIC DRAMA.

Eye rhyme, 75 See RHYME.

Fable, 273. A short tale in which the characters are usually animals and the theme often suggests a moral. Aesop's fables are among the best known. When the fable form is extended so that all the characters form an overall symbolic system, the result is a type of ALLEGORY such as George Orwell's *Animal Farm*.

Factual writing, 145. See CREATIVE WRITING.

Falling action, 340. See PLOT.

Falling meter. See METER.

Fantasy, 275, Highly imaginative fiction based on a self-contained imaginary world.

Farce, 399. See COMEDY.

Feminine rhyme, 76. See RHYME.

Fiction, 145ff., 151ff. A NARRATIVE (characters doing something) in PROSE in which the author's primary commitment is to the creation of an art form even though actual events, places, or people may be used directly or in modified form. (See CREATIVE WRITING.) It may be SIMPLE, as with most COMMERCIAL WRITING or SOPHISTICATED. Fiction is also subdivided loosely by length: *Short-short* stories (see page 152) are usually 3 to 6 typed, double-spaced pages; *short stories* are most often about 7 to 24 pages; *novellas* tend to be 50 to 150 pages; *novels* are commonly 250 pages upward. Complexity of PLOT tends to increase with length.

Figurative language, 62, 281. See IMAGE.

Figure of speech, 59ff., 62, 281. See IMAGE.

First-person narration, 194ff. See PERSON.

Fixed forms, 94ff. Traditional VERSE forms that follow certain CONVENTIONS in METER, RHYME scheme, or syllabics (see RHYTHM). Examples: the BALLAD, SONNET, and HAIKU.

Flashback, 202ff. See PLOT.

Flash-forward, 203, 258. See PLOT.

Flat character, 256, 371. See CHARACTERIZATION.

Focus, 196. The character or characters who are the primary concern of a story. When it is a single individual, he or she is also referred to as the PROTAGONIST. In first-person fiction, however, the focus may be on a character other than the NARRATOR.

Foil, 347. A secondary character in FICTION or DRAMA who sets off a primary character by contrast in attitude, appearance, or in other ways. Not to be confused with the ANTAGONIST, who is an opponent of the PROTAGONIST.

Foot, 88ff. See METER.

Forewarning. The technique in FICTION of preparing the reader for a shift in TONE or for some turn of PLOT. Informally referred to as a *pre-echo*.

Formalism, 5. See NEW FORMALISM.

Formula, 149. Popular CONVENTIONS that characterize SIMPLE FICTION and DRAMA. These conventions are usually patterns of PLOT combined with STOCK CHARACTERS. Sample: The-sincere-brunette who competes with The-scheming-blonde for the attentions of The-rising-young-executive who at first is "blind to the truth" but who finally "sees the light."

Frame story, 204. See PLOT.

Free-form rhythms, 84. An informal synonym for FREE VERSE.

Free verse, 5, 105ff. VERSE that is written without METER, relying instead on RHYTHMICAL patterns derived from TYPOGRAPHY, syntactical elements, the repetition of words and phrases, syllabics (see RHYTHM), or so-called breath units (see RHYTHM). Free verse contains no regular RHYME, depending instead on SOUND DEVICES such as assonance, consonance, and alliteration.

Genre, 1, 316. Any of several types of imaginative writing. In common usage, genres refer to FICTION, POETRY, DRAMA, and CREATIVE NONFICTION. Subdivisions of popular fiction such as "mysteries," "Westerns," and "science fiction" are confusingly referred to as *genre writing*.

Gimmick, 157, 197, An unusual twist of PLOT or CHARACTERIZATION. A colloquial term, it is generally used in a pejorative sense to describe contrived, attention-getting details.

Hackneyed language, 64ff., 150. A broad term that includes CLICHES as well as non-metaphorical phrases and words that have been weakened by overuse such as "tried and true." Such language is often found in SIMPLE WRITING.

Haiku, 5, 85ff. Originally a Japanese VERSE form. In English it is usually written as a three-line poem containing five syllables in the first LINE, seven in the second, and five in the third. Traditionally, the haiku draws on some aspect of nature and either states or implies a particular season.

Heptameter, 90. See LINE.

Hero, 218, 345. See PROTAGONIST.

Heroic couplet. Rhyming couplets (see LINE) in iambic pentameter (see METER).

Hexameter, 90. See LINE.

Hook, 221, 339. See DRAMATIC QUESTION.

Hyperbole, 62. A figure of speech (see IMAGE) employing extreme exaggeration not to be taken literally, often in the form of a simile or METAPHOR. Example: "you a wonder/ you a city / of a woman."

Iambic foot, 88ff. The most popular type of METER in English: ta-*TUM*.

Identity, 75. See RHYME.

Image, 3, 57ff., 67. An item that can be perceived by one of the five senses. The most common are visual details. Images, especially visual ones, are called *concrete words* as opposed to those that are ABSTRACT. When several closely related images are used near each other, they are called an *image cluster* (page 124). Images may be used literally or as a SYMBOL, or in a figure of speech (see METAPHOR). A figure of speech (also called *figurative language*) uses an image in a stated or implied comparison. METAPHORS are the most common figures of speech. Other figures of speech include similes, PUNS, HYPERBOLE, and SYNECDOCHE.

Image cluster, 68ff., 124. See IMAGE.

Imaginative writing, 145. Same as CREATIVE WRITING.

In medias res, 221. Literally, "in the middle of things." It refers to a work of FICTION that begins abruptly in the middle of an ongoing plot.

Indirect discourse, 240ff. See DIALOGUE.

Interior monologue, 241ff. See DIALOGUE.

Internal rhyme, 95, 110. See RHYME.

Irony, 132ff., 305, 400. A reversal in which (a) a literal statement is knowingly or unknowingly the opposite from the intended meaning, or (b) an event is surprisingly or dramatically different from reasonable expectations. The first general type deals with words and can take two forms. One is *verbal* or *conscious* irony, in which the author or a character makes a statement that he or she knows is the opposite of the intended meaning (like saying, "Great day for a sail" during a hurricane). It is similar to sarcasm. The second is *dramatic irony,* in which a character *unknowingly* makes a statement that is the opposite of the true situation or events to come. *Cosmic irony* or *irony of fate,* deals with a reversal of expected events, not words (like the firefighter who dies from smoking in bed).

Italian sonnet, 98. See SONNET.

Legitimate theater, 315. Plays performed by actors on a stage as contrasted with cinema, television DRAMA, and the like.

Level of usage, 298. The degree of formality or informality in PROSE or VERSE. It runs from formal word choice and grammatical construction to colloquial phrasing and slang.

Line, 2, 89ff. A unit of VERSE that when printed usually appears without being broken, the length of which is determined by the poet alone. The inclusion of the line as a part of the art form rather than merely a printer's concern is one of the fundamental distinctions between VERSE and PROSE. In METERED VERSE, lines usually contain the same number of *feet* (see METER); in *sprung rhythm* and *alliterative* VERSE, lines are linked by having the same number of stressed syllables; and in FREE VERSE, the length of lines is more of a visual concern (see TYPOGRAPHY). The following terms describe most line lengths in metered verse: (1) monometer (one foot), (2) dimeter (two feet), (3) trimeter (three feet), (4) tetrameter (four feet), (5) pentameter (five feet), (6) hexameter (six feet), (7) heptameter (seven feet), (8) octometer (eight feet). Trimeter, tetrameter, and pentameter are by far the most frequently used.

Literary, 8, 145. See LITERATURE.

Literature, 8, 145. PROSE or VERSE in which style, suggestion, and implication are developed with some degree of conscious care. Literary writing is differentiated from purely factual and utilitarian writing such as reports, news items, and scientific articles, as well as from personal writing such as diaries, letters, and journals. In this text, the term SOPHISTICATED WRITING is often used as a synonym for *literary writing* to avoid implying a value judgment.

Local color, 232. See REGIONALISM.

Lyric, 73, 89. A relatively brief, subjective poem expressing a strongly felt emotion. Thus, poems of love, deep feeling, observation, and contemplation are *lyrics* in contrast with BALLADS and other types of NARRATIVE POETRY. *Lyrical* is often used loosely to describe poetry that sounds musical because of its SOUND DEVICES and RHYTHM. *Lyric* is derived from a Greek term for VERSE to be accompanied by a lyre.

Means of perception, 189ff. The agent through whose eyes a piece of FICTION appears to be presented. This character is also the one whose thoughts are revealed directly. The term is synonymous with *point of view* and *viewpoint.* It is generally limited to a single character in short fiction.

Melodrama, 137, 156ff., 223, 343ff. SIMPLE WRITING (usually DRAMA or FICTION) that is dominated by SUSPENSE and exaggerated forms of dramatic TENSION. It usually makes use of STOCK CHARACTERS. SOPHISTICATED LITERATURE also uses conflict but keeps it from dominating the THEME or CHARACTERIZATION.

Metafiction, 276. FICTION in which the theme deals with the act of writing itself. It is generally less concerned with realism and CHARACTERIZATION than with commentary on the genre. John Barth's story "Lost in the Funhouse" is a classic and entertaining example.

Metamorphosis, 163. Same as TRANSFORMATION.

Metaphor and Simile, 16, 281. A *simile* is a figure of speech (see IMAGE) in which one item (usually an abstraction) is compared with another (usually a concrete noun) that is different in all but a few significant respects. The comparison (a type of *analogy*) uses *like* or *as*. Thus, "She fought like a lion" suggests courage but not the use of claws and teeth. The item being described (the woman) is called the *tenor*, and the item introduced merely for comparison (the lion) is the *vehicle*. A *metaphor* implies rather than states a similar comparison without using *like* or *as*—"She was a lion when fighting for civil rights." A *controlling simile* (or *dominant metaphor*) is a figure of speech that dominates a poem. (Not to be confused with SYMBOL.)

Meter, 87ff. See table on page 89. A system of STRESSED and unstressed syllables that creates RHYTHM in certain types of verse. The CONVENTIONALIZED units of stressed and unstressed syllables are known as *feet*. Metered verse normally contains the same number of feet in each LINE and basically the same type of foot throughout the poem. The effect is usually muted by occasionally substituting other types of feet. If the pattern ends on a stressed syllable, it is called *rising meter;* if the pattern ends on an unstressed syllable, it is called *falling meter.*

Mixed metaphor, 61. A METAPHOR that is internally confusing or illogical because the two vehicles (see METAPHOR) are contradictory. Example: "The bitter taste of rejection rang in his ears."

Modes, 150, 301ff. See NARRATIVE MODES.

Monologue, 244, 347. See DIALOGUE.

Multiple flashback, 203. See PLOT.

Narrative, 34, 85, 122ff. Any work that tells a story; that is, characters doing something. It can take the form of FICTION, CREATIVE NONFICTION, DRAMA, NARRATIVE POETRY.

Narrative modes, 150, 301ff. The five methods by which FICTION can be presented: DIALOGUE, thoughts, action, description, and exposition. Most writers use all five in varying proportions. Unusual emphasis on any one affects the STYLE.

Narrative poetry, 95, 122ff. VERSE that tells a story. This may take the form of the BALLAD, the EPIC, or a tale in verse such as Hecht's "Lizards and Snakes" (page 33).

Narrator, 122ff., 195. A character who appears to be telling a story, novel, or narrative poem. He or she may be clearly identified as in first-person writing (see MEANS OF PERCEPTION) or implied as in most third-person writing. A narrator is often but not always the PROTAGONIST.

New formalism, 5. A recent poetic movement (starting in the 1980s and '90s) reflecting a renewed interest in metrical forms and, often, innovative use of such forms. Also called *neo-formalism.*

Nonrealistic drama, 356ff. See REALISTIC DRAMA.

Nonrecurrent stanzas, 108. STANZAS of unequal length often used in FREE VERSE. They serve some of the same functions as paragraphs in PROSE.

Novel, 152. See FICTION.

Novella, 152. See FICTION.

Occasion, 36. In poetry, the incident or cause that appears to have initiated the narrator's concern. Not all poems have an occasion stated or implied, but some make it clear, as in Robert Frost's "Design" (page 15) and Mary Oliver's "The Black Snake" (page 26).

Occasional verse, 8, 75. VERSE written for a particular occasion such as an anniversary, birthday, death, or dedication. Many are literarily simple and comic, but others are serious.

Octave, 99. An eight-lined STANZA in METERED VERSE. Also, the first eight lines of a SONNET.

Octometer, 90. See LINE.

Ode, A LYRIC poem, usually metered and serious, commemorating or honoring a person, place, or event.

Off rhyme, 78. See RHYME.

Omniscient point of view, 93. The MEANS OF PERCEPTION in which the author enters the minds of all major characters. *Limited omniscience* restricts the means of perception to certain characters. Most short FICTION and many novels limit the means of perception to a single character.

Onomatopoeia, 74. See SOUND DEVICES.

Orientation, 226ff. The sense in FICTION, DRAMA, or NARRATIVE POETRY of being somewhere specific. A more general term than SETTING, it includes awareness of geography (real or invented), historical period, season, and time.

Overtone, 10, 37, 297. See CONNOTATION.

Overwriting, 299. FICTION or VERSE that is overblown, excessive in phrasing, or overly modified. It strikes the reader as artificial or affected. Informally called *purple prose*. It is the opposite of a sparse or economical STYLE.

Oxymoron. An apparent contradiction presented either as a figure of speech (see IMAGE), as in Roethke's "I wake to sleep," or as a simple phrase, such as "a silent scream" or "cruel kindness."

Pace, 206, 244, 340ff., 400. The reader's sense that a story or play either moves rapidly or drags. This is determined by the RATE OF REVELATION and by the STYLE.

Pantoum, 100ff. A VERSE form in quatrains. The type of meter and length is up to the poet. The traditional rhyme is *abab, bcbc, cdcd*. The the stanzas interlock through repetition: lines 2 and 4 of each stanza become lines 1 and 3 of the next. The last stanza of the poem can take one of two patterns: a couplet made up of lines 1 and 3 in reverse order or a concluding quatrain using lines 1 and 3 of the first stanza as lines 4 and 2 respectively. Example: "Always the One Who Loves His Father Most" by Clement Long (page 23).

Parable, 130. A short, usually ALLEGORICAL story used to illustrate some moral lesson or religious principle.

Paradox, 127. A statement that on one level is logically absurd yet on another level implies a reasonable assertion. Example from Heller's *Catch 22*: "The Texan turned out to be good-natured, generous, and likable. In three days no one could stand him."

Parody, A satiric (see SATIRE) imitation of a work of FICTION, VERSE, or DRAMA or of a writer's style designed to ridicule the original.

Passive voice. Grammatical construction in which the subject is hidden: "Mistakes were made" as opposed to the active construction, "I made a mistake." Use of passive construction tends to weaken one's STYLE.

Pathos. Work that evokes a feelings of sympathy or pity. Unsuccessful, excessive, or insincere pathos produces *bathos.*

Pentameter, 90. See LINE.

Person, 194ff. Any of several methods of presenting fiction: (a) First person ("I") gives the illusion of a story being told directly by a character either in an inconspicuous STYLE or "as-if-told." (b) Third person ("he" or "she") is equally popular. (c) The "you" form reads as if the reader is being addressed directly. It is rarely used. (d) The "they" form is used least of all. *Person is how* a story is presented; the MEANS OF PERCEPTION is *who* appears to present it.

Persona, 135, 146ff. The narrator, implied or identified, in a work of fiction or a poem. It distinguishes the fictional character from the author or poet.

Personification. Attributing human characteristics to inanimate objects, as in "the enraged sea."

Petrarchan sonnet, 98ff. See SONNET.

Plot, 149, 202ff., 405. The sequence of events, often divided into SCENES, in FICTION, DRAMA, or NARRATIVE POETRY. It may be chronological, or it may be nonchronological in any of four ways: by *flashback* (inserting an earlier scene), by *multiple flashbacks*, by a *flash-forward* (rare), or by using a *frame* (beginning and ending with the same scene). *Base line* refers to the primary plot from which flashbacks and, less often, flash-forwards depart. A *subplot* is a secondary plot that echoes or amplifies the main plot or provides *comic relief.* In traditional tragedies the increasing complications are called *rising action*, the turning point is the *climax,* followed by *falling action,* which in turn leads to the final *catastrophe* (also called the *denouement*), often the death of the PROTAGONIST. Contemporary drama (and some fiction) often follows modified versions of this structure, frequently treating the death in a symbolic rather than literal manner.

Poetic, 73ff., 115. In addition to being an adjective for *poetry* (see VERSE), this term is used to describe fiction or drama that makes special use of RHYTHM, SOUND DEVICES, figurative language (see IMAGE), SYMBOL, and compression of meaning and implication.

Poetry, 1ff. See VERSE.

Point of view, 189ff. See MEANS OF PERCEPTION.

Postmodern fiction, 276. A fairly recent stylistic approach that emphasizes ingenuity of language itself and often focuses on writing as writing. It makes little or in some cases no use of plot and traditional characterization. Reader interest is often (but not always) sustained with wit and verbal inventiveness.

Private symbols, 68, 283. See SYMBOL.

Proscenium arch, 374. See STAGE DESIGNS.

Prose, 1. Writing in which the length of the LINES is not determined by the author and so is not a part of the art form. As a result, the sentence, not the line, is the basic organizing unit. Prose also tends to be less concerned with RHYTHM, SOUND DEVICES, and compression of statement than is VERSE.

Prose poetry, 115. A hybrid literary form in which the writer maintains control over line length, as in VERSE, but generally ignores other poetic devices such as a regular RHYTHMICAL SYSTEM, SOUND DEVICES, and figurative language (see IMAGE).

Prose rhythm, 83. RHYTHM in PROSE writing achieved through SYNTAX (sentence length and type), paragraph length, and most often by ANAPHORA, repetition of words or phrases.

Prosody. The construction of a poem (see VERSE) including SCANSION (metrical scheme), stanzaic patterns (see STANZA), DICTION, phrasing, and the like. Don't confuse this with PROSE.

Protagonist, 122, 218, 345. The main character in a piece of FICTION, a play, or a NARRATIVE POEM. This character is often opposed by an *antagonist*. The term is broader than *hero*, which suggests greatness. Protagonists who are base or ignoble are sometimes referred to as *antiheroes*.

Public symbols, 67, 283. See SYMBOL.

Pun, 62. A figure of speech (see IMAGE) in which two different but significantly related meanings are attached to a single word. Most SOPHISTICATED uses of the pun are a form of METAPHOR with a vehicle (see METAPHOR) that has two meanings, as in Dylan Thomas' "some grave truth."

Purple prose, 299. A colloquial synonym for OVERWRITING.

Pyrrhic foot, 89. See METER.

Quatrain, 96. See STANZA.

Rate of revelation, 206. In FICTION or DRAMA, the rate at which new information or insights regarding CHARACTER, THEME, or PLOT are given to the reader or audience. It is one of the primary factors that determine PACE of such work.

Realism, 271. NARRATIVE in which characters, events, and settings are similar to those in everyday life. In fiction this is contrasted with *fantasy*, *science fiction*, ALLEGORICAL fiction, most METAFICTION, and POSTMODERN work. Some prefer the word *verisimilitude*, the *illusion* of reality. Thus, Kafka's dreamlike scenes "seem real" (have verisimilitude) without being conventionally realistic.

Realistic drama, 356. DRAMA in which, like realistic fiction, characters, events, and settings are similar to those in everyday life. Costume, set, and PLOT conform to what we see in daily life. This is opposed to *nonrealistic drama*, which creates its own world in somewhat the same manner as a dream. *Expressionism* is sometimes used as a synonym for nonrealistic drama, but more strictly it refers to a dramatic school culminating in the 1920s and 1930s with the works of O'Neill, Rice, and others.

Refrain, 125. A phrase, LINE, or STANZA that is repeated periodically in a poem.

Regionalism, 232. FICTION and VERSE that draw on the customs, traditions, attitudes, and, occasionally, the DICTION of a particular geographic region. It is a more contemporary term than *local color* writing, a term that is tainted by certain 19th century authors who adopted the patronizing TONE of an outsider.

Resonance, 124. That aspect of TONE in SOPHISTICATED WRITING that is created by the use of suggestive details such as SYMBOLS, figurative language (see IMAGE), and other layers of meaning. It is a complexity of suggestion not found in SIMPLE WRITING. Resonance adds to the DENSITY of a work.

Rhyme, 74ff. Two or more words in poetry (see VERSE) that are linked because their final syllables sound alike. In *true rhyme* the matching sounds must be identical from the accented vowel to the end of the word, and the sound preceding the accented vowels in each word must be unlike. (If the sounds preceding the accented vowel in each word are the same, the pair is known as an *identity*, not a rhyme.) *Slant rhyme* and *off-rhyme* use similar rather than identical vowel sounds. *Double rhyme*, also called *feminine rhyme*, is a two-syllable rhyme as in "running" and "sunning." In an *eye rhyme* (also called *sight rhyme*) the words look alike but sound different (like *have* and *grave*). *Internal rhyme* links two or more rhyming words within the same line.

Rhyme royal, 97. A seven-line STANZA in iambic pentameter (see LINE) with a RHYME SCHEME of *ababbcc*.

Rhyme scheme, 94ff. A recurring pattern of rhymed endings repeated regularly in each STANZA of rhymed and METERED VERSE.

Rhythm, 5, 83ff., 116. A systematic variation in the flow of sound. Traditional rhythms include established patterns such as METER, ALLITERATIVE VERSE, and *syllabic* verse. Unique rhythms are those created uniquely for a particular poem as in FREE VERSE. In METERED VERSE rhythm is achieved through a repeated pattern of stressed and unstressed syllables. In ALLITERATIVE VERSE the pattern is determined by the number of stresses in each line without regard for the unstressed syllables. In syllabic verse, the number of syllables in any one line matches the number in the corresponding line of each of the other STANZAS. In FREE VERSE, rhythms are achieved by TYPOGRAPHY, repeated syntactical patterns, and breath units. Rhythms in PROSE are achieved by repeating key words or phrases (ANAPHORA) and SYNTACTICAL patterns.

Rising action, 340. See PLOT.

Rising meter. See METER.

Rondeau, 99. A 15-line, three-STANZA poem in syllabics (see RHYTHM) unified with a REFRAIN. The first STANZA has five lines; the second has four lines; and the third has six lines. There is one REFRAIN that appears in the opening of the first line and is repeated at the end of the second and third stanzas. With R standing for the refrain, the RHYME SCHEME is aabba; aabR; aabbaR.

Round character, 256, 371. See CHARACTERIZATION.

Run-on line, 76. Same as ENJAMBMENT.

SASE, 431. "Self-addressed stamped envelope," which should accompany any submission you wish returned.

Satire, 134ff., 306ff., 399ff. A form of wit in which a distorted view of characters, places, or institutions is used for the purpose of criticism or ridicule. At least some measure of exaggeration (if only through a biased selection of details) is necessary for satire to be effective.

Scanning. The analysis of METER in metered VERSE, identifying the various feet (see METER) and the type of LINE used.

Scansion, 91. The noun that refers to SCANNING.

Scene, 200ff., 208, 335ff. In DRAMA, (a) a formal subdivision of an *act* marked in the script and indicated to the audience by lowering the curtain or dimming the lights or (b) a more subtle subdivision of the PLOT suggested by the exit or the entrance of a character. In this text the former are called *primary scenes* and the latter *secondary*. In FICTION, the scene is a less precise unit of action marked either by a shift in the number of characters or a shift in time or place.

Script, 315. The written text of a play (see DRAMA) including the dialogue and brief notations on the action. The script is not to be confused with a performance.

Sentimentality, 54, 136. A form of SIMPLE WRITING that is dominated by a blunt appeal to the emotions of pity and love. It does so at the expense of subtlety and literary sophistication (see SOPHISTICATED WRITING). Popular subjects are puppies, grandparents, and young lovers.

Septet, 97. A seven-line STANZA in METERED VERSE. It is the stanza form used in RHYME ROYAL.

Sestet, 99. A six-line STANZA in METERED VERSE. Also the last six lines of the SONNET.

Set, 373ff. In DRAMA the set includes everything the audience sees except the actors themselves. There are three basic approaches to set design. Most sets are realistic in that they create the illusion of an actual place. (The realistic set design of *The Collection* appears on page 376.) Sets can also be symbolic, adopting dreamlike distortions. Occasionally the set is a bare stage, relying, as Shakespeare did, on the imagination of the audience.

Setting, 150, 226ff. Strictly, the geographic area in which a PLOT takes place; but more generally, the time of day, the season, and the social environment as well. In DRAMA the setting is usually specified briefly at the beginning of the script.

Shaped verse, 110. VERSE in which TYPOGRAPHY is employed to make the lines, words, and word fragments suggest a shape or picture that becomes of greater importance than RHYTHM or sound. Also called *concrete poetry.*

Short-short story, 152. See FICTION.

Short story, 152. See FICTION.

Simile, 60ff. See METAPHOR.

Simple writing, 7ff., 147ff. Writing in which the THEME is blatant or a TRUISM, the STYLE is limited to a single effect, and/or the TONE is limited to a single emotion. It includes the adventure and horror story (MELODRAMA), many love stories, most greeting-card verse (SENTIMENTALITY), most patriotic VERSE and politically partisan FICTION and DRAMA (propaganda), and that which is single-mindedly sexual or sadistic (pornography). It also includes work that is so personal or so obscure that it remains unintelligible even to conscientious readers. Antonyms for *simple* are SOPHISTICATED and LITERARY.

Slant rhyme, 78. See RHYME.

Slapstick, 348, 371, 403.

Sonnet, 98ff. A METERED and RHYMED poem of fourteen LINES usually in iambic pentameter (see LINE). The Italian or Petrarchan sonnet is often rhymed *abba, abba; cde, cde.* The first eight lines are known as the OCTAVE and the last six as the SESTET. The Elizabethan sonnet (see Shakespeare's "Sonnet 29," page 18) is thought of as three quatrains and a final rhyming couplet: *abab, cdcd, efef gg.*

Sophisticated writing, 7ff., 147ff. Writing in which the THEME is fresh and insightful, the STYLE makes rich use of the techniques available, and the TONE provides some measure of RESONANCE. A value-free synonym for LITERARY WRITING, it is the opposite of SIMPLE WRITING. Not to be confused with the popular use of *sophisticated.*

Sound devices, 4, 72ff. The technique of linking two or more words by *alliteration* (similar initial sounds), *assonance* (similar vowel sounds), *consonance* (similar consonantal sounds), *onomatopoeia* (similarity between the sound of the word and the object or action it describes), or RHYME. In addition, *sound clusters* link groups of words with related vowel sounds that are too disparate to be called true samples of assonance.

Spondaic foot, 89. See METER.

Stage business, 382. Minor action or facial expressions on the part of an actor.

Stage designs, 373ff. The *conventional stage* has a raised playing area that is located behind a *proscenium arch* from which a curtain is lowered between acts and SCENES. It resembles a picture frame. A *thrust stage* has no arch and no single picture effect because it extends into the audience and is open on three sides. The curtain is replaced by a dimming of the lights. *Theater in the round* or *arena theater* extends this concept further by having the audience encircle the playing area as it does in a circus tent.

Stanza, 94ff. In METERED poetry a regularly recurring group of lines usually separated by spaces and unified by LINE length, metrical system, and often by a RHYME scheme. Common forms include the *couplet* (two lines); *tercet* or *triplet* (three lines); quatrain (four lines); *cinquain* (five lines); SESTET (six lines); *septet* (seven lines); OCTAVE (eight lines). The term is occasionally applied to irregular units in FREE VERSE, which are used more like paragraphs in PROSE.

Stereotype, 346, 348. See STOCK CHARACTER.

Stock character, 151, 223. Characters in FICTION or DRAMA that are SIMPLE and also conform to one of a number of types that have appeared over such a long period and in so many different works that they are familiar to readers and audiences. Their DIALOGUE is often HACKNEYED. Minor characters are often stock types, but when major characters appear so, the work as a whole may be SIMPLE as opposed to SOPHISTICATED. Also known as *stereotypes* or *"flat"* as opposed to *"round"* characters.

Stock situation. A situation in FICTION or DRAMA that is too familiar to have freshness or impact.

Story, 152. See FICTION.

Stream of consciousness, 159, 275. FICTION appearing to resemble a character's thoughts quoted directly without exposition. Although wandering and disjointed, such passages are designed to reveal character. This is in sharp contrast with *automatic writing*, in which the writer's goal is not CHARACTERIZATION (or even FICTION) but undirected self-expression.

Stress, 84. In metered VERSE, the relative force or emphasis placed on a particular syllable. In "awake," for example, the second syllable is stressed. See METER.

Style, 295ff. The manner in which a work is written. It is determined by the author's decisions, both conscious and unconscious, regarding DICTION (the type of words used), SYNTAX (the type of sentences), NARRATIVE MODE (relative importance of DIALOGUE, thoughts, action, description, and EXPOSITION), and PACE (the reader's sense of progress). It is closely connected with TONE. *Inconspicuous style* is that in which no one technique is noticeable.

Subplot, 341ff. See PLOT.

Substitution, 191ff. The technique in METERED VERSE of occasionally replacing a foot (see METER) that has become the standard in a particular poem with some other type of foot. Example: Using a trochee for emphasis in a poem that is iambic.

Suspense, 223. A heightened form of curiosity that creates excitement and a sense of drama. In moderation, it provides effective TENSION. When it dominates the work, the result is MELODRAMA.

Syllabics, 85ff. See RHYTHM.

Symbol, 65ff., 67, 283ff. Any detail such as an object, action, or state that has a range of meaning beyond and usually larger than itself. *Public symbols* are those that have become a part of the general consciousness—the flag, the cross, Uncle Sam, and the like. *Private* (or *unique*) symbols are those devised by individual writers for a particular work. Usually the *vehicle* (see METAPHOR) is introduced directly as a detail in the story or poem and the *tenor* is implied indirectly. This is in contrast with FIGURES OF SPEECH, such as similes and METAPHORS, in which the vehicle is introduced merely to serve as a comparison and has no other function. In Robley Wilson's "On a Maine Beach" (page 29) the phrase "beach rhythms" (line 15) is a symbol for our own life cycle, while "like worn change" (line 1) is a simile describing an aspect of the rocks.

Synecdoche, 63. A FIGURE OF SPEECH in which a part is used for the whole. "Many hands," for example, suggests many people; "bread for the poor" suggests food generally.

Syntactical rhythm, 111ff. See RHYTHM.

Syntax, 113, 298ff. Sentence structure; the arrangement of words in the sentence. It is sometimes used to create RHYTHM in FREE VERSE and less often in PROSE.

Tag, 239. See DIALOGUE TAG.

Tenor, 61, 282. See METAPHOR.

Tense, 302ff. The various forms a verb can take. The past tense ("She ran to the window") is traditional in fiction, but the present tense ("She runs to the window") is increasingly popular. The past perfect ("She had run to the window shortly before the explosion") is often used briefly to introduce a flashback (see PLOT).

Tension, 217ff. A force and a counterforce within a work of LITERATURE. In FICTION, DRAMA, and NARRATIVE POETRY, it can be created through conflict between a character and another character, a group, an aspect of nature, or an inner struggle. It can also be generated when the writer withholds information to arouse the reader's curiosity or a sense of suspense. In VERSE tension is more often generated by a contrast or conflict in THEME, TONE, or both. Tension provides a sense of vitality in a work.

Tercet, 96. See STANZA.

Terza rima, 96. A traditional VERSE form consisting of iambic pentameter tercets (see STANZA) in which each stanza is linked to the next through an interlocking rhyme scheme of *aba, bcb, cdc,* etc.

Tetrameter, 90. See LINE.

Theater in the round, 374. See STAGE DESIGNS.

Theater of the absurd, 357, 363. A somewhat loosely defined dramatic "school" in the *expressionistic* (see REALISTIC DRAMA) tradition beginning in the 1950s. Shared convictions: that life is "absurd" in the sense of lacking ultimate meaning and that the intellect cannot determine truth. Shared techniques: the use of nonrealistic situations, SATIRE, and a tendency to develop a static quality rather than a DRAMATIC PLOT. Examples include works by Ionesco, Beckett, Pinter.

Theme, 121ff., 150, 287ff., 405ff. The portion of a LITERARY work that comments on the human condition. It is the primary statement, suggestion, or implication of the work. The term is used interchangeably with *central concern.* It does not have the moral implications of *message* nor the didactic element of *thesis.* A thesis states or clearly implies a particular conviction or recommends a specific course of action. Theses are often propagandistic. Most SOPHISTICATED WRITING is unified loosely by a theme rather than a thesis.

Thesis, 411ff. See THEME.

Third-person narration, 194ff. See PERSON.

Thrust stage, 374. See STAGE DESIGNS

Tone, 127ff., 278, 303ff., 397ff. The emotional quality of a LITERARY work itself and of the author's implicit attitude toward the work as well. Some critics prefer to separate the two aspects of this definition, but most writers tend to think of them as two forms of the same quality. Tone is described with adjectives like "exciting," "sad," "merry," or "eerie," as well as "satiric," "sardonic," and "ironic."

Tragedy, 340. DRAMA that is generally serious in TONE and focuses on a PROTAGONIST who in most cases faces a climax and an eventual downfall, often death.

Transformation, 163ff., 176, 235. Radical alteration of an experience or of an early outline of a story or play in order to create a fresh LITERARY work. (Also called *metamorphosis*.) It often precedes the first draft and so is far more basic than *revision.* The process can be either conscious or unconscious. Its function is to clarify existing patterns, to break up patterns that appear to be contrived, or to help a writer regain control over an experience that is still too personal to develop in LITERARY form.

Trimeter, 90. See LINE.

Triplet, 96. See STANZA.

Trochaic foot, 88. See METER.

True rhyme, 174. See RHYME.

Truism, 9, 53, 289. A statement that reiterates a well-known truth; a platitude.

Typography, 106ff. The technique in VERSE (and particularly FREE VERSE) of arranging words, phrases, and lines on the printed page to create a RHYTHMICAL effect. When used to an extreme degree to create a picture, it is called SHAPED POETRY.

Unique rhythm, 109. See RHYTHM.

Vanity press, 435. A commercial publisher that charges the author a part or, more often, all of the printing costs. *Cooperative presses,* in contrast, are usually non-profit and share the expense with the author or poet. Regular commercial publishers assume all costs themselves and pay the author an advance and a percentage (generally between 10 and 15 percent) of the sales.

Vehicle, 61, 282. See METAPHOR.

Verbal irony, 132, 305. See IRONY.

Verisimilitude, 274. See REALISM.

Verse, 1ff. The form of LITERARY writing that uses line length as an aspect of the art form and is typically concerned with SOUND, RHYTHM, and compression of language. *Verse* is occasionally used as a synonym for LINE, STANZA, or REFRAIN. Although *verse* is often a general synonym for *poetry,* many prefer that the word *poetry* be limited to SOPHISTICATED verse.

Viewpoint, 189ff. See MEANS OF PERCEPTION.

Villanelle, 101ff. A French verse form of 19 lines in iambic pentameter (see LINE) divided into five tercets (see STANZA) and a final four-line STANZA. The poem has only two rhymes. They are arranged in this pattern: *aba aba aba aba aba abaa.* Line 1 is a REFRAIN that is repeated entirely as lines 6, 12, and 18; and line 3 is repeated to form lines 9, 15, and 19. The effect is to give subtly different meanings to the repeated lines. An example: "The Waking" by Theodore Roethke, page 29.

Visual rhythm, 106ff. See TYPOGRAPHY.

Voice, 295. Sometimes used as a broad and unneeded synonym for STYLE. More specifically, it describes styles that are pronounced, especially those presented through a first-person narrator. The voice often contributes to CHARACTERIZATION, as in "Gotta Dance" (page 291). Voice can also refer to the author's attitude toward his or her work as in a *serious, flippant,* or *satiric* voice.

Vowel, 73. A letter sounded with the lips open and without obstruction or constriction in the flow of air: *a, e, i, o, u,* and sometimes *y.* All the rest are *consonants,* letters in which the flow of air is restricted with the lips or tongue. An important distinction in the analysis of RHYME.